Mathematics for Stability and Optimization of Economic Systems

ECONOMIC THEORY AND MATHEMATICAL ECONOMICS

Consulting Editor: Karl Shell

UNIVERSITY OF PENNSYLVANIA
PHILADELPHIA, PENNSYLVANIA

Franklin M. Fisher and Karl Shell. **The Economic Theory of Price Indices:** ***Two Essays on the Effects of Taste, Quality, and Technological Change***

Luis Eugenio Di Marco (Ed.). **International Economics and Development:** ***Essays in Honor of Raúl Presbisch***

Erwin Klein. **Mathematical Methods in Theoretical Economics:** ***Topological and Vector Space Foundations of Equilibrium Analysis***

Paul Zarembka (Ed.). **Frontiers in Econometrics**

George Horwich and Paul A. Samuelson (Eds.). **Trade, Stability, and Macroeconomics:** ***Essays in Honor of Lloyd A. Metzler***

W. T. Ziemba and R. G. Vickson (Eds.). **Stochastic Optimization Models in Finance**

Steven A. Y. Lin (Ed.). **Theory and Measurement of Economic Externalities**

David Cass and Karl Shell (Eds.). **The Hamiltonian Approach to Dynamic Economics**

R. Shone. **Microeconomics:** ***A Modern Treatment***

C. W. J. Granger and Paul Newbold. **Forecasting Economic Time Series**

Michael Szenberg, John W. Lombardi, and Eric Y. Lee. **Welfare Effects of Trade Restrictions:** ***A Case Study of the U.S. Footwear Industry***

Haim Levy and Marshall Sarnat (Eds.). **Financial Decision Making under Uncertainty**

Yasuo Murata. **Mathematics for Stability and Optimization of Economic Systems**

In preparation

Alan S. Blinder and Philip Friedman (Eds.). **Natural Resources, Uncertainty, and General Equilibrium Systems:** ***Essays in Memory of Rafael Lusky***

Jerry S. Kelly. **Arrow Impossibility Theorems**

Mathematics for Stability and Optimization of Economic Systems

Yasuo Murata

NAGOYA CITY UNIVERSITY
FACULTY OF ECONOMICS
MIZUHOCHIO, MIZUHOKU
NAGOYA, JAPAN

ACADEMIC PRESS New York San Francisco London 1977
A Subsidiary of Harcourt Brace Jovanovich, Publishers

ACADEMIC PRESS, INC.
111 Fifth Avenue, New York, New York 10003

United Kingdom Edition published by
ACADEMIC PRESS, INC. (LONDON) LTD.
24/28 Oval Road, London NW1

Library of Congress Cataloging in Publication Data

Murata, Yasuo, Date
Mathematics for stability and optimization of economic systems.

(Economic theory and mathematical economics series)
Includes bibliographies.
1. Economics, Mathematical. I. Title.
HB135.M87 330'.01'51 76-27449
ISBN 0-12-511250-5

PRINTED IN THE UNITED STATES OF AMERICA

To My Parents

Contents

Preface xi
Acknowledgments xv
Notation and Symbols xvii

Part I LINEAR STRUCTURE AND STABILITY OF ECONOMIC SYSTEMS

Chapter 1 **Fundamentals of Square Matrices**

1.1 Determinants, Inversion of Matrices, and Partitioned Matrices 3
1.2 Eigenvalues, Eigenvectors, and the Generalized Eigenvalue Problem 13
1.3 Matrices with Dominant Diagonals and P-Matrices 21
Exercises 30
References and Further Reading 31

Chapter 2 **Linear Equations and Related Topics with Reference to Economics**

2.1 Vector Spaces and Convex Sets 32
2.2 Linear Transformations 39
2.3 Rank and Nullity 43
2.4 Elementary Operations and Hawkins–Simon Conditions 48
2.5 Symmetric Matrices, Stable Matrices, and the Lyapunov Theorem 53
Exercises 64
References and Further Reading 64

Chapter 3 **Linear Dynamic Systems and Stability**

3.1 Linear Differential Equations 66
3.2 Jordan Form of a Square Matrix 71
3.3 Difference Equations and Dynamic Multipliers 79
3.4 Modified Routh–Hurwitz Conditions for Stability 87
3.5 Sufficient Conditions for the Tinbergenian 96
Exercises 102
References and Further Reading 103

Chapter 4 Nonnegative Square Matrices and Stability in Economic Systems

4.1 Frobenius Theorems 105
4.2 Solow Conditions, Stability, and Comparative Statics in Leontief–Hicks–Metzler Systems 115
4.3 Primitivity, the Kakeya Theorem, and Relative Stability 129
4.4 Price Systems of Leontief Type, the Fundamental Marxian Theorem, and Dual Stability 140
4.5 Generalization of the Hicks–Metzler System and Global Stability 151
Exercises 159
References and Further Reading 160

Part II OPTIMIZATION METHODS FOR ECONOMIC SYSTEMS

Chapter 5 Preliminary Mathematical Concepts

5.1 Normed Spaces and Inner Product Spaces 165
5.2 Closedness and Continuity 171
5.3 Banach Spaces and Hilbert Spaces 175
5.4 Separable Sets and Isomorphisms 179
5.5 Bounded Linear Functionals and Dual Spaces 184
5.6 Minkowski Functionals and the Hahn–Banach Theorem 189
Exercises 195
References and Further Reading 196

Chapter 6 Projection and Generalized Inverse with Reference to Economics

6.1 Projection Theorems and the Gauss–Markov Theorem 198
6.2 Adjoint Operators 204
6.3 Generalized Inverse (Pseudoinverse) 208
6.4 Generalization of the Gauss–Markov Theorem 218
6.5 Generalized Linear Equation Economic Systems 228
Exercises 235
References and Further Reading 236

Chapter 7 Optimization under Economic Equation Constraints

7.1 Differentials and Extrema 238
7.2 The Euler Equation, the Ramsey Path, and Concave Functionals 243
7.3 Contraction Mappings, the Implicit Function Theorem, Univalence Theorems, and a Nonlinear Price System 252
7.4 The Lagrange Multiplier Theory under Equality Constraints 260
7.5 Second-Order Conditions for Local Maxima and Demand Laws 263
Exercises 271
References and Further Reading 272

Chapter 8 **Optimization in Inequality Economic Systems**

8.1 Hyperplanes and Separation Theorems 273
8.2 Dual Linear Relations and Gale–Nikaido Theorems 283
8.3 The von Neumann Economic System and Maximal Paths 291
8.4 Kuhn–Tucker Theorems, Concave and Quasi-Concave Programming 306
8.5 Duality in Linear Programming, the Morishima Turnpike Theorem, and Other Related Problems 323
Exercises 337
References and Further Reading 340

Chapter 9 **Optimal Control of Dynamical Economic Systems**

9.1 Pontryagin Maximum Principle: Necessity and Sufficiency 343
9.2 Optimal Accumulation of Nontransferable Capital 355
9.3 Controllability of Linear Dynamical Economic Systems: Generalization of the Static Tinbergen Theory of Policy 361
9.4 Optimal Stabilization Policy for Linear Dynamical Economic Systems with Quadratic Cost Criteria 371
9.5 Realization of Controllable and Observable Linear Dynamical Systems 390
Exercises 402
References and Further Reading 403

Author Index 407
Subject Index 411

Preface

The aim of this book is to supply mathematical theorems (with rigorous proof) sufficient to develop and generalize important economic systems, such as Keynesian dynamic models, Leontief input–output systems, Hicks–Metzler multiple-market systems, Gauss–Markov estimation models, the Ramsey optimal accumulation model, von Neumann expanding economic systems, and Tinbergen economic policy models. Our two main concerns are stability aspects and optimization methods relevant to these economic systems. Thus the book is divided accordingly, though the latter is related to the former.

Part I covers most of the stability problems of linear economic systems, in which we adopt algebraic approaches. Chapter 1 provides useful theorems on matrices (and partitioned matrices), eigenvalue problems, and, in particular, matrices with dominant diagonals and P-matrices. Corresponding to matrices, Chapter 2 deals with linear transformations on vector spaces, proceeds to the Hawkins–Simon theorem concerning nonnegative linear systems, and discusses various stability matrices and the Lyapunov theorem via positive (or negative) difiniteness of symmetric matrices.

Stability conditions for dynamic economic systems are presented in Chapter 3. Linear differential equation systems are taken up first, and their general solutions are provided in Section 3.1. Section 3.4 is devoted to a necessary and sufficient stability condition for these systems, which we term "the modified Routh–Hurwitz conditions." Linear difference equation systems are discussed in Section 3.3 with reference to Keynesian multiplier models. Various sufficient conditions for their stability are given in Section 3.5.

Chapter 4 begins with a complete proof of the Frobenius theorem regarding nonnegative matrices. This is a revised version of the elementary proof developed by the present author. (See Murata (1972) in the references of Chapter 4.) In the other sections, with the help of a thorough survey of the literature, we discuss stability and comparative statics of Leontief systems, Hicks–Metzler systems, and related or generalized systems.

Part II is concerned with optimization methods applicable to economic systems. In preparation, we introduce norms and other topological concepts into vector spaces. Chapter 5 reviews some basic mathematics needed for subsequent developments toward optimization problems. The reader may skip this chapter at first and return to it later, as necessary. For example, the Hahn–Banach theorem, which is proved for complex separable sets in Section 5.6, will be found relevant in proving a theorem in Section 8.1.

In Chapter 6, making full use of projection theorems and the existence and properties of the Penrose generalized inverse, we develop the Gauss–Markov theory and other theorems on estimation (Section 6.4) and generalized economic equation systems in which the number of activities exceeds that of commodities (Section 6.5).

In Chapter 7, the Euler equation and Lagrange multiplier theory under equality constraints are established together with second-order maximum conditions and their applications to a Ramsey optimal accumulation model in a two-sector economy and the behavior of a firm engaged in joint production. Furthermore, we deal with properties of concave functionals in Section 7.2 and with contraction mappings, the implicit function theorem, and univalence theorems with an application to nonlinear price systems in Section 7.3.

Chapter 8 assembles dual linear relations and optimization methods applicable to inequality economic systems. Starting with geometric apparatus such as hyperplanes, half-spaces, and separation theorems, we prove the Farkas lemma, go through many theorems on dual linear systems, and reach a nonlinear extension. As a typical dual economic system, the von Neumann expanding economy is discussed fully in Section 8.3; the section concludes with an introduction to maximal paths. Section 8.4 is devoted to Kuhn–Tucker theorems and the related concave and quasi-concave programming. From these nonlinear programming theories, various duality theorems of linear programming follow easily. Their applications to the Morishima turnpike theorem and other interesting economic problems are also presented.

Chapter 9 provides powerful optimal control methods for dynamical systems. One is the Pontryagin maximum principle, which is proved in detail, from Luenberger's approach for its necessity and from Mangasarian's approach for its sufficiency. As an important application, we discuss optimal accumulation of capital along the lines of the Ramsey model. The next two sections are devoted to generalizations of the Tinbergen theory of economic policy formation and of the Phillips stabilization policy model, from a control systems point of view. Controllability conditions and optimal control values are examined both for linear differential systems and for linear difference systems. We show in the last section that any linear dynamical system can be converted into a controllable and observable system.

The author has attempted to verify theorems in as elementary a manner as possible so that an undergraduate student should be able to follow this self-contained book if he or she proceeds step by step. Selected exercises, which include important problems not covered in the text, are appended to each chapter.

Acknowledgments

The author is indebted to many articles, books, and persons. Relevant literature sources appear at the end of each chapter for reference as well as for further research.

I owe much to Professors K. J. Arrow, E. Klein, K. Mizutani, M. Morishima, E. A. Thompson, and H. Uzawa who have profoundly influenced my mathematical thinking in economics.

Thanks are due Professor H. Myoken for useful suggestions and materials on optimal control. I express my appreciation to Professors T. Hayashi, R. Iwahashi, H. Iyemoto, Y. Kimura, D. G. Luenberger, Y. Maruyama, S. L. Mehndiratta, N. Okishio, U. L. G. Rao, W. R. Sutherland, Y. Uekawa, and K. Watanabe, and to my graduate students for kind advice and comments.

I thank Professor K. Shell for welcoming my work into the series of which he is the consulting editor and for his suggestions.

Finally, I express my thanks to Miss Y. Mizutori for her excellent typing of the manuscript.

Notation and Symbols

BLUE	best linear unbiased estimator
d.d.	dominant diagonal
diag	diagonal matrix
dim X	dimension of X
exp	exponential
inf	infimum (= greatest lower bound)
lim	limit
ln	natural logarithm
max	maximum
min	minimum
sgn(a)	sign of number a
sup	supremum (= least upper bound)
q.d.d.	quasi-dominant diagonal
Q.E.D.	completion of a proof
$\{a\}$	set consisting of a single element a
$\bar{a}$	conjugate of complex number a
$\|a\|$	modulus of number a
$[a_{ij}]$	matrix whose (i, j)th component is a_{ij}
A^{-1}	inverse of square matrix A
A^{T}	transpose of matrix A
A^{+}	generalized inverse of A
$\|A\|$ or det A	determinant of square matrix A
adj A	adjoint of square matrix A
$\|\|A\|\|$	norm of matrix A
$[a, b]$	interval between a and b with a, b included
$[a, b)$	interval between a and b with b excluded
$(a, b]$	interval between a and b with a excluded
(a, b)	interval between a and b with a, b excluded
$B(X, Y)$	normed space of bounded linear transformations mapping from X into Y
$C[a, b]$	set of all continuous real-valued functions on $[a, b]$
Cov(p, q)	covariance between p and q

C^n	complex n-space
D	differential operator
$E(p)$	expectation of p
E^n	Euclidean n-space
E^n_+	nonnegative orthant of E^n
E^n_-	nonpositive orthant of E^n
$f(x)$ or $[x;f]$	value of functional f at x
$f'(x)$ or $\nabla f(x)$	gradient of functional f at x
$f''(x)$	Hessian of functional f at x
f/v	division of f by v
$df(x)/dx$	derivative of f with respect to x
$f_i(x)$ or $\partial f(x)/\partial x_i$	partial derivative of f with respect to x_i
$F: X \to Y$	transformation F mapping X into Y
F^{-1}	inverse transformation of F
F^*	adjoint of transformation F
F_x or $F'(x)$	derivative of F with respect to x
$\delta F(x;h)$	Gateaux differential of F at x with increment h
G	difference operator
i	$(-1)^{1/2}$
I	identity matrix (or operator)
$k \times m$	having k rows and m columns
$n!$	factorial of n $(= 1 \cdot 2 \cdot 3 \cdot \cdots \cdot n)$
$o(\cdot)$	Landau's o-symbol
$N(F)$	nullspace of F
$\mathrm{Re}(a)$	real part of number a
$R(F)$	range of F
$\mathrm{rk}(A)$	rank of matrix A
R^n	real n-space
$\bar{S}$	closure of set S
$\mathring{S}$	interior of set S
S^c	complement of set S
$S^\perp$	orthogonal complement of set S
$\mathrm{tr}(A)$	trace of square matrix A
$V(p)$	variance of p
$V \equiv W$	V is identically (or by definition) equal to W
$V \Rightarrow W$	V implies W
$x \to y$	x approaches y
x^{T}	transpose of vector x
$\dot{x}$	derivative of x with respect to time
$\|x\|$	norm of vector x
$\{x_n\}$	sequence $x_1, x_2, \ldots, x_n, \ldots$
X^*	dual (space) of X
$(x_1, \ldots, x_n)$	row n-vector whose ith component is x_i
$\{x_1, \ldots, x_n\}$	column n-vector whose jth component is x_j
$\{x: P\}$	set of all x having property P
$x \in X$	x is an element of set X
$x \notin X$	x is not an element of set X
$\|x - y\|$	distance between x and y
$x \perp y$	x is orthogonal to y
$(x \mid y)$	inner product of x and y

$x \neq y$	some component of x is different from the corresponding component of y
$x \leqq y$	x is not larger than y, componentwise
$x < y$	x is less than y, componentwise
$x \leq y$	$x \leqq y$ and $x \neq y$
$x + y$	componentwise addition of x and y
$x - y$	componentwise subtraction of y from x
$X + Y$	sum of sets X and Y
$X \oplus Y$	direct sum of sets X and Y
$X \times Y$	Cartesian product of spaces X and Y
$X \cap Y$	intersection of sets X and Y
$X \cup Y$	union of sets X and Y
$X \subset Y$	set X is included in set Y
0	numerical zero, or zero matrix
θ	null (zero) vector
$\emptyset$	empty set
Σ_i	summation over index i
Π_i	multiplication over index i
$\cap_i$	intersection over index i
$\cup_i$	union over index i
∞	infinity
$\int$	integration

Part I

LINEAR STRUCTURE AND STABILITY OF ECONOMIC SYSTEMS

Chapter 1

Fundamentals of Square Matrices

1.1 Determinants, Inversion of Matrices, and Partitioned Matrices

This section is intended to provide fundamental relations concerning determinants and inversion of square matrices, which have frequent applicability in subsequent chapters.

DEFINITION 1 We denote by A a square matrix of order n ($\geqq 2$) with a_{ij} as its (i, j)th component, and by $|A|$ or $\det A$ the *determinant* of A defined as

$$|A| \equiv \sum(-1)^{P(s)} \prod_{i=1}^{n} a_{is(i)}, \tag{1}$$

where the sequence $\{s(1), s(2), \ldots, s(n)\} \equiv S$ stands for a combination of n integers $1, 2, \ldots, n$; $P(s)$ is the frequency of interchanges of the numbers required to reach the sequence S starting from $N \equiv \{1, 2, \ldots, n\}$, the sequence of the first n integers in increasing order; and the summation covers all $n!$ cases of these different combinations of the integers.

Example When $n = 3$, $|A|$ is equal to

$$a_{11}a_{22}a_{33} - a_{12}a_{21}a_{33} + a_{12}a_{23}a_{31} - a_{13}a_{22}a_{31} + a_{13}a_{21}a_{32} - a_{11}a_{23}a_{32},$$

which may be rearranged as

$$a_{11}a_{22}a_{33} - a_{21}a_{12}a_{33} + a_{21}a_{32}a_{13} - a_{31}a_{22}a_{13} + a_{31}a_{12}a_{23} - a_{11}a_{32}a_{23}.$$

The above example suggests that $|A|$ may be redefined as

$$|A| = \sum(-1)^{P(r)} \prod_{j=1}^{n} a_{r(j)j}, \tag{2}$$

where the sequence $\{r(1), r(2), \ldots, r(n)\} \equiv R$ stands for a combination of

$1, 2, \ldots, n$. The second definition (2) of determinant is found to be equivalent to the first definition (1) applied to A^{T}, the transpose of A, since the (i, j)th component of A^{T} is a_{ji}. Thus we know

$$|A^{\mathrm{T}}| = |A|. \tag{3}$$

If two rows (or columns) are interchanged in matrix A, there occurs an interchange of two subscripts $s(i)$ in (1) (or $r(j)$ in (2)) and hence its determinant is equal to $-|A|$. From this fact it follows that if two rows (or columns) of a matrix A are identical, its determinant vanishes.

Let a_i denote the ith row of A and $A[k : a_i]$ the matrix A with the kth row replaced by a_i. Then for an arbitrary scalar c,

$$\det A[k : ca_i] = \begin{cases} c|A| & \text{if} \quad k = i, \\ 0 & \text{if} \quad k \neq i. \end{cases} \tag{4}$$

If each component of A is multiplied by c, then

$$|cA| = c^n |A|. \tag{5}$$

By definition (1),

$$\det A[k : a_i + a_h] = \det A[k : a_i] + \det A[k : a_h]. \tag{6}$$

From (4) and (6) it follows that for arbitrary scalars c_i,

$$\det A[k : a_k + \sum_{i \neq k} c_i a_i] = |A|, \tag{7}$$

$$\det A[k : \sum_{i \neq k} c_i a_i] = 0. \tag{8}$$

(8) implies that if one row is linearly dependent on the other rows, the determinant must vanish. Notice that the above discussion is also applicable to the cases in which columns instead of rows are interchanged.

Let A, B be real square matrices of order n with a^i denoting the ith column of A and b_{ij} the (i, j)th component of B. Then, $AB = [a^1, \ldots, a^n]B = [\sum_{i=1}^n b_{i1} a^i, \ldots, \sum_{i=1}^n b_{in} a^i]$. In view of (6) and (8),

$$|AB| = \sum |b_{r(1)1} a^{r(1)}, \ldots, b_{r(n)n} a^{r(n)}|,$$

where $\{r(1), \ldots, r(n)\}$ is a combination of $1, 2, \ldots, n$, and the summation covers all $n!$ cases of the distinct combinations. Taking account of (4) and (2), we have

$$\begin{aligned} |AB| &= \sum \prod_{j=1}^n b_{r(j)j} |a^{r(1)}, \ldots, a^{r(n)}| \\ &= b_{11} b_{22} \cdots b_{nn} |A| + b_{21} b_{12} b_{33} \cdots b_{nn} (-1) |A| + \cdots \\ &= \sum (-1)^{P(r)} \prod_{j=1}^n b_{r(j)j} |A| = |A| \; |B|. \end{aligned} \tag{9}$$

Let b^i be the ith column of B. By (6),

$$|A + B| = |a^1 + b^1, a^2 + b^2, \ldots, a^n + b^n| = \sum |v^1, v^2, \ldots, v^n|, \tag{10}$$

where v^i represents a^i or b^i and the summation covers the 2^n cases of all distinct combinations of the representation.

Using the above properties of determinants, we show a relation concerning a special type of determinant.

THEOREM 1 For arbitrary scalars c_i $(i = 1, 2, \ldots, n)$

$$\begin{vmatrix} 1 & 1 & \cdots & 1 \\ c_1 & c_2 & & c_n \\ c_1^2 & c_2^2 & & c_n^2 \\ \vdots & \vdots & & \vdots \\ c_1^{n-1} & c_2^{n-1} & \cdots & c_n^{n-1} \end{vmatrix} = \prod_{k>i} (c_k - c_i), \qquad \begin{array}{l} i = 1, 2, \ldots, n-1, \\ k = 2, 3, \ldots, n, \end{array} \tag{11}$$

where the left-hand side is called the *Vandermonde determinant* of order n.

PROOF Let $\Delta(c_1, \ldots, c_n)$ denote the above Vandermonde determinant. Subtracting the first column from all the other columns yields

$$\Delta(c_1, \ldots, c_n) = \begin{vmatrix} 1 & 0 & \cdots & 0 \\ c_1 & c_2 - c_1 & & c_n - c_1 \\ \vdots & \vdots & & \vdots \\ c_1^{n-1} & c_2^{n-1} - c_1^{n-1} & \cdots & c_n^{n-1} - c_1^{n-1} \end{vmatrix}$$

$$= \begin{vmatrix} c_2 - c_1 & \cdots & c_n - c_1 \\ \vdots & & \vdots \\ c_2^{n-1} - c_1^{n-1} & \cdots & c_n^{n-1} - c_1^{n-1} \end{vmatrix}.$$

Applying the operation (row i) $-$ c_1 (row $i - 1$) for each row, we get

$$\Delta(c_1, \ldots, c_n) = \begin{vmatrix} c_2 - c_1 & \cdots & c_n - c_1 \\ (c_2 - c_1)c_2 & & (c_n - c_1)c_n \\ \vdots & & \vdots \\ (c_2 - c_1)c_2^{n-2} & \cdots & (c_n - c_1)c_n^{n-2} \end{vmatrix}$$

$$= \prod_{k=2}^{n} (c_k - c_1) \begin{vmatrix} 1 & \cdots & 1 \\ c_2 & & c_n \\ \vdots & & \vdots \\ c_2^{n-2} & \cdots & c_n^{n-2} \end{vmatrix} = \prod_{k=2}^{n} (c_k - c_1) \cdot \Delta(c_2, \ldots, c_n).$$

Proceeding in the same manner, we have

$$\Delta(c_2, \ldots, c_n) = \prod_{k=3}^{n} (c_k - c_2) \cdot \Delta(c_3, \ldots, c_n),$$

$$\vdots$$

$$\Delta(c_{n-1}, c_n) = (c_n - c_{n-1}).$$

(11) follows from these results. Q.E.D.

Let A_{ij} denote the cofactor of a_{ij} in A; i.e.,

$$A_{ij} \equiv (-1)^{i+j} |S_{ij}|, \tag{12}$$

where S_{ij} stands for the submatrix of A after deleting its ith row and jth column. Then, the determinant of A can be expanded as

$$|A| = \sum_{i=1}^{n} a_{ij} A_{ij} = \sum_{j=1}^{n} a_{ij} A_{ij}. \tag{13}$$

This is named the *Laplace expansion* with respect to column j or with respect to row i, respectively. (13) can be verified by definition (1) or (2) of determinant, and by taking (12) into consideration. We remark that $\sum_{i=1}^{n} a_{ij} A_{it}$ for $t \neq j$ and $\sum_{j=1}^{n} a_{ij} A_{kj}$ for $k \neq i$ must vanish since these are the cases where A contains two identical columns and two identical rows, respectively. Let adj A designate the adjoint of A; i.e.,

$$\text{adj } A \equiv \begin{bmatrix} A_{11} & A_{21} & \cdots & A_{n1} \\ A_{12} & A_{22} & \cdots & A_{n2} \\ \vdots & \vdots & & \vdots \\ A_{1n} & A_{2n} & \cdots & A_{nn} \end{bmatrix}. \tag{14}$$

Then, from (13) and the above remark it follows that

$$A[\text{adj } A] = [\text{adj } A]A = \underbrace{\begin{bmatrix} |A| & 0 & \cdots & 0 \\ 0 & |A| & & 0 \\ \vdots & & \ddots & \\ 0 & 0 & & |A| \end{bmatrix}}_{(n)} = |A| \cdot I, \tag{15}$$

where I stands for the identity matrix of order n.

THEOREM 2 Denote by adj $A_m[{}^{1}_{1} {}^{\cdots}_{\cdots} {}^{m}_{m}]$ the square matrix of order m composed of the first m rows and m columns of adj A, and by $A_{n-m}[{}^{m+1}_{m+1} {}^{\cdots}_{\cdots} {}^{n}_{n}]$ the square matrix of order $n - m$ composed of the last $n - m$ rows and $n - m$ columns of A. Then for m, $1 \leqq m \leqq n$ (with $A_0 \equiv 1$),

$$\left| \text{adj } A_m \begin{bmatrix} 1 & \cdots & m \\ 1 & \cdots & m \end{bmatrix} \right| = |A|^{m-1} \cdot \left| A_{n-m} \begin{bmatrix} m+1 & \cdots & n \\ m+1 & \cdots & n \end{bmatrix} \right|. \tag{16}$$

PROOF

$$A \cdot \begin{bmatrix} A_{11} & \cdots & A_{m1} & 0 & \cdots & 0 \\ \vdots & & \vdots & \vdots & \ddots & \vdots \\ A_{1m} & \cdots & A_{mm} & 0 & \cdots & 0 \\ A_{1m+1} & \cdots & A_{mm+1} & 1 & \cdots & 0 \\ \vdots & & \vdots & \vdots & \ddots & \vdots \\ A_{1n} & \cdots & A_{mn} & 0 & \cdots & 1 \end{bmatrix} = \begin{bmatrix} |A| & \cdots & 0 & a_{1m+1} & \cdots & a_{1n} \\ \vdots & \ddots & \vdots & \vdots & & \vdots \\ 0 & \cdots & |A| & a_{mm+1} & \cdots & a_{mn} \\ 0 & \cdots & 0 & a_{m+1m+1} & \cdots & a_{m+1n} \\ \vdots & \ddots & \vdots & \vdots & & \vdots \\ 0 & \cdots & 0 & a_{nm+1} & \cdots & a_{nn} \end{bmatrix}.$$

Taking determinants on both sides of this relation yields (16). Q.E.D.

The following corollary is a generalized version of (16), which can be verified in a similar manner.

COROLLARY 1 Select two sequences $\{i_1, \ldots, i_m\}$ and $\{j_1, \ldots, j_m\}$ independently from $\{1, 2, \ldots, n\} \equiv N$ and denote the rest of N after the selections as the sequences $\{i_{m+1}, \ldots, i_n\}$ and $\{j_{m+1}, \ldots, j_n\}$, respectively. Let $\operatorname{adj} A_m \left[\begin{smallmatrix} j_1 & \cdots & j_m \\ i_1 & \cdots & i_m \end{smallmatrix}\right]$ be the square matrix of order m composed of rows $j_1, \ldots, j_m$ and columns $i_1, \ldots, i_m$ of $\operatorname{adj} A$, and let $A_{n-m} \left[\begin{smallmatrix} i_{m+1} & \cdots & i_n \\ j_{m+1} & \cdots & j_n \end{smallmatrix}\right]$ be the square matrix of order $n - m$ composed of rows $i_{m+1}, \ldots, i_n$ and columns $j_{m+1}, \ldots, j_n$ of A. Then for m, $1 \leqq m \leqq n$,

$$(-1)^{i_1+\cdots+i_m+j_1+\cdots+j_m} \left| \operatorname{adj} A_m \begin{bmatrix} j_1 & \cdots & j_m \\ i_1 & \cdots & i_m \end{bmatrix} \right| = |A|^{m-1} \cdot \left| A_{n-m} \begin{bmatrix} i_{m+1} & \cdots & i_n \\ j_{m+1} & \cdots & j_n \end{bmatrix} \right|. \tag{17}$$

Setting $m = 2$ and $i_1 = i, i_2 = h, j_1 = k, j_2 = j$ in (17), we obtain a useful theorem frequently applied to economic theory, Jacobi's theorem.

COROLLARY 2 (*Jacobi's ratio theorem*) Let $A_{ik,hj}$ be the cofactor of a_{hj} in A_{ik}. Then

$$\begin{vmatrix} A_{ik} & A_{hk} \\ A_{ij} & A_{hj} \end{vmatrix} = |A| \cdot A_{ik,hj} \qquad \text{for} \quad h \neq i \quad \text{and} \quad k \neq j, \tag{18}$$

or by setting $i = j$, we have

$$A_{ii}A_{hk} - A_{hi}A_{ik} = -|A|A_{ik,hi} = |A|A_{ii,hk} \qquad \text{for} \quad h, k \neq i. \tag{19}$$

COROLLARY 3 Consider the case where A is partitioned as

$$A = \begin{bmatrix} A_{(m)} & H \\ 0 & A_{(n-m)} \end{bmatrix},$$

where 0 stands for a matrix composed of all zeros, $A_{(n-m)} \equiv A_{n-m} \left[\begin{smallmatrix} m+1 & \cdots & n \\ m+1 & \cdots & n \end{smallmatrix}\right]$ and $A_{(m)} \equiv A_m \left[\begin{smallmatrix} 1 & \cdots & m \\ 1 & \cdots & m \end{smallmatrix}\right]$. Then for m, $1 \leqq m < n$,

$$|A| = |A_{(m)}| \, |A_{(n-m)}|. \tag{20}$$

PROOF In this case

$$\left[\operatorname{adj} A_m \begin{bmatrix} 1 & \cdots & m \\ 1 & \cdots & m \end{bmatrix} \right] \cdot A_{(m)} = \underbrace{\begin{bmatrix} |A| & & 0 \\ & \ddots & \\ 0 & & |A| \end{bmatrix}}_{(m)}$$

(a diagonal matrix). Thus, from (16) it follows that

$$|A|^m = |A|^{m-1} \cdot |A_{(n-m)}| \cdot |A_{(m)}|. \qquad \text{Q.E.D.}$$

Now we turn to inversion of square matrices.

DEFINITION 2 A square matrix A is said to be *nonsingular* or *regular* unless its determinant vanishes, and in this case the *inverse* of A, denoted by A^{-1}, is defined as

$$A^{-1} \equiv \frac{1}{|A|} [\text{adj } A]. \tag{21}$$

From this definition it follows that

$$[A^{\mathrm{T}}]^{-1} = \frac{1}{|A^{\mathrm{T}}|} [\text{adj } A^{\mathrm{T}}] = \frac{1}{|A|} [\text{adj } A]^{\mathrm{T}} = [A^{-1}]^{\mathrm{T}}. \tag{22}$$

It is clear by definition (21) and (15) that

$$A^{-1}A = AA^{-1} = I. \tag{23}$$

(9) implies $|AA^{-1}| = |A|\,|A^{-1}|$, and hence

$$|A^{-1}| = |A|^{-1}. \tag{24}$$

Considering (24) and $[\text{adj } A^{-1}]\, A^{-1} = |A^{-1}|I$, we have

$$[A^{-1}]^{-1} = \frac{1}{|A^{-1}|} [\text{adj } A^{-1}] = |A|\,|A^{-1}|A = A. \tag{25}$$

Let A and B be nonsingular matrices of order n. Then

$$[AB]^{-1} = B^{-1}A^{-1}, \tag{26}$$

since $ABB^{-1}A^{-1} = I$.

Consider a linear system

$$Ax = b, \tag{27}$$

where A stands for an $n \times n$ matrix, b a column n-vector, and x a column n-vector to be determined. If A is nonsingular,

$$x = A^{-1}b = \frac{1}{|A|} [\text{adj } A]\, b.$$

The ith component of x is then written as

$$x_i = \frac{1}{|A|} [\text{adj } A]_i b = \frac{1}{|A|} \det A[i : b], \tag{28}$$

where $[\text{adj } A]_i$ denotes the ith row of adj A, and $\det A[i : b]$ the determinant of A after substituting b for its ith column. (28) is termed *Cramer's rule.* Suppose b is a null vector in (27). Then, in case A is nonsingular, x must be null because of Cramer's rule. Therefore, in order for x satisfying

$$Ax = \theta \tag{29}$$

to be nonzero, matrix A must be singular. Note θ denotes a null vector.

The following theorem shows how a matrix of large order can be inverted by means of a partition.

THEOREM 3 Suppose a square matrix A is partitioned as

$$A = \begin{bmatrix} B & C \\ L & D \end{bmatrix}, \tag{30}$$

where B and D are square matrices. If B is nonsingular,

$$A^{-1} = \begin{bmatrix} B^{-1} + B^{-1}CD^*LB^{-1} & -B^{-1}CD^* \\ -D^*LB^{-1} & D^* \end{bmatrix}, \quad \text{where} \quad D^* \equiv [D-LB^{-1}C]^{-1}. \tag{31}$$

If D is nonsingular,

$$A^{-1} = \begin{bmatrix} B^* & -B^*CD^{-1} \\ -D^{-1}LB^* & D^{-1} + D^{-1}LB^*CD^{-1} \end{bmatrix}, \quad \text{where} \quad B^* \equiv [B - CD^{-1}L]^{-1}. \tag{32}$$

PROOF A straightforward multiplication AA^{-1} verifies the above statements. Q.E.D.

THEOREM 4 Suppose A is partitioned as in (30). If B is nonsingular, we have

$$|A| = |B| \cdot |D - LB^{-1}C|, \tag{33}$$

and if D is nonsingular, we get

$$|A| = |D| \cdot |B - CD^{-1}L|. \tag{34}$$

PROOF Let the orders of B and D be m and $n - m$, respectively. Then, D is rewritten as $A_{n-m}\left[\begin{smallmatrix} m+1 & \cdots & n \\ m+1 & \cdots & n \end{smallmatrix}\right]$ in Theorem 2, and hence (16) holds, i.e.,

$$|\text{adj } A_{(B)}| = |A|^{m-1} \cdot |D|, \tag{$*$}$$

where $\text{adj } A_{(B)} \equiv \text{adj } A_m\left[\begin{smallmatrix} 1 & \cdots & m \\ 1 & \cdots & m \end{smallmatrix}\right]$. On the other hand, comparison of (32) with (21) yields

$$\text{adj } A_{(B)} = |A| \, [B - CD^{-1}L]^{-1}.$$

Taking the determinant of this matrix equation, we get

$$|\text{adj } A_{(B)}| = |A|^m \cdot |B - CD^{-1}L|^{-1}. \tag{$**$}$$

(34) follows from ($*$) and ($**$). (33) can be verified similarly. Q.E.D.

As a corollary to Theorem 3, we remark that if L is a zero matrix 0 in the partition (30), then (31) and (32) reduce to

$$\begin{bmatrix} B & C \\ 0 & D \end{bmatrix}^{-1} = \begin{bmatrix} B^{-1} & -B^{-1}CD^{-1} \\ 0 & D^{-1} \end{bmatrix}. \tag{35}$$

Moreover if $C = 0$, then (35) is further reduced to

$$\begin{bmatrix} B & 0 \\ 0 & D \end{bmatrix}^{-1} = \begin{bmatrix} B^{-1} & 0 \\ 0 & D^{-1} \end{bmatrix}. \tag{36}$$

Thus, the inverse of a diagonal matrix is the diagonal matrix composed of the inverses of the diagonal components.

If $C = 0$ and $L \neq 0$, then (31) and (32) reduce to

$$\begin{bmatrix} B & 0 \\ L & D \end{bmatrix}^{-1} = \begin{bmatrix} B^{-1} & 0 \\ -D^{-1}LB^{-1} & D^{-1} \end{bmatrix}. \tag{37}$$

THEOREM 5 Let I be the identity matrix of order n, 0 a zero matrix of the same order, and k a real scalar. Then for $r \geqq 1$

$$\underbrace{\begin{bmatrix} kI & -I & 0 & \cdots & 0 \\ 0 & kI & -I & \ddots & 0 \\ \vdots & & \ddots & & -I \\ 0 & 0 & & & kI \end{bmatrix}}_{(r\times n)}{}^{-1} = \begin{bmatrix} k^{-1}I & k^{-2}I & k^{-3}I & \cdots & k^{-r}I \\ 0 & k^{-1}I & k^{-2}I & & k^{-r+1}I \\ \vdots & & & \ddots & \\ 0 & 0 & & & k^{-1}I \end{bmatrix}. \tag{38}$$

PROOF We apply a mathematical induction on order r. For $r = 1$, (38) holds trivially. Assume (38) holds for order $r - 1$ ($r \geqq 2$). Then, applying (35) to the partitioned matrix

$$\begin{bmatrix} B & C \\ 0 & D \end{bmatrix} \equiv \left[\begin{array}{c|cccc} kI & -I & 0 & \cdots & 0 \\ \hline 0 & kI & -I & \ddots & 0 \\ \vdots & & \ddots & & -I \\ 0 & 0 & & & kI \end{array}\right],$$

and taking account of the induction assumption, we obtain (38) since

$$-B^{-1}C = [k^{-1}I \quad 0 \cdot \cdot \cdot 0]. \qquad \text{Q.E.D.}$$

In a similar way, the following can be proved.

COROLLARY For I, 0, k, and r defined as in Theorem 5,

$$\begin{bmatrix} kI & I & 0 & \cdots & 0 \\ 0 & kI & I & \ddots & 0 \\ \vdots & & \ddots & & I \\ 0 & 0 & & & kI \end{bmatrix}^{-1} = \begin{bmatrix} k^{-1}I & -k^{-2}I & k^{-3}I & \cdots & (-1)^{r-1}k^{-r}I \\ 0 & k^{-1}I & -k^{-2}I & & \\ \vdots & & & \ddots & -k^{-2}I \\ 0 & 0 & & & k^{-1}I \end{bmatrix}. \tag{39}$$

THEOREM 6 Let A_i ($i = 0, 1, \ldots, r$) be square matrices of order n, and I and 0 the identity and zero matrices of the same order respectively, and

k a real scalar. Then for $r \geqq 1$,

$$\underbrace{\begin{vmatrix} kI & -I & 0 & \cdots & 0 & 0 \\ 0 & kI & -I & & 0 & 0 \\ \vdots & & & \ddots & & \vdots \\ & & \ddots & & -I & 0 \\ 0 & 0 & & & kI & -I \\ A_0 & A_1 & \cdots & & A_{r-1} & A_r \end{vmatrix}}_{((r+1)\times n)} = |k^r A_r + k^{r-1}A_{r-1} + \cdots + kA_1 + A_0|. \tag{40}$$

PROOF We partition the matrix on the left-hand side of (40) as

$$\left[\begin{array}{cccccc|c} kI & -I & 0 & \cdots & & 0 & 0 \\ 0 & kI & -I & & & 0 & 0 \\ & & & & \ddots & & \vdots \\ \vdots & & & \ddots & & -I & 0 \\ 0 & 0 & & & & kI & -I \\ \hline A_0 & A_1 & & \cdots & & A_{r-1} & A_r \end{array}\right] \equiv \left[\begin{array}{c|c} B & C \\ \hline L & D \end{array}\right]. \tag{***}$$

Then B^{-1} is equivalent to the left-hand side of (38), $|B| = k^{rn}$, and

$$-LB^{-1}C = k^{-r}A_0 + k^{-r+1}A_1 + \cdots + k^{-1}A_{r-1}.$$

By (33) we get the determinant of (***) as

$$\begin{aligned} |B| \cdot |D - LB^{-1}C| &= k^{rn}|k^{-r}A_0 + k^{-r+1}A_1 + \cdots + k^{-1}A_{r-1} + A_r| \\ &= |A_0 + kA_1 + \cdots + k^{r-1}A_{r-1} + k^r A_r|. \end{aligned}$$

Q.E.D.

Putting $r = 1$ in (40) yields

$$\begin{vmatrix} kI & -I \\ A_0 & A_1 \end{vmatrix} = |kA_1 + A_0|. \tag{40$'$}$$

COROLLARY 1 Assume the same notation as in Theorem 6. Then

$$\underbrace{\begin{vmatrix} kI & -I & 0 & \cdots & 0 \\ 0 & kI & -I & & \vdots \\ \vdots & & \ddots & & 0 \\ 0 & 0 & & kI & -I \\ A_0 & A_1 & \cdots & A_{r-2} & kI + A_{r-1} \end{vmatrix}}_{(r\times n)} = |k^r I + k^{r-1}A_{r-1} + \cdots + kA_1 + A_0|. \tag{41}$$

PROOF Replace A_r in (40) by $kI + A_r$ and reduce the order to $r - 1$.

Q.E.D.

COROLLARY 2 If $n = 1$ in the above corollary, then

$$\begin{vmatrix} k & -1 & 0 & \cdots & 0 \\ 0 & k & -1 & & \vdots \\ \vdots & & \ddots & \ddots & 0 \\ 0 & 0 & & k & -1 \\ a_0 & a_1 & \cdots & a_{r-2} & k + a_{r-1} \end{vmatrix} = k^r + k^{r-1}a_{r-1} + \cdots + ka_1 + a_0 \equiv \phi(k), \tag{42}$$

where a_i ($i = 0, 1, \ldots, r - 1$) are scalars.

In general, the following matrix is said to be the *companion matrix* of $\phi(k)$:

$$\begin{bmatrix} 0 & 1 & 0 & \cdots & 0 \\ 0 & 0 & 1 & & \vdots \\ \vdots & & \ddots & \ddots & 0 \\ 0 & 0 & \cdots & 0 & 1 \\ -a_0 & -a_1 & \cdots & -a_{r-2} & -a_{r-1} \end{bmatrix}$$

Putting $r = 2$ in (41) yields

$$\begin{vmatrix} kI & -I \\ A_0 & kI + A_1 \end{vmatrix} = |k^2I + kA_1 + A_0|. \tag{41'}$$

THEOREM 7 Let A_i ($i = 0, 1, \ldots, r$) be square matrices of order n, I the identity matrix, and 0 the zero matrix of the same order. Then for $r \geqq 1$,

$$\begin{vmatrix} -I & I & 0 & \cdots & 0 \\ 0 & -I & I & & \vdots \\ \vdots & & \ddots & \ddots & 0 \\ 0 & 0 & & -I & I \\ A_0 & A_1 & \cdots & A_{r-1} & A_r \end{vmatrix} = (-1)^{rn}|A_0 + A_1 + \cdots + A_r|. \tag{43}$$

PROOF We partition the matrix associated with the determinant on the left-hand side of (43) as

$$\left[\begin{array}{cccc:c} -I & I & 0 & \cdots & 0 \\ 0 & -I & I & & \vdots \\ \vdots & & \ddots & \ddots & 0 \\ 0 & 0 & & -I & I \\ \hdashline A_0 & A_1 & \cdots & A_{r-1} & A_r \end{array}\right] = \left[\begin{array}{c:c} B & C \\ \hdashline L & D \end{array}\right].$$

Then, $|B| = (-1)^{rn}$, and by setting $k = -1$ in (39) we have

$$B^{-1} = \underbrace{\begin{bmatrix} -I & -I & -I & \cdots & -I \\ 0 & -I & -I & \cdots & -I \\ \vdots & & \ddots & \ddots & \vdots \\ & & & & -I \\ 0 & 0 & \cdots & 0 & -I \end{bmatrix}}_{(r\times n)}.$$

Thus, applying formula (33) yields (43). Q.E.D.

When $r = 1$, (43) is reduced to

$$\begin{vmatrix} -I & I \\ A_0 & A_1 \end{vmatrix} = (-1)^n |A_0 + A_1|. \tag{43'}$$

1.2 Eigenvalues, Eigenvectors, and the Generalized Eigenvalue Problem

This section is concerned with eigenvalue problems that are particularly essential for the study of the operation of linear economic systems.

DEFINITION 3 The scalars λ satisfying the characteristic equation (44) below of a square matrix A are termed the *eigenvalues* (or *characteristic roots*) of A.

$$|\lambda I - A| = 0. \tag{44}$$

Let λ_i be an eigenvalue of A. Then, the solutions v_i of

$$[\lambda_i I - A]v_i = \theta \tag{45}$$

are said to be the *eigenvectors* (or *characteristic vectors*) of A associated with λ_i. (We denote by θ a zero (null) vector throughout the book.)

Note that any eigenvalue of A is a continuous function of the elements of A.

THEOREM 8 For any nonsingular matrix P of the same order as a square matrix A, $P^{-1}AP \equiv B$ and A have identical eigenvalues. B and A are said to be *similar* to each other.

PROOF Taking determinants on both sides of

$$[\lambda I - P^{-1}AP] = P^{-1}[\lambda I - A]P$$

yields

$$|\lambda I - P^{-1}AP| = |P|^{-1}|\lambda I - A||P| = |\lambda I - A|. \qquad \text{Q.E.D.}$$

Let A and B be square matrices of the same order, and suppose one of them, say A, is nonsingular. Then, since $A^{-1}ABA = BA$, the products AB and BA have identical eigenvalues in view of Theorem 8.

In this section A is assumed to be a real square matrix of order $n \geqq 2$ with a_{ij} as its (i, j)th component. We shall show that for matrix A there always exists a nonsingular matrix P such that

$$P^{-1}AP = \begin{bmatrix} 0 & 1 & 0 & \cdots & 0 \\ 0 & 0 & 1 & & \vdots \\ \vdots & \vdots & & \ddots & 0 \\ 0 & 0 & \cdots & 0 & 1 \\ -a_0 & -a_1 & \cdots & -a_{n-2} & -a_{n-1} \end{bmatrix}, \tag{46}$$

where

$$\begin{aligned} a_{n-1} &\equiv -\sum_{i=1}^{n} a_{ii}, \\ a_{n-2} &\equiv (-1)^2 \sum_{i,j=1,\ i<j}^{n} \begin{vmatrix} a_{ii} & a_{ij} \\ a_{ji} & a_{jj} \end{vmatrix}, \\ &\ \ \vdots \\ a_r &\equiv (-1)^{n-r} \sum_{\substack{i,j,\ldots,k=1, \\ i<j<\cdots<k}}^{n} \underbrace{\begin{vmatrix} a_{ii} & a_{ij} & \cdots & a_{ik} \\ a_{ji} & a_{jj} & \cdots & a_{jk} \\ \vdots & \vdots & & \\ a_{ki} & a_{kj} & \cdots & a_{kk} \end{vmatrix}}_{(n-r)}, \\ &\ \ \vdots \\ a_0 &\equiv (-1)^n |A|. \end{aligned} \tag{47}$$

Example In case $n = 2$,

$$P \equiv \begin{bmatrix} a_{12} & 0 \\ -a_{11} & 1 \end{bmatrix} \quad \text{transforms} \quad A \equiv \begin{bmatrix} a_{11} & a_{12} \\ a_{21} & a_{22} \end{bmatrix}$$

into

$$P^{-1}AP = \begin{bmatrix} 0 & 1 \\ a_{12}a_{21} - a_{11}a_{22} & a_{11} + a_{22} \end{bmatrix}, \quad \text{where} \quad P^{-1} \equiv \begin{bmatrix} 1/a_{12} & 0 \\ a_{11}/a_{12} & 1 \end{bmatrix}.$$

The verification of the existence of a matrix P satisfying (46) will be given by a corollary to the following theorem.

THEOREM 9 The characteristic polynomial of A can be expanded as

$$|\lambda I - A| = \lambda^n + a_{n-1}\lambda^{n-1} + \cdots + a_1\lambda + a_0, \tag{48}$$

where the coefficients a_i $(i = 0, 1, \ldots, n-1)$ are those defined by (47).

PROOF Let a^i be the ith column vector of A and e^i the column unit n-vector with one as the ith component and zeros otherwise. Then

$$|A - \lambda I| = |a^1 - \lambda e^1, a^2 - \lambda e^2, \ldots, a^n - \lambda e^n| = \sum |b^1, b^2, \ldots, b^n|, \tag{49}$$

where b^i represents a^i or $-\lambda e^i$, and the summation covers all 2^n cases of different combinations. Consider two determinants among these combinations:

$$|a^1, \ldots, a^r, -\lambda e^{r+1}, \ldots, -\lambda e^n| = \begin{vmatrix} a_{11} & \cdots & a_{1r} \\ \vdots & & \vdots \\ a_{r1} & \cdots & a_{rr} \end{vmatrix} (-\lambda)^{n-r},$$

and

$$|a^1, \ldots, a^{r-1}, -\lambda e^r, a^{r+1}, -\lambda e^{r+2}, \ldots, -\lambda e^n|$$

$$= \begin{vmatrix} a_{11} & \cdots & a_{1,r-1} & a_{1,r+1} \\ \vdots & & & \vdots \\ a_{r-1,1} & \cdots & & a_{r-1,r+1} \\ a_{r+1,1} & \cdots & & a_{r+1,r+1} \end{vmatrix} (-\lambda)^{n-r}.$$

These two determinants indicate that any determinant in (49) involving $n-r$ unit vectors must be $(-\lambda)^{n-r}$ times a principal minor (of A) of order r. Thus

$$|A - \lambda I| = \sum_{r=0}^{n} (-\lambda)^{n-r} M_{n-r},$$

where M_{n-r} stands for the sum of all the principal minors of A of order r, with $M_0 \equiv |A|$ and $M_n \equiv 1$. Hence

$$\begin{aligned} |\lambda I - A| &= (-1)^n |A - \lambda I| \\ &= \sum_{r=0}^{n} (-1)^r \cdot M_{n-r} \lambda^{n-r} \\ &= \lambda^n + (-1) \sum_{i=1}^{n} a_{ii} \lambda^{n-1} + (-1)^2 \sum_{i<j} \begin{vmatrix} a_{ii} & a_{ij} \\ a_{ji} & a_{jj} \end{vmatrix} \lambda^{n-2} \\ &\quad + \cdots + (-1)^n |A|. \end{aligned}$$

Q.E.D.

COROLLARY By (42) in the preceding section, we have

$$|\lambda I - A| = \lambda^n + a_{n-1}\lambda^{n-1} + \cdots + a_1 \lambda + a_0$$

$$= \begin{vmatrix} \lambda & -1 & 0 & \cdots & 0 \\ 0 & \lambda & -1 & & \vdots \\ \vdots & & \ddots & \ddots & 0 \\ 0 & 0 & & \lambda & -1 \\ a_0 & a_1 & \cdots & a_{n-2} & \lambda + a_{n-1} \end{vmatrix},$$

which implies the existence of a nonsingular matrix P such that (46) holds, in view of Theorem 8.

Let λ_i $(i = 1, \ldots, n)$ be the eigenvalues of matrix A. Then

$$|\lambda I - A| = \prod_{i=1}^{n} (\lambda - \lambda_i), \tag{49'}$$

and hence, in view of (48), the trace of A equals the sum of the λ's:

$$\sum_{i=1}^{n} a_{ii} = \sum_{i=1}^{n} \lambda_i, \qquad \text{and} \qquad |A| = \prod_{i=1}^{n} \lambda_i. \tag{47'}$$

It is clear that if λ is a complex eigenvalue of a matrix A, then its conjugate is also an eigenvalue of A. Let λ be represented by $\alpha + i\beta$ where α and β are real scalar and $i \equiv \sqrt{-1}$. Then its conjugate is expressed as $\bar{\lambda} = \alpha - i\beta$. The eigenvector v of A associated with λ must be complex, say $v = p + iq$, where p and q are real vectors. Then the eigenvector u of A associated with $\bar{\lambda}$ is $u = p - iq$.

THEOREM 10 Let λ be a real eigenvalue of a real square matrix A. Then, the eigenvector associated with λ can be real.

PROOF Suppose $v \equiv p + iq$ is the eigenvector of A associated with real λ. Since $Av = \lambda v$, we have $Ap = \lambda p$ and $Aq = \lambda q$. Obviously, p and q are real eigenvectors associated with λ. Q.E.D.

As we shall see in Section 2.3, the rank k of matrix A is equal to the highest order of its minors that do not vanish. Thus, if k is less than n, the order of A, then $a_0 = a_1 = \cdots = a_{n-k+1} = 0$ in (48), and hence (48) reduces to

$$|\lambda I - A| = \lambda^{n-k}(\lambda^k + a_{n-1}\lambda^{k-1} + \cdots + a_{n-k}), \tag{48'}$$

which implies that at least $n - k$ eigenvalues of A must be zero, or equivalently that there are at most k nonzero eigenvalues.

THEOREM 11 Let A be a nonsingular matrix, λ_i a real eigenvalue of A, and v the associated nontrivial eigenvector. Then λ_i^{-1} is an eigenvalue of A^{-1} and v is the associated eigenvector.

PROOF λ_i is nonzero because $0 \neq |A| = \prod_{i=1}^{n} \lambda_i$. Premultiply $\lambda_i v = Av$ by $\lambda_i^{-1}A^{-1}$. Then we have $[A^{-1} - \lambda_i^{-1}I]v = 0$. Since $v \neq 0$, λ_i^{-1} is an eigenvalue of A^{-1}. Q.E.D.

Let $\psi(\alpha)$ be a polynomial of a real scalar α:

$$\psi(\alpha) \equiv c_0\alpha^p + c_1\alpha^{p-1} + \cdots + c_{p-1}\alpha + c_p.$$

Define a polynomial of a real square matrix A corresponding to $\psi(\alpha)$ as

$$\psi(A) \equiv c_0A^p + c_1A^{p-1} + \cdots + c_{p-1}A + c_pI. \tag{50}$$

Then, we have a relation between the eigenvalues of A and $\psi(A)$.

THEOREM 12 Let λ be an eigenvalue of A. Then $\psi(\lambda)$ is an eigenvalue of $\psi(A)$, where ψ stands for a polynomial.

PROOF Since $\lambda^r I - A^r = (\lambda I - A)(\lambda^{r-1} I + \lambda^{r-2} A + \cdots + \lambda A^{r-2} + A^{r-1})$,

$$\begin{aligned}|\psi(\lambda)I - \psi(A)| &= |c_0(\lambda^p I - A^p) + c_1(\lambda^{p-1} I - A^{p-1}) + \cdots \\ &\qquad + c_{p-1}(\lambda I - A)| \\ &= |\lambda I - A| \cdot F(\lambda, A) = 0,\end{aligned}$$

where $F(\lambda, A)$ denotes the determinant after $|\lambda I - A|$ is factored out.

Q.E.D.

COROLLARY Let λ be an eigenvalue of A, and v the associated eigenvector of A. Then for any positive integer r and any scalar c, $(c\lambda)^r$ is an eigenvalue of $(cA)^r$ and v is the associated eigenvector.

PROOF $c^r \lambda^r v = c^r \lambda^{r-1} \lambda v = c^r A \lambda^{r-1} v = c^r A \lambda^{r-2} \lambda v = c^r A^2 \lambda^{r-2} v = \cdots = c^r A^r v$. Q.E.D.

For convenience we briefly define here the concept of linear independence of vectors. (For a more complete definition, refer to Section 2.1.) If none of the vectors $x_1, x_2, \ldots, x_n$, all of the same dimension, can be represented as a linear combination of the others, these vectors are said to be linearly independent. Otherwise they are linearly dependent.

THEOREM 13 Let $\lambda_1, \ldots, \lambda_k$ be distinct eigenvalues of A, and v_j an eigenvector associated with λ_j $(j = 1, \ldots, k)$. Then, these eigenvectors are linearly independent.

PROOF Suppose that the maximum number of linearly independent eigenvectors is h which is less than k, and that these vectors are $v_1, \ldots, v_h$. Then, there are scalars $c_1, \ldots, c_h$ not all equal to zero such that $v_q = \sum_{j=1}^h c_j v_j$ for q, $h < q \leqq k$. Premultiplying it by A, we have

$$Av_q = \sum_{j=1}^h c_j A v_j = \sum_{j=1}^h c_j \lambda_j v_j,$$

since $Av_j = \lambda_j v_j$. Also $Av_q = \lambda_q v_q = \lambda_q \sum_{j=1}^h c_j v_j$. Thus

$$\sum_{j=1}^h c_j(\lambda_q - \lambda_j) v_j = 0.$$

By assumption, $\lambda_q - \lambda_j \neq 0$ for $j = 1, \ldots, h$. Hence, $v_1, \ldots, v_h$ are linearly dependent, which is a contradiction. Q.E.D.

THEOREM 14 Let λ_1, λ_2 be two distinct eigenvalues of A, and let v_i and u_i be the eigenvectors of A and of A^{T}, respectively, associated with λ_i $(i = 1, 2)$. (We sometimes call v_i the *right eigenvector* and u_i^{T} the *left eigenvector* of A.) Then we have

$$u_1^T v_2 = u_2^T v_1 = 0. \tag{51}$$

PROOF $Av_i = \lambda_i v_i$, $A^T u_i = \lambda_i u_i$ for $i = 1, 2$. Thus

$$u_1^T A v_2 = u_1^T \lambda_2 v_2 = \lambda_2 u_1^T v_2.$$

On the other hand, $u_1^T A v_2 = (A^T u_1)^T v_2 = \lambda_1 u_1^T v_2$. Hence, we get $(\lambda_2 - \lambda_1) \times u_1^T v_2 = 0$ with $\lambda_2 \neq \lambda_1$, which implies $u_1^T v_2 = 0$. Similarly for $u_2^T v_1 = 0$. Q.E.D.

As in (51), when the inner product of two vectors vanishes, they are said to be *orthogonal* to each other.

THEOREM 15 If all the eigenvalues λ_i $(i = 1, \ldots, n)$ of A are distinct, then the following holds for the associated eigenvectors v_i and u_i, respectively, of A and A^T:

$$u_i^T v_i \neq 0 \qquad \text{for} \quad i = 1, 2, \ldots, n. \tag{52}$$

PROOF Suppose, to the contrary, $u_i^T v_i = 0$. Then, taking account of (51), we have $[u_1, \ldots, u_n]^T v_i = \theta$. Since v_i is nonzero, the matrix $[u_1, \ldots, u_n]$ must be singular, i.e., its rank is less than n. This means that vectors $u_1, \ldots, u_n$ are linearly dependent, contradicting the statement of Theorem 13. Q.E.D.

Each eigenvector has a unique proportionality in its components, but its length can be arbitrary. Usually, we normalize eigenvectors such that (52) is equal to one.

THEOREM 16 Assume that all the eigenvalues $\lambda_1, \ldots, \lambda_n$ of A are distinct. Let v_i and u_i be the eigenvectors of A and A^T, respectively, associated with λ_i. Normalizing these eigenvectors such that

$$u_i^T v_i = 1 \qquad \text{for all} \quad i, \tag{53}$$

we have the transformation matrices $M = [v_1, \ldots, v_n]$ and $M^{-1} = [u_1, \ldots, u_n]^T$ by which A is diagonalized as

$$M^{-1}AM = \begin{bmatrix} \lambda_1 & & & 0 \\ & \lambda_2 & & \\ & & \ddots & \\ 0 & & & \lambda_n \end{bmatrix}, \tag{54}$$

where off-diagonal elements are all zero.

PROOF In view of (51) and (53), we have

$$[u_1, \ldots, u_n]^T [v_1, \ldots, v_n] = I$$

and

$$u_i^T A v_j = \lambda_i u_i^T v_j = \begin{cases} \lambda_i & \text{for} \quad i = j, \\ 0 & \text{for} \quad i \neq j. \end{cases} \qquad \text{Q.E.D.}$$

THEOREM 17 For any square matrix A, there exists a nonsingular matrix M such that

$$M^{-1}AM = \Delta, \tag{55}$$

where Δ is a triangular matrix with the eigenvalues of A on its principal diagonal.

PROOF Let $n\,(\geqq 2)$ be the order of A, $\lambda_i\,(i = 1, \ldots, n)$ be its eigenvalues, and v_1 be the normalized eigenvector of A associated with λ_1. Define a nonsingular square matrix M_1 whose first column is v_1. Then the first column of AM_1 is $Av_1 = \lambda_1 v_1$, and hence the first column of $M_1^{-1}AM_1$ becomes

$$M_1^{-1}Av_1 = \lambda_1 M_1^{-1}v_1 = \lambda_1[1, 0, \ldots, 0]^{\mathrm{T}}.$$

Therefore

$$M_1^{-1}AM_1 = \begin{bmatrix} \lambda_1 & B_1 \\ \theta & A_1 \end{bmatrix},$$

where A_1 is a square matrix of order $n - 1$. Since $M_1^{-1}AM_1$ is similar to A, the eigenvalues of the former are the same as those of the latter. From the preceding expression it follows that

$$|\lambda I - M_1^{-1}AM_1| = (\lambda - \lambda_1)|\lambda I - A_1|.$$

Thus, $\lambda_2, \ldots, \lambda_n$ are the eigenvalues of A_1. Let v_2 be the normalized eigenvector of A_1 associated with λ_2, and define a nonsingular square matrix M_2 of order $n - 1$ whose first column is v_2. Then

$$M_2^{-1}A_1M_2 = \begin{bmatrix} \lambda_2 & B_2 \\ \theta & A_2 \end{bmatrix}.$$

Perform a similar transformation on A_2, and we have

$$M_3^{-1}A_2M_3 = \begin{bmatrix} \lambda_3 & B_3 \\ \theta & A_3 \end{bmatrix}.$$

Repeating this procedure $n - 1$ times, we define

$$M \equiv M_1 \begin{bmatrix} I_1 & 0 \\ 0 & M_2 \end{bmatrix} \begin{bmatrix} I_2 & 0 \\ 0 & M_3 \end{bmatrix} \cdots \begin{bmatrix} I_{n-2} & 0 \\ 0 & M_{n-1} \end{bmatrix}, \tag{56}$$

where I_i stands for the identity matrix of order i. M defined in (56) is the matrix that triangularizes A as Δ in (55). Q.E.D.

Consider the generalized eigenvalue problem

$$[\lambda I - A]\,V = \theta, \tag{57}$$

where

$$A \equiv \begin{bmatrix} 0 & I & 0 & \cdots & 0 \\ 0 & 0 & I & & 0 \\ \vdots & \vdots & & \ddots & \\ 0 & 0 & \cdots & 0 & I \\ A_0 & A_1 & \cdots & A_{r-2} & A_{r-1} \end{bmatrix}, \tag{58}$$

and submatrix A_i has order n $(i = 0,1, \ldots, r-1)$. Then

$$|\lambda I - A| = \begin{vmatrix} \lambda I & -I & 0 & \cdots & 0 \\ 0 & \lambda I & -I & & 0 \\ \vdots & & \ddots & \ddots & \\ 0 & 0 & & \lambda I & -I \\ -A_0 & -A_1 & \cdots & -A_{r-2} & \lambda I - A_{r-1} \end{vmatrix} = |B(\lambda)|,$$

where $B(\lambda) \equiv [\lambda^r I - \lambda^{r-1} A_{r-1} - \cdots - \lambda A_1 - A_0]$. Let λ_i be an eigenvalue of A, i.e., $|B(\lambda_i)| = 0$, and define the right eigenvectors of B associated with λ_i as the solutions v_i of $B(\lambda_i)v_i = \mathit{0}$ and its left eigenvectors as the solutions u_i^{T} of $u_i^{\mathrm{T}} B(\lambda_i) = \mathit{0}^{\mathrm{T}}$. We shall study the relation that these vectors bear to the eigenvectors of A defined in (58). The generalized right eigenvector of A associated with an eigenvalue λ_i is given by

$$V_i \equiv \begin{bmatrix} v_i \\ \lambda_i v_i \\ \lambda_i^2 v_i \\ \vdots \\ \lambda_i^{r-1} v_i \end{bmatrix},$$

and the generalized left eigenvectors of A are found to be

$$\begin{aligned} U_i^{\mathrm{T}} \equiv [&\lambda_i^{r-1} u_i^{\mathrm{T}} - \lambda_i^{r-2} u_i^{\mathrm{T}} A_{r-1} - \cdots - u_i^{\mathrm{T}} A_1; \\ &\lambda_i^{r-2} u_i^{\mathrm{T}} - \lambda_i^{r-3} u_i^{\mathrm{T}} A_{r-1} - \cdots - u_i^{\mathrm{T}} A_2; \\ &\cdots; \lambda_i^2 u_i^{\mathrm{T}} - \lambda_i u_i^{\mathrm{T}} A_{r-1} - u_i^{\mathrm{T}} A_{r-2}; \lambda_i u_i^{\mathrm{T}} - u_i^{\mathrm{T}} A_{r-1}; u_i^{\mathrm{T}}]. \end{aligned}$$

Assuming that all eigenvalues λ_i $(i = 1, 2, \ldots, rn)$ of A are distinct, we collect all V_i and U_i^{T} as follows:

$$V_* \equiv \begin{bmatrix} V \\ V\Lambda \\ V\Lambda^2 \\ \vdots \\ V\Lambda^{r-1} \end{bmatrix} = [V_1, V_2, \ldots, V_{rn}], \tag{59}$$

$$\begin{aligned}U_*^{\mathrm{T}} \equiv [&\Lambda^{r-1}U^{\mathrm{T}} - \Lambda^{r-2}U^{\mathrm{T}}A_{r-1} - \cdots - U^{\mathrm{T}}A_1;\\ &\Lambda^{r-2}U^{\mathrm{T}} - \Lambda^{r-3}U^{\mathrm{T}}A_{r-1} - \cdots - U^{\mathrm{T}}A_2;\\ &\ldots; \Lambda^2U^{\mathrm{T}} - \Lambda U^{\mathrm{T}}A_{r-1} - U^{\mathrm{T}}A_{r-2}; \Lambda U^{\mathrm{T}} - U^{\mathrm{T}}A_{r-1}; U^{\mathrm{T}}]\\ = [&U_1, U_2, \ldots, U_{rn}]^{\mathrm{T}},\end{aligned} \tag{60}$$

where

$$\Lambda \equiv \begin{bmatrix} \lambda_1 & & & 0 \\ & \lambda_2 & & \\ & & \ddots & \\ 0 & & & \lambda_{rn} \end{bmatrix}, \qquad U^{\mathrm{T}} \equiv \begin{bmatrix} u_1^{\mathrm{T}} \\ u_2^{\mathrm{T}} \\ \vdots \\ u_{rn}^{\mathrm{T}} \end{bmatrix}, \qquad \text{and} \qquad V \equiv [v_1, v_2, \ldots, v_{rn}].$$

Then $AV_* = V_*\Lambda$, and $U_*^{\mathrm{T}}A = \Lambda U_*^{\mathrm{T}}$.

Noting that $U_i^{\mathrm{T}}V_j = 0$ $(i \neq j)$ and $U_i^{\mathrm{T}}V_i \neq 0$, we normalize V_* and U_*^{T} such that

$$U_*^{\mathrm{T}}V_* = I, \tag{61}$$

and hence we have

$$U_*^{\mathrm{T}}AV_* = \Lambda. \tag{62}$$

An application of the generalized eigenvalue problem is seen at the end of Section 3.3.

1.3 Matrices with Dominant Diagonals and P-Matrices

This section is devoted to matrices with dominant diagonals and other related matrices. Throughout this section matrices A and B are supposed to be of dimension $n \times n$ with $n \geqq 2$; a_{ij} and b_{ij} denote the (i, j)th components of A and B, respectively.

DEFINITION 4 Matrix $A = [a_{ij}]$ is said to have a *column dominant diagonal* or a *column dominance* if there are positive scalars d_i $(i = 1, \ldots, n)$ such that

$$d_j|a_{jj}| > \sum_{i=1, i\neq j}^{n} d_i|a_{ij}| \qquad \text{for} \quad j = 1, \ldots, n, \tag{63}$$

where $|a_{ij}|$ stands for the modulus of a_{ij}. If there are positive scalars d_j $(j = 1, \ldots, n)$ such that

$$|a_{ii}|d_i > \sum_{j=1, j\neq i}^{n} |a_{ij}|d_j \qquad \text{for} \quad i = 1, \ldots, n, \tag{64}$$

then matrix A is said to have a *row dominant diagonal* or a *row dominance*.

Henceforth, dominant diagonal is abbreviated as d.d.; we are concerned with matrices having a column d.d.

Remark If matrix A has a column d.d., it has a row d.d. since $y > \theta$ such that $yB > \theta$ implies $x > \theta$ such that $Bx > \theta$ (see Theorem 30 in Section 2.4), where the (i, j)th entry of B is $-|a_{ij}|$ for $i \neq j$ and the (i, i)th is $|a_{ii}|$.

It is clear by definition that if matrix A has a column d.d., then every principal submatrix of A has a column d.d. and all the diagonal elements of A are nonzero.

DEFINITION 5 An $n \times n$ matrix $B = [b_{ij}]$ with $n \geqq 2$ is said to be a *Hadamard matrix* if it has the property

$$|b_{jj}| > \sum_{i=1, i \neq j}^{n} |b_{ij}| \qquad \text{for} \quad j = 1, \ldots, n. \tag{65}$$

Let D be the diagonal matrix of order n composed of the d_i satisfying (63). Obviously, matrix DA is a Hadamard matrix.

THEOREM 18 A Hadamard matrix is nonsingular.

PROOF Let B be an $n \times n$ Hadamard matrix. Suppose, to the contrary, that B is singular. Then the homogeneous equation system $yB = \theta$ has a nonzero solution $y = (y_1, \ldots, y_n)$. Thus $y_j b_{jj} = -\sum_{i \neq j} y_i b_{ij}$ for $j = 1, \ldots, n$. Hence

$$|y_j|\,|b_{jj}| = |y_j b_{jj}| = \Big|\sum_{i \neq j} y_i b_{ij}\Big| \leqq \sum_{i \neq j} |y_i|\,|b_{ij}| \qquad \text{for all} \quad j.$$

Let k be the subscript for which $|y_k| \geqq |y_i|$ for all i. Then

$$|y_k|\,|b_{kk}| \leqq \sum_{i \neq k} |y_i|\,|b_{ik}| \leqq \sum_{i \neq k} |y_k|\,|b_{ik}|,$$

or

$$|b_{kk}| \leqq \sum_{i \neq k} |b_{ik}|,$$

which is a contradiction. Q.E.D.

COROLLARY Any matrix A having a column d.d. is nonsingular.

PROOF Let D be the diagonal matrix composed of the d_i satisfying (63). Then, DA is nonsingular since DA is a Hadamard matrix. $|D|\,|A| \neq 0$ implies $|A| \neq 0$. Q.E.D.

THEOREM 19 Let λ denote any eigenvalue of matrix A, and N the set of indices $1, 2, \ldots, n$. Then

$$|\lambda| \leqq \max_{j \in N} \sum_{i=1}^{n} |a_{ij}|, \tag{66}$$

and

$$|\lambda| \leqq \max_{i \in N} \sum_{j=1}^{n} |a_{ij}|. \tag{67}$$

PROOF Suppose, to the contrary, that $|\lambda| > \sum_i |a_{ij}|$ for all j. Then, for all j,

$$|\lambda - a_{jj}| \geqq |\lambda| - |a_{jj}| > \textstyle\sum_i |a_{ij}| - |a_{jj}| = \displaystyle\sum_{i \neq j} |a_{ij}|.$$

Hence $[\lambda I - A]$ is a Hadamard matrix and nonsingular, contradicting that λ is an eigenvalue of A. This completes the proof of (66). (67) may be proved in a similar manner. Q.E.D.

THEOREM 20 If B is a Hadamard matrix with negative (main) diagonal, then all of its eigenvalues have negative real parts.

PROOF Suppose, to the contrary, that B has some eigenvalue $\lambda \equiv \alpha + i\beta$ with $\alpha \geqq 0$. Taking $b_{jj} < 0$ into account, we get

$$|\lambda - b_{jj}| = ((\alpha - b_{jj})^2 + \beta^2)^{1/2} \geqq \alpha - b_{jj} = \alpha + |b_{jj}| \geqq |b_{jj}|.$$

Since $|b_{jj}| > \sum_{i \neq j} |b_{ij}|$ for all j, we have $|\lambda - b_{jj}| > \sum_{i \neq j} |b_{ij}|$ for all j, which implies that $[\lambda I - B]$ is a Hadamard matrix, and hence nonsingular. Thus, such λ cannot be an eigenvalue of B. Q.E.D.

McKenzie (1960) generalized the concept of dominant diagonal to the concept of quasi-dominant diagonal as follows. (See Uekawa, 1971.)

DEFINITION 6 Matrix $A = [a_{ij}]$ is said to have a *quasi-dominant diagonal,* abbreviated q.d.d., if there exist positive scalars d_j ($j = 1, \ldots, n$) such that for any nonempty subset J of indices from $N \equiv \{1, \ldots, n\}$,

$$d_j |a_{jj}| \geqq \sum_{i \in J, i \neq j} d_i |a_{ij}| \qquad \text{for} \quad j \in J, \tag{68}$$

with strict inequality for some $j \in J$.

It is clear that if A has a q.d.d., then all the diagonal components of A are nonzero; and that if A has a column d.d., then A has a q.d.d.

THEOREM 21 A matrix A having a q.d.d. is nonsingular.

PROOF Denote $d_i a_{ij}$ in (68) by b_{ij}. Then for any $J \subset N$,

$$|b_{jj}| \geqq \sum_{i \in J, i \neq j} |b_{ij}| \qquad \text{for} \quad j \in J, \tag{69}$$

with strict inequality for some $j \in J$. Let B denote the square matrix whose (i, j)th entry is b_{ij}. Now suppose, to the contrary of the statement, that A is singular. Then B must be singular, and hence there exists a nonzero vector $q \equiv (q_1, \ldots, q_n)^{\mathrm{T}}$ such that $Bq = \theta$. Define the set of indices $P \equiv \{i : q_i \neq 0\}$ and

$$|q_k| \equiv \max_{i \in P} |q_i|. \tag{70}$$

Consider

$$q_j b_{jj} + \sum_{i\in P, i\neq j} q_i b_{ij} = 0 \qquad \text{for} \quad j \in P. \tag{71}$$

It follows from (70) and (71) that

$$|q_k|\,|b_{kk}| = |q_k b_{kk}| = \Big|\sum_{i\in P, i\neq k} q_i b_{ik}\Big| \leqq \sum_{i\in P, i\neq k} |q_i|\,|b_{ik}| \leqq \sum_{i\in P, i\neq k} |q_k|\,|b_{ik}|,$$

or

$$|b_{kk}| \leqq \sum_{i\in P, i\neq k} |b_{ik}|, \tag{72}$$

which contradicts (69) with strict inequality for some $j \in J$, since (72) does not allow $|b_{kk}| > \sum_{i\in P, i\neq k} |b_{ik}|$. Q.E.D.

THEOREM 22 If a matrix A with negative diagonal has a q.d.d., then all of its eigenvalues have negative real parts.

PROOF Suppose that A has an eigenvalue $\lambda \equiv \alpha + i\beta$ with $\alpha \geqq 0$. Then

$$|\lambda - a_{jj}| = ((\alpha - a_{jj})^2 + \beta^2)^{1/2} \geqq \alpha - a_{jj} \geqq |a_{jj}|. \tag{73}$$

Since A has a q.d.d., there exist $d_j > 0$ ($j = 1, \ldots, n$) satisfying (68) with strict inequality for some $j \in J$. It follows from (73) and (68) that there exist $d_j > 0$ ($j = 1, \ldots, n$) such that for any $J \subset N$

$$d_j |\lambda - a_{jj}| \geqq \sum_{i\in J, i\neq j} d_i |a_{ij}| \qquad \text{for} \quad j \in J,$$

with strict inequality for some $j \in J$. This means that $[\lambda I - A]$ has a q.d.d., and that it is nonsingular by Theorem 21. Hence λ cannot be an eigenvalue of A. Q.E.D.

THEOREM 23 Let A be an $n \times n$ real matrix with $a_{ii} > 0$, $a_{ij} \leqq 0$ for $i \neq j$. A necessary and sufficient condition for $Ax = y$ to have a unique solution $x \geqq \theta$ for *any* $y \geqq \theta$ is that A have a q.d.d.

PROOF *Sufficiency* Assume that there exist $d_i > 0$ ($i = 1, \ldots, n$) for which conditions (68) are satisfied. By Theorem 21, A is nonsingular, and a unique solution $x \equiv (x_1, \ldots, x_n)^{\mathrm{T}}$ exists to $Ax = y$. Suppose there are two subsets of indices P, Q of $N \equiv \{1, \ldots, n\}$ such that $P \cap Q = \varnothing$, $P \cup Q = N$, $x_j < 0$ for $j \in P \subset N$, and $x_j \geqq 0$ for $j \in Q \subset N$. Multiplying

$$\sum_{j\in Q} a_{ij} x_j + \sum_{j\in P} a_{ij} x_j = y_i \geqq 0 \qquad \text{for} \quad i \in P$$

by $d_i > 0$ and summing yield

$$\sum_{i\in P}\sum_{j\in Q} d_i a_{ij} x_j + \sum_{j\in P}\sum_{i\in P} d_i a_{ij} x_j = \sum_{i\in P} d_i y_i \geqq 0, \tag{74}$$

where the first term on the left is nonpositive. By the assumed signs of components of A and by (68), we have $\sum_{i\in P} d_i a_{ij} \geqq 0$ for $j \in P$, with strict inequality for some $j \in P$. Taking $x_j < 0$ for $j \in P$ into account, we know that the second term on the left is negative. This contradicts inequality (74), implying that P is empty.

Necessity Suppose $Ax = y$ has a unique $x \geqq \theta$ for *some* $y \geqq \theta$. Then by the assumed signs of a_{ij}, the solution to $Ax = y > \theta$ must be $x \equiv (x_1, \ldots, x_n)^{\mathrm{T}} > \theta$, that is,

$$a_{ii}x_i > \sum_{j=1, j\neq i}^{n} |a_{ij}|x_j \qquad \text{for} \quad i = 1, \ldots, n,$$

which means that A^{T} has a column d.d., and hence that A^{T} has a q.d.d. Then, by the above sufficiency proof, for every $u \geqq \theta$, $A^{\mathrm{T}}v = u$ is solved for a unique $v \geqq \theta$. Thus, for some $u > \theta$, $A^{\mathrm{T}}v = u$ has a unique solution $v \equiv (v_1, \ldots, v_n)^{\mathrm{T}} > \theta$, i.e.,

$$v_j a_{jj} > \sum_{i=1, i\neq j}^{n} v_i |a_{ij}| \qquad \text{for} \quad j = 1, \ldots, n,$$

which means that A has a column d.d., and hence A has a q.d.d.

Note that there is a loop such that "A has a q.d.d." ⇒ "$Ax = y$ has a unique $x \geqq \theta$ for *every* $y \geqq \theta$" ⇒ "$Ax = y$ has a unique $x \geqq \theta$ for *some* $y \geqq \theta$" ⇒ "A^{T} has a column d.d." ⇒ "A^{T} has a q.d.d." ⇒ "A has a column d.d." ⇒ "A has a q.d.d." Q.E.D.

COROLLARY Let A be an $n \times n$ real matrix with $a_{ii} > 0$, $a_{ij} \leqq 0$ for $i \neq j$. A necessary and sufficient condition for $Ax = y$ to have a unique solution $x \geqq \theta$ for *some* $y \geqq \theta$ is that A and/or A^{T} have a q.d.d. or a column d.d.

THEOREM 24 A real matrix A has a q.d.d. if and only if A has a column d.d.

PROOF Since the "if" part is obvious, we prove below the "only if" part. Assume A has a q.d.d. Writing $b_{jj} \equiv |a_{jj}|$ and $b_{ij} \equiv -|a_{ij}|$, we have from (68) for any nonempty $J \subset N$

$$\sum_{i\in J} d_i b_{ij} \geqq 0 \qquad \text{for} \quad j \in J, \tag{68'}$$

with strict inequality for some $j \in J$. Setting $J = N$ in (68′) yields $B^{\mathrm{T}}d \geq \theta$ (semipositive) with $d \equiv (d_1, \ldots, d_n)^{\mathrm{T}} > \theta$, where B is the $n \times n$ matrix whose (i, j)th component is b_{ij}. Since $b_{jj} > 0$ and $b_{ij} \leqq 0$ for $i \neq j$, by the corollary to Theorem 23, B has a column d.d., i.e., there exist $d_j > 0$ ($j = 1, \ldots, n$) such that

$$d_j b_{jj} > \sum_{i=1, i\neq j}^{n} d_i |b_{ij}| \qquad \text{for} \quad j = 1, \ldots, n,$$

or equivalently

$$d_j |a_{jj}| > \sum_{i=1, i\neq j}^{n} d_i |a_{ij}| \qquad \text{for} \quad j = 1, \ldots, n. \qquad \text{Q.E.D.}$$

From Theorem 22 and Theorem 24 we obtain at once

THEOREM 22′ If a real square matrix with negative diagonal has a column d.d., then all of its eigenvalues have negative real parts.

We shall abbreviate a matrix with negative diagonal having a column d.d. as "a matrix having negative d.d."

THEOREM 23′ Let $A = [a_{ij}]$ be an $n \times n$ nonnegative matrix. A necessary and sufficient condition for $x = Ax + y$ to have a unique solution $x \geqq \theta$ for any $y \geqq \theta$ is that there be $d_1, \ldots, d_n > 0$ such that

$$\sum_{i=1}^{n} d_i a_{ij} < d_j \qquad \text{for} \quad j = 1, \ldots, n. \tag{75}$$

PROOF Since $a_{ij} \geqq 0$ for all i, j, (75) is equivalent to saying that

$$d_j |1 - a_{jj}| > \sum_{i=1, i \neq j}^{n} d_i |a_{ij}| \qquad \text{for} \quad j = 1, \ldots, n,$$

i.e., $[I - A]$ has a d.d. Then, Theorems 23 and 24 are taken into consideration. Q.E.D.

Similarly we have the following symmetric result.

COROLLARY Let $A = [a_{ij}]$ be an $n \times n$ nonnegative matrix. A necessary and sufficient condition for $p = A^{\mathrm{T}}p + v$ to have a unique solution $p \geqq \theta$ for any $v \geqq \theta$ is that there be $d_1, \ldots, d_n > 0$ such that

$$\sum_{j=1}^{n} a_{ij} d_j < d_i \qquad \text{for} \quad i = 1, \ldots, n. \tag{75′}$$

Consider a dynamic system

$$x(t) = Ax(t-1) + y \tag{76}$$

where A is an $n \times n$ real matrix, y is a constant n-vector, and $x(t)$ is the variable n-vector in period t. We say that system (76) is *stable* if $x(t)$ converges to a unique limit as t goes to infinity, irrespective of the initial value $x(0)$.

THEOREM 25 The dynamic system (76) with real A is stable and $x(t)$ converges to

$$\lim_{t \to \infty} x(t) = [I - A]^{-1} y, \tag{77}$$

as t tends to infinity if there are positive scalars $d_1, \ldots, d_n$ such that

$$\sum_{i=1}^{n} d_i |a_{ij}| < d_j \qquad \text{for} \quad j = 1, \ldots, n. \tag{78}$$

PROOF By an iterative substitution, we get from (76)

$$x(t) = A^t x(0) + [I - A]^{-1}[I - A^t] y. \tag{76′}$$

Let λ be any eigenvalue of A. By virtue of Theorems 8 and 19,

$$|\lambda| \leqq \frac{\sum_{i=1}^{n} d_i |a_{ij}|}{d_j} \qquad \text{for} \quad j = 1, \ldots, n.$$

Thus, if (78) holds, $|\lambda| < 1$, and hence (76′) converges to (77) in view of Theorem 7 in Section 3.3. Q.E.D.

COROLLARY The dynamic system (76) with nonnegative A is stable and the limit (77) is nonnegative for any $y \geqq \theta$ if there are positive scalars $d_1, \ldots, d_n$ for which (75) holds.

PROOF This result follows immediately from Theorems 25 and 23′. Q.E.D.

It may be convenient to know some special matrices related to matrices with dominant diagonals.

DEFINITION 7 A square matrix with positive diagonal entries and nonpositive off-diagonal ones is called a *Minkowski matrix* if every row (or column) sum of the matrix is positive.

LEMMA 1 All the principal minors of a Minkowski matrix are positive.

PROOF Let B be a Minkowski matrix. Then $B\{1\} > \theta$, where $\{1\}$ stands for a column vector composed of all ones. Take account of Corollary 1 to Theorem 30 in Section 2.4 in the above inequality system. Q.E.D.

DEFINITION 8 Let b_{ij} be the (i, j)th component of a square matrix B and define a new matrix B^* of the same order such that

$$\text{the } (i, j)\text{th component of } B^* = \begin{cases} b_{ij} & \text{if} \quad i = j, \\ -|b_{ij}| & \text{if} \quad i \neq j. \end{cases}$$

The matrix B is referred to as an *H-matrix* if its diagonal entries are positive and if all the principal minors of B^* are positive.

THEOREM 26 A Hadamard matrix with positive diagonal entries is an H-matrix.

(The proof is similar to that of Lemma 1.)

DEFINITION 9 A real square matrix is said to be a *P-matrix* if all of its principal minors are positive.

A Minkowski matrix is a P-matrix.

DEFINITION 9′ A real square matrix is said to be an *NP-matrix* if all its principal minors of odd orders are negative and those of even orders positive.

THEOREM 27 An $n \times n$ real matrix B with positive (or negative) d.d. is a P-matrix (or an NP-matrix, respectively).

PROOF Let B_i be an mth order principal submatrix of B having negative d.d. and consider a polynomial of ρ, $f(\rho) \equiv |\rho I - B_i|$. Since $f(\rho) = 0$ has no nonnegative root by virtue of Theorem 22′ and since $f(\rho)$ takes a positive value for a large ρ, $(-1)^m|B_i| = f(0) > 0$. Thus, $|B_i| < 0$ for odd m and $|B_i| > 0$ for even m. (If B has positive d.d., $-B$ has negative d.d. and hence B is a P-matrix.) Q.E.D.

There is an equivalent condition for a P-matrix.

DEFINITION 10 An $n \times n$ real matrix A is said to *reverse the sign* of a column real n-vector x if

$$x_i[Ax]_i \leqq 0 \qquad \text{for all} \quad i = 1, \ldots, n,$$

where x_i and $[Ax]_i$ stand for the ith components of x and Ax, respectively.

THEOREM 28 (Gale and Nikaido, 1965) For an $n \times n$ real matrix A to be a P-matrix, it is necessary and sufficient that A reverses the sign of no column real n-vector other than the null vector.

PROOF *Sufficiency* Suppose that there is a principal submatrix of A, denoted C, whose determinant is nonpositive. Then C must have one real nonpositive eigenvalue λ and its associated nonzero real eigenvector y since the determinant of C equals the product of all its eigenvalues, among which complex eigenvalues occur as conjugate pairs. Let J be the set of indices of the columns of C and construct a column n-vector x such that $x_i = y_i$ for $i \in J$, and $x_i = 0$ for $i \notin J$. Thus

$$x_i[Ax]_i = \begin{cases} y_i[Cy]_i & \text{for} \quad i \in J, \\ 0 & \text{otherwise.} \end{cases}$$

Since $y_i[Cy]_i = \lambda y_i^2 \leqq 0$, A reverses the sign of the nonzero vector x.

Necessity Let A be an $n \times n$ P-matrix, reversing the sign of a nonzero real n-vector x. If $x \ngeq \theta$, then let E be the diagonal matrix obtained from the identity matrix I of order n by replacing its ith column e^i by $-e^i$ for all i for which $x_i < 0$. Then $D \equiv EAE$ is again a P-matrix and

$$[Ex]_i[DEx]_i = [Ex]_i[EAx]_i = x_i[Ax]_i.$$

Hence, whenever A reverses the sign of a nonzero vector x, D reverses the sign of nonnegative vector Ex. So we may assume from the outset that A reverses the sign of a nonnegative vector x. Consider the set $H \equiv \{i\colon x_i > 0\}$, and suppose it is nonempty. Letting A^* be the principal submatrix of A obtained by deleting its ith row and column for every $i \notin H$ and letting x^* be the corresponding strictly positive vector obtained from x, we know that A^* is again a P-matrix and that it reverses the sign of x^*, implying $A^*x^* \leq \theta$. Thus, by virtue of Theorem 16 in Section 8.2, x^* must be null; i.e., H must be empty. Q.E.D.

A necessary and sufficient condition for a nonnegative matrix to be a P-matrix is found. (See also Fiedler and Pták (1962) listed in Chapter 2.)

DEFINITION 11 An $n \times n$ real matrix $A \equiv [a_{ij}]$ is said to satisfy the *U-1 condition* if for any nonempty proper subset J of indices $N \equiv \{1, 2, \ldots, n\}$, there exists a strictly positive n-vector $x_J \equiv (x_{1J}, \ldots, x_{nJ})$ such that

$$\sum_{i \in J} x_{iJ} a_{ij} + \sum_{i \notin J} x_{iJ}(-a_{ij}) > 0 \qquad \text{for} \quad j \in J, \tag{79-1}$$

$$\sum_{i \in J} x_{iJ}(-a_{ij}) + \sum_{i \notin J} x_{iJ} a_{ij} > 0 \qquad \text{for} \quad j \notin J. \tag{79-2}$$

Inequalities (79-1) and (79-2) together can be rewritten as

$$x_J[E_J A E_J] > \theta, \tag{80}$$

where E_J is the diagonal matrix obtained from the identity matrix of order n by replacing its ith column e^i by $-e^i$ for $i \in J$.

Remark If $A \geqq 0$ satisfies the U-1 condition, its main diagonal entries are all positive; as special instances $J = \{i\}$ $(i = 1, \ldots, n)$.

THEOREM 29 (Uekawa, 1971) For an $n \times n$ nonnegative matrix $A \equiv [a_{ij}]$ to be a P-matrix, it is necessary and sufficient that A satisfies the U-1 condition.

PROOF *Sufficiency* Suppose that nonnegative matrix A satisfies the U-1 condition and that A is not a P-matrix. Then by the Gale–Nikaido theorem (Theorem 28) A reverses the sign of some nonzero vector $z \equiv (z_1, \ldots, z_n)$, i.e.,

$$z_i \sum_{j=1}^{n} a_{ij} z_j \leqq 0 \qquad \text{for all} \quad i. \tag{81}$$

Let $J \equiv J_1 \cup J_2$, where $J_1 \equiv \{i : z_i < 0, \sum_{j=1}^{n} a_{ij} z_j \geqq 0\}$ and $J_2 \equiv \{i : z_i = 0, \sum_{j=1}^{n} a_{ij} z_j > 0\}$. J cannot be equal to N since $\sum_{j=1}^{n} a_{ij} z_j > 0$ requires some positive z_j. We shall show that $J \neq \varnothing$. If $J_1 = \varnothing$, then all nonzero components of z $(\neq \theta)$ are positive and hence there is some i such that $\sum_{j=1}^{n} a_{ij} z_j > 0$ in view of the fact that $a_{ij} \geqq 0$ for all i, j and $a_{ii} > 0$ for all i (by the above remark). For such an i, z_i must be zero in order that (81) holds. Thus J_2 is nonempty. Conversely if $J_2 = \varnothing$, then $J_1 \neq \varnothing$. Therefore, we see that J is a nonempty proper subset of N. From (81) we have

$$\begin{aligned} \sum_{j \in J} a_{ij} y_{Jj} + \sum_{j \notin J} (-a_{ij}) y_{Jj} &\leqq 0 \qquad \text{for} \quad i \in J, \\ \sum_{j \in J} (-a_{ij}) y_{Jj} + \sum_{j \notin J} a_{ij} y_{Jj} &\leqq 0 \qquad \text{for} \quad i \notin J, \end{aligned} \tag{82}$$

where $y_{Jj} \equiv -z_j \geqq 0$ for $j \in J$ and $y_{Jj} \equiv z_j \geqq 0$ for $j \notin J$. Inequalities (82) imply that

$$[E_J A E_J]\, y \leqq \theta \tag{83}$$

has a semipositive solution $y_J \equiv \{y_{J1}, \ldots, y_{Jn}\}$. Applying the corollary to Theorem 12 in Section 8.2, we know that inequality (80) has no semipositive solution, contradicting that A satisfies the U-1 condition. Hence A must be a P-matrix.

Necessity Suppose A is a P-matrix. Then there is no semipositive solution $y \equiv \{y_1, \ldots, y_n\}$ such that (83) holds, for otherwise,

$$[E_J y]_i [A E_J y]_i = y_i [[E_J A E_J] y]_i \leqq 0 \qquad \text{for all} \quad i,$$

where $[\cdot]_i$ denotes the ith component of the vector in question, implying that A reverses the sign of $E_J y \neq \theta$, which contradicts the hypothesis in view of the Gale–Nikaido theorem. Applying again the corollary to Theorem 12 (in Section 8.2) to (83), we know that system (80) has a semipositive x_J, and hence a strictly positive x_J as can be easily verified. (Note that the necessity proof does not require nonnegativity of A.) Q.E.D.

One sufficient condition for a P-matrix is supplied concerning a nonnegative matrix.

DEFINITION 12 An $n \times n$ real matrix $A \equiv [a_{ij}]$ is said to satisfy the the *U-2 condition* if for any nonempty proper subset J of indices $N \equiv \{1, 2, \ldots, n\}$, there exists a strictly positive n-vector $x_J \equiv \{x_{J1}, \ldots, x_{Jn}\}$ such that

$$\sum_{j \in J} a_{ij} x_{Jj} + \sum_{j \in J} (-a_{kj}) x_{Jj} > 0 \qquad \text{for} \quad i \in J \text{ and } k \notin J. \tag{84}$$

THEOREM 30 (Uekawa, 1971) If an $n \times n$ nonnegative matrix $A \equiv [a_{ij}]$ satisfies the U-2 condition, A is a P-matrix.

(For the proof, refer to Uekawa (1971).)

For an application of P-matrices and their related matrices to economics, the reader may refer to Uekawa *et al.* (1973).

EXERCISES

1. Let A and B be nonsingular square matrices of the same order; verify

$$\begin{aligned}[A + B]^{-1} &= A^{-1}[I + BA^{-1}]^{-1} = B^{-1}[AB^{-1} + I]^{-1} \\ &= [I + A^{-1}B]^{-1}A^{-1} = [B^{-1}A + I]^{-1}B^{-1} \\ &= A^{-1}[B^{-1} + A^{-1}]^{-1}B^{-1} = B^{-1}[B^{-1} + A^{-1}]^{-1}A^{-1}.\end{aligned}$$

2. Let x and y be column vectors of the same dimension; verify

$$|I - xy^{\mathrm{T}}| = 1 - y^{\mathrm{T}}x.$$

3. Let A be an $n \times n$ matrix, let b, c be n-dimensional column vectors; verify

$$\begin{vmatrix} I - A & -b \\ -c^{\mathrm{T}} & 1 \end{vmatrix} = |I - A - bc^{\mathrm{T}}|.$$

4. Let $x = (x_1, \ldots, x_n)$ and $y = (y_1, \ldots, y_n)$, where x_i, y_i are real scalars; prove the following Cauchy–Schwarz inequality for real numbers:

$$\left(\sum_{i=1}^{n} x_i y_i\right)^2 \leqq \left(\sum_{i=1}^{n} x_i^2\right)\left(\sum_{i=1}^{n} y_i^2\right),$$

where equality holds if and only if y is the null vector or y is a scalar multiplication of x.

5. Prove Jacobi's ratio theorem more directly than is done in the text.

6. Let A and B be $m \times n$ matrices, and let λ be a nonzero eigenvalue of AB^{T}. Show that λ is also an eigenvalue of $B^{\mathrm{T}}A$.

7. A square matrix A is said to be an *orthogonal matrix* if $A^{\mathrm{T}} = A^{-1}$. Show that any permutation matrix is an orthogonal matrix.

8. Let $A \equiv [a_{ij}]$ be an $n \times n$ matrix. Show that if $d_1, \ldots, d_n$ are positive scalars such that

$$d_j |a_{jj}| > \sum_{i=1, i \neq j}^{n} d_i |a_{ij}| \qquad \text{for} \quad j = 1, \ldots, n$$

and

$$d_j |a_{jj}| > \sum_{i=1, i \neq j}^{n} d_i |a_{ji}| \qquad \text{for} \quad j = 1, \ldots, n,$$

then, for the same $d_1, \ldots, d_n$,

$$2d_j |a_{jj}| > \sum_{i=1, i \neq j}^{n} d_i |a_{ij} + a_{ji}| \qquad \text{for} \quad j = 1, \ldots, n,$$

viz., $A + A^{\mathrm{T}}$ has a column dominant diagonal.

9. Prove Theorem 26.

10. Prove Theorem 30.

REFERENCES AND FURTHER READING

Aitkens, A. C. (1946). *Determinants and Matrices*, rev. ed. Oliver & Boyd, Edinburgh.

Gale, D., and Nikaido, H. (1965). "The Jacobian Matrix and Global Univalence of Mappings," *Mathematishe Annalen* **159**, 81–93; (1968). in *Readings in Mathematical Economics* (P. Newman, ed.), Vol. I. Johns Hopkins Press, Baltimore, Maryland.

Gantmacher, F. R. (1959). *The Theory of Matrices* (English translation), Vol. I. Chelsea, New York.

Hadley, G. (1961). *Linear Algebra*. Addison-Wesley, Reading, Massachusetts.

Lancaster, K. (1968). *Mathematical Economics*. Macmillan, New York.

Lang, S. (1971). *Linear Algebra*, 2nd ed. Addison-Wesley, Reading, Massachusetts.

McKenzie, L. W. (1960). "Matrices with Dominant Diagonals and Economic Theory," in *Mathematical Methods in the Social Sciences 1959* (K. J. Arrow, S. Karlin, and P. Suppes, eds.), pp. 47–62. Stanford Univ. Press, Stanford, California.

Uekawa, Y. (1971). "Generalization of the Stolper–Samuelson Theorem," *Econometrica* **39**, 197–217.

Uekawa, Y., Kemp, M. C., and Wegge, L. L. (1973). "*P*- and *PN*-Matrices, Minkowski- and Metzler-Matrices, and Generalizations of the Stolper–Samuelson and Samuelson–Rybczynski Theorems," *Journal of International Economics* **3**, 53–76.

Chapter 2

Linear Equations and Related Topics with Reference to Economics

2.1 Vector Spaces and Convex Sets

DEFINITION 1 A *field* is defined as a set L of scalars satisfying the conditions:

(1) For any $\alpha, \beta \in L$, $\alpha + \beta$ is an element of L.
(2) For any $\alpha, \beta \in L$, $\alpha\beta$ is an element of L.
(3) L contains 0 (zero).
(4) L contains 1 (one).
(5) For each $\alpha \in L$, $-\alpha$ is an element of L.
(6) For each nonzero $\alpha \in L$, $1/\alpha$ is an element of L.

Examples The set R of all real numbers, the set C of all complex numbers, or the set Q of all rational numbers constitutes a field.

DEFINITION 2 A nonempty set X of objects, each of which consists of number(s) in a given field L, is said to be a *vector space* (or *linear space*) over the field and its elements are called *vectors* if the following three groups I, II, III of axioms hold for any elements x, y, z of the set X.

I. The addition $x + y$ determines a unique element belonging to X, or equivalently

$$x + y \in X \qquad \text{(vector addition)}$$

and the operation of vector addition satisfies

$$x + y = y + x,$$

$$(x + y) + z = x + (y + z);$$

a null vector θ exists in X such that $x + \theta = x$ for each $x \in X$, and $-x$ exists in X such that $x + (-x) = \theta$ for each $x \in X$.

II. For arbitrary scalars α, β from the field L,

$$\alpha x \in X \qquad \text{(scalar multiplication)}$$

and the operation of scalar multiplication satisfies

$$(\alpha\beta)x = \alpha(\beta x), \qquad 1x = x.$$

III. Vector addition and scalar multiplication are connected with each other by

$$\alpha(x + y) = \alpha x + \alpha y, \qquad (\alpha + \beta)x = \alpha x + \beta x.$$

Remark Let θ be the null vector in a vector space X over a field L. For any $x \in X$ and $0, 1, \alpha \in L$, we obtain by Definition 2

(i) $0x = \theta$,
(ii) $(-1)x = -x$,
(iii) $\alpha\theta = \theta$.

PROOF (i) $x = 1x = (1 + 0)x = 1x + 0x = x + 0x$. Adding $-x$ to both sides yields $x - x = x + 0x - x$, that is, $\theta = 0x$.
(ii) $x + (-1)x = 1x - 1x = (1 - 1)x = 0x = \theta$.
(iii) $\alpha\theta = \alpha(x + (-1)x) = \alpha x + \alpha(-x) = \alpha x + (-\alpha x) = \theta$. Q.E.D.

It follows from Definition 2 that every linear combination of elements of a vector space X over a field L belongs to X, provided all the coefficients in the linear combination are from L. According to whether the field L is real or complex, the vector space will be termed a real vector space or a complex vector space.

Example 1 An object x composed of an ordered sequence of n scalars ξ_i $(i = 1, 2, \ldots, n)$ from a field L is said to be an *n-tuple* in the field and denoted as

$$x = \{\xi_1, \xi_2, \ldots, \xi_n\}.$$

We define an *n-space* over a field L as the set X consisting of all the n-tuples in the field together with the axioms in Definition 2. Hence an n-space is a vector space and its elements will be called *n-vectors*. We shall denote the real n-space by R^n and the complex n-space by C^n.

Example 2 The set X of all continuous real-valued functions defined on a closed interval $[a, b]$ of the real line, where $a < b$, together with the following two operations constitutes a vector space over the real field R: For any $x, y \in X$ and any real scalar α,

$$(x + y)(t) = x(t) + y(t) \qquad \text{for all } t \in [a, b],$$
$$(\alpha x)(t) = \alpha x(t) \qquad \text{for all } t \in [a, b].$$

This set X will be denoted as $C[a, b]$. Note that θ in $C[a, b]$ is the function that is identically zero on the interval $[a, b]$.

DEFINITION 3 A nonempty subset M of a vector space X over a field L is called a (*linear*) *subspace* of X if for any $x, y \in M$ and any $\alpha, \beta \in L$, the following holds:

$$\alpha x + \beta y \in M. \tag{7}$$

When M is a subspace of an n-space, any element of M is an n-vector. By definition M must contain θ. The subset $\{\theta\}$ of a vector space X is a subspace. The entire vector space X is also a subspace of itself. A subspace neither equal to θ nor to the entire vector space is said to be a *proper subspace*. Any subspace is found to be a vector space by definition. Henceforth the field over which a vector space or subspace is defined will not be specified explicitly unless confusion may occur.

DEFINITION 4 Let $x_1, x_2, \ldots, x_r$ be elements of a vector space. These vectors are said to be *linearly dependent* if one of them, say x_r, can be represented as a linear combination of the remaining vectors, i.e.,

$$x_r = \sum_{i=1}^{r-1} \mu_i x_i,$$

or equivalently

$$\theta = \sum_{i=1}^{r} \mu_i x_i, \tag{8}$$

where not all coefficients μ_i are zero. If Eq. (8) holds true only when every coefficient μ_i is zero, then $x_1, x_2, \ldots, x_r$ are said to be *linearly independent*.

THEOREM 1 If $x_1, x_2, \ldots, x_r$ are linearly independent vectors, and if $\sum_{i=1}^r \alpha_i x_i = \sum_{i=1}^r \beta_i x_i$, then $\alpha_i = \beta_i$ for all $i = 1, 2, \ldots, r$.

PROOF If $\sum_{i=1}^r \alpha_i x_i = \sum_{i=1}^r \beta_i x_i$, then $\sum_{i=1}^r (\alpha_i - \beta_i) x_i = \theta$. Since $x_1, \ldots, x_r$ are linearly independent, $\alpha_i = \beta_i$ for all $i = 1, \ldots, r$. Q.E.D.

DEFINITION 5 Let $x_1, x_2, \ldots, x_r$ be elements of a vector space X. The set of all linear combinations of these vectors constitutes a subpsace of X, which is called the (*linear*) *subspace generated* (or *spanned*) by $x_1, x_2, \ldots, x_r$. Let $S \equiv S(x_1, \ldots, x_r)$ be the subspace generated by $x_1, \ldots, x_r$. If these vectors are linearly independent, they are said to be a *basis* for S. Note that there can be other bases for S besides $x_1, \ldots, x_r$.

DEFINITION 6 Let M be a subspace of a vector space X. If M has a basis consisting of a finite number of vectors of X, we say that M is *finite dimensional*.

THEOREM 2 Any two bases for a finite-dimensional subspace contain the same number of linearly independent vectors.

PROOF Suppose that x_i $(i = 1, 2, \ldots, m)$ and y_j $(j = 1, 2, \ldots, n)$ are bases for a subspace M of a vector space, where m and n are finite natural numbers.

The vector y_n can be uniquely expressed as a linear combination of the vectors x_i in the first basis, say

$$y_n = \sum_{i=1}^{m} \alpha_i x_i, \tag{1*}$$

where not all the coefficients α_i are zero. By rearranging the x_i if necessary, we assume that $\alpha_m \neq 0$. Then it will be shown that x_i $(i = 1, 2, \ldots, m - 1)$ and y_n are linearly independent. For if they were linearly dependent,

$$\sum_{i=1}^{m-1} \beta_i x_i + \beta y_n = \theta$$

holds for β_i $(i = 1, \ldots, m - 1)$ and β not all equal to zero. $\beta \neq 0$ must hold since if $\beta = 0$, $\sum_{i=1}^{m-1} \beta_i x_i = \theta$ for some β_i $(i = 1, \ldots, m - 1)$ not all equal to zero, contradicting the assumption of linear independence of x_i $(i = 1, \ldots, m - 1)$. Thus we have $y_n = -\sum_{i=1}^{m-1} \beta_i x_i/\beta$. Substituting this for (1*) yields

$$\sum_{i=1}^{m-1} (\beta\alpha_i + \beta_i)x_i + \beta\alpha_m x_m = \theta,$$

where $\beta\alpha_m \neq 0$, which contradicts the assumption of linear independence of the x_i $(i = 1, \ldots, m)$.

Next we show that x_i $(i = 1, \ldots, m - 1)$ and y_n constitute a basis for M. Let x be an arbitrary element of M. Then it is uniquely represented as

$$x = \sum_{i=1}^{m} \lambda_i x_i.$$

When x_m in this equation is replaced by $x_m = (1/\alpha_m)(y_n - \sum_{i=1}^{m-1} \alpha_i x_i)$ obtained from (1*), we get

$$x = \sum_{i=1}^{m-1} \left(\lambda_i - \frac{\alpha_i}{\alpha_m} \lambda_m\right) x_i + \frac{1}{\alpha_m} \lambda_m y_n,$$

where the coefficients are unique since all the α_i and λ_i are unique. Thus $x_1, x_2, \ldots, x_{m-1}, y_n$ constitute a basis for M. Therefore, y_{n-1} has a unique representation in terms of this new basis:

$$y_{n-1} = \sum_{i=1}^{m-1} \mu_i x_i + \mu y_n, \tag{2*}$$

where all the coefficients are not zero. $\mu_j \neq 0$ for some $j = 1, \ldots, m - 1$, for if $\mu_j = 0$ for all $j = 1, \ldots, m - 1$, we have $y_{n-1} = \mu y_n$ for some $\mu \neq 0$, a contradiction. We may assume that $\mu_{m-1} \neq 0$. Then in the same way as before it can be shown that x_i $(i = 1, 2, \ldots, m - 2)$ and y_{n-1}, y_n constitute a basis for M. Substituting y vectors for x vectors one by one in this manner, we finally reach a stage where x_i $(i = 1, 2, \ldots, m - n)$ and y_j $(j = 1, 2, \ldots,$

n) constitute a basis or only y_j ($j = 1, 2, \ldots, n$) constitute it, implying that $m \geqq n$. For otherwise in the above substitution process the term involving x vectors (e.g., the second term of Eq. (2*)) will disappear, which contradicts the linear dependence of y_j ($j = 1, \ldots, n$).

If we reverse the order of substitution, i.e., if we substitute x vectors for y vectors one by one, then we end up with $n \geqq m$. Thus we know that $m = n$. Q.E.D.

DEFINITION 7 A subspace M with a basis consisting of r vectors is said to be *r-dimensional*. Hence the maximum number of mutually linearly independent vectors in M is referred to as the *dimension* of M, and represented as dim M.

THEOREM 3 An n-space X has dimension n.

PROOF X has a basis consisting of $e_1, e_2, \ldots, e_n$ where e_i is the ith unit vector, viz., the vector whose ith component is unity and the others are all zero for each $i = 1, \ldots, n$. Q.E.D.

THEOREM 4 Let S_1 and S_2 be subspaces of a vector space X. Then their intersection $S_1 \cap S_2$ is a subspace of X.

PROOF Since $\theta \in S_1$ and $\theta \in S_2$, we know $\theta \in S_1 \cap S_2$, and hence the intersection is nonempty.

For any vectors $x, y \in S_1 \cap S_2$, $x, y \in S_1$ and $x, y \in S_2$;

$$\Rightarrow \alpha x + \beta y \in S_1 \text{ and } \alpha x + \beta y \in S_2 \qquad \text{for any scalars } \alpha, \beta;$$

$$\Rightarrow \alpha x + \beta y \in S_1 \cap S_2. \qquad \text{Q.E.D.}$$

DEFINITION 8 The translation of a subspace of a vector space X is said to be a *linear variety* (or *affine subspace*) and is expressed as

$$V = x_0 + M \equiv \{v : v = x_0 + m, \ \ m \in M\},$$

where M is a subspace and x_0 a vector in X and not in M. (If x_0 were in M, V would reduce to M. Our definition excludes such an incident.)

For any $x, y \in V$, there exist $x_1, y_1 \in M$ such that $x = x_0 + x_1$, $y = x_0 + y_1$ and by definition of M, $\alpha x_1 + \beta y_1 \in M$ for any scalars α, β. We have $\alpha x + \beta y = x_0 + \alpha x_1 + \beta y_1 \in x_0 + M = V$ if and only if $\alpha + \beta = 1$. Thus a linear variety V can be defined as a subset in a vector space such that for any $x, y \in V$ and any scalars α, β satisfying $\alpha + \beta = 1$, the following holds:

$$\alpha x + \beta y \in V.$$

DEFINITION 9 Let S be a nonempty subset in a vector space X, and V_i ($i \in J$) all the linear varieties in X that contain S. Then

$$v(S) \equiv \bigcap_{i \in J} V_i$$

is called the *linear variety generated* by S.

THEOREM 5 Let S be a nonempty subset in a vector space X. Then $v(S)$ defined above is a linear variety.

PROOF For any $x, y \in v(S)$ and any scalars α, β such that $\alpha + \beta = 1$,

$$x, y \in V_i \text{ and } \alpha x + \beta y \in V_i \qquad (i \in J);$$

$$\Rightarrow \alpha x + \beta y \in v(S). \qquad \text{Q.E.D.}$$

DEFINITION 10 Let x and y be two points in a vector space. The set

$$Z = \{z : z = \alpha x + (1 - \alpha) y \text{ for } \alpha \in [0,1]\}$$

is termed the *segment* joining x and y. A subset K of a vector space is said to be *convex* if segment Z defined above belongs to K for any $x, y \in K$.

THEOREM 6 The intersection of an arbitrary collection of convex sets is convex.

PROOF Let x, y be elements of $K \equiv \bigcap_{i \in J} K_i$, where K_i is a convex set. The segment joining x and y belongs to K_i for each $i \in J$, where J stands for an arbitrary collection of indices. Hence the segment belongs to K. Q.E.D.

DEFINITION 11 Let S be an arbitrary set in a vector space. The intersection of all the convex sets containing S is called the *convex hull* (or *convex cover*) of S.

The convex hull of a set S is the smallest convex set containing S.

THEOREM 7 Subspaces and linear varieties are convex sets.

PROOF (1) Let M be a subspace of a vector space;

$\Rightarrow$ for $x, y \in M$ and scalars α, β, we have $\alpha x + \beta y \in M$;
$\Rightarrow$ for α, $0 \leqq \alpha \leqq 1$, we have $\alpha x + (1 - \alpha)y \in M$.

(2) Let V be a linear variety in a vector space X, i.e., $V = x_0 + M$, where $x_0 \in X$ and M is a subspace of X;

$\Rightarrow$ for $x, y \in V$, there exist $x_1, y_1 \in M$ such that $x = x_0 + x_1$, $y = x_0 + y_1$;
$\Rightarrow$ for α, β such that $\alpha + \beta = 1$, we have $\alpha x + \beta y = x_0 + \alpha x_1 + \beta y_1 \in V$;
$\Rightarrow$ for α such that $0 \leqq \alpha \leqq 1$, we have $\alpha x + (1 - \alpha)y = x_0 + \alpha x_1 + (1 - \alpha)y_1 \in V$. Q.E.D.

THEOREM 8 Let K be a convex set in a vector space. Then a set $\alpha K \equiv \{x : x = \alpha k \text{ for } k \in K\}$ is convex for any scalar α.

PROOF For $x, y \in K$, $k \equiv \beta x + (1 - \beta)y \in K$ for β, $0 \leqq \beta \leqq 1$. Thus, $\alpha x \in \alpha K$, $\alpha y \in \alpha K$ and $\beta\alpha x + (1 - \beta)\,\alpha y = \alpha k \in \alpha K$. Q.E.D.

DEFINITION 12 A set C in a vector space is said to be a *cone* with vertex at the origin if $x \in C$ implies that $\alpha x \in C$ for all $\alpha \geqq 0$.

THEOREM 9 Any subspace is a cone with vertex at the origin.

PROOF Let M be a subspace of a vector space. Then for any $x \in M$, we have $\alpha x = \alpha x + \beta\theta \in M$ for $\alpha \geqq 0$ and any scalar β. Q.E.D.

Thus, a subspace is a *convex cone* with vertex at the origin.

DEFINITION 13 Let C be a cone with vertex at the origin in a vector space X and p be a vector in X. Then $C_p \equiv p + C$ is called a cone with vertex p.

THEOREM 10 Let M be a subspace of a vector space X and x_0 a vector in X. Then the linear variety $V = x_0 + M$ is a convex cone with vertex x_0.

PROOF We already know that V is convex. Since M is a cone with vertex at the origin, V is obviously a cone with vertex x_0. Q.E.D.

DEFINITION 14 An *extreme point* in a convex set is a point in the set that does not lie on a segment joining any two other points in the set. A *convex polyhedron* is a convex set containing a finite number of extreme points.

A cone C generated by a convex polyhedron K such that

$$C = \{x : x = \alpha k \quad \text{for} \quad k \in K \text{ and } \alpha \geqq 0\}$$

is called a *convex polyhedral cone* (or *finite convex cone*).

THEOREM 11 Let k_i ($i = 1, 2, \ldots, n$) be fixed points in a vector space X. Then the set of all linear combinations

$$x = \sum_{i=1}^{n} \lambda_i k_i \qquad \text{for all} \quad \lambda_i \geqq 0$$

represents the convex polyhedral cone in X generated by these points.

PROOF Any point in the convex polyhedron generated by the given points can be represented by a convex combination

$$k = \sum_{i=1}^{n} \mu_i k_i \qquad \text{for} \quad \mu_i \text{ such that } 0 \leqq \mu_i \leqq 1 \quad \text{and} \quad \sum_{i=1}^{n} \mu_i = 1.$$

x can be rewritten as

$$x = \sum_{j=1}^{n} \lambda_j \Big(\sum_{i=1}^{n} \mu_i k_i \Big) = \alpha k,$$

where $\mu_i \equiv \lambda_i / \sum_{j=1}^{n} \lambda_j$, and $\alpha \equiv \sum_{j=1}^{n} \lambda_j \geqq 0$. Q.E.D.

DEFINITION 15 Let S, T be subsets in a vector space. The *sum* of S and T is defined as

$$S + T = \{x \, : \, x = s + t \text{ for } s \in S \text{ and } t \in T\}.$$

THEOREM 12 Let M, N be subspaces of a vector space X. Then $M + N$ is a subspace of X.

PROOF (1) $\theta \in M$ and $\theta \in N$ imply $\theta \in M + N$.

(2) For any $x, y \in M + N$, there exist $m_1, m_2 \in M$ and $n_1, n_2 \in N$ such that $x = m_1 + n_1$ and $y = m_2 + n_2$. Thus, for any scalars α and β, $\alpha m_1 + \beta m_2 \in M$ and $\alpha n_1 + \beta n_2 \in N$. Hence $\alpha x + \beta y = \alpha m_1 + \beta m_2 + \alpha n_1 + \beta n_2 \in M + N$. Q.E.D.

THEOREM 13 Let K, G be convex sets in a vector space. Then, $K + G$ is a convex set.

PROOF $k_0 \equiv \alpha k_1 + (1 - \alpha)k_2 \in K$ and $g_0 \equiv \alpha g_1 + (1 - \alpha)g_2 \in G$ for $k_1, k_2 \in K$, $g_1, g_2 \in G$, and scalar α such that $0 \leqq \alpha \leqq 1$. Thus, we have, for $k_1 + g_1$, $k_2 + g_2 \in K + G$,

$$\alpha(k_1 + g_1) + (1 - \alpha)(k_2 + g_2) = k_0 + g_0 \in K + G. \qquad \text{Q.E.D.}$$

DEFINITION 16 Let V, W be subspaces of a vector space X. If $X = V + W$ and $V \cap W = \theta$, then X is said to be the *direct sum* of V and W. In this case, any element x of X has a unique representation:

$$x = v + w \qquad \text{for unique} \quad v \in V \text{ and } w \in W.$$

Symbolically, the above relation is expressed as

$$X = V \oplus W.$$

The only difference between the sum and the direct sum of two subspaces of a vector space is the *unique* representation of an element in the latter.

THEOREM 14 If $X = V \oplus W$, where V, W are subspaces of a finite-dimensional vector space X, then

$$\dim X = \dim V + \dim W.$$

PROOF By definition, every element x of X has a unique representation $x = v + w$. Let $\{v_1, \ldots, v_p\}$ be a basis of V, and $\{w_1, \ldots, w_q\}$ a basis of W. Then, each element v of V is represented uniquely as a linear combination of these v's and each element w of W as that of these w's. Hence, x has a unique representation as the sum of unique linear combinations of these v's and w's, which implies that $\{v_1, \ldots, v_p, w_1, \ldots, w_q\}$ constitutes a basis of X, proving the assertion. Q.E.D.

2.2 Linear Transformations

DEFINITION 17 Let X, Y be arbitrary sets and D a subset in X. A rule F that associates an element $y \in Y$ to each element x of D is said to be a *transformation* (or *mapping*) from X into (or to) Y with domain D, and we write

$$y = F(x) \qquad \text{for} \quad x \in D \subset X \text{ and } y \in Y,$$

or

$$F: X \to Y.$$

If a domain is not explicitly specified with respect to a transformation defined on a set X, it should be understood that the domain is X itself.

DEFINITION 18 A transformation (or mapping) F from a set X into a set Y is called a *linear transformation* (or *linear mapping*) if

$$F(cx + z) = cF(x) + F(z) \tag{9}$$

for $x, z \in X$ and any scalar c. Note that $F(\theta) = \theta$.

DEFINITION 19 Let F be a transformation from a set X into a set Y. Assuming the domain of F is X, we define the *range* of F as the set

$$R(F) = \{y : y \in Y, y = F(x) \text{ for some } x \in X\},$$

and the *nullspace* (or *kernel*) of F as the set

$$N(F) = \{x : x \in X \text{ and } F(x) = \theta\}.$$

THEOREM 15 Let X and Y be vector spaces over a field L, and let F be a linear transformation from X into Y. Then, the range and the nullspace of F are subspaces of Y and X, respectively.

PROOF (1) Let y_1, y_2 be elements of $R(F)$. Then there exist some $x_1, x_2 \in X$ such that $y_1 = F(x_1)$ and $y_2 = F(x_2)$. Hence for any scalar c in L, we have $cy_1 + y_2 = F(cx_1 + x_2) \in R(F)$.

(2) Let x_1, x_2 be elements of $N(F)$, i.e., $F(x_1) = \theta$ and $F(x_2) = \theta$. Then for any scalar b in L, we have $F(bx_1 + x_2) = \theta$. Q.E.D.

THEOREM 16 Let X and Y be vector spaces over a field L, and let $\{x_1, \ldots, x_n\}$ be a basis for X and $y_1, \ldots, y_n$ be any vectors in Y. Then, there exists a unique linear transformation F from X into Y such that $F(x_i) = y_i$ for $i = 1, \ldots, n$.

PROOF For any x in X, there is a unique set of constants $a_1, \ldots, a_n$ in L satisfying

$$x = \sum_{i=1}^{n} a_i x_i.$$

We define F such that $F(x) = \Sigma_{i=1}^{n} a_i y_i$. Then it is clear that $F(x)$ belongs to Y and hence F is a transformation from X into Y. Choosing x as x_i, we have $F(x_i) = y_i$ for each i.

To see that F is linear, let $z = \sum_{i=1}^{n} b_i x_i \in X$. For any scalar c, $cx + z = \sum_{i=1}^{n}(ca_i + b_i)x_i$, and hence by definition, $F(cx + z) = \sum_i (ca_i + b_i)y_i$. On the other hand, $cF(x) + F(z) = c\sum_i a_i y_i + \sum_i b_i y_i$. Thus F is linear.

Let G be another linear transformation from X into Y with $G(x_i) = y_i$ for every $i = 1, \ldots, n$. Then for the vector $x = \sum_i a_i x_i$ we have $G(x) = \sum_i a_i G(x_i) = \sum_i a_i y_i$. So G turns out to be identical with F. Q.E.D.

THEOREM 17 Let X and Y be vector spaces over a field L, and let $\{x_1,$

$\ldots, x_n\}$ be a basis for X and $\{y_1, \ldots, y_m\}$ a basis for Y. Then, (1) any linear transformation $F\colon X \to Y$, determines a unique $m \times n$ matrix $A = [a_{ij}]$ such that

$$F(x_j) = \sum_{i=1}^{m} a_{ij} y_i \qquad \text{for} \quad j = 1, \ldots, n, \tag{10}$$

where $a_{ij} \in L$, and (2) conversely, an $m \times n$ matrix A determines a unique linear transformation F such that (10) holds.

PROOF (1) $F(x_j) \in Y$ is represented by a unique linear combination of the basis vectors of Y.

(2) Let x, z be elements of X, which are uniquely represented as

$$x = \sum_{i=1}^{n} b_i x_i \qquad \text{and} \qquad z = \sum_{i=1}^{n} c_i x_i.$$

Define $G(x) = \sum_{j=1}^{n} b_j F(x_j)$ and $G(z) = \sum_{j=1}^{n} c_j F(x_j)$, where $F(x_j) = \sum_{i=1}^{n} a_{ij} y_i$ (unique for each j). Then for any scalar λ we have $\lambda G(x) + G(z) = \sum_j (\lambda b_j + c_j) F(x_j) = G(\lambda x + z)$, implying that G is a linear transformation. Moreover, setting $x = x_j$, we find $G(x_j) = F(x_j)$. Therefore, G turns out to be identical with F. Q.E.D.

COROLLARY Assume the same situation as in Theorem 17. Then the coordinates of the image vector $F(x)$ of $x = \sum_{j=1}^{n} b_j x_j$ are given by

$$d_i = \sum_{j=1}^{n} a_{ij} b_j \qquad \text{for} \quad i = 1, \ldots, m. \tag{11}$$

PROOF $F(x) = \sum_{j=1}^{n} b_j F(x_j) = \sum_j^n b_j \sum_{i=1}^{m} a_{ij} y_i = \sum_i^m \sum_j^n a_{ij} b_j y_i$. Q.E.D.

We have learned that given a pair of bases for vector spaces X and Y over a field, the image of a vector $x \in X$ under a linear transformation F from X into Y,

$$y = F(x)$$

can be represented by a system of linear equations

$$d = Ab,$$

where A is a matrix and b, d stand for the column vectors composed of the coordinates of x, y, respectively, relative to the given pair of bases. We shall inquire what happens if these bases change.

DEFINITION 20 Let $\{x_1, \ldots, x_n\}$ and $\{v_1, \ldots, v_n\}$ be two bases for a vector space X over a field L. Then x_j is uniquely represented as

$$x_j = \sum_{i=1}^{n} q_{ij} v_i \qquad \text{for} \quad j = 1, \ldots, n,$$

where q_{ij} are in L. The square matrix composed of these q's

$$Q \equiv \begin{bmatrix} q_{11} & q_{12} & \cdots & q_{1n} \\ \vdots & \vdots & & \vdots \\ q_{n1} & q_{n2} & \cdots & q_{nn} \end{bmatrix}$$

is said to be the *transition matrix* from a basis $\{v_1, \ldots, v_n\}$ to another basis $\{x_1, \ldots, x_n\}$.

THEOREM 18 Let $\{x_1, \ldots, x_n\}$, $\{v_1, \ldots, v_n\}$, and $\{u_1, \ldots, u_n\}$ be three bases for a vector space X over a field L. Let Q and K be transition matrices from $\{v_1, \ldots, v_n\}$ to $\{x_1, \ldots, x_n\}$ and from $\{u_1, \ldots, u_n\}$ to $\{v_1, \ldots, v_n\}$, respectively. Then the transition matrix from $\{u_1, \ldots, u_n\}$ to $\{x_1, \ldots, x_n\}$ is KQ.

PROOF Let q_{ij} and k_{ij} be the (i, j)th components of Q and K, respectively. Then x_j is uniquely represented in terms of u as follows:

$$x_j = \sum_i q_{ij} v_i = \sum_i q_{ij} \sum_h k_{hi} u_h = \sum_h \sum_i k_{hi} q_{ij} u_h,$$

where $\sum_i k_{hi} q_{ij}$ is the (h, j)th component of matrix KQ. Q.E.D.

COROLLARY A transition matrix is nonsingular.

PROOF Let the basis $\{u_1, \ldots, u_n\}$ for a vector space X be identical with the basis $\{x_1, \ldots, x_n\}$ in Theorem 18. Then we have $KQ = I$, which implies nonsingularity of Q and K. Q.E.D.

Now we are in a position to clarify the effects of basis changes.

THEOREM 19 Let y be a vector belonging to a vector space Y represented in terms of a basis $\{y_1, \ldots, y_m\}$ as $y = \sum_{j=1}^m d_j y_j$, and also represented in terms of another basis $\{v_1, \ldots, v_m\}$ as $y = \sum_{i=1}^m c_i v_i$, and suppose Q is the transition matrix from $\{v_1, \ldots, v_m\}$ to $\{y_1, \ldots, y_m\}$. Then

$$d = Q^{-1} c, \qquad \text{where} \quad d \equiv \begin{bmatrix} d_1 \\ \vdots \\ d_m \end{bmatrix} \quad \text{and} \quad c \equiv \begin{bmatrix} c_1 \\ \vdots \\ c_m \end{bmatrix}. \tag{12}$$

PROOF $y = \sum_j d_j y_j = \sum_j d_j \sum_i q_{ij} v_i = \sum_i \sum_j q_{ij} d_j v_i$. Since the representation is unique, $\sum_j q_{ij} d_j = c_i$, or $Qd = c$. Hence (12) follows. Q.E.D.

As was remarked before, to a given matrix A, there corresponds a unique linear transformation $F\colon X \to Y$ such that

$$y = F(x) \tag{13}$$

can be represented by

$$d = Ab, \tag{14}$$

where b and d stand for the column vectors composed of the coordinates of $x \in X$ and $y \in Y$, respectively, relative to a given pair of bases for X and Y.

By Theorem 19, if the basis for Y is replaced by another basis, system (14) will change into

$$c = QAb, \tag{15}$$

where Q is the associated transition matrix and $c \equiv Qd$. Given F and y in (13), therefore, interchanging bases for Y affects the corresponding representative matrix of F simply by premultiplying matrix A by Q, leaving the coordinate vector b of x intact. We shall utilize this fact to solve a system of linear equations such as (14) in subsequent sections.

To conclude this section, we provide an obvious extension of the above remark.

Let $F\colon X \to X$ be a linear transformation, where X is a vector space over a field L, and let y be the image of $x \in X$ under F. In terms of a basis u for X, $y = F(x)$ has a unique matrix expression $d = Ab$, where A is a square matrix and b, d are the coordinate vectors of x, y, respectively, in terms of u. In terms of another basis v for X, the same $F(x) = y$ has a different matrix representation $c = Bh$, where h, c are the coordinate vectors of x, y, respectively, in terms of v, and matrix B has the following relation with A and the transition matrix Q from v to u:

$$B = QAQ^{-1}. \tag{16}$$

Any square matrices A and B connected by the form (16) are said to be similar. Clearly the determinants of A and B are identical since

$$|B| = |Q|\,|A|\,|Q|^{-1} = |A|.$$

Likewise, the characteristic polynomial of B is equal to that of A since

$$|\lambda I - B| = |\lambda I - QAQ^{-1}| = |Q[\lambda I - A]Q^{-1}| = |\lambda I - A|.$$

Thus, an eigenvalue of a linear transformation $F\colon X \to X$, which is the same as that of its associated representative matrix (A or B above), is invariant of the basis chosen for X.

2.3 Rank and Nullity

DEFINITION 21 The *rank* of a matrix A is defined as the maximum number of linearly independent column vectors of A, and is denoted as $\mathrm{rk}(A)$.

THEOREM 20 Let r be the highest order of the minors of a matrix A that do not vanish. Then $r = \mathrm{rk}(A)$.

PROOF Suppose there are k linearly independent column vectors in A. Then some square matrix of order k made from these vectors is nonsingular. Hence $k \leq r$. On the other hand, an rth order nonvanishing minor of A contains r linearly independent column vectors. Hence $r \leq \mathrm{rk}(A)$. Q.E.D.

Owing to the following theorem, the rank of a matrix can be defined as the maximum number of linearly independent row vectors of the matrix.

THEOREM 21 (*rank theorem*) Let V(rows of A) denote the subspace generated by all the row vectors of a matrix A. Then

$$\dim V(\text{rows of } A) = \text{rk}(A). \tag{17}$$

PROOF Suppose $\dim V(\text{rows of } A) = k$. Then, any square submatrix of A whose order is higher than k is singular. Hence, the highest order of non-vanishing minors of A must not be larger than k, i.e.,

$$\text{rk}(A) \leqq k. \tag{$*$}$$

Let r be $\text{rk}(A)$, M an rth order square submatrix of A whose determinant does not vanish, and D the $(r+1)$th order minor of A containing M in its first r rows and r columns, i.e.,

$$D = \left| \begin{array}{ccc:c} & & & a_{1t} \\ & M & & \vdots \\ & & & a_{rt} \\ \hdashline a_{s1} & \cdots & a_{sr} & a_{st} \end{array} \right|$$

for $s = 1, \ldots, m$ and $t = 1, \ldots, n$. Obviously $D = 0$. Let A_{ij} be the cofactor of a_{ij} in D. Then

$$\sum_{i=1}^{r} a_{it}A_{it} + a_{st}|M| = 0 \qquad \text{for} \quad t = 1, \ldots, n.$$

Since $|M| \neq 0$, we have for all $t = 1, \ldots, n$,

$$a_{st} = \sum_{i=1}^{r} b_i a_{it} \qquad \text{with} \quad b_i \equiv -A_{it}/|M|.$$

Thus, row $s = \sum_{i=1}^{r} b_i$(row i) for $s = 1, \ldots, m$, where row i stands for the ith row of A. Hence

$$\dim V(\text{rows of } A) = \dim V(\text{rows 1 to } r \text{ of } A) \leqq r. \tag{$**$}$$

(17) follows from ($*$) and ($**$). Q.E.D.

COROLLARY Let $a^1, \ldots, a^r$ be linearly independent column m-vectors. Then there exists a row m-vector y such that for given scalars $\alpha_1, \ldots, \alpha_r$,

$$ya^i = \alpha_i \qquad \text{for} \quad i = 1, \ldots, r.$$

PROOF Let A be an $m \times r$ matrix with columns $a^1, \ldots, a^r$ and rows $a_1, \ldots, a_m$. By Theorem 21 (rank theorem), there are r linearly independent row vectors in A, say $a_1, \ldots, a_r$, and a row r-vector $\alpha = (\alpha_1, \ldots, \alpha_r)$ can be represented as a linear combination of the row vectors; i.e.,

$$\alpha = \sum_{j=1}^{r} \eta_j a_j = yA = y[a^1, \ldots, a^r],$$

where $y = (\eta_1, \ldots, \eta_r, 0, \ldots, 0)$. Q.E.D.

THEOREM 22 Let A be an $m \times q$ matrix and B a $q \times n$ matrix. Then

$$\text{rk}(AB) \leqq \min\{\text{rk}(A), \text{rk}(B)\}. \tag{18}$$

PROOF Let k be rk(B). Then, any $k + 1$ column vectors of B are linearly dependent. Hence, denoting by B_1 the matrix composed of an arbitrary $k + 1$ columns of B, we get $B_1 x = \theta$ for some nonzero $(k + 1)$-tuple vector x. Let y be the n-tuple vector composed of x and zeros otherwise. Then we have $By = \theta$, which is premultiplied by A to obtain $ABy = \theta$. We know, therefore, that any $k + 1$ column vectors of AB are linearly dependent, and hence $\text{rk}(AB) \leqq k = \text{rk}(B)$. Similarly, we obtain $\text{rk}(AB) \leqq \text{rk}(A)$. Q.E.D.

THEOREM 23 For any matrix A

$$\text{rk}(A^{\text{T}}A) = \text{rk}(A). \tag{19}$$

PROOF By Theorem 22, $\text{rk}(A^{\text{T}}A) \leqq \text{rk}(A)$. Let A be an $m \times n$ matrix with rank r and assume without loss of generality that its first r columns are linearly independent. Suppose $\text{rk}(A^{\text{T}}A) < r$; namely, any r column vectors of $A^{\text{T}}A$ are supposed to be linearly dependent. Let B be the $n \times r$ matrix composed of the first r columns of $A^{\text{T}}A$. Then there exists a nonzero column vector $x = \{x_1, \ldots, x_r\}$ such that $Bx = \theta$. Let y denote the n-vector consisting of x in its first r components and of zeros otherwise. Then $A^{\text{T}}Ay = \theta$ and hence $y^{\text{T}}A^{\text{T}}Ay = 0$. Vector Ay whose inner product vanishes must be a null vector, i.e.,

$$a^1 x_1 + \cdots + a^r x_r = \theta,$$

where a^i stands for the ith column of A. Since x is a nonzero vector, the above equation implies that $a^1, \ldots, a^r$ are linearly dependent, contradicting our previous assumption. Q.E.D.

THEOREM 24 Let A and B be matrices such that AB can be defined. Then (i) $\text{rk}(AB) = \text{rk}(A)$ if B is a nonsingular square matrix and (ii) $\text{rk}(AB) = \text{rk}(B)$ if A is a nonsingular square matrix.

PROOF Set $q = n$ in Theorem 22. In (i) by assumption B is a nonsingular square matrix. Assume $\text{rk}(AB) = k$ and $\text{rk}(A) = r$. Inequality (18) implies $k \leqq r$. On the other hand, $A = (AB)B^{-1}$ and Theorem 22 imply $r \leqq k$. Hence statement (i) follows. Similarly, by setting $q = m$, we can verify statement (ii). Q.E.D.

Next we shall be concerned with the relationships between the rank of a matrix and the dimension of the range or the nullspace of the associated linear transformation.

THEOREM 25 Let X and Y be vector spaces over a field, and let F be a linear transformation from X into Y. If A is the $m \times n$ matrix representing F relative to a chosen pair of bases for X and Y, then

$$\dim R(F) = \text{rk}(A). \tag{20}$$

PROOF Let y be an element of $R(F)$, namely, $F(x) = y$ for some $x \in X$. Let b and d be column vectors composed of coordinates of x and y, respectively, relative to a chosen pair of bases $\{x_1, \ldots, x_n\} \subset X$ and $\{y_1, \ldots, y_m\} \subset Y$. Hence $Ab = d$. Let M be the square matrix of order m whose columns are $y_1, \ldots, y_m$. Then we have $y = Md = MAb$. Since M is nonsingular, $\text{rk}(MA) = \text{rk}(A) \equiv r$, i.e., MA contains r linearly independent columns. Denote the jth column vector of MA by v_j and assume the first r columns are linearly independent. Then y can be expressed as $y = \sum_{j=1}^{r} \lambda_j v_j$, which means that y belongs to an r-dimensional subspace of Y. Q.E.D.

As we remarked in Section 2.2, corresponding to a given $m \times n$ matrix A, there is a unique linear transformation $F: X \to Y$ (where $\dim X = n$ and $\dim Y = m$) such that

$$F(x) = \theta \qquad \text{for} \quad x \in X, \tag{21}$$

and

$$Ab = \theta, \tag{22}$$

where b is a column vector composed of the coordinates of x relative to a basis for X. The set of solutions b satisfying (22) may be termed the *nullspace* of matrix A and is denoted $N(A)$. Clearly the dimension of $N(A)$ is equal to the dimension of $N(F)$, which is called the *nullity* of F. We shall establish a fundamental relation concerning the nullity of F.

THEOREM 26 Let X and Y be vector spaces over a field L, and let F be a linear transformation from X into Y. Then

$$\dim N(F) = \dim X - \dim R(F). \tag{23}$$

PROOF Assume $\dim X = n$ and $\dim N(F) = n - k$. Since $N(F) \subset X$, a basis $\{x^{k+1}, x^{k+2}, \ldots, x^n\}$ of $N(F)$ can be extended to a basis $\{x^1, \ldots, x^k, x^{k+1}, \ldots, x^n\}$ of X. The set $\{F(x^1), \ldots, F(x^k)\}$ is found to be linearly independent since if the set were linearly dependent, we would have

$$\theta = \sum_{i=1}^{k} \alpha_i F(x^i) = F\left(\sum_{i=1}^{k} \alpha_i x^i\right)$$

for some not-all-zero scalars $\alpha_i \in L$ $(i = 1, \ldots, k)$. This would mean that $\sum_{i=1}^{k} \alpha_i x^i$ lies in $N(F)$ and hence $\{x^1, \ldots, x^k, x^{k+1}, \ldots, x^n\}$ would be linearly dependent, contradicting our assumption that it is linearly independent. Next we shall show that the linearly independent set $\{F(x^1), \ldots, F(x^k)\}$ generates $R(F)$. For any $F(x)$ for $x \in X$, there are scalars $\beta_i \in L$

$(i = 1, \ldots, n)$ such that

$$F(x) = F\left(\sum_{i=1}^{n} \beta_i x^i\right) = \sum_{i=1}^{n} \beta_i F(x^i) = \sum_{i=1}^{k} \beta_i F(x^i)$$

since x^i $(i = k + 1, \ldots, n)$ lie in $N(F)$. That is, every vector in $R(F)$ is represented as a linear combination of vectors $F(x^1), \ldots, F(x^k)$. Thus, $\dim R(F) = k$. Q.E.D.

In view of Theorems 25 and 26, the solution space for system (22), which is the nullspace of A, has dimension equal to the number of columns of A minus its rank; i.e., letting n denote the number of columns of A, we have

$$\dim N(A) = n - \mathrm{rk}(A). \tag{24}$$

By utilizing relation (24), we prove the following theorem.

THEOREM 27 For a square matrix A, there exists a nonzero vector x satisfying $Ax = \theta$ if and only if A is singular.

PROOF Let n be the order of A. In case $n = 1$, the above statement holds trivially. Assume $n \geqq 2$. If $|A| = 0$, then $\mathrm{rk}(A) \leqq n - 1$. Hence, by taking (24) into account, we know $\dim N(A) \geqq 1$, which implies the existence of a nonzero vector x satisfying $Ax = \theta$. If $|A| \neq 0$, then $\dim N(A) = 0$, implying that the only solution to $Ax = \theta$ is a null vector. Q.E.D.

Next we shall study a nonhomogeneous system of linear equations

$$Ax = d, \tag{25}$$

where A is an $m \times n$ matrix, d is a nonzero column m-vector, and x is an unknown n-vector to be determined. If $\mathrm{rk}(A) = m$, then (25) has a solution x for any d since $\mathrm{rk}[A|d] = m$. If $\mathrm{rk}(A) < m$, some m-vector d cannot be represented by any linear combination of the columns of A. Thus

THEOREM 28 System (25) has a solution for an arbitrary d if and only if $\mathrm{rk}(A) = m$.

THEOREM 28′ The solution space S for system (25) is the translation of $N(A)$ by a particular solution $x^0 \in X$, where X is a vector space with dimension n; i.e.,

$$S = N(A) + x^0. \tag{26}$$

PROOF (1) For $x \in S$, $A(x - x^0) = Ax - Ax^0 = d - d = \theta$. Hence $x - x^0$ belongs to $N(A)$. Thus, $S - x^0 \subset N(A)$. (2) For $y \in N(A)$, $A(y + x^0) = \theta + Ax^0 = d$, and hence $y + x^0$ is an element of S. Thus $N(A) + x^0 \subset S$. Q.E.D.

Since x^0 in Theorem 28′ does not belong to $N(A)$,

$$\dim S = \dim N(A) + 1 = n + 1 - \mathrm{rk}(A), \tag{27}$$

in view of (24). In a limiting case where A is a square matrix of full rank, $\dim S = 1$ since $\text{rk}(A) =$ the order of A; and in this case system (25) has a unique solution

$$x = A^{-1}d \tag{28}$$

since $\dim N(A) = 0$, i.e., $N(A)$ is nothing but a null vector θ.

To conclude this section, we add a theorem concerning the solvability of linear equations.

THEOREM 29 Exactly one of the following alternatives holds. Either system (25) has a solution x or there exists a solution y to the following system

$$yA = \theta \qquad \text{and} \qquad yd = 1, \tag{29}$$

where y is a row m-vector.

PROOF If system (25) has a solution, system (29) cannot have any solution, for then we have a contradiction:

$$0 = yAx = yd = 1.$$

Suppose system (25) has no solution. Let $a^1, \ldots, a^r$ be column vectors of A constituting a basis for the subspace V(columns of A) generated by all columns of A. Then these vectors together with d are linearly independent since otherwise d would be represented by a linear combination of the a^i ($i = 1, \ldots, r$) giving a solution of system (25). By the corollary to Theorem 21 (rank theorem), there exists a vector y such that

$$ya^i = 0 \quad \text{for} \quad i = 1, \ldots, r, \qquad \text{and} \qquad yd = 1.$$

Since a^k ($k = r + 1, \ldots, n$) can be represented as a linear combination of $a^1, \ldots, a^r$, say $a^k = \sum_{i=1}^r \beta_i a^i$, we have

$$ya^k = \sum_{i=1}^{r} \beta_i ya^i = 0 \qquad \text{for} \quad k = r + 1, \ldots, n. \qquad \text{Q.E.D.}$$

In order to verify the insolubility of system (25), one need only produce a solution y to system (29).

2.4 Elementary Operations and Hawkins–Simon Conditions

So far we have studied the theoretical aspects of linear equations. This section first deals with the computation of linear equations over the real field and secondly, as an application, with a fundamental theorem concerning a multisectoral production system.

Given an $m \times n$ matrix A and an m-vector d, we want to solve its associated system of linear equations:

$$Ax = d. \tag{30}$$

Premultiplying (30) by a nonsingular square matrix M of order m results in

$$MAx = Md. \tag{31}$$

Clearly, any solution x of system (30) must satisfy system (31); and conversely, any solution x of system (31) must satisfy (30) since (31) can be transformed into (30) by premultiplying by M^{-1}. Thus systems (30) and (31) yield identical solutions, and the one system is said to be equivalent to the other. Selecting matrix M such that the resulting matrix MA takes a convenient form, we may easily compute solution x of system (31) and hence of system (30). Elementary row operations introduced below will serve for such a transformation of linear equations.

There are three types of elementary row operations on a matrix A: (i) to multiply a row of matrix A by a nonzero scalar λ; (ii) to add a row of matrix A multiplied by a nonzero scalar λ to another row of A; and (iii) to interchange two rows in matrix A. Each of these operations is characterized by premultiplication of matrix A by a nonsingular square matrix M, which will be illustrated as follows in the case where A is a $3 \times n$ matrix. (i) To multiply row 2 of A by λ ($\neq 0$) is equivalent to MA where $M = M_1$ defined below; (ii) to add row 2 of A multiplied by λ ($\neq 0$) to row 3 is equivalent to MA where $M = M_2$ defined below; and (iii) to interchange rows 2 and 3 in A is equivalent to MA where $M = M_3$ defined below.

$$M_1 \equiv \begin{bmatrix} 1 & 0 & 0 \\ 0 & \lambda & 0 \\ 0 & 0 & 1 \end{bmatrix}, \qquad M_2 \equiv \begin{bmatrix} 1 & 0 & 0 \\ 0 & 1 & 0 \\ 0 & \lambda & 1 \end{bmatrix}, \qquad M_3 \equiv \begin{bmatrix} 1 & 0 & 0 \\ 0 & 0 & 1 \\ 0 & 1 & 0 \end{bmatrix}.$$

Matrix B obtained after having performed a finite number of elementary row operations on matrix A is said to be *row-equivalent* to A. Let $[B\,|\,z]$ be the resulting matrix after such operations on the augmented matrix $[A\,|\,d]$. Then system $Bx = z$ is obviously equivalent to system (30). In general, a finite number of elementary row operations reduces any matrix to the form

$$\begin{bmatrix} + & * & * & & & & \cdots & * \\ 0 & + & * & & & & \cdots & * \\ 0 & 0 & \ddots & & & & & \vdots \\ \vdots & \vdots & & + & * & * & \cdots & * \\ 0 & 0 & \cdots & 0 & + & * & \cdots & * \end{bmatrix}, \tag{32}$$

where $^+$ stands for one or zero and $*$ any scalar. (32) is termed a *row-reduced echelon* matrix.

Let A be an $m \times n$ matrix with rank r and consider the associated homogeneous system of linear equations

$$Ax = \theta. \tag{33}$$

Applying a finite number of elementary row operations, we can transform system (33) into

$$Bx = \theta, \tag{34}$$

where the resulting matrix B is of a row-reduced echelon form. Note that $\text{rk}(B) = \text{rk}(A) = r$. Thus B can be expressed as

$$B = \begin{bmatrix} b_{11} & \cdots & b_{1r} & \cdots & b_{1n} \\ \vdots & & \vdots & & \vdots \\ b_{r1} & \cdots & b_{rr} & \cdots & b_{rn} \\ 0 & \cdots & 0 & \cdots & 0 \\ \vdots & & \vdots & & \vdots \\ 0 & \cdots & 0 & \cdots & 0 \end{bmatrix} \left.\begin{matrix} \\ \\ \\ \\ \\ \\ \end{matrix}\right\} (m - r) \tag{35}$$

Hence system (34) is rewritten as

$$\begin{bmatrix} b_{11} & \cdots & b_{1r} \\ \vdots & & \vdots \\ b_{r1} & \cdots & b_{rr} \end{bmatrix} \begin{bmatrix} x_1 \\ \vdots \\ x_r \end{bmatrix} = - \begin{bmatrix} b_{1,r+1} & \cdots & b_{1n} \\ \vdots & & \vdots \\ b_{r,r+1} & \cdots & b_{rn} \end{bmatrix} \begin{bmatrix} x_{r+1} \\ \vdots \\ x_n \end{bmatrix}, \tag{36}$$

where x_i stands for the ith component of n-vector x. Given the $n - r$ components $x_{r+1}, \ldots, x_n$ of x, the rest $x_1, \ldots, x_r$ are determined uniquely by (36). Conventionally, by setting $x_k = 1$ for one k and $x_j = 0$ for any $j \neq k$ such that

$$r + 1 \leqq k, \qquad j \leqq n,$$

we determine $\{x_1, \ldots, x_r\}$, say $\{x_1^{(k-r)}, \ldots, x_r^{(k-r)}\}$. The set of all the solutions $\{x_1, \ldots, x_r, x_{r+1}, \ldots, x_n\}$ obtained in this way is

$$\begin{aligned} &\{x_1^{(1)}, \ldots, x_r^{(1)}, 1, 0, \ldots, 0\} \\ &\{x_1^{(2)}, \ldots, x_r^{(2)}, 0, 1, \ldots, 0\} \\ &\vdots \\ &\{x_1^{(n-r)}, \ldots, x_r^{(n-r)}, 0, 0, \ldots, 1\}. \end{aligned} \tag{37}$$

These are linearly independent vectors forming a basis for nullspace $N(A)$ of A. Thus, any vector belonging to $N(A)$ is represented by a linear combination of vectors in (37), which is the so-called general solution of system (33).

Example Let matrix A and vector d in system (30) be given as

$$[A \mid d] = \left[\begin{array}{ccccc|c} 3 & -2 & 2 & 2 & 1 & 4 \\ 1 & -1 & 2 & -1 & -2 & 1 \\ 1 & 0 & -1 & 4 & 5 & 1 \end{array}\right].$$

First perform three stages of elementary row operations indicated by (I), (II), and (III) on $[A \mid d]$ in order to obtain a row-reduced echelon matrix:

$$[A|d] \xrightarrow{\text{(I)}} \left[\begin{array}{ccccc|c} 0 & 1 & -4 & 5 & 7 & 1 \\ 1 & -1 & 2 & -1 & -2 & 1 \\ 0 & 1 & -3 & 5 & 7 & 0 \end{array}\right] \xrightarrow{\text{(II)}} \left[\begin{array}{ccccc|c} 0 & 1 & -4 & 5 & 7 & 1 \\ 1 & -1 & 2 & -1 & -2 & 1 \\ 0 & 0 & 1 & 0 & 0 & -1 \end{array}\right]$$

$$\xrightarrow{\text{(III)}} \left[\begin{array}{ccccc|c} 1 & -1 & 2 & -1 & -2 & 1 \\ 0 & 1 & -4 & 5 & 7 & 1 \\ 0 & 0 & 1 & 0 & 0 & -1 \end{array}\right],$$

where the last matrix is designated as $[B|z]$ and each stage of elementary row operations is the following: (I) to add $(-3) \times$ row 2 to row 1 and to add $(-1) \times$ row 2 to row 3; (II) to add $(-1) \times$ row 1 to row 3; and (III) to interchange row 1 and row 2. Then, it follows from the transformed system $Bx = z$ that

$$\begin{aligned} x_1 &= x_2 - 2x_3 + x_4 + 2x_5 + 1, \\ x_2 &= 4x_3 - 5x_4 - 7x_5 + 1, \\ x_3 &= -1. \end{aligned}$$

Setting $x_4 = x_5 = 0$ in the above equations, we have a particular solution $x^0 = \{0, -3, -1, 0, 0\}$. Since $\text{rk}(A) = 3$, $\dim N(A) = 2$ $(= 5 - 3)$. We have, therefore, two vectors forming a basis for $N(A)$: $x^1 = \{-3, -5, 0, 1, 0\}$ and $x^2 = \{-5, -7, 0, 0, 1\}$, and the general solution of nonhomogeneous system (30) is obtained by

$$x = c_1x^1 + c_2x^2 + x^0,$$

where c_1 and c_2 are arbitrary scalars.

Now, utilizing elementary row operations, we shall verify a fundamental theorem concerning a multisectoral production system represented by

$$x_i = \sum_{j=1}^{n} a_{ij}x_j + y_i \qquad \text{for} \quad i = 1, \ldots, n, \tag{38}$$

where a_{ij} stands for the input coefficient of good i in sector j, y_i the final demand for good i, and x_i the total output of good i to meet the bill of goods finally demanded. System (38) is the so-called Leontief production system where each sector is supposed to produce a single good and each a_{ij} is assumed nonnegative. By denoting $b_{ij} \equiv -a_{ij}$ for $i \neq j$ and $b_{ii} \equiv 1 - a_{ii}$, we rewrite system (38) in matrix form

$$Bx = y, \tag{39}$$

where

$$B \equiv \begin{bmatrix} b_{11} & b_{12} & \cdots & b_{1n} \\ b_{21} & b_{22} & \cdots & b_{2n} \\ \vdots & \vdots & & \vdots \\ b_{n1} & b_{n2} & \cdots & b_{nn} \end{bmatrix}, \qquad x \equiv \begin{bmatrix} x_1 \\ x_2 \\ \vdots \\ x_n \end{bmatrix}, \qquad \text{and} \qquad y \equiv \begin{bmatrix} y_1 \\ y_2 \\ \vdots \\ y_n \end{bmatrix}.$$

THEOREM 30 (*Hawkins–Simon theorem*) Solution x of system (39) is semipositive for any semipositive y if and only if all the principal minors of B are positive; i.e.,

$$b_{ii} > 0, \qquad \begin{vmatrix} b_{ii} & b_{ij} \\ b_{ji} & b_{jj} \end{vmatrix} > 0, \qquad \begin{vmatrix} b_{ii} & b_{ij} & b_{ik} \\ b_{ji} & b_{jj} & b_{jk} \\ b_{ki} & b_{kj} & b_{kk} \end{vmatrix} > 0, \qquad \ldots, \qquad |B| > 0,$$

for $i \neq j \neq k \in \{1, 2, \ldots, n\}$. The set of all these conditions are said to be the *Hawkins–Simon conditions*, abbreviated henceforth as H-S conditions.

(*Remark* In view of Theorem 23 in Section 1.3, that a real matrix B fulfills the H-S conditions is equivalent to saying that B has a q.d.d.)

PROOF The sufficiency and necessity of this theorem will both be proved by applying a mathematical induction on the dimension n. The semipositivity of a vector v will be denoted as "$v \geq 0$." Numbering is arbitrary.

Sufficiency We show that the H-S conditions imply $x \geq 0$ in system (39) for any $y \geq 0$. In case $n = 1$, system (39) reduces to $b_{11}x_1 = y_1$, where we have $x_1 > 0$ for any $y_1 > 0$ since $b_{11} > 0$. Next, after reducing the dimension of system (39) by one, we assume that the H-S conditions imply $x \geq 0$ for any $y \geq 0$ in the reduced system. The original system (39) can be transformed into an equivalent system (40) below by the elementary row operations that (row i) – b_{i1}(row 1)/b_{11} for $i = 2, 3, \ldots, n$:

$$\begin{bmatrix} b_{11} & b_{12} & \cdots & b_{1n} \\ 0 & b_{22}^* & \cdots & b_{2n}^* \\ \vdots & \vdots & & \vdots \\ 0 & b_{n2}^* & \cdots & b_{nn}^* \end{bmatrix} \begin{bmatrix} x_1 \\ x_2 \\ \vdots \\ x_n \end{bmatrix} = \begin{bmatrix} y_1 \\ y_2^* \\ \vdots \\ y_n^* \end{bmatrix}, \tag{40}$$

where $b_{ij}^* \equiv b_{ij} - b_{i1}b_{1j}/b_{11} \leqq b_{ij}$ and $y_i^* \equiv y_i - b_{i1}y_1/b_{11} \geqq y_i$ for $i, j = 2, 3, \ldots, n$. System (40) is divided into two subsystems:

$$\begin{bmatrix} b_{22}^* & \cdots & b_{2n}^* \\ \vdots & & \vdots \\ b_{n2}^* & \cdots & b_{nn}^* \end{bmatrix} \begin{bmatrix} x_2 \\ \vdots \\ x_n \end{bmatrix} = \begin{bmatrix} y_2^* \\ \vdots \\ y_n^* \end{bmatrix} \tag{41}$$

and

$$b_{11}x_1 = y_1 - \sum_{j=2}^{n} b_{1j}x_j. \tag{42}$$

Because of the elementary row operations mentioned above, we have

$$\begin{vmatrix} b_{22}^* & \cdots & b_{2k}^* \\ \vdots & & \vdots \\ b_{k2}^* & \cdots & b_{kk}^* \end{vmatrix} = \frac{1}{b_{11}} \begin{vmatrix} b_{11} & \cdots & b_{1k} \\ \vdots & & \vdots \\ b_{k1} & \cdots & b_{kk} \end{vmatrix} > 0 \quad \text{for} \quad k = 2, 3, \ldots, n, \tag{43}$$

i.e., the H-S conditions hold for the coefficient matrix of system (41). By the induction assumption, therefore, all solutions of system (41) must be semipositive for any $\{y_2^*, \ldots, y_n^*\} \geq \theta$, which is implied by any $y \geq \theta$ and $b_{i1} < 0$ for some $i = 2, 3, \ldots, n$. Hence from (42) we have $x_1 \geqq 0$ for any $y \geq \theta$. (In case $y_1 > 0$ and $y_2 = y_3 = \cdots = y_n = 0$, $b_{21} \doteq b_{31} = \cdots = b_{n1} = 0$ implies $b_{ij}^* = b_{ij}$ and $y_i^* = y_i$ for $i, j = 2, 3, \ldots, n$. Hence system (41) produces only a null vector as its solution and Eq. (42) yields $x_1 > 0$.)

Necessity It suffices to verify that $x \geq \theta$ for *some* $y \geq \theta$ in system (39) implies the H-S conditions because the sufficiency proved above ensures that the H-S conditions imply $x \geq \theta$ for any $y \geq \theta$ in (39), and because $x \geq \theta$ for any $y \geq \theta$ in (39) implies $x \geq \theta$ for some $y \geq \theta$.

In case $n = 1$, the necessity statement mentioned above is verified trivially. $x \geq \theta$ for some $y \geq \theta$ in (39) implies that not all b_{ii} $(i = 1, \ldots, n)$ can be nonpositive. (If all b_{ii} were nonpositive, a contradiction would obviously occur in (39).) So we may assume $b_{11} > 0$ without loss of generality. Consider the case where $x \geq \theta$ for some $y \geq \theta$ in system (39). Then, clearly the solution of system (41) is semipositive for the $\{y_2^*, \ldots, y_n^*\}$ corresponding to the y, which in turn implies that the H-S conditions hold for the coefficient matrix in system (41) in view of the induction assumption. Thus we have, from (43),

$$\begin{vmatrix} b_{11} & b_{12} & \cdots & b_{1k} \\ b_{21} & b_{22} & \cdots & b_{2k} \\ \vdots & \vdots & & \vdots \\ b_{k1} & b_{k2} & \cdots & b_{kk} \end{vmatrix} = b_{11} \begin{vmatrix} b_{22}^* & \cdots & b_{2k}^* \\ \vdots & & \vdots \\ b_{k2}^* & \cdots & b_{kk}^* \end{vmatrix} > 0 \qquad \text{for} \quad k = 2, \ldots, n. \qquad \text{Q.E.D.}$$

COROLLARY 1 Solution x of system (39) is semipositive for some $y \geq \theta$ if and only if the H-S conditions hold for matrix B.

COROLLARY 2 The H-S conditions hold for matrix B if and only if B^{-1} is a nonnegative matrix with positive main diagonal entries.

PROOF There exists B^{-1} since the H-S conditions hold for B. $x = B^{-1}y \geq \theta$ for any $y \geq \theta$ if and only if B^{-1} is nonnegative and nonzero. Q.E.D.

2.5 Symmetric Matrices, Stable Matrices, and the Lyapunov Theorem

In this section we prove some important theorems concerning real symmetric matrices and related matrices.

THEOREM 31 Every eigenvalue of a real symmetric matrix is real.

PROOF Let A be a real symmetric matrix. Suppose λ were a complex eigenvalue of A. Then, its conjugate $\bar{\lambda}$ must be an eigenvalue of A. Let v and $\bar{v}$

denote the eigenvectors of A associated with λ and $\bar{\lambda}$, respectively; i.e., $Av = \lambda v$, $A\bar{v} = \bar{\lambda}\bar{v}$. Notice that $v^{\mathrm{T}}\bar{v}$ is a real scalar. From these equations it follows that

$$\bar{v}^{\mathrm{T}}Av - v^{\mathrm{T}}A\bar{v} = (\lambda - \bar{\lambda})v^{\mathrm{T}}\bar{v}.$$

Since A is symmetric, the left-hand side of this equation is zero. Hence, $\lambda = \bar{\lambda}$. Q.E.D.

THEOREM 32 The eigenvectors associated with distinct eigenvalues of a real symmetric matrix are orthogonal to each other.

PROOF Let λ_1 and λ_2 be distinct eigenvalues of a real symmetric matrix A and v_i be the eigenvector of A associated with λ_i ($i = 1, 2$). Then

$$\lambda_2 v_1^{\mathrm{T}} v_2 = v_1^{\mathrm{T}} A v_2 = v_2^{\mathrm{T}} A v_1 = \lambda_1 v_2^{\mathrm{T}} v_1.$$

Since $\lambda_1 \neq \lambda_2$, we have $v_1^{\mathrm{T}} v_2 = 0$. Q.E.D.

It will be shown in Section 3.2 that there are exactly w_i linearly independent eigenvectors associated with an eigenvalue λ_i of a real square matrix with multiplicity w_i. These eigenvectors can be orthonormalized. Let v_i ($i = 1, \ldots, n$) represent the orthonormalized eigenvectors of a real symmetric matrix A of order n. Then, in view of Theorem 32, by defining $V \equiv [v_1, \ldots, v_n]$, we have

$$V^{\mathrm{T}}V = I \qquad \text{(identity matrix)}, \tag{44}$$

and

$$V^{\mathrm{T}}AV = \begin{bmatrix} \lambda_1 & & \\ & \ddots & \\ & & \lambda_n \end{bmatrix} \equiv \Lambda \tag{45}$$

since $v_i^{\mathrm{T}}Av_i = \lambda_i v_i^{\mathrm{T}} v_i = \lambda_i$ and $v_i^{\mathrm{T}}Av_j = \lambda_j v_i^{\mathrm{T}} v_j = 0$ for $i \neq j$.

In general, a square matrix M is said to be *orthogonal* if

$$M^{-1} = M^{\mathrm{T}}. \tag{46}$$

Obviously, V defined above is an orthogonal matrix.

There are other diagonalizations of a symmetric matrix besides (45). Let $A \equiv [a_{ij}]$ be a symmetric matrix of order n satisfying

$$A_1 \equiv a_{11} \neq 0, \qquad A_2 \equiv \begin{vmatrix} a_{11} & a_{12} \\ a_{12} & a_{22} \end{vmatrix} \neq 0, \qquad A_3 \equiv \begin{vmatrix} a_{11} & a_{12} & a_{13} \\ a_{12} & a_{22} & a_{23} \\ a_{13} & a_{23} & a_{33} \end{vmatrix} \neq 0, \ldots,$$

$$A_{n-1} \equiv \begin{vmatrix} a_{11} & a_{12} & \cdots & a_{1,n-1} \\ a_{12} & a_{22} & \cdots & a_{2,n-1} \\ \vdots & & & \vdots \\ a_{1,n-1} & & \cdots & a_{n-1,n-1} \end{vmatrix} \neq 0. \tag{47}$$

Then we have a transformation matrix C such that

$$C^{\mathrm{T}}AC = \begin{bmatrix} \beta_1 & 0 & \cdots & 0 \\ 0 & \beta_2 & & \vdots \\ \vdots & & \ddots & 0 \\ 0 & \cdots & 0 & \beta_n \end{bmatrix}, \tag{48}$$

where

$$\beta_r \equiv A_r/A_{r-1} \qquad \text{for} \quad r = 2,3, \ldots, n\text{–}1;$$

$$\beta_n \equiv |A|/A_{n-1}; \qquad \beta_1 \equiv A_1; \tag{49}$$

$$C \equiv \begin{bmatrix} 1 & c_{12} & c_{13} & \cdots & c_{1n} \\ 0 & 1 & c_{23} & \cdots & c_{2n} \\ 0 & 0 & \ddots & & \vdots \\ \vdots & & & & c_{n-1,n} \\ 0 & & \cdots & 0 & 1 \end{bmatrix}, \tag{50}$$

whose components are determined in the following way:

$$\begin{bmatrix} a_{11} & a_{12} & \cdots & a_{1r} \\ a_{12} & a_{22} & \cdots & a_{2r} \\ \vdots & \vdots & & \vdots \\ a_{1r} & a_{2r} & \cdots & a_{rr} \end{bmatrix} \begin{bmatrix} c_{1,r+1} \\ c_{2,r+1} \\ \vdots \\ c_{r,r+1} \end{bmatrix} = - \begin{bmatrix} a_{1,r+1} \\ a_{2,r+1} \\ \vdots \\ a_{r,r+1} \end{bmatrix} \qquad \text{for} \quad r = 1, 2, \ldots, n-1.$$

Clearly the β's in (48) are the eigenvalues of $C^{\mathrm{T}}AC$.

DEFINITION 22 Let A be a symmetrix matrix of order n. Then a functional Q defined by

$$Q(x) \equiv x^{\mathrm{T}}Ax, \tag{51}$$

where x is a column n-vector, is said to be a *quadratic form* corresponding to A. When the components of A are real, Q defined by (51) is called a real quadratic form. We restrict the following discussion to real quadratic forms. If x is transformed into $y \equiv \{y_1, \ldots, y_n\}$ by

$$V^{\mathrm{T}}x = y, \tag{52}$$

where $V \equiv [v_1, \ldots, v_n]$ as defined above, then in view of (44) and (45)

$$Q(x) = \sum_{i=1}^{n} \lambda_i y_i^2, \tag{53}$$

where $y^{\mathrm{T}}y = x^{\mathrm{T}}x$. (53) is termed the canonical quadratic form.

DEFINITION 23 Let A be a real symmetric matrix of order n, p the number of positive eigenvalues λ_i of A, and k the rank of A. Assume $k \geqq 1$.

(i) If $p = k \leqq n$, A or its associated quadratic form Q is said to be *positive semidefinite* (or *nonnegative definite*) since then $Q(x) \geqq 0$ for all $x \in R^n$. [Note $Q(x) = 0$ for some $x \neq \theta$ if and only if $k < n$.]

(ii) If $p = k = n$, i.e., if all eigenvalues of A are positive, then $Q(x) > 0$ for all $x \neq \theta$, and A or Q is said to be *positive definite*.

(iii) If $0 = p < k \leqq n$, A is said to be *negative semidefinite* (or *nonpositive definite*) since then $Q(x) \leqq 0$ for all $x \in R^n$. [The note in (i) applies.]

(iv) If $0 = p < k = n$, i.e., if all eigenvalues of A are negative, then $Q(x) < 0$ for all $x \neq \theta$, and A or Q is said to be negative definite.

Obviously, if A is positive (semi-) definite, then $-A$ is negative (semi-) definite, and vice versa.

Note that for a positive definite matrix A of order n, $|A| > 0$ and $\sum_{i=1}^{n} a_{ii} > 0$, where a_{ii} stands for the ith principal diagonal element of A.

THEOREM 33 Let A be a real symmetric matrix of order n. (i) A necessary and sufficient condition for A to be positive semidefinite with $rk(A) < n$ is that there exist an $n \times n$ real singular matrix B such that $B^T B = A$. (ii) A necessary and sufficient condition for A to be positive definite is that there exist as $n \times n$ real nonsingular matrix B such that $B^T B = A$.

PROOF *Sufficiency* $x^T A x = (Bx)^T (Bx) \geqq 0$ for every $x \neq \theta$. In case (i), $|B| = 0$, implying the existence of a nonzero x such that $Bx = \theta$, or $x^T A x = 0$. In case (ii), $|B| \neq 0$, implying the nonexistence of any nonzero x for which $Bx = \theta$. Thus for every $x \neq \theta$ we have $Bx \neq \theta$ and hence $x^T A x > 0$.

Necessity Assume that A is positive (semi-) definite. There is, by (45), an orthogonal matrix V such that $V^T A V = \Lambda$. Since all eigenvalues are nonnegative, $A = V\Lambda^{1/2}\Lambda^{1/2}V^T$, where $\Lambda^{1/2}$ is the diagonal matrix consisting of $\lambda_i^{1/2}$ $(i = 1, \ldots, n)$. Set $B = \Lambda^{1/2}V^T$. In case (i), $\text{rk}(\Lambda^{1/2}) < n$ and hence $\text{rk}(B) < n$. In case (ii), $\text{rk}(\Lambda^{1/2}) = n$ and hence $\text{rk}(B) = n$. Q.E.D.

THEOREM 34 Let A be an $n \times n$ real symmetric positive (or negative) definite matrix. Then its principal submatrices of any order are nonsingular.

PROOF Make a partition of A such that

$$A = \begin{bmatrix} A_{11} & A_{12} \\ A_{21} & A_{22} \end{bmatrix}$$

where A_{11} and A_{22} are square matrices of order m $(< n)$ and $n - m$, respectively. There is an orthogonal matrix V such that $V^T A V = \Lambda$, where Λ is the diagonal matrix with the eigenvalues λ_i $(i = 1, \ldots, n)$ of A at diagonal entries. Set $B = \Lambda^{1/2}V^T$, where $\Lambda^{1/2}$ is the diagonal matrix consisting of $\lambda_i^{1/2}$ $(i = 1, \ldots, n)$, and make a partition of B such that $B = [B_1, B_2]$, where B_1 and B_2 are $n \times m$ and $n \times (n - m)$ matrices, respectively. Then $A_{11} = B_1^T B_1$ and $A_{22} = B_2^T B_2$. Since B is nonsingular, we have $\text{rk}(A_{11}) = \text{rk}(B_1^T B_1) = \text{rk}(B_1) = m$, and $\text{rk}(A_{22}) = \text{rk}(B_2^T B_2) = \text{rk}(B_2) = n - m$. Q.E.D.

THEOREM 35 Let A be a real symmetric matrix. A is positive definite if and only if all the principal minors of A are positive, i.e., A is a P-matrix.

PROOF *Sufficiency* Let n be the order of $A \equiv [a_{ij}]$.

$$|A - \lambda I| = (-1)^n |\lambda I - A|$$

$$= (-\lambda)^n + \sum_{i=1}^{n} a_{ii}(-\lambda)^{n-1} + \sum_{i,j=1,i<j}^{n} \begin{vmatrix} a_{ii} & a_{ij} \\ a_{ji} & a_{jj} \end{vmatrix} (-\lambda)^{n-2} + \cdots + |A|.$$

Notice that all eigenvalues of a real symmetric matrix are real. Thus, if all the principal minors of A are positive, $|A - \lambda I| = 0$ requires that $-\lambda$ takes on a negative value for each eigenvalue λ, i.e., that λ takes on a positive value.

Necessity Positive definite A implies that there is an $n \times n$ real nonsingular matrix B such that $B^T B = A$. Conditions (47) are fulfilled by A in view of Theorem 34. Thus we have matrix C defined by (50) for which $C^T AC = C^T B^T BC$. Set $G \equiv BC$, which is nonsingular. By Theorem 33, therefore, $C^T AC$ is found to be positive definite. Hence its eigenvalues $\beta_i > 0$ $(i = 1, \ldots, n)$, implying, in view of (49), that

$$a_{11} > 0, \qquad \begin{vmatrix} a_{11} & a_{12} \\ a_{12} & a_{22} \end{vmatrix} > 0, \qquad \begin{vmatrix} a_{11} & a_{12} & a_{13} \\ a_{12} & a_{22} & a_{23} \\ a_{13} & a_{23} & a_{33} \end{vmatrix} > 0, \qquad \ldots, \qquad |A| > 0.$$

Q.E.D.

COROLLARY Let A be a real symmetric matrix. A is negative definite if and only if every principal minor of odd order takes on a negative value and every principal minor of even order is positive, i.e., A is an NP-matrix.

PROOF *Sufficiency* Let n be the order of $A \equiv [a_{ij}]$. Since

$$|\lambda I - A| = \lambda^n - \sum_{i=1}^{n} a_{ii}\lambda^{n-1} + \sum_{i<j} \begin{vmatrix} a_{ii} & a_{ij} \\ a_{ji} & a_{jj} \end{vmatrix} \lambda^{n-2} + \cdots + (-1)^n |A|,$$

all these coefficients are positive when the conditions stated above are fulfilled. Hence every root of $|\lambda I - A| = 0$ must be negative.

Necessity Assume that A is negative definite or equivalently that $-A$ is positive definite. Then by a similar procedure, we have $-\beta_i > 0$ $(i = 1, \ldots, n)$, implying that

$$a_{11} < 0, \qquad \begin{vmatrix} a_{11} & a_{12} \\ a_{12} & a_{22} \end{vmatrix} > 0, \qquad \begin{vmatrix} a_{11} & a_{12} & a_{13} \\ a_{12} & a_{22} & a_{23} \\ a_{13} & a_{23} & a_{33} \end{vmatrix} < 0, \qquad \ldots, \qquad (-1)^n |A| > 0.$$

Q.E.D.

It is clear that if a real symmetric matrix A is positive (or negative) definite, then its principal submatrix of any order is positive (or negative) definite.

THEOREM 36 Let A be a real symmetric matrix of order n, and B an $m \times n$ real matrix of rank m with $m < n$. Define a square matrix D_r of order r $(m + 1 \leqq r \leqq n)$ such that

$$D_r \equiv \begin{bmatrix} \Theta & B_r \\ B_r^{\mathrm{T}} & A_r \end{bmatrix},$$

where Θ stands for the square zero matrix of order m, $B_r \equiv [B_m, B_{r-m}]$, with a nonsingular $m \times m$ matrix B_m consisting of m columns of B and an $m \times (r - m)$ matrix B_{r-m} consisting of any other $r - m$ columns of B, and A_r the $r \times r$ principal submatrix of A comformable with B_r and B_r^{T}, the transpose of B_r. Then

$$u^{\mathrm{T}}Au > 0 \qquad \text{for all } u \in R^n \text{ satisfying } Bu = \theta, \tag{54}$$

if and only if

$$\text{in case } m \text{ is odd,} \qquad |D_r| < 0 \qquad \text{for} \quad r = m + 1, \ldots, n; \tag{55}$$

$$\text{in case } m \text{ is even,} \qquad |D_r| > 0 \qquad \text{for} \quad r = m + 1, \ldots, n. \tag{56}$$

And

$$u^{\mathrm{T}}Au < 0 \qquad \text{for all } u \in R^n \text{ satisfying } Bu = \theta, \tag{57}$$

if and only if

$$(-1)^r |D_r| > 0 \qquad \text{for} \quad r = m + 1, \ldots, n. \tag{58}$$

PROOF Define a transformation matrix of order n:

$$C \equiv \begin{bmatrix} B \\ \hline 0_m \quad I_{n-m} \end{bmatrix}^{-1},$$

where 0_m is the $(n - m) \times m$ matrix composed of all zeros and I_{n-m} is the identity matrix of order $n - m$. Transform u into y such that

$$y \equiv C^{-1}u = \begin{bmatrix} \theta_m \\ u_* \end{bmatrix}$$

since $Bu = \theta$, where $\theta_m \equiv$ the column vector of m zeros and $u_* \equiv (u_{m+1}, \ldots, u_n)^{\mathrm{T}}$. Thus

$$u^{\mathrm{T}}Au = y^{\mathrm{T}}C^{\mathrm{T}}ACy = u_*^{\mathrm{T}}P_{n-m}u_*,$$

where P_{n-m} is the principal submatrix of $C^{\mathrm{T}}AC$ after deleting the first m rows and columns. Hence

$$u_*^{\mathrm{T}}P_{n-m}u_* > 0 \qquad \text{for all} \quad u_* \in R^{n-m} \tag{59}$$

is equivalent to (54), and

$$u_*^{\mathrm{T}}P_{n-m}u_* < 0 \qquad \text{for all} \quad u_* \in R^{n-m} \tag{60}$$

is equivalent to (57).

Define

$$C_r \equiv \begin{bmatrix} B_r \\ \hdashline 0_m \quad I_{r-m} \end{bmatrix}^{-1}, \qquad S_r \equiv \left[\begin{array}{c:c} I_m & 0 \\ \hdashline 0 & C_r \end{array}\right],$$

$$M_r \equiv S_r^{\mathrm{T}} D_r S_r = \left[\begin{array}{c:c} 0 & B_r C_r \\ \hdashline C_r^{\mathrm{T}} B_r^{\mathrm{T}} & C_r^{\mathrm{T}} A_r C_r \end{array}\right], \tag{61}$$

where

$$B_r C_r = [B_m,\ B_{r-m}] \left[\begin{array}{c:c} B_m^{-1} & -B_m^{-1} B_{r-m} \\ \hdashline 0_m & I_{r-m} \end{array}\right] = [I_m,\ 0].$$

Denoting by P_{r-m} the principal submatrix of $C_r^{\mathrm{T}} A_r C_r$ after deleting the first m rows and columns, we rewrite M_r as

$$M_r = \begin{bmatrix} 0 & I_m & 0 \\ I_m & (*_1) & (*_2) \\ 0 & (*_3) & P_{r-m} \end{bmatrix},$$

where $(*_1)$, $(*_2)$, and $(*_3)$ stand for some submatrices of $C_r^{\mathrm{T}} A_r C_r$. Then

$$(-1)^m |M_r| = \begin{vmatrix} I_m & 0 & 0 \\ (*_1) & I_m & (*_2) \\ (*_3) & 0 & P_{r-m} \end{vmatrix} = |P_{r-m}|. \tag{62}$$

Since $|S_r| = |C_r| = |B_m|^{-1}$, we have from (61)

$$|M_r| = |D_r|\,|S_r|^2 = |D_r|\,|B_m|^{-2}. \tag{63}$$

It follows from (62) and (63) that

$$\operatorname{sgn} |P_{r-m}| = \operatorname{sgn}(-1)^m |M_r| = \operatorname{sgn}(-1)^m |D_r|. \tag{64}$$

Thus, $|P_{r-m}| > 0$ if and only if $\operatorname{sgn}|D_r| = \operatorname{sgn}(-1)^m$. Therefore, in view of Theorem 35, (59) holds if and only if (55) and (56) are fulfilled. By the corollary to Theorem 35 and (64), (60) holds if and only if $(-1)^m |D_r| < 0$ for odd $r - m$ and $(-1)^m |D_r| > 0$ for even $r - m$; or equivalently if and only if (58) is satisfied. Q.E.D.

COROLLARY. When there is only one constraint, that is, in case $m = 1$ in Theorem 36, we have the following:

(i) $u^{\mathrm{T}} A u > 0$ for all $u \in R^n$ satisfying $bu \equiv \sum_{i=1}^n b_i u_i = 0$ if and only if

$$\begin{vmatrix} 0 & b_1 & b_2 \\ b_1 & a_{11} & a_{12} \\ b_2 & a_{12} & a_{22} \end{vmatrix}, \quad \begin{vmatrix} 0 & b_1 & b_2 & b_3 \\ b_1 & a_{11} & a_{12} & a_{13} \\ b_2 & a_{12} & a_{22} & a_{23} \\ b_3 & a_{13} & a_{23} & a_{33} \end{vmatrix}, \quad \ldots, \quad \begin{vmatrix} 0 & b \\ b^{\mathrm{T}} & A \end{vmatrix} \tag{65}$$

take on all negative values.

(ii) $u^T A u < 0$ for all $u \in R^n$ satisfying $bu = 0$ if and only if all the determinants of odd order in (65) take on positive values and all the determinants of even order in (65) take on negative values.

Regarding a positive semidefinite matrix, we have the following theorems parallel to Theorems 35 and 36.

THEOREM 35′ Let A be a real symmetric matrix. A is positive semidefinite if and only if all the principal minors of A are nonnegative.

PROOF *"If" part* Let λ be an eigenvalue of A and suppose, to the contrary, that λ be negative. Then, in view of the expansion of $|A - \lambda I|$ shown in the proof of Theorem 35, $|A - \lambda I|$ would be positive, contradicting that λ is an eigenvalue of A.

"Only if" part Let λ_i $(i = 1, \ldots, n)$ be eigenvalues of A. Then

$$|A| = \prod_{i=1}^{n} \lambda_i \geqq 0.$$

Since every principal submatrix of A is positive semidefinite, we know that every principal minor of A is nonnegative by a similar argument. Q.E.D.

COROLLARY Let A be a real symmetric matrix. A is negative semidefinite if and only if every principal minor of odd order takes on a nonpositive value and every principal minor of even order takes on a nonnegative value.

THEOREM 36′ We adopt the same notations as in Theorem 36. Then

$$u^T A u \geqq 0 \qquad \text{for all } u \in R^n \text{ satisfying } Bu = \mathit{0}, \tag{54′}$$

if and only if

$$\text{in case } m \text{ is odd,} \qquad |D_r| \leqq 0 \qquad \text{for} \quad r = m + 1, \ldots, n; \tag{55′}$$

$$\text{in case } m \text{ is even,} \qquad |D_r| \geqq 0 \qquad \text{for} \quad r = m + 1, \ldots, n. \tag{56′}$$

And

$$u^T A u \leqq 0 \qquad \text{for all} \quad u \in R^n \text{ satisfying } Bu = \mathit{0}, \tag{57′}$$

if and only if

$$(-1)^r \, |D_r| \geqq 0 \qquad \text{for} \quad r = m + 1, \ldots, n. \tag{58′}$$

COROLLARY When there is only one constraint, that is, in case $m = 1$ in Theorem 36′, we have the following:

(i) $u^T A u \geqq 0$ for all $u \in R^n$ satisfying $bu \equiv \sum_{i=1}^{n} b_i u_i = 0$ if and only if all the determinants in (65) are nonpositive.

(ii) $u^T A u \leqq 0$ for all $u \in R^n$ satisfying $bu = 0$ if and only if all the determinants of odd order in (65) take on nonnegative values and all the determinants of even order in (65) take on nonpositive values.

We turn now to matrices that are not required to be symmetric, but are related to definiteness.

DEFINITION 24 An $n \times n$ real matrix A is said to be *positive* (or *negative*) *quasi-definite* if $x^{\mathrm{T}}Ax$ is positive (or negative) for any real nonzero column n-vector x, or equivalently, if $A + A^{\mathrm{T}}$ is positive (or negative) definite since

$$x^{\mathrm{T}}Ax = x^{\mathrm{T}}(A + A^{\mathrm{T}})x/2.$$

Obviously, if A is positive quasi-definite, $-A$ is negative quasi-definite.

Definiteness of a matrix A is the special case of quasi-definiteness where A is symmetric.

THEOREM 37 If matrix A is positive or negative quasi-definite, it is nonsingular and its inverse is also positive or negative quasi-definite, respectively.

PROOF Quasi-definiteness implies that $Ax = \theta$ has no nonzero x, which is equivalent to saying that A is nonsingular, in view of Theorem 27 in Section 2.3.

$$x^{\mathrm{T}}A^{-1}x = x^{\mathrm{T}}(A^{-1})^{\mathrm{T}}A^{\mathrm{T}}A^{-1}x = y^{\mathrm{T}}A^{\mathrm{T}}y = y^{\mathrm{T}}Ay,$$

where $x = Ay \neq \theta$ for any real nonzero vector y. Q.E.D.

THEOREM 38 Let A be an $n \times n$ real matrix with positive diagonal entries. If $A + A^{\mathrm{T}}$ has a column d.d., then $A + A^{\mathrm{T}}$ is positive definite; i.e., A is positive quasi-definite.

PROOF By Theorem 27 in Section 1.3, $A + A^{\mathrm{T}}$ is a P-matirx, i.e., all of its principal minors are positive. Then, by Theorem 35 above, $A + A^{\mathrm{T}}$ is positive definite. Q.E.D.

COROLLARY Let A be an $n \times n$ real matrix with positive diagonal entries. If there are positive numbers $d_1, \ldots, d_n$ for which A has a column d.d. and a row d.d., then A is positive quasi-definite.

PROOF We can easily see that $A + A^{\mathrm{T}}$ has a column d.d. for the same $d_1, \ldots, d_n$. (Refer to Exercise 8 in Chapter 1.) Q.E.D.

THEOREM 38′ Let A be an $n \times n$ real matrix with negative diagonal entries. If there are positive numbers $d_1, \ldots, d_n$ for which A has a column d.d. and a row d.d., then A is negative quasi-definite.

PROOF Since $A + A^{\mathrm{T}}$ with negative diagonal entries has a column d.d., all eigenvalues of $A + A^{\mathrm{T}}$ are negative, in view of Theorem 22′ in Section 1.3 and real symmetricalness of $A + A^{\mathrm{T}}$; viz., $A + A^{\mathrm{T}}$ is negative definite. Q.E.D.

THEOREM 39 Let A be a negative quasi-definite matrix, and let S be any real symmetric and positive definite matrix having the same dimension as A. Then all eigenvalues of SA or AS have negative real parts.

PROOF If λ is an eigenvalue of SA (or AS), there is a nonzero eigenvector x such that $\lambda x = SAx$ (or $\lambda x = SA^{\mathrm{T}}x$). Premultiply both sides by $\bar{x}^{\mathrm{T}}S^{-1}$, where $\bar{x}$ denotes the complex conjugate of x:

$$\lambda\bar{x}^{\mathrm{T}}S^{-1}x = \bar{x}^{\mathrm{T}}Ax \qquad (\text{or} \quad \lambda\bar{x}^{\mathrm{T}}S^{-1}x = \bar{x}^{\mathrm{T}}A^{\mathrm{T}}x). \tag{66}$$

Write $x = y + iz$, $\lambda = \alpha + i\beta$, where y, z are real vectors and α, β are real scalars. Equating real parts of (66), we have

$$\alpha(y^{\mathrm{T}}S^{-1}y + z^{\mathrm{T}}S^{-1}z) = y^{\mathrm{T}}Ay + z^{\mathrm{T}}Az < 0$$

because A is negative quasi-definite. Hence $\alpha < 0$. Q.E.D.

In the next chapter, we shall define a real square matrix as a stable matrix if all its eigenvalues have negative real parts. Thus, by setting $S = I$, Theorem 39 implies that any negative quasi-definite matrix is stable. In view of Theorem 38′, therefore, if an $n \times n$ real matrix A with negative diagonal entries has both a column d.d. and a row d.d. for a set of n positive numbers, then A is stable. Furthermore, by introducing special types of stable matrices, we can restate Theorem 39 as below.

DEFINITION 25 A real square matrix A is said to be *S-stable* if SA or AS is stable for any real symmetric and positive definite matrix S. (In defining this, we take account of the fact that SA and AS are similar since $SA = S(AS)S^{-1}$.)

DEFINITION 26 A real square matrix A is said to be *D-stable* if DA or AD is stable for any diagonal matrix D with positive diagonal entries.

Obviously, S-stability implies D-stability, and the latter implies stability.

THEOREM 39′ (Arrow and McManus, 1958) Any negative quasi-definite matrix is S-stable.

COROLLARY Any negative quasi-definite matrix is D-stable.

We add another class of D-stable matrices.

THEOREM 40 A square matrix A having a negative d.d. is D-stable.

PROOF $y > \theta$ such that $yB > \theta$ implies

$$yD^{-1} > \theta \qquad \text{such that} \qquad yD^{-1}DB > \theta$$

for any diagonal matrix D with positive diagonal entries, where the (i, j)th entry of B is $-|a_{ij}|$ for $i \neq j$ and the (i, i)th is $|a_{ii}|$. Thus DB has a negative d.d. and hence all its eigenvalues have negative real parts. (See Theorem 22′ in Section 1.3.) Q.E.D.

Lastly, an important necessary and sufficient condition for a stable matrix is stated.

THEOREM 41 (*Lyapunov theorem*) A real square matrix A is stable if and only if the matrix equation

$$A^{\mathrm{T}}B + BA = -Q \qquad \text{(for each real symmetric positive definite } Q) \tag{67}$$

has as its solution B a symmetric positive definite matrix.

PROOF *"If" part* By the Arrow–McManus theorem (Theorem 39′), BA is S-stable. Then, in view of Definition 25, $A = B^{-1}BA$ is stable. (Note that B^{-1} is positive definite.)

"Only if" part Suppose

$$\dot{x} \equiv dx/dt = Ax \qquad \text{(with constant } x(0)) \tag{68}$$

is a stable system. The general solution of (68) is

$$x = e^{At}C, \tag{69}$$

where C is an arbitrary constant vector and

$$e^{At} \equiv I + \sum_{k=1}^{\infty} \frac{1}{k!}(At)^k. \tag{70}$$

Since system (68) is stable,

$$e^{At} \to 0 \qquad \text{as} \quad t \to \infty. \tag{71}$$

For an arbitrary positive definite matrix Q, we define

$$B \equiv \int_0^{\infty} e^{A^{\mathrm{T}}t}Qe^{At}\,dt.$$

Thus, in view of (71),

$$-Q = e^{A^{\mathrm{T}}t}\,Qe^{At}\Big]_0^{\infty} = \int_0^{\infty} \frac{d}{dt}\left(e^{A^{\mathrm{T}}t}Qe^{At}\right) dt$$

$$= \int_0^{\infty} \left(A^{\mathrm{T}}e^{A^{\mathrm{T}}t}Qe^{At} + e^{A^{\mathrm{T}}t}Qe^{At}A\right) dt = A^{\mathrm{T}}B + BA. \quad \text{Q.E.D.}$$

Remark A bounded positive definite quadratic form $V(x)$ is said to be a *Lyapunov function* with respect to a system of differential equations, if $\dot{V} \equiv dV/dt$ is negative for all nonequilibrium x satisfying the system.

COROLLARY If a Lyapunov function $V(x)$ exists with respect to a linear differential equation system (68), then the system is stable.

PROOF Define $V(x) \equiv x^{\mathrm{T}}Bx$ for a positive definite matrix B. Then

$$0 > \dot{V}(x) = \dot{x}^{\mathrm{T}}Bx + x^{\mathrm{T}}B\dot{x} = x^{\mathrm{T}}(A^{\mathrm{T}}B + BA)x \qquad \text{for} \quad x \neq \mathit{0}.$$

Thus $A^{\mathrm{T}}B + BA$ is negative definite and hence, by the Lyapunov theorem, system (68) is stable. Q.E.D.

EXERCISES

1. Show that the set Y defined by (57) in Section 8.3 is a convex polyhedral cone with vertex at the origin.

2. Let V_1, V_2, and V_3 be vector spaces over a field, and let F and G be linear transformations from V_1 into V_2 and from V_2 into V_3, respectively. Show that $GF(x) = G(F(x))$ is a linear transformation from V_1 into V_3.

3. Verify that for any real square matrix A, the nullspace of A is equal to that of A^TA.

4. Let A and B be $m \times n$ and $n \times q$ matrices. Prove the following *Sylvester inequality:*

$$\text{rk}(A) + \text{rk}(B) - n \leqq \text{rk}(AB) \leqq \min\{\text{rk}(A), \text{rk}(B)\}.$$

5. Show that an $m \times n$ matrix A of rank r can be factored such that $A = BC$, where B is an $m \times r$ matrix and C is an $r \times n$ matrix, both having rank r.

6. A square matrix A is said to be an *idempotent matrix* if $A^2 = A$. Show that an idempotent matrix has rank equal to its trace.

7. Let x_k $(k = 1, 2, \ldots, m)$ be column real n-vectors, and verify the following propositions. The $n \times n$ matrix

$$M \equiv \sum_{k=1}^{m} x_k x_k^T$$

is positive semidefinite; if $x_1, x_2, \ldots, x_m$ are linearly independent, the above matrix M is positive definite.

8. Prove the following propositions.

(i) Let A be a real symmetric positive definite matrix. Then there is a positive definite matrix B such that $A = B^2$.

(ii) Let A be an $n \times n$ real symmetric positive semidefinite matrix of rank r $(< n)$. Then there is a positive semidefinite matrix B of rank r such that $A = B^2$.

9. Let A be an $n \times k$ real matrix. Show that the rank of A equals k if and only if A^TA is positive definite.

10. A real square matrix is said to be an *M-matrix* if all its off-diagonal entries are nonpositive and all its principal minors are positive. Show that an M-matrix is D-stable.

REFERENCES AND FURTHER READING

Arrow, K. J., and McManus, M. (1958). "A Note on Dynamic Stability," *Econometrica* **26**, 448–454.

Bellman, R. (1970). *Introduction to Matrix Analysis*, 2nd ed. McGraw-Hill, New York.

Black, J., and Morimoto, Y. (1968). "A Note on Quadratic Forms Positive Definite under Linear Constraints," *Economica* **35**, 205–206.

Bodewig, E. (1959). *Matrix Calculus*, 2nd ed. North-Holland Publ., Amsterdam.

Debreu, G. (1952). "Definite and Semidefinite Quadratic Forms," *Econometrica* **20**, 295–300.

Fiedler, M., and Pták, V. (1962). "On Matrices with Nonpositive Offdiagonal Elements and Positive Principal Minors," *Czechoslovak Mathematical Journal* **12**, 382–400.

Gantmacher, F. R. (1959). *The Theory of Matrices* (English translation), Vol. I. Chelsea, New York.

Hawkins, D., and Simon, H. A. (1949). "Note: Some Conditions of Macroeconomic Stability," *Econometrica* **17**, 245–248.

Hoffman, K., and Kunze, R. (1961). *Linear Algebra*. Prentice-Hall, Englewood Cliffs, New Jersey.

Johnson, C. R. (1974). "Sufficient Conditions for *D*-Stability," *Journal of Economic Theory* **9**, 53–62.

La Salle, J., and Lefschetz, S. (1961). *Stability by Liapunov's Direct Method with Applications*. Academic Press, New York.

Mann, H. B. (1943). "Quadratic Forms with Linear Constraints," *American Mathematical Monthly* **50**, 430–433; (1968), in *Readings in Mathematical Economics* (P. Newman, ed.), Vol. I. Johns Hopkins Press, Baltimore, Maryland.

Nikaido, H. (1970). *Introduction to Sets and Mappings in Modern Economics* (English translation). North-Holland Publ., Amsterdam.

Shilov, G. E. (1961). *An Introduction to the Theory of Linear Spaces* (English translation). Prentice-Hall, Englewood Cliffs, New Jersey.

Yaari, M. E. (1971). *Linear Algebra For Social Sciences*. Prentice-Hall, Englewood Cliffs, New Jersey.

Chapter 3

Linear Dynamic Systems and Stability

3.1 Linear Differential Equations

This section is intended to provide the general solution to a linear differential equation system.

A linear differential equation of order r ($\geqq 1$) with constant coefficients is expressed for continuous time t as

$$P(D)x(t) = b(t), \tag{1}$$

where $P(D) \equiv \sum_{i=0}^{r} a_i D^i$, $D \equiv d/dt$ (differential operator) with $D^0 \equiv 1$, a_i ($i = 0, 1, \ldots, r$) are constants, $a_r \neq 0$, b is a known function of t, and x an unknown function of t to be determined. (1) is called a nonhomogeneous equation if and only if $b(t)$ is not identically zero. Its associated homogeneous equation is

$$P(D)x(t) = 0. \tag{2}$$

Since Eq. (1) is a linear function in x, its general solution must be the sum of a particular solution of (1) and a linear combination of the basis solutions satisfying Eq. (2), where the basis solutions mean the linearly independent solutions that can generate the solution space of (2). Let $x_1, x_2, \ldots, x_r$ be solutions to (2). These solutions are linearly independent when

$$\sum_{i=1}^{r} \alpha_i x_i(t) = 0 \qquad \text{for all } t$$

holds true only if all the coefficients α_i are zeros.

THEOREM 1 Let $x_1, \ldots, x_r$ be solutions of Eq. (2). They are linearly independent if and only if the following determinant $\tilde{D}(t)$ is not identically zero:

$$\tilde{D}(t) \equiv \begin{vmatrix} x_1(t) & x_2(t) & \cdots & x_r(t) \\ Dx_1(t) & Dx_2(t) & \cdots & Dx_r(t) \\ \vdots & \vdots & & \vdots \\ D^{r-1}x_1(t) & D^{r-1}x_2(t) & \cdots & D^{r-1}x_r(t) \end{vmatrix}. \tag{3}$$

PROOF If $\tilde{D}(t) \neq 0$, the system of equations $\sum_{i=1}^{r} \alpha_i D^j x_i(t) = 0$ ($j = 0, 1, \ldots, r-1$) holds true only if $\alpha_i = 0$ ($i = 1, \ldots, n$). If $\tilde{D}(t) \equiv 0$, there can exist nonzero α_i satisfying the above system of equations. Q.E.D.

Let λ be a constant. Then

$$P(D)e^{\lambda t} = P(\lambda)e^{\lambda t}.$$

Thus $P(D)e^{\lambda t} = 0$ if and only if

$$P(\lambda) \equiv a_0 + a_1\lambda + \cdots + a_{r-1}\lambda^{r-1} + a_r\lambda^r = 0, \tag{4}$$

which is said to be the characteristic equation of (1). Denoting the roots of (4) by λ_i ($i = 1, \ldots, r$), we have a set of solutions to Eq. (2):

$$x_i(t) = \exp\{\lambda_i t\} \qquad \text{for} \quad i = 1, \ldots, r. \tag{5}$$

Substitution from (5) into (3) yields

$$\tilde{D}(t) = \exp\left\{\sum_{i=1}^{r} \lambda_i t\right\} \tilde{D}(0), \tag{6}$$

where

$$\tilde{D}(0) \equiv \begin{vmatrix} 1 & 1 & \cdots & 1 \\ \lambda_1 & \lambda_2 & \cdots & \lambda_r \\ \vdots & \vdots & & \vdots \\ \lambda_1^{r-1} & \lambda_2^{r-1} & \cdots & \lambda_r^{r-1} \end{vmatrix} \qquad \text{(Vandermonde determinant)} \tag{7}$$

$$= \prod_{i,j=1;i<j}^{r-1} (\lambda_j - \lambda_i).$$

If the characteristic roots λ_i ($i = 1, \ldots, r$) of (4) are all distinct, then $\tilde{D}(t) \neq 0$, and hence the set of solutions (5) constitutes a basis for the solution space of the homogeneous system (2). Therefore, the general solution of (2) is expressed as

$$x^{\mathrm{c}}(t) = \sum_{i=1}^{r} c_i \exp\{\lambda_i t\}, \tag{8}$$

where the c_i are arbitrary constants.

Suppose there exist multiple roots λ_i with multiplicity w_i among the characteristic roots mentioned above, then

$$x_{s_i}(t) \equiv t^{s_i} \exp\{\lambda_i t\} \qquad (s_i = 0, 1, \ldots, w_i - 1) \tag{9}$$

are found to be linearly independent. (The proof is left to the reader.) Let λ_i $(i = 1, \ldots, k)$ be the distinct characteristic roots of (4) with multiplicity w_i fulfilling $\sum_{i=1}^{k} w_i = r$. Then the general solution of (2) is represented as

$$x^c(t) = \sum_{i=1}^{k} g_i(t) \exp\{\lambda_i t\}, \tag{10}$$

where $g_i(t) \equiv \sum_{s_i=0}^{w_i-1} c_{is_i} t^{s_i}$ and c_{is_i} stands for an arbitrary constant $(i = 1, \ldots, k)$. Thus, once we obtain a particular solution $x_p(t)$, the general solution of (1) is given by

$$x(t) = x_p(t) + \sum_{i=1}^{k} g_i(t) \exp\{\lambda_i t\}. \tag{11}$$

The constants c_{is_i} in (11) will be uniquely determined by r boundary conditions. If the characteristic roots of (4) are all distinct, (11) is reduced to

$$x(t) = x_p(t) + \sum_{i=1}^{r} c_i \exp\{\lambda_i t\}. \tag{11'}$$

Before entering into a system of linear differential equations, we shall verify that a linear differential equation (1) of any order can be converted into a system of linear differential equations of order one. Noticing $a_r \neq 0$ and defining

$$X \equiv \begin{bmatrix} x \\ Dx \\ \vdots \\ D^{r-1}x \end{bmatrix}, \quad B(t) \equiv \begin{bmatrix} 0 \\ \vdots \\ 0 \\ b(t)/a_r \end{bmatrix}, \quad A \equiv \begin{bmatrix} 0 & 1 & 0 & \cdots & 0 \\ 0 & 0 & 1 & & 0 \\ \vdots & \vdots & & \ddots & \\ 0 & 0 & & & 1 \\ -a_0/a_r & -a_1/a_r & \cdots & & -a_{r-1}/a_r \end{bmatrix}$$

we can express (1) as

$$DX = AX + B(t), \tag{12}$$

which will be called the canonical form of (1). The associated characteristic equation is

$$|\lambda I - A| = 0, \tag{13}$$

where

$$|\lambda I - A| = \begin{vmatrix} \lambda & -1 & 0 & \cdots & 0 \\ 0 & \lambda & -1 & & 0 \\ \vdots & & \ddots & \ddots & \\ 0 & 0 & & \lambda & -1 \\ a_0/a_r & a_1/a_r & \cdots & a_{r-2}/a_r & \lambda + a_{r-1}/a_r \end{vmatrix}$$

$$= \frac{a_0}{a_r} + \frac{a_1}{a_r}\lambda + \ldots + \frac{a_{r-2}}{a_r}\lambda^{r-2} + \frac{a_{r-1}}{a_r}\lambda^{r-1} + \lambda^r.$$

Thus, (13) is equivalent to (4).

Now we shall be concerned with a system of linear differential equations of order r ($\geqq 1$) with constant coefficients:

$$P(D)x = b(t), \tag{14}$$

where

$$P(D) \equiv \begin{bmatrix} P_{11}(D) & \cdots & P_{1n}(D) \\ \vdots & & \vdots \\ P_{n1}(D) & \cdots & P_{nn}(D) \end{bmatrix}, \qquad x \equiv \begin{bmatrix} x_1 \\ \vdots \\ x_n \end{bmatrix}, \qquad b(t) \equiv \begin{bmatrix} b_1(t) \\ \vdots \\ b_n(t) \end{bmatrix},$$

$P_{hj}(D) \equiv \sum_{i=0}^{r} a_i^{(hj)} D^i$ ($h, j = 1, \ldots, n$), $a_i^{(hj)}$ is a constant, at least one of $a_r^{(hj)}$ must be nonzero, and $b_j(t)$ is a known function of t. We shall convert system (14) into a canonical form. By defining

$$a_i \equiv \begin{bmatrix} a_i^{(11)} & \cdots & a_i^{(1n)} \\ \vdots & & \vdots \\ a_i^{(n1)} & \cdots & a_i^{(nn)} \end{bmatrix} \qquad \text{for} \quad i = 0, 1, \ldots, r,$$

(14) is represented as

$$a_0 x + a_1 Dx + a_2 D^2 x + \cdots + a_r D^r x = b(t). \tag{15}$$

Note that a_r may be singular. Following the same procedure as before, we get the canonical form of (15):

$$\tilde{I} DX = \tilde{A} X + B(t), \tag{16}$$

where

$$X \equiv \begin{bmatrix} x \\ Dx \\ \vdots \\ D^r x \end{bmatrix}, \qquad B(t) \equiv \begin{bmatrix} 0 \\ \vdots \\ 0 \\ b(t) \end{bmatrix}, \qquad \tilde{A} \equiv \begin{bmatrix} 0 & I & 0 & \cdots & 0 \\ 0 & 0 & I & & 0 \\ \vdots & \vdots & & \ddots & \\ 0 & 0 & & & I \\ -a_0 & -a_1 & \cdots & & -a_r \end{bmatrix},$$

and

$$\tilde{I} \equiv \begin{bmatrix} I & 0 & \cdots & 0 \\ 0 & I & & 0 \\ \vdots & & \ddots & \vdots \\ 0 & & I & 0 \\ 0 & \cdots & 0 & 0 \end{bmatrix}.$$

The characteristic equation of (16) is

$$0 = |\lambda\tilde{I} - \tilde{A}| = \begin{vmatrix} \lambda I & -I & 0 & \cdots & 0 \\ 0 & \lambda I & -I & & 0 \\ \vdots & & \ddots & \ddots & \vdots \\ 0 & 0 & & \lambda I & -I \\ a_0 & a_1 & \cdots & a_{r-1} & a_r \end{vmatrix} \tag{17}$$

$$= |a_0 + \lambda a_1 + \ldots + \lambda^{r-1} a_{r-1} + \lambda^r a_r| \equiv |P(\lambda)|.$$

There should be $n \times r$ roots satisfying (17) as a whole. If a_r is nonsingular, the characteristic polynomial $|P(\lambda)|$ is represented as

$$|P(\lambda)| = |\lambda I - A|\,|a_r|, \tag{18}$$

where

$$A \equiv \begin{bmatrix} 0 & I & 0 & \cdots & 0 \\ 0 & 0 & I & & 0 \\ \vdots & \vdots & & \ddots & \\ 0 & 0 & & & I \\ A_0 & A_1 & & \cdots & A_{r-1} \end{bmatrix}$$

with $A_i \equiv -a_r^{-1} a_i$ $(i = 0, 1, \ldots, r-1)$.

Let λ be a constant and v a nonzero column n-vector independent of t. Then

$$P(D) v e^{\lambda t} = P(\lambda) v e^{\lambda t}, \tag{19}$$

where $P(\lambda)$ is a square matrix of constants. Let $P^*(\lambda)$ be the adjoint of $P(\lambda)$, i.e.,

$$P^*(\lambda) = P(\lambda)^{-1} |P(\lambda)|. \tag{20}$$

In view of (19) and (20), we get

$$P(D) e^{\lambda t} P^*(\lambda) = e^{\lambda t} P(\lambda) P^*(\lambda) = e^{\lambda t} |P(\lambda)| I.$$

Choosing λ_i as a root of

$$|P(\lambda)| = 0, \tag{21}$$

we have $P(D) \exp\{\lambda_i t\} P^*(\lambda_i) = 0$. Thus, denoting by v_i an arbitrary column of $P^*(\lambda_i)$, we know that $\exp\{\lambda_i t\} v_i$ is a solution x of the homogeneous system

$$P(D) x = \theta. \tag{22}$$

Notice that the roots of (21) are identical with those of (17).

Suppose there are k distinct roots λ_i $(i = 1, \ldots, k)$ with each multiplicity w_i fulfilling $\sum_{i=1}^{k} w_i = r \times n$. In a similar manner to a single equation, we have the general solution of nonhomogeneous system (14) as follows:

$$x(t) = x_p(t) + \sum_{i=1}^{k} \sum_{s_i=0}^{w_i-1} c_{is_i} v_{s_i} t^{s_i} \exp\{\lambda_i t\}\,, \tag{23}$$

where $x_p(t)$ is a particular solution of (14), c_{is_i} stands for an arbitrary scalar and v_{s_i} ($s_i = 0, 1, \ldots, w_i - 1$) are linearly independent column vectors of $P^*(\lambda_i)$. It will be shown in Section 3.2 that if λ_i is a multiple root with multiplicity w_i, then there exist w_i linearly independent columns in $P^*(\lambda_i)$ in the case where matrix a_r is nonsingular and hence the characteristic polynomial $|P(\lambda)|$ can be represented as (18). We shall henceforth confine our discussion to such a case. Lastly, it is clear that if all the roots of (21) are distinct, (23) is reduced to

$$x(t) = x_p(t) + \sum_{i=1}^{rn} c_i v_i \exp\{\lambda_i t\}\,, \tag{23$'$}$$

where v_i satisfies $[P(\lambda_i)]v_i = \theta$ or equivalently $[\lambda_i I - A]v_i = \theta$.

To conclude this section, we provide the general solution to a system of linear differential equations of order one with constant coefficients:

$$Dx(t) = Ax(t) + b(t) \tag{12$'$}$$

with initial condition $x(t_0) = x_0$ (constant), where x and b are n-vectors as denoted in (14) and A is an $n \times n$ constant matrix. Define

$$e^{At} \equiv I + \sum_{k=1}^{\infty} \frac{1}{k!}(At)^k \qquad \text{for a finite scalar } t.$$

It is noted that the right-hand side of the above converges. Then

$$D(e^{-A\tau}x(\tau)) = e^{-A\tau}(Dx(\tau) - Ax(\tau)) = e^{-A\tau}b(\tau).$$

Integrating this equation from t_0 to t yields

$$e^{-At}x(t) - e^{-At_0}x_0 = \int_{t_0}^{t} e^{-A\tau}b(\tau)\,d\tau.$$

Hence, we have the solution to (12′):

$$x(t) = e^{A(t-t_0)}x_0 + \int_{t_0}^{t} e^{A(t-\tau)}b(\tau)\,d\tau. \tag{24}$$

Obviously, in case $b(t) = \theta$ in (12′), (24) reduces to

$$x(t) = e^{A(t-t_0)}x_0. \tag{24$'$}$$

$e^{A(t-t_0)}$ in (24′) is called the *fundamental matrix* of differential system (12′) and is found to be nonsingular.

3.2 Jordan Form of a Square Matrix

It is shown in this section that any square matrix can be transformed into a similar quasi-diagonal matrix, which will be convenient for examining the behavior of a linear equation system.

We begin by defining an annihilating polynomial for a square matrix. Let A be an $n \times n$ matrix that determines a unique linear transformation $F: X \to X$, relative to a given basis for the n-space X over the real field. (Throughout this section A, F, and X are supposed to be the matrix, the linear transformation, and the relevant space, respectively, as defined just now.) Given a matrix A, the (monic) polynomial

$$\Phi(z) \equiv z^p + c_{p-1}z^{p-1} + \cdots + c_1 z + c_0 \tag{25}$$

such that for a vector $x \in X$

$$\Phi(A)x \equiv [A^p + c_{p-1}A^{p-1} + \cdots + c_1 A + c_0 I]x \tag{26}$$

vanishes is called an *annihilating polynomial* of x. And the polynomial that has the least degree among all the annihilating polynomials of x is said to be the *minimal polynomial* of x. If (26) vanishes for every $x \in X$, Φ is an annihilating polynomial for the entire space X and the annihilating polynomial for X that has the least degree is termed the minimal polynomial for X.

THEOREM 2 (*Cayley–Hamilton theorem*) Let $\Phi(\lambda)$ be the characteristic polynomial of a square matrix A, i.e.,

$$\Phi(\lambda) = |\lambda I - A|.$$

Then Φ is an annihilating polynomial for the relevant space X mentioned above.

PROOF Let $B(\lambda)$ be the adjoint of $[\lambda I - A]$. Then

$$B(\lambda)[\lambda I - A] = |\lambda I - A| I. \tag{$*$}$$

$B(\lambda)$ can be expanded as

$$B(\lambda) = \lambda^{n-1}I + \lambda^{n-2}B_1 + \lambda^{n-3}B_2 + \cdots + \lambda B_{n-2} + B_{n-1},$$

where B_i $(i = 1, \ldots, n-1)$ are square matrices. Likewise, $|\lambda I - A|$ is expanded

$$|\lambda I - A| = \lambda^n + a_1\lambda^{n-1} + a_2\lambda^{n-2} + \cdots + a_{n-1}\lambda + a_n.$$

Substituting these expansions into ($*$) yields

$$\begin{aligned}\lambda^n I + \lambda^{n-1}(B_1 - A) + \lambda^{n-2}(B_2 - B_1 A) + \cdots + \lambda(B_{n-1} - B_{n-2}A)\\ + (-B_{n-1}A)\\ = \lambda^n I + a_1\lambda^{n-1}I + a_2\lambda^{n-2}I + \cdots + a_{n-1}\lambda I + a_n I.\end{aligned}$$

Comparing both sides term by term, we have

$$\begin{aligned} I &= I,\\ B_1 - A &= a_1 I,\\ B_2 - B_1 A &= a_2 I,\\ &\vdots \end{aligned}$$

$$B_{n-1} - B_{n-2}A = a_{n-1}I,$$
$$-B_{n-1}A = a_nI.$$

Postmultiply these equations in this order by A^n, A^{n-1}, A^{n-2}, . . ., A, I, respectively, and sum. Then

$$0 = A^n + a_1A^{n-1} + a_2A^{n-2} + \cdots + a_{n-1}A + a_nI \equiv \Phi(A). \qquad \text{Q.E.D.}$$

In order to proceed to the next theorem, it is necessary to introduce the so-called "Euclidean algorithm."

LEMMA 1 (*Euclidean algorithm*) For arbitrary polynomials f and g ($\deg g \geqq 0$) over the field L, there exist unique polynomials q and r over L such that

$$f(z) = q(z)g(z) + r(z) \qquad (0 \leqq \deg r < \deg g), \tag{27}$$

where q is a quotient, r is a residue, and $\deg g$ denotes the degree of g. If f and g are relatively prime, then there exist polynomials x and y such that

$$1 = f(z)x(z) + g(z)y(z). \tag{28}$$

(For the proof of Lemma 1, refer to, for example, Lang (1971, pp. 281–285).)

THEOREM 3 For a square matrix A, every annihilating polynomial of $x \in X$ is divisible by the minimal polynomial of x.

PROOF Let $\Phi(z)$ be an annihilating polynomial of x and $\phi(z)$ the minimal polynomial. Let $q(z)$ be the quotient of $\Phi(z)$ with respect to $\phi(z)$ and $r(z)$ the residue. Then by (27)

$$\Phi(z) = q(z)\phi(z) + r(z).$$

Replacing z by A and postmultiplying by x, we have

$$\Phi(A)x = q(A)\phi(A)x + r(A)x.$$

Since $\Phi(A)x = \theta$ and $\phi(A)x = \theta$, $r(A)x$ must vanish. If $r(z)$ were not identically zero, a contradiction would occur, for then the degree of $r(z)$ would be lower than that of the minimal polynomial $\phi(z)$ of x. Q.E.D.

THEOREM 4 Let A be an $n \times n$ matrix. λ is a root of the minimal polynomial ϕ for the n-space X if and only if λ is an eigenvalue of A.

PROOF (1) *"If" part* Let λ be an eigenvalue of A, and x its associated nonzero eigenvector, i.e., $Ax = \lambda x$. Then for any polynomial f, we have $f(\lambda)x = f(A)x$ since $A^ix = A^{i-1}\lambda x = A^{i-2}\lambda^2x = \cdots = \lambda^ix$. In particular $\phi(\lambda)x = \phi(A)x = \theta$. Since x is nonzero, $\phi(\lambda) = 0$.

(2) *"Only if" part* Let λ be a root of $\phi(z) = 0$. Then

$$\phi(z) = (z - \lambda)\Gamma(z),$$

where Γ is not an annihilating polynomial for X since $\phi(z)$ is its minimal polynomial. Therefore, there exists a nonzero vector $x \in X$ such that $\Gamma(A)x = y \neq \theta$. Hence

$$\theta = \phi(A)x = [A - \lambda I]\,\Gamma(A)x = [A - \lambda I]y.$$

Thus we have $|A - \lambda I| = 0$. Q.E.D.

Let A be an $n \times n$ matrix whose distinct eigenvalues are λ_i with multiplicity w_i $(i = 1, \ldots, k)$. By Theorems 2–4, we know that the minimal polynomial for X takes the form

$$\phi(z) = \prod_{i=1}^{k} (z - \lambda_i)^{q_i},$$

where $1 \leqq q_i \leqq w_i$. $(z - \lambda_i)^{q_i}$ is called an *elementary divisor* of A.

THEOREM 5 Let A be a square matrix with its distinct eigenvalues λ_i $(i = 1, \ldots, k)$ and let $(z - \lambda_i)^{q_i}$ be one of its elementary divisors. Define

$$\phi_i(A) \equiv [A - \lambda_i I]^{q_i}, \tag{29}$$

and hence $\phi(A) \equiv \prod_{i=1}^{k} \phi_i(A)$. Let X_i be the nullspace of $\phi_i(A)$; i.e.,

$$X_i \equiv \{x : \phi_i(A)x = \theta\}, \qquad i = 1, \ldots, k. \tag{30}$$

Observe that the relevant space X becomes $X = \{x : \phi(A)x = \theta\}$. Then X is the direct sum of X_i $(i = 1, \ldots, k)$, i.e.,

$$X = X_1 \oplus X_2 \oplus \cdots \oplus X_k. \tag{31}$$

PROOF We shall prove the case where $k = 2$. Since $\phi_1(z)$ and $\phi_2(z)$ are relatively prime, by (28) of the Euclidean algorithm there exist polynomials $p_1(z)$ and $p_2(z)$ satisfying

$$1 = p_1(z)\phi_1(z) + p_2(z)\phi_2(z).$$

Replacing z in this equation by A yields

$$I = p_1(A)\phi_1(A) + p_2(A)\phi_2(A). \tag{32}$$

Thus, for $x \in X$ we have $x = x_2 + x_1$, where $x_2 \equiv p_1(A)\phi_1(A)x$ and $x_1 \equiv p_2(A)\phi_2(A)x$. Then it follows that

$$\phi_1(A)x_1 = \phi_1(A)p_2(A)\phi_2(A)x = p_2(A)\phi(A)x = \theta,$$

and similarly $\phi_2(A)x_2 = \theta$, which implies that x_i belongs to X_i $(i = 1, 2)$.

Suppose that $x \in X$ is represented as $x = x_1' + x_2'$, where $x_i' \in X_i$ $(i = 1, 2)$. Then, by (32)

$$\begin{aligned} x_1' &= p_1(A)\phi_1(A)x_1' + p_2(A)\phi_2(A)x_1' = p_2(A)\phi_2(A)(x - x_2') \\ &= p_2(A)\phi_2(A)x = x_1. \end{aligned}$$

Likewise, we obtain $x_2' = x_2$. Thus we have verified the uniqueness of the representation of $x \in X$ in terms of vectors in X_1 and X_2. Q.E.D.

We shall show that the dimension of space X_i in Theorem 5 is equal to the multiplicity of λ_i. (29) and (30) imply that $(z - \lambda_i)^{q_i}$ is an annihilating polynomial for space X_i, and in fact its minimal polynomial. Choose a nonzero vector x_1 from X_i and consider the vectors (by setting $q_i = q$ for the sake of brevity)

$$x_1^1 \equiv [A - \lambda_i I]^{q-1}x_1, \quad x_1^2 \equiv [A - \lambda_i I]^{q-2}x_1, \quad \ldots, \quad x_1^q \equiv x_1. \tag{33}$$

These vectors $x_1^1, x_1^2, \ldots, x_1^q$ are linearly independent since otherwise there would be an annihilating polynomial for x of degree less than q, which is impossible. Now we note that

$$[A - \lambda_i I]x_1^1 = \theta, \quad [A - \lambda_i I]x_1^2 = x_1^1, \quad \ldots \quad, [A - \lambda_i I]x_1^q = x_1^{q-1},$$

or equivalently

$$Ax_1^1 = \lambda_i x_1^1, \quad Ax_1^2 = \lambda_i x_1^2 + x_1^1, \quad \ldots \quad, Ax_1^q = \lambda_i x_1^q + x_1^{q-1},$$

which can be expressed as (by setting back $q = q_i$)

$$A[x_1^1, x_1^2, \ldots, x_1^{q_i}] = [x_1^1, x_1^2, \ldots, x_1^{q_i}]B_{i1}, \tag{34}$$

where

$$B_{i1} \equiv \begin{bmatrix} \lambda_i & 1 & 0 & \cdots & 0 \\ 0 & \lambda_i & 1 & & 0 \\ \vdots & & \ddots & & \\ 0 & 0 & & & \lambda_i \end{bmatrix}, \tag{35}$$

whose order is q_i. If there exists a nonzero vector $x_2 \in X_i$ that is linearly independent of the vectors in (33), then we shall get another matrix B_{i2} of the same type as B_{i1}. Suppose we obtain all matrices B_{is_i} ($s_i = 1, 2, \ldots, m_i$) of type (35) in this way. Then (34) is extended as

$$A\{x_i\} = \{x_i\}B_i, \tag{36}$$

where $\{x_i\} \equiv [x_1^1, \ldots, x_1^{q_i}; x_2^1, \ldots, x_2^{q_i}; \ldots; x_{m_i}^1, \ldots, x_{m_i}^{q_i}]$ and

$$B_i \equiv \begin{bmatrix} B_{i1} & 0 & \cdots & 0 \\ 0 & B_{i2} & & 0 \\ \vdots & & \ddots & \\ 0 & 0 & & B_{im_i} \end{bmatrix},$$

whose order is $m_i q_i$.

Since subscript i covers from 1 to k, we finally obtain

$$A\{x\} = \{x\}B, \tag{37}$$

where $\{x\} \equiv [\{x_1\}, \{x_2\}, \ldots, \{x_k\}]$ and

$$B \equiv \begin{bmatrix} B_1 & 0 & \cdots & 0 \\ 0 & B_2 & & 0 \\ \vdots & & \ddots & \\ 0 & 0 & & B_k \end{bmatrix},$$

whose order is $\sum_{i=1}^{k} m_i q_i$. Since A is a matrix representing a linear transformation F: $X \to X$ with $\dim X = n$, the dimension of $\{x\}B$ in (37) must be n, which implies $\dim\{x\} = n$ since B is nonsingular. Thus, we have $\sum_{i=1}^{k} m_i q_i = n$. Therefore, $\{x\}$ is a nonsingular square matrix, and hence $B = \{x\}^{-1} A \{x\}$, which implies

$$|\lambda I - B| = |\lambda I - A|. \tag{38}$$

Since $|\lambda I - B| = \prod_{i=1}^{k} |\lambda I - B_i| = \prod_{i=1}^{k} (\lambda - \lambda_i)^{m_i q_i}$, it follows from (38) that for an arbitrary scalar λ

$$\prod_{i=1}^{k} (\lambda - \lambda_i)^{m_i q_i} = \prod_{i=1}^{k} (\lambda - \lambda_i)^{w_i},$$

which in turn implies that $m_i q_i = w_i$, and hence that $\{x_i\}$ in (36) consists of w_i linearly independent vectors in X_i. Thus we have $\dim X_i \geqq w_i$. However, in view of (31),

$$\sum_{i=1}^{k} w_i = n = \dim X = \sum_{i=1}^{k} \dim X_i.$$

Therefore, $\dim X_i = w_i$.

The above analysis is summarized as follows.

THEOREM 6 (*Jordan form of a square matrix*) Let A be an $n \times n$ matrix and λ_i $(i = 1, \ldots, k)$ be its all distinct eigenvalues with multiplicity w_i. Then the nullspace

$$X_i \equiv \{x : [\lambda_i I - A]x = \theta\}$$

has dimension w_i, and there exists a nonsingular matrix M of order n such that

$$B = M^{-1} A M, \tag{39}$$

where M is called the Jordan transformation matrix of A,

$$B \equiv \begin{bmatrix} B_1 & 0 & \cdots & 0 \\ 0 & B_2 & & 0 \\ \vdots & & \ddots & \\ 0 & 0 & & B_k \end{bmatrix}, \qquad B_i \equiv \begin{bmatrix} \lambda_i & * & 0 & \cdots & 0 \\ 0 & \lambda_i & * & & 0 \\ \vdots & & & \ddots & \\ 0 & 0 & & & \lambda_i \end{bmatrix},$$

each asterisk stands for one or zero, and the order of B_i is w_i.

COROLLARY Let A be an $n \times n$ matrix with n distinct eigenvalues. Then there exists a nonsingular matrix M of order n such that

$$B = M^{-1}AM, \tag{39'}$$

where B is the diagonal matrix composed of λ_i as its ith diagonal element for $i = 1, \ldots, n$. The nonsingular matrix M that diagonalizes A by (39′) is $M = [v_1, v_2, \ldots, v_n]$, where v_i is the eigenvector of A associated with λ_i; i.e., v_i satisfies $[\lambda_i I - A]v_i = \theta$. Note that in this case $M^{-1} = [u_1, u_2, \ldots, u_n]^{\mathrm{T}}$, where u_i is the eigenvector of A^{T} associated with λ_i, i.e., $[\lambda_i I - A^{\mathrm{T}}]u_i = \theta$.

To conclude this section, we illustrate how to transform a square matrix A of order 3 into its Jordan form. Let A be

$$A = \begin{bmatrix} a_{11} & a_{12} & a_{13} \\ a_{21} & a_{22} & a_{23} \\ a_{31} & a_{32} & a_{33} \end{bmatrix}$$

with eigenvalues λ_1, λ_2, and λ_3, not necessarily distinct. In the beginning, A will be transformed into a triangular matrix A_1 with the help of a nonsingular matrix M_* which will be defined below:

$$A_1 \equiv M_*^{-1}AM_* = \begin{bmatrix} \lambda_1 & * & * \\ 0 & \lambda_2 & * \\ 0 & 0 & \lambda_3 \end{bmatrix}, \tag{40}$$

where each asterisk in the last matrix stands for a constant. Let b^i be the ith column of $[\lambda_1 I - A]$. Since $[\lambda_1 I - A]$ is singular, b^1 is represented as a linear combination of b^2 and b^3, say $b^1 = \alpha_2 b^2 + \alpha_3 b^3$. Defining

$$M_0 \equiv \begin{bmatrix} 1 & 0 & 0 \\ -\alpha_2 & 1 & 0 \\ -\alpha_3 & 0 & 1 \end{bmatrix},$$

we get

$$M_0^{-1}[\lambda_1 I - A]M_0 = [0, M_0^{-1}b^2, M_0^{-1}b^3],$$

or

$$M_0^{-1}AM_0 = \left[\begin{array}{c|cc} \lambda_1 & * & * \\ \hline 0 & \multicolumn{2}{c}{\multirow{2}{*}{B_1}} \\ 0 & & \end{array}\right].$$

Note that $|\lambda I - A| = |\lambda I - M_0^{-1}AM_0| = (\lambda - \lambda_1)|\lambda I - B_1|$. Let c^1 and c^2 be the first and second columns of $[\lambda_2 I - B_1]$, respectively. Since $[\lambda_2 I - B_1]$ is singular, $c^1 = \alpha_4 c^2$ for some constant α_4. Defining

$$N_1 \equiv \begin{bmatrix} 1 & 0 \\ -\alpha_4 & 1 \end{bmatrix},$$

we have

$$N_1^{-1} B_1 N_1 = \begin{bmatrix} \lambda_2 & * \\ 0 & \lambda_3 \end{bmatrix}$$

because the following must hold:

$$|\lambda I - B_1| = |\lambda I - N_1^{-1} B_1 N_1| = (\lambda - \lambda_2)(\lambda - \lambda_3).$$

Again defining

$$M_1 \equiv \left[\begin{array}{c|cc} 1 & 0 & 0 \\ \hline 0 & \multicolumn{2}{c}{\multirow{2}{*}{N_1}} \\ 0 & & \end{array}\right],$$

and $M_* \equiv M_0 M_1$, we obtain (40). Then we transform (40) into its Jordan form. Suppose $\lambda_2 = \lambda_3$ and specify elements $*$ in (40), say

$$A_1 = \begin{bmatrix} \lambda_1 & \alpha & \beta \\ 0 & \lambda_2 & \gamma \\ 0 & 0 & \lambda_2 \end{bmatrix}.$$

Define

$$M_2 \equiv \begin{bmatrix} 1 & \mu_2 & 0 \\ 0 & 1 & 0 \\ 0 & 0 & 1 \end{bmatrix},$$

where $\mu_2 \equiv \alpha/(\lambda_2 - \lambda_1)$. Then

$$A_2 \equiv M_2^{-1} A_1 M_2 = \begin{bmatrix} \lambda_1 & 0 & \delta \\ 0 & \lambda_2 & \gamma \\ 0 & 0 & \lambda_2 \end{bmatrix},$$

where $\delta \equiv \beta - \gamma\mu_2$. Define

$$M_3 \equiv \begin{bmatrix} 1 & 0 & \mu_3 \\ 0 & 1 & 0 \\ 0 & 0 & 1 \end{bmatrix},$$

where $\mu_3 \equiv \delta/(\lambda_2 - \lambda_1)$. Then

$$A_3 \equiv M_3^{-1} A_2 M_3 = \begin{bmatrix} \lambda_1 & 0 & 0 \\ 0 & \lambda_2 & \gamma \\ 0 & 0 & \lambda_2 \end{bmatrix}.$$

If $\gamma = 0$, then A_3 is the Jordan form of A. If $\gamma \neq 0$, then defining

$$M_4 \equiv \begin{bmatrix} 1 & 0 & 0 \\ 0 & 1 & 0 \\ 0 & 0 & 1/\gamma \end{bmatrix},$$

we get the Jordan form

$$A_4 \equiv M_4^{-1} A_3 M_4 = \begin{bmatrix} \lambda_1 & 0 & 0 \\ 0 & \lambda_2 & 1 \\ 0 & 0 & \lambda_2 \end{bmatrix}.$$

Formerly speaking, by redefining $M \equiv M_0 M_1 M_2 M_3 M_4$, we have the Jordan form of A as $M^{-1}AM$.

3.3 Difference Equations and Dynamic Multipliers

This section concerns the working of linear difference equation systems and various types of the dynamic Keynesian multipliers within the systems.

A linear difference equation of order r ($\geqq 1$) with constant coefficients is expressed for discrete time t as

$$P(G)x(t) = b(t), \tag{41}$$

where $P(G) \equiv \sum_{i=0}^{r} a_i G^i$, G is the difference operator such that

$$Gx(t) = x(t+1) \qquad \text{with} \qquad G^0 \equiv 1, \tag{42}$$

a_i ($i = 0, 1, \ldots, r$) are constants, $a_r \neq 0$, b is a known function of t, and x an unknown function of t. Equation (41) is nonhomogeneous if and only if $b(t)$ is not identically zero, and its general solution is obtained analogously to that of a linear differential equation discussed in Section 3.1; i.e.,

$$x(t) = x_p(t) + \sum_{i=1}^{k} \sum_{s_i=0}^{w_i-1} c_{is_i} t^{s_i} \lambda_i^t, \tag{43}$$

where $x_p(t)$ is a particular solution of Eq. (41), λ_i ($i = 1, \ldots, k$) stand for all distinct roots of the characteristic equation

$$P(\lambda) \equiv a_0 + a_1\lambda + \cdots + a_{r-1}\lambda^{r-1} + a_r\lambda^r = 0 \tag{44}$$

with multiplicity w_i fulfilling $\sum_{i=1}^{k} w_i = r$, and c_{is_i} for arbitrary constants.

As an application of the solution (43), we shall analyze an economic problem entitled "the interaction between the multiplier analysis and the acceleration principle," which is due to Samuelson (1939) and Hicks (1950). A set of notations is introduced as follows: Y, national income; C, consumption; I, investment; K, stock of capital; v, capital coefficient; s, marginal propensity to save; $\bar{C}$, a fixed level of consumption; g, the rate of growth of autonomous investment; and t, an arbitrary discrete time period.

Neglecting government activity and foreign trade, we set national income definitionally equal to the sum of consumption and investment:

$$Y_t = C_t + I_t. \tag{45}$$

Consumption and investment are supposed to depend upon variables in the previous period in the following manner:

$$C_t = (1 - s)Y_{t-1} + \bar{C} \tag{46}$$

with the assumption $1 - s > 0$,

$$I_t = vY_{t-1} - K_{t-1} + \alpha(1 + g)^t, \tag{47}$$

where α is a constant. Another definitional identity is

$$K_t = K_{t-1} + I_t. \tag{48}$$

Substituting from (47) to (48) and then considering one period lag, we have

$$K_{t-1} = vY_{t-2} + \alpha(1 + g)^{t-1},$$

which is substituted back into (47) to give

$$I_t = v(Y_{t-1} - Y_{t-2}) + \alpha g(1 + g)^{t-1}. \tag{49}$$

And substitution of (46) and (49) into (45) yields a linear difference equation of order two:

$$Y_t - (1 - s + v)Y_{t-1} + vY_{t-2} = \bar{C} + \alpha g(1 + g)^{t-1}. \tag{50}$$

This nonhomogeneous equation will be solved as indicated by solution (43). First we deal with the associated homogeneous equation of (50):

$$Y_t - (1 - s + v)Y_{t-1} + vY_{t-2} = 0. \tag{51}$$

The characteristic equation of (51) is obviously given by

$$\lambda^2 - (1 - s + v)\lambda + v = 0,$$

whose roots are

$$\lambda_1 = \tfrac{1}{2}(1 - s + v + [(1 - s + v)^2 - 4v]^{1/2}),$$
$$\lambda_2 = \tfrac{1}{2}(1 - s + v - [(1 - s + v)^2 - 4v]^{1/2}).$$

Since $\lambda_1\lambda_2 > 0$ and $\lambda_1 + \lambda_2 > 0$, the following three cases are distinguished.

Case 1: λ_1 and λ_2 are distinct, real and positive.
Case 2: $\lambda_1 = \lambda_2$ is real and positive.
Case 3: λ_1 is a complex number and λ_2 is its conjugate.

These cases will be briefly examined one by one.

Case 1 comprises two subcases: Case 1a and Case 1b. In Case 1a, $v > (1 + s^{1/2})^2$ and hence $\lambda_1 > 1$, $\lambda_2 > 1$. Thus

$$Y_t = c_1\lambda_1^t + c_2\lambda_2^t \tag{52}$$

will monotonically increase or eventually tend to zero depending on initial conditions. In Case 1b, $v < (1 - s^{1/2})^2$ and hence both λ_1 and λ_2 are less than one, implying that Y_t in (52) converges monotonically to zero.

Case 2 also comprises two subcases: Case 2a and Case 2b. In Case 2a, $v = (1 + s^{1/2})^2$ and hence $\lambda_1 = \lambda_2 > 1$. Thus the behavior of Y_t is of the same kind as Case 1a. In Case 2b where $v = (1 - s^{1/2})^2$, there occurs a similar situation to Case 1b.

In Case 3, $(1 - s^{1/2})^2 < v < (1 + s^{1/2})^2$. Let $\lambda_1 = \alpha + i\beta$ and $\lambda_2 = \alpha - i\beta$, where $\alpha \equiv \frac{1}{2}(1 - s + v)$ and $\beta \equiv \frac{1}{2}[4v - (1 - s + v)^2]^{1/2}$. Since $\alpha \pm i\beta = \rho(\cos \omega \pm i \sin \omega)$, where $\rho \equiv (\alpha^2 + \beta^2)^{1/2} = v^{1/2}$ and ω is the angle between λ_1 and the real axis, the solution of (51) becomes

$$Y_t = (v^{1/2})^t(c_1 \cos t\omega + c_2 \sin t\omega), \tag{53}$$

where c_1 and c_2 are real constants. Thus if $v = 1$, Y_t in (53) oscillates with a fixed amplitude; if $v > 1$, Y_t oscillates with an expanding amplitude; and if $v < 1$, Y_t oscillates with a shrinking amplitude.

In summary, we have five different cases: (a) Y_t converges monotonically to zero in case $v \leqq (1 - s^{1/2})^2$; (b) Y_t oscillates with a shrinking amplitude in case $(1 - s^{1/2})^2 < v < 1$; (c) Y_t oscillates with a fixed amplitude in case $v = 1$; (d) Y_t oscillates with an expanding amplitude in case $1 < v < (1 + s^{1/2})^2$; (e) Y_t expands monotonically or tends eventually to zero depending on initial conditions in case $(1 + s^{1/2})^2 \leqq v$.

So far we have analyzed the behavior of Y_t in the homogeneous equation (51). Next, a particular solution of Eq. (50) is sought. We split the equation into two:

$$Y_t - (1 - s + v)Y_{t-1} + vY_{t-2} = \bar{C}, \tag{50a}$$

$$Y_t - (1 - s + v)Y_{t-1} + vY_{t-2} = \alpha g(1 + g)^{t-1}. \tag{50b}$$

Y_t satisfying (50a) is equal to a constant: $\bar{Y} \equiv \bar{C}/s$. Setting $Y_t = z(1 + g)^{t-1}$ in (50b), we get $z = \alpha g/(s + sg + g - vg + g^2)$. Hence we have a particular solution of Eq. (50) as follows:

$$\bar{Y}_t = \frac{\bar{C}}{s} + \frac{\alpha g(1 + g)^{t+1}}{s + (1 + s - v)g + g^2} \tag{54}$$

which can be regarded as a dynamic equilibrium path. Finally, the general solution of Eq. (50) is obtained by adding (54) to (52) or to (53). The first term of (54) gives the *long-run equilibrium* level to which national income approaches in case Y_t in (52) is convergent, while the second term of (54) is said to be the *supermultiplier* which raises the long-run equilibrium level at a constant rate.

Now we turn to a system of linear difference equations of order r ($\geqq 1$) with constant coefficients which can in general be expressed as

$$P(G)x(t) = b(t), \tag{55}$$

where G is the difference operator defined by (42),

$$P(G) \equiv \begin{bmatrix} P_{11}(G) & \cdots & P_{1n}(G) \\ \vdots & & \vdots \\ P_{n1}(G) & \cdots & P_{nn}(G) \end{bmatrix}, \qquad x(t) \equiv \begin{bmatrix} x_1(t) \\ \vdots \\ x_n(t) \end{bmatrix}, \qquad b(t) \equiv \begin{bmatrix} b_1(t) \\ \vdots \\ b_n(t) \end{bmatrix},$$

$P_{hj}(G) \equiv \sum_{i=0}^{r} a_i^{(hj)} G^i$ $(h, j = 1, \ldots, n)$, $a_i^{(hj)}$ is a constant, at least one of $a_r^{(hj)}$ must be nonzero, b_j is a known function of t, and x_j is an unknown function of t. The general solution of Eq. (55) takes the form

$$x(t) = x_{\mathrm{p}}(t) + \sum_{i=1}^{k} \sum_{s_i=0}^{w_i-1} c_{is_i} v_{s_i} t^{s_i} \lambda_i^t, \tag{56}$$

where $x_{\mathrm{p}}(t)$ is a particular solution of (55), c_{is_i} $(i = 1, \ldots, k)$ stand for arbitrary constants, λ_i is a root of the characteristic equation

$$|P(\lambda)| \equiv |a_0 + \lambda a_1 + \cdots + \lambda^{r-1} a_{r-1} + \lambda^r a_r| = 0, \tag{57}$$

with multiplicity w_i fulfilling $\sum_{i=1}^{k} w_i = r \times n$,

$$a_i \equiv \begin{bmatrix} a_i^{(11)} & \cdots & a_i^{(1n)} \\ \vdots & & \vdots \\ a_i^{(n1)} & \cdots & a_i^{(nn)} \end{bmatrix} \qquad (i = 0, 1, \ldots, r)$$

and v_{s_i} $(s_i = 0, 1, \ldots, w_i - 1)$ stand for linearly independent eigenvectors of A defined below associated with λ_i; i.e., those vectors v satisfying

$$[\lambda_i I - A]v = \theta,$$

in which A is defined as

$$A \equiv \begin{bmatrix} 0 & I & 0 & \cdots & 0 \\ 0 & 0 & I & & 0 \\ \vdots & \vdots & & \ddots & \\ 0 & 0 & & & I \\ A_0 & A_1 & \cdots & & A_{r-1} \end{bmatrix} \tag{58}$$

with $A_i \equiv -a_r^{-1} a_i$ $(i = 0, 1, \ldots, r - 1)$ on the assumption that a_r is nonsingular. Clearly, system (55) is equivalent to

$$a_0 x(t) + a_1 x(t+1) + a_2 x(t+2) + \cdots + a_r x(t+r) = b(t). \tag{55$'$}$$

As an example of system (55), consider the following Keynesian system (59), where C, V, F, Y, and R denote consumption, investment, other effective demand, national income, and interest rate, respectively, and subscript t designates a time period.

$$C_t = 0.4 Y_t + 0.3 C_{t-1},$$

$$V_t = 0.1Y_t + 0.5(Y_{t-1} - Y_{t-2}) - 2R_t, \tag{59}$$
$$Y_t = C_t + V_t + F_t.$$

This system of equations can be rewritten as

$$\begin{bmatrix} 1 & 0 & -.4 \\ 0 & 1 & -.1 \\ -1 & -1 & 1 \end{bmatrix} \begin{bmatrix} C_t \\ V_t \\ Y_t \end{bmatrix} = \begin{bmatrix} .3 & 0 & 0 \\ 0 & 0 & .5 \\ 0 & 0 & 0 \end{bmatrix} \begin{bmatrix} C_{t-1} \\ V_{t-1} \\ Y_{t-1} \end{bmatrix} + \begin{bmatrix} 0 & 0 & 0 \\ 0 & 0 & -.5 \\ 0 & 0 & 0 \end{bmatrix} \begin{bmatrix} C_{t-2} \\ V_{t-2} \\ Y_{t-2} \end{bmatrix}$$
$$+ \begin{bmatrix} 0 & 0 \\ -2 & 0 \\ 0 & 1 \end{bmatrix} \begin{bmatrix} R_t \\ F_t \end{bmatrix},$$

which is of the form of (55′) with a time lag of two periods. Premultiplying this system by the inverse of the coefficient matrix on the left-hand side, we get

$$x(t) = A_1 x(t-1) + A_0 x(t-2) + Nz(t), \tag{60}$$

where

$$x(t) \equiv \begin{bmatrix} C_t \\ V_t \\ Y_t \end{bmatrix}, \quad A_1 \equiv \begin{bmatrix} .54 & 0 & .4 \\ .06 & 0 & .6 \\ .6 & 0 & 1 \end{bmatrix}, \quad A_0 \equiv \begin{bmatrix} 0 & 0 & -.4 \\ 0 & 0 & -.6 \\ 0 & 0 & -1 \end{bmatrix}, \quad N \equiv \begin{bmatrix} -1.6 & .8 \\ -2.4 & .2 \\ -4 & 2 \end{bmatrix},$$

$$z(t) \equiv \begin{bmatrix} R_t \\ F_t \end{bmatrix}.$$

Defining

$$X(t) \equiv \begin{bmatrix} x(t-1) \\ x(t) \end{bmatrix}, \quad A \equiv \begin{bmatrix} 0 & I \\ A_0 & A_1 \end{bmatrix}, \quad W \equiv \begin{bmatrix} \theta & 0 \\ \theta & N \end{bmatrix}, \quad \text{and} \quad Z(t) \equiv \begin{bmatrix} 0 \\ z(t) \end{bmatrix},$$

we transform (60) into its canonical form:

$$X(t) = AX(t-1) + WZ(t). \tag{61}$$

An iterative substitution performed on (61) yields

$$X(t) = A^t X(0) + \sum_{s=0}^{t-1} A^s WZ(t-s). \tag{62}$$

Thus we have the dynamic multiplier effects on X of Z as follows:

$$\partial X(t)/\partial Z(t-s) = A^s W \qquad \text{for} \quad s = 0, 1, 2, \ldots, t-1;$$

or equivalently the multiplier effects on x of z are

$$\frac{\partial x(0)}{\partial z(0)} \equiv \begin{bmatrix} \partial C_0/\partial R_0 & \partial C_0/\partial F_0 \\ \partial V_0/\partial R_0 & \partial V_0/\partial F_0 \\ \partial Y_0/\partial R_0 & \partial Y_0/\partial F_0 \end{bmatrix} = N \qquad \text{(the impact multiplier)},$$

$$\frac{\partial x(1)}{\partial z(0)} = A_1 N \qquad \text{(the one-period lagged multiplier)},$$

$$\frac{\partial x(2)}{\partial z(0)} = (A_0 + A_1^2)N \qquad \text{(the two-period lagged multiplier)},$$

$$\frac{\partial x(3)}{\partial z(0)} = A_0 \frac{\partial x(1)}{\partial z(0)} + A_1 \frac{\partial x(2)}{\partial z(0)} \qquad \text{(the three-period lagged multiplier)},$$

$$\vdots$$

$$\frac{\partial x(t)}{\partial z(0)} = A_0 \frac{\partial x(t-2)}{\partial z(0)} + A_1 \frac{\partial x(t-1)}{\partial z(0)} \qquad \text{(the } t\text{-period lagged multiplier)}.$$

If the autonomous variable vector $z(t)$ remains constant over time t, the cumulated multiplier effect of $Z(0)$ on $X(t)$ will be

$$[I + A + A^2 + \cdots + A^{t-1}]W = [I - A]^{-1}[I - A^t]W. \tag{63}$$

Whether the series in (63) is convergent or not is our next concern.

Let λ be an eigenvalue of an $n \times n$ matrix A. Then λ^q is an eigenvalue of A^q where q stands for an arbitrary positive integer. Denote by b_{ij} the (i, j)th element of A^q. Since

$$|\lambda|^q = |\lambda^q| \leqq \max_j \sum_{i=1}^{n} |b_{ij}|,$$

if A^q tends to a zero matrix as q approaches infinity, every eigenvalue of A will be less than unity in modulus. The converse also holds as is verified below.

For a given square matrix A, there is a nonsingular matrix M such that $J \equiv M^{-1}AM$ takes a Jordan canonical form; i.e., J is partitioned into the diagonal blocks

$$J_i \equiv \underbrace{\begin{bmatrix} \lambda_i & 1 & & 0 \\ & \ddots & \ddots & \\ & & \ddots & 1 \\ 0 & & & \lambda_i \end{bmatrix}}_{(w_i)} = \lambda_i I + E_i, \tag{64}$$

and zero off-diagonal blocks, where λ_i denotes an eigenvalue of A with multiplicity w_i $(i = 1, \ldots, k)$, and

$$E_i \equiv \underbrace{\begin{bmatrix} 0 & 1 & & 0 \\ & \ddots & \ddots & \\ & & \ddots & 1 \\ 0 & & & 0 \end{bmatrix}}_{(w_i)}.$$

We note that some of the ones in J_i and E_i could be zeros, but this does not influence the subsequent analysis in any substance. Conformably to the transformation of A into J, system (62) will become

$$X^*(t) = J^t X^*(0) + \sum_{s=0}^{t-1} J^s Z^*(t-s), \tag{65}$$

where $X^* \equiv M^{-1}X$ and $Z^* \equiv M^{-1}WZ$. Note that J^t has the diagonal blocks J_i^t and zero off-diagonal blocks. In view of (64),

$$J_i^t = \lambda_i^t I + t\lambda_i^{t-1}E_i + \frac{1}{2}t(t-1)\lambda_i^{t-2}E_i^2 + \frac{1}{3!}t(t-1)(t-2)\lambda_i^{t-3}E_i^3 + \cdots$$

$$+ \frac{1}{(w_i - 1)!} f_i(t) E^{w_i - 1},$$

where $f_i(t) \equiv \prod_{s_i=0}^{w_i-2} (t - s_i)\lambda_i^{t-w_i+1}$. For example, if $w_i = 3$,

$$J_i^t = \begin{bmatrix} \lambda_i^t & t\lambda_i^{t-1} & \frac{1}{2}t(t-1)\lambda_i^{t-2} \\ 0 & \lambda_i^t & t\lambda_i^{t-1} \\ 0 & 0 & \lambda_i^t \end{bmatrix}.$$

Since

$$\frac{f_i(t+1)}{f_i(t)} = \frac{1 + 1/t}{1 - (w_i - 2)/t}\lambda_i,$$

$|f_i(t+1)|/|f_i(t)|$ tends to $|\lambda_i|$ as t approaches infinity. Thus, if $|\lambda_i| < 1$, there exists an integer t_0 such that for $t \geqq t_0$, $|f_i(t+1)|/|f_i(t)| < \delta$, or equivalently $|f_i(t+1)| < \delta|f_i(t)|$, where $\delta \in (|\lambda_i|, 1)$. In general, for an arbitrary positive integer τ we have $|f_i(t+\tau)| < \delta^\tau |f_i(t)|$ for $t \geqq t_0$. Since $0 < \delta < 1$, $|f_i(t+\tau)|$ tends to zero as τ increases. Therefore, when λ_i is smaller than unity in modulus, $f_i(t)$ tends to zero and hence J_i^t converges to a zero matrix as t approaches infinity. If $|\lambda_i| < 1$ for every i, J^t and hence A^t converges to a zero matrix since $A^t = MJ^tM^{-1}$. By the above analysis we have a theorem on matrix stability:

THEOREM 7 Let A be a real square matrix. Then $\lim_{t\to\infty} A^t = 0$ if and only if every eigenvalue of A is less than unity in modulus.

COROLLARY Let A be a real square matrix. The series $I + A + A^2 + A^3 + \cdots$ converges to $[I - A]^{-1}$ if and only if every eigenvalue of A is less than unity in modulus.

Accordingly, if the modulus of each eigenvalue of A is less than unity with a fixed $Z(t)$ in (61) for all t, say Z_0, the level of $X(t)$ converges to an equilibrium

$$[I - A]^{-1}WZ_0, \tag{66}$$

which will be termed the *long-run equilibrium multiplier*. In a similar sense, system (55) of linear difference equations is said to be stable if every characteristic root of (57) is less than unity in modulus.

We show an easy formula for computing $[I - A]^{-1}$ when A takes the general form (58) and in case its eigenvalues are all distinct. Referring to the generalized eigenvalue problem in Section 1.2 and using the same notation, we have

$$I - A = V_*[I - \Lambda]U_*^{\mathrm{T}},$$

where V_* and U_*^{T} stand for the square matrices composed of all the right and left generalized eigenvectors of A respectively. Since $V_*^{-1} = U_*^{\mathrm{T}}$,

$$[I - A]^{-1} = V_* \operatorname{diag}\left[\frac{1}{1-\lambda}\right]U_*^{\mathrm{T}}, \tag{67}$$

where $\operatorname{diag}[1/(1 - \lambda)]$ stands for the rnth order diagonal matrix whose ith diagonal element is $1/(1 - \lambda_i)$. Partitioning $[I - A]^{-1}$ into $r \times r$ submatrices, each of order n, we know that its (k, j)th submatrix is found to be

$$\begin{aligned} V\Lambda^{k-1} &\operatorname{diag}\left[\frac{1}{1-\lambda}\right][\Lambda^{r-j}U^{\mathrm{T}} - \Lambda^{r-j-1}U^{\mathrm{T}}A_{r-1} - \cdots - \Lambda U^{\mathrm{T}}A_{j+1} - U^{\mathrm{T}}A_j] \\ &= V\left[\operatorname{diag}\left(\frac{\lambda^{k+r-j-1}}{1-\lambda}\right)U^{\mathrm{T}} - \operatorname{diag}\left(\frac{\lambda^{k+r-j-2}}{1-\lambda}\right)U^{\mathrm{T}}A_{r-1} - \cdots \right. \\ &\quad \left. - \operatorname{diag}\left(\frac{\lambda^{k}}{1-\lambda}\right)U^{\mathrm{T}}A_{j+1} - \operatorname{diag}\left(\frac{\lambda^{k-1}}{1-\lambda}\right)U^{\mathrm{T}}A_j\right], \end{aligned} \tag{68}$$

where every power should not be less than $k - 1$, otherwise the involved and the subsequent terms should be disregarded. For the previous example where $r = 2$, we have

$$[1 - A]^{-1} = \begin{bmatrix} V\left[\operatorname{diag}\left(\frac{\lambda}{1-\lambda}\right)U^{\mathrm{T}} - \operatorname{diag}\left(\frac{1}{1-\lambda}\right)U^{\mathrm{T}}A_1\right], & V\operatorname{diag}\left[\frac{1}{1-\lambda}\right]U^{\mathrm{T}} \\ V\left[\operatorname{diag}\left(\frac{\lambda^2}{1-\lambda}\right)U^{\mathrm{T}} - \operatorname{diag}\left(\frac{\lambda}{1-\lambda}\right)U^{\mathrm{T}}A_1\right], & V\operatorname{diag}\left[\frac{\lambda}{1-\lambda}\right]U^{\mathrm{T}} \end{bmatrix}$$

Lastly we see how the solution of difference equation system (55′) is expressible in terms of the generalized eigenvectors of A mentioned above. The system can be transformed into the following canonical form:

$$X(t + r) = AX(t + r - 1) + B(t),$$

or equivalently

$$X(t) = AX(t - 1) + B(t - r), \tag{69}$$

where A is defined as (58),

$$X(t) \equiv \begin{bmatrix} x(t - r + 1) \\ \vdots \\ x(t - 1) \\ x(t) \end{bmatrix} \quad \text{and} \quad B(t) \equiv \begin{bmatrix} \theta \\ \vdots \\ \theta \\ a_r^{-1}b(t) \end{bmatrix}.$$

By an iterative substitution, we get from (69)

$$X(t) = A^t X(0) + \sum_{s=0}^{t-1} A^s B(t - r - s).$$

Supposing all the eigenvalues of A are distinct, we follow the discussion about the generalized eigenvalue problem and know that $A = V_* \Lambda U_*^{\mathrm{T}}$. Hence $A^t = V_* \Lambda^t U_*^{\mathrm{T}}$. Since

$$\sum_{s=0}^{t-1} \Lambda^s = [I - \Lambda]^{-1}[I - \Lambda^t] = \mathrm{diag}\left(\frac{1 - \lambda^t}{1 - \lambda}\right),$$

by assuming $b(t - r - s) = b_0$(constant) for $s = 0, 1, \ldots, t - 1$, we obtain

$$X(t) = V_* \,\mathrm{diag}(\lambda^t) U_*^{\mathrm{T}} X(0) + V_* \,\mathrm{diag}\left(\frac{1 - \lambda^t}{1 - \lambda}\right) U^{\mathrm{T}} a_r^{-1} b_0,$$

from which it follows that the general solution is represented as

$$x(t) = V \,\mathrm{diag}(\lambda^{t+r-1}) U_*^{\mathrm{T}} X(0) + V \,\mathrm{diag}\left(\frac{\lambda^{r-1}(1 - \lambda^t)}{1 - \lambda}\right) U^{\mathrm{T}} a_r^{-1} b_0. \tag{70}$$

For the previous example where $r = 2$, $U_*^{\mathrm{T}} = [\Lambda U^{\mathrm{T}} - U^{\mathrm{T}} A_1,\ U^{\mathrm{T}}]$ and (70) reduces to

$$x(t) = V\Bigg[\mathrm{diag}(\lambda^{t+2}) U^{\mathrm{T}} x(-1) + \mathrm{diag}(\lambda^{t+1}) U^{\mathrm{T}} (a_2^{-1} a_1 x(-1) + x(0))$$
$$+ \,\mathrm{diag}\left(\frac{\lambda(1 - \lambda^t)}{1 - \lambda}\right) U^{\mathrm{T}} a_2^{-1} b_0\Bigg].$$

3.4 Modified Routh–Hurwitz Conditions for Stability

In the preceding section we dealt with the stability condition for a system of linear difference equations; this condition was summarized by Theorem 7 and its corollary. Our main concern in the present section is to establish a stability condition for a linear differential equation system, as termed the modified Routh–Hurwitz conditions. The last part of this section will touch upon a comparative-statics problem related to the stability conditions.

Consider a linear differential-equation system similar to (15) in Section 3.1:

$$k_0 x + k_1 D x + k_2 D^2 x + \cdots + k_r D^r x = b(t), \tag{15'}$$

where x and $b(t)$ are column h-vectors, k_i is an $h \times h$ matrix of constants ($i = 1, \ldots, h$), and D denotes differential operator d/dt. Assuming that k_r is nonsingular, we rewrite (15′) as

$$DX = AX + B(t), \tag{71}$$

where

$$X \equiv \begin{bmatrix} x \\ Dx \\ \vdots \\ D^{r-1}x \end{bmatrix}, \qquad B(t) \equiv \begin{bmatrix} \theta \\ \vdots \\ \theta \\ k_r^{-1}b(t) \end{bmatrix}, \qquad A \equiv \begin{bmatrix} 0 & I & 0 & \cdots & 0 \\ 0 & 0 & I & & 0 \\ \vdots & \vdots & & \ddots & \\ 0 & 0 & & & I \\ A_0 & A_1 & \cdots & & A_{r-1} \end{bmatrix}$$

with $A_i \equiv -k_r^{-1}k_i$ $(i = 0, 1, \ldots, r-1)$. If the solution of system (71) approaches a particular solution determined by nonhomogeneous term $B(t)$ as t goes to infinity, the system is said to be *stable*. In other words, if and only if the solution of the associated homogeneous system

$$DX = AX \tag{72}$$

tends to zero as t goes to infinity regardless of initial conditions, nonhomogeneous system (71) is stable, and A is referred to as a *stable matrix*. We have the following fundamental theorem concerning the stability.

THEOREM 8 A necessary and sufficient condition for the stability of system (71) or (72) is that every eigenvalue of matrix A have a negative real part. [We denote the real part of a number s as $\mathrm{Re}(s)$.]

PROOF Let λ_i $(i = 1, \ldots, n)$ be the eigenvalues of matrix A. A can be transformed into a triangular matrix by a nonsingular matrix Q:

$$Q^{-1}AQ = \begin{bmatrix} \lambda_1 & b_{12} & \cdots & b_{1n} \\ 0 & \lambda_2 & & b_{2n} \\ \vdots & & \ddots & \\ 0 & 0 & & \lambda_n \end{bmatrix} \equiv B,$$

where $n \equiv rh$. Accordingly, system (72) is transformed into

$$DY = BY,$$

where $Y \equiv Q^{-1}X$, and its ith component is denoted by y_i. Or

$$Dy_n = \lambda_n y_n, \tag{73}$$

$$Dy_{n-1} = \lambda_{n-1}y_{n-1} + b_{n-1,n}y_n, \tag{74}$$

$$\vdots$$

$$Dy_1 = \lambda_1 y_1 + b_{12}y_2 + \cdots + b_{1n}y_n.$$

Solving (73), we have $y_n(t) = c_n e^{\lambda_n t}$, where $c_n \equiv y_n(0)$. Hence y_n tends to zero as t goes to infinity if and only if $\mathrm{Re}(\lambda_n) < 0$. Next solve (74) for y_{n-1}. Letting m denote $n-1$, we get

$$y_m(t) = c_m e^{\lambda_m t} + e^{\lambda_m t}\int_0^t e^{-\lambda_m s} b_{mn} y_n(s)\, ds, \tag{75}$$

where $c_m \equiv y_m(0)$. The second term on the right can be rewritten as

$$c_n b_{mn} e^{\lambda_m t} \int_0^t e^{(\lambda_n - \lambda_m)s}\, ds = \begin{cases} c_n b_{mn} t e^{\lambda_m t} & \text{for} \quad \lambda_m = \lambda_n, \\ \dfrac{c_n b_{mn}}{\lambda_n - \lambda_m}(e^{\lambda_n t} - e^{\lambda_m t}) & \text{for} \quad \lambda_m \neq \lambda_n. \end{cases}$$

Hence y_m tends to zero as t goes to infinity if and only if $\text{Re}(\lambda_m) < 0$ and $\text{Re}(\lambda_n) < 0$. Operate similarly one by one on the remaining $n - 2$ roots, $\lambda_{n-2}, \ldots, \lambda_1$. Q.E.D.

Henceforth, we consider an arbitrary real square matrix A of order n and say that A is a *stable* (or *stability*) *matrix* if

$$\text{every eigenvalue of matrix } A \text{ has a negative real part.} \tag{76}$$

We want to obtain some simple conditions that are equivalent to the stability condition (76) for matrix A. Let us express the characteristic equation of matrix A as

$$|\lambda I - A| = \lambda^n + a_{n-1}\lambda^{n-1} + \cdots + a_1\lambda + a_0 = 0, \tag{77}$$

where the coefficients are those in (47) in Section 1.2. Let λ_i $(i = 1, \ldots, n)$ be the eigenvalues of A. Then, there is the associated equation

$$\mu^p + b_{p-1}\mu^{p-1} + \cdots + b_1\mu + b_0 = 0, \tag{78}$$

whose roots are given by

$$\mu = \lambda_i + \lambda_j \qquad (i = 2, 3, \ldots, n; \quad j = 1, 2, \ldots, i - 1), \tag{79}$$

and whose degree is $p = 1 + 2 + \cdots + (n - 1) = \frac{1}{2}n(n - 1)$.

THEOREM 9 Assume Eq. (77) has real coefficients. A necessary and sufficient condition for the roots of (77) to have all their real parts negative is that $a_0, a_1, \ldots, a_{n-1}$ in (77) and $b_0, b_1, \ldots, b_{p-1}$ in (78) be all positive.

PROOF Represent the real roots of (77) by $\alpha_1, \alpha_2, \ldots$ and the complex roots by $\beta_1 \pm i\gamma_1, \beta_2 \pm i\gamma_2, \ldots$. Then (77) is rewritten as

$$(\lambda - \alpha_1)(\lambda - \alpha_2) \cdots (\lambda^2 - 2\beta_1\lambda + \beta_1^2 + \gamma_1^2)(\lambda^2 - 2\beta_2\lambda + \beta_2^2 + \gamma_2^2) \cdots = 0. \tag{80}$$

Necessity If $\alpha_1, \alpha_2, \ldots$ and $\beta_1, \beta_2, \ldots$ are all negative, the factors in (80) are all polynomials (of degree 0, 1, or 2) with positive coefficients. Thus when multiplied out, (80) becomes a polynomial with positive coefficients, i.e., the coefficients $a_0, a_1, \ldots, a_{n-1}$ in (77) are all positive. On the other hand, if the real parts of the roots of (77) are all negative, so are the real parts of the roots of (78) in view of (79). By the same reasoning as above, therefore, $b_0, b_1, \ldots, b_{p-1}$ should be all positive.

Sufficiency If $a_0, a_1, \ldots, a_{n-1}$ are all positive, then (77) has no positive or zero real roots. Similarly, if $b_0, b_1, \ldots, b_{p-1}$ are all positive, (78) has no positive or zero real roots. But from (79) the roots of (78) include the values $2\beta_1, 2\beta_2, \ldots$, i.e., twice the real parts of the complex roots of (77). Hence if $a_0, a_1, \ldots, a_{n-1}, b_0, b_1, \ldots, b_{p-1}$ are all positive, the real parts of the roots of (77) are all negative. Q.E.D.

Next we shall find a matrix whose eigenvalues are identical with the roots of (78). (Refer to Fuller (1968).)

DEFINITION 1 Let A and B be $n \times n$ matrices whose (i, j)th components are denoted a_{ij} and b_{ij}, respectively. By the *bialternate product* of A and B, denoted $A \cdot B$, we mean the square matrix of order $p = \frac{1}{2}n(n-1)$ such that its rows are labeled gk $(g = 2, 3, \ldots, n;\ k = 1, 2, \ldots, g-1)$ and its columns are labeled rs $(r = 2, 3, \ldots, n;\ s = 1, 2, \ldots, r-1)$ and whose (gk, rs)th component is

$$\frac{1}{2}\left[\begin{vmatrix} a_{gr} & a_{gs} \\ b_{kr} & b_{ks} \end{vmatrix} + \begin{vmatrix} b_{gr} & b_{gs} \\ a_{kr} & a_{ks} \end{vmatrix}\right]. \tag{81}$$

The (gk, rs)th component $c_{gk,rs}$ of $2A \cdot I$, where I is an identity matrix, is represented as

$$c_{gk,rs} = \begin{vmatrix} a_{gr} & a_{gs} \\ \delta_{kr} & \delta_{ks} \end{vmatrix} + \begin{vmatrix} \delta_{gr} & \delta_{gs} \\ a_{kr} & a_{ks} \end{vmatrix} \qquad \text{for} \quad g > k, \quad r > s, \tag{82}$$

where $\delta_{ij} = 1$ for $i = j$ and $\delta_{ij} = 0$ for $i \neq j$. Hence (82) can be rewritten as follows, with $g > k$, $r > s$ taken into account:

$$c_{gk,rs} = \begin{cases} -a_{gs} & \text{if} \quad r = k \quad (s < k) \\ a_{gr} & \text{if} \quad s = k \text{ and } r \neq g \quad (r > k) \\ a_{ks} & \text{if} \quad r = g \text{ and } s \neq k \quad (s < g) \\ -a_{kr} & \text{if} \quad s = g \quad (r > g) \\ a_{gg} + a_{kk} & \text{if} \quad r = g \text{ and } s = k \\ 0 & \text{otherwise.} \end{cases} \tag{82'}$$

THEOREM 10 The eigenvalues of the matrix

$$C \equiv 2A \cdot I \tag{83}$$

are the $p \equiv \frac{1}{2}n(n-1)$ values

$$\lambda_i + \lambda_j \qquad (i = 2, 3, \ldots, n;\quad j = 1, 2, \ldots, i-1).$$

PROOF Let $v^i = (v_1^i, v_2^i, \ldots, v_n^i)$ be an eigenvector of A associated with λ_i, i.e., $\lambda_i v^i = Av^i$, or equivalently

$$\lambda_i v_k^i = a_{k1}v_1^i + a_{k2}v_2^i + \cdots + a_{kn}v_n^i \qquad (k = 1, \ldots, n). \tag{84}$$

Similarly,

$$\lambda_j v_k^j = a_{k1}v_1^j + a_{k2}v_2^j + \cdots + a_{kn}v_n^j \qquad (k = 1, \ldots, n), \tag{84'}$$

where the eigenvector $v^j = (v_1^j, v_2^j, \ldots, v_n^j)$ is assumed to be linearly independent of v^i. Note that even if $\lambda_i = \lambda_j$ with multiplicity w, there are w linearly independent eigenvectors associated with λ_i. (See Section 3.2.)

Define

$$x_{gk}^{ij} \equiv \begin{vmatrix} v_g^i & v_g^j \\ v_k^i & v_k^j \end{vmatrix} \qquad \begin{matrix}(i = 2, 3, \ldots, n;\ j = 1, 2, \ldots, i-1; \\ g = 1, 2, \ldots, n;\ k = 1, 2, \ldots, n).\end{matrix} \tag{85}$$

Then

$$x_{gk}^{ij} = -x_{kg}^{ij}, \qquad x_{gg}^{ij} = 0, \tag{86}$$

and

$$(\lambda_i + \lambda_j)x_{gk}^{ij} = \begin{vmatrix} \lambda_i v_g^i & \lambda_j v_g^j \\ v_k^i & v_k^j \end{vmatrix} + \begin{vmatrix} v_g^i & v_g^j \\ \lambda_i v_k^i & \lambda_j v_k^j \end{vmatrix}. \tag{87}$$

Substituting (84) and (84′) into (87) and taking account of (86) yield

$$\begin{aligned}
(\lambda_i + \lambda_j)x_{gk}^{ij} &= \begin{vmatrix} \sum_{r=1}^{n} a_{gr}v_r^i & \sum_{r=1}^{n} a_{gr}v_r^j \\ v_k^i & v_k^j \end{vmatrix} + \begin{vmatrix} v_g^i & v_g^j \\ \sum_{s=1}^{n} a_{ks}v_s^i & \sum_{s=1}^{n} a_{ks}v_s^j \end{vmatrix} \\
&= \sum_{r=1}^{n} a_{gr} \begin{vmatrix} v_r^i & v_r^j \\ v_k^i & v_k^j \end{vmatrix} + \sum_{s=1}^{n} a_{ks} \begin{vmatrix} v_g^i & v_g^j \\ v_s^i & v_s^j \end{vmatrix} \\
&= \sum_{r=1, r\neq k}^{n} a_{gr}x_{rk}^{ij} + \sum_{s=1, s\neq g}^{n} a_{ks}x_{gs}^{ij} \\
&= -\sum_{r=1}^{k-1} a_{gr}x_{kr}^{ij} + \sum_{r=k+1}^{n} a_{gr}x_{rk}^{ij} + \sum_{s=1}^{g-1} a_{ks}x_{gs}^{ij} - \sum_{s=g+1}^{n} a_{ks}x_{sg}^{ij} \\
&= -\sum_{s=1}^{k-1} a_{gs}x_{ks}^{ij} + \sum_{r=k+1}^{n} a_{gr}x_{rk}^{ij} + \sum_{s=1}^{g-1} a_{ks}x_{gs}^{ij} - \sum_{r=g+1}^{n} a_{kr}x_{rg}^{ij}.
\end{aligned} \tag{88}$$

The coefficient of x_{rs}^{ij} on the extreme right of (88) is identical to $c_{gk,rs}$ in (82′), with $g > k$ and $r > s$. Therefore, we have

$$(\lambda_i + \lambda_j)x_{gk}^{ij} = \sum_{rs} c_{gk,rs}x_{rs}^{ij} \qquad \text{with} \quad g > k \text{ and } r > s, \tag{89}$$

or equivalently

$$(\lambda_i + \lambda_j)x^{ij} = Cx^{ij}, \tag{89′}$$

where x^{ij} is defined as a column vector with $\frac{1}{2}n(n-1)$ components x_{gk}^{ij} $(g = 2, 3, \ldots, n; k = 1, 2, \ldots, g-1)$. (89′) holds for $i = 2, 3, \ldots, n$ and $j = 1, 2, \ldots, i-1$. Thus, the eigenvectors of C are x^{ij}, and the eigenvalues of C are $\lambda_i + \lambda_j$. Q.E.D.

Noticing that (78) is equivalent to

$$|\mu I - C| = 0, \tag{90}$$

where C is defined as (83), one obtains what we call the modified *Routh–Hurwitz* theorem by Theorems 9 and 10.

THEOREM 11 (*the modified Routh–Hurwitz theorem*) Let A be an $n \times n$ real matrix whose (i, j)th component is denoted a_{ij}, and let C be the square matrix of order $p \equiv \frac{1}{2}n(n-1)$ defined as (83), with rows labeled gk ($g = 2, 3, \ldots, n$; $k = 1, 2, \ldots, g-1$), columns labeled rs ($r = 2, 3, \ldots, n$; $s = 1, 2, \ldots, r-1$), and components given by (82) or equivalently by (82′). Then for the eigenvalues of matrix A to have all their real parts negative, it is necessary and sufficient that all the coefficients in expansion forms of $|\lambda I - A|$ and $|\mu I - C|$ are positive, including constant terms.

The conditions stated in Theorem 11, which will be called the *modified Routh–Hurwitz conditions*, are easier to deal with than the original Routh–Hurwitz conditions (91) described below in Theorem 12 since the latter involves determinants within determinants.

THEOREM 12 Let A be an $n \times n$ real matrix, and express its characteristic equation as (77). Then for the roots of (77) to have all real parts negative, it is necessary and sufficient that

$$a_{n-1} > 0, \qquad \begin{vmatrix} a_{n-1} & a_{n-3} \\ 1 & a_{n-2} \end{vmatrix} > 0, \qquad \begin{vmatrix} a_{n-1} & a_{n-3} & a_{n-5} \\ 1 & a_{n-2} & a_{n-4} \\ 0 & a_{n-1} & a_{n-3} \end{vmatrix} > 0, \qquad \ldots, \qquad D > 0, \tag{91}$$

where D stands for the determinant of order n defined as

$$D \equiv \begin{vmatrix} a_{n-1} & a_{n-3} & a_{n-5} & a_{n-7} & \cdots & a_0 & 0 & \cdots & 0 \\ 1 & a_{n-2} & a_{n-4} & & \cdots & a_1 & 0 & & \\ 0 & a_{n-1} & a_{n-3} & & & a_2 & a_0 & 0 & \vdots \\ 0 & 1 & a_{n-2} & & & a_3 & a_1 & 0 & \\ \vdots & 0 & & & & & & & 0 \\ 0 & \vdots & & & & & & & a_0 \end{vmatrix} \quad \text{for an odd } n, \tag{92a}$$

and

$$D \equiv \begin{vmatrix} a_{n-1} & a_{n-3} & a_{n-5} & a_{n-7} & \cdots & a_1 & 0 & \cdots & 0 \\ 1 & a_{n-2} & a_{n-4} & & \cdots & a_2 & a_0 & 0 & \\ 0 & a_{n-1} & a_{n-3} & & & a_3 & a_1 & 0 & \vdots \\ 0 & 1 & a_{n-2} & & & a_4 & a_2 & a_0 & \\ \vdots & 0 & & & & & & & 0 \\ 0 & \vdots & & & & & & & a_0 \end{vmatrix} \quad \text{for an even } n. \tag{92b}$$

Note that the coefficients $a_{n-1}, \ldots, a_2, a_1, a_0$ involve determinants of submatrices of A. (For details, see Gantmacher (1960, pp. 190–196).)

Example 1 When the order of matrix A is two, i.e.,

$$A = \begin{bmatrix} a_{11} & a_{12} \\ a_{21} & a_{22} \end{bmatrix},$$

there will be no difficulty in obtaining conditions (91) of Theorem 12 or the modified Routh–Hurwitz conditions. Those are both reduced to

$$a_{11} + a_{22} < 0 \qquad \text{and} \qquad |A| > 0. \tag{93}$$

Example 2 When the order of matrix A is three, i.e.,

$$A = \begin{bmatrix} a_{11} & a_{12} & a_{13} \\ a_{21} & a_{22} & a_{23} \\ a_{31} & a_{32} & a_{33} \end{bmatrix},$$

it would be better to apply the modified Routh–Hurwitz conditions rather than conditions (91) since the latter involve

$$\begin{vmatrix} -(a_{11} + a_{22} + a_{33}) & -|A| \\ 1 & \begin{vmatrix} a_{11} & a_{12} \\ a_{21} & a_{22} \end{vmatrix} + \begin{vmatrix} a_{11} & a_{13} \\ a_{31} & a_{33} \end{vmatrix} + \begin{vmatrix} a_{22} & a_{23} \\ a_{32} & a_{33} \end{vmatrix} \end{vmatrix} > 0,$$

while the former are reduced to the following nonredundant conditions:

$$a_{11} + a_{22} + a_{33} < 0, \qquad |A| < 0, \qquad \text{and} \qquad |2A \cdot I| < 0. \tag{94}$$

Application 1 Assume that each of three target variables X_1, X_2, X_3 is a function of three policy instruments S_1, S_2, S_3:

$$X_i = X_i(S_1, S_2, S_3) \qquad \text{for} \quad i = 1, 2, 3.$$

Given a set of target values X_i^* $(i = 1, 2, 3)$, the corresponding equilibrium values of S_j $(j = 1, 2, 3)$ are supposed to be uniquely determined by the above equations and are represented as S_j^* $(j = 1, 2, 3)$. Furthermore, assume that the discrepancy of X_i from X_i^* is small enough to be approximated linearly by

$$x_i = k_{i1}s_1 + k_{i2}s_2 + k_{i3}s_3 \qquad \text{for} \quad i = 1, 2, 3,$$

where $x_i \equiv X_i - X_i^*$, $s_j \equiv S_j - S_j^*$, and $k_{ij} \equiv \partial X_i/\partial S_j$. Let us postulate that the speed of adjustment for each instrument responds to one of the discrepancies mentioned above such that

$$ds_i/dt = \gamma_i x_i \qquad \text{for} \quad i = 1, 2, 3,$$

where t stands for the time for adjustment and the γ's are constants. Thus we have a system of linear differential equations:

$$ds/dt = \Gamma K s,$$

where

$$s \equiv \begin{bmatrix} s_1 \\ s_2 \\ s_3 \end{bmatrix}, \qquad \Gamma \equiv \begin{bmatrix} \gamma_1 & 0 & 0 \\ 0 & \gamma_2 & 0 \\ 0 & 0 & \gamma_3 \end{bmatrix}, \qquad K \equiv \begin{bmatrix} k_{11} & k_{12} & k_{13} \\ k_{21} & k_{22} & k_{23} \\ k_{31} & k_{32} & k_{33} \end{bmatrix}.$$

Then, the stability conditions for this system are obtained as follows by applying (94) and taking (82′) into consideration:

$$\gamma_1\gamma_2\gamma_3|K| < 0, \qquad \gamma_1 k_{11} + \gamma_2 k_{22} + \gamma_3 k_{33} < 0,$$

$$\begin{vmatrix} \gamma_1 k_{11} + \gamma_2 k_{22} & \gamma_2 k_{23} & -\gamma_1 k_{13} \\ \gamma_3 k_{32} & \gamma_1 k_{11} + \gamma_3 k_{33} & \gamma_1 k_{12} \\ -\gamma_3 k_{31} & \gamma_2 k_{21} & \gamma_2 k_{22} + \gamma_3 k_{33} \end{vmatrix} < 0.$$

Now we turn to the study of relationships between stability of differential equations and that of difference equations, and to a comparative-statics problem.

Let A be an $n \times n$ real matrix and $X(t)$ a column n-vector of variables. In view of Theorem 7 in Section 3.3, a linear difference equation system

$$X(t) = AX(t-1) \tag{95}$$

has the stability property, i.e., $X(t)$ in (95) approaches zero as the integer t goes to infinity, regardless of any initial condition, if and only if every eigenvalue λ of A is less than unity in modulus:

$$|\lambda| < 1 \qquad \text{for all } \lambda, \tag{96}$$

which is termed the *Tinbergenian* condition by Samuelson (1947). Condition (96) implies

$$\mathrm{Re}(\lambda - 1) < 0 \qquad \text{for all } \lambda. \tag{97}$$

Since $\lambda - 1$ is an eigenvalue of matrix $A - I$, we can assert that if the difference equation system (95) is stable, the following differential equation system

$$dX/dt = [A - I]X$$

is also stable. Obviously the converse is not true.

Application 2 Consider a system of linear difference equations

$$x(t+r) + B_{r-1}x(t+r-1) + \cdots + B_2 x(t+2) + B_1 x(t+1) + B_0 x(t) = z \tag{98}$$

where $x(t)$ stands for a column h-vector to be determined, z a column h-vector of constants, and B_i $(i = 0, 1, \ldots, r-1)$ $h \times h$ coefficient matrices. (98) can be rewritten as

$$X(t+1) = BX(t) + Z, \tag{98′}$$

where

$$B \equiv \begin{bmatrix} 0 & I & 0 & \cdots & 0 \\ 0 & 0 & I & & 0 \\ \vdots & & & \ddots & \\ 0 & 0 & & & I \\ -B_0 & -B_1 & \cdots & & -B_{r-1} \end{bmatrix}, \qquad X(t) \equiv \begin{bmatrix} x(t) \\ x(t+1) \\ \vdots \\ x(t+r-1) \end{bmatrix}, \qquad Z \equiv \begin{bmatrix} \theta \\ \vdots \\ \theta \\ z \end{bmatrix}.$$

Suppose system (98) or equivalently (98′) is stable. Then the eigenvalues of $A \equiv B - I$ have all negative real parts, and it follows from Theorem 11 that all the coefficients, including a_0, in

$$|\lambda I - A| = \lambda^n + a_{n-1}\lambda^{n-1} + \cdots + a_1\lambda + a_0,$$

where $n \equiv rh$, should be positive. In particular

$$a_0 \equiv (-1)^n |A| > 0,$$

which can be rewritten as

$$|I + B_{r-1} + \cdots + B_1 + B_0| > 0, \tag{99}$$

because

$$(-1)^n|A| = |-A| = |I - B|$$
$$= \begin{vmatrix} I & -I & 0 & \cdots & 0 \\ 0 & I & -I & & 0 \\ \vdots & & \ddots & \ddots & \\ 0 & 0 & & I & -I \\ B_0 & B_1 & \cdots & B_{r-2} & I + B_{r-1} \end{vmatrix},$$

to which formula (41) in Section 1.1 is applied.

In equilibrium $x(t+r) = \cdots = x(t+1) = x(t) \equiv x^*$ holds, and system (98) reduces to $Hx^* = z$, where $H \equiv I + B_{r-1} + \cdots + B_1 + B_0$. A change in z will shift the position of equilibrium x^*. The effect of a change in the ith component z_i of z upon x^* is represented as

$$\frac{\partial}{\partial z_i} x^* = \frac{1}{H} [\operatorname{adj} H] e^i, \tag{100}$$

where e^i stands for the ith column vector of identity matrix I. In (100) we know that $|H| > 0$ by the result (99) from the stability conditions. The property that comparative statics is linked with stability conditions is termed the *correspondence principle* by Samuelson (1947).

In case $h = 1$ in (98), it becomes a single difference equation and H is simply a scalar. Hence, (100) is now reduced to

$$dx^*/dz = 1/H > 0. \tag{100′}$$

3.5 Sufficient Conditions for the Tinbergenian

The present section is a direct continuation of Section 3.3, where we established a necessary and sufficient condition for stability of a linear difference equation system. Now we want to provide various sufficient conditions for system stability.

Consider a system of linear difference equations of order one:

$$x(t) = Ax(t-1) + y, \tag{101}$$

where A is an $n \times n$ matrix of constants, y is a column n-vector of constants, and $x(t)$ denotes a column n-vector of variables in period t. We know that the Tinbergenian condition (96) is necessary and sufficient for the system (101) to be stable in the sense that $x(t)$ converges to a unique limit:

$$\lim_{t\to\infty} x(t) = [I - A]^{-1}y, \tag{102}$$

as t goes to infinity. Easy methods of checking stability will be obtained from simple sufficient conditions for the Tinbergenian condition (96). Let us list some sufficient conditions.

According to Theorem 19 in Section 1.3, any eigenvalue of an $n \times n$ matrix A cannot exceed either its row sums or its column sums of elements in modulus, whence a sufficient condition for the Tinbergenian condition (96) is

$$\sum_{i=1}^{n} |a_{ij}| < 1 \qquad \text{for} \quad j = 1, \ldots, n, \tag{103}$$

or

$$\sum_{j=1}^{n} |a_{ij}| < 1 \qquad \text{for} \quad i = 1, \ldots, n, \tag{104}$$

where $|a_{ij}|$ stands for the modulus of the (i, j)th component a_{ij} of matrix A. Another sufficient condition for (96) is the following which is to be derived in relation to contraction mappings in Section 7.3 (see Example 2):

$$\sum_{i=1}^{n} \sum_{j=1}^{n} |a_{ij}|^2 < 1. \tag{105}$$

Condition (103) may be termed the *column-sum condition*, (104) the *row-sum condition*, and (105) the *sum-of-squares condition*. It is obvious that

$$\sum_{i=1}^{n} \sum_{j=1}^{n} |a_{ij}| < 1 \tag{106}$$

is a stronger sufficient condition for (96), which may be called the *element-sum condition*.

Theorem 25 in Section 1.3 provides the following sufficient condition for the system (101) with real A: There are $d_1, \ldots, d_n > 0$ such that

$$\sum_{i=1}^{n} d_i |a_{ij}| < d_j \qquad \text{for} \quad j = 1, \ldots, n; \tag{107}$$

or equivalently

$$[d_1, \ldots, d_n] \begin{bmatrix} 1-|a_{11}| & -|a_{12}| & \cdots & -|a_{1n}| \\ -|a_{21}| & 1-|a_{22}| & & -|a_{2n}| \\ \vdots & & & \vdots \\ -|a_{n1}| & -|a_{n2}| & & 1-|a_{nn}| \end{bmatrix} > \theta; \qquad (107')$$

in other words, $[I - A^*]$ has a positive dominant diagonal (d.d. for short), meaning that it has all positive diagonal entries and a column d.d., where $A^* \equiv [|a_{ij}|]$. In the case that A is real and $0 \leqq a_{jj} < 1$ for all j, the condition is reduced to: There are $d_1, \ldots, d_n > 0$ such that

$$d_j|1 - a_{jj}| > \sum_{i=1, i\neq j}^{n} d_i|a_{ij}| \qquad \text{for} \quad j = 1, \ldots, n; \qquad (108)$$

in other words, $[I - A]$ has a column d.d. If A is nonnegative in system (101), condition (107) is found to be equivalent to the Tinbergenian condition (96).

THEOREM 13 The system (101) with nonnegative A is stable and the unique limit (102) is nonnegative for any nonnegative y if and only if there are positive scalars $d_1, \ldots, d_n$ such that

$$\sum_{i=1}^{n} d_i a_{ij} < d_j \qquad \text{for} \quad j = 1, \ldots, n; \qquad (109)$$

in other words,

$$[I - A] \text{ has a positive d.d.} \qquad (109')$$

PROOF By virtue of Theorem 24 in Section 1.3 and the remark on Theorem 30 in Section 2.4, condition (109′) is equivalent to the H-S conditions for $[I - A]$; while the latter is equivalent to the Tinbergenian condition (96) in view of Theorem 1 and Lemma 2 in Section 4.1 below. Note that nonnegativity of $[I - A]^{-1}$ is assured by the H-S conditions. Q.E.D.

Theorem 13 above is regarded as the dynamic counterpart of Theorem 23′ in Section 1.3. The following corollary is immediate from Theorem 13.

COROLLARY For a nonnegative square matrix A, condition (109′) is equivalent to saying that $[I - A]$ is a P-matrix.

Note that in case A is real and not nonnegative, condition (109′) is only sufficient for $[I - A]$ to be a P-matrix. (See Theorem 27 in Section 1.3.)

Now consider the model of distributed lags

$$x(t) = \sum_{i=1}^{r} A_i x(t - i) + y, \qquad (110)$$

where A_i is an $n \times n$ real matrix, or equivalently

$$X(t) = AX(t - 1) + Y, \qquad (110')$$

where

$$X(t) \equiv \begin{bmatrix} x(t-r+1) \\ x(t-r+2) \\ \vdots \\ x(t-1) \\ x(t) \end{bmatrix}, \qquad A \equiv \begin{bmatrix} 0 & I & 0 & \cdots & 0 \\ 0 & 0 & I & & 0 \\ \vdots & & & \ddots & \\ 0 & 0 & & & I \\ A_r & A_{r-1} & & \cdots & A_1 \end{bmatrix}, \qquad Y \equiv \begin{bmatrix} \theta \\ \theta \\ \vdots \\ \theta \\ y \end{bmatrix}.$$

We are interested in the stability of system (110) in relation to its first-order aggregated system

$$x(t) = \bar{A}x(t-1) + y, \tag{111}$$

where $\bar{A} \equiv \sum_{i=1}^{r} A_i$.

LEMMA 2 (Bear, 1966) Assume A_i $(i = 1, \ldots, r)$ are $n \times n$ nonnegative matrices, let $\bar{A} = \sum_{i=1}^{r} A_i$, and let A be as defined in (110′). Then $[I - A]$ has a positive d.d. if and only if $[I - \bar{A}]$ has a positive d.d.

PROOF *Necessity* That $[I - A]$ has a positive d.d. can be restated as follows: There are r strictly positive row n-vectors $\delta_1, \ldots, \delta_r$ such that

$$\delta_1 - \delta_r A_r > \theta,$$

$$\delta_{r-i+1} - \delta_{r-i} - \delta_r A_i > \theta \qquad \text{for} \quad i = 1, \ldots, r-1.$$

Summing these inequalities over i yields $\delta_r[I - \bar{A}] > \theta$, meaning that $[I - \bar{A}]$ has a positive d.d. (see (109)).

Sufficiency Define

$$q_1 \equiv \delta_1[I - \bar{A}] > \theta,$$

where δ_1 is a given positive row n-vector, and define

$$\delta_i \equiv \delta_1 \sum_{p=i}^{r} A_p + q_i \qquad \text{for} \quad i = 1, \ldots, r,$$

where

$$q_i \equiv \frac{r+1-i}{r} q_1 > \theta \qquad \text{for} \quad i = 1, \ldots, r.$$

Then, $q_r = q_1/r$ and $q_i = q_{i+1} + q_r$ $(i = 1, \ldots, r-1)$. Thus

$$\begin{aligned} \delta_i &= \delta_1 A_i + \delta_1 \sum_{p=i+1}^{r} A_p + q_{i+1} + q_r \\ &= \delta_1 A_i + \delta_{i+1} + q_r \qquad \text{for} \quad i = 1, \ldots, r-1, \end{aligned}$$

and

$$\delta_r = \delta_1 A_r + q_r.$$

These equations put together are shown by

$$(\delta_r, \delta_{r-1}, \ldots, \delta_1)[I - A] = (q_r, q_r, \ldots, q_r) > \theta,$$

meaning that $[I - A]$ has a column d.d. Lastly, note that the main diagonal entries of $[I - A_1]$ are all positive since $A_1 \leqq \bar{A}$. Q.E.D.

THEOREM 14 (Bear, 1963) Assume $A_i \geqq 0$ in system (110). Then, the system is stable if and only if its first-order aggregated system (111) is stable.

PROOF By Theorem 13, system (110′) is stable if and only if $[I - A]$ has a positive d.d., which is equivalent to saying that $[I - \bar{A}]$ has a positive d.d. by virtue of Lemma 2, meaning that system (111) is stable. Q.E.D.

We remark that in the case where A_i in system (110) are all nonnegative scalars and not all zero,

$$\sum_{i=1}^{r} A_i < 1 \tag{112}$$

is necessary and sufficient for the equation (110) to be stable in view of (99) in Section 3.4 and Theorem 12 (Solow theorem) in Section 4.2 below.

When the A_i $(i = 1, \ldots, n)$ in system (110) are not all nonnegative, define $A_i^* \equiv [|a_{kj}|]$, where a_{kj} stands for the (k, j)th component of A_i, $\bar{A}^* \equiv \sum_{i=1}^{r} A_i^*$ and

$$A^* \equiv \begin{bmatrix} 0 & I & 0 & \cdots & 0 \\ 0 & 0 & I & & 0 \\ \vdots & & & \ddots & \\ 0 & 0 & & & I \\ A_r^* & A_{r-1}^* & & \cdots & A_1^* \end{bmatrix}.$$

Then, in view of condition (107), we have the following

THEOREM 15 System (110) is stable if $[I - A^*]$ has a positive d.d., or equivalently (see Lemma 2) if $[I - \bar{A}^*]$ has a positive d.d.

The condition that $[I - A^*]$ has a positive d.d. reduces to the requirement that there be r strictly positive row n-vectors $\delta_1, \ldots, \delta_r$ such that

$$\delta_r A_r^* < \delta_1 \quad \text{and} \quad \delta_r A_i^* < \delta_{r-i+1} - \delta_{r-i} \quad \text{for} \quad i = 1, \ldots, r-1. \tag{113}$$

Condition (113) may be difficult to use to check the stability of system (110). An easy stability check for such a distributed-lag model is given next.

THEOREM 16 (Conlisk, 1973) System (110) is stable and has a unique limit if

$$\sum_{i=1}^{r} \|A_i\| < 1, \tag{114}$$

where $\|A_i\|$ is defined as either one of the following:

$$\|A_i\| = \max_{1 \leqq j \leqq n} \sum_{k=1}^{n} |a_{kj}| \qquad \text{(column-sum norm)} \tag{115}$$

$$\|A_i\| = \max_{1 \leqq k \leqq n} \sum_{j=1}^{n} |a_{kj}| \qquad \text{(row-sum norm)} \tag{116}$$

where a_{kj} stands for the (k, j)th component of A_i.

Remark Let B and C be $n \times n$ complex matrices. Then, norm $f(B) = \|B\|$ defined by (115) or (116) satisfies:

(i) $f(B) \geqq 0$, where equality holds if and only if $B = 0$.
(ii) $f(\alpha B) = |\alpha| f(B)$ for any scalar α.
(iii) $f(B + C) \leqq f(B) + f(C)$.
(iv) $f(BC) \leqq f(B)f(C)$.

Any real-valued function f of a matrix fulfilling the four axioms (i)–(iv) is called a *matrix norm*. There are forms of norms other than those defined by (115) and (116). We adopt the norms defined by (115) and (116) in this section simply because they are convenient for our purposes. (Cf. Section 5.5.)

Some lemmas about matrix norms are useful for the proof of Theorem 16.

LEMMA 3 Let $f(B)$ be a matrix norm of a square matrix B and let $\mu(B)$ be the modulus of an eigenvalue of B having maximum modulus. Then

$$\mu(B) \leqq f(B).$$

PROOF Let λ be an eigenvalue of B having maximum modulus with nontrivial eigenvector x. Let X be the square matrix $X \equiv (x, \theta, \ldots, \theta)$. Then, since $\lambda X = BX$,

$$\mu(B) = |\lambda| = f(\lambda X)/f(X) = f(BX)/f(X) \leqq f(B). \qquad \text{Q.E.D.}$$

The next lemma can be verified easily.

LEMMA 4 If $f(B)$ is a matrix norm of B, then $g(B) \equiv f(P^{-1}BP)$ is a matrix norm of B for any nonsingular matrix P.

LEMMA 5 Let f be a matrix norm having the property $f(B) \leqq f(C)$ whenever $0 \leqq B \leqq C$, and let g be any matrix norm. Partitioning a square matrix B into r^2 square blocks B_{ij} $(i, j = 1, \ldots, r)$, we define a function h of B as $h(B) = f(G(B))$, where

$$G(B) \equiv \begin{bmatrix} g(B_{11}) & \cdots & g(B_{1r}) \\ \vdots & & \vdots \\ g(B_{r1}) & \cdots & g(B_{rr}) \end{bmatrix}.$$

Then h is a matrix norm of B.

PROOF Axioms (i)–(iii) are obviously fulfilled by h. Axiom (iv) is also satisfied as may be seen below.

$$h(BC) = f\begin{bmatrix} g(\sum_j B_{1j}C_{j1}) & \cdots & g(\sum_j B_{1j}C_{jr}) \\ \vdots & & \vdots \\ g(\sum_j B_{rj}C_{j1}) & \cdots & g(\sum_j B_{rj}C_{jr}) \end{bmatrix} \leqq f(G(B)G(C)) \leqq h(B)h(C). \quad \text{Q.E.D.}$$

PROOF OF THEOREM 16 We shall show that condition (114) implies $\mu(A) < 1$ for the matrix A defined in (110′). Noticing that $\|I\| = 1$, we take the column sum norm or row sum norm of each block of the matrix A, i.e.,

$$G(A) \equiv \begin{bmatrix} 0 & 1 & \cdots & 0 \\ 0 & 0 & & 0 \\ \vdots & & \ddots & \\ 0 & & & 1 \\ \|A_r\| & & \cdots & \|A_1\| \end{bmatrix}.$$

By an $r \times r$ diagonal matrix $P = \operatorname{diag}(p_1, \cdots, p_r)$ such that

$$p_1 > p_2 > \cdots > p_{r-1} > p_r > 0,$$

we define the matrix norm of A, in view of Lemmas 4 and 5, as follows:

$$h(A) = f(P^{-1}G(A)P),$$

where f is the row sum norm. A choice of P as above and condition (114) assure that the row sums of matrix $[P^{-1}G(A)P]$ are all less than one. Thus, $h(A) < 1$, which implies $\mu(A) < 1$ by virtue of Lemma 3. Q.E.D.

Sometimes it is more convenient to deal with the distributed-lag model with a contemporary term in addition to the terms in system (110).

COROLLARY (Conlisk, 1973) Consider the dynamic system

$$x(t) = \sum_{i=0}^{r} A_i x(t-i) + y, \tag{117}$$

where A_i is an $n \times n$ real matrix. This system is stable and has a unique limit if

$$\sum_{i=0}^{r} \|A_i\| < 1, \tag{114′}$$

where $\|A_i\|$ is the column sum norm or the row sum norm.

PROOF System (117) can be rewritten as

$$X(t) = AX(t-1) + BX(t) + Y, \tag{117′}$$

where $X(t)$, A, and Y are as defined in (110′) and

$$B \equiv \begin{bmatrix} 0 & \cdots & 0 & 0 \\ \vdots & & \vdots & \vdots \\ 0 & & 0 & 0 \\ 0 & \cdots & 0 & A_0 \end{bmatrix} \qquad \text{(matrix of } r^2 \text{ blocks).}$$

Define

$$h(A) = f(P^{-1}G(A)P) \qquad \text{and} \qquad h(B) = f(G(B)),$$

where G, P, and f are as in the proof of Theorem 16. Then (114′) implies $h(A) + h(B) < 1$. It suffices to show that $h(A) + h(B) < 1$ implies $h([I - B]^{-1}A) < 1$. In view of Lemma 3 above and Theorem 7 in Section 3.3, A_0^t and thereby B^t converge to zero as t goes to infinity. Hence we have $[I - B]^{-1} = \sum_{t=0}^{\infty} B^t$.

$$\begin{aligned} h([I - B]^{-1}A) &\leqq h\left(\sum_{t=0}^{\infty} B^t\right)h(A) \leqq \left(1 + \sum_{t=1}^{\infty} h(B^t)\right)h(A) \leqq (1 - h(B))^{-1}h(A) \\ &= 1 - (1 - h(B))^{-1}(1 - h(B) - h(A)) < 1. \qquad \text{Q.E.D.} \end{aligned}$$

Lastly, we remark that the above observations of Conlisk may be useful for a generalization of the concept of matrices with dominant diagonals defined in Section 1.3 (see Pearce (1974)).

EXERCISES

1. Show that $x_{s_i}(t)$ ($s_i = 0, 1, \ldots, w_i - 1$) in (9) are linearly independent.

2. Let y be a function of t, and solve

$$\frac{d^2y}{dt^2} - 4\frac{dy}{dt} - + 4y = ce^{nt} \qquad (c,\ n \text{ constants})$$

with initial conditions $y(0) = 10$ and $y(1) = 15e^2$.

3. Verify that

$$P(D)g(t)e^{\lambda t} = e^{\lambda t}P(D + \lambda)g(t),$$

where $P(D)$ is as in (14), λ is a complex number,

$$g(t) \equiv \{g_1(t), \ldots, g_n(t)\} \qquad \text{(column } n\text{-vector)},$$

and the $g_i(t)$ ($i = 1, \ldots, n$) are arbitrary functions differentiable successively for relevant times.

4. Show that the fundamental matrix of the differential system (12′) is nonsingular.

5. Prove Lemma 1.

6. Prove the following theorem. Let A be an $n \times n$ real matrix and let ψ be its minimal polynomial. When two polynomials p_1 and p_2 are expressed as $p_i = q_i\psi + r_i$ $(i = 1, 2)$, where q_i is the quotient and r_i is the residue, the statements $p_1(A) = p_2(A)$ and $r_1 = r_2$ are equivalent.

7. Let $r = 3$ in (69), and write out its general solution in terms of V, U, and λ.

8. Prove that a second degree polynomial

$$x^2 + bx + c = 0$$

has two roots whose real parts are negative if and only if its coefficients b and c are both positive. (Refer to Samuelson (1947, pp. 430–431).)

9. Prove Lemma 4.

10. Let B and C be $n \times n$ complex matrices and define the *spectral norm* of B, denoted $f(B)$, as

$$f(B) \equiv \max\ (\mu(B^*B))^{1/2},$$

where B^* stands for the conjugate transpose of B (so $B^* = B^{\mathrm{T}}$ for real B), and $\mu(A)$ represents an eigenvalue of matrix A. Show that Lemma 5 holds for the spectral norm f.

REFERENCES AND FURTHER READING

Barnett, S., and Storey, C. (1970). *Matrix Methods in Stability Theory.* Barnes and Noble, New York, and Nelson, London.

Bear, D. (1963). "The Matrix Multiplier and Distributed Lags," *Econometrica* **31**, 514–529.

Bear, D. (1966). "Distributed Lags and Economic Theory," *Review of Economic Studies* **33**, 235–243.

Bellman, R. (1970). *Introduction to Matrix Analysis*, 2nd ed. McGraw-Hill, New York.

Benavie, A. (1971). "The Correspondence Principle and Distributed Lags," *Journal of Economic Theory* **3**, 335–340.

Bowden, R. (1972). "The Generalized Characteristic Equation of a Linear Dynamic System," *Econometrica* **40**, 201–203.

Conlisk, J. (1973). "Quick Stability Checks and Matrix Norms," *Economica* **40**, 402–409.

Fuller, A. T. (1968). "Conditions for a Matrix to Have Only Characteristic Roots with Negative Real Parts," *Journal of Mathematical Analysis and Applications* **23**, 71–98.

Gandolfo, G. (1971). *Mathematical Methods and Models in Economic Dynamics.* North-Holland Publ., Amsterdam.

Gantmacher, F. R. (1960). *The Theory of Matrices* (English translation), Vol. II. Chelsea, New York.

Goldberg, S. (1958). *Introduction to Difference Equations.* Wiley, New York.

Hicks, J. R. (1950). *A Contribution to the Theory of Trade Cycle.* Oxford Univ. Press, London and New York.

Keynes, J. M. (1936). *The General Theory of Employment, Interest and Money.* Harcourt, New York.

Lang, S. (1971). *Linear Algebra*, 2nd ed. Addison-Wesley, Reading.

Pearce, I. F. (1974). "Matrices with Dominating Diagonal Blocks," *Journal of Economic Theory* **9**, 159–170.

Pontryagin, L. S. (1962). *Ordinary Differential Equations* (English translation). Addison–Wesley, Reading, Massachusetts.

Samuelson, P. A. (1939). "Interactions between the Multiplier Analysis and the Principle of Acceleration," *Review of Economics and Statistics* **21**, 75–78.

Samuelson, P. A. (1947). *Foundations of Economic Analysis*. Harvard Univ. Press, Cambridge, Massachusetts.

Chapter 4

Nonnegative Square Matrices and Stability in Economic Systems

4.1 Frobenius Theorems

The so-called Frobenius theorems regarding a nonnegative (and nonzero) square matrix will be established, based on the following lemma which is to be proved by the utilization of elementary relations between submatrices.

LEMMA 1 Let $A = [a_{ij}]$ be an $n \times n$ nonnegative matrix with $n > 1$; $L(\lambda) = |\lambda I - A|$; $L_{ij}(\lambda) =$ the cofactor of $\lambda\delta_{ij} - a_{ij}$ in $L(\lambda)$, where $\delta_{ij} = 0$ $(i \neq j)$ and $\delta_{ii} = 1$; $r_n =$ the largest real eigenvalue of A; $M(\lambda) = L_{11}(\lambda)$ where we may choose any i as 1 after an appropriate permutation; and $r_{n-1} =$ the largest real root of $M(\lambda) = 0$. Then we can assert that there is a nonnegative $r_n \geqq r_{n-1}$ and that $L_{ij}(\lambda)$ is nonnegative for $\lambda \geqq r_n$ and in particular $L_{ii}(\lambda)$ is positive for $\lambda > r_n$ $(i, j = 1, \ldots, n)$.

PROOF We apply the method of mathematical induction to the assumption that the lemma holds true for a matrix of order $n - 1$ and show that the lemma then holds for a matrix of order n. It will also be shown that the lemma holds for matrices of order two. Throughout the proof, we suppose that $i, j = 2, 3, \ldots, n$.

Define $M_{ij}(\lambda)$ to be the cofactor of $\lambda\delta_{ij} - a_{ij}$ in $M(\lambda)$. Then we have the Laplace expansions

$$L_{1j}(\lambda) = \sum_{i=2}^{n} a_{i1} M_{ij}(\lambda) \tag{1}$$

and

$$L_{i1}(\lambda) = \sum_{j=2}^{n} a_{1j} M_{ij}(\lambda). \tag{2}$$

Thus $L(\lambda)$ takes the following form of expansion in terms of the first row:

$$L(\lambda) = (\lambda - a_{11}) M(\lambda) - \sum_{i=2}^{n} \sum_{j=2}^{n} a_{i1}a_{1j} M_{ij}(\lambda). \tag{3}$$

Since the lemma holds true for a matrix of order $n - 1$,

$$r_{n-1} \text{ is real and nonnegative,} \tag{4}$$

and

$$M_{ij}(\lambda) \geqq 0 \qquad \text{for} \quad \lambda \geqq r_{n-1}, \tag{5}$$

$$M_{ii}(\lambda) > 0 \qquad \text{for} \quad \lambda > r_{n-1}. \tag{5$'$}$$

Setting $\lambda = r_{n-1}$ in Eq. (3) yields

$$L(r_{n-1}) = -\sum_{i=2}^{n} \sum_{j=2}^{n} a_{i1}a_{1j}M_{ij}(r_{n-1}).$$

It follows from (5) that

$$L(r_{n-1}) \leqq 0. \tag{6}$$

Let $\lambda_1, \lambda_2, \ldots, \lambda_n$ be the roots of $L(\lambda) = 0$. Since $L(\lambda) = \prod_{i=1}^{n}(\lambda - \lambda_i)$, (6) implies that there is a real root r_n of $L(\lambda) = 0$ such that $r_n \geqq r_{n-1}$. Let $\rho_1, \ldots, \rho_{n-1}$ be the roots of $M(\lambda) = 0$. Then, by the definition of r_{n-1}, we have

$$M(\lambda) = \prod_{i=1}^{n-1} (\lambda - \rho_i) > 0 \qquad \text{for} \quad \lambda > r_{n-1}. \tag{7}$$

Also we know the following from relations (1), (2), and (5):

$$\left.\begin{aligned} L_{1j}(\lambda) \geqq 0 \qquad \text{for} \quad \lambda \geqq r_n \geqq r_{n-1}, \\ L_{i1}(\lambda) \geqq 0 \qquad \text{for} \quad \lambda \geqq r_n \geqq r_{n-1}. \end{aligned}\right. \tag{8}$$

Now, for any square matrix L the following equation holds

$$L_{11}L_{ij} - L_{i1}L_{1j} = L \cdot L_{11,ij},$$

so that in our notation ($M = L_{11}$ and $M_{ij} = L_{11,\,ij}$), we get

$$L_{ij}(\lambda) = (L(\lambda)M_{ij}(\lambda) + L_{i1}(\lambda)L_{1j}(\lambda)) \,/M(\lambda) \geqq 0 \qquad \text{for any} \quad \lambda > r_n,$$

$$L_{ii}(\lambda) > 0 \qquad \text{for} \quad \lambda > r_n$$

because of (5), (5$'$), (7), (8), and $L(\lambda) > 0$ for $\lambda > r_n$. Furthermore, $L_{ij}(r_n) \geqq 0$ since $M(r_n)\, L_{ij}(r_n) = L_{i1}(r_n)\, L_{1j}(r_n) \geqq 0$ and $M(r_n) \geqq 0$.

Consider a nonnegative square matrix A of order two:

$$A = \begin{bmatrix} a_{11} & a_{12} \\ a_{21} & a_{22} \end{bmatrix}.$$

Then, since $((a_{11} - a_{22})^2 + 4a_{12}a_{21})^{1/2} \geqq |a_{11} - a_{22}| \geqq a_{11} - a_{22}$, the largest real eigenvalue is

$$r_2 = \{a_{11} + a_{22} + ((a_{11} - a_{22})^2 + 4a_{12}a_{21})^{1/2}\}/2 \geqq a_{11} \geqq 0.$$

Since

$$L(\lambda) = \begin{vmatrix} \lambda - a_{11} & -a_{12} \\ -a_{21} & \lambda - a_{22} \end{vmatrix},$$

we know $L_{12}(\lambda) = a_{21} \geqq 0$, $L_{21}(\lambda) = a_{12} \geqq 0$, $L_{22}(\lambda) = \lambda - a_{11} \geqq 0$ for $\lambda \geqq r_2$, and

$$L_{11}(r_2) = r_2 - a_{22} = \{a_{11} - a_{22} + ((a_{11} - a_{22})^2 + 4a_{12}a_{21})^{1/2}\}/2 \geqq 0$$

implies that $L_{11}(\lambda) \geqq 0$ for $\lambda \geqq r_2$. Lastly $L_{ii}(\lambda) > 0$ for $\lambda > r_2$ $(i = 1, 2)$. Q.E.D.

DEFINITION 1 Let $\lambda_1, \lambda_2, \ldots, \lambda_n$ be the eigenvalues of A which is any nonnegative square matrix of order n with a_{ij} as its (i, j)th element. The largest real eigenvalue among these λ_i is called the *Frobenius* (or *Perron*) *root* of A and denoted henceforth by λ_1.

λ_1 is nonnegative by Lemma 1.

PROPOSITION 1 When A is a nonnegative square matrix, $[\lambda I - A]^{-1} \geqq 0$ for any λ larger than λ_1, and its diagonal elements are all positive.

PROOF The (i, j)th element of $[\lambda I - A]^{-1}$ is $L_{ji}(\lambda)/L(\lambda)$, which is nonnegative for $\lambda > \lambda_1$ because $L_{ji}(\lambda) \geqq 0$ for $\lambda \geqq \lambda_1$ and because $L_{ii}(\lambda) > 0$, $L(\lambda) > 0$ for $\lambda > \lambda_1$ (see Lemma 1). Q.E.D.

THEOREM 1 When $A = [a_{ij}]$ is an $n \times n$ nonnegative matrix, we have $\lambda_1 \geqq |\lambda|$ for any other eigenvalue λ of A, where $|\lambda|$ stands for the modulus of λ.

PROOF Let x be a nonzero eigenvector associated with λ, let x^* be the vector each component of which is the modulus of the corresponding component of x, and let ξ_i be the ith component of x. Note that x^* is semipositive, denoted $x^* \geq \theta$. Since

$$|\lambda||\xi_i| = |\lambda\xi_i| \leqq \sum_{j=1}^{n} a_{ij}|\xi_j|,$$

we have $Bx^* \leqq \theta$, where $B \equiv |\lambda|I - A$. By the corollary to Theorem 12 in Section 8.2, exactly one of the following alternatives holds: either $Bx^* \leqq \theta$ has a semipositive solution or $zB > \theta$ has a semipositive solution. If $|\lambda| > \lambda_1$, it would follow from Lemma 1 that $x = yB^{-1} > \theta$ for any positive vector y and hence that $xB > \theta$ would have a positive solution, which is a contradiction. Q.E.D.

Thus, $\lambda_1 \geqq |\lambda| \geqq \text{Re}(\lambda)$ for any eigenvalue λ of A. Hence the Frobenius root λ_1 could be defined as the eigenvalue having the maximal real part among all eigenvalues of A.

THEOREM 2 When A is a nonnegative square matrix, the eigenvector x_1 of A associated with the Frobenius root λ_1 can be semipositive.

PROOF By Lemma 1, $\operatorname{adj}[\lambda_1 I - A] = [L_{ij}(\lambda_1)]^T$ is a nonnegative matrix. In case $\operatorname{rk}[\lambda_1 I - A] = n - 1$, we apply a duality, Theorem 13 in Section 8.2, viz., exactly one of the following alternatives holds: either the equality $[\lambda_1 I - A]x = \theta$ has a semipositive solution or the inequality $y[\lambda_1 I - A] > \theta$ has a solution. In the present case there is no solution y satisfying $y[\lambda_1 I - A] > \theta$, for, if such a solution y existed, then we would have the following contradiction:

$$\theta = y[\lambda_1 I - A] \cdot \operatorname{adj}[\lambda_1 I - A] = z \cdot \operatorname{adj}[\lambda_1 I - A] \geq \theta$$

for any $z > \theta$ since there are indices i and j such that $L_{ij}(\lambda_1) > 0$.

In case $\operatorname{rk}[\lambda_1 I - A] < n - 1$, we apply mathematical induction on n. $\operatorname{adj}[\lambda_1 I - A] = 0$ implies in particular $L_{ii}(\lambda_1) = 0$ for $i = 1, \ldots, n$, and hence λ_1 is the Frobenius root of A_{ii} in view of $\lambda_1 \geqq r_{n-1}^i$ in Lemma 1, where A_{ii} stands for a submatrix of A after deleting its ith row and column, and r_{n-1}^i its Frobenius root. Since $[\lambda_1 I - A]$ is singular, one of its rows, say its kth row, can be represented as a linear combination of the other rows. By virtue of the induction assumption, there exists a semipositive eigenvector x of A_{kk} associated with λ_1:

$$x = \{\xi_1, \ldots, \xi_{k-1}, \xi_{k+1}, \ldots, \xi_n\}.$$

Defining $\hat{x} = \{\xi_1, \ldots, \xi_{k-1}, 0, \xi_{k+1}, \ldots, \xi_n\}$, we obtain

$$[\lambda_1 I - A]\hat{x} = \theta,$$

which completes the proof since when $n = 2$ vector x reduces to a positive scalar. Q.E.D.

Replacing matrix A in the above proof by A^T, we obtain

COROLLARY When A is a nonnegative square matrix, the eigenvector of A^T associated with the Frobenius root λ_1 can be semipositive.

PROPOSITION 2 When A is a nonnegative square matrix, $[\lambda I - A]^{-1} \geqq 0$ implies $\lambda > \lambda_1$.

PROOF According to Theorem 2, there exists $x_1 \geq \theta$ such that $Ax_1 = \lambda_1 x_1$. If $[\lambda I - A^T]^{-1}$ is nonnegative, we have for any positive vector y, $x = [\lambda I - A^T]^{-1} y \geq \theta$ or $[\lambda I - A^T]x = y > \theta$. Hence $\lambda x > A^T x$. Therefore we know that

$$\lambda x_1^T x > x_1^T A^T x = x^T A x_1 = \lambda_1 x^T x_1,$$

which implies $\lambda > \lambda_1$ because $x_1^T x \geqq 0$. Q.E.D.

Propositions 1 and 2 merge in

THEOREM 3 When A is a nonnegative square matrix, $[\lambda I - A]^{-1} \geqq 0$ if and only if $\lambda > \lambda_1$.

LEMMA 2 (*Metzler lemma*) When A is a nonnegative square matrix, a necessary and sufficient condition for λ to be larger than the Frobenius root λ_1 is that any principal minor of $[\lambda I - A]$ take on a positive value.

PROOF *Necessity* Suppose $\lambda > \lambda_1$. Choose any principal submatrix of A and let r be the largest real root among all the eigenvalues of that submatrix. Due to Lemma 1, $\lambda > \lambda_1 \geqq r$. The characteristic polynomial of that submatrix is apparently positive for $\lambda > r$.

Sufficiency Set $z \equiv \lambda_1 - \lambda$. Then

$$|\lambda_1 I - A| = |zI - [A - \lambda I]|$$

$$= z^n + (-1) \sum_i (a_{ii} - \lambda)z^{n-1} + (-1)^2 \sum_{i,j;i<j} \begin{vmatrix} a_{ii} - \lambda & a_{ij} \\ a_{ji} & a_{jj} - \lambda \end{vmatrix} z^{n-2}$$

$$+ \cdots + (-1)^n |A - \lambda I|.$$

All the principal minors of $[\lambda I - A]$ being positive implies that all the coefficients, including the constant term, of the above polynomial take positive values. Thus, in order to have $|\lambda_1 I - A| = 0$, z must be negative. Q.E.D.

Theorem 3 coupled with the Metzler lemma yields

THEOREM 4 When A is a nonnegative square matrix, $[\lambda I - A]^{-1} \geqq 0$ if and only if $[\lambda I - A]$ satisfies the Hawkins–Simon conditions.

THEOREM 5 Let A be a nonnegative square matrix. If an element of A increases, its Frobenius root will be nondecreasing.

PROOF Let λ_1 be the Frobenius root of A, whose order is supposed to be n. By the corollary to Theorem 2, there is the associated semipositive eigenvector x_1 of A^{T}. Let $B = [b_{ij}]$ be a nonnegative square matrix of order n such that at least one element of B is smaller than the corresponding element of A and the other elements are equal, i.e., $A \geq B \geqq 0$. Let ρ be an eigenvalue of B and let $y = \{\eta_1, \ldots, \eta_n\} \neq \theta$ be its associated eigenvector. Then, since $By = \rho y$,

$$\sum_{j=1}^{n} b_{ij}|\eta_j| \geqq |\rho|\,|\eta_i| \qquad \text{for} \quad i = 1, \ldots, n,$$

or

$$By^* \geqq |\rho|y^*,$$

where $y^* = \{|\eta_1|, \ldots, |\eta_n|\} \geq \theta$. Thus

$$\lambda_1 x_1^{\mathrm{T}} y^* = x_1^{\mathrm{T}} A y^* \geqq x_1^{\mathrm{T}} B y^* \geqq |\rho| x_1^{\mathrm{T}} y^*,$$

which implies $\lambda_1 \geqq |\rho|$ in view of $x_1^{\mathrm{T}} y^* \geqq 0$. Q.E.D.

So far we have shown that the following statements hold true for any nonnegative (and nonzero) square matrix A of order n with $n > 1$:

(a) Matrix A has nonnegative Frobenius root which is not less than any other eigenvalue of A in modulus.

(b) The eigenvectors of A (and of A^{T}) associated with its Frobenius root can be semipositive.

(c) The Frobenius root of A does not decrease when an element of A increases.

(d) $[\lambda I - A]^{-1} \geqq 0$ if and only if λ is larger than the Frobenius root of A, or alternatively if and only if $[\lambda I - A]$ satisfies the Hawkins–Simon conditions.

(e) The Frobenius root of A is not less than that of any principal submatrix of A.

If nonnegative square matrix A is indecomposable as defined below, all the above five statements are strengthened as follows:

(a′) A has positive Frobenius root which is a simple eigenvalue and which is not less than any other eigenvalue of A in modulus.

(b′) The eigenvector of A (or of A^{T}) associated with its Frobenius root is a unique positive vector, and no other eigenvalue of A has an associated semipositive eigenvector.

(c′) The Frobenius root of A increases when an element of A increases.

(d′) $[\lambda I - A]^{-1} > 0$ if and only if λ is larger than the Frobenius root of A, or alternatively if and only if $[\lambda I - A]$ satisfies the Hawkins–Simon conditions.

(e′) The Frobenius root of A is larger than that of any principal submatrix of A.

DEFINITION 2 A square matrix A is said to be *decomposable* if it can be partitioned as follows by a permutation matrix P:

$$PAP^{\mathrm{T}} = \begin{bmatrix} B_1 & B_{12} \\ 0 & B_2 \end{bmatrix}, \tag{9}$$

where B_1, B_2 are square matrices and 0 stands for a zero matrix. If A cannot be partitioned as (9) by any permutation matrix P, A is said to be *indecomposable*.

A permutation matrix P is composed of all different unit vectors. For example, in the case where the order of matrix A is three, the following P is a permutation matrix:

$$P = \begin{bmatrix} 0 & 0 & 1 \\ 1 & 0 & 0 \\ 0 & 1 & 0 \end{bmatrix}.$$

By operation PAP^T, columns of A are interchanged at the same time as the corresponding rows are interchanged. In the above example,

$$PAP^T = \begin{bmatrix} 0 & 0 & 1 \\ 1 & 0 & 0 \\ 0 & 1 & 0 \end{bmatrix} \begin{bmatrix} a_{11} & a_{12} & a_{13} \\ a_{21} & a_{22} & a_{23} \\ a_{31} & a_{32} & a_{33} \end{bmatrix} \begin{bmatrix} 0 & 1 & 0 \\ 0 & 0 & 1 \\ 1 & 0 & 0 \end{bmatrix} = \begin{bmatrix} a_{33} & a_{31} & a_{32} \\ a_{13} & a_{11} & a_{12} \\ a_{23} & a_{21} & a_{22} \end{bmatrix}.$$

If $a_{23} = a_{21} = 0$ or $a_{13} = a_{23} = 0$ in this example, A is decomposable. Thus we can redefine the decomposability of matrix as follows.

DEFINITION 2′ Let $A = [a_{ij}]$ be an $n \times n$ matrix. If there exist non-empty subsets N_1, N_2 of index set $N \equiv \{1, 2, \ldots, n\}$ such that

$$N_1 \cup N_2 = N, \qquad N_1 \cap N_2 = \varnothing,$$

and $a_{ij} = 0$ for every $i \in N_1$ and $j \in N_2$, matrix A is said to be decomposable. Otherwise, A is indecomposable.

We remark that if an $n \times n$ matrix $A = [a_{ij}]$ is indecomposable, there exists an index $k \neq i$ such that $a_{ik} \neq 0$ for each $i = 1, \ldots, n$ and there exists an index $h \neq j$ such that $a_{hj} \neq 0$ for each $j = 1, \ldots, n$. Thus, if an indecomposable matrix A is nonnegative, each row and column of A is a semipositive vector.

One example of an indecomposable matrix is a positive square matrix, whose Frobenius root has the following properties.

LEMMA 3 Let $A = [a_{ij}]$ be an $n \times n$ positive matrix with $n > 1$; $L(\lambda) = |\lambda I - A|$; $L_{ij}(\lambda) =$ the cofactor of $\lambda\delta_{ij} - a_{ij}$ in $L(\lambda)$, where $\delta_{ij} = 0\,(i \neq j)$ and $\delta_{ii} = 1$; $r_n =$ the largest real eigenvalue of A; $r_{n-1} =$ the largest real root of $L_{11}(\lambda) = 0$ where we may choose any i as 1 after an appropriate permutation. Then we may assert that there is a positive $r_n > r_{n-1}$ and that $L_{ij}(\lambda)$ is positive for $\lambda \geqq r_n$ $(i, j = 1, \ldots, n)$.

(The proof proceeds in a similar manner to that of Lemma 1, *mutatis mutandis*.)

LEMMA 4 (*Lancaster lemma*) Let A be an $n \times n$ indecomposable nonnegative matrix and let $Z(x)$ be the number of zero components of the column n-vector x. If x is semipositive and not strictly positive, $Z((I + A)x) < Z(x)$.

PROOF Let $y = (I + A)x$. Since $I + A \geqq I$, we have $Z(y) \leqq Z(x)$. It suffices to rule out the equality case. Suppose equality did hold. Then the zeros in y must occupy the same positions as those of x because $y \geqq x$. We may suppose the zeros to occupy the last s components, so that we could partition vectors y and x as

$$y = \begin{bmatrix} \hat{y} \\ \theta \end{bmatrix}, \qquad x = \begin{bmatrix} \hat{x} \\ \theta \end{bmatrix},$$

where $\hat{y}$ and $\hat{x}$ are positive vectors. Partitioning matrix $I + A$ conformably with the partition of y and x, we have

$$\begin{bmatrix} \hat{y} \\ \theta \end{bmatrix} = \begin{bmatrix} I + A_{11} & A_{12} \\ A_{21} & I + A_{22} \end{bmatrix} \begin{bmatrix} \hat{x} \\ \theta \end{bmatrix},$$

from which it follows that $\theta = A_{21}\hat{x}$. This implies $A_{21} = 0$, contradicting the assumption of indecomposability of A. Thus we cannot have $Z(y) = Z(x)$. Q.E.D.

COROLLARY 1 Let A be an indecomposable nonnegative matrix and x be a semipositive vector having some zero components. There is an index j such that $\operatorname{sgn}(Ax)_j > 0$, $\operatorname{sgn} x_j = 0$, and $\operatorname{sgn}(Ax)_h \geqq 0$ for $h \neq j$, where $(Ax)_j$ and x_j stand for the jth components of Ax and x, respectively.

COROLLARY 2 Let A be an $n \times n$ indecomposable nonnegative matrix. There is some power $p \leqq n - 1$ such that $(I + A)^p > 0$.

PROOF Taking an arbitrary semipositive vector x and applying Lemma 4 repeatedly, we can eliminate all zero components of $(I + A)^p x$ for some $p \leqq n - 1$. Since x is arbitrary, $(I + A)^p > 0$. Q.E.D.

THEOREM 6 Let A be an $n \times n$ indecomposable nonnegative matrix with $n > 1$, r_n be the Frobenius root of A, and r_{n-1} be the Frobenius root of one of the $(n - 1) \times (n - 1)$ principal submatrices of A. Then

$$r_n > r_{n-1} \geqq 0. \tag{10}$$

PROOF By Corollary 2 to Lemma 4, there is some power $p \leqq n - 1$ such that $(I + A)^p > 0$. Let μ_n be the Frobenius root of $B \equiv (I + A)^p$. Then, by Lemma 3, μ_n is larger than the Frobenius root $\mu_{n-1}(> 0)$ of any $(n - 1) \times (n - 1)$ principal submatrix, say B_1, of B. Since $(1 + r_n)^p = \mu_n$, we have $r_n > (\mu_{n-1})^{1/p} - 1$. Let A_1 be the $(n - 1) \times (n - 1)$ principal submatrix of A corresponding to B_1, and r_{n-1} be the Frobenius root of A_1, a nonnegative matrix not necessarily indecomposable. It is already known that r_{n-1} is nonnegative. Since $B_1 \geqq (I + A_1)^p$, $\mu_{n-1} \geqq (1 + r_{n-1})^p$. Thus we have (10). Q.E.D.

THEOREM 7 The Frobenius root of an indecomposable nonnegative square matrix is a simple root.

PROOF Let A be an $n \times n$ indecomposable nonnegative matrix with $n > 1$, λ_1 be its Frobenius root, and μ_1 be the Frobenius root of $B \equiv (I + A)^p$, a positive matrix. Since $(1 + \lambda_1)^p = \mu_1$, it suffices to show that μ_1 is a simple root.

Let w_i be the multiplicity of an eigenvalue μ_i of B, and suppose that there are k distinct roots as a whole. Since

$$L(\mu) = |\mu I - B| = (\mu - \mu_1)^{w_1} \prod_{i=2}^{k} (\mu - \mu_i)^{w_i},$$

we know that $L'(\mu_1) \neq 0$ in case $w_1 = 1$ and that $L'(\mu_1) = 0$ in case $w_1 \geqq 2$. On the other hand, it follows from Lemma 3 that

$$L'(\mu_1) = \sum_{i=1}^{n} |\mu_1 I - B_{ii}| = \sum_{i=1}^{n} L_{ii}(\mu_1) > 0,$$

where B_{ii} is the square matrix of order $n - 1$ obtained from B by deleting the ith row and the ith column, and $L_{ii}(\mu) = |\mu I - B_{ii}|$. Q.E.D.

Note that if a nonnegative square matrix A is decomposable, its Frobenius root λ_1 is nonnegative and not necessarily a simple root of A because

$$L'(\lambda_1) = \sum_{i=1}^{n} L_{ii}(\lambda_1) \geqq 0 \qquad \text{(see Lemma 1).}$$

THEOREM 8 Let A be an indecomposable nonnegative square matrix. Then $[\lambda I - A]^{-1} > 0$ if and only if $\lambda > \lambda_1$, where λ_1 is the Frobenius root of A.

PROOF *Sufficiency* We show that $y \geq \theta$ implies $x = [\lambda I - A]^{-1} y > \theta$. By Lemma 1, $x \geqq \theta$ for nonnegative A. If x had some zero components, we may suppose the last components of x are zeros, and partition our system of equations as

$$\begin{bmatrix} \lambda I - A_1 & -A_{12} \\ -A_{21} & \lambda I - A_2 \end{bmatrix} \begin{bmatrix} \hat{x} \\ \theta \end{bmatrix} = y,$$

where $\hat{x} > \theta$. Therefore, $-A_{21}\hat{x} \geqq \theta$, and hence $A_{21} = 0$, violating the indecomposability of A. (The proof is due to Debreu and Herstein (1953).)

Necessity has already been proved since $[\lambda I - A]^{-1} > 0$ implies $[\lambda I - A]^{-1} \geqq 0$ and since $[\lambda I - A]^{-1} \geqq 0$ holds if and only if $\lambda > \lambda_1$. Q.E.D.

Theorem 8 coupled with the Metzler lemma yields the following.

COROLLARY Let A be an indecomposable nonnegative square matrix. Then $[\lambda I - A]^{-1} > 0$ if and only if $[\lambda I - A]$ satisfies the Hawkins–Simon conditions.

THEOREM 9 Let $A = [a_{ij}]$ be an $n \times n$ indecomposable nonnegative matrix. (i) The eigenvector of A associated with its Frobenius root must be strictly positive and unique except for a proportionality factor. (ii) No other eigenvalue of A has an associated semipositive eigenvector.

PROOF (i) Define a functional g by

$$g(x, \lambda) \equiv \min_{1 \leqq i \leqq n} \sum_{j=1}^{n} (\lambda \delta_{ij} - a_{ij}) \xi_j$$

for $x = \{\xi_1, \ldots, \xi_n\} \in S$ and $\lambda \in R^1$, where $\delta_{ij} = 0\ (i \neq j)$, $\delta_{ii} = 1$, and $S \equiv \{x : \sum_{i=1}^{n} \xi_i = 1,\ \xi_i \geqq 0\ (i = 1, \ldots, n)\}$. Given λ, the functional g is continuous with respect to $x \in S$. Since S is a closed and bounded set, g achieves a maximum on S. (See Theorem 19 in Section 5.2.) So a function f is well defined as follows:

$$f(\lambda) \equiv \max_{x \in S} g(x, \lambda).$$

$f(\lambda)$ is continuous with respect to λ, and we can select real numbers λ_0, λ_2 for which $f(\lambda_0) < 0$ and $f(\lambda_2) > 0$. Hence there is a real λ^* for which $f(\lambda^*) = 0$. Let $x^* = \{\xi_1^*, \ldots, \xi_n^*\}$ be its associated x in the expression of $f(\lambda^*)$, i.e.,

$$f(\lambda^*) = \min_i \sum_j (\lambda^* \delta_{ij} - a_{ij})\xi_j^* = 0. \tag{11}$$

If $\xi_i^* = 0$ for all $i \in J$, where J stands for some nonempty subset of indices from $\{1, 2, \ldots, n\}$, then due to the indecomposability of A,

$$\sum_{j=1}^{n} (\lambda^* \delta_{ij} - a_{ij})\xi_j^* = \sum_{j \notin J} (-a_{ij}\xi_j^*) < 0 \qquad \text{for some} \quad i \in J.$$

This contradicts (11). Thus x^* must be a positive vector.

Next we show that λ^* is an eigenvalue of A and that x^* is the associated eigenvector, i.e.,

$$\eta_i \equiv \lambda^* \xi_i^* - \sum_{j=1}^{n} a_{ij}\xi_j^* = 0 \qquad \text{for all} \quad i = 1, \ldots, n.$$

By (11), we have $\eta_i \geqq 0\ (i = 1, \ldots, n)$ with equality for at least one i. If $\eta_i > 0$ for some i, then $[\lambda^* I - A]$ has a q.d.d. since $x^* > \theta$. Due to the indecomposability of A,

$$(\lambda^* - a_{ii})\xi_i^* = \sum_{j \neq i} a_{ij}\xi_j^* > 0 \qquad \text{for all } i,$$

and hence $\lambda^* - a_{ii} > 0$ for all i. Therefore, it follows from Theorem 23 in Section 1.3 that $[\lambda^* I - A]x = y$ has a unique solution $x \geqq \theta$ for every $y \geqq \theta$, or in view of the indecomposability of A that $[\lambda^* I - A]^{-1} > 0$. In other words, there is a positive vector x, say x^{**}, such that $[\lambda^* I - A]x^{**} > \theta$, and x^{**} may be chosen in S. Then, $\max_{x \in S} g(x, \lambda^*) \geqq g(x^{**}, \lambda^*) > 0$, contradicting $f(\lambda^*) = 0$. Thus $\eta_i = 0$ must hold for each $i = 1, \ldots, n$, and hence λ^* is an eigenvalue of A and x^* is the associated eigenvector.

Lastly, we show that λ^* is the Frobenius root of A, i.e., that $\lambda^* \geqq |\lambda|$ for any eigenvalue λ of A. Suppose, to the contrary, that $\lambda^* < |\lambda|$. Then $|\lambda - a_{ii}| \geqq |\lambda| - a_{ii} > \lambda^* - a_{ii}$ for all i. Hence

$$|\lambda - a_{ii}|\xi_i^* > (\lambda^* - a_{ii})\xi_i^* = \sum_{j \neq i} a_{ij}\xi_j^* \qquad \text{for all } i.$$

Thus $[\lambda I - A]$ has a d.d. and it is nonsingular, implying that λ cannot be an eigenvalue of A. (The above proof is due to McKenzie (1960).)

Since λ^* is a simple root, the nullspace of $[\lambda^* I - A]$ has dimension one; in other words, any eigenvector of A associated with λ^* must be equal to a scalar multiplication of the x^* mentioned above.

(ii) Let x_1 be the eigenvector of A^{T} associated with λ^*. x_1 is found to be strictly positive in the same way as x^*. Let λ be any eigenvalue of A other than λ^*, and x be a nontrivial eigenvector of A associated with λ. Then

$$x_1^{\mathrm{T}}\lambda x = x_1^{\mathrm{T}}Ax = x^{\mathrm{T}}A^{\mathrm{T}}x_1 = x^{\mathrm{T}}\lambda^* x_1 \qquad \text{with} \quad \lambda \neq \lambda^*,$$

which implies $x^{\mathrm{T}}x_1 = 0$. Thus x cannot be semipositive. Q.E.D.

(For a nonlinear extension of Theorem 9, see Morishima and Fujimoto (1974).)

THEOREM 10 Let A be an indecomposable nonnegative square matrix. If an element of A increases, its Frobenius root will increase.

PROOF Let λ be any eigenvalue of $A = [a_{ij}]$, whose order is supposed to be n, and let $x = \{\xi_1, \ldots, \xi_n\}$ be its associated eigenvector of A. Then

$$|\lambda|\,|\xi_i| = |\lambda\xi_i| \leqq \sum_{j=1}^{n} a_{ij}|\xi_j| \qquad \text{for} \quad i = 1, \ldots, n,$$

or

$$|\lambda| x^* \leqq Ax^*,$$

where $x^* = \{|x_1|, \ldots, |x_n|\}$. Let B be a nonnegative square matrix of order n such that at least one element is larger than the corresponding element of A and the other elements are equal, i.e., $B \geq A$. Let ρ be the Frobenius root of B and y be its associated positive eigenvector of B^{T}. Then

$$\rho y = B^{\mathrm{T}}y \qquad \text{and} \qquad Bx^* \geq Ax^*.$$

Thus $\rho y^{\mathrm{T}}x^* = y^{\mathrm{T}}Bx^* > y^{\mathrm{T}}Ax^* \geqq |\lambda| y^{\mathrm{T}}x^*$, from which it follows that $\rho > |\lambda|$. Q.E.D.

4.2 Solow Conditions, Stability, and Comparative Statics in Leontief–Hicks–Metzler Systems

Nonnegative square matrices recur in Leontief's input–output models and the multiple markets theory of Hicks and Metzler. Thus the Frobenius theorems presented in Section 4.1 are an important mathematical arsenal for these multisectoral analyses. In the present section we are concerned with other mathematical developments of these economic systems.

In a Leontief model we assume that a single good is obtainable as an output by a fixed combination of production factors. Denoting by a_{ij} the quantity in physical units of good i consumed in the production process of good j per unit of its output, by y_i the final demand for good i, and by x_i the output of good i, we represent the system of supply = demand equations for an n-good economy as

$$x_i = \sum_{j=1}^{n} a_{ij}x_j + y_i \qquad (i = 1, \ldots, n).$$

Let A be an $n \times n$ nonnegative matrix whose (i, j)th element is a_{ij}. Then the above system is rewritten as

$$[I - A]x = y, \tag{12}$$

where x and y stand for column n-vectors $\{x_1, \ldots, x_n\}$ and $\{y_1, \ldots, y_n\}$, respectively. Given $y \geq \theta$, (12) is solved for x as

$$x = [I - A]^{-1}y \geq \theta,$$

provided $[I - A]$ satisfies the Hawkins–Simon conditions. First, we introduce a theorem concerning an expansion of $[I - A]^{-1}$, the Leontief inverse.

THEOREM 11 Let A be a nonnegative square matrix.

$$[I - A]^{-1} = \sum_{t=0}^{\infty} A^t, \qquad \text{where} \quad A^0 \equiv I, \tag{13}$$

if and only if the Frobenius root of A is less than unity.

PROOF *"If" part* Let λ_1 be the Frobenius root of A. $\lambda_1 < 1$ implies $|\lambda| < 1$ for any eigenvalue λ of A. Then by Theorem 7 in Section 3.3,

$$\lim_{\tau \to \infty} A^\tau = 0,$$

which, together with the identity

$$\sum_{t=0}^{\tau-1} A^t = [I - A]^{-1}[I - A^\tau],$$

implies (13).

"Only if" part Since A is nonnegative, (13) implies that $[I - A]^{-1}$ is nonnegative. Hence by Proposition 2, $\lambda_1 < 1$. Q.E.D.

COROLLARY Let A be a nonnegative square matrix, let λ_1 be the Frobenius root of A, and assume that $\lambda > \lambda_1$. The larger λ is, the smaller will be all positive elements of $[I - (1/\lambda)A]^{-1}$ except the diagonal elements equal to unity.

PROOF For $\lambda > \lambda_1$,

$$\left[I - \frac{1}{\lambda} A\right]^{-1} = \left(\frac{1}{\lambda}[\lambda I - A]\right)^{-1} \geqq 0,$$

which implies that the Frobenius root of $(1/\lambda)A$ is less than unity. Hence we have the expansion

$$\left[I - \frac{1}{\lambda} A\right]^{-1} = \sum_{t=0}^{\infty} \left(\frac{1}{\lambda} A\right)^t, \qquad \text{where} \quad A^0 \equiv I,$$

from which the above assertion follows. Q.E.D.

THEOREM 12 (*Solow theorem*) Let $A = [a_{ij}]$ be a nonnegative square matrix of order n, and λ_1 its Frobenius root. A sufficient condition for $\lambda_1 < 1$ is that either:

(i) $\sum_{i=1}^{n} a_{ij} \leqq 1$ for $j = 1, \ldots, n$ with strict inequality for some j; or
(ii) $\sum_{j=1}^{n} a_{ij} \leqq 1$ for $i = 1, \ldots, n$ with strict inequality for some i.

These conditions are referred to as the *Solow conditions*.

PROOF First assume A is indecomposable. Let $x \equiv \{x_1, \ldots, x_n\}$ be the eigenvector of A associated with λ_1. Then $\lambda_1 x_i = \sum_{j=1}^{n} a_{ij} x_j$ for $i = 1, \ldots, n$. Summing over i, we have

$$\lambda_1 \sum_i x_i = \sum_i \sum_j a_{ij} x_j = \sum_j x_j (\sum_i a_{ij}),$$

or

$$\lambda_1 = \sum_j \left(\frac{x_j}{\sum_i x_i} \sum_i a_{ij}\right).$$

In view of $x > \theta$, condition (i) implies $\lambda_1 < 1$.

Next let $y \equiv \{y_1, \ldots, y_n\}$ be the eigenvector of A^{T} associated with λ_1. Note that $y > \theta$. Proceeding in a similar manner to the above, *mutatis mutandis,* we obtain

$$\lambda_1 = \sum_i \left(\frac{y_i}{\sum_j y_j} \sum_j a_{ij}\right) < 1,$$

provided condition (ii) holds.

When A is decomposable, it can be partitioned as

$$A = \begin{bmatrix} A_1 & A_{12} & \cdots & A_{1m} \\ 0 & A_2 & & A_{2m} \\ \vdots & & \ddots & \\ 0 & 0 & & A_m \end{bmatrix},$$

where diagonal blocks A_i ($i = 1, \ldots, m$) are all square and indecomposable or zero. Then

$$|\lambda I - A| = \prod_{i=1}^{m} |\lambda I - A_i|.$$

Thus the Frobenius root of A is the dominant root among all the roots satisfying

$$|\lambda_i I - A_i| = 0 \qquad (i = 1, \ldots, m).$$

If Solow condition (i) or (ii) holds for A, then it also holds for A_i for each i, and hence the dominant eigenvalue of A_i is less than unity. Q.E.D.

Theorem 11 coupled with the Solow theorem yields the following.

COROLLARY If nonnegative square matrix A has each column sum (or row sum) not greater than unity and at least one column sum (or row sum) less than unity, then Eq. (13) holds.

THEOREM 13 Let A be an indecomposable nonnegative square matrix satisfying Solow condition (i) or (ii). If an element of A increases without violating the Solow condition, then all elements of $[I - A]^{-1}$ will increase.

PROOF Let B be a nonnegative square matrix of the same order as A such that at least one element of B is larger than the corresponding element of A and the other elements are equal, i.e., $B \geq A$. By the Solow theorem, the Frobenius roots of A and B are both less than unity. Hence $[I - A]^{-1}$ and $[I - B]^{-1}$ are both positive matrices. Since $[I - B]^{-1}[I - B] = [I - A]^{-1}[I - A]$, we have

$$\begin{aligned}[I - B]^{-1} - [I - A]^{-1} &= [I - B]^{-1}B - [I - A]^{-1}A \\ &= [I - B]^{-1}[B - A] + ([I - B]^{-1} - [I - A]^{-1})A \\ &= [I - B]^{-1}[B - A][I - A]^{-1}.\end{aligned}$$

In view of $B - A \geq 0$, $[I - B]^{-1}[B - A]$ has at least one column strictly positive, and hence $[I - B]^{-1}[B - A][I - A]^{-1}$ is found to be a positive matrix. Q.E.D.

Proceeding in a similar manner, we can prove

COROLLARY Let A be a nonnegative square matrix satisfying Solow condition (i) or (ii). If an element of A increases without violating the Solow condition, then all elements of $[I - A]^{-1}$ will be nondecreasing.

THEOREM 14 Let $A = [a_{ij}]$ be a nonnegative square matrix and assume that its Frobenius root is less than unity. Let A_1 be the submatrix of A after deleting its first row and column, where we may choose any i as 1 after an appropriate permutation. Then each element of $[I - A_1]^{-1}$ is not larger than the corresponding element of $[I - A]^{-1}$.

PROOF Denote $L = |I - A|$, $L_{11} = |I - A_1|$, $L_{ij} =$ the cofactor of $\delta_{ij} - a_{ij}$ in $[I - A]$, $L_{11,ij} =$ the cofactor of $\delta_{ij} - a_{ij}$ in $[I - A_1]$, where $\delta_{ij} = 0$ $(i \neq j)$ and $\delta_{ii} = 1$ for all i, j. Then by Jacobi's ratio theorem,

$$L_{11}L_{ij} - L_{i1}L_{1j} = LL_{11,ij} \qquad \text{for} \quad i, j \neq 1,$$

from which it follows that

$$\frac{L_{11,ij}}{L_{11}} = \frac{L_{ij}}{L} - \left(\frac{L_{i1}}{L}\frac{L_{1j}}{L}\right)\Big/\frac{L_{11}}{L} \qquad \text{for} \quad i, j \neq 1,$$

where $L_{11} > 0$, $L_{ij} \geqq 0$ $(i \neq j)$, and $L > 0$ since the Frobenius root is less than unity. The first term on the right-hand side of this equation represents the (j, i)th element of $[I - A]^{-1}$ while the left-hand side is the corresponding element of $[I - A_1]^{-1}$. Q.E.D.

COROLLARY 1 If A is indecomposable in addition to the other assumptions in Theorem 14, then each element of $[I - A_1]^{-1}$ is less than the corresponding element of $[I - A]^{-1}$.

Note that in Theorem 14 and its Corollary 1 the assumption that the Frobenius root of A is less than unity can be replaced by the assumption that $[I - A]$ satisfies the Hawkins–Simon conditions.

COROLLARY 2 (*Samuelson theorem on the Leontief inverse*) Let A be an $n \times n$ nonnegative matrix and assume that $[I - A]$ satisfies the Hawkins–Simon conditions. Denote by $A_1, A_2, \ldots, A_k$ $(k < n)$ the submatrices of A after deleting its first row and column, after deleting its first two rows and columns, . . ., after deleting its first k rows and columns, respectively. Let B^{ij} stand for the (j, i)th element of $[I - A]^{-1}$, and let $B_1^{ij}, B_2^{ij}, \ldots, B_k^{ij}$ stand for the corresponding elements of $[I - A_1]^{-1}, [I - A_2]^{-1}, \ldots, [I - A_k]^{-1}$, respectively, for $i, j = k + 1, \ldots, n$. Then

$$B^{ij} \geqq B_1^{ij} \geqq B_2^{ij} \geqq \cdots \geqq B_k^{ij} \geqq 0 \qquad \text{for} \quad i, j = k + 1, \ldots, n. \tag{14}$$

(The result of Corollary 2 follows at once from Theorem 14 by induction.)

In the context of the Leontief system (12), inequalities (14) have the implication that the increment in output of good j resulting from an increase in the final demand for good i is not larger if outputs of a number of goods are held constant than it would be if some of them are permitted to vary since from (12) we have

$$\begin{bmatrix} x_{k+1} \\ \vdots \\ x_n \end{bmatrix} = [I - A_k]^{-1} \begin{bmatrix} y_{k+1} \\ \vdots \\ y_n \end{bmatrix} + [I - A_k]^{-1} \begin{bmatrix} a_{k+1,1} & \cdots & a_{k+1,k} \\ \vdots & & \vdots \\ a_{n1} & \cdots & a_{nk} \end{bmatrix} \begin{bmatrix} \bar{x}_1 \\ \vdots \\ \bar{x}_k \end{bmatrix} \tag{15}$$

where $\bar{x}_i$ is the output of good i held constant $(i = 1, \ldots, k)$.

THEOREM 15 Let $A = [a_{ij}]$ be a nonnegative square matrix of order $n > 1$, and denote $|I - A|$ by L and the cofactor of $\delta_{ij} - a_{ij}$ in L by L_{ij}, where $\delta_{ii} = 1$ and $\delta_{ij} = 0$ $(i \neq j)$. If A satisfies Solow condition (i), viz., if each column sum of A is not greater than unity and at least one column sum is less than unity, then for each $j = 1, \ldots, n$, we have

$$L_{jj}/L > L_{ij}/L \qquad \text{for} \quad i \neq j; \quad i = 1, \ldots, n. \tag{16}$$

If A satisfies Solow condition (ii), viz., if each row sum of A is not greater than unity and at least one row sum is less than unity, then for each $i = 1, \ldots, n$, we have

$$L_{ii}/L > L_{ij}/L \qquad \text{for} \quad j \neq i; \quad j = 1, \ldots, n. \tag{17}$$

PROOF Without loss of generality, it suffices to verify (16) for $j = 1$. Notice that $L > 0$, $L_{jj} > 0$, and $L_{ij} \geqq 0$ $(i \neq j)$ since the Frobenius root of A is less than unity.

$$L_{i1} = \begin{vmatrix} 0 & -a_{12} & \cdots & -a_{1n} \\ 0 & 1 - a_{22} & \cdots & -a_{2n} \\ \vdots & \vdots & & \vdots \\ 1 & -a_{i2} & \cdots & -a_{in} \\ \vdots & \vdots & & \vdots \\ 0 & -a_{n2} & \cdots & 1-a_{nn} \end{vmatrix} = (-1) \begin{vmatrix} 1 - a_{22} & \cdots & -a_{2n} \\ \vdots & & \vdots \\ -a_{12} & \cdots & -a_{1n} \\ \vdots & & \vdots \\ -a_{n2} & \cdots & 1-a_{nn} \end{vmatrix}.$$

Hence

$$L_{11} - L_{i1} = \begin{vmatrix} 1 - a_{22} & \cdots & -a_{2n} \\ \vdots & & \vdots \\ -a_{i2} - a_{12} & \cdots & -a_{in} - a_{1n} \\ \vdots & & \vdots \\ -a_{n2} & \cdots & 1 - a_{nn} \end{vmatrix} > 0$$

since each column sum of the matrix associated with the determinant on the right-hand side of the above equation is nonnegative and at least one column sum is positive. Thus (16) holds for $j = 1$.

(17) will be proved in a similar manner. Q.E.D.

In the context of the Leontief system (12), property (17) can be expressed as

$$\partial x_i/\partial y_i > \partial x_j/\partial y_i \qquad \text{for} \quad j \neq i; \quad j = 1, \ldots, n. \tag{17'}$$

In other words, an increase in the final demand for good i brings forth larger effects on the output of the good than on the output of any other good. (17′) may be termed the *Metzlerian law*.

The following theorem is due to Morishima and Nosse (1972).

THEOREM 16 Let A be an indecomposable nonnegative square matrix of order n and assume that its Frobenius root is less than unity. Denote by B^{ij} the (j, i)th element of $[I - A]^{-1}$. Then for an arbitrary positive n-vector $z \equiv \{z_1, \ldots, z_n\}$ the following inequalities hold:

$$\frac{B^{ii}}{\sum_{k=1}^{n} z_k B^{ki}} > \frac{B^{ij}}{\sum_{k=1}^{n} z_k B^{kj}} \qquad \text{for all} \quad i \neq j; \quad i, j = 1, \ldots, n. \tag{18}$$

PROOF Suppose, to the contrary, that for some $z > \theta$ there is a set of indices $J \equiv \{j_1, \ldots, j_s\}$ such that

$$\frac{B^{ii}}{\sum_k z_k B^{ki}} \leqq \frac{B^{ip}}{\sum_k z_k B^{kp}} \qquad \text{for} \quad p = j_1, \ldots, j_s.$$

Let j be the index from J such that

$$\frac{B^{ij}}{\sum_k z_k B^{kj}} = \max_{p \in J} \frac{B^{ip}}{\sum_k z_k B^{kp}}.$$

Then for the index j,

$$\frac{B^{ih}}{\sum_k z_k B^{kh}} \leqq \frac{B^{ij}}{\sum_k z_k B^{kj}} \qquad \text{for all} \quad h \neq j; \quad h = 1, \ldots, n. \tag{1*}$$

From $[I - A]\,[I - A]^{-1} = I$ it follows that

$$B^{ii} = \sum_{h=1}^{n} a_{ih} B^{ih} + 1 \tag{2*}$$

$$B^{ki} = \sum_{h=1}^{n} a_{ih} B^{kh} \qquad (k \neq i). \tag{3*}$$

Note that $B^{ij} > 0$ for all i, j. Multiplying (3*) by $\sum_k z_k B^{kj}/B^{ij}$ yields

$$\sum_k z_k B^{kj} = \sum_h a_{jh} \left(\frac{B^{ih}/\sum_k z_k B^{kh}}{B^{ij}/\sum_k z_k B^{kj}} \right) \sum_k z_k B^{kh}.$$

Due to (1*), the term inside of the parentheses on the right-hand side of the above equation does not exceed unity for all h. Hence

$$\begin{aligned} \sum_k z_k B^{kj} &\leqq \sum_k \sum_h a_{jh} z_k B^{kh} \\ &= \sum_{k \neq j} \sum_h a_{jh} z_k B^{kh} + \sum_h a_{jh} z_j B^{jh} \\ &= \sum_{k \neq j} z_k B^{kj} + (B^{jj} - 1) z_j \qquad \text{(in view of (2*), (3*))} \\ &= \sum_k z_k B^{kj} - z_j. \end{aligned}$$

This is a contradiction since $z_j > 0$. Q.E.D.

Consider Leontief system (12), where matrix A is assumed to be indecomposable. Furthermore we assume that final demand vector $y = \{y_1, \ldots, y_n\}$ is strictly positive. In the context of this Leontief system, (18) is expressed as

$$\frac{[\partial x_i/\partial y_i]}{x_i} > \frac{[\partial x_j/\partial y_i]}{x_j} \qquad \text{for all} \quad i \neq j \tag{19}$$

since $x_i = \sum_{k=1}^{n} y_k B^{ki}$. (19) means that if the final demand for good i rises, the final demand for all the other goods remaining unchanged, then the output of good i will increase by the largest percentage. (19) is obviously a stronger assertion than (17′). (19) may be called the *Hicksian law*. Moreover, from (19) we have the following *elasticity law*:

$$\frac{\partial x_j/x_j}{\partial y_i/y_i} < \frac{\partial x_i/x_i}{\partial y_i/y_i} = \frac{y_i B^{ii}}{\sum_k y_k B^{ki}} < 1, \tag{20}$$

which implies that the elasticity of the output of good j with respect to the final demand for good i is less than unity for all i, j.

Next we turn to the stability analysis of multiple markets in an n-good economy. The numeraire is out of our picture at first. When the supply of and demand for each good are equalized, we say that all the markets are cleared and that the prices prevailing in this situation are the equilibrium prices. Denoting by p_i the price of good i and by $\bar{p}_i$ its equilibrium price, we can express the equilibrium situation as

$$D_i(\bar{p}_1 \bar{p}_2, \ldots, \bar{p}_n) = 0 \qquad \text{for} \quad i = 1, \ldots, n, \tag{21}$$

where D_i denotes an excess demand for good i. If the price of a good falls in the equilibrium, an excess demand for the good will be created immediately and then the other markets will be affected subsequently. The adjustment in the other markets will also bring about some repercussions to the market where the original fall in price took place. The adjustment in prices will be formulated as

$$\dot{p}_i = S_i(D_i(p_1, \ldots, p_n)) \qquad \text{for} \quad i = 1, \ldots, n, \tag{22}$$

where $\dot{p}_i$ denotes the derivative of p_i with respect to time t, and S_i the adjustment function depending on excess demand such that for each i,

$$S_i(0) = 0, \tag{23}$$

and

$$s_i \equiv dS_i/dD_i > 0. \tag{24}$$

(23) implies that there is no change in p_i when the supply and demand for good i are equal. (24) means that if an excess demand for good i becomes larger, the speed of adjustment in p_i will increase.

Confining ourselves to the study of price adjustment in the vicinity of an equilibrium characterized by (21), we can approximate Eq. (22) by the linear equation

$$\dot{p}_i = s_i \sum_{k=1}^{n} b_{ik}(p_k - \bar{p}_k) \qquad \text{for} \quad i = 1, \ldots, n, \tag{25}$$

where b_{ik} is the partial derivative of D_i with respect to p_k evaluated at the equilibrium prices, and s_i is also evaluated in the same manner. Define

$$\hat{S}_n = \begin{bmatrix} s_1 & & & 0 \\ & s_2 & & \\ & & \ddots & \\ 0 & & & s_n \end{bmatrix}, \qquad B_n = \begin{bmatrix} b_{11} & b_{12} & \cdots & b_{1n} \\ b_{21} & b_{22} & \cdots & b_{2n} \\ \vdots & \vdots & & \vdots \\ b_{n1} & b_{n2} & \cdots & b_{nn} \end{bmatrix}. \tag{26}$$

System (25) is a set of differential equations, which is stable in the sense that its solution converges to the set of equilibrium prices if and only if the eigenvalues of matrix $\hat{S}_n B_n$ have all negative real parts.

Hicks (1939) describes stability of multiple markets without relying on the speed of adjustment; i.e., a market is said by Hicks to be *perfectly stable* at an equilibrium price if a fall in the price of the good traded there below the equilibrium price creates an excess demand for that good after any subset of the prices of the other goods is adjusted so that their supplies are again equalized to their demands, with all the remaining prices held constant.

The above definition by Hicks may be mathematically expressed as follows: Assume that p_1 has fallen below $\bar{p}_1$ at first and that $p_2, \ldots, p_m$ change subsequently. Market 1 is perfectly stable if for $dp_1 < 0$ and for every m, $1 \leqq m \leqq n$,

$$\begin{aligned} 0 < dD_1 &= b_{11}\,dp_1 + b_{12}\,dp_2 + \cdots + b_{1m}\,dp_m, \\ 0 = dD_2 &= b_{21}\,dp_1 + b_{22}\,dp_2 + \cdots + b_{2m}\,dp_m, \\ &\vdots \\ 0 = dD_m &= b_{m1}\,dp_1 + b_{m2}\,dp_2 + \cdots + b_{mm}\,dp_m, \end{aligned} \tag{27}$$

where dp_i $(i = 1, \ldots, m)$ stand for price changes and dD_i $(i = 1, \ldots, m)$ the resulting change in D_i. System (27) is solved for the dp_i:

$$\begin{bmatrix} dp_1 \\ \vdots \\ dp_m \end{bmatrix} = \frac{1}{|B_m|} \begin{bmatrix} B_m^{11} \\ \vdots \\ B_m^{1m} \end{bmatrix} dD_1,$$

where

$$B_m \equiv \begin{bmatrix} b_{11} & b_{12} & \cdots & b_{1m} \\ b_{21} & b_{22} & \cdots & b_{2m} \\ \vdots & \vdots & & \vdots \\ b_{m1} & b_{m2} & \cdots & b_{mm} \end{bmatrix}$$

and B_m^{1j} is the cofactor of b_{1j} in B_m. Hence, (27) implies

$$0 > b_{11} \tag{28}$$

and

$$0 > d\dot{D}_1/dp_1 = |B_m|/B_m^{11} \qquad \text{for} \quad m = 2, 3, \ldots, n. \tag{29}$$

These inequalities (28) and (29) are equivalent to

$$b_{11} < 0, \quad |B_2|/b_{22} < 0, \quad |B_3|/B_3^{11} < 0, \quad \ldots, \quad |B_n|/B_n^{11} < 0. \tag{30}$$

(30) may be called the *Hicks conditions* for perfect stability of market 1. Therefore, the Hicks conditions for perfect stability of all markets are that for every $i = 1, \ldots, n$ and $j \neq k \neq i$,

$$b_{ii} < 0, \quad \begin{vmatrix} b_{ii} & b_{ij} \\ b_{ji} & b_{jj} \end{vmatrix} > 0, \quad \begin{vmatrix} b_{ii} & b_{ij} & b_{ik} \\ b_{ji} & b_{jj} & b_{jk} \\ b_{ki} & b_{kj} & b_{kk} \end{vmatrix} < 0, \ldots, \quad (-1)^n |B_n| > 0;$$

i.e., B_n is an NP-matrix. (31)

THEOREM 17 (*Metzler, first theorem*) If all the eigenvalues of matrix $\hat{S}_n B_n$ have negative real parts for all possible values of s_i $(i = 1, \ldots, n)$, then the Hicks conditions (31) for perfect stability hold true. In other words, the stability of multiple markets cannot be independent of speeds of adjustment, unless the Hicks conditions for perfect stability are satisfied.

PROOF First assume all $s_i > 0$ $(i = 1, \ldots, n)$. Let λ_i $(i = 1, \ldots, n)$ be eigenvalues of matrix $\hat{S}_n B_n$. Since

$$|\hat{S}_n B_n| = \prod_{i=1}^{n} \lambda_i,$$

if each λ_i has negative real part, then

$$\operatorname{sgn} |\hat{S}_n B_n| = \operatorname{sgn}(-1)^n.$$

For in case λ_j is complex, its conjugate $\bar{\lambda}_j$ is also an eigenvalue and $\lambda_j \bar{\lambda}_j > 0$. Hence

$$\operatorname{sgn}(\prod_i \lambda_i) = \operatorname{sgn}(-1)^{n-q},$$

where q is the number of complex eigenvalues, which is even. Since all $s_i > 0$, $\operatorname{sgn} |\hat{S}_n B_n| = \operatorname{sgn} |B_n|$. Therefore we have

$$(-1)^n |B_n| > 0.$$

If the market system is to be stable for any set of speeds of adjustment, it must be stable when some s_i are quite small relative to others in the set. Thus the system must be stable even when any subgroup of prices is completely inflexible, e.g., when $s_i = 0$ for $i = m + 1, \ldots, n$. Then system (25) becomes a system of order m in the variables p_i $(i = 1, \ldots, m)$. From the preceding analysis it follows that the stability requires

$$\operatorname{sgn} |\hat{S}_m B_m| = \operatorname{sgn}(-1)^m,$$

and taking into account that $s_i > 0$ $(i = 1, \ldots, m)$, we have

$$(-1)^m |B_m| > 0.$$

The above argument holds for any integer m, $1 \leqq m \leqq n - 1$. Q.E.D.

By virtue of Theorems 39′ and 40 in Section 2.5, if matrix B_n has negative d.d. or is negative quasi-definite, it is D-stable, and hence it satisfies the Hicks conditions (31) in view of Theorem 17.

Now we introduce the concept of gross substitutes.

DEFINITION 3 Denote as before

$$b_{ij} \equiv \left.\frac{\partial D_i}{\partial p_j}\right|_{p=\bar{p}},$$

with income effect taken into account as well as substitution effect. (Refer to Hicks (1939).) Namely, b_{ij} stands for all impact effect on excess demand for good i of a change in the price of good j, with the other prices held constant, at the equilibrium price vector $\bar{p}$. If $b_{ij} > 0$ for $i \neq j$, goods i and j are said to be gross substitutes. When

$$b_{ij} > 0 \qquad \text{for} \quad i \neq j; \quad i, j = 1, \ldots, n; \tag{32}$$

we say that all goods are *strong gross substitutes* of one another. When

$$b_{ij} \geqq 0 \qquad \text{for} \quad i \neq j; \quad i, j = 1, \ldots, n, \tag{33}$$

we say that all goods are *weak gross substitutes* of one another.

Suppose all the speeds of adjustment s_i are positive and choose the unit of good i such that $s_i = 1$ for all i. Then we shall show that system (25) is stable if and only if B_n satisfies the Hicks conditions (31), under the assumption that all goods are weak gross substitutes.

LEMMA 1* Let $A = [a_{ij}]$ be a square matrix with nonnegative off-diagonal elements of order n with $n > 1$; $L_{ij}(\lambda)$ = the cofactor of $\lambda\delta_{ij} - a_{ij}$ in $|\lambda I - A|$; r_n = the largest real eigenvalue of A; r_{n-1}^i = the largest real root of $L_{ii}(\lambda) = 0$. Then $r_n \geqq r_{n-1}^i$, $L_{ij}(\lambda) \geqq 0$ for $\lambda \geqq r_n$ and $L_{ii}(\lambda) > 0$ for $\lambda > r_n$ $(i, j = 1, \ldots, n)$.

(The proof is similar to that of Lemma 1.)

LEMMA 5 Let A be a square matrix with nonnegative off-diagonal elements and λ_1 be its largest real eigenvalue. Then

$$\lambda_1 \geqq \operatorname{Re}(\lambda) \qquad \text{for every eigenvalue } \lambda \text{ of } A.$$

PROOF Let s be a sufficiently large positive scalar such that

$$M \equiv sI + A \geqq 0.$$

Let μ_1 be the largest real eigenvalue of M. Then

$$\mu_1 \geqq |\mu| \qquad \text{for every eigenvalue } \mu \text{ of } M.$$

Since $\mu = \lambda + s$,

$$|\mu| \geqq \operatorname{Re}(\mu) = \operatorname{Re}(\lambda) + s.$$

Hence $\lambda_1 = \mu_1 - s \geqq \operatorname{Re}(\lambda)$. Q.E.D.

We recall that B_n is a stability matrix, or equivalently system (25) with $s_i = 1$ for all i is stable if and only if

$$\mathrm{Re}(\lambda) < 0 \qquad \text{for every eigenvalue } \lambda \text{ of } B_n. \tag{34}$$

(Refer to Theorem 8 in Section 3.4.)

THEOREM 18 (*Metzler, second theorem*) The Hicks conditions (31) for perfect stability are necessary and sufficient for (34) to hold, on the assumption that all goods are weak gross substitutes.

PROOF *Sufficiency*:

$$0 = |\lambda I - B_n|$$

$$= \lambda^n + (-1) \sum_i b_{ii}\lambda^{n-1} + \sum_{i<j}\sum \begin{vmatrix} b_{ii} & b_{ij} \\ b_{ji} & b_{jj} \end{vmatrix} \lambda^{n-2} + \cdots + (-1)^n |B_n|.$$

Take conditions (31) into consideration in the above equation. Then all coefficients on its right-hand side assume positive values. Hence any eigenvalue of B_n cannot have nonnegative real part.

Necessity In view of (34), we have $(-1)^n|B_n| > 0$. (Refer to the proof of Theorem 17.) Let ρ_1 be the largest real eigenvalue of B_{n-1}. Since B_n is a square matrix with nonnegative off-diagonal elements, we apply Lemma 1* and Lemma 5, and get

$$0 > \lambda_1 \geqq \rho_1 \geqq \mathrm{Re}(\rho) \qquad \text{for every eigenvalue } \rho \text{ of } B_{n-1}.$$

Hence $(-1)^{n-1}|B_{n-1}| > 0$. By induction we obtain all the conditions (31).

Q.E.D.

To conclude this section, we examine the correspondence principle between stability conditions and comparative statics in the analysis of multiple markets.

Consider a shift parameter α of demand explicitly in the excess demand function D_i, viz.,

$$D_i(p_1, \ldots, p_n; \alpha) = 0 \qquad \text{for} \quad i = 1, \ldots, n. \tag{35}$$

A change in α at an equilibrium results in

$$b_{i1}\frac{dp_1}{d\alpha} + \cdots + b_{in}\frac{dp_n}{d\alpha} + \frac{\partial D_i}{\partial \alpha} = 0 \qquad \text{for} \quad i = 1, \ldots, n, \tag{36}$$

or

$$Bp_\alpha + D_\alpha = \theta \tag{36$'$}$$

where B is the same matrix as B_n in (26), and p_α and D_α stand for column n-vectors whose ith components are $dp_i/d\alpha$ and $\partial D_i/\partial\alpha$, respectively. The solution of (36′) is

$$\frac{dp_j}{d\alpha} = -\sum_{i=1}^{n} \frac{B_{ij}}{|B|}\frac{\partial D_i}{\partial \alpha} \qquad \text{for} \quad j = 1, \ldots, n, \tag{37}$$

where B_{ij} is the cofactor of b_{ij} in B.

THEOREM 19 (*Mosak theorem*) Assume that all goods are weak gross substitutes. The Hicks conditions (31) hold for B if and only if

$$B_{ij}/|B| \leqq 0 \qquad \text{for} \quad i \neq j; \quad i,j = 1, \ldots, n, \tag{38}$$

and

$$B_{jj}/|B| < 0 \qquad \text{for} \quad j = 1, \ldots, n. \tag{39}$$

PROOF By our assumption, conditions (31) for B are equivalent to the Hawkins–Simon conditions for $-B$ since the off-diagonal elements of $-B$ are nonpositive and the diagonal elements are positive. Thus $[-B]^{-1} \geqq 0$ by Corollary 2 to the Hawkins–Simon theorem in Section 2.4. Hence

$$(-1)^{n-1}B_{ij}/|-B| \geqq 0 \qquad \text{for all} \quad i, j,$$

or equivalently

$$B_{ij}/|B| \leqq 0 \qquad \text{for all } i, j.$$

In particular,

$$B_{jj}/|B| < 0 \qquad \text{for all } j. \qquad \text{Q.E.D.}$$

Thus, in view of (37), we can assert that if all goods are weak gross substitutes and if the Hicks conditions (31) hold for B, then a shift of demand from the numeraire to good j raises the price of good j and the prices of the other goods are nondecreasing.

Now we introduce an identity called the *Walras law:*

$$\sum_{i=1}^{n} p_i D_i + p_0 D_0 \equiv 0, \tag{40}$$

where good 0 designates the numeraire. Differentiating (40) with respect to p_j at an equilibrium yields

$$\sum_{i=1}^{n} \bar{p}_i b_{ij} + D_j + \bar{p}_0 b_{0j} = 0, \tag{41}$$

where $b_{0j} = \partial D_0/\partial p_j$ evaluated at the equilibrium prices $\{\bar{p}_0, \bar{p}_1, \ldots, \bar{p}_n\}$. Since $D_j = 0$ at an equilibrium, if the unit of each good is chosen such that $\bar{p}_i = 1$ for $i = 0, 1, \ldots, n$, (41) reduces to

$$\sum_{i=1}^{n} b_{ij} + b_{0j} = 0. \tag{41$'$}$$

We may assume that $b_{0j} > 0$. Hence it follows from (41′) that

$$\sum_{i=1}^{n} b_{ij} < 0 \qquad (j = 1, \ldots, n). \tag{42}$$

THEOREM 20 If all goods are weak gross substitutes and if $b_{0j} > 0$ and $a_{jj} \equiv 1 + b_{jj} < 1$ for all j, then

$$B_{jj}/|B| < B_{ij}/|B| \qquad \text{for} \quad i \neq j; \quad i, j = 1, \ldots, n. \tag{43}$$

PROOF $-B$ can be rewritten as

$$-B = \begin{bmatrix} 1 - a_{11} & -b_{12} & \cdots & -b_{1n} \\ -b_{21} & 1 - a_{22} & \cdots & -b_{2n} \\ \vdots & \vdots & & \vdots \\ -b_{n1} & -b_{n2} & \cdots & 1 - a_{nn} \end{bmatrix}$$

Due to (42), $a_{jj} + \sum_{i \neq j} b_{ij} = 1 + \sum_{i=1}^{n} b_{ij} < 1$ for all j. Thus, by Theorem 15

$$(-1)^{n-1} B_{jj} / |-B| > (-1)^{n-1} B_{ij} / |-B| \qquad \text{for all} \quad i \neq j.$$

Hence we get (43). Q.E.D.

Set $\partial D_k / \partial \alpha = 1$, $\partial D_j / \partial \alpha = -1$ and $\partial D_i / \partial \alpha = 0$ for $i \neq j, k$ in (37). Then, by virtue of (43)

$$\frac{dp_j}{d\alpha} = \frac{B_{jj}}{|B|} - \frac{B_{kj}}{|B|} < 0.$$

Likewise,

$$\frac{dp_k}{d\alpha} = \frac{B_{jk}}{|B|} - \frac{B_{kk}}{|B|} > 0.$$

These inequalities imply that if all goods are weak gross substitutes with $b_{0j} > 0$ for at least one j and if the Hicks conditions (31) hold for B, then a shift of demand from good j to good k lowers the price of good j and raises that of good k.

We can derive an inequality symmetric to (43). Assume that function D_i in (35) is homogeneous of degree zero in $p_0, p_1, \ldots, p_n$. Then, by virtue of the Euler theorem (Lemma 6 below),

$$\sum_{j=1}^{n} p_j b_{ij} + p_0 b_{i0} = 0 \qquad \text{for} \quad i = 1, \ldots, n. \tag{44}$$

Choose the unit of each good such that $p_j = 1$ for all j, and assume $b_{i0} > 0$. Then

$$\sum_{j=1}^{n} b_{ij} < 0 \qquad (i = 1, \ldots, n).$$

THEOREM 20′ If all goods are weak gross substitutes and if $b_{i0} > 0$ and $a_{ii} \equiv 1 + b_{ii} < 1$ for all i, then

$$B_{ii} / |B| < B_{ij} / |B| \qquad \text{for} \quad i \neq j; \quad i, j = 1, \ldots, n. \tag{45}$$

(The proof is similar to that of Theorem 20.)

Set $\partial D_k / \partial \alpha > 0$ and $\partial D_i / \partial \alpha = 0$ for all $i \neq k$ in (37). Then, in view of (45), we have

$$\frac{dp_k}{d\alpha} - \frac{dp_j}{d\alpha} = \frac{\partial D_k}{\partial \alpha} \left[\frac{B_{kj}}{|B|} - \frac{B_{kk}}{|B|} \right] > 0 \qquad \text{for} \quad j \neq k,$$

which implies that if all goods are weak gross substitutes with $b_{i0} > 0$ for at least one i and if the Hicks conditions (31) hold for B, then a shift of demand from the numeraire to good k raises the price of good k more than any other price.

LEMMA 6 (*Euler theorem on homogeneous functions*) Let $f: E^n \to E^m$ be a transformation defined on a cone C (with vertex at the origin) in E^n. If for any $x \equiv (x_1, \ldots, x_n) \in C$ and $\alpha > 0$

$$f(\alpha x) = \alpha^h f(x) \qquad \text{for an integer } h,$$

then f is said to be (*positively*) *homogeneous* of degree h on C. In particular, when $h = 1$, f is termed a *linear homogeneous function*. For a homogeneous function f of degree h, we have

(i) $\partial f(\alpha x)/\partial(\alpha x_i) = \alpha^{h-1}\, \partial f(x)/\partial x_i$,

(ii) $\sum_{i=1}^{n} x_i\, \partial f(x)/\partial x_i = hf(x)$.

(The proof is left to the reader.)

Lastly, assuming the homogeneity of excess demand functions with respect to all prices, we prove a theorem related to the second Metzler theorem (Theorem 18).

THEOREM 21 (Negishi, 1958) If all goods are weak gross substitutes and if each excess demand function is homogeneous of degree zero in all prices, then the Hicks conditions (31) hold for matrix B.

PROOF · From (44), it follows that

$$\sum_{j=1}^{n} (-b_{ij})p_j = b_{i0}p_0 > 0 \qquad (i = 1, \ldots, n),$$

or equivalently

$$-Bp > \theta,$$

where $p \equiv \{p_1, \ldots, p_n\} > \theta$. Thus, by virtue of the Hawkins–Simon theorem (Theorem 30 in Section 2.4), all the principal minors of $-B$ are positive, i.e., B satisfies the Hicks conditions (31). Q.E.D.

Remark Closely parallel results to Theorem 21 were obtained by Hahn (1958) and by Arrow and Hurwicz (1958), making use of the Walras law instead of the homogeneity of excess demand functions.

4.3 Primitivity, the Kakeya Theorem, and Relative Stability

In this section we study indecomposable nonnegative matrices further in terms of primitivity, which is found to be related to some stability problems.

DEFINITION 4 Let A be an indecomposable square matrix of order $n > 1$. If there is a permutation matrix P of the same order such that

$$B \equiv PAP^{-1} = \begin{bmatrix} 0 & A_{12} & 0 & \cdots & 0 \\ 0 & 0 & A_{23} & \cdots & 0 \\ \vdots & \vdots & 0 & \ddots & \\ 0 & 0 & & \ddots & A_{h-1,h} \\ A_{h1} & 0 & 0 & \cdots & 0 \end{bmatrix} \qquad (h > 1), \tag{46}$$

where 0 stands for a zero submatrix and A_{kj} a nonzero submatrix of A, with square zero submatrices on the main diagonal, then A is said to be *imprimitive*. A partition in the form (46) may not be unique for an imprimitive matrix A. If A cannot be transformed into form (46) by any simultaneous permutation of its rows and columns, A is called *primitive*.

Clearly an indecomposable square matrix having a nonzero main diagonal element is primitive.

Example The following matrix A is imprimitive:

$$A = \begin{bmatrix} 0 & a_{12} & 0 & a_{14} & 0 \\ a_{21} & 0 & a_{23} & 0 & a_{25} \\ 0 & a_{32} & 0 & a_{34} & 0 \\ a_{41} & 0 & a_{43} & 0 & a_{45} \\ 0 & a_{52} & 0 & a_{54} & 0 \end{bmatrix}$$

since

$$PAP^{-1} = \begin{bmatrix} 0 & 0 & 0 & a_{14} & a_{12} \\ 0 & 0 & 0 & a_{54} & a_{52} \\ 0 & 0 & 0 & a_{34} & a_{32} \\ a_{41} & a_{45} & a_{43} & 0 & 0 \\ a_{21} & a_{25} & a_{23} & 0 & 0 \end{bmatrix} \quad \text{for} \quad P = P^{-1} = \begin{bmatrix} 1 & 0 & 0 & 0 & 0 \\ 0 & 0 & 0 & 0 & 1 \\ 0 & 0 & 1 & 0 & 0 \\ 0 & 0 & 0 & 1 & 0 \\ 0 & 1 & 0 & 0 & 0 \end{bmatrix}.$$

A straightforward computation from the form (46) ensures

THEOREM 22 Let A be an indecomposable square matrix of order $n > 1$ and be transformed into form (46). Then A raised to the power h can be expressed as

$$PA^hP^{-1} = \begin{bmatrix} A_{12}A_{23} \cdots A_{h1} & 0 & \cdots & 0 \\ 0 & A_{23}A_{34} \cdots A_{12} & & 0 \\ \vdots & & \ddots & \\ 0 & 0 & & A_{h1}A_{12} \cdots A_{h-1,h} \end{bmatrix}$$

where P is the permutation matrix in (46).

Therefore, A^h is decomposable if A is indecomposable and imprimitive.

Next we shall clarify the most fundamental relationship between imprimitivity and the Frobenius root of an indecomposable nonnegative matrix.

PROPOSITION 3 Let A be an indecomposable nonnegative square matrix of order $n > 1$, λ_1 be its Frobenius root, and x_1 be the associated positive eigenvector of A. If A is transformed into the form (46), there are at least h different eigenvalues, say $\lambda_1, \lambda_2, \ldots, \lambda_h$, each of which has modulus equal to λ_1, and they can be represented as

$$\lambda_s = \lambda_1 e^{2\pi(s-1)i/h} \qquad \text{for} \quad s = 1, 2, \ldots, h, \tag{47}$$

where $i \equiv \sqrt{-1}$.

PROOF Since $B \equiv PAP^{-1}$ has identical eigenvalues with A, the Frobenius root of B is λ_1 and the associated positive eigenvector of B is Px_1. Conformably with the partition in (46), we partition Px_1 as

$$Px_1 = \{\xi^1, \xi^2, \ldots, \xi^h\} \qquad \text{(a column vector)},$$

where ξ^s stands for the components of Px_1 corresponding to submatrix $A_{s-1,s}$. Hence, in view of $\lambda_1 Px_1 = BPx_1$, we have

$$\begin{aligned} \lambda_1\xi^1 &= A_{12}\xi^2 \\ \lambda_1\xi^2 &= A_{23}\xi^3 \\ &\vdots \\ \lambda_1\xi^h &= A_{h1}\xi^1. \end{aligned} \tag{48}$$

Let q be $e^{2\pi(s-1)i/h}$ for an integer $s \in [1, h]$. Multiplying the rth equation in (48) by q^r, we have

$$\begin{aligned} \lambda_1 q\xi^1 &= A_{12}q\xi^2 \\ \lambda_1 qq\xi^2 &= A_{23}q^2\xi^3 \\ &\vdots \\ \lambda_1 qq^{h-1}\xi^h &= A_{h1}q^h\xi^1, \end{aligned} \tag{49}$$

where

$$q^h = e^{2\pi(s-1)i} = \cos 2\pi(s-1) + i \sin 2\pi(s-1) = 1.$$

Thus, system (49) is rewritten as

$$\rho y = By, \tag{49'}$$

where $\rho \equiv \lambda_1 q$ and $y \equiv \{\xi^1, q\xi^2, \ldots, q^{h-1}\xi^h\}$. Obviously, ρ is an eigenvalue of B (and hence of A), and y is the associated eigenvector. Q.E.D.

PROPOSITION 4 Let A be an indecomposable nonnegative square matrix of order $n > 1$, and λ_1 be its Frobenius root. If A has k different eigenvalues of modulus λ_1, A can be transformed into the form (46) with h replaced by k.

PROOF Let λ_j be an eigenvalue of A and x_j be a nontrivial eigenvector of A associated with λ_j. Then

$$|\lambda_j|x_j^* \leqq Ax_j^*, \tag{50}$$

where x_j^* stands for the vector each component of which consists of the modulus of the corresponding element of x_j. Let λ_s be an eigenvalue of modulus λ_1 and x_s be its associated eigenvector for $s = 1, 2, \ldots, k$. Then due to (50),

$$\lambda_1 x_s^* = |\lambda_s|x_s^* \leqq Ax_s^* \qquad (s = 1, 2, \ldots, k). \tag{51}$$

Denote by y the positive eigenvector of A associated with λ_1, and by z that of A^{T} associated with λ_1. Then, since $\lambda_1 z^{\mathrm{T}} = z^{\mathrm{T}}A$, it follows from (51) that

$$\lambda_1 z^{\mathrm{T}} x_s^* \leqq z^{\mathrm{T}} A x_s^* = \lambda_1 z^{\mathrm{T}} x_s^*.$$

Hence

$$\lambda_1 z^{\mathrm{T}} x_s^* = z^{\mathrm{T}} A x_s^* \qquad \text{for} \quad s = 1, \ldots, k,$$

from which we know

$$\lambda_1 x_s^* = A x_s^* \qquad \text{for} \quad s = 1, \ldots, k \tag{52}$$

since $z > \mathit{0}$. On the other hand, the eigenvector y must be unique (except for a proportionality factor). Therefore, $x_s^* = y > \mathit{0}$. Thus x_s can be represented as

$$x_s = D_s y \qquad \text{for} \quad s = 1, \ldots, k,$$

where

$$D_s \equiv \begin{bmatrix} \delta_{1s} & & & 0 \\ & \delta_{2s} & & \\ & & \ddots & \\ 0 & & & \delta_{ns} \end{bmatrix}, \qquad |\delta_{js}| = 1 \qquad \text{for} \quad j = 1, \ldots, n; \quad s = 1, \ldots, k.$$

Hence $D_s^* = I$, where D_s^* stands for the diagonal matrix whose jth element is $|\delta_{js}|$ ($j = 1, \ldots, n$; $s = 1, 2, \ldots, k$).

Since $|e^{it}| = 1$ and $e^{i(t+2\pi)} = e^{it}$, λ_s can be expressed as

$$\lambda_s = \lambda_1 e^{it_s} \qquad \text{for} \quad s = 1, \ldots, k,$$

where $0 = t_1 < t_2 < \cdots < t_k < 2\pi$. Thus $\lambda_s x_s = Ax_s$ is rewritten as

$$\lambda_1 e^{it_s} D_s y = AD_s y \qquad \text{for} \quad s = 1, \ldots, k, \tag{53}$$

or equivalently

$$\lambda_1 y = C_s y \qquad \text{for} \quad s = 1, \ldots, k, \tag{54}$$

where $C_s \equiv e^{-it_s} D_s^{-1} A D_s$. Then $C_s^* \equiv |e^{-it_s}| D_s^{*-1} A D_s^* = A$. Thus (52) can be rewritten as

$$\lambda_1 y = C_s^* y. \tag{55}$$

Comparing (54) with (55), we know $C_s y = C_s^* y$ for every s. Since $y > \theta$, we have $C_s = C_s^* = A$, i.e.,

$$e^{-it_s} D_s^{-1} A D_s = A \qquad \text{for} \quad s = 1, \ldots, k, \tag{56}$$

from which it follows that

$$A = e^{it_s} D_s A D_s^{-1} \qquad \text{for} \quad s = 1, \ldots, k. \tag{56'}$$

In view of (56) and (56′)

$$A = e^{i(t_s + t_r)} D_s D_r A D_r^{-1} D_s^{-1} \qquad \text{for} \quad r, s = 1, \ldots, k, \tag{57}$$

and

$$A = e^{i(t_s - t_r)} D_s D_r^{-1} A D_r D_s^{-1} \qquad \text{for} \quad r, s = 1, \ldots, k. \tag{57'}$$

$$\begin{aligned} \lambda_1 e^{i(t_s+t_r)} D_s D_r y &= e^{it_s} D_s \lambda_1 e^{it_r} D_r y \\ &= e^{it_s} D_s A D_r y \qquad \text{(in view of (53))} \\ &= A D_s D_r y. \qquad \text{(in view of (56′))} \\ \lambda_1 e^{i(t_s-t_r)} D_s D_r^{-1} y &= e^{i(t_s-t_r)} D_s D_r^{-1} \lambda_1 y \\ &= e^{i(t_s-t_r)} D_s D_r^{-1} A y \qquad \text{(in view of (55))} \\ &= e^{i(t_s-t_r)} D_s D_r^{-1} e^{it_r} D_r A D_r^{-1} y \\ &= e^{it_s} D_s A D_r^{-1} y \\ &= A D_s D_r^{-1} y. \qquad \text{(in view of (56′))} \end{aligned}$$

In short

$$\lambda_1 e^{i(t_s \pm t_r)} D_s D_r^{\pm 1} y = A D_s D_r^{\pm 1} y, \tag{58}$$

where vector $D_s D_r^{\pm 1} y$ is an eigenvector of A associated with the eigenvalue $\lambda_1 e^{i(t_s \pm t_r)}$. Therefore we have for some integers $u, v \in \{1, \ldots, k\}$,

$$e^{i(t_s+t_r)} = e^{it_u}, \qquad e^{i(t_s-t_r)} = e^{it_v}; \tag{59}$$

and

$$D_s D_r = D_u, \qquad D_s D_r^{-1} = D_v. \tag{60}$$

Thus the number e^{it_s} ($s = 1, \ldots, k$) and the corresponding diagonal matrices D_s ($s = 1, \ldots, k$) form two isomorphic multiplicative abelian groups, respectively. (Refer to, for example, Klein (1973, pp. 145–147).)

Define a set

$$\Gamma = \{e^{\pm it_s}\colon s = 1, \ldots, k;\ \ 0 = t_1 < t_2 < \cdots < t_k < 2\pi\}.$$

In view of (59), if $\gamma \in \Gamma$, then $\gamma^\nu \in \Gamma$ for $\nu = 0, \pm 1, \pm 2, \pm 3, \ldots$. We shall show that $\gamma^k = 1$ for each $\gamma \in \Gamma$. If $\gamma = 1$, obviously $\gamma^k = 1$. Assume henceforth $\gamma \neq 1$. Let p be the smallest positive integer such that $\gamma^p = 1$. Then $\gamma^\nu \neq 1$ for $\nu = 1, 2, \ldots, p-1$. It suffices to show that k/p is an integer, for then $\gamma^k = (\gamma^p)^{k/p} = 1$. Define

$$\Gamma_0 = \{1, \gamma, \gamma^2, \ldots, \gamma^{p-1}\}.$$

Apparently $\Gamma_0 \subset \Gamma$. A variation of the Euclidean algorithm (Lemma 1 in Section 3.2) ensures that for an integer ν ($\nu = 0, \pm 1, \pm 2, \ldots$) there is a unique set of integers q and r such that

$$\nu = pq + r \qquad (0 \leqq r < p).$$

Hence $\gamma^\nu = (\gamma^p)^q \gamma^r = \gamma^r \in \Gamma_0$. If $\Gamma_0 \neq \Gamma$, select α_1 in Γ but not in Γ_0 and define

$$\Gamma_1 = \{\alpha_1, \alpha_1\gamma^{\pm 1}, \alpha_1\gamma^{\pm 2}, \ldots, \alpha_1\gamma^{\pm(p-1)}\}.$$

Then $\Gamma_1 \subset \Gamma$. Moreover $\Gamma_0 \cap \Gamma_1 = \varnothing$, for if there were integers $\mu, \nu \in (0, p)$ for which $\gamma^{\pm\nu} = \alpha_1\gamma^{\pm\mu}$, then $\alpha_1 = \gamma^{\pm(\nu-\mu)} \in \Gamma_0$. Furthermore, if $\Gamma_0 \cup \Gamma_1 \neq \Gamma$, select α_2 in Γ but not in $\Gamma_0 \cup \Gamma_1$ and define

$$\Gamma_2 = \{\alpha_2, \alpha_2\gamma^{\pm 1}, \alpha_2\gamma^{\pm 2}, \ldots, \alpha_2\gamma^{\pm(p-1)}\}.$$

Then $\Gamma_2 \subset \Gamma$, $\Gamma_0 \cap \Gamma_2 = \varnothing$, and $\Gamma_1 \cap \Gamma_2 = \varnothing$. Proceeding in this manner, we end up with

$$\Gamma = \bigcup_{\nu=0}^{N} \Gamma_\nu, \qquad \text{where} \quad \Gamma_\nu \cap \Gamma_\mu = \varnothing \quad (\nu \neq \mu),$$

for some finite nonnegative integer N since Γ is a finite set. Clearly, all the elements of Γ_ν ($\nu = 0, 1, \ldots, N$) are different from one another. Thus $k = p(N+1)$, i.e., k/p is an integer. In short, if $\gamma \in \Gamma$, then $\gamma^k = 1$. Hence each element of Γ is the kth root of unity; viz.,

$$e^{it_s} = e^{2\pi(s-1)i/k} \qquad \text{for} \quad s = 1, \ldots, k. \tag{61}$$

Note that $e^{-it_s} = e^{2\pi(k-s+1)i/k}$ for each s, and hence $e^{-it_1} = e^{it_1}$, $e^{-it_2} = e^{it_k}$, $e^{-it_3} = e^{it_{k-1}}, \ldots, e^{-it_k} = e^{it_2}$.

Isomorphism of a multiplicative group e^{it_s} ($s = 1, \ldots, k$) and that of D_s ($s = 1, \ldots, k$) together with (61) imply

$$D_s = D^{s-1} \qquad \text{for} \quad s = 1, \ldots, k, \tag{62}$$

where $D \equiv D_2$ and $D_1 = I$. Then $D^k = I$ and hence each element of D is the kth root of unity. By a permutation of A (and hence of D) we can rearrange D as

$$D = \begin{bmatrix} I_1\eta_1 & & & \\ & I_2\eta_2 & & \\ & & \ddots & \\ & & & I_m\eta_m \end{bmatrix}, \qquad \text{where} \quad \eta_j \equiv e^{2\pi n_j i/k} \quad \text{for} \quad j = 1, \ldots, m, \tag{63}$$

$$n_j \text{ is an integer,} \qquad 0 = n_1 < n_2 < \cdots < n_m < k, \tag{64}$$

and I_j is an identity matrix of an appropriate order ($j = 1, \ldots, m$). Note that (64) implies $m \leq k$.

Conformably with (63), A is partitioned blockwise as

$$A = \begin{bmatrix} A_{11} & A_{12} & \cdots & A_{1m} \\ A_{21} & A_{22} & \cdots & A_{2m} \\ \vdots & \vdots & & \vdots \\ A_{m1} & A_{m2} & \cdots & A_{mm} \end{bmatrix}. \tag{65}$$

Substitution of (62)–(65) into (56) yields

$$e^{2\pi(s-1)(n_j-n_h)i/k}A_{hj} = e^{2\pi(s-1)i/k}A_{hj} \qquad \text{for} \quad h, j = 1, \ldots, m. \tag{66}$$

Thus for every h and j, one of the followings holds: either

$$e^{2\pi(n_j-n_h)i/k} = e^{2\pi i/k} \qquad \text{or} \qquad A_{hj} = 0. \tag{67}$$

Put $h = 1$ in (66) and note that $n_1 = 0$. $A_{12}, A_{13}, \ldots, A_{1m}$ cannot vanish simultaneously since A is indecomposable. Hence at least one of the numbers

$$e^{2\pi n_j i/k} \qquad (j = 2, 3, \ldots, m)$$

must be equal to $e^{2\pi i/k}$. In view of (64), this is possible only for $n_2 = 1$. Then $\eta_2 = e^{2\pi i/k}$ and $A_{11} = A_{13} = \cdots = A_{1m} = 0$.

Next put $h = 2$ in (66) and note that $n_2 = 1$. All $A_{21}, A_{23}, \ldots, A_{2m}$ cannot vanish, so that at least one of the numbers

$$e^{2\pi(n_j-1)i/k} \qquad (j = 1, 3, 4, \ldots, m)$$

must be equal to $e^{2\pi i/k}$. In view of (64) again, this is possible only for $n_3 = 2$. Then $\eta_3 = e^{4\pi i/k}$ and $A_{21} = A_{22} = A_{24} = \cdots = A_{2m} = 0$. Proceeding in this way until $h = m - 1$, we obtain

$$A = \begin{bmatrix} 0 & A_{12} & 0 & \cdots & 0 \\ 0 & 0 & A_{23} & & 0 \\ \vdots & \vdots & & \ddots & \\ 0 & 0 & 0 & & A_{m-1,m} \\ A_{m1} & A_{m2} & A_{m3} & \cdots & A_{mm} \end{bmatrix}$$

and $n_j = j - 1$ ($j = 1, \ldots, m$). Lastly at least one of the numbers

$$e^{2\pi(n_j-n_m)i/k} = e^{2\pi(j-m)i/k} \qquad (j = 1, 2, \ldots, m),$$

must be equal to $e^{2\pi i/k}$. This is possible if $j = 1$ and $m = k$, and impossible for $j = 2, 3, \ldots, m$. Thus $A_{m2} = A_{m3} = \cdots = A_{mm} = 0$ and hence matrix A can be transformed into form (46) with h replaced by k. Q.E.D.

Proposition 4 coupled with Proposition 3 yields the following theorem.

THEOREM 23 Let A be an indecomposable nonnegative square matrix of order $n > 1$. A is imprimitive and can be transformed into the form (46) if and only if A has at least h (> 1) different eigenvalues of modulus equal to its Frobenius root λ_1. Furthermore, these eigenvalues are represented as (47).

COROLLARY Let A be an indecomposable nonnegative square matrix of order $n > 1$. A is primitive if and only if its Frobenius root is larger than any other eigenvalue of A in modulus.

PROOF If k in Proposition 4 is equal to unity, $m \leqq k = 1$. Hence A is primitive. If $k \geqq 2$, A is transformed into the form (46) with h replaced by k, implying that A is imprimitive. Q.E.D.

The above theorem and its corollary are useful to prove the subsequent theorems. (Refer to Sato (1970) and Karlin (1959, p. 248).)

THEOREM 24 (*generalized Kakeya theorem*) If the polynomial of order r

$$f(\lambda) \equiv \lambda^r + c_{r-1}\lambda^{r-1} + \cdots + c_1\lambda + c_0 \tag{68}$$

has coefficients c_j ($0 \leqq j \leqq r-1$) satisfying

$$1 > c_{r-1} \geqq \cdots \geqq c_1 \geqq c_0 > 0, \tag{69}$$

then the modulus of each root of $f(\lambda) = 0$ is less than unity. If the coefficients satisfy

$$1 \geqq c_{r-1} \geqq \cdots \geqq c_1 \geqq c_0 > 0, \tag{69$'$}$$

then the modulus of any root of $f(\lambda) = 0$ does not exceed unity.

PROOF Assume condition (69) is satisfied by the coefficients of $f(\lambda)$. Then $f(\lambda) = 0$ has no roots that are real and positive. Hence

$$(\lambda - 1)\sum_{j=0}^{r} c_j\lambda^j = 0 \qquad (c_r \equiv 1) \tag{70}$$

has only one positive real root that is equal to unity. The remaining r roots of Eq. (70) are identical with roots of $f(\lambda) = 0$. Define

$$b_j \equiv c_j - c_{j-1} \quad (j = 1, \ldots, r) \qquad \text{and} \qquad b_0 \equiv c_0. \tag{71}$$

Then by condition (69), $b_0 > 0$, $b_j \geqq 0$ ($j = 1, \ldots, r-1$), and $b_r > 0$. Equation (70) is now rewritten as

$$\lambda^{r+1} - \sum_{j=0}^{r} b_j\lambda^j = 0, \tag{72}$$

or equivalently, by Corollary 2 to Theorem 6 in Section 1.1,

$$|\lambda I - B| = 0, \tag{72$'$}$$

where

$$B \equiv \begin{bmatrix} 0 & 1 & 0 & \cdots & 0 \\ 0 & 0 & 1 & & \vdots \\ \vdots & \vdots & & \ddots & 0 \\ 0 & 0 & \cdots & 0 & 1 \\ b_0 & b_1 & \cdots & b_{r-1} & b_r \end{bmatrix}$$

Thus the roots of Eq. (70) are identical with the eigenvalues of matrix B, which is nonnegative, indecomposable, and primitive. Hence B has Frobenius root that is greater than any other eigenvalue of B in modulus, by the corollary to Theorem 23. Since Eq. (70) has only one positive root equal to unity, the Frobenius root is equal to unity, and any other eigenvalue of B is less than unity in modulus.

If the coefficients of $f(\lambda)$ satisfy condition (69′), then $b_r \geqq 0$ in the coefficients redefined by (71). Hence matrix B can be imprimitive and each eigenvalue of B does not exceed the Frobenius root ($= 1$). Q.E.D.

Application 1 Consider a distributed-lag system characterized by the difference equation

$$y_t = a_{r-1}y_{t-1} + \cdots + a_1 y_{t-r+1} + a_0 y_{t-r}, \tag{73}$$

where

$$a_{r-1} \geqq \cdots \geqq a_1 \geqq a_0 > 0. \tag{74}$$

The characteristic equation corresponding to (73) is

$$\lambda^r - a_{r-1}\lambda^{r-1} - \cdots - a_1\lambda - a_0 = 0, \tag{75}$$

or equivalently

$$|\lambda I - A| = 0, \tag{75′}$$

where

$$A \equiv \begin{bmatrix} 0 & 1 & 0 & \cdots & 0 \\ 0 & 0 & 1 & & \vdots \\ \vdots & \vdots & & \ddots & 0 \\ 0 & 0 & \cdots & 0 & 1 \\ a_0 & a_1 & \cdots & a_{r-2} & a_{r-1} \end{bmatrix}.$$

Since A is indecomposable nonnegative, its Frobenius root λ_1 is positive and is not less than any other eigenvalue of A in modulus. By factoring out $\lambda - \lambda_1$, we rewrite (75) as

$$(\lambda - \lambda_1)(\lambda^{r-1} + \alpha_{r-2}\lambda^{r-2} + \cdots + \alpha_1\lambda + \alpha_0) = 0, \tag{75″}$$

where

$$\alpha_j = (\lambda_1^j a_j + \cdots + \lambda_1 a_1 + a_0)/\lambda_1^{j+1} > 0 \qquad (j = 0, 1, \ldots, r-2). \quad (76)$$

Then

$$\alpha_j - \alpha_{j-1} = \frac{\lambda_1^j(a_j - a_{j-1}) + \cdots + \lambda_1(a_1 - a_0) + a_0}{\lambda_1^{j+1}} > 0$$

$$(j = 1, 2, \ldots, r-1),$$

where $\alpha_{r-1} = 1$. Hence

$$1 = \alpha_{r-1} > \alpha_{r-2} > \cdots > \alpha_1 > \alpha_0 > 0. \quad (77)$$

Applying Theorem 24, therefore, we know that the modulus of each root of

$$\lambda^{r-1} + \alpha_{r-2}\lambda^{r-2} + \cdots + \alpha_1\lambda + \alpha_0 = 0$$

is less than unity. In other words, Eq. (75) has at least $r - 1$ roots lying within a unit circle. Note that λ_1 is real. Thus the oscillations caused by imaginary parts of complex roots of the characteristic equation (75) are damped; i.e., our distributed-lag system is stable in the sense that $y_t \to \lambda_1^t y_0$ as t goes to infinity.

THEOREM 25 Let A be an indecomposable nonnegative square matrix, λ_1 be its Frobenius root, and x_1, z_1 be the associated eigenvectors of A, A^{T}, respectively; viz.,

$$[\lambda_1 I - A]x_1 = \theta, \qquad z_1[\lambda_1 I - A] = \theta^{\mathrm{T}}.$$

Normalize x_1, z_1 such that $z_1 x_1 = 1$, and define a positive square matrix $Q \equiv x_1 z_1$. Then

(1) $Q^2 = Q$.
(2) $QA = AQ = \lambda_1 Q$.
(3) If A is primitive, then $(A/\lambda_1)^t \to Q$ as $t \to \infty$.

PROOF (1) $Q^2 = x_1 z_1 x_1 z_1 = x_1 z_1 = Q$.

(2) $QA = x_1 z_1 A = \lambda_1 x_1 z_1 = \lambda_1 Q$. Similarly for $AQ = \lambda_1 Q$.

(3) Define $B \equiv A - \lambda_1 Q$. We verify that each nonzero eigenvalue of B is an eigenvalue of A and that λ_1 cannot be an eigenvalue of B. Let λ be a nonzero eigenvalue of B and $y \neq \theta$ be the associated eigenvector; i.e.,

$$\lambda y = By.$$

Premultiplying both sides of this equation by Q yields

$$\lambda Q y = QBy = \theta$$

since $QB = QA - \lambda_1 Q^2 = \lambda_1 Q - \lambda_1 Q = 0$. Thus $Qy = \theta$ since $\lambda \neq 0$. Hence

$$\lambda y = By = (B + \lambda_1 Q)y = Ay,$$

which implies that λ is an eigenvalue of A. In particular, set $\lambda = \lambda_1$. Then $\lambda_1 y = By$ would yield $\lambda_1 y = Ay$, where y must be a nonzero multiple of

$x_1 > \theta$; i.e., $y = cx_1$ with a nonzero scalar c. Then $Qy = cx_1z_1x_1 = cx_1 \neq \theta$, contradicting $Qy = \theta$. Thus λ_1 cannot be an eigenvalue of B. In short, each nonzero eigenvalue $\lambda(B)$ of B is an eigenvalue of A other than λ_1. By the corollary to Theorem 23, therefore,

$$|\lambda(B)| < \lambda_1 \qquad \text{for all} \quad \lambda(B),$$

or in view of $\lambda_1 > 0$,

$$|\lambda(B)/\lambda_1| < 1 \qquad \text{for all} \quad \lambda(B).$$

Since $\lambda(B)/\lambda_1$ is an eigenvalue of B/λ_1,

$$B^t/\lambda_1^t \to 0 \qquad \text{as} \quad t \to \infty.$$

Lastly we know that $B^t = A^t - \lambda_1^t Q$ for $t = 1, 2, 3, \ldots$. Thus

$$\frac{B^t}{\lambda_1^t} = \frac{A^t}{\lambda_1^t} - Q. \qquad \text{Q.E.D.}$$

COROLLARY Let A be an indecomposable nonnegative square matrix. There is some positive integer k such that

$$A^k > 0$$

if and only if A is primitive.

PROOF If A is imprimitive, there is no such k in view of Theorem 22. If A is primitive, $(A/\lambda_1)^t$ converges to a positive matrix by Theorem 25, where λ_1 is the Frobenius root (> 0) of A. Thus there is some positive integer k such that $A^k > 0$. Q.E.D.

Application 2 Consider a homogeneous difference equation system

$$x(t) = Ax(t-1), \tag{78}$$

where x is an n-vector, A is an $n \times n$ indecomposable and primitive nonnegative matrix, and t indicates a period in time. An iterative substitution starting from $t = 1$ in (78) yields

$$x(t) = A^t x(0).$$

Since $A \geqq 0$ is primitive, there exists a positive integer k such that $A^k > 0$, and the Frobenius root λ_1 of A is larger than any other eigenvalue in modulus. Thus, given semipositive $x(0)$, we have $x(t) > \theta$ for some t and

$$x(t) \to c\lambda_1^t x_1 \qquad \text{as} \quad t \to \infty, \tag{79}$$

where x_1 is the positive eigenvector of A associated with λ_1 and c is a constant dependent on $x(0)$. Clearly c is positive. Letting ξ_i^* and $\xi_i(t)$ be the ith components of x_1 and $x(t)$, respectively, we rewrite (79) as

$$\xi_i(t)/\lambda_1^t\xi_i^* \to c \qquad \text{for all } i \qquad \text{as} \quad t \to \infty, \tag{79'}$$

which implies that each component of $x(t)$ tends to grow proportionately relative to the balanced growth path characterized by $\lambda_1^t x_1$, regardless of any initial condition $x(0) \geq \theta$. This convergence in (79) or (79′) may be termed a *relative stability* in the large, as opposed to a simple stability in the usual sense.

4.4 Price Systems of Leontief Type, the Fundamental Marxian Theorem, and Dual Stability

In Section 4.2 we touched on a simple quantity system of Leontief type, putting stress on its relations to the surrounding mathematics. The corresponding price system will now be taken up as an appropriate economics topic to which the foregoing mathematical apparatus is applicable in many respects. We start our analysis with the relations between prices and labor content of commodities.

In this section, let A be an $n \times n$ nonnegative matrix whose (i, j)th component a_{ij} represents the quantity of good i consumed in the process of production of good j per unit of output, and let l_j (> 0) be the *direct* labor requirement per unit of output of good j. Then, the total quantity of standard labor presently necessary to reproduce one unit of good j, denoted λ_j ($j = 1, 2, \ldots, n$), must satisfy the system of equations

$$\Lambda = L + \Lambda A, \tag{80}$$

where $L \equiv (l_1, l_2, \ldots, l_n)$ and $\Lambda \equiv (\lambda_1, \lambda_2, \ldots, \lambda_n)$. We may call Λ the *labor-value vector*, which is uniquely determined by system (80):

$$\Lambda = L[I - A]^{-1}. \tag{81}$$

We assume that $[I - A]$ fulfills the Hawkins–Simon (H-S) conditions. Therefore, Λ is strictly positive and not less than L componentwise since Eq. (81) can be expressed as

$$\Lambda = L + LA + LA^2 + \cdots. \tag{81′}$$

We seek to find some relationship between the labor value and the price of each commodity. To begin, we confine ourselves to the economy where no fixed capital exists. Denote by p_j the price of good j and by w the money wage rate. When the price of each good is equal to its full cost,

$$p_j = \sum_{i=1}^{n} p_i a_{ij} + w l_j \qquad \text{for} \quad j = 1, \ldots, n, \tag{82}$$

or in matrix form

$$p = pA + wL, \tag{82′}$$

where $p = (p_1, \ldots, p_n)$. Since we adopt the full-cost pricing principle, prices are given as the solution of (82′):

$$p = wL[I - A]^{-1} = w\Lambda. \tag{83}$$

The relation (83) implies that the full-cost prices are exactly proportional to the labor content of goods in our no-fixed-capital economy.

Let us introduce profits into our model, and denote by r_i the rate of profit per unit of output of good i. Now the prices will be determined by

$$p_j = \sum_{i=1}^{n} p_i a_{ij} + wl_j + r_j, \qquad \text{for} \quad j = 1, \ldots, n, \tag{84}$$

or in matrix form

$$p = pA + wL + R, \tag{84'}$$

where $R \equiv (r_1, \ldots, r_n)$. Given w and R, prices are determined by

$$\begin{aligned} p &= (wL + R)[I - A]^{-1} = w\Lambda + R[I - A]^{-1} \\ &= w\Lambda + R + RA + RA^2 + \cdots + RA^m + \cdots. \end{aligned}$$

Suppose that the wage rate is at the subsistence level, so that it is just enough to reproduce a unit of labor. In other words,

$$w = \sum_{i=1}^{n} p_i c_i = pC, \tag{85}$$

where $C \equiv \{c_1, \ldots, c_n\}$ is a column vector whose ith component represents the average quantity of good i consumed by an average laborer to survive. Substitution of (85) in (84′) yields

$$p[I - A - CL] = R. \tag{86}$$

On the other hand, corresponding to the price system (86) we consider its dual quantity system

$$[I - A - CL]x = z, \tag{87}$$

where x stands for the "total output" vector and z the "surplus output" vector since CLx designates the consumption goods necessary to reproduce total labor input.

Consider the case where $z \geq \theta$. Then $[I - A]^{-1}z \geq \theta$. In order to have semipositive solution x to system (87) for an arbitrary $z \geq \theta$, it is necessary and sufficient that $[I - A - CL]$ fulfills the H-S conditions. This fulfillment is in turn necessary and sufficient for p in (86) to be semipositive for an arbitrary $R \geq \theta$. Thus we can state

PROPOSITION 5 p in system (86) is semipositive for an arbitrary $R \geq \theta$ if and only if x in system (87) is semipositive for an arbitrary $z \geq \theta$. In this case

$$|I - A - CL| > 0. \tag{88}$$

Note that

$$\begin{aligned} |I - C\Lambda| &= |I - CL[I - A]^{-1}| = |I - A - CL| \cdot |I - A|^{-1} \\ &= |I - A|^{-1} \cdot |I - A - CL| = |I - [I - A]^{-1}CL| \\ &= |I - qL|, \end{aligned} \tag{89}$$

where $q \equiv [I - A]^{-1}C$ is the output vector necessary to reproduce one unit of labor. Also note that $|I - A| > 0$. (Cf. the H-S conditions.) Thus (88) implies

$$|I - C\Lambda| > 0 \qquad \text{and/or} \qquad |I - qL| > 0, \tag{90}$$

and vice versa. We know that

$$|I - C\Lambda| = 1 - \Lambda C \equiv \mu \tag{91}$$

and

$$|I - qL| = 1 - Lq \equiv \mu. \tag{91'}$$

μ is termed the surplus labor per unit of labor input. Therefore, (88) implies that there exists a positive surplus labor for an average laborer. Multiplying (91) by L, we have

$$L = \Lambda CL + \mu L = \Lambda CL\left(1 + \frac{\mu}{1 - \mu}\right) \tag{92}$$

since $\Lambda CL = (1 - \mu)L$. Substitution of (92) for L in (80) yields

$$\Lambda = \Lambda[A + \nu CL], \tag{93}$$

where $\nu \equiv 1 + \mu/(1 - \mu) = 1/(1 - \mu)$, which may be termed the labor exploitation factor ($= 1 +$ the rate of labor exploitation). (93) can be regarded as the value system with reference to an *extending reproduction* scheme because without positive μ system (87) cannot have $x \geq \theta$ for an arbitrary semipositive surplus output. Indeed, $\mu = 0$ implies

$$\Lambda = \Lambda[A + CL], \tag{94}$$

in which $\Lambda \geq \theta$ is possible if and only if

$$|I - A - CL| = 0. \tag{95}$$

Note that (95) is also a necessary and sufficient condition for

$$p[I - A - CL] = \theta \tag{96}$$

and/or

$$[I - A - CL]\, x = \theta \tag{96'}$$

to have nonzero solutions.

It is easy to see that $\mu > 0$ is sufficient for

$$p[I - C\Lambda] = R[I - A]^{-1} \tag{86'}$$

and/or

$$[I - qL]\, x = [I - A]^{-1} z \tag{87'}$$

to have semipositive solutions p and x, respectively, for arbitrary $R \geq \theta$ and $z \geq \theta$ since $\mu > 0$ implies

$$1 > \sum_i \lambda_i c_i \qquad \text{and} \qquad 1 > \sum_i q_i l_i$$

for summation over any subset of indices $\{1, 2, \ldots, n\}$, meaning that every principal minor of $[I - C\Lambda]$ and $[I - qL]$ is positive. Thus, in view of Proposition 5, we have

THEOREM 26 Positive μ is necessary and sufficient for systems (86) and/or (87) to have semipositive solutions p and x, respectively, for arbitrary semipositive R and z. In this case, total profit equals surplus output in money value:

$$Rx = pz. \tag{97}$$

In fact, plausible prices determined by (86′) are all positive as shown below.

PROPOSITION 6 Assume $w = pC$. Let $\mu > 0$, $C_m \equiv \{c_1, \ldots, c_m\} > \theta$, $c_{m+1} = \cdots = c_n = 0$, $R_m \equiv (r_1, \ldots, r_m) \geq \theta$ with $R \geq \theta$. Then all the prices take on positive values.

PROOF $p[I - C\Lambda] = R[I - A]^{-1}$ is partitioned as

$$(p_{(m)}, p_{(n-m)}) \begin{bmatrix} [I - C_m \Lambda_m], & -C_m \Lambda_{n-m} \\ 0 & I \end{bmatrix} = (\gamma_{(m)}, \gamma_{(n-m)}),$$

or

$$p_{(m)} = \gamma_{(m)} [I - C_m \Lambda_m]^{-1} \qquad \text{and} \qquad p_{(n-m)} = p_{(m)} C_m \Lambda_{n-m} + \gamma_{(n-m)},$$

where $\Lambda_m \equiv (\lambda_1, \ldots, \lambda_m)$, $\Lambda_{n-m} \equiv (\lambda_{m+1}, \ldots, \lambda_n)$, $p_{(m)} \equiv (p_1, \ldots, p_m)$, $p_{(n-m)} \equiv (p_{m+1}, \ldots, p_n)$, $\gamma_{(m)} \equiv (\gamma_1, \ldots, \gamma_m)$, $\gamma_{(n-m)} \equiv (\gamma_{m+1}, \ldots, \gamma_n)$, $\gamma_k \equiv \sum_{i=1}^n r_i \alpha_{ik} \geqq r_k$, $\alpha_{ik} \equiv$ the (i, k) element of $[I - A]^{-1}$. Since $C_m \Lambda_m > 0$ and $\mu > 0$, $[I - C_m \Lambda_m]^{-1} > 0$ and hence $p_{(m)} > \theta$. Thus $p_{(n-m)}$ is also a positive vector. Q.E.D.

Now we relax the assumption $w = \sum_{i=1}^n c_i p_i$ and instead assume

$$w \geqq \sum_{i=1}^n p_i c_i = pC. \tag{98}$$

Then we seek the condition for the existence of positive w and p_i ($i = 1, \ldots, n$) such that (98) and

$$p[I - A] \geq wL \tag{99}$$

are satisfied. Putting (98) and (99) together, we have

$$(p, w) \begin{bmatrix} I - A & -C \\ -L & 1 \end{bmatrix} = (R, s), \tag{100}$$

where $R \geq \theta$ and $s \equiv w - pC \geqq 0$. This system has a semipositive vector (p, w) if and only if the coefficient matrix on the left-hand side of (100) satisfies H-S conditions. System (100) is composed of $n + 1$ equations, so that if one half of the all $2(n + 1)$ variables $p_1, \ldots, p_n, w, r_1, \ldots, r_n, s$ is given a priori, then the other $n + 1$ variables may be uniquely determined by (100).

Suppose (R, s) is fixed a priori and assume $\mu > 0$. Then (p, w) will be

$$(p, w) = (R, s)\begin{bmatrix} H + (HCA/\mu) & HC/\mu \\ A/\mu & 1/\mu \end{bmatrix}, \tag{101}$$

where $H \equiv [I - A]^{-1}$. Note that $HC = q$. Equation (101) implies

$$w\mu = RHC + s, \tag{101$'$}$$

which indicates that s is a part of the money value of the surplus labor $w\mu$. In particular if $R = \theta$, then $s = w\mu$.

PROPOSITION 7 Consider the system (100) with $s > 0$. Then (p, w) is strictly positive for an arbitrary $R \geqq \theta$ if and only if $\mu > 0$.

PROOF "If" part is obvious from (101). "Only if" part is shown by the following:

$$0 < \begin{vmatrix} I - A & -C \\ -L & 1 \end{vmatrix} = |I - A - CL| = |I - CA| \cdot |I - A|$$
$$= (1 - AC)|I - A|$$

with $|I - A| > 0$. Q.E.D.

Let us introduce the net own-rate of return γ_i of capital good i, and consider

$$p = wL + pA + p\hat{\gamma}B, \tag{102}$$

where $B = [b_{ij}]$ is the matrix of capital coefficients and $\hat{\gamma} \equiv \text{diag}(\gamma_1, \ldots, \gamma_n)$, denoting the diagonal matrix consisting of $\gamma_1, \ldots, \gamma_n$. The solution to (102) is given by

$$p = wL[I - A - \hat{\gamma}B]^{-1} = wA[I - \hat{\gamma}B[I - A]^{-1}]^{-1}. \tag{103}$$

PROPOSITION 8 (Burmeister and Dobell, 1970) Consider the system (102) with $w > 0$ and $L > \theta$. $p > \theta$ if and only if $[I - A - \hat{\gamma}B]^{-1} \geq 0$.

PROOF The "if" part is immediate from (103) because $[I - A - \hat{\gamma}B]^{-1} \geq 0$ is equivalent to saying that $[I - A - \hat{\gamma}B]$ fulfills the H-S conditions and hence

$$[I - A - \hat{\gamma}B]^{-1} = \sum_{t=0}^{\infty} (A + \hat{\gamma}B)^t.$$

"Only if" part Let $p > \theta$ in (103) and define $H \equiv A + \hat{\gamma}B = [h_{ij}]$, $\hat{p} \equiv$

$\text{diag}(p_1, \ldots, p_n)$, $e \equiv (1, \ldots, 1) \in R^n$, $H^* \equiv \hat{p}H\hat{p}^{-1} = [h_{ij}p_i/p_j] \equiv [h_{ij}^*]$ and $L^* \equiv wL\hat{p}^{-1} = (wl_i/p_i)$. Then (102) can be expressed as

$$e\hat{p}[I - H] = wL \qquad \text{or} \qquad e[I - H^*] = L^*,$$

of which the jth component is

$$1 - \left(\sum_i p_i h_{ij}\right)/p_j = wl_j/p_j > 0.$$

Thus, the column sums of H^* satisfy Solow condition (i), ensuring $[I - H^*]^{-1} \geq 0$. Hence

$$[I - H]^{-1} = \hat{p}^{-1}[I - H^*]^{-1}\hat{p} \geq 0. \qquad \text{Q.E.D.}$$

We seek a simple sufficient condition for $[I - A - \hat{\gamma}B]^{-1} \geq 0$, for which two lemmas are provided.

LEMMA 7 Let γ_0 be a positive scalar. $[I - A - \gamma_0 B]^{-1} \geq 0$ if and only if $1/\gamma_0 > \rho^*$, where ρ^* is the Frobenius root of $B[I - A]^{-1}$.

PROOF

$$[I - A - \gamma_0 B]^{-1} = \frac{1}{\gamma_0}[I - A]^{-1}\left[\frac{1}{\gamma_0}I - B[I - A]^{-1}\right]^{-1},$$

in which we take into consideration $[I - A]^{-1} \geq 0$ and the fact that

$$\left[\frac{1}{\gamma_0}I - B[I - A]^{-1}\right]^{-1} \geq 0 \quad \Leftrightarrow \quad \frac{1}{\gamma_0} > \rho^*. \qquad \text{Q.E.D.}$$

LEMMA 8 Let γ_0 be the maximum among $\gamma_1, \gamma_2, \ldots, \gamma_n$. Then

$$[I - A - \gamma_0 B]^{-1} \geq 0 \qquad \text{implies} \qquad [I - A - \hat{\gamma}B]^{-1} \geq 0.$$

PROOF Let ρ^0 be the Frobenius root of $A + \gamma_0 B$, and $\hat{\rho}$ be that of $A + \hat{\gamma}B$. Then $\rho^0 \geqq \hat{\rho}$. Hence

$$[I - A - \gamma_0 B]^{-1} \geq 0 \Leftrightarrow 1 > \rho^0 \Rightarrow 1 > \hat{\rho} \Leftrightarrow [I - A - \hat{\gamma}B]^{-1} \geq 0. \quad \text{Q.E.D.}$$

By the above two lemmas and Proposition 8, we get the following at once.

PROPOSITION 9 (Burmeister and Dobell, 1970) Let ρ^* be the Frobenius root of $B[I - A]^{-1}$ and assume $\rho^* > 0$. Then, the price vector p in the system (102) with $w > 0$ and $L > \theta$ is strictly positive if

$$0 < \gamma_i < 1/\rho^* \qquad \text{for} \quad i = 1, \ldots, n. \tag{104}$$

It is presumed that capitalists tend to shift their capital from one industry to another until the resulting scarcity relationships have established a price system where rates of return of all capitals are equalized:

$$\gamma_1 = \gamma_2 = \cdots = \gamma_n \equiv \gamma. \tag{105}$$

Then, (102) is reduced to

$$p[I - A - \gamma B] = wL. \tag{102'}$$

In view of Proposition 9, p in (102′) takes on a strictly positive value for γ such that

$$0 < \gamma < 1/\rho^*. \tag{104′}$$

Obviously, zero is the lower bound and $1/\rho^*$ is the upper bound for the uniform rate of return γ compatible with $p > \theta$.

So far we have been concerned with the rate of return of each capital good. Next we are interested in the rate of profit in each sector per unit of capital. First, we consider the turnover of circulating capital. Circulating capital is the monetary value of current inputs of materials and labor. Given total stock of circulating capital K_{cj} in sector j and its annual output x_j, under our fixed-proportion production functions, the annual turnover τ_j of the capital is defined as

$$\tau_j = \left(\sum_{i=1}^{n} p_i a_{ij} + wl_j\right) x_j / K_{cj}. \tag{106}$$

Let us take account of the existence of fixed capital as well and denote by K_{fj} the stock of fixed capital in sector j. The annual rate of profit π_j in sector j per unit of capital is defined as

$$\pi_j = \left(p_j - \sum_{i=1}^{n} p_i a_{ij} - wl_j - \sum_{i=1}^{n} p_i \delta_{ij} b_{ij}\right) x_j / K_j, \tag{107}$$

where $K_j \equiv K_{cj} + K_{fj}$ is total stock of capital in sector j, δ_{ij} denotes the depreciation rate of capital good i in sector j, and b_{ij} is the so-called "capital coefficient," i.e., the stock of good i needed to produce a unit of output in sector j in a period. We suppose that fixed capital K_{fj} is equal to $\sum_i p_i b_{ij} x_j$, i.e., the total amount of stocks of goods required in sector j. Substituting this supposition together with (106) in (107) yields

$$\pi_j\left(\sum_i p_i b_{ij} + \left(\sum_i p_i a_{ij} + wl_j\right)\tau_j^{-1}\right) = p_j - \sum_i p_i a_{ij} - wl_j - \sum_i p_i d_{ij}, \tag{108}$$

for $j = 1, \ldots, n$, or in matrix form,

$$(pB + (pA + wL)\hat{\tau}^{-1})\,\hat{\pi} = p[I - A - D] - wL, \tag{108′}$$

where $B = [b_{ij}]$, $d_{ij} \equiv \delta_{ij} b_{ij}$, $D = [d_{ij}]$, $\hat{\pi} = \text{diag}(\pi_1, \ldots, \pi_n)$, and $\hat{\tau} = \text{diag}(\tau_1, \ldots, \tau_n)$. Given the rate of profit and the turnover of circulating capital in every sector together with money wage rate and technological coefficients, the prices are to be determined uniquely from (108′) in the following manner:

$$p = wL[I + \hat{\pi}\hat{\tau}^{-1}]\,[I - A[I + \hat{\pi}\hat{\tau}^{-1}] - D - B\hat{\pi}]^{-1}. \tag{109}$$

Now consider the equilibrium situation where a uniform annual rate of profit π prevails over the whole economy, i.e., $\pi_1 = \cdots = \pi_n \equiv \pi$, and assume the wage rate kept at subsistence level. Then, Eq. (108′) is reduced to

$$\pi p[B + [A + CL]\hat{\tau}^{-1}] = p[I - A - CL - D], \tag{110}$$

from which we obtain

$$p\left[\frac{1}{\pi} I - M\right] = \theta, \tag{111}$$

where $M \equiv G[I - E]^{-1}$, $G \equiv B + [A + CL]\hat{\tau}^{-1}$, and $E \equiv A + CL +$ D. Assume E is indecomposable. Then $[I - E]^{-1} > 0$ and hence $M > 0$. Applying the Frobenius Theorem 9, we assert that a strictly positive vector p is associated only with the positive Frobenius root of M; whence π must be the reciprocal of the unique root, and p is the associated positive eigenvector that is unique up to proportionality. When one of the τ_j increases, some elements of M will decrease, and hence the uniform rate of profit π is to rise. Moreover, if one of the coefficients a_{ij}, b_{ij}, δ_{ij}, l_j, or c_i decreases, *ceteris paribus*, π will rise.

In a simplified case where we neglect fixed capital and assume $\tau_1 = \cdots = \tau_n \equiv 1$ and $\pi_1 = \cdots = \pi_n \equiv \pi$, (109) reduces to

$$p = (1 + \pi)wL[I - (1 + \pi)A]^{-1}. \tag{112}$$

This is the price system formulated by von Weizsäcker and Samuelson (1971). Assuming $w = pC$ in (112) results in

$$p\left[\frac{1}{1 + \pi} I - A - CL\right] = \theta. \tag{113}$$

Morishima (1973) proposed the following theorem with reference to (113).

THEOREM 26′ (*fundamental Marxian theorem*) Assume matrix $[A + CL]$ is indecomposable. Then, π determined by system (113) with a positive price vector p is positive if and only if $\mu > 0$.

PROOF In view of Theorem 26,

$$\mu > 0 \Leftrightarrow [I - A - CL]^{-1} \geqq 0 \qquad (\neq 0),$$

which is equivalent to the fact that the Frobenius root of $A + CL$ ($\geqq 0$), denoted σ^*, is less than unity. On the other hand, p is strictly positive in (113) if and only if $1/(1 + \pi)$ is equal to σ^*. Q.E.D.

In view of the above proof, system (113) with $p > \theta$ is rewritten as

$$p = (1 + \pi^*)p[A + CL], \tag{113′}$$

where $1 + \pi^*$ is equal to the reciprocal of the Frobenius root of the indecomposable matrix $A + CL$. Then $E^* \equiv (1 + \pi^*)[A + CL]$ is a nonnegative matrix whose largest positive eigenvalue is unity. Consider the dynamic system (see Morishima, 1974)

$$p_t = p_{t-1}E^*. \tag{113″}$$

Provided E^* is primitive, from Application 2 in Section 4.3, it follows that the unique positive eigenvector of E^* associated with the largest eigenvalue 1 becomes the limit to which p_t in (113″) converges, starting from an arbitrary semipositive initial price vector.

Another simplified version of system (109) is obtained by neglecting circulating capital, viz.,

$$p = wL + pA + pB\hat{\pi}, \tag{114}$$

where A is the input coefficient matrix of *all* current material consumed in production process including depreciation of durable capital goods, and hence the A is equivalent to A plus D in (109). Since system (114) resembles system (102), it is natural to expect that similar propositions to Propositions 8 and 9 will be able to be established with reference to (114).

PROPOSITION 8′ The price vector p is strictly positive in the system (114) with $w > 0$ and $L > \theta$ assumed if and only if $[I - A - B\hat{\pi}]^{-1}$ is nonnegative and nonzero.

PROPOSITION 9′ Let ρ^* be the Frobenius root of $[I - A]^{-1} B$ and assume $\rho^* > 0$. Then, the price vector p in system (114) with $w > 0$ and $L > \theta$ assumed is strictly positive if

$$0 < \pi_i < 1/\rho^* \qquad \text{for} \quad i = 1, \ldots, n. \tag{115}$$

When a uniform rate of profit π prevails over all sectors, system (114) will coincide with system (102′), i.e.,

$$p = wL + pA + \pi pB. \tag{114′}$$

Hence, the lower and upper bounds for π compatible with $p > \theta$ are the same as those for γ shown by (104′):

$$0 < \pi < 1/\rho^*. \tag{104″}$$

In a dynamic situation where prices vary from time to time, capital gains (or losses) should be considered as well. Let p_{it} denote the price of good i, w_t the wage rate, and r_{it} the rate of profit in sector i, in time period t. We may take as one period a year, a month, or any other arbitrary length of time. Suppose that production activity takes place all through period t and that the performance of the activity is evaluated at the beginning of period $t + 1$. Confining ourselves to the economy where no circulating capital exists, with the total stock of capital amounting to $k_{jt} = \sum_{i=1}^{n} p_{it} b_{ij}$, we expect the following profit factor ($= 1 +$ the rate of profit) in period $t + 1$:

$$1 + \pi_{jt} = \left(p_{j,t+1} - \sum_{i=1}^{n} p_{i,t+1} a_{ij} - w_{t+1} l_j + k_{j,t+1}\right) / k_{jt}, \tag{116}$$

or equivalently

$$p_{j,t+1} = \sum_{i} p_{i,t+1} a_{ij} + w_{t+1} l_j + k_{jt}\pi_{jt} - (k_{j,t+1} - k_{jt}), \tag{116′}$$

for all $j = 1, \ldots, n$. That is, the price of each good is equal to its production cost plus profits minus capital gains (or plus capital losses). Let p_t denote the price vector in period t, i.e., $p_t = (p_{1t}, \ldots, p_{nt})$, and $\hat{\pi}_t = \text{diag}(\pi_{1t}, \ldots, \pi_{nt})$. Furthermore, by imposing another assumption that profit rates and wage rate are independent of time period, i.e.,

$$\hat{\pi}_t = \hat{\pi} \qquad \text{and} \qquad w_t = w \qquad \text{for all} \quad t, \tag{117}$$

we obtain the following dynamic price system from (116′):

$$p_{t+1}[I - A + B] = p_t B[I + \hat{\pi}] + wL. \tag{118}$$

Through competition, profit rates may tend to be equalized in all sectors. So in equilibrium where $\pi_1 = \cdots = \pi_n = \pi$, system (118) reduces to the so-called Solow dynamic price system (see Solow (1959)):

$$p_{t+1}[I - A + B] = (1 + \pi)p_t B + wL. \tag{118′}$$

If system (118′) converges to a stationary equilibrium described by (114′) above, as t tends to infinity, irrespective of an arbitrary initial value of p_t, then system (118′) is said to be globally stable. We may assume nonsingularity of matrix $[I - A + B]$. Then, in view of Theorem 7 and its corollary in Section 3.3, system (118′) is globally stable if and only if every eigenvalue of matrix $(1 + \pi)B[I - A + B]^{-1}$ is less than unity in modulus. (The verification is left to the reader as an exercise.) Given the technology characterizing input coefficient matrices A and B, the rate of profit π should play a vital role in the system to determine its dynamic property.

We assume that $[I - A + B]$ and $H \equiv [I - A + B]^{-1}B$ are nonsingular, that $[I - A]$ fulfills the Hawkins–Simon conditions and hence $[I - A]^{-1}$ is nonnegative, and that $[I - A]^{-1}B$ is indecomposable. System (118′) is now rewritten as

$$p_{t+1} = (1 + \pi)p_t K + W, \tag{119}$$

where W stands for $wL[I - A + B]^{-1}$ and K denotes $B[I - A + B]^{-1} = [k_{ij}]$.

PROPOSITION 10 Assume $w > 0$ and $L > \theta$. System (119) is globally stable and price vector converges to a unique positive solution of system (114′):

$$p^* = wL[I - A - \pi B]^{-1} \tag{120}$$

if π satisfies

$$0 < \pi < \frac{1}{\max_{1 \leqq j \leqq n} \sum_i |k_{ij}|} - 1. \tag{121}$$

PROOF If inequality (121) holds, every eigenvalue of $(1 + \pi)K$ is less than unity in modulus and hence system (119) is globally stable. It remains to show only that $[I - A - \pi B]^{-1} \geqq 0$. Let $v(K)$ and $v(H)$ be eigenvalues of K and H, respectively, and let z be an eigenvalue of $[I - A]^{-1}B$. Then for any $v(H) \neq 1$, $|v(H)I - H| = 0$ implies

$$|v(H)/(1 - v(H))I - [I - A]^{-1}B| = 0,$$

i.e., $v(H)/(1 - v(H)) = z$. Thus, for the Frobenius root z^* of $[I - A]^{-1}B$, there exists $v^*(H) < 1$ such that $v^*(H)/(1 - v^*(H)) = z^*$ since $z^* > 0$. In view of the fact that H and K are similar matrices, there is an eigenvalue $v^*(K)$ of K equal to $v^*(H)$. Therefore, we have

$$z^*/(1 + z^*) = |v^*(H)| = |v^*(K)| \leqq \max_j \sum_i |k_{ij}|. \tag{122}$$

(121) and (122) imply $0 < \pi < 1/z^*$, which guarantees $[I - A - \pi B]^{-1} \geqq 0$, and hence $\geqq I$ since

$$[I - A - \pi B]^{-1} = \frac{1}{\pi}\left[\frac{1}{\pi} I - [I - A]^{-1}B\right]^{-1}[I - A]^{-1}. \qquad \text{Q.E.D.}$$

Now we consider a dual quantity system corresponding to price system (118′):

$$[I - A + B]X_t = (I + g)^2 BX_{t-1} + y_t, \tag{123}$$

where $X_t = \{x_{1t}, \ldots, x_{nt}\}$ is the column vector of outputs in period t, $y_t = \{y_{1t}, \ldots, y_{nt}\}$ the column vector of consumption, and g a uniform rate of growth of capital goods. The economic implication of system (123) will become clearer when it is rewritten as

$$X_t - AX_t - y_t = B((1 + g)^2 X_{t-1} - X_t); \tag{123′}$$

i.e., commodities are produced such that net investment (on the left-hand side of (123′)) fills the gap in output capacity between periods t and $t + 1$ when the output level in period $t + 1$ is supposed to reach $(1 + g)^2 X_{t-1}$ for a given rate of growth g. This myopic investment policy will guarantee a global stability for system (123) if the value of g is restricted as suggested below.

PROPOSITION 11 If growth rate g is a positive number not exceeding $(1 + \pi)^{1/2} - 1$ for π fulfilling inequality (121) and if consumption y_t ($\geq \theta$) grows at g, then quantity system (123) as well as price system (118′) is globally stable, and output vector regulated by system (123) converges to a unique semipositive growing equilibrium:

$$X_t^* = [I - A - gB]^{-1} y_t. \tag{124}$$

PROOF Rewrite (123) as

$$X_t = (1 + g)^2 HX_{t-1} + Y_t, \tag{123″}$$

where $Y_t = [I - A + B]^{-1} y_t$. Let $\bar{v}(H)$ and $\bar{v}(K)$ be the dominant eigenvalues of H and K, respectively. They are identical with each other since H and K are similar matrices. Thus, inequality (121) and $g \leqq (1 + \pi)^{1/2} - 1$ imply

$$|v(H)| = |v(K)| \leqq \max_j \sum_i |k_{ij}| < \frac{1}{1+\pi} \leqq \left(\frac{1}{1+g}\right)^2;$$

or in short,

$$|(1+g)^2 v(H)| < 1 \qquad \text{for all } v(H),$$

which is equivalent to

$$\lim_{t\to\infty} [(1+g)^2 H]^t = 0. \tag{125}$$

After an iterative substitution, we obtain from (123″)

$$X_t = (1+g)^{2t} H^t X_0 + [I - (1+g)H]^{-1} [I - (1+g)^t H^t] Y_t,$$

which will converge to, in view of (125) and $(1+g)^2 > 1+g$ for $g > 0$,

$$\lim_{t\to\infty} X_t = [I - (1+g)H]^{-1} Y_t = X_t^*.$$

On the other hand,

$$\frac{1}{1+g} > \max_j \sum_i |k_{ij}| \geqq \frac{z^*}{1+z^*}$$

implies $g < 1/z^*$ which, with $g > 0$, ensures $[I - A - gB]^{-1} \geq 0$. Q.E.D.

Symmetric to the above two propositions are the following, which can be verified in a similar manner.

PROPOSITION 10′ System (123) is globally stable and the output vector converges to the growing equilibrium X_t^* if growth rate g satisfies

$$0 < g < \frac{1}{(\max_{1\leqq i\leqq n} \sum_j |h_{ij}|)^{1/2}} - 1. \tag{126}$$

where h_{ij} denotes the (i, j)th component of matrix H, and if y_t grows at g.

PROPOSITION 11′ If profit rate π is a positive number not exceeding $g(2+g)$ for g fulfilling (126), price system (118′) as well as output system (123) are globally stable.

4.5 Generalization of the Hicks–Metzler System and Global Stability

In this section we aim to review further developments in stability of economic systems involving complementary relations among commodities and other attempts of generalization of the foregoing theories. We shall begin with a discussion concerning the so-called Morishima matrices.

Good i is said to be a complement of good j if b_{ij} is negative, where b_{ij} is that denoted in Definition 3 of Section 4.2. We assume that if good i is a substitute of a substitute (or a complement of a complement) of good j, then good i is a substitute of good j and that if good i is a complement of a substitute (or a substitute of a complement) of good j, then good i is complementary with good j. These assumptions can be formally written as

$$\operatorname{sgn}(b_{ik}b_{kj}) = \operatorname{sgn} b_{ij} \qquad \text{for distinct} \quad i, k, j. \tag{127}$$

Note that (127) implies $\operatorname{sgn} b_{kj} = \operatorname{sgn} b_{jk}$ for $k \neq j$.

DEFINITION 5 A square matrix is termed a *Metzlerian matrix* if all its (main) diagonal entries are negative and all its off-diagonal entries are nonnegative. A square matrix B is called a *Morishima matrix* if B can be permuted into the form

$$PBP^{-1} = \left[\begin{array}{c:c} B_{11} & B_{12} \\ \hdashline B_{21} & B_{22} \end{array}\right] \tag{128}$$

where P is a permutation matrix, diagonal blocks B_{11}, B_{22} on the right-hand side are Metzlerian matrices, and off-diagonal blocks B_{12}, B_{21} are nonpositive matrices.

Observe that any square matrix obeying assumption (127) and having negative main diagonal elements is a Morishima matrix.

Considering a Morishima matrix, we have the following generalized Frobenius theorem due to Morishima (1952).

THEOREM 27 (*a generalized Frobenius theorem*) Let an $n \times n$ real matrix $A \equiv [a_{ij}]$ with $n > 1$ satisfy

$$a_{ii} > 0 \qquad \text{for all} \quad i, \tag{129-1}$$

$$\operatorname{sgn} a_{ij} = \operatorname{sgn} a_{ji} \qquad \text{for all} \quad i \neq j, \tag{129-2}$$

$$\operatorname{sgn}(a_{ik}a_{kj}) = \operatorname{sgn} a_{ij} \qquad \text{for distinct} \quad i, k, j. \tag{129-3}$$

(i) There is an eigenvalue r_n of A that is real, positive, and not less in modulus than any eigenvalue of A (we may call r_n the *quasi-Frobenius root* of A); and the cofactor of $\lambda\delta_{ij} - a_{ij}$ in $[\lambda I - A]$ has the same sign as a_{ij} for $\lambda \geqq r_n$. Moreover, $r_n \geqq a_{ii}$ for any i and $r_n \geqq r_{n-1}$, where r_{n-1} is the quasi-Frobenius root of A_{ii}, the matrix obtained from A by deleting its ith row and column for any i.

(ii) In particular, if A is indecomposable, r_n is a simple eigenvalue, $r_n > r_{n-1}$, and the diagonal blocks of $[\lambda I - A]^{-1}$ corresponding to B_{11}, B_{22} in (128) are strictly positive and its off-diagonal blocks corresponding to B_{12}, B_{21} are strictly negative for $\lambda \geqq r_n$.

(The proof of (i) proceeds in a similar manner to that of Lemma 1 in Section 4.1, *mutatis mutandis*. For the proof of (ii), refer to the proofs of Theorems 6–8 in Section 4.1.)

First, we are concerned with the stability of a Morishima matrix. In view of Theorem 40 in Section 2.5, we can state

THEOREM 28 Let B be a Morishima matrix. If B has a column dominant diagonal, B is D-stable.

Metzler's second theorem (Theorem 18 in Section 4.2) states that when B is a Metzlerian matrix, B is stable if and only if B is Hicksian (i.e., B satisfies the Hicks conditions (31)). This statement can be generalized as follows.

THEOREM 29 (Morishima, 1952) Let B be a Morishima matrix. B is stable if and only if B is Hicksian.

PROOF Let E_1 be the diagonal matrix obtained from the identity matrix I by replacing its ith column e^i by $-e^i$ for $i \in \{1, \ldots, n_1\}$ where n_1 is the order of square matrix B_{11} in (128). Then

$$E_1 PBP^{-1}E_1 \equiv C$$

is a Metzlerian matrix. By Lemma 5 in Section 4.2, the largest real eigenvalue ρ^* of C is not less than $\mathrm{Re}(\rho)$, where ρ stands for an eigenvalue of C. Since $E_1CE_1 = PBP^{-1}$ and since $|\rho I - E_1CE_1| = 0$, ρ is also an eigenvalue of PBP^{-1} and hence of B. Thus ρ^* is equal to the largest real eigenvalue μ^* of B such that

$$\mu^* \geqq \mathrm{Re}(\mu) \qquad \text{for any eigenvalue } \mu \text{ of } B. \tag{130}$$

By the second Metzler theorem, matrix C is Hicksian if and only if C is stable. Since $\mu \equiv \rho$, C is stable (i.e., $\mathrm{Re}(\rho) < 0$) if and only if B is stable (i.e., $\mathrm{Re}(\mu) < 0$). The determinant of any principal submatrix of C is equal to that of the corresponding principal submatrix of E_1CE_1, so that C is Hicksian if and only if B is Hicksian. Thus we have completed the proof of the present theorem. Q.E.D.

We now turn to comparative statics problems related to a stable Morishima matrix, in terms of which the Mosak theorem (Theorem 19 in Section 4.2) and its relevant propositions are modified as follows.

THEOREM 30 (Morishima, 1952) Let $B \equiv [b_{ij}]$ be a stable Morishima matrix of order n. Then, (i) inequalities (39) in Section 4.2 hold true and hence, as an impact effect, a shift of demand to a good from the numeraire raises the price of the good; and (ii) a shift of demand to good i from the numeraire raises the prices of those goods that are substitutes of good i and lowers the prices of those goods that are complements of good i, as impact effects.

PROOF (i) follows immediately from Theorem 29.

(ii) Put $A \equiv [a_{ij}] \equiv B + bI$, where $b > \max_i |b_{ii}|$. Let μ denote an eigenvalue of B and put $\lambda \equiv \mu + b$. Then

$$\mu I - B = \lambda I - A.$$

Since B is stable, $\mathrm{Re}(\mu) < 0$ for any eigenvalue μ of B, and hence $b > \lambda^*$, where λ^* is the quasi-Frobenius root of A. By Theorem 27 above, therefore, the cofactor of $b\delta_{ij} - a_{ij}$ in $[bI - A] \equiv -B$ has the same sign as $a_{ij} = b_{ij}$ $(i \neq j)$; i.e.,

$$\operatorname{sgn}(-1)^{n-1}B_{ij} = \operatorname{sgn} b_{ij} \qquad \text{for} \quad i \neq j.$$

On the other hand, B is Hicksian by Theorem 29. Hence

$$|-B| = (-1)^n |B| > 0.$$

Thus, in view of (37), we have

$$\operatorname{sgn} \frac{\partial p_j}{\partial \alpha} = \operatorname{sgn}\left(-\frac{B_{ij}}{|B|}\frac{\partial D_i}{\partial \alpha}\right) = \operatorname{sgn}\left(b_{ij}\frac{\partial D_i}{\partial \alpha}\right). \tag{131}$$

Statement (ii) follows from (131). Q.E.D.

Theorem 29 could be applicable in the entire system including the numeraire. In this case, if the numeraire is a complement of some good, the relevant Morishima matrix corresponding to the entire system will not be Hicksian and hence the system will be dynamically unstable.

THEOREM 31 (Kennedy, 1970) Postulate that each excess demand function is homogeneous of degree zero in all prices. The extended Morishima matrix relevant to the entire system including the numeraire as good 0 is not Hicksian, provided the numeraire is a complement of some good.

PROOF We confine ourselves to the effects on a subset of prices, say of goods 0, 1, . . ., m $(< n)$, where good 0 (the numeraire) is complementary with all the other goods 1 to m, and these goods are supposed to be gross substitutes of one another. By the homogeneity postulate,

$$\sum_{j=1}^{m} (-b_{ij})\, p_j^* = b_{i0}\, p_0^* \qquad \text{for} \quad i = 1, \ldots, m, \tag{132}$$

where p_j^* $(j = 0, 1, \ldots, m)$ are the equilibrium prices taking positive values. Since $b_{i0} < 0$ and $b_{ij} \geqq 0$ $(i \neq j;\ i, j = 1, \ldots, m)$, (132) can be rewritten as

$$-B_{11}\, p^* < \theta, \tag{132$'$}$$

where p^* is a positive column m-vector and B_{11} is a Metzlerian matrix as in (128).

If B_{11} is Hicksian, all the principal minors of $-B_{11}$ are positive, and hence, by Corollary 2 to the Hawkins–Simon theorem (Theorem 30 in Section 2.4), $[-B_{11}]^{-1}$ is nonnegative and nonzero. This is incompatible with inequality system (132$'$). Q.E.D.

Remark The extended Morishima matrix $\bar{B}$ mentioned in Theorem 31 must be singular because

$$p^{\mathrm{T}}\bar{B} = \theta \tag{133}$$

follows from the Walras law. (Refer to (41) in Section 4.2.) p in (133) is the $(n+1)$-vector consisting of positive equilibrium prices. Thus, by saying that $\bar{B}$ is Hicksian, we mean that each principal minor of $\bar{B}$, except the singular $\bar{B}$ itself, takes the sign $(-1)^k$, where k is the order of the minor.

Consequently, we adopt the following definition as to whether $\bar{B}$ is stable or not.

DEFINITION 6 A square singular matrix is said to be *stable* if the real parts of all its nonzero eigenvalues are negative and zero is a simple eigenvalue.

A case of stability in the sense just defined will be referred to in Theorem 32 below.

LEMMA 9 Let A be an indecomposable Metzlerian matrix. Then there is a real simple eigenvalue λ_1 of A with an associated positive eigenvector. No other eigenvalue of A has an associated semipositive eigenvector, and

$$\lambda_1 > \mathrm{Re}(\lambda) \qquad \text{for every eigenvalue } \lambda \text{ of } A. \tag{134}$$

(The proof proceeds in a similar manner to those of Theorems 7 and 9 in Section 4.1 and Lemma 5 in Section 4.2, *mutatis mutandis.*)

THEOREM 32 (Mukherji, 1972) Let $\bar{B}$ be a matrix satisfying (133) with a strictly positive p. Then $\bar{B}$ is stable in the sense of Definition 6 if there is a nonsingular matrix S such that $\bar{A} \equiv S\bar{B}S^{-1}$ is an indecomposable Metzlerian matrix and either S or S^{-1} is nonnegative.

PROOF Let $S^{-1} \geqq 0$. From (133), we have

$$y\bar{A} = \theta, \tag{133$'$}$$

where $y \equiv p^{\mathrm{T}}S^{-1} > \theta$. By virtue of Lemma 9, (133′) implies that zero is a simple eigenvalue of $\bar{A}$ with y as its associated eigenvector. By (134), all the other eigenvalues of $\bar{A}$ have negative real parts. Since $\bar{B}$ is similar to $\bar{A}$, they have identical eigenvalues. (See Theorem 8 in Section 1.2.) Q.E.D.

When we postulate zero-degree homogeneity of every excess demand function, is an original Morishima matrix stable? To this problem, the sign symmetric relations in the matrix will not be sufficient to provide any definite answer, as may be seen below.

Let $\bar{B}$ be the $(n+1)\times(n+1)$ Jacobian matrix (evaluated at equilibrium prices) of the excess demand functions of all goods including the numeraire (good 0), and let B be the $n \times n$ matrix obtained from $\bar{B}$ by deleting the first row and column. Assume that $\bar{B} = [b_{ij}]$ is sign symmetric, i.e.,

$$\operatorname{sgn} b_{ij} = \operatorname{sgn} b_{ji} \qquad \text{for all} \quad i \neq j, \tag{135}$$

that each excess demand function is homogeneous of degree zero in all prices, whence we have

$$\bar{B}p = \theta, \tag{136}$$

where $p > \theta$, and that the units of measurement for goods are so chosen that equilibrium prices are all unity. The last assumption implies that

$$\sum_{i=0}^{n} b_{ij} = 0 \qquad \text{for} \quad j = 0, 1, \ldots, n, \tag{137}$$

which follows from (133); and that

$$\sum_{j=0}^{n} b_{ij} = 0 \qquad \text{for} \quad i = 0, 1, \ldots, n, \tag{138}$$

which follows from (136).

We introduce the notion of qualitative stability. (Refer to Quirk (1970).)

DEFINITION 7 Let $A = [a_{ij}]$ and $C = [c_{ij}]$ be real square matrices of order n and let

$$Q_A = \{C : \operatorname{sgn} c_{ij} = \operatorname{sgn} a_{ij} \text{ for every } i, j = 1, \ldots, n\}.$$

In other words, Q_A is the family of matrices all with the same sign pattern as matrix A. Given $\bar{B}$ (the matrix of order $n + 1$ defined in the preceding paragraph), let

$$S_{\bar{B}} = \left\{\bar{C} = [c_{ij}] : \bar{C} \in Q_{\bar{B}} \text{ and } \sum_{i=0}^{n} c_{ij} = 0 \; (j = 0, 1, \ldots, n), \right.$$
$$\left. \sum_{j=0}^{n} c_{ij} = 0 \; (i = 0, 1, \ldots, n)\right\}.$$

Then B (the matrix of order n defined in the preceding paragraph) is said to be *qualitatively stable* under (137) and (138) if

$$\bar{C} \in S_{\bar{B}} \Rightarrow C \text{ is a stable matrix}, \tag{139}$$

where C is the matrix obtained from $\bar{C}$ by deleting the first row and column. Similarly, B is *qualitatively D-stable* under (137) and (138) if

$$\bar{C} \in S_{\bar{B}} \Rightarrow C \text{ is a } D\text{-stable matrix}. \tag{139'}$$

LEMMA 10 (Quirk, 1970) Let $\bar{B}$ and B be the sign-symmetric matrices defined above. If B is qualitatively stable under (137) and (138), then

$$\bar{C} \in S_{\bar{B}} \Rightarrow C \text{ is negative quasi-definite}. \tag{140}$$

PROOF $\bar{C} + \bar{C}^{\mathrm{T}}$ satisfies

$$\sum_{i=0}^{n} (c_{ij} + c_{ji}) = 0 \qquad \text{for} \quad j = 0, 1, \ldots, n,$$
$$\sum_{j=0}^{n} (c_{ij} + c_{ji}) = 0 \qquad \text{for} \quad i = 0, 1, \ldots, n,$$
$$\operatorname{sgn}(c_{ij} + c_{ji}) = \operatorname{sgn} c_{ij}.$$

Thus, in view of (139)

$$\bar{C} \in S_{\bar{B}} \Rightarrow \bar{C} + \bar{C}^{\mathrm{T}} \in S_{\bar{B}} \Rightarrow C + C^{\mathrm{T}} \text{ is a stable matrix,}$$

i.e., $x^{\mathrm{T}}(C + C^{\mathrm{T}})x < 0$ for any nonzero $x \in R^n$. Q.E.D.

THEOREM 33 (Quirk, 1970) Let $\bar{B}$ and B be the sign-symmetric matrices defined above. If B contains any negative off-diagonal entries, B is not qualitatively stable under (137) and (138).

PROOF Suppose that B is qualitatively stable under (137) and (138). Then, by Lemma 10, (140) holds; viz., $\Lambda \equiv C + C^{\mathrm{T}}$ is negative definite. Assume a pair of goods i, j exhibit complementarity in B and consider the principal submatrix of order 2 of $\Lambda = [\gamma_{ij}]$ involving the ith and jth rows and columns. Hence

$$\operatorname{sgn} \gamma_{ij} = \operatorname{sgn} \gamma_{ji} < 0.$$

By the corollary to Theorem 35 in Section 2.5, Λ is an NP-matrix, so that

$$\gamma_{ii} < 0, \qquad \gamma_{jj} < 0, \qquad \gamma_{ii}\gamma_{jj} - \gamma_{ij}^2 > 0.$$

Let $\alpha_i \equiv \gamma_{ii} + \gamma_{ij} < 0$ and $\alpha_j \equiv \gamma_{ij} + \gamma_{jj} < 0$. Consider $\bar{E} \in Q_{\bar{B}}$, where all entries of $\bar{E} = [e_{ij}]$ are identical to those of $\bar{\Lambda} \equiv \bar{C} + \bar{C}^{\mathrm{T}}$ except that

$$e_{ii} = \frac{\alpha_i^2}{\alpha_i + \alpha_j} + \delta, \qquad e_{jj} = \frac{\alpha_j^2}{\alpha_i + \alpha_j} + \delta, \qquad e_{ij}\,(= e_{ji}) = \frac{\alpha_i\alpha_j}{\alpha_i + \alpha_j} - \delta,$$

where δ is such a positive scalar that $e_{ii} < 0$, $e_{jj} < 0$, $e_{ij} = e_{ji} < 0$. Here $e_{ii} + e_{ij} = \alpha_i$ and $e_{ij} + e_{jj} = \alpha_j$. Thus clearly $\bar{E} \in S_{\bar{B}}$. But we get

$$e_{ii}e_{jj} - e_{ij}^2 = \delta(\alpha_i + \alpha_j) < 0,$$

so that $\bar{E}$ is not an NP-matrix and consequently B is not qualitatively stable under (137) and (138). Q.E.D.

COROLLARY Let $\bar{B}$ and B be the sign-symmetric matrices defined above. Then B is qualitatively stable (and qualitatively D-stable) under (137) and (138) only if B is a weak gross substitute matrix.

PROOF D-stability follows from Lemma 10 since any negative quasi-definite matrix is D-stable, by virtue of Theorem 39′ in Section 2.5. Q.E.D.

Theorem 33 implies that, "if one considers substitutability and complementarity to be symmetric relations, the presence of complementarity precludes the demonstration of the stability of equilibrium, unless some information of a quantitative nature is also available" (Mukherji, 1972).

Now we turn to the global stability of equilibrium in a weak gross substitute trading system.

Assume that price change of each good is proportional to its excess demand for any relevant prices:

$$dp_i/dt = s_i D_i(p) \qquad \text{for} \quad i = 0, 1, \ldots, n, \tag{141}$$

where s_i is a positive constant and $p \equiv (p_0, p_1, \ldots, p_n)$. (141) is a special case of (22) in Section 4.2. Choosing the units of measurement of all goods so that $s_i = 1$ for all i, we reduce (141) to

$$\dot{p}_i = D_i(p) \qquad \text{for} \quad i = 0, 1, \ldots, n, \tag{141'}$$

where we adopt the convention that $\dot{x}$ denotes dx/dt for an arbitrary x. Define

$$V \equiv \tfrac{1}{2} \sum_{i \in K} D_i^2, \tag{142}$$

where $K \equiv \{i : D_i(p) > 0\}$. We shall show that V in (142) is a Lyapunov function with respect to (141′), provided each D_i is homogeneous of degree zero in p.

Differentiation of V in (142) with respect to t yields, in view of (141′),

$$\dot{V} = \sum_{i \in K} \sum_{j=0}^{n} D_i b_{ij} D_j, \tag{143}$$

where b_{ij} denotes $\partial D_i/\partial p_j$. We assume $b_{ij} \geqq 0$ for all $i \neq j$ in an arbitrary vicinity of equilibrium. Hence

$$\sum_{i \in K} \sum_{j \notin K} D_i b_{ij} D_j \leqq 0. \tag{144}$$

Differentiating the Walras law (40) with respect to p, we have

$$\sum_{i \in K} p_i b_{ij} = -\sum_{i \notin K} p_i b_{ij} - D_j \qquad \text{for} \quad j = 0, 1, \ldots, n.$$

Take $b_{ij} \geqq 0$, $D_j > 0$ (for $j \in K$), and $p_i > 0$ (for all i) into account, and we obtain from the above equation

$$\sum_{i \in K} p_i b_{ij} < 0 \qquad \text{for} \quad j \in K. \tag{145}$$

Thus, $G \equiv [b_{ij}]$ $(i, j \in K)$ has a dominant diagonal. Further, by assuming the homogeneity of degree zero of D_i in all prices, we have (136), from which it follows that

$$\sum_{j \in K} b_{ij} p_j = -\sum_{j \notin K} b_{ij} p_j \leqq 0 \qquad \text{for} \quad i \in K. \tag{146}$$

Combining (145) and (146),

$$g^{\mathrm{T}} G^* < \theta, \tag{147}$$

where g^{T} is the row vector consisting of all p_i for $i \in K$, and $G^* \equiv (G + G^{\mathrm{T}})/2$. Also from (147) one gets

$$p_i b_{ii} < -\sum_{j \in K, j \neq i} \tfrac{1}{2} p_j (b_{ij} + b_{ji}) \leqq 0 \qquad \text{for} \quad i \in K,$$

and hence $b_{ii} < 0$ for $i \in K$. Thus G^* is a real symmetric matrix having a negative dominant diagonal. In view of Theorem 22′ in Section 1.3 and of Theorem 31 in Section 2.5, all the eigenvalues of G^* are negative; i.e., G^* is negative definite. Therefore, considering that $q^{\mathrm{T}} G q = q^{\mathrm{T}} G^{\mathrm{T}} q$, we have

$$q^{\mathrm{T}}Gq = \tfrac{1}{2}(q^{\mathrm{T}}Gq + q^{\mathrm{T}}Gq) = q^{\mathrm{T}}G^*q < 0 \qquad \text{for} \quad q \neq \theta; \tag{148}$$

viz., G is negative quasi-definite. In view of (143), (144), and (148), we know

$$\dot{V} < 0 \qquad \text{for any} \quad D_i > 0. \tag{149}$$

Then by the Walras law, (149) entails the convergence of all D_i to zero as t goes to infinity. But V is positive definite. Thus V is a Lyapunov function.

The above analysis is summarized in

THEOREM 34 (McKenzie, 1960) Postulate that each excess demand function is homogeneous of degree zero in all prices. If price changes are proportional to excess demands in the weak gross substitute case, the equilibrium of an exchange system is stable in the large.

A result parallel to Theorem 34 was originally obtained by Arrow *et al.* (1959), including the verification of the unique existence of a positive equilibrium price vector, though in the strong gross substitute case. (Refer to Negishi (1962).)

Lastly we state without proof one theorem of global stability closely related to Theorem 28 of local stability.

THEOREM 35 (Arrow *et al.*, 1959) Let $B = [b_{ij}]$ be "the excess demand matrix" corresponding to an exchange system, where b_{ij} stands for denotes that in Definition 3 in Section 4.2 but evaluated at arbitrary positive prices. If B has always negative diagonal entries and a row-dominant diagonal for a fixed set of positive constants, then the exchange system is stable in the large.

The reader may refer to Uzawa (1961) for a generalization of the Arrow, Block, and Hurwicz (1959) result. A unified treatment of the local and global stability problems of the so-called tâtonnement process we have been concerned with is found in Arrow and Hahn (1971, Chapters 11 and 12).

EXERCISES

1. Prove the corollary to Theorem 13.

2. Prove Lemma 1*.

3. Prove Theorem 20′.

4. Utilizing Theorem 20, verify the following proposition: A shift of demand from all other goods onto good k raises the price of k and lowers the prices of all other goods in terms of k. (Refer to Mundell (1965).)

5. Prove Lemma 6.

6. Prove Proposition 10′.

7. Prove Proposition 11′.

8. Prove Theorem 27.

9. Prove Lemma 9.

10. Show that a Morishima matrix is stable if and only if it has a quasi-dominant diagonal. (Refer to Mukherji (1972).)

REFERENCES AND FURTHER READING

Arrow, K. J., Block, H. D., and Hurwicz, L. (1959). "On the Stability of Competitive Equilibrium, II," *Econometrica* **27**, 82–109.

Arrow, K. J., and Hahn, F. H. (1971). *General Competitive Analysis*. Holden-Day, San Francisco, California.

Arrow, K. J., and Hurwicz, L. (1958). "On the Stability of Competitive Equilibrium, I," *Econometrica* **26**, 522–552.

Burmeister, E., and Dobell, A. R. (1970). *Mathematical Models of Economic Growth*. Macmillan, New York.

Chitre, V. (1974). "A Note on the Three Hicksian Laws of Comparative Statics for the Gross Substitute Case," *Journal of Economic Theory* **8**, 397–400.

Debreu, G., and Herstein, I. N. (1953). "Nonnegative Square Matrices," *Econometrica* **21**, 596–607.

Fisher, F. M. (1962). "An Alternative Proof and Extension of Solow's Theorem on Nonnegative Square Matrices," *Econometrica* **30**, 349–350.

Gale, D. (1960). *The Theory of Linear Economic Models*. McGraw-Hill, New York.

Gantmacher, F. R. (1960). *The Theory of Matrices* (English translation), Vol. II. Chelsea, New York.

Hahn, F. H. (1958). "Gross Substitutes and the Dynamic Stability of General Equilibrium," *Econometrica* **26**, 169–170.

Hicks, J. R. (1939). *Value and Capital*. Oxford Univ. Press, London and New York.

Horwich, G., and Samuelson, P. A. (eds.) (1974). *Trade, Stability, and Macroeconomics*. Academic Press, New York.

Jorgenson, D. W. (1960). "A Dual Stability Theorem," *Econometrica* **28**, 892–899.

Karlin, S. (1959). *Mathematical Methods and Theory in Games, Programming and Economics*, Vol. I. Addison-Wesley, Reading, Massachusetts.

Kennedy, C. (1970). "The Stability of the 'Morishima System'," *Review of Economic Studies* **37**, 173–175.

Klein, E. (1973). *Mathaemtical Methods in Theoretical Economics*. Academic Press, New York.

Lancaster, K. (1968). *Mathematical Economics*. Macmillan, New York.

Leontief, W. W. (1951). *The Structure of American Economy, 1919–39*. Oxford Univ. Press, London and New York.

Leontief, W. W. (1953). "Dynamic Analysis," in *Studies in the Structure of the American Economy* (W. W. Leontief *et al.*, eds.), pp. 53–90. Oxford Univ. Press, London and New York.

McKenzie, L. W. (1960). "Matrices with Dominant Diagonals and Economic Theory," in *Mathematical Methods in the Social Sciences 1959* (K. J. Arrow, S. Karlin, and P. Suppes, eds.), pp. 47–62. Stanford Univ. Press, Stanford, California.

Marx, K. (1867). *Das Kapital*, Vol. I; (1893). Vol. II; (1894). Vol. III. Verlag von Otto Meissner, Hamburg. [English translation, (1967). *Capital*, International Publ., New York.]

Metzler, L. A. (1945). "Stability of Multiple Markets: The Hicks Conditions," *Econometrica* **13**, 277–292; (1968), in *Readings in Mathematical Economics* (P. Newman, ed.), Vol. I. Johns Hopkins Press, Baltimore, Maryland.
Metzler, L. A. (1950). "A Multiple-Region Theory of Income and Trade," *Econometrica* **18**, 329–354.
Metzler, L. A. (1951). "A Multiple-Country Theory of Income Transfers," *Journal of Political Economy* **59**, 14–29.
Morishima, M. (1952). "On the Laws of Change of the Price-System in an Economy Which Contains Complementary Commodities," *Osaka Economic Papers* **1**, 101–113.
Morishima, M. (1964). *Equilibrium Stability and Growth.* Oxford Univ. Press, London and New York.
Morishima, M. (1970). "A Generalization of the Gross Substitute System," *Review of Economic Studies* **37**, 177–186.
Morishima, M. (1973). *Marx's Economics.* Cambridge Univ. Press, London and New York.
Morishima, M. (1974). "Marx in the Light of Modern Economic Theory," *Econometrica* **42**, 611–632.
Morishima, M., and Fujimoto, T. (1974). "The Frobenius Theorem, Its Solow–Samuelson Extension and the Kuhn–Tucker Theorem," *Journal of Mathematical Economics* **1**, 199–205.
Morishima, M., and Nosse, T. (1972). "Input–Output Analysis of the Effectiveness of Fiscal Policies for the United Kingdom, 1954," in *The Working of Econometric Models* (M. Morishima *et al.*, eds.), pp. 71–143. Cambridge Univ. Press, London and New York.
Mosak, J. L. (1944). *General Equilibrium Theory in International Trade.* Principia Press, Bloomington, Illinois.
Mukherji, A. (1972). "On Complementarity and Stability," *Journal of Economic Theory* **4**, 442–457.
Mundell, R. A. (1965). "The Homogeneity Postulate and the Laws of Comparative Statics in the Walrasian and Metzleric Systems," *Econometrica* **33**, 349–356.
Murata, Y. (1972). "An Alternative Proof of the Frobenius Theorem," *Journal of Economic Theory* **5**, 285–291.
Negishi, T. (1958). "A Note on the Stability of an Economy Where All Goods Are Gross Substitutes," *Econometrica* **26**, 445–447.
Negishi, T. (1962). "The Stability of a Competitive Economy: A Survey Article," *Econometrica* **30**, 635–669.
Nikaido, H. (1968). *Convex Structures and Economic Theory.* Academic Press, New York.
Okishio, N. (1963). "A Mathematical Note on Marxian Theorems," *Weltwirtschaftliches Archiv* **91**, 287–299.
Quirk, J. (1970). "Complementarity and Stability of Equilibrium," *American Economic Review* **60**, 358–363.
Quirk, J., and Saposnik, R. (1968). *Introduction to General Equilibrium Theory and Welfare Economics.* McGraw-Hill, New York.
Samuelson, P. A. (1947). *Foundations of Economic Analysis.* Harvard Univ. Press, Cambridge, Massachusetts.
Samuelson, P. A. (1960). "An Extension of LeChatelier Principle," *Econometrica* **28**, 368–379.
Sato, R. (1970). "A Further Note on a Difference Equation Recurring in Growth Theory," *Journal of Economic Theory* **2**, 95–102.
Sato, R. (1972). "The Stability of the Competitive System Which Contains Gross Complementary Goods," *Review of Economic Studies* **39**, 495–499.
Seneta, E. (1973). *Non-Negative Matrices.* Allen and Unwin, London.

Seton, F. (1957). "The Transformation Problem," *Review of Economic Studies* **24**, 149–160.

Solow, R. M. (1952). "On the Structure of Linear Models," *Econometrica* **20**, 29–46.

Solow, R. M. (1959). "Competitive Valuation in a Dynamic Input–Output System," *Econometrica* **27**, 30–53.

Solow, R. M., and Samuelson, P. A. (1953). "Balanced Growth under Constant Returns to Scale," *Econometrica* **21**, 412–424.

Tsukui, J. (1961). "On a Theorem of Relative Stability," *International Economic Review* **2**, 229–230.

Uzawa, H. (1961). "The Stability of Dynamic Processes," *Econometrica* **29**, 617–631.

Walras, L. (1954). *Elements of Pure Economics* (English translation). Irwin, Homewood.

von Weizsäcker, C. C., and Samuelson, P. A. (1971). "A New Labor Theory of Value for Rational Planning through Use of the Bourgeois Profit Rate," *Proc. Nat. Acad. Sci. U.S.* **68**, 1192–1194.

Wolfstetter, E. (1973). "Surplus Labour, Synchronised Labour Costs and Marx's Labour Theory of Value," *Economic Journal* **83**, 787–809.

Part II

OPTIMIZATION METHODS FOR ECONOMIC SYSTEMS

Chapter 5

Preliminary Mathematical Concepts

5.1 Normed Spaces and Inner Product Spaces

DEFINITION 1 A *normed (vector) space* is a vector space X on which a real-valued transformation is defined such that it assigns to each element $x \in X$ a real number $\|x\|$ called the *norm* of x, which satisfies the following axioms:

(1) $\|x\| \geqq 0$ for all $x \in X$, where equality holds if and only if $x = \theta$.

(2) $\|x + y\| \leqq \|x\| + \|y\|$ for each $x, y \in X$ (triangle inequality).

(3) $\|ax\| = |a| \, \|x\|$ for all $x \in X$ and scalar a, where $|a|$ stands for the modulus of a, i.e., for $a = \alpha + i\beta$ and $\bar{a} = \alpha - i\beta$, $|a|^2 = a\bar{a} = \alpha^2 + \beta^2$.

Example 1 Let X be an n-space whose element is represented by $x = \{x_1, \ldots, x_n\}$. Then $\|x\|$ defined as

$$\|x\| = \max_{1 \leqq i \leqq n} |x_i| \qquad \text{or} \qquad \|x\| = \sum_{i=1}^{n} |x_i|$$

satisfies the above axioms for norm. We inspect only axiom (2) for the first case:

$$\|x + y\| = \max_i |x_i + y_i| = |x_p + y_p| \leqq |x_p| + |y_p|$$

$$\leqq \max_i |x_i| + \max_i |y_i| = \|x\| + \|y\|.$$

Example 2 The set $C[a,b]$ with the norm of an element x in $C[a,b]$ defined as

$$\|x\| = \max_{a \leqq t \leqq b} |x(t)|,$$

constitutes a normed space since the proposed norm satisfies the required axioms; i.e., for $x, y \in C[a,b]$ and any real scalar α,

$$\|x\| = \max_t |x(t)| \geqq 0 \qquad \text{where equality holds if and only if } x = \theta;$$

$$\|x + y\| = \max_t |x(t) + y(t)| \leqq \max_t |x(t)| + \max_t |y(t)| = \|x\| + \|y\|;$$

$$\|\alpha x\| = \max_t |\alpha x(t)| = |\alpha| \max_t |x(t)|.$$

Example 3 The real n-space R^n with the norm of an element $x = \{\xi_1, \xi_2, \ldots, \xi_n\}$ in R^n defined as

$$\|x\| = \left(\sum_{i=1}^{n} \xi_i^2\right)^{1/2} \qquad \text{(Euclidean norm)}$$

constitutes a normed space called *Euclidean* n-space, denoted E^n, since the proposed norm satisfies the required axioms (1) and (3) obviously and (2) with the following proof: For $x = \{\xi_1, \ldots, \xi_n\}$ and $y = \{\eta_1, \ldots, \eta_n\}$ in R^n,

$$\begin{aligned} \|x + y\|^2 &= \sum(\xi_i + \eta_i)^2 = \sum\xi_i^2 + 2\sum\xi_i\eta_i + \sum\eta_i^2 \\ &= \|x\|^2 + 2\sum\xi_i\eta_i + \|y\|^2. \\ (\|x\| + \|y\|)^2 &= \|x\|^2 + 2\,\|x\|\,\|y\| + \|y\|^2 \\ &= \|x\|^2 + 2((\sum\xi_i^2)(\sum\eta_i^2))^{1/2} + \|y\|^2. \end{aligned}$$

By the Cauchy–Schwarz inequality for real numbers,

$$(\sum\xi_i\eta_i)^2 \leqq (\sum\xi_i^2)(\sum\eta_i^2).$$

Thus

$$\|x + y\| \leqq \|x\| + \|y\|.$$

THEOREM 1 Axioms (2) and (3) imply

$$\|x - y\| \leqq \|x\| + \|y\|. \tag{4}$$

PROOF $\|x + (-y)\| \leqq \|x\| + \|-y\| = \|x\| + |-1|\,\|y\|$. Q.E.D.

THEOREM 2 In a normed space X

$$\|x\| - \|y\| \leqq \|x - y\| \qquad \text{for each} \quad x, y \in X. \tag{5}$$

PROOF $\|x\| - \|y\| = \|x - y + y\| - \|y\| \leqq \|x - y\| + \|y\| - \|y\|$. Q.E.D.

COROLLARY $\|w - u\| \leqq \|w - v\| + \|v - u\|$.

PROOF Put $x = w - u$ and $y = v - u$ in (5). Q.E.D.

DEFINITION 2 An *inner product space* is a vector space X together with an *inner product* defined on $X \times X$ as follows: Corresponding to each pair of vectors x, y in X, the inner product $(x|y)$ of x and y is a scalar satisfying the four axioms:

(i) $(x|y) = \overline{(y|x)}$, where $\overline{(y|x)}$ represents the complex conjugate of $(y|x)$.
(ii) $(x + y|z) = (x|z) + (y|z)$ for $z \in X$.
(iii) $(ax|y) = a(x|y)$ for scalar a.
(iv) $(x|x) \geqq 0$, where equality holds if and only if $x = \theta$.

Remark From the above axioms, we derive:

(v) $(x|y + z) = \overline{(y + z|x)} = \overline{(y|x)} + \overline{(z|x)} = (x|y) + (x|z)$,
(vi) $(x|ay) = \overline{(ay|x)} = \bar{a}\overline{(y|x)} = \bar{a}(x|y)$.

THEOREM 3 In an inner product space, $(x|y) = 0$ for all $y \in X$ implies $x = \theta$.

PROOF Put $y = x$. Then $(x|x) = 0$. By axiom (iv), $x = \theta$. Q.E.D.

Example 1 *Unitary* n-space, denoted U^n, is the n-space C^n over the complex field together with the inner product defined as follows: For $x = \{\xi_1, \ldots, \xi_n\}$, $y = \{\eta_1, \ldots, \eta_n\} \in C^n$,

$$(x|y) = \sum_{k=1}^{n} \xi_k \bar{\eta}_k, \qquad (y|x) = \sum_{k=1}^{n} \bar{\xi}_k \eta_k, \qquad (x|x) = \sum_{k=1}^{n} \xi_k \bar{\xi}_k.$$

Let $\xi_k = \alpha_k + i\beta_k$, $\bar{\xi}_k = \alpha_k - i\beta_k$, $\eta_k = \sigma_k + i\delta_k$, and $\bar{\eta}_k = \sigma_k - i\delta_k$. The inner product defined above is found to be compatible with the required axioms. We shall verify this only for axiom (i). By substitutions, we get

$$(x|y) = \sum(\alpha\sigma + \beta\delta) + i\sum(\beta\sigma - \alpha\delta), \quad (y|x) = \sum(\alpha\sigma + \beta\delta) - i\sum(\beta\sigma - \alpha\delta)$$

where the summation varies from 1 to n and the subscripts are omitted. Hence $(x|y) = \overline{(y|x)}$. Note that Euclidean n-space E^n is a special case of U^n, where the relevant field is real.

Example 2 Let A be a real symmetric positive definite matrix of order n. For any column vectors x, y in real n-space R^n, define an inner product

$$(x|y) = x^{\mathrm{T}}Ay,$$

where superscript T indicates transpose. Then we see that the proposed inner product satisfies the required axioms: For x, y, $z \in R^n$ and any real scalar a,

$$(x|y) = x^{\mathrm{T}}Ay = y^{\mathrm{T}}A^{\mathrm{T}}x = y^{\mathrm{T}}Ax = (y|x);$$
$$(x + y|z) = (x^{\mathrm{T}} + y^{\mathrm{T}})Az = x^{\mathrm{T}}Az + y^{\mathrm{T}}Az = (x|z) + (y|z);$$
$$(ax|y) = ax^{\mathrm{T}}Ay = a(x|y);$$
$$(x|x) = x^{\mathrm{T}}Ax \begin{cases} > 0 & \text{for} \quad x \neq \theta, \\ = 0 & \text{if and only if} \quad x = \theta. \end{cases}$$

We shall show that the quantity $(x|x)^{1/2}$ plays the role of norm $\|x\|$

in any inner product space, and thereby any inner product space becomes a normed space. Axioms (1) and (3) in the definition of a norm are apparently satisfied by the quantity. The following lemma will facilitate verifying the rest.

LEMMA 1 (*the Cauchy–Schwarz inequality*) In an inner product space X

$$|(x|y)| \leqq \|x\|\|y\| \qquad \text{for} \quad x, y \in X, \tag{6}$$

where equality holds if and only if $x = ay$ for scalar a or $y = \theta$.

PROOF (a) If $x = ay$, then, since $|(x|y)|^2 = (x|y)\overline{(x|y)} = (x|y)(y|x)$, we know that

$$|(ay|y)| = ((ay|y)(y|ay))^{1/2} = (a \cdot \bar{a})^{1/2}(y|y) = |a| \, \|y\|^2,$$

and $\|ay\| \, \|y\| = |a| \, \|y\|^2$.

(b) If $y = \theta$, inequality (6) above holds trivially.

(c) Assume $y \neq \theta$. For any scalar b,

$$\begin{aligned} 0 \leqq (x + by|x + by) &= (x|x + by) + (by|x + by) \\ &= (x|x) + (x|by) + (by|x) + (by|by) \\ &= \|x\|^2 + \bar{b}(x|y) + b(y|x) + \bar{b} \cdot b(y|y). \end{aligned}$$

Set $b = -(x|y)/(y|y)$. Then $\bar{b} = -(y|x)/(y|y)$. Thus,

$$0 \leqq \|x\|^2 - (x|y)(y|x)/(y|y) = \|x\|^2 - |(x|y)|^2/\|y\|^2.$$

Therefore, $|(x|y)| \leqq \|x\|\|y\|$. Q.E.D.

THEOREM 4 In an inner product space X, the transformation $\|x\| = (x|x)^{1/2}$ satisfies axiom (2) (triangle inequality) of norm.

PROOF For any $x, y \in X$,

$$\|x + y\|^2 = (x + y|x + y) = (x|x) + (x|y) + (y|x) + (y|y).$$

Since $(x|y) + (y|x) = 2 \operatorname{Re}(x|y) \leqq 2|(x|y)|$, we have

$$\begin{aligned} \|x + y\|^2 &\leqq \|x\|^2 + 2|(x|y)| + \|y\|^2 \\ &\leqq \|x\|^2 + 2\|x\| \, \|y\| + \|y\|^2 \\ &= (\|x\| + \|y\|)^2. \qquad \text{Q.E.D.} \end{aligned}$$

THEOREM 5 In an inner product space X, for $x, y \in X$,

$$\|x - y\|^2 = \|x\|^2 + \|y\|^2 - (x|y) - (y|x).$$

PROOF $\|x - y\|^2 = (x - y|x - y) = (x|x) - (x|y) - (y|x) + (y|y).$

Q.E.D.

Example In Euclidean space E^n, for any elements $x, y \in E^n$, $x \neq \theta$, $y \neq \theta$, $\|x\|^2 = (x|x) = \sum_k \xi_k^2$, and $\|x - y\|^2 = \sum_k (\xi_k - \eta_k)^2$, where x

$= \{\xi_1, \ldots, \xi_n\}$, $y = \{\eta_1, \ldots, \eta_n\}$. Thus, $||x||$ means the "length" of x and $||x - y||$ the "distance" between x and y. (See the illustration in Fig. 1 for E^2 space.)

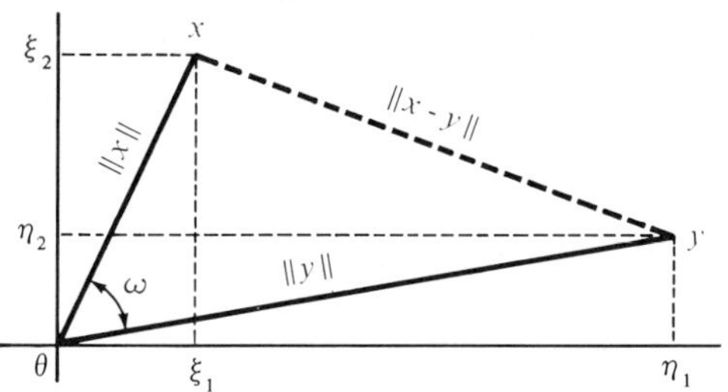

FIGURE 1. E^2 space.

Taking Theorem 5 and

$$||x - y||^2 = ||x||^2 + ||y||^2 - 2||x|| \, ||y|| \cos \omega$$

into consideration, we have in a Euclidean space

$$\cos \omega = \frac{(x|y)}{||x|| ||y||} \tag{7}$$

since $(x|y) = (y|x)$. Then we observe $(x|y) > 0$, $= 0$, or < 0, according as the angle between x and y is less than, equal to, or larger than 90 degrees, respectively.

THEOREM 6 In Euclidean n-space E^n, for $x, y \in E^n$,

$$x \geqq y \Leftrightarrow (x|m) \geqq (y|m) \qquad \text{for} \quad m \geqq \theta, \quad m \in E^n.$$

PROOF Let $x = \{\xi_1, \ldots, \xi_n\}$, $y = \{\eta_1, \ldots, \eta_n\}$, and $m = \{\mu_1, \ldots, \mu_n\}$.

Necessity $\xi_i \geqq \eta_i \Rightarrow \xi_i\mu_i \geqq \eta_i\mu_i$ for $\mu_i \geqq 0$, $i = 1, \ldots, n$;

$$\Rightarrow \sum \xi_i\mu_i \geqq \sum \eta_i\mu_i \Rightarrow (x|m) \geqq (y|m) \quad \text{for} \quad m \geqq 0.$$

Sufficiency $(x|m) \geqq (y|m)$ for $m \geqq 0$;

$$\Rightarrow (x|u_i) \geqq (y|u_i) \qquad \text{for } u_i \text{, the } i\text{th unit vector;}$$

$$\Rightarrow \xi_i \geqq \eta_i \qquad \text{for} \quad i = 1, \ldots, n. \quad \text{Q.E.D.}$$

THEOREM 7 (*the parallelogram law*) In an inner product space X, for any $x, y \in X$,

$$||x + y||^2 + ||x - y||^2 = 2||x||^2 + 2||y||^2. \tag{8}$$

PROOF

$$||x + y||^2 = (x + y|x + y) = ||x||^2 + (x|y) + (y|x) + ||y||^2,$$

and

$$\|x - y\|^2 = (x - y \,|\, x - y) = \|x\|^2 - (x \,|\, y) - (y \,|\, x) + \|y\|^2.$$

The addition of these equations yields statement (8). Q.E.D.

DEFINITION 3 In an inner product space X, elements $x, y \in X$ are said to be *orthonormal* to each other if $(x \,|\, y) = 0$, $(x \,|\, x) = 1$, and $(y \,|\, y) = 1$.

DEFINITION 4 Let $\{e_1, \ldots, e_r\}$ be a basis for subspace M of an inner product space X. If

$$(e_i \,|\, e_j) = \begin{cases} 0 & \text{for} \quad i \neq j, \\ 1 & \text{for} \quad i = j, \end{cases}$$

then the basis is called an *orthonormal basis* of M.

THEOREM 8 Let $\{x_1, \ldots, x_r\}$ be a basis for subspace M of an inner product space X. Then it can be converted to an orthonormal basis of M.

PROOF First, define $e_1 = x_1/\|x_1\|$. Then

$$(e_1 \,|\, e_1) = (1/\|x_1\|)^2 \, (x_1 \,|\, x_1) = 1.$$

Secondly, set $v_2 = x_2 - (x_2 \,|\, e_1)e_1$. Clearly $(v_2 \,|\, e_1) = 0$. By assumption e_1 and x_2 are linearly independent, and hence v_2 cannot be a null vector. Thus we define $e_2 = v_2/\|v_2\|$ and set $v_3 = x_3 - (x_3 \,|\, e_1)e_1 - (x_3 \,|\, e_2)e_2$. Clearly, $(v_3 \,|\, e_1) = 0$ and $(v_3 \,|\, e_2) = 0$. Since e_1, e_2, and x_3 are linearly independent, $v_3 \neq \theta$. Thus we define $e_3 = v_3/\|v_3\|$. Proceeding in this way, we define in general

$$e_j = v_j/\|v_j\| \qquad \text{for} \quad j = 2, 3, \ldots, r,$$

where $v_j = x_j - \sum_{i=1}^{j-1} (x_j \,|\, e_i)e_i \neq \theta$ since $e_1, e_2, \ldots, e_{j-1}$, and x_j are linearly independent. Then

$$(e_j \,|\, e_j) = (1/\|v_j\|)^2 (v_j \,|\, v_j) = 1 \qquad \text{for} \quad j = 2, 3, \ldots, r,$$

and

$$\begin{aligned} (v_j \,|\, e_h) &= (x_j \,|\, e_h) - \sum_{i=1}^{j-1} (x_j \,|\, e_i)(e_i \,|\, e_h) \\ &= - \sum_{i \neq h}^{j-1} (x_j \,|\, e_i)(v_i \,|\, e_h)/\|v_i\| \\ &= 0 \qquad \text{for} \quad h < j = 2, 3, \ldots, r \end{aligned}$$

since we know already $(v_2 \,|\, e_1) = (v_3 \,|\, e_1) = (v_3 \,|\, e_2) = 0$. Q.E.D.

The above procedure by which we obtain an orthonormal basis $\{e_1, \ldots, e_r\}$ is called the *Gram–Schmidt procedure*.

We shall see a relationship between a set of linearly independent vectors and nonsingularity of a matrix.

DEFINITION 5 Let $y_1, y_2, \ldots, y_n$ be elements of an inner product space; then we call the following $n \times n$ matrix the *Gram matrix* of $y_1, \ldots, y_n$:

$$G(y_1, y_2, \ldots, y_n) = \begin{bmatrix} (y_1|y_1) & (y_1|y_2) & \cdots & (y_1|y_n) \\ (y_2|y_1) & (y_2|y_2) & \cdots & (y_2|y_n) \\ \vdots & \vdots & & \vdots \\ (y_n|y_1) & (y_n|y_2) & \cdots & (y_n|y_n) \end{bmatrix}. \tag{9}$$

The determinant of the Gram matrix, denoted $g(y_1, \ldots, y_n)$, is referred to as the *Gram determinant.*

If $y_1, \ldots, y_n$ are all real vectors, the Gram matrix will be a symmetric matrix.

THEOREM 9 The Gram determinant $g(y_1, \ldots, y_n)$ does not vanish if and only if the vectors $y_1, \ldots, y_n$ are linearly independent.

PROOF An equivalent statement is that $g(y_1, \ldots, y_n) = 0$ if and only if $y_1, \ldots, y_n$ are linearly dependent. (i) Suppose that the y_i are linearly dependent, i.e., that there are constants a_i, not all zero, such that $\sum_{i=1}^n a_i y_i = \theta$. Then the rows (or columns) in the Gram determinant have a corresponding linear dependency and hence the determinant becomes nil. (ii) Suppose that the Gram determinant is zero, or equivalently that there is a linear dependency among its rows (and its columns). Then there are constants a_i, not all zero, such that

$$\sum_{i=1}^n a_i(y_i|y_j) = 0 \qquad \text{for all} \quad j = 1, \ldots, n,$$

which implies $(\sum_i a_i y_i | y_j) = 0$ for all j, whence

$$\sum_{j=1}^n \bar{a}_j\Big(\sum_i a_i y_i \,\Big|\, y_j\Big) = \Big(\sum_i a_i y_i \,\Big|\, \sum_j a_j y_j\Big) = \Big\|\sum_i a_i y_i\Big\|^2 = 0.$$

Thus $\sum_{i=1}^n a_i y_i = \theta$, i.e., $y_1, y_2, \ldots, y_n$ are linearly dependent. Q.E.D.

5.2 Closedness and Continuity

DEFINITION 6 Let S be a subset of a normed space X. Given $s \in S$ and $\delta > 0$, the set $U(s; \delta) \equiv \{x: x \in X, \|x - s\| < \delta\}$ is called a *sphere* (or *neighborhood*) centered at s with radius δ.

DEFINITION 7 Let S be a subset of a normed space X. The point $s \in S$ is said to be an *interior point* of S if there is a positive scalar δ for which a sphere $U(s; \delta)$ is contained in S. The collection of all interior points of S is called the *interior* of S and is denoted $\mathring{S}$.

DEFINITION 8 A set S in a normed space X is said to be *open* if $\mathring{S} = S$.

Examples (1) The entire normed space X is an open set. (2) The unit sphere $\{x: x \in X, \|x\| < 1\}$ is an open set.

THEOREM 10 The union of an arbitrary collection of open sets is open.

PROOF Let x be an element of $\tilde{S} \equiv \bigcup_{i \in J} S_i$, where S_i is an open set for each $i \in J$ (J = an arbitrary collection of indices). x belongs to at least one of these S's, say $x \in S_j$. Then there is a sphere $U(x; \delta)$ in S_j and hence in $\tilde{S}$. Thus x is an interior point of $\tilde{S}$. Q.E.D.

THEOREM 11 The intersection of a *finite* number of open sets is open.

PROOF Let x be an element of $\hat{S} \equiv \bigcap_{i=1}^{n} S_i$, where S_i is an open set for each i ($i = 1, \ldots, n$). Then there is a sphere centered at x, $U_i(x; \delta) \equiv \{y : \|y - x\| < \delta, \delta > 0\}$ in S_i for each i. The smallest of these spheres is contained in $\hat{S}$. Q.E.D.

The finiteness in Theorem 11 is necessary because, for example, if $a_i = a - (1/i)$, $b_i = b + (1/i)$ (where a, b, i are real scalars and $a < b$), then the intersection of an infinite collection of open intervals (a_i, b_i) is equal to the closed interval $[a, b]$.

DEFINITION 9 Let S be a subset of a normed space X. A point $x \in X$ is said to be an *adherent point* (or a *closure point*) of S if for any $\delta > 0$ there exists $s \in S$ such that $\|x - s\| < \delta$, or equivalently if every sphere centered at x contains a point of S. The collection of all adherent points of S is called the *closure* of S and is denoted $\bar{S}$. It is clear that $S \subset \bar{S}$.

DEFINITION 10 A set S in a normed space X is said to be *closed* if $S = \bar{S}$.

Examples (1) A single point is a closed set. (2) The entire normed space X is a closed set (as well as an open set). (3) The unit sphere $\{x : \|x\| \leqq 1\}$ is a closed set.

DEFINITION 11 Let A be a subset of a set B. The set $\{x: x \in B, x \notin A\}$ is said to be the *complement* of A in B, and denoted $B \setminus A$. If B is the entire space, it will be called simply the complement of A and is denoted A^c.

THEOREM 12 (i) The complement of an open set S in a normed space X is a closed set. (ii) Conversely, if S is closed, then its complement is open.

PROOF (i) Assume that S is open and let x be an adherent point of its complement S^c. If $x \notin S^c$, then $x \in S$ and hence there is some sphere centered at x contained in S. But, being a subset of S, this sphere can contain no points of S^c, contradicting the fact that x is an adherent point of S^c. Therefore $x \in S^c$ and hence S^c is closed.

(ii) Assume that S is closed and let $x \in S^c$. Then $x \notin S$ and hence x cannot be an adherent point of S. Thus there exists a sphere centered at x that has no points of S and contains only points of S^c. That is, the sphere is a subset of S^c and hence S^c is open. Q.E.D.

Example The empty set is open as well as closed since it is the complement of the entire normed space.

Remark The following hold:

(1) $(A^c)^c = A$.
(2) $(A \cap B)^c = A^c \cup B^c$.
(3) $(A \cup B)^c = A^c \cap B^c$.

The last two are called *De Morgan's formulas*.

THEOREM 13 The union of a *finite* number of closed sets is closed.

PROOF Let $P = \bigcup_{i=1}^{n} P_i$, where P_i is a closed set for each i. By De Morgan's formula, $P^c = \bigcap_{i=1}^{n} P_i^c$, where P_i^c is open. Thus P^c is open and hence $P = (P^c)^c$ is closed. Q.E.D.

THEOREM 14 The intersection of an arbitrary collection of closed sets is closed.

PROOF Let $P \equiv \bigcap_{i \in J} P_i$, where P_i is a closed set for each $i \in J$ ($J =$ an arbitrary collection of indices). By one of De Morgan's formulas, $P^c = \bigcup_{i \in J} P_i^c$, where P_i^c is open. Thus P^c is open and hence P is closed. Q.E.D.

DEFINITION 12 Let S be a subset of a normed space X. A point $x \in X$ is said to be an *accumulation point* of S if for any $\delta > 0$ there exists a point $s \in S$ distinct from x such that $\|x - s\| < \delta$. Let S' be the set of accumulation points of S. Then it is clear that $\bar{S} = S \cup S'$.

DEFINITION 13 Let S be a subset of a normed space. Any point of S but an accumulation point of S is said to be an *isolated point* of S. In other words, if there exists a sphere centered at $x \in S$ with some radius $\delta > 0$ that contains no other point of S, x is an isolated point of S.

DEFINITION 14 In a normed vector space an infinite sequence of vectors $\{x_n\}$ is said to converge to a vector x if the sequence $\{\|x_n - x\|\}$ of real numbers converges to zero. In this case we write $x_n \to x$ (as $n \to \infty$).

In a unitary space, a sequence of vectors converges if and only if each component of the vectors converges since

$$\|x_n - x\|^2 = \sum_k (\xi_{nk} - \xi_k)(\bar{\xi}_{nk} - \bar{\xi}_k) \to 0$$

if and only if $\xi_{nk} \to \xi_k$ for each k, where ξ_{nk} and ξ_k stand for the kth components of x_n and x, respectively.

THEOREM 15 A subset S of a normed space is closed if and only if every convergent sequence of vectors from S has its limit in S.

PROOF If S is closed, the limit of a convergent sequence from S is obviously an accumulation point of S and must be contained in S. (The converse is left as an exercise to the reader.) Q.E.D.

DEFINITION 15 A subset M of a normed space X is said to be *bounded* if there is a finite positive number r such that M is contained in the closed sphere centered at θ with radius r:

$$S(\theta; r) = \{x : x \in X, \|x\| \leqq r\}.$$

DEFINITION 16 Let X and Y be normed spaces over a field and F be a transformation from X into Y. F is said to be *continuous* at $x_0 \in X$, if for every $\varepsilon > 0$, there exists $\delta > 0$ such that

$$\|F(x) - F(x_0)\| < \varepsilon \qquad \text{for} \quad \|x_0 - x\| < \delta.$$

If F is continuous at every point of X, then F is said to be *continuous everywhere*, or simply *continuous* on X.

Example An eigenvalue of a square matrix over the real field is a continuous function of its elements.

THEOREM 16 Let F be a transformation from X into Y, where X and Y are normed spaces over a field. F is continuous at $x_0 \in X$ if and only if $x_n \to x_0$ implies $F(x_n) \to F(x_0)$.

PROOF Since the sufficiency of the statement is obvious, we shall prove only the necessity. Suppose $\{x_n\}$ is a sequence such that $x_n \to x_0$ and $F(x_n) \not\to F(x_0)$. Then for some $\varepsilon > 0$ and any integer N, there exists an $n > N$ such that $\|F(x_n) - F(x_0)\| \geqq \varepsilon$. Since $x_n \to x_0$, this implies that for each $\delta > 0$, there exists x_n with $\|x_n - x_0\| < \delta$ and $\|F(x_n) - F(x_0)\| > \varepsilon$. Hence F is not continuous at x_0. Q.E.D.

THEOREM 17 (*continuity of an inner product*) Let $\{x_n\}$ and $\{y_n\}$ be convergent sequences in an inner product space, i.e.,

$$x_n \to x \qquad \text{and} \qquad y_n \to y.$$

Then $(x_n \mid y_n) \to (x \mid y)$.

PROOF Since the sequence $\{x_n\}$ is convergent, it is bounded above; i.e., there exists a positive number P such that $\|x_n\| \leqq P$. Then

$$\begin{aligned} |(x_n \mid y_n) - (x \mid y)| &= |(x_n \mid y_n) - (x_n \mid y) + (x_n \mid y) - (x \mid y)| \\ &= |(x_n \mid y_n - y) + (x_n - x \mid y)| \\ &\leqq |(x_n \mid y_n - y)| + |(x_n - x \mid y)| \\ &\leqq \|x_n\| \, \|y_n - y\| + \|x_n - x\| \, \|y\| \\ &\leqq P\|y_n - y\| + \|x_n - x\| \, \|y\| \to 0 \end{aligned}$$

since $\|y\|$ is finite. Q.E.D.

COROLLARY In an inner product space, if $\{x_n\}$ is a convergent sequence, the norm $\|x_n\|$ is continuous.

PROOF If $x_n \to x$, then $(x_n | x_n) \to (x | x)$. Since $\|x_n\| = (x | x)^{1/2}$, $\|x_n\| \to \|x\|$. Q.E.D.

THEOREM 18 Let F be a linear transformation from X into Y, where X and Y are normed spaces over a field. If F is continuous at a single point $x_0 \in X$, then it is continuous everywhere on X.

PROOF We shall show that $\|F(x_n) - F(x)\| \to 0$ as $x_n \to x \in X$. Let $\{x_n\}$ be a sequence from X convergent to $x \in X$. Then, by the linearity of F, $\|F(x_n) - F(x)\| = \|F(x_n - x + x_0) - F(x_0)\|$. However, since $x_n - x + x_0 \to x_0$ and since F is continuous at x_0, we have $F(x_n - x + x_0) \to F(x_0)$. Q.E.D.

COROLLARY Let F be a continuous linear transformation defined on a normed space X. Then its nullspace $N(F)$ is a closed set.

PROOF Let $\{x_n\}$ be an arbitrary convergent sequence from $N(F)$, and let x_0 be its limit. Since F is continuous everywhere on X, $0 = F(x_n) \to F(x_0)$ as $n \to \infty$. Hence x_0 belongs to $N(F)$. Q.E.D.

Lastly, we state without proof an important property of a real-valued function and two additional theorems regarding some specific open or closed sets.

THEOREM 19 A real-valued continuous function defined on a bounded and closed subset M of Euclidean n-space E^n can achieve a maximum and a minimum.

(For a proof, see for example Apostol (1957, p. 73).)

THEOREM 20 Let F be a nonnegative-valued functional on a normed space X. If F is continuous on X, then the set

$$S_1 \equiv \{x : x \in X,\ F(x) \leqq 1\}$$

is closed, and the set

$$S_2 \equiv \{x : x \in X,\ F(x) < 1\}$$

is open.

THEOREM 21 Let K be a convex set in a normed space. Then its interior $\mathring{K}$ and its closure $\bar{K}$ are convex.

(The proofs of the above two theorems are left to the reader.)

5.3 Banach Spaces and Hilbert Spaces

DEFINITION 17 A sequence of vectors $\{x_n\}$ in a normed space is said to be a *Cauchy sequence* if

$$||x_n - x_m|| \to 0 \qquad \text{as} \quad n, m \to \infty;$$

or more precisely, if given $\varepsilon > 0$ there exists an integer N such that

$$||x_n - x_m|| < \varepsilon \qquad \text{for} \quad n, m > N.$$

THEOREM 22 In a normed space, every convergent sequence is a Cauchy sequence.

PROOF If $x_n \to x$ (and hence $x_m \to x$), then

$$||x_n - x_m|| = ||x_n - x + x - x_m|| \leqq ||x_n - x|| + ||x - x_m|| \to 0.$$

Q.E.D.

THEOREM 23 A Cauchy sequence is bounded above.

PROOF Let $\{x_n\}$ be a Cauchy sequence, and put $\varepsilon = 1$ in Definition 17. Then there exists an integer N such that $||x_n - x_m|| < 1$ for n, $m > N$. Assuming $n > m$ without loss of generality, we can choose an m such that $m > N$. Letting M denote this m, we have $||x_n - x_M|| < 1$ for $n > M$; and hence

$$||x_n|| = ||x_n - x_M + x_M|| \leqq ||x_M|| + ||x_n - x_M|| < ||x_M|| + 1$$
$$\text{for} \quad n > M.$$

Q.E.D.

COROLLARY Every convergent sequence in a normed space is bounded above.

PROOF The statement follows immediately from Theorems 22 and 23.

Q.E.D.

THEOREM 24 If a sequence converges in a normed space, its limit is unique.

PROOF Suppose $x_n \to x$ and $x_n \to y$. Then

$$||x - y|| = ||x - x_n + x_n - y|| \leqq ||x - x_n|| + ||x_n - y|| \to 0.$$

Q.E.D.

DEFINITION 18 A subset S of a normed space is said to be *complete* if every Cauchy sequence from S has a limit in S and hence is convergent in S.

DEFINITION 19 A complete normed space is called a *Banach space*.

Example The set of all real scalars R is apparently complete.

THEOREM 25 Euclidean n-space E^n is complete.

PROOF Let $\{x_t\}$ be a Cauchy sequence from E^n, i.e., for any $\varepsilon > 0$ there exists an integer N such that $||x_p - x_q|| < \varepsilon$ for p, $q > N$. Letting $x_t = \{\xi_{t1}, \ldots, \xi_{tn}\}$, we say that there exists N such that

$$\sum_{k=1}^{n} (\xi_{pk} - \xi_{qk})^2 < \varepsilon^2 \qquad \text{for} \quad p, q > N.$$

Since $(\xi_{pi} - \xi_{qi})^2 \leqq \sum_k (\xi_{pk} - \xi_{qk})^2$ for $i = 1, \ldots, n$, we can state for each i that given $\varepsilon > 0$, there exists N such that $|\xi_{pi} - \xi_{qi}| < \varepsilon$ for $p, q > N$. $\{\xi_{ti}\}$ is therefore a Cauchy sequence from the set of real scalars R for each i. Since R is complete, we have $\lim_{t\to\infty} \xi_{ti} = \xi_i$, and hence $\lim_{t\to\infty} x_t = x$, where $x = \{\xi_1, \ldots, \xi_n\}$. Q.E.D.

COROLLARY Unitary 1-space U^1 is complete.

PROOF U^1 can be treated as E^2 because any $x, y \in U^1$ can be represented as

$$x = \xi_1 + i\xi_2 \qquad \text{and} \qquad y = \eta_1 + i\eta_2.$$

Hence, $\|x - y\|^2 = (\xi_1 - \eta_1)^2 + (\xi_2 - \eta_2)^2$, which is equivalent to the content of $\|x - y\|^2$ in the case where x and y belong to E^2. Q.E.D.

DEFINITION 20 A complete vector space X together with an inner product defined on $X \times X$ is called a *Hilbert space*.

THEOREM 26 In a Banach space, a subset is complete if and only if it is closed.

PROOF (1) If a subset is complete, every Cauchy sequence from it has a limit in it. Thus it is closed. (2) Every Cauchy sequence from a closed subset of a Banach space has a limit in the Banach space. By closure, the limit must be in the subset. Hence the subset is complete. Q.E.D.

THEOREM 27 In a normed space, any finite-dimensional subspace is complete.

PROOF We apply the method of mathematical induction to the assumption that the theorem holds true for any $(N - 1)$-dimensional subspace and show that the theorem holds for an N-dimensional subspace. At first a one-dimensional subspace is found to be complete in a normed space. Define a set $L_y = \{x : x = \alpha y \text{ for a scalar } \alpha\}$ for a fixed vector y. The convergence of a sequence of vectors $\{\alpha_n y\}$ is equivalent to that of scalars $\{\alpha_n\}$. Thus, the completeness of L_y follows from that of U^1.

Let X be a normed space and M an N-dimensional subspace of X. Assume that the theorem holds for any subspace of dimension $N - 1$. Let $\{y_1, \ldots, y_N\}$ be a basis for M, and define a subspace of M generated by $N - 1$ y_i $(i \neq k)$ as

$$M_k \equiv \{x : x = \sum_{i\neq k} \alpha_i y_i \quad \text{for arbitrary scalars } \alpha_i\},$$

and the distance between y_k and M_k as

$$d_k = \inf \|y_k - \sum_{i\neq k} \alpha_i y_i\| \qquad \text{for the given basis.}$$

M_k is complete by assumption, and hence every Cauchy sequence from M_k has a limit in it. Furthermore, no sequence from M_k converges to y_k

since y_k is linearly independent of the other y_i. Therefore, d_k takes a positive value for each $k = 1, \ldots, N$. Define $d = \min_k d_k$ and let $\{x_n\}$ be a Cauchy sequence from M. Since each x_n is uniquely represented as

$$x_n = \sum_{i=1}^{N} b_{ni} y_i,$$

we have for arbitrary integers n and m,

$$\begin{aligned} \|x_n - x_m\| &= \left\| \sum_i (b_{ni} - b_{mi}) y_i \right\| \\ &= \left\| c_{nmk}\left(y_k - \frac{\sum_{i \neq k}(-c_{nmi}) y_i}{c_{nmk}} \right) \right\|, \end{aligned}$$

where $c_{nmi} \equiv b_{ni} - b_{mi}$. Thus,

$$\|x_n - x_m\| \geqq |c_{nmk}| d_k \geqq |c_{nmk}| d \qquad \text{for} \quad k = 1, \ldots, N.$$

Since $\{x_n\}$ is a Cauchy sequence, $|b_{nk} - b_{mk}| \to 0$ for $k = 1, \ldots, N$. This implies that for each k, $\{b_{nk}\}$ is a Cauchy sequence from U^1 and hence it is convergent to a scalar b_k. Let $x = \sum_{k=1}^{N} b_k y_k$. Then clearly $x \in M$. For each n,

$$\begin{aligned} \|x_n - x\| &= \left\| \sum_{k=1}^{n} (b_{nk} - b_k) y_k \right\| \leqq \sum_k \|(b_{nk} - b_k) y_k\| \\ &= \sum_k |b_{nk} - b_k| \, \|y_k\| \leqq N |b_{nh} - b_h| \, \|y_h\|, \end{aligned}$$

where $|b_{nh} - b_h| \, \|y_h\| \equiv \max_k |b_{nk} - b_k| \, \|y_k\|$. Therefore, we know that $x_n \to x \in M$, in view of the fact that $b_{nh} \to b_h$. Q.E.D.

COROLLARY Any finite-dimensional subspace in a Banach space is closed.

PROOF In a Banach space, any finite-dimensional subspace is complete and any complete subset is closed. Q.E.D.

To conclude this section, we shall show that the set of all continuous real-valued functions defined on a closed real interval is a Banach space.

THEOREM 28 Let a, b be real constants such that $a < b$. The set $C[a, b]$ is a Banach space.

PROOF Since we have shown that the set $C[a, b]$ is a normed vector space, it is necessary to verify only that it is complete, i.e., that every Cauchy sequence from $C[a, b]$ has a limit in it.

(1) Suppose $\{x_n\}$ is a Cauchy sequence from $C[a, b]$, i.e.,

$$\|x_n - x_m\| \to 0 \qquad \text{as} \quad n, m \to \infty.$$

In view of the norm $\|x\| = \max_{a \leqq t \leqq b} |x(t)|$ of an element x of $C[a, b]$,

$$|x_n(t) - x_m(t)| \leqq \|x_n - x_m\| \to 0 \qquad \text{for each} \quad t \in [a, b].$$

Thus, sequence $\{x_n(t)\}$ for a fixed t in $[a, b]$ is a Cauchy sequence of real numbers. Since the set R of real numbers is complete, therefore, $x_n(t)$ converges to a limit $x(t)$ in R for the fixed t.

(2) For an arbitrary positive number α, choose a positive integer N such that

$$\|x_n - x_m\| < \alpha/2 \qquad \text{for} \quad n, m > N.$$

Since $x_m(t)$ converges to $x(t)$ for each t in $[a, b]$, choose m sufficiently large such that

$$|x_m(t) - x(t)| < \alpha/2 \qquad \text{for all} \quad t \in [a, b].$$

Then for $n > N$

$$\begin{aligned} |x_n(t) - x(t)| &\leqq |x_n(t) - x_m(t)| + |x_m(t) - x(t)| \\ &\leqq \|x_n - x_m\| + \alpha/2 < \alpha, \end{aligned}$$

i.e., sequence $\{x_n(t)\}$ converges to $x(t)$ for all t in $[a, b]$. In other words, $\{x_n\}$ is a convergent sequence.

(3) Lastly, we prove the limit function x is continuous. Since $\{x_n(t)\}$ is convergent to $x(t)$ for all t in $[a, b]$, for an arbitrary positive number α, n can be selected such that

$$|x_n(t) - x(t)| < \alpha/3 \qquad \text{and} \qquad |x(t+\delta) - x_n(t+\delta)| < \alpha/3$$

for all t and $t + \delta$ in $[a, b]$. Then δ may be chosen to make

$$|x_n(t+\delta) - x_n(t)| < \alpha/3,$$

in view of the continuity of the function x_n. Thus there exists δ such that

$$\begin{aligned} |x(t+\delta) - x(t)| \leqq |x(t+\delta) - x_n(t+\delta)| + |x_n(t+\delta) - x_n(t)| \\ + |x_n(t) - x(t)| < \alpha \end{aligned}$$

for all t in $[a, b]$, i.e., x is continuous. Moreover, by the continuity of norm, the sequence $\{x_n\}$ converges to x in the norm of $C[a, b]$. Hence the limit function belongs to $C[a, b]$. Q.E.D.

5.4 Separable Sets and Isomorphisms

Since our relevant spaces are all to be separable in the sense defined later, we shall introduce some fundamental concepts and theorems related to separability of sets in this section.

DEFINITION 21 Let F be a transformation from a set X into a set Y (with domain X); i.e., F is a rule that assigns to each $x \in X$ a unique element $y \in Y$. If for every $y \in Y$ there is at most one $x \in X$ for which $F(x) = y$, i.e., if $F(x_1) = F(x_2)$ only when $x_1 = x_2$, then the transformation F is said to be *one-to-one* or *univalent*. If for every $y \in Y$ there is at least one $x \subset X$ for which $F(x) = y$, or equivalently if the range of F is equal to Y itself, then the transformation F is said to be *onto*, or F is said to map X onto Y. If transformation $F: X \to Y$ is one-to-one and onto, we say that F is a *one-to-one correspondence* of X with Y.

DEFINITION 22 When F is a one-to-one transformation from a set X into a set Y, there is a transformation F^{-1}, called the *inverse* of F, such that $F^{-1}(F(x)) = x$ for every $x \in X$. If F is a one-to-one correspondence of a set X with a set Y, then X and Y have the same number of elements, and hence $F^{-1}(F(x)) = x$ and $F(F^{-1}(y)) = y$ for every $x \in X$ and $y \in Y$.

DEFINITION 23 Set A is said to be *countably infinite* or simply *countable* if there exists a one-to-one correspondence of set A with the set of all natural numbers N.

Examples (1) The set of all integers is countable, because we have the following correspondence:

$$\begin{array}{ccccc} 0, & -1, & 1, & -2, & 2, \ldots \\ \updownarrow & \updownarrow & \updownarrow & \updownarrow & \updownarrow \\ 1, & 2, & 3, & 4, & 5, \ldots \end{array}$$

(2) The set of all positive and negative rational numbers is countable. (The verification is left to the reader.)

THEOREM 29 Every subset of a countable set is either a finite set or a countable set.

PROOF Let B be a subset of a countable set A, whose elements are arranged as $a_1, a_2, a_3, \ldots$. Elements of B are picked from among these a_i and rearranged as $b_1, b_2, b_3, \ldots$. If there is a largest index of the b_i, B is a finite set; otherwise it is a countable set. Q.E.D.

THEOREM 30 Let N be the set of all natural numbers. Then the Cartesian product $N \times N$ is a countable set.

PROOF Define a transformation f on $N \times N$ as

$$f(x, y) = p_1^x p_2^y \qquad \text{for} \quad (x, y) \in N \times N,$$

where p_1 and p_2 are different prime numbers, such as 2, 3, 5, 7, etc. Then f is one-to-one on $N \times N$ because $p_1^r p_2^s = p_1^x p_2^y$ implies $(r, s) = (x, y)$. And the range of f is a subset of N without upper bound, i.e., the range of f is a countable set. Thus f is a one-to-one correspondence of $N \times N$ with N. Q.E.D.

THEOREM 31 The set of all finite sequences from a countable set is countable.

PROOF Let A be a countable set. Then A can be put into a one-to-one correspondence with the set N of natural numbers. Thus it suffices to prove that the set S of all finite sequences of natural numbers is countable. Each x in N has a unique factorization in terms of prime numbers: $x = 2^{\xi_1} 3^{\xi_2} \cdots p_k^{\xi_k}$, where $\xi_i \in N_0 \equiv N_k \cup \{0\}$ and $\xi_k > 0$. Let f be a transformation on N assigning to the natural number x a finite sequence $\{\xi_1, \ldots, \xi_k\}$ from N_0. Hence each natural number corresponds to a unique finite sequence from N_0, and vice versa. Thus the set S' of all finite sequences from N_0 has a one-to-one correspondence with N, and hence is countable. The set S is a subset of S' and is not finite. Therefore, S is countable. Q.E.D.

THEOREM 32 The union of countable collection of countable sets is countable, i.e., $\bigcup_{i=1}^{\infty} A_i$, where A_i is a countable set, is countable.

PROOF Let a_j^i be the jth element of set A_i and arrange $A_1, A_2, A_3, \ldots$ as

$$
\begin{array}{rcccccccc}
A_1 = & \{a_1^1 & & a_2^1 & \rightarrow & a_3^1 & & a_4^1 & \ldots\} \\
 & \downarrow & \nearrow & & \swarrow & & \nearrow & & \\
A_2 = & \{a_1^2 & & a_2^2 & & a_3^2 & & a_4^2 & \ldots\} \\
 & & \swarrow & & \nearrow & & & & \\
A_3 = & \{a_1^3 & & a_2^3 & & a_3^3 & & a_4^3 & \ldots\} \\
 & \downarrow & \nearrow & & & & & & \\
A_4 = & \{a_1^4 & & a_2^4 & & a_3^4 & & a_4^4 & \ldots\} \\
 & \vdots & & & & & & &
\end{array}
$$

Then we count all the elements, starting from a_1^1, following the direction of arrows and skipping identical elements that have been counted once. This counting procedure shows the existence of a one-to-one correspondence of the union of countable collection of A_i with the set of all natural numbers.

Q.E.D.

DEFINITION 24 A subset D of a normed vector space X is said to be *dense* in X, if $\bar{D} = X$ where $\bar{D}$ is the closure of D, or equivalently if for given $x \in X$ and $\delta > 0$ there exists an element d of D such that $\|x - d\| < \delta$.

Example The set of all rationals is a dense subset of the real line E^1 with norm $\|x\| = (x^2)^{1/2}$.

DEFINITION 25 A normed vector space X is said to be *separable* if it contains a subset that comprises a countable number of points and is dense in X.

Examples (1) The real line E^1 is a separable set since the set of all rational numbers is a countable and dense subset of E^1. (2) Euclidean n-space E^n is separable since the collection of vectors $x = \{\xi_1, \ldots, \xi_n\}$, where each component is rational, is regarded as a subset (not finite) of all finite sequences from the set of rational numbers and hence countable, and since it is dense in E^n.

THEOREM 33 A Hilbert space is separable if and only if it has a finite basis or a countable basis.

PROOF (1) Assume that a Hilbert space H is separable, and hence that there is a sequence $X \equiv \{x_n\}_{n=1}^{\infty}$ that is dense in H. Let y_1 be the x_n ($\neq 0$) with the smallest index n, let y_2 be the x_n ($\neq 0$) that is linearly independent of y_1 with the second smallest index n, let y_3 be the x_n($\neq 0$) that is linearly independent of y_1 and y_2 with the third smallest index n, and so on. Continuing this procedure as long as possible, we select a subsequence $Y \equiv \{y_m\}_{m=1}^{k}$ where $k < \infty$ or $k = \infty$. Obviously every vector x_n $(1 \leqq n < \infty)$ is a linear combination of these y_i. Let $Z \equiv \{e_m\}_{m=1}^{k}$ be an orthonormal sequence obtained from Y. Then every vector $x_n (1 \leqq n < \infty)$ is a linear combination of some elements of Z. Thus if there is an element x of H such that x is orthogonal to e_m for all $e_m \in Z$, then x is orthogonal to x_n for all $x_n \in X$. Since X is dense in H, there is a subsequence $\{x_n'\}_{n=1}^{\infty}$ from X such that $x = \lim_{n\to\infty} x_n'$. Therefore, $(x\,|\,x) = \lim_{n\to\infty} (x\,|\,x_n') = 0$, implying that the x must be a null vector. Thus Z constitutes a basis for H.

(2) Suppose $Z \equiv \{e_m\}_{m=1}^{k}$ is a finite or countable basis for H, where the e_m are orthonormal vectors. Then H is identical with the subspace M generated by this basis. Let M' be the subset of M consisting of all finite linear combinations of vectors in Z with rational coefficients. Then M' is countable. We shall show that M' is dense in M. For any given $x \in M$ and $\delta > 0$, choose $y = \sum_{k=1}^{n} \alpha_k e_k \in M$ such that $\|x - y\| < \delta/2$. Next for integer k with $1 \leqq k \leqq n$, choose a rational number α_k' such that $|\alpha_k - \alpha_k'| < \delta/2n$. For $y' = \sum_{k=1}^{n} \alpha_k' e_k \in M'$, we get

$$\|x - y'\| \leqq \|x - y\| + \|y - y'\| \leqq \delta/2 + \sum_{k=1}^{n} |\alpha_k - \alpha_k'| < \delta. \qquad \text{Q.E.D.}$$

In order to show that the set $C[a, b]$ of all real-valued continuous functions defined on a closed real interval $[a, b]$ is separable, we need a lemma.

LEMMA 2 (*Weierstrass approximation theorem*) Let f be a real-valued continuous function on a closed real interval $[a, b]$. Given $\delta > 0$, there is a polynomial p such that.

$$|f(t) - p(t)| < \delta \qquad \text{for} \quad t \in [a, b].$$

(For a proof, see for example Apostol (1957, pp. 481–482).)

THEOREM 34 The space $C[a, b]$ is separable.

PROOF Let x be an element of $C[a, b]$. By the Weierstrass approximation theorem, for given $\delta > 0$ there is a polynomial $p \equiv \pi_n t^n + \pi_{n-1} t^{n-1} + \cdots + \pi_1 t + \pi_0$ such that

$$|x(t) - p(t)| < \delta/2 \qquad \text{for} \quad t \in [a, b].$$

We can have another polynomial $r \equiv \rho_n t^n + \rho_{n-1} t^{n-1} + \cdots + \rho_1 t + \rho_0$ with rational coefficients such that

$$|p(t) - r(t)| \leqq \sum_{i=1}^{n} |\pi_i - \rho_i|\,|t^i| < \sum_{i=1}^{n} \delta|t^i|/(2n \max_{0 \leq j \leq n} |t^i|) \leqq \delta/2.$$

Thus

$$\|x - r\| = \max_t |x(t) - r(t)| \leqq \max|x(t) - p(t)| + \max|p(t) - r(t)| < \delta.$$

Denote by D the countable set of all polynomials $r(t)$ with rational coefficients for all $t \in [a, b]$. From the above it follows that D is dense in $C[a, b]$. Q.E.D.

Now we turn to isomorphic spaces. As was mentioned before, if transformation F is a one-to-one correspondence of a set X with a set Y, the inverse F^{-1} is defined such that if $F(x) = y$, then $F^{-1}(y) = x$ for $x \in X$ and $y \in Y$. When F is linear and X, Y are vector spaces, F^{-1} will be linear and become an isomorphism as discussed below.

THEOREM 35 Let X, Y be vector spaces over a field L and let F be a one-to-one linear transformation from X onto Y. Then its inverse F^{-1} is linear.

PROOF Suppose $x_i \in X$ and $y_i \in Y$ satisfy $F(x_i) = y_i$ for each $i = 1, 2$. Then for scalars $\alpha_1, \alpha_2 \in L$

$$F(\alpha_1 x_1 + \alpha_2 x_2) = \alpha_1 F(x_1) + \alpha_2 F(x_2) = \alpha_1 y_1 + \alpha_2 y_2 \in Y.$$

By the definition of inverse,

$$F^{-1}(\alpha_1 y_1 + \alpha_2 y_2) = \alpha_1 x_1 + \alpha_2 x_2 = \alpha_1 F^{-1}(y_1) + \alpha_2 F^{-1}(y_2). \qquad \text{Q.E.D.}$$

DEFINITION 26 If there exists a one-to-one linear transformation F from a vector space X onto a vector space Y, F is called an *isomorphism* of X onto Y, and X is said to be *isomorphic* to Y. By the above theorem, the inverse F^{-1} becomes an isomorphism of Y onto X. Hence we may say that X and Y are isomorphic.

THEOREM 36 Let X, Y be isomorphic vector spaces over a field. Then, $\dim X = \dim Y$.

PROOF Let $\{x_1, \ldots, x_n\}$ be a basis for X and $\{y_1, \ldots, y_m\}$ a basis for Y. Let F be the corresponding one-to-one linear transformation from X onto Y. By Theorem 17 in Section 2.2, F determines a unique $m \times n$ matrix $A = [a_{ij}]$ such that

$$F(x_j) = \sum_{i=1}^{m} a_{ij} y_i \qquad \text{for} \quad j = 1, \ldots, n.$$

For the inverse F^{-1}, we have in view of its linearity

$$\sum_{i=1}^{m} a_{ij} F^{-1}(y_i) = F^{-1}\left(\sum_i a_{ij} y_i\right) = x_j \qquad \text{for} \quad j = 1, \ldots, n,$$

and a unique $n \times m$ matrix $B = [b_{ki}]$ such that

$$F^{-1}(y_i) = \sum_{k=1}^{n} b_{ki}x_k \qquad \text{for} \quad i = 1, \ldots, m.$$

It follows that

$$\sum_{i=1}^{m} a_{ij} \sum_{k=1}^{n} b_{ki}x_k = x_j \qquad \text{for} \quad j = 1, \ldots, n,$$

or equivalently

$$\{x\}\, BA = \{x\},$$

where $\{x\} \equiv (x_1, \ldots, x_n)$, implying $BA = I_n$ (identity matrix of order n). Likewise, starting from F^{-1}, we obtain $AB = I_m$, which in turn implies, together with $BA = I_n$, that $B = A^{-1}$ and hence $n = m$. Q.E.D.

COROLLARY Let X, Y be vector spaces isomorphic via a linear transformation F. Then F is represented by a unique nonsingular square matrix A and the inverse F^{-1} of F is represented by the inverse matrix A^{-1} of A.

5.5 Bounded Linear Functionals and Dual Spaces

We shall introduce the dual space of a normed space in this section. For this purpose bounded linear functionals are essential. We begin with the concept of boundedness of a linear transformation.

DEFINITION 27 Let X, Y be normed (vector) spaces and F be a linear transformation from X into Y. F is said to be *bounded* if there exists a finite positive number M such that

$$\|F(x)\| \leqq M\|x\| \qquad \text{for all} \quad x \in X.$$

THEOREM 37 A linear transformation F from a normed space X into a normed space Y is bounded if and only if it is continuous on X.

PROOF (a) Suppose F is bounded, i.e., there exists a constant M such that $\|F(x)\| \leqq M\|x\|$ for all $x \in X$. If $x_n \to \theta$, we have $\|F(x_n)\| \leqq M\|x_n\| \to 0$. Thus F is continuous at $\theta \in X$, and hence continuous everywhere on X.

(b) Assume F is continuous at θ. By Definition 16 in Section 5.2, there is $\delta > 0$ such that $\|F(x) - F(\theta)\| < 1$ for $\|x - \theta\| \leqq \delta$, or $\|F(x)\| < 1$ for $\|x\| \leqq \delta$. For any nonzero vector $x \in X$, $\delta x/\|x\|$ has a norm equal to δ, since

$$\left\|\frac{\delta x}{\|x\|}\right\| = \frac{\delta}{\|x\|}\,\|x\| = \delta.$$

Thus we have $\|F(\delta x/\|x\|)\| < 1$, and hence

$$\|F(x)\| = \frac{\delta}{\|x\|}\,\|F(x)\|\,\frac{\|x\|}{\delta} = \left\|F\left(\frac{\delta x}{\|x\|}\right)\right\|\frac{\|x\|}{\delta} < \frac{\|x\|}{\delta}.$$

$1/\delta$ serves as a bound for F. Q.E.D.

DEFINITION 28 The norm of a bounded linear transformation F on a normed space X is defined as

$$\|F\| = \inf_M \{M\colon \|F(x)\| \leqq M\|x\| \text{ for } x \in X\} = \sup_{x\neq\theta} \frac{\|F(x)\|}{\|x\|},$$

since $\|F\|\,\|x\| \geqq \|F(x)\|$ and since $x = \theta$ has no effect on M.

The normed space of all bounded linear transformations from a normed space X into a normed space Y is henceforth denoted $B(X, Y)$, where the norm is defined as

$$\|F\| = \sup_{x\in X, x\neq\theta} \frac{\|F(x)\|}{\|x\|} \quad \text{for} \quad F \in B(X, Y). \tag{10}$$

THEOREM 38 Let $G \in B(X, Y)$ and $F \in B(Y, Z)$, and define $FG\colon X \to Z$ such that $(FG)(x) = F(G(x))$ for $x \in X$. Then

$$\|FG\| \leqq \|F\|\,\|G\|.$$

PROOF Since

$$\|F\| = \sup_{y\in Y, y\neq\theta} \frac{\|F(y)\|}{\|y\|} \quad \text{and} \quad \|G\| = \sup_{x\in X, x\neq\theta} \frac{\|G(x)\|}{\|x\|},$$

we have

$$\|F\|\,\|G\| \geqq \frac{\|F(G(x))\|}{\|G(x)\|}\frac{\|G(x)\|}{\|x\|} = \frac{\|(FG)(x)\|}{\|x\|}$$

for all nonzero $x \in X$. Hence

$$\|F\|\,\|G\| \geqq \sup_{x\in X, x\neq\theta} \frac{\|(FG)(x)\|}{\|x\|} = \|FG\|. \qquad \text{Q.E.D.}$$

THEOREM 39 Let F be a bounded linear transformation on a normed space X. Then

$$\|F\| = \sup_{\|x\|=1} \|F(x)\| = \sup_{\|x\|\leqq 1} \|F(x)\| \qquad \text{for all} \quad x \in X. \tag{11}$$

PROOF

$$\sup_{x\neq\theta} \frac{\|F(x)\|}{\|x\|} = \sup_{x\neq\theta} \left\| F\left(\frac{x}{\|x\|}\right)\right\| \leqq \sup_{\|x\|=1} \|F(x)\| \leqq \sup_{\|x\|\leqq 1} \|F(x)\|$$
$$\leqq \sup_{0<\|x\|\leqq 1} \frac{\|F(x)\|}{\|x\|} \leqq \sup_{x\neq\theta} \frac{\|F(x)\|}{\|x\|},$$

of which the first inequality holds true because $y \equiv x/\|x\|$ yields $\|y\| = 1$, implying that y is a special case of x such that $\|x\| = 1$; and the third inequality holds since $\|F(x)\| \leqq \|F(x)\|/\|x\|$ for $x \neq \theta$ satisfying $\|x\| \leqq 1$.

DEFINITION 29 A transformation f from a multidimensional vector space X into a one-dimensional space is called a *functional* on X; and if the functional f is linear for $x \in X$, it is said to be a *linear functional* on X.

The norm of a bounded linear functional f on a normed space X is defined as $\|f\| = \inf_M \{M : |f(x)| \leqq M\|x\| \text{ for } x \in X\}$, and the following relations hold:

$$\|f\| = \sup_{x \neq \theta} \frac{|f(x)|}{\|x\|} = \sup_{\|x\|=1} |f(x)| = \sup_{\|x\| \leqq 1} |f(x)|. \tag{11'}$$

We are now in a position to define the dual space of a normed (vector) space. First, we introduce the algebraic dual of a vector space.

DEFINITION 30 The space generated by all the linear functionals on a vector space X such that for any two elements f_1 and f_2 of this space and for an arbitrary scalar c, $cf_1 + f_2$ is an element of it, where $[cf_1 + f_2](x) = cf_1(x) + f_2(x)$ for $x \in X$, is called the *algebraic dual* of X.

THEOREM 40 Let X be a finite-dimensional vector space. Then, its algebraic dual X^{d} is finite-dimensional and

$$\dim X^{\mathrm{d}} = \dim X.$$

PROOF Let $\{x_1, \ldots, x_n\}$ be a basis for X. According to Theorem 16 in Section 2.2, for each $i = 1, \ldots, n$, there exists a unique functional f_i such that

$$f_i(x_j) = \delta_{ij} \qquad \text{for} \quad j = 1, \ldots, n,$$

where $\delta_{ij} = 0\,(i \neq j)$ and $\delta_{ii} = 1$. These n functionals are found to be linearly independent because from their linear combination $f = \sum_{k=1}^{n} c_k f_k$, we have

$$f(x_j) = \sum_k c_k f_k(x_j) = \sum_k c_k \delta_{kj} = c_j \qquad \text{for each } j.$$

Thus, if f is a null functional, $f(x_j) = 0$ for every j, entailing $c_j = 0$ for every j. For given $g \in X^{\mathrm{d}}$, define $c_i = g(x_i)$. We contend that $g = \sum_{i=1}^{n} c_i f_i$. For each i, $\sum_{k=1}^{n} c_k f_k(x_i) = \sum_k c_k \delta_{ki} = c_i$. Therefore, g and $\sum_k c_k f_k$ assume identical values on all the basis vectors, and hence on any linear combination of them, implying that g and $\sum_k c_k f_k$ assume identical values on X. Thus $f_1, \ldots, f_n$ generate the dual X^{d}. Q.E.D.

The following stems immediately from the above proof.

COROLLARY Let X be a finite-dimensional vector space and $\{x_1, \ldots, x_n\}$ be a basis for X. Then, linear functionals $f_1, \ldots, f_n$ such that $f_i(x_j) = \delta_{ij}$ for $i, j = 1, \ldots, n$, form a basis for the algebraic dual of X, where $\delta_{ij} = 0$ $(i \neq j)$ and $\delta_{ii} = 1$.

DEFINITION 31 The space generated by all the bounded linear functionals f on a normed (vector) space X in the same way as the algebraic dual, with the norm for that space defined as $\|f\| = \sup_{\|x\| \leq 1} |f(x)|$, is called the *dual space* or simply the *dual* of X, and denoted X^*.

An element f of X^* assumes a value $f(x)$ at $x \in X$. This value $f(x)$ will alternatively be expressed as $[x; f]$ in this book.

PROPOSITION 1 The dual X^* of a normed space X is a normed space.

PROOF X^* is a special algebraic dual of X, and an algebraic dual is a vector space by definition. It suffices to show that the norm of an element f of X^* satisfies the usual requirements of a norm. (Assume the sup is taken over $\|x\| \leqq 1$ for $x \in X$ in the following.)

(1) $\|f\| = \sup |f(x)| \geqq 0$ and equality holds if and only if $f = \theta$.

(2) $\|cf\| = |c| \cdot \sup |f(x)| = |c| \, \|f\|$ for any scalar c.

(3) $\|f_1 + f_2\| = \sup |f_1(x) + f_2(x)| \leqq \sup |f_1(x)| + \sup |f_2(x)|$
$= \|f_1\| + \|f_2\|$ for $f_1, f_2 \in X^*$. Q.E.D.

THEOREM 41 The dual space X^* of any normed space X is a Banach space, i.e., a complete normed space.

PROOF Since, by Proposition 1, X^* is known to be a normed space, it remains only to show that X^* is complete, i.e., that a Cauchy sequence in X^* is convergent with limit in X^*.

(a) First, we shall show that a Cauchy sequence $\{f_n\}$ in X^* is convergent to a limit for each $x \in X$.

$$\|f_n - f_m\| \to 0 \qquad \text{as} \quad n, m \to \infty,$$

where $f_n - f_m$ is an element of X^* since it is a vector space. By the definition of norm, for given $x \in X$,

$$|f_n(x) - f_m(x)| \leqq \|f_n - f_m\| \, \|x\| \to 0 \qquad \text{as} \quad n, m \to \infty.$$

Hence $\{f_n(x)\}$ is a Cauchy sequence of scalars, which is convergent since E^1 is complete. Thus, there exists a limit $f(x)$ of $\{f_n(x)\}$ for each $x \in X$.

(b) The functional f (on X) obtained in this way is linear because for $x, y \in X$ and any scalar α

$$f(\alpha x + y) = \lim_{n \to \infty} f_n(\alpha x + y) = \alpha \lim f_n(x) + \lim f_n(y) = \alpha f(x) + f(y).$$

(c) Since $\{f_n\}$ is Cauchy, for given $\delta > 0$, there exists an integer M such that $\|f_n - f_m\| < \delta$ for $n, m > M$, or in view of the definition of norm, $|f_n(x) - f_m(x)| < \delta \|x\|$ for $n, m > M$. Choose n as large as possible, and $f_n(x) \to f(x)$. Then we have $|f(x) - f_m(x)| < \delta \|x\|$ for $m > M$ and $x \in X$, because $|f_n(x) - f_m(x)| = |f_n(x) - f(x) + f(x) - f_m(x)|$. Thus, for $m > M$ and $x \in X$,

$$|f(x)| = |f(x) - f_m(x) + f_m(x)|$$
$$\leqq |f(x) - f_m(x)| + |f_m(x)| < (\delta + \|f_m\|)\|x\|.$$

Hence, f is bounded.

(d) By (b) and (c) above, we know that f is an element of X^*. Lastly, we show that the f is a limit of the sequence $\{f_m\}$.

$$|f(x) - f_m(x)| < \delta\|x\| \qquad \text{for} \quad m > M \quad \text{and} \quad x \in X$$

implies that $\|f - f_m\| < \delta$ for $m > M$ since $\|f - f_m\| = \sup_{x \neq \theta} |f(x) - f_m(x)|/\|x\|$. Choosing δ close to zero yields $f_m \to f$. Q.E.D.

A Hilbert space has a one-to-one correspondence with its dual, as is implied by the following theorem.

THEOREM 42 (i) For each vector y in a Hilbert space H, a bounded linear functional f can be defined on H such that

$$f(x) = (x|y) \quad \text{for any } x \in H \qquad \text{and} \qquad \|f\| = \|y\|. \tag{12}$$

(ii) Conversely, corresponding to every bounded linear functional f defined on H, there exists a unique vector y in H such that (12) holds.

PROOF (i) For fixed $y \in H$, define a functional f_y by $f_y(x) = (x|y)$ for $x \in H$. Then f_y is linear since

$$f_y(\alpha x_1 + x_2) = (\alpha x_1 + x_2|y) = \alpha(x_1|y) + (x_2|y) = \alpha f_y(x_1) + f_y(x_2)$$

for $x_1, x_2 \in H$ and any scalar α. Moreover, the Cauchy–Schwarz inequality guarantees the boundedness of f_y since $|(x|y)| \leqq \|x\|\,\|y\|$ where y is fixed.

$$|f_y(x)| = |(x|y)| \leqq \|x\|\,\|y\|$$

for fixed $y \in H$ and any $x \in H$ implies that

$$\|f_y\| \equiv \sup_{x \neq \theta} \frac{|f_y(x)|}{\|x\|} \leqq \|y\|.$$

Putting x equal to y in $f_y(x)$ and considering the definition $\|y\| = (y|y)^{1/2}$, we have

$$|f_y(y)| = |(y|y)| = \|y\|^2 \qquad \text{or} \qquad |f_y(y)|/\|y\| = \|y\|.$$

Hence $\|f_y\| = \|y\|$.

(ii) When $f \equiv \theta$, statement (ii) holds for $y = \theta$. Assume henceforth that f is a nonzero functional, and define

$$Z = \{z : z \in H, \quad f(z) = 0\}.$$

Obviously Z is a proper subspace of H. Z is closed since a sequence $\{z_n\}$ from Z convergent to $z_0 \in H$ implies

$$0 = f(z_n) \to f(z_0)$$

by virtue of the continuity of f. (Cf. Theorem 37 in this section.) Thus Z is a closed proper subspace of H and hence, by Theorem 7 in Section 6.1, $H = Z \oplus Z^\perp$, where $Z^\perp$ is a nonempty subspace. Let q be a nonzero elemcnt of $Z^\perp$ such that $f(q) \neq 0$. Then $p \equiv q/f(q)$ is a nonzero vector in $Z^\perp$ and $f(p) = 1$. Hence

$$f[x - f(x)p] = f(x) - f(x)f(p) = 0 \qquad \text{for} \quad x \in H.$$

Thus, $x - f(x)p \in Z$. Therefore,

$$(x - f(x)p\,|\,p) = 0 \qquad \text{or} \qquad (x\,|\,p) = f(x)\,\|p\|^2.$$

Defining $y = p/\|p\|^2$, we get $f(x) = (x\,|\,y)$. Such a y must be unique because if y' were another vector satisfying $f(x) = (x\,|\,y')$ for any $x \in H$, then we would have $(x\,|\,y) - (x\,|\,y') = 0$ for any $x \in H$, implying that $y - y' = \theta$.

Q.E.D.

In particular, the dual of Euclidean n-space E^n is nothing but E^n itself, as may be seen in the following example.

Example Let $x \equiv \{\xi_1, \ldots, \xi_n\}$ be an element of E^n, e_i be the ith unit vector in E^n, and f be a linear functional on E^n. Then

$$f(x) = f\left(\sum_{i=1}^{n} \xi_i e_i\right) = \sum_i \xi_i f(e_i) = \sum_i \xi_i \eta_i, \tag{13}$$

where $\eta_i \equiv f(e_i)$. $y \equiv \{\eta_1, \ldots, \eta_n\}$ will be shown to be the unique vector in E^n such that (12) holds. By the Cauchy–Schwarz inequality,

$$|f(x)|^2 = \left|\sum_i \eta_i \xi_i\right|^2 \leqq \sum_i \eta_i^2 \cdot \sum_i \xi_i^2 = \sum_i \eta_i^2\,\|x\|^2 \qquad \text{for} \quad x \in E^n.$$

Hence f is bounded. If $x = y$, the equality sign holds in this inequality. Thus the norm of f is

$$\|f\| = \left(\sum_i \eta_i^2\right)^{1/2}. \tag{14}$$

Conversely, for each $y = \{\eta_1, \ldots, \eta_n\} \in E^n$, a bounded linear functional f is defined by (13) with norm defined by (14). Since all linear functionals in the dual of E^n are formed in this way, the dual can be regarded as E^n.

5.6 Minkowski Functionals and the Hahn–Banach Theorem

This section is devoted to the complete proofs of a theorem concerning the so-called Minkowski functional and of the Hahn–Banach theorem. Both of these theorems are useful and powerful in the subsequent analysis.

DEFINITION 32 A nonnegative-valued functional p on a vector space X is said to be a *sublinear functional* on X if

$$p(x + y) \leqq p(x) + p(y) \qquad \text{for} \quad x, y \in X;$$

and

$$p(\alpha x) = |\alpha|\, p(x) \qquad \text{for} \quad x \in X \quad \text{and any scalar } \alpha.$$

Example Any norm is a sublinear functional.

DEFINITION 33 Let K be a convex set in a normed space X and assume that the null vector θ is an interior point of K. Then we define the *Minkowski functional* p_K of K on X as

$$p_K(x) = \inf\{r : x/r \in K, r > 0\} \qquad \text{for} \quad x \in X. \tag{15}$$

The set of r (> 0) satisfying $x/r \in K$ in (15) is an open interval, and its infimum does not belong to the set.

Examples $p_K(\theta) = 0 \notin \{r > 0 : \theta/r \in K\}$. If K is equal to a unit sphere $\{k : \|k\| < 1\}$, then $p_K(x) = \inf\{r : r > \|x\|\} = \|x\|$.

THEOREM 43 Let K be a convex set in a normed space X and assume that the null vector θ is an interior point of K. Then the Minkowski functional p_K of K on X is a continuous sublinear functional; i.e.,

(1) $0 \leqq p_K(x) < \infty$ for $x \in X$,
(2) $p_K(\alpha x) = \alpha p_K(x)$ for $x \in X$ and $\alpha \geqq 0$,
(3) $p_K(x + y) \leqq p_K(x) + p_K(y)$ for $x, y \in X$,
(4) p_K is continuous on X.

Furthermore,

(5) $\{x : p_K(x) < 1\} = \mathring{K}$, and $\{x : p_K(x) \leqq 1\} = \bar{K}$.

PROOF (1) Since θ is an interior point of K, there is a $\delta > 0$ such that the sphere $U(\theta; \delta) = \{x : \|x\| < \delta\}$ is contained in K. Given $x \in K$, there exists $r > 0$ for which $\|x\|/r < \delta$. For such an r, x/r belongs to $U(\theta; \delta)$. Since $U(\theta\ ;\ \delta) \subset K$,

$$\begin{aligned} p_K(x) &\equiv \inf\{r : x/r \in K, r > 0\} \\ &\leqq \inf\{r : x/r \in U(\theta;\ \delta),\ r > 0\} \\ &\leqq \inf\{r : \|x\|/r < \delta, r > 0\} = \|x\|/\delta < \infty. \end{aligned}$$

$p_K(x) \geqq 0$ is apparent by definition (15).

(2) If $\alpha = 0$, Eq. (2) holds trivially. Let $r^* \equiv r/\alpha$ for $\alpha > 0$. Then

$$\begin{aligned} p_K(\alpha x) &= \inf\{r\colon \alpha x/r \in K, r > 0\} \\ &= \inf\{\alpha r^* : x/r^* \in K,\ r^* > 0\} \\ &= \alpha \inf\{r^* : x/r^* \in K, r^* > 0\} = \alpha p_K(x). \end{aligned}$$

(3) Given $x_1, x_2 \in X$ and $\delta > 0$, we choose positive numbers r_1, r_2 such that $p_K(x_i) < r_i < p_K(x_i) + \delta$ for $i = 1, 2$. Then by the above statement (2),

$$1 > p_K(x_i)/r_i = p_K(x_i/r_i) = \inf\{w_i : x_i/(r_i w_i) \in K,\ w_i > 0\},$$

implying that $x_i/(r_i w_i) \in K$ for some $w_i \in (0, 1]$. Since K is a convex set containing θ, for such a w_i

$$x_i/r_i = w_i x_i/(r_i w_i) + (1 - w_i)\,\theta \in K \qquad \text{for} \quad i = 1, 2.$$

Let $r \equiv r_1 + r_2$. By the convexity of K,

$$(x_1 + x_2)/r = (x_1/r_1)(r_1/r) + (x_2/r_2)(r_2/r) \in K.$$

Then $(x_1 + x_2)/rq \in K$ for $q \geqq 1$ in view of the fact that $\theta \in K$. Thus

$$1 \geqq \inf\{v\colon\ (x_1 + x_2)/rv \in K,\ v > 0\} = p_K((x_1 + x_2)/r) = p_K(x_1 + x_2)/r.$$

Hence $p_K(x_1 + x_2) \leqq r < p_K(x_1) + p_K(x_2) + 2\delta$. Since δ is arbitrary, we get $p_K(x_1 + x_2) \leqq r = p_K(x_1) + p_K(x_2)$.

(4) Let δ be a positive number such that the closed sphere $S(\theta;\ \delta) \equiv \{x : \|x\| \leqq \delta\}$ is contained in K. Since for each nonzero $x \in X$, $\|\,\delta x/\|x\|\,\| = \delta$, we have $\delta x/\|x\| \in S(\theta;\ \delta) \subset K$, which implies $(\delta x/\|x\|)/q \in K$ for $q \geqq 1$. Hence

$$1 \geqq \inf\{v : (\delta x/\|x\|)/v \in K, v > 0\} = p_K(\delta x/\|x\|) = p_K(x)(\delta/\|x\|),$$

i.e., $p_K(x) \leqq \|x\|/\delta$. Thus $p_K(x) \to 0$ as $x \to \theta$.

It follows from the above statement (3) that

$$p_K(y) = p_K(y - x + x) \leqq p_K(y - x) + p_K(x)$$

and

$$p_K(x) \leqq p_K(x - y) + p_K(y);$$

or in short

$$-p_K(x - y) \leqq p_K(y) - p_K(x) \leqq p_K(y - x).$$

Since $p_K(x_n - x) \to 0$ as $x_n \to x$, we know $p_K(x_n) \to p_K(x)$ as $x_n \to x$ for each $x \in X$.

(5) Since p_K is continuous on X, the set $B_1 \equiv \{x : p_K(x) < 1\}$ is open and the set $B_2 \equiv \{x : p_K(x) \leqq 1\}$ is closed. (See Theorem 20 in Section 5.2.) For $x, y \in B_1$ and $\alpha \in [0, 1]$,

$$p_K(\alpha x + (1 - \alpha)y) \leqq \alpha p_K(x) + (1 - \alpha)p_K(y) < 1.$$

Hence B_1 is convex. Similarly, B_2 is convex. Let x be an element of $\mathring{K}$. Then $x/c \in \mathring{K}$ for $c \geqq 1$ in view of the fact that $\theta \in \mathring{K}$. Since $\mathring{K} \subset K$,

$$1 > \inf\{r :\ x/r \in K,\ r > 0\} = p_K(x). \tag{16}$$

Hence $\mathring{K} \subset B_1$. Conversely, let x be an element of B_1. Then, by (16), $x/r \in \mathring{K}$ for some $r \in (0, 1)$. Since $\mathring{K}$ is a convex set, in view of Theorem 21 in Section 5.2, containing θ,

$$x = rx/r + (1 - r)\,\theta \in \mathring{K} \qquad \text{for such an } r,$$

implying that $B_1 \subset \mathring{K}$. Hence $B_1 \equiv \mathring{K}$.

Similarly for $B_2 \equiv \bar{K}$. Q.E.D.

Now we turn to the Hahn–Banach theorem, where a sublinear functional plays a role. First, we shall prove the Hahn–Banach theorem in the case where the relevant space is real, and then by utilizing the result we verify the theorem in general circumstances. (The presentation of the following proof is parallel to the relevant parts of Kolmogorov and Fomin (1957), Yoshida (1965), and Luenberger (1969).)

THEOREM 44 (*Hahn–Banach theorem—the real case*) Let p be a continuous sublinear functional on a *real* normed vector space X, and f a linear functional on a subspace M of X satisfying

$$f(m) \leqq p(m) \qquad \text{for} \quad m \in M.$$

Then there is a bounded linear functional F on X such that

$$F(x) \leqq p(x) \qquad \text{for} \quad x \in X,$$

$$F(m) = f(m) \qquad \text{for} \quad m \in M.$$

In this case F is called an *extension* of f from M to X.

PROOF Although this theorem holds for the case where X is not separable, we suppose that X is separable in proving the theorem, simply because all the spaces to which this theorem is to be applied in this book are separable.

Let y be an element of X and not an element of M, define a linear variety $V \equiv y + M = \{v : v = y + m, m \in M\}$ and generate the subspace (of real space X) by V:

$$[V] = \{x : x = \alpha v + \beta w \quad \text{for} \quad v, w \in V \quad \text{and any } \textit{real } \alpha, \beta\}.$$

Then an element x of $[V]$ is uniquely represented by

$$x = \sum_{i=1}^{k} b_i v_i = by + m,$$

where $v_i = y + m_i$, $\{m_1, \ldots, m_k\}$ is a basis for M, $b \equiv \sum_i b_i$, all the b_i are real, and $m \equiv \sum_i b_i m_i$. An extension g of f from M to $[V]$ has the form,

$$g(x) = bg(y) + f(m),$$

where $g(x) = f(x)$ for $x \in M$ and g is found to be linear in x. Thus the extension becomes definite by prescribing the constant $g(y)$. We shall show that this constant can be chosen so that $g(x) \leqq p(x)$ on $[V]$.

For $m, n \in M$ we have

$$f(m) + f(n) = f(m + n) \leqq p(m + n) \leqq p(m - y) + p(n + y),$$

or

$$f(m) - p(m - y) \leqq p(n + y) - f(n),$$

and hence

$$\sup_{m \in M} [f(m) - p(m - y)] \leqq \inf_{m \in M} [p(m + y) - f(m)].$$

Therefore, there is a constant c such that

$$\sup_{m} [f(m) - p(m - y)] \leqq c \leqq \inf_{m} [p(m + y) - f(m)]. \tag{17}$$

For $x = by + m \in [V]$, we define $g(x) = bc + f(m)$. Then

$$g(by + m) \leqq p(by + m) \qquad \text{for any real } b$$

because, if $b > 0$, then in view of the second inequality in (17)

$$\begin{aligned} bc + f(m) &= b[c + f(m/b)] \leqq b[p(y + m/b) - f(m/b) + f(m/b)] \\ &= p(by + m), \end{aligned}$$

and if $b = -\beta < 0$, then in view of the first inequality in (17)

$$\begin{aligned} -\beta c + f(m) &= \beta[-c + f(m/\beta)] \\ &\leqq \beta[p(-y + m/\beta) - f(m/\beta) + f(m/\beta)] = p(by + m). \end{aligned}$$

Thus g is an extension of f from M to $[V]$.

Let $\{x_1, x_2, \ldots, x_n, \ldots\}$ be a countable dense set in X and from this set select a subset $\{y_1, y_2, \ldots\}$ whose vectors are linearly independent mutually and independent of M. Then the set $\{y_1, y_2, \ldots\}$ together with M generates a subspace S (of X) that is dense in X. The functional f can be extended to a functional g on the subspace S by extending f from M to $[M + y_1]$, then to $[[M + y_1] + y_2]$, and so on until all the y's are exhausted. Then the resulting g can be extended from the dense set S to the space X because for an x in X there is a sequence $\{s_n\}$ in S convergent to x, and

$$p(s_n) \to p(x)$$

since by assumption p is a continuous functional on X, which together with $g(x) \leqq p(x)$ for $x \in X$ guarantees that g is a *bounded* linear functional and hence continuous on X, implying that

$$g(s_n) \to F(x) \equiv \lim_{n \to \infty} g(s_n),$$

where F is a linear functional defined on X since g is so. Thus we get, by taking into account that $g(s_n) \leqq p(s_n)$,

$$F(x) \leqq p(x) \qquad \text{on } X.$$

Lastly, F is bounded because p is continuous on X. Q.E.D.

THEOREM 45 (*Hahn–Banach theorem—the complex case*) Let p be a continuous sublinear functional on a complex normed vector space X, and f a linear functional on a subspace M of X satisfying

$$|f(m)| \leqq p(m) \qquad \text{for} \quad m \in M.$$

Then there is a bounded linear functional F on X such that

$$|F(x)| \leqq p(x) \qquad \text{for} \quad x \in X,$$
$$F(m) = f(m) \qquad \text{for} \quad m \in M.$$

PROOF When X is regarded as real, we denote X by X_r and M by M_r. Let f be a linear functional on M of the complex form

$$f(m) \equiv f_r(m) - if_r(im) \qquad \text{for} \quad m \in M, \quad \text{where} \quad i \equiv (-1)^{1/2},$$

with $|f(m)| \leqq p(m)$ for $m \in M$. For an element h in M_r, $f(h) = \operatorname{Re}[f(h)] = f_r(h)$ since $f_r(ih)$ is irrelevant to M_r. Thus $|f_r(h)| = |f(h)| \leqq p(h)$ for $h \in M_r$, which implies

$$f_r(h) \leqq p(h) \qquad \text{for} \quad h \in M_r.$$

By the Hahn–Banach theorem (real case), there exists a bounded linear functional F_r such that

$$F_r(y) \leqq p(y) \qquad \text{for} \quad y \in X_r,$$
$$F_r(h) = f_r(h) \qquad \text{for} \quad h \in M_r.$$

Since $-F_r(y) = F_r(-y) \leqq p(-y) = p(y)$, we have

$$-p(y) \leqq -F_r(y) \leqq p(y),$$

or equivalently

$$|F_r(y)| \leqq p(y) \qquad \text{for} \quad y \in X_r. \tag{18}$$

Define $F(x) \equiv F_r(x) - iF_r(ix)$ for $x \in X$, where X is complex. For $y \in X_r$, $F(y) = \operatorname{Re}[F(y)] = F_r(y)$; and for $h \in M_r$, $F(h) = \operatorname{Re}[F(h)] = F_r(h) = f_r(h)$ since $F_r(iy)$ and $F_r(ih)$ are irrelevant to real spaces. For $m \in M$, $F(m) = F_r(m) - iF_r(im) = f_r(m) - if_r(im) = f(m)$.

It will be verified that $|F(x)| \leqq p(x)$ for $x \in X$. Suppose to the contrary that $|F(x_0)| > p(x_0)$ for some $x_0 \in X$. Complex number $F(x_0) = \gamma e^{-ib}$, where $\gamma > 0$. (Recall that a complex $c = \alpha + i\beta = |c|e^{it}$ with $|e^{it}| = 1$.) Define $z \equiv e^{ib}x_0 \in X$. Then

$$F_r(z) = \operatorname{Re}[F(z)] = \operatorname{Re}[e^{ib}F(x_0)] = \gamma = |F(x_0)| > p(x_0) = p(z).$$

This inequality must hold also for the case where X is real. In that case $X = X_r$ and $F_r(z) > p(z)$, contradicting (18) above. Q.E.D.

COROLLARY (*Hahn–Banach theorem—the simple version*) Let f be a bounded linear functional on a subspace M of a normed vector space X. There exists a bounded linear functional F on X that is an extension of f and has norm equal to that of f on M, i.e.,

$$\|F\| = \|f\|_M \equiv \sup_{m \in M} \frac{|f(m)|}{\|m\|}.$$

PROOF Take $p(x) = \|f\|_M \|x\|$ in the Hahn–Banach theorem (complex case). Then there is an extension F of f from M to X such that $|F(x)| \leqq$

$\|f\|_M \, \|x\|$ for $x \in X$. Define

$$\|F\| \equiv \sup_{x \in X} \frac{|F(x)|}{\|x\|}.$$

Then, since $F(m) = f(m)$ for $m \in M$,

$$\sup_{x \in X} \frac{|F(x)|}{\|x\|} \leqq \|f\|_M = \sup_{m \in M} \frac{|f(m)|}{\|m\|} = \sup_{m \in M} \frac{|F(m)|}{\|m\|} \leqq \sup_{x \in X} \frac{|F(x)|}{\|x\|}.$$

Thus $\|F\| = \|f\|_M$. Q.E.D.

THEOREM 46 Let x be an element of a normed vector space X. Then there is a nonzero bounded linear functional F on X such that $F(x) = \|F\| \, \|x\|$.

PROOF If $x = \theta$, any bounded linear functional will do. Assume $x \neq \theta$, and generate by x the one-dimensional subspace:

$$S_x = \{s : s = \beta x \text{ for any scalar } \beta\}.$$

On S_x we define a functional f such that $f(\beta x) = \beta\|x\|$. f is linear and continuous. The norm of f defined on S_x is

$$\|f\| \equiv \sup_{s \neq \theta} \frac{|f(s)|}{\|s\|} = \sup_{\beta \neq 0} \frac{|\beta| \, \|x\|}{|\beta| \, \|x\|} = 1.$$

Thus f is a bounded linear functional with norm equal to one. By the corollary above, therefore, there is a bounded linear functional F on X with $\|F\| = \|f\| = 1$. Since F is an extension of f from S_x to X, we have

$$F(\beta x) = f(\beta x) = \beta\|x\|,$$

and hence

$$F(x) = \|x\| = \|F\| \, \|x\|. \qquad \text{Q.E.D.}$$

The bounded linear functional F defined in Theorem 46 is obviously an element of the dual of X.

EXERCISES

1. Verify the De Morgan formulas:

$$(A \cap B)^c = A^c \cup B^c, \qquad (A \cup B)^c = A^c \cap B^c.$$

2. Show that the set of optimal strategies for each player of a matrix game described in Section 8.3 is convex and closed.

3. Prove the "if" part of Theorem 15.

4. Prove Theorem 20.

5. Prove Theorem 21.

6. Let M be a subspace of a vector space X. Two vectors $x, y \in X$ are said to be *congruent* (or *equivalent*) *modulo* M if and only if $y - x \in M$. In this case we write

$$x \equiv y \pmod{M},$$

signifying that x and y differ by a vector in M. For the subspace $M \subset X$ and a given vector $x \in X$, the set

$$[x]_M = \{k : k \in X, x \equiv k \pmod{M}\}$$

is called the *coset* of M with respect to x. Henceforth $[x]_M$ will be abbreviated as $[x]$.

The concept of congruence defined above possesses the following properties: For $x, y, z \in X$,

(i) $x \equiv x \pmod{M}$;
(ii) if $x \equiv y \pmod{M}$, then $y \equiv x \pmod{M}$;
(iii) if $x \equiv y \pmod{M}$ and $y \equiv z \pmod{M}$, then $x \equiv z \pmod{M}$.

The presence of these properties ensures the disjointness of cosets of M. Note that cosets of M except $[\theta]$ are the linear varieties that are distinct translates of M. Define the *quotient space* of X modulo M, denoted X/M, as the family of all cosets of M in X. Show that quotient space X/M can be treated as a vector space whose elements are cosets of M, and that if dim $X = n$ and dim $M = m$, then dim $X/M = n - m$.

7. Let $[x]$ be a coset of a closed subspace M of a normed space X and define

$$\|[x]\| = \inf_{m \in M} \|x + m\|. \tag{$*$}$$

Verify that this satisfies all the requirements for a norm.

8. Let M be a closed subspace of a Banach space X, and X/M be the quotient space with norm defined by $(*)$ above. Then prove X/M is a Banach space.

9. Show that the set of all positive and negative rational numbers is countable.

10. Let f be a functional defined on a space X and denote the value of f at a point $x \in X$ by $f(x)$, or alternatively by $[x; f]$. When f is a functional defined on the dual X^* of a normed vector space X, we define a functional g_x on X^* for each given $x \in X$ such that

$$g_x(f) = [x; f] \qquad \text{for} \quad f \in X^*.$$

Verify that given x in a normed vector space X, the above defined functional g_x is bounded and linear on X^* and preserves norm, i.e., $\|g_x\| = \|x\|$.

REFERENCES AND FURTHER READING

Apostol, T. M. (1957). *Mathematical Analysis*. Addison-Wesley, Reading, Massachusetts.
Berge, C. (1963). *Topological Spaces* (English translation). Oliver & Boyd, Edinburgh.

Dunford, N., and Schwartz, J. T. (1958). *Linear Operators*, Part I. Wiley(Interscience), New York.

Helmberg, G. (1969). *Introduction to Spectral Theory in Hilbert Space*. North-Holland Publ., Amsterdam.

Klein, E. (1973). *Mathematical Methods in Theoretical Economics*. Academic Press, New York.

Kolmogorov, A. N., and Fomin, S. V. (1957). *Elements of the Theory of Functional Analysis* (English translation), Vol. I. Graylock Press, Rochester, New York.

Lancaster, P. (1969). *Theory of Matrices*. Academic Press, New York.

Luenberger, D. G. (1969). *Optimization by Vector Space Methods*. Wiley, New York.

Simmons, G. F. (1963). *Introduction to Topology and Modern Analysis*. McGraw-Hill, New York.

Yoshida, K. (1965). *Functional Analysis*. Springer-Verlag, Berlin and New York.

Chapter 6

Projection and Generalized Inverse with Reference to Economics

6.1 Projection Theorems and the Gauss–Markov Theorem

We begin with some preliminary concepts and theorems.

DEFINITION 1 Vectors x and y belonging to an inner product space are said to be *orthogonal* if $(x|y) = 0$. We symbolize this by $x \perp y$.

THEOREM 1 (*Pythagorean theorem*) If x is orthogonal to y in an inner product space, then

$$\|x \pm y\|^2 = \|x\|^2 + \|y\|^2.$$

PROOF

$$\|x \pm y\|^2 = \|x\|^2 \pm (x|y) \pm (y|x) + \|y\|^2 = \|x\|^2 + \|y\|^2$$

since $(x|y) = 0$. Q.E.D.

DEFINITION 2 Let S be a subset of an inner product space X. The set of all vectors in X orthogonal to every element of S is called the *orthogonal complement* of S and is denoted $S^\perp$, i.e.,

$$S^\perp \equiv \{x : x \in X, (x|y) = 0 \text{ for every } y \in S\}.$$

Clearly, each $y \in S$ is orthogonal to every $x \in S^\perp$.

THEOREM 2 For any subset S of an inner product space, $S^\perp$ is a closed subspace.

PROOF For any $x, z \in S^\perp$ and scalars α, β,

$$(\alpha x + \beta z|y) = \alpha(x|y) + \beta(z|y) = 0 \qquad \text{for} \quad y \in S.$$

Hence $S^\perp$ is a subspace. Let $\{x_n\}$ be a sequence from $S^\perp$ convergent to x. Then, because of the continuity of inner product,

$$0 = (x_n \mid s) \to (x \mid s) \qquad \text{for} \quad s \in S.$$

Thus $(x \mid s) = 0$, which implies $x \in S^\perp$, and hence $S^\perp$ is closed. Q.E.D.

THEOREM 3 Let S, T be subsets of an inner product space X such that $S \subset T$. Then $S^\perp \supset T^\perp$.

PROOF Let x be an element of $T^\perp \equiv \{x : x \in X, (x \mid y) = 0 \text{ for every } y \in T\}$. Since $S \subset T$, $(x \mid s) = 0$ for any $s \in S$. Hence $x \in S^\perp$. Q.E.D.

THEOREM 4 For any subset S of an inner product space X,

$$S \subset S^{\perp\perp} \equiv \{z : z \in X,\ (z \mid y) = 0 \text{ for every } y \in S^\perp\}.$$

PROOF Any $x \in S$ is orthogonal to every $y \in S^\perp$. Hence $x \in S^{\perp\perp}$. Q.E.D.

Now we provide a lemma to verify the most fundamental theorem.

LEMMA 1 Let M be a subspace of an inner product space X and x be an element of X. (i) If there exists $m_0 \in M$ such that

$$\|x - m_0\| \leqq \|x - m\| \qquad \text{for any} \quad m \in M, \tag{$*$}$$

then m_0 is a unique vector; i.e., $\|x - m_0\| < \|x - m\|$ for $m \neq m_0$. (ii) m_0 is a unique minimizing vector in M if and only if

$$(x - m_0 \mid m) = 0 \quad \text{for any} \quad m \in M. \tag{$**$}$$

PROOF If $x \in M$, then $m_0 = x$. In the following we assume $x \notin M$.

(a) First, we shall prove that $(*)$ implies $(**)$. Suppose to the contrary that there exists an $m \in M$ such that $(x - m_0 \mid m) = \delta \neq 0$. We can normalize this m such that $\|m\| = 1$. Since M is a subspace, $m_1 \equiv m_0 + \delta m \in M$. Then,

$$\begin{aligned}
\|x - m_1\|^2 &= \|x - m_0 - \delta m\|^2 = (x - m_0 - \delta m \mid x - m_0 - \delta m) \\
&= (x - m_0 \mid x - m_0) - \delta(m \mid x - m_0) - \bar{\delta}(x - m_0 \mid m) + (\delta m \mid \delta m) \\
&= \|x - m_0\|^2 - 2\delta\bar{\delta} + \delta\bar{\delta}\|m\|^2 = \|x - m_0\|^2 - |\delta|^2 \\
&< \|x - m_0\|^2.
\end{aligned}$$

Hence, there exists $m_1 \in M$ such that $\|x - m_1\| < \|x - m_0\|$, entailing a contradiction.

(b) Next we shall prove that $(**)$ implies that m_0 is a unique minimizing vector. Since $(x - m_0 \mid m_0) = (x - m_0 \mid m) = 0$,

$$\|x - m\|^2 = \|x - m_0 + m_0 - m\|^2 = \|x - m_0\|^2 + \|m_0 - m\|^2.$$

Thus, $\|x - m\| > \|x - m_0\|$ for $m \neq m_0$.

(a) and (b) prove statement (i). The loop that "m_0 is a unique minimizing vector" $\Rightarrow (*) \Rightarrow (**) \Rightarrow$ "m_0 is a unique minimizing vector," proves statement (ii). Q.E.D.

THEOREM 5 (*projection theorem on a subspace*) Let M be a closed subspace of a Hilbert space H and x be an element of H. Then, there is a unique $m_0 \in M$ such that $\|x - m_0\| \leqq \|x - m\|$ for $m \in M$, and m_0 is the unique minimizing vector if and only if $x - m_0$ is orthogonal to M.

PROOF If $x \in M$, then $m_0 = x$ and the above statement holds trivially. Assume $x \notin M$ henceforth. The uniqueness and orthogonality established in the preceding lemma applies to the present case where $M \subset H$.

We need only establish the existence of the minimizing vector for a closed subspace M. Let $\{m_i\}$ be a sequence of vectors in M such that

$$\|x - m_i\| \to \delta \equiv \inf_{m \in M} \|x - m\|.$$

$$\begin{aligned}\|m_j - m_i\|^2 + \|m_j - 2x + m_i\|^2 &= \|(m_j - x) + (x - m_i)\|^2 + \|(m_j - x) \\ &\quad - (x - m_i)\|^2 \\ &= 2\|m_j - x\|^2 + 2\|x - m_i\|^2.\end{aligned}$$

Taking into account the facts that $\|m_j - 2x + m_i\|^2 = 4\|x - (m_i + m_j)/2\|^2$ and that $\|x - (m_i + m_j)/2\| \geqq \delta$ since $(m_i + m_j)/2 \in M$, we have

$$\begin{aligned}\|m_j - m_i\|^2 &= 2\|m_j - x\|^2 + 2\|x - m_i\|^2 - 4\|x - (m_i + m_j)/2\|^2 \\ &\leqq 2\|m_j - x\|^2 + 2\|x - m_i\|^2 - 4\delta^2.\end{aligned}$$

Therefore, $\|x - m_i\| \to \delta$ (as $i \to \infty$) implies that

$$\|m_j - m_i\|^2 \to 0 \qquad \text{as} \quad i, j \to \infty.$$

That is, $\{m_i\}$ is a Cauchy sequence in $M \subset H$. So it is also convergent to a limit in H. Since M is closed, the sequence has a limit in M; i.e., there exists a limit $m_0 \in M$ such that $\|x - m_0\| \leqq \|x - m\|$ for $m \in M$. Q.E.D.

Theorem 5 implies that there is a unique decomposition of x:

$$x = m_0 + \tilde{x}$$

where $m_0 \in M$ and $\tilde{x} \perp M$. The vector m_0 is called the projection of x on M.

THEOREM 6 (Albert, 1972) For any $n \times n$ real symmetric matrix A, real $\alpha \neq 0$, and any vector $y \in R^n$, the following limit exists:

$$\lim_{\alpha \to 0} (A + \alpha I)^{-1} A y = y_0,$$

where y_0 is the projection of y on $\bar{R}(A)$.

PROOF For the matrix A, there is a square matrix V such that

$$A = V \Lambda V^{\mathrm{T}} \qquad \text{and} \qquad V V^{\mathrm{T}} = I,$$

where Λ is the diagonal matrix consisting of the eigenvalues of A. Thus

$$A + \alpha I = V(\Lambda + \alpha I)\, V^{\mathrm{T}}.$$

Let λ be the nonzero eigenvalue of A having the smallest modulus. Then for any α with $0 < |\alpha| < |\lambda|$, $\Lambda + \alpha I$ is nonsingular and hence $A + \alpha I$ is nonsingular for such α's.

Any vector $y \in R^n$ can be decomposed as

$$y = y_0 + \tilde{y},$$

where $y_0 \in \bar{R}(A)$ and $\tilde{y} \in R(A)^{\perp} = N(A)$ in view of Corollary 2 to Theorem 16 in Section 6.2 and of the fact that $A^{\mathrm{T}} = A$. Hence

$$Ay = Ay_0,$$

and $y_0 = Ax_0$ for some $x_0 \in R^n$. Therefore

$$(A + \alpha I)^{-1} Ay = (A + \alpha I)^{-1} A^2 x_0 = V(\Lambda + \alpha I)^{-1} \Lambda^2 V^{\mathrm{T}} x_0.$$

Since it is easily seen that

$$\lim_{\alpha \to 0} (\Lambda + \alpha I)^{-1} \Lambda^2 = \Lambda,$$

we have

$$\lim_{\alpha \to 0} (A + \alpha I)^{-1} Ay = V\Lambda V^{\mathrm{T}} x_0 = Ax_0 = y_0. \qquad \text{Q.E.D.}$$

THEOREM 7 Let M be a closed subspace of a Hilbert space H. Then, (i) $H = M \oplus M^{\perp}$ and (ii) $M = M^{\perp\perp}$.

PROOF (i) Let $x \in H$. By the preceding projection theorem, there exists a unique $m_0 \in M$ such that $\|x - m_0\| \leqq \|x - m\|$ for $m \in M$, and $n_0 \equiv x - m_0 \in M^{\perp}$. Hence $x = m_0 + n_0$ for $m_0 \in M$ and $n_0 \in M^{\perp}$. In order to show that this representation is unique, suppose $x = m_1 + n_1$ for $m_1 \in M$ and $n_1 \in M^{\perp}$. Then, $\theta = m_1 - m_0 + n_1 - n_0$ and $(m_1 - m_0) \perp (n_1 - n_0)$ since M and $M^{\perp}$ are subspaces. Thus, by the Pythagorean theorem,

$$\|\theta\|^2 = \|m_1 - m_0\|^2 + \|n_1 - n_0\|^2,$$

which means that $m_1 = m_0$ and $n_1 = n_0$.

(ii) Since $M \subset M^{\perp\perp}$ is known, it is only necessary to show that $M^{\perp\perp} \subset M$. Let x be a vector in $M^{\perp\perp}$. Because $H = M^{\perp} \oplus M^{\perp\perp}$, x is an element of H, and hence $x = m + n$ with unique $m \in M$ and $n \in M^{\perp}$. Since $m \in M \subset M^{\perp\perp}$, $n = x - m \in M^{\perp\perp}$. Thus, $n \perp n$, which implies $n = \theta$, entailing $x = m \in M$. Q.E.D. (The proof is due to Luenberger (1969).)

COROLLARY Let N, M be closed subspaces of a Hilbert space H such that $N \supset M$. Then $N = M \oplus (N \cap M^{\perp})$.

PROOF $N \cap M^{\perp} = \{n : n \in N, n \perp M\}$ is the closed orthogonal complement of M in N. Replacing H in Theorem 7 by N yields the result stated above. Q.E.D.

THEOREM 8 Let S be a subset of a Hilbert space, and $[\bar{S}]$ the smallest closed subspace containing S. Then $S^{\perp\perp} = [\bar{S}]$.

PROOF Let S_i $(i \in J)$ be all the closed subspaces containing S. Then $[\bar{S}]$ must be defined as $[\bar{S}] \equiv \bigcap_{i \in J} S_i$ because the intersection of an arbitrary collection of closed sets is closed and because the intersection of any two subspaces is a subspace. Since $S^{\perp\perp}$ is a closed subspace containing S (by Theorems 2 and 4), we have $S^{\perp\perp} \supset [\bar{S}]$. On the other hand, $[\bar{S}]^{\perp\perp} \subset [\bar{S}]$ by the proof of Theorem 7. Also $S \subset [\bar{S}]$ implies $S^{\perp} \supset [\bar{S}]^{\perp}$, which in turn implies $S^{\perp\perp} \subset [\bar{S}]^{\perp\perp}$ (by Theorem 3). Thus, we obtain

$$S^{\perp\perp} \subset [\bar{S}]^{\perp\perp} \subset [\bar{S}]. \qquad \text{Q.E.D.}$$

The projection theorem stated on a subspace can be extended to one on a linear variety.

THEOREM 9 (*projection theorem on a linear variety*) Let M be a closed subspace of a Hilbert space H and x an element of H. Define a linear variety $V = x + M$. Then, (i) there exists a unique vector $x_0 \in V$ such that $\|x_0\| \leqq \|v\|$ for $v \in V$, and (ii) x_0 is a unique minimizing vector if and only if $x_0 \perp M$.

PROOF The projection theorem on a subspace states that there is a unique $m_0 \in M$ such that $\|x - m_0\| \leqq \|x - m\|$ for $m \in M$ and that m_0 is the unique minimizing vector, i.e., $\|x - m_0\| < \|x - m\|$ for $m \neq m_0$ if and only if $(x - m_0) \perp M$ (see Fig. 2). Put $x_0 = x - m_0$, and $v = x - m$. Then restate the theorem as follows: (i′) there exists $x - x_0 \in M$ such that $\|x_0\| \leqq \|v\|$ for $v \in M$ and (ii) $\|x_0\| < \|v\|$ for $v \neq x_0$ if and only if $x_0 \perp M$. In (i′) above $x - x_0 \in M$ implies $x_0 \in x + M = V$ since $x_0 - x \in M$. Q.E.D.

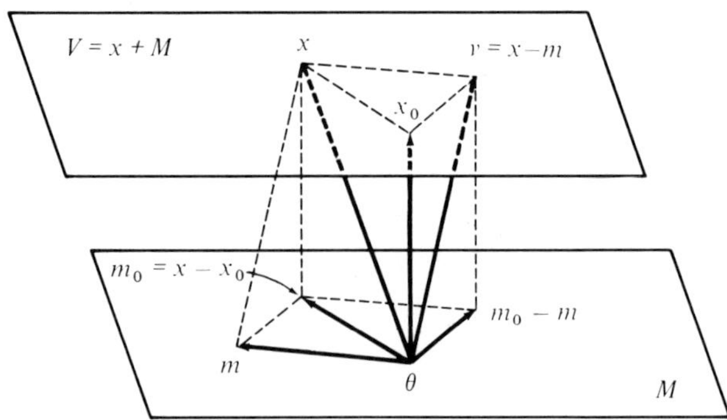

FIGURE 2. Projection.

The following theorem, which can be regarded as a corollary to the preceding projection theorem, is particularly useful for estimiatng parameters in a stochastic linear system. (Refer to Luenberger (1969).)

THEOREM 10 Let $y_1, \ldots, y_n$ be linearly independent vectors in a Hilbert space H, and x^0 be the vector having minimum norm among all vectors $x \in H$ satisfying the constraints

$$(x \mid y_j) = c_j \qquad \text{for} \quad j = 1, \ldots, n, \tag{$*$}$$

where $c_1, \ldots, c_n$ are constants. Then we know that

$$x^0 = \sum_{i=1}^{n} b_i y_i, \tag{$**$}$$

where the coefficients b_i are uniquely determined by the equations

$$\sum_{i=1}^{n} (y_i \mid y_j) b_i = c_j \qquad (j = 1, \ldots, n). \tag{$***$}$$

PROOF Let M be the subspace generated by the vectors $y_1, \ldots, y_n$. Clearly M is closed. If every c_j is zero, the set of x satisfying the constraints $(*)$ is the subspace $M^\perp$. Given nonzero values of the c_j, the sum of any vector x satisfying the constraints $(*)$ and an element of $M^\perp$ will also fulfill the constraints. Thus the space satisfying the constraints $(*)$ is a linear variety $V = x + M^\perp$, where x is any vector satisfying the constraints. Since $M^\perp$ is closed, the existence and uniqueness of a minimum norm vector follow from Theorem 9. Furthermore, by the same theorem, such a vector x^0 is orthogonal to $M^\perp$, i.e., x^0 belongs to $M^{\perp\perp}$. Since M is closed, $M^{\perp\perp} = M$. (See Theorem 7.) Therefore, x^0 is an element of M, which can be represented by a linear combination $(**)$ of y's. Substituting x^0 for x in $(*)$ yields $(***)$. Since all the y's are linearly independent, the Gram matrix of these y's is nonsingular. (Refer to Theorem 9 in Section 5.1.) Hence the b's in $(***)$ are uniquely determined. Q.E.D.

Application 1 (*Gauss-Markov theorem*) We show the unique existence of the so-called Gauss–Markov estimator. The *Gauss–Markov model* is composed of

$$y = X\beta + \varepsilon,$$

where y and ε are n-tuple column vectors, X is an $n \times k$ matrix with linearly independent columns, and β is a k-tuple column vector of unknown constants, all over the field of real numbers, with the following properties about the expectations of ε and $\varepsilon\varepsilon^{\mathrm{T}}$:

$$E(\varepsilon) = \theta \qquad \text{and} \qquad E(\varepsilon\varepsilon^{\mathrm{T}}) = Q,$$

where Q is assumed to be positive definite. We seek the linear unbiased estimator $\hat{\beta}$ of β in the Gauss–Markov model that minimizes $E(\|\hat{\beta} - \beta\|^2)$ where the norm is Euclidean. The linearity of the estimator means that $\hat{\beta}$ is expressed as $\hat{\beta} = Py$ where P is a $k \times n$ matrix, and the linear unbiasedness requires $PX = I$ since

$$\beta = E(\hat{\beta}) = E(Py) = E(PX\beta + P\varepsilon) = PX\beta.$$

Let s_{ij} be the (i, j)th component of matrix $P^{\mathrm{T}}P$ and $E(\varepsilon_i \varepsilon_j)$ be that of matrix $E(\varepsilon\varepsilon^{\mathrm{T}})$.

$$\begin{aligned} E(\|\hat{\beta} - \beta\|^2) &= E(\|Py - \beta\|^2) = E(\|P\varepsilon\|^2) = E(\varepsilon^{\mathrm{T}}P^{\mathrm{T}}P\varepsilon) \\ &= E(\sum_i \sum_j s_{ij}\varepsilon_i\varepsilon_j) = \sum_i \sum_j s_{ij}E(\varepsilon_i\varepsilon_j) = \mathrm{tr}(P^{\mathrm{T}}PQ) = \mathrm{tr}(PQP^{\mathrm{T}}), \end{aligned}$$

where $\mathrm{tr}(A)$ stands for the trace of square matrix A, i.e., the sum of the principal diagonal elements of A. Thus the problem is to select P such that $\mathrm{tr}(PQP^{\mathrm{T}})$ is minimized under the constraint $PX = I$. By p_i and x_i we denote the ith column vectors of P^{T} and X, respectively. Then the present problem is found to be decomposed into k subproblems, the ith of which is to minimize $p_i^{\mathrm{T}}Qp_i$ subject to $p_i^{\mathrm{T}}x_j = \delta_{ij}$ $(j = 1, \ldots, k)$, where $\delta_{ii} = 1$ and $\delta_{ij} = 0$ $(i \neq j)$. Defining an inner product as $(v\,|\,w) = v^{\mathrm{T}}Qw$, the ith subproblem is rewritten as: Minimize $(p_i\,|\,p_i)$ subject to $(p_i\,|\,Q^{-1}x_j) = \delta_{ij}$ for $j = 1, \ldots, k$. For this, Theorem 10 is applied. Thus the optimal p_i is represented as

$$p_i = \sum_{h=1}^{k} b_h Q^{-1} x_h = Q^{-1} Xb,$$

where column vector $b \equiv \{b_1, \ldots, b_k\}$ satisfies the equations

$$\sum_{h=1}^{k} (Q^{-1} x_h\,|\,Q^{-1} x_j)\, b_h = \delta_{ij} \qquad \text{for} \quad j = 1, \ldots, k.$$

Since the left-hand sides of the above equations as a whole for all j can be expressed as $X^{\mathrm{T}}Q^{-1}Xb$, we obtain

$$P^{\mathrm{T}} = (p_1, \ldots, p_k) = Q^{-1}X(X^{\mathrm{T}}Q^{-1}X)^{-1}.$$

Hence the *best linear unbiased estimator* $\hat{\beta}$ is computed as

$$\hat{\beta} = Py = (X^{\mathrm{T}}Q^{-1}X)^{-1}X^{\mathrm{T}}Q^{-1}y$$

with the corresponding error covariance

$$E[(\hat{\beta} - \beta)(\hat{\beta} - \beta)^{\mathrm{T}}] = E(P\varepsilon\varepsilon^{\mathrm{T}}P^{\mathrm{T}}) = PQP^{\mathrm{T}} = (X^{\mathrm{T}}Q^{-1}X)^{-1}.$$

6.2 Adjoint Operators

This section is devoted to adjoint operators; these have intimate relationships with the properties of the generalized inverse introduced in the next section.

Let $F \in B(X, Y)$; i.e., let F be a bounded linear transformation from a normed space X into a normed space Y over a field L. Denote by X^* and Y^*

the dual spaces of X and Y, respectively. Given a linear functional $y^* \in Y^*$, the quantity

$$Q(x) \equiv y^*(F(x)) = [F(x);\, y^*]$$

is a scalar for each $x \in X$, and hence Q is a functional on X. Q is found to be linear on X because in view of the linearity of F

$$[F(\alpha x_1 + \beta x_2);\, y^*] = \alpha[F(x_1);\, y^*] + \beta[F(x_2);\, y^*]$$

for $x_1, x_2 \in X$ and scalars $\alpha, \beta \in L$. Thus Q is a linear functional on X. This line of thought justifies the existence of a transformation $F^*\colon Y^* \to X^*$ such that $F^*(y^*) = Q$.

DEFINITION 3 Let X, Y be normed spaces and assume $F \in B(X, Y)$. A transformation $F^*\colon Y^* \to X^*$ such that

$$[x;F^*(y^*)] = [F(x);y^*] \qquad \text{for} \quad x \in X \quad \text{and} \quad y^* \in Y^*,$$

is called the *adjoint* (*operator*) of F.

F^* defined above is unique, for if there were another transformation $G^*\colon Y^* \to X^*$ such that $G^*(y^*) = Q$, then $[F(x);\, y^*] \equiv [G(x);\, y^*]$ for each $x \in X$, i.e., $[(F - G)(x);\, y^*] \equiv 0$ for each $x \in X$, implying $F \equiv G$.

When X, Y are finite-dimensional Euclidean spaces, their duals are X, Y themselves. Therefore, the adjoint operator of $F \in B(X, Y)$ is the transformation $F^*\colon Y \to X$ such that

$$(x\,|\,F^*(y)) = (F(x)\,|\,y) \qquad \text{for} \quad x \in X \quad \text{and} \quad y \in Y.$$

If A is the matrix representing F relative to a given pair of bases for X and Y, then it will be shown that the matrix representing F^* is the transpose A^{T} of A. (The proof is left to the reader.) Consequently, the norm of F^* is defined in the same manner as that of F in this case.

THEOREM 11 Let X, Y be finite-dimensional Euclidean spaces and let $F \in B(X, Y)$. Then $F^{**} = F$.

PROOF F^{**} maps from X into Y, and

$$(y\,|\,F^{**}(x)) = (F^*(y)\,|\,x) = (x\,|\,F^*(y)) = (F(x)\,|\,y) = (y\,|\,F(x)). \qquad \text{Q.E.D.}$$

A discussion of properties of adjoint operators is in order.

THEOREM 12 Let X, Y be normed spaces over a field L and let $F \in B(X, Y)$. Then its adjoint F^* is linear and bounded on Y^*.

PROOF *Linearity* Given $x \in X$,

$$\begin{aligned}[x;\, F^*(\alpha y^* + \beta z^*)] &= [F(x);\, \alpha y^* + \beta z^*] = [F(x);\, \alpha y^*] + [F(x);\, \beta z^*]\\ &= \alpha[F(x);\, y^*] + \beta[F(x);\, z^*]\\ &= \alpha[x;\, F^*(y^*)] + \beta[x;\, F^*(z^*)]\end{aligned}$$

for $y^*, z^* \in Y^*$ and scalars $\alpha, \beta \in L$.

Boundedness In view of the norms $\|y^*\|$ and $\|F\|$,

$$|[F(x); y^*]| \leqq \|y^*\| \, \|F(x)\| \leqq \|y^*\| \, \|F\| \, \|x\|.$$

Since $F^*(y^*)$ is an element of X^*,

$$\|F^*(y^*)\| = \sup_{x \in X, x \neq \theta} \frac{|[x; F^*(y^*)]|}{\|x\|} = \sup \frac{|[F(x); y^*]|}{\|x\|} \leqq \|F\| \, \|y^*\|,$$

where $\|F\|$ is finite due to the boundedness of F. Q.E.D.

Note that if X, Y are Euclidean spaces and $F \in B(X, Y)$, then $F^* \in B(Y, X)$.

THEOREM 13 Let X, Y be normed spaces, let $F \in B(X, Y)$ and assume F has an inverse. Then $(F^*)^{-1} = (F^{-1})^*$.

PROOF First, we show that the adjoint F^* is a one-to-one and onto transformation, i.e., that for each $x^* \in X^*$ there exist at most one $y^* \in Y^*$ and at least one $y^* \in Y^*$ for which $F^*(y^*) = x^*$. Let y^* and z^* be different elements of Y^*. Then

$$[x; F^*(y^*)] - [x; F^*(z^*)] = [x; \ F^*(y^* - z^*)] = [F(x); y^* - z^*] \neq 0$$

for some $x \in X$. Hence $F^*(y^*) \neq F^*(z^*)$, implying that F^* is one-to-one. If $F(x) = y$, we have $x = F^{-1}(y)$ by assumption. Thus

$$\begin{aligned}[x; x^*] &= [F^{-1}(y); x^*] = [y; (F^{-1})^*(x^*)] = [F(x); (F^{-1})^*(x^*)] \\ &= [x; F^*((F^{-1})^*(x^*))].\end{aligned}$$

Hence $x^* = F^*((F^{-1})^*(x^*))$, implying $(F^{-1})^*(x^*) \in Y^*$, which in turn implies that F^* is onto. Therefore, there is an inverse of F^*. Since $F^*(F^{-1})^* = I$ (an identity operator), we get $(F^{-1})^* = (F^*)^{-1}$. Q.E.D.

THEOREM 14 Let X, Y, Z be normed spaces.

(i) If I is the identity operator on X, then $I^* = I$.
(ii) If $F \in B(X, Y)$ and α is a real scalar, then $(\alpha F)^* = \alpha F^*$.
(iii) If $F, G \in B(X, Y)$, then $(F + G)^* = F^* + G^*$.
(iv) If $F \in B(X, Y)$ and $G \in B(Y, Z)$, then $(GF)^* = F^*G^*$.

PROOF (i) $[x; I^*(y^*)] = [I(x); y^*] = [x; I(y^*)]$.

(ii) $[x; (\alpha F)^*(y^*)] = [\alpha F(x); y^*] = \alpha[x; F^*(y^*)] = [x; \alpha F^*(y^*)]$.

(iii) $$\begin{aligned}[x; (F + G)^*(y^*)] &= [(F + G)(x); y^*] = [F(x); y^*] + [G(x); y^*] \\ &= [x; F^*(y^*)] + [x; G^*(y^*)] = [x; (F^* + G^*)(y^*)].\end{aligned}$$

(iv) $[x; (GF)^*(y^*)] = [GF(x); y^*] = [F(x); G^*(y^*)] = [x; F^*G^*(y^*)]$.

Q.E.D.

THEOREM 15 Let X, Y be finite-dimensional Euclidean spaces and let $F \in B(X, Y)$. Suppose $G \in B(Y, X)$ such that for given nonzero $y \in Y$

$$\|FG(y) - y\| \leqq \|F(x) - y\| \qquad \text{for all} \quad x \in X. \tag{1}$$

Then

$$FGF = F; \tag{2}$$

$$(FG)^* = FG. \tag{3}$$

PROOF Denote $w \equiv x - G(y)$. Then (1) is rewritten as

$$\|FG(y) - y\| \leqq \|FG(y) - y + F(w)\| \qquad \text{for all } w.$$

$$\Rightarrow \|FG(y) - y\|^2 \leqq \|FG(y) - y\|^2 + \|F(w)\|^2 + 2(FG(y) - y \,|\, F(w))$$
$$\text{for all } w.$$

$$\Rightarrow 0 = (F(w) \,|\, FG(y) - y) = (w \,|\, F^*(FG - I)(y)) \qquad \text{for all } w.$$

Thus we have

$$F^*FG = F^*,$$

from which it follows that $F^*FGF = F^*F$ and hence (2). (3) is derived from the following:

$$(FG)^*F = (FG)^*F^{**} = (F^*FG)^* = F^{**} = F = FGF. \qquad \text{Q.E.D.}$$

COROLLARY Assume the same situation as in the above theorem. Let A and C be the matrices representing F and G, respectively, relative to a chosen pair of bases for X and Y. Then $\text{rk}(CA) = \text{rk}(A)$.

PROOF In view of (2), $ACA = A$. Hence

$$\text{rk}(A) \geqq \text{rk}(CA) \geqq \text{rk}(ACA) = \text{rk}(A). \qquad \text{Q.E.D.}$$

Next we shall present fundamental relations concerning the nullspace and range of an adjoint operator. Let us recall the notation: $R(F) \equiv$ the range of F and $N(F) \equiv$ the nullspace of F, where F is a transformation.

THEOREM 16 Let X, Y be normed spaces and let $F \in B(X, Y)$. Then $R(F)^\perp = N(F^*)$.

PROOF Let $y^* \in N(F^*)$ and $y \in R(F)$. Then $F^*(y^*) = \theta$ and $y = F(x)$ for some $x \in X$. Hence

$$[y; y^*] = [F(x); y^*] = [x; F^*(y^*)] = [x; \theta] = 0,$$

meaning that $y^* \in R(F)^\perp$.

Let $y^* \in R(F)^\perp$. Then $[y; y^*] = 0$ for all $y \in R(F)$. Thus $[x; F^*(y^*)] = [F(x); y^*] = 0$ for all $x \in X$, implying that $F^*(y^*) = \theta$. Hence $y^* \in N(F^*)$. Q.E.D.

COROLLARY 1 Let X, Y be Hilbert spaces and let $F \in B(X, Y)$. Then $\bar{R}(F) = N(F^*)^\perp$, where $\bar{R}(F)$ stands for the closure of $R(F)$.

PROOF From the above theorem it follows that $N(F^*)^\perp = R(F)^{\perp\perp} = \bar{R}(F)$. Q.E.D.

COROLLARY 2 Let X, Y be finite-dimensional Euclidean spaces and let $F \in B(X, Y)$. Then $N(F) = R(F^*)^{\perp}$ and $N(F)^{\perp} = \bar{R}(F^*)$.

PROOF Since $F^* \in B(Y, X)$, we obtain $R(F^*)^{\perp} = N(F^{**}) = N(F)$ in view of the above theorem and $F^{**} = F$. $N(F)^{\perp} = R(F^*)^{\perp\perp} = \bar{R}(F^*)$. Q.E.D.

Lastly, we provide a general solution to a minimizer of Euclidean distance, which will be employed to define a generalized inverse.

THEOREM 17 Let X, Y be finite-dimensional Euclidean spaces with $\dim X = n$, and let $F \in B(X, Y)$. Suppose $G \in B(Y, X)$ such that for given nonzero $y \in Y$, $x_1 = G(y)$ is a solution of

$$\|F(x_1) - y\| \leqq \|F(x) - y\| \qquad \text{for} \quad x \in X. \tag{4}$$

Then the general solution of (4) is represented as

$$x_1 = G(y) + (I - GF)(x) \qquad \text{for} \quad x \in X. \tag{5}$$

PROOF By Theorem 15, $F(I - GF) = \theta$; i.e., $(I - GF)(x) \in N(F)$ for $x \in X$. Thus we define

$$M \equiv \{x_2 : x_2 = (I - GF)(x) \text{ for some } x \in X\},$$

which is a closed subspace (of X) contained in $N(F)$. Let A, C be matrices representing F, G respectively relative to a chosen pair of bases for X and Y. By the corollary to Theorem 15 with idempotent CA,

$$\dim M = \dim R(I - GF) = \operatorname{rk}(I - CA) = \operatorname{tr}(I - CA) = n - \operatorname{rk}(A).$$

On the other hand, in view of $X = N(F) \oplus N(F)^{\perp}$,

$$\dim N(F) = n - \dim N(F)^{\perp} = n - \dim \bar{R}(F^*) = n - \operatorname{rk}(A^{\mathrm{T}}).$$

Hence, $\dim M = \dim N(F)$. Moreover, both M and $N(F)$ are closed subspaces, each of which contains the other. Therefore, $M = N(F)$, and the entire solution space of (4) is equal to the translation of M by $G(y)$, i.e., $G(y) + M$, whose elements are represented as in (5). Q.E.D.

6.3 Generalized Inverse (Pseudoinverse)

We are now in a position to define a generalized inverse in Euclidean spaces.

Let X, Y be finite-dimensional Euclidean spaces and let $F \in B(X, Y)$ with closed $R(F)$. Then by the projection theorem on a subspace, for given nonzero $y_0 \in Y$ there is a unique vector y_1 in $R(F)$ such that

$$\|y_1 - y_0\| \leqq \|y - y_0\| \qquad \text{for} \quad y \in R(F), \tag{6}$$

which implies that there is an $x_1 \in X$ satisfying

$$\|F(x_1) - y_0\| \leqq \|F(x) - y_0\| \qquad \text{for} \quad x \in X. \tag{7}$$

The x_1 may not be unique. So let X_1 be the set of solutions x_1 of (7) satisfying $F(x_1) = y_1$ for the unique y_1. By Theorem 17, X_1 is a translation of $N(F)$ that is a closed subspace of X. By the projection theorem on a linear variety, there exists a unique vector x_0 of minimum norm in X_1 and $x_0 \in N(F)^\perp$. The operator F restricted to $N(F)^\perp$ is regarded as a transformation from $N(F)^\perp$ onto $R(F)$. Besides, $x_0 \in N(F)^\perp$ satisfying $F(x_0) = y_1$ for each $y_1 \in R(F)$ is unique. Thus, transformation F is one-to-one and onto, implying that there is a linear "inverse" operator from $R(F)$ onto $N(F)^\perp$. The domain of the transformation can be extended from $R(F)$ to Y by assigning to every $y_2 \in R(F)^\perp$ the null vector θ.

DEFINITION 4 Let X, Y be finite-dimensional Euclidean spaces and let $F \in B(X, Y)$ with closed $R(F)$. Then we define the *generalized inverse* or *pseudoinverse* of F, denoted F^+, as the bounded linear transformation from Y onto $N(F)^\perp$ such that it assigns to each $y_0 \in Y$ a unique $x_0 \in N(F)^\perp$ by

$$F^+(y_0) = F^+(y_1 + y_2) = F^+(y_1) = x_0, \tag{8}$$

where $y_1 \in R(F)$ satisfying (6), $y_2 \in R(F)^\perp$, and x_0 is the vector of minimum norm among all vectors x_1 satisfying (7). (8) implies $F^+(y_2) = \theta$ for $y_2 \in R(F)^\perp$.

We remark that

$$R(F^+) = \bar{R}(F^*) \tag{9}$$

since $N(F)^\perp = \bar{R}(F^*)$, where F^* stands for the adjoint operator of F.

THEOREM 18 Let X, Y be finite-dimensional Euclidean spaces and let F^+ be the generalized inverse of $F \in B(X, Y)$. Then the following relations hold:

$$FF^+F = F \tag{10}$$

$$(FF^+)^* = FF^+ \tag{11}$$

$$F^+FF^+ = F^+ \tag{12}$$

$$(F^+F)^* = F^+F. \tag{13}$$

PROOF Given nonzero $y \in Y$, $\|F^+(y)\| \leqq \|x_1\|$ for x_1 satisfying

$$\|F(x_1) - y\| \leqq \|F(x) - y\| \qquad \text{for all} \quad x \in X. \tag{$*$}$$

(10) and (11) follow immediately from Theorem 15 in the preceding section. By Theorem 17, the general solution of ($*$) is

$$x_1 = F^+(y) + (I - F^+F)(x) \qquad \text{for arbitrary} \quad x \in X.$$

Hence $\|F^+(y)\| \leqq \|F^+(y) + (I - F^+F)(x)\|$ for arbitrary $x \in X$.

$$\Rightarrow 0 = ((I - F^+F)(x) \mid F^+(y)) = (x \mid (I - F^+F)^*F^+(y)) \qquad \text{for} \quad x \in X$$

$$\Rightarrow (I - (F^+F)^*)F^+ = \theta,$$

i.e.,

$$F^+ = (F^+F)^*F^+ \tag{**}$$

$$\Rightarrow (F^+)^* = (F^*(F^+)^*F^+)^* = (F^+)^*F^+F$$

$$\Rightarrow (F^+)^*F^+ = (F^+)^*F^+FF^+ \Rightarrow (12).$$

(**) and (12) $\Rightarrow$ (13). Q.E.D.

Note that if F has an inverse F^{-1}, then F^{-1} plays the role of F^+ in relations (10)–(13).

COROLLARY 1 Let X, Y be finite-dimensional Euclidean spaces and denote by A the matrix representing $F \in B(X, Y)$ relative to a given pair of bases for X and Y. Then the generalized inverse A^+ of A satisfies

$$AA^+A = A \tag{10$'$}$$

$$(AA^+)^{\mathrm{T}} = AA^+ \tag{11$'$}$$

$$A^+AA^+ = A^+ \tag{12$'$}$$

$$(A^+A)^{\mathrm{T}} = A^+A. \tag{13$'$}$$

Equations (10′)–(13′) are the fundamentals from which various properties of A^+ will be deduced. If, given a real number $\alpha \neq 0$, αA and $\alpha^{-1}A^+$ are substituted for A and A^+ respectively, then these equations hold as they are. Therefore, for a real number $\alpha \neq 0$,

$$(\alpha A)^+ = \alpha^{-1}A^+. \tag{14}$$

COROLLARY 2 Let A be a real matrix. Then AA^+, A^+A, $I - AA^+$, $I - A^+A$ are all symmetric idempotent.

PROOF

$$(I - AA^+)^{\mathrm{T}} = I - (AA^+)^{\mathrm{T}} = I - AA^+.$$

$$(I - AA^+)^2 = I - 2AA^+ + A(A^+AA^+) = I - 2AA^+ + AA^+ = I - AA^+.$$

Hence $I - AA^+$ is symmetric idempotent. Similarly for the others. Q.E.D.

COROLLARY 3 Let A be a real matrix. Then

$$\mathrm{rk}(A^+) = \mathrm{rk}(A) = \mathrm{rk}(AA^+) = \mathrm{rk}(A^+A).$$

PROOF $\mathrm{rk}(A) = \mathrm{rk}(AA^+A) \leqq \mathrm{rk}(AA^+) \leqq \mathrm{rk}(A^+) = \mathrm{rk}(A^+AA^+) \leqq \mathrm{rk}(A^+A) \leqq \mathrm{rk}(A)$. Q.E.D.

THEOREM 19 (*Penrose, first theorem*) The four equations

$$AZA = A \tag{1$'$}$$

$$(AZ)^{\mathrm{T}} = AZ \tag{2$'$}$$

$$ZAZ = Z \tag{3$'$}$$

$$(ZA)^{\mathrm{T}} = ZA \tag{4$'$}$$

have a unique solution Z for any matrix A. Hence the generalized inverse A^+ of matrix A is unique.

PROOF Such a solution Z exists since A^+ is known to be a solution to the equations. To show that Z is unique, we suppose that S satisfies (2*) and (4*) below, which are obtained respectively by substituting (2′) into (1′) and (4′) into (3′); i.e.,

$$A^{\mathrm{T}}AS = A^{\mathrm{T}}, \tag{2*}$$

$$A^{\mathrm{T}}S^{\mathrm{T}}S = S. \tag{4*}$$

Equations (2′) and (3′) together are found to be equivalent to

$$ZZ^{\mathrm{T}}A^{\mathrm{T}} = Z, \tag{3*}$$

because (2′) and (3′) $\Rightarrow$(3*) $\Rightarrow AZ(AZ)^{\mathrm{T}} = AZ \Rightarrow (AZ(AZ)^{\mathrm{T}})^{\mathrm{T}} = (AZ)^{\mathrm{T}}$ $\Rightarrow AZ(AZ)^{\mathrm{T}} = (AZ)^{\mathrm{T}} \Rightarrow$(2′); and because substituting (2′) into (3*) yields (3′). Similarly, Eqs. (1′) and (4′) together are equivalent to

$$AA^{\mathrm{T}}Z^{\mathrm{T}} = A \quad \text{or} \quad ZAA^{\mathrm{T}} = A^{\mathrm{T}}. \tag{1*}$$

Now

$$\begin{aligned} Z &= ZZ^{\mathrm{T}}A^{\mathrm{T}} = ZZ^{\mathrm{T}}A^{\mathrm{T}}AS = Z(AZ)^{\mathrm{T}}AS = ZAZAS = ZAS \\ &= ZAA^{\mathrm{T}}S^{\mathrm{T}}S = A^{\mathrm{T}}S^{\mathrm{T}}S = S. \qquad \text{Q.E.D.} \end{aligned}$$

COROLLARY 1 Given matrix A, by solving

$$AA^{\mathrm{T}}Z^{\mathrm{T}} = A \qquad \text{for} \quad Z^{\mathrm{T}}, \tag{1*}$$

$$A^{\mathrm{T}}AS = A^{\mathrm{T}} \qquad \text{for} \quad S, \tag{2*}$$

we can compute A^+ from

$$A^+ = ZAS.$$

PROOF Using $(AS)^{\mathrm{T}} = AS$, $(ZA)^{\mathrm{T}} = ZA$, and $AZA = A = ASA$, we observe that the four equations (10′)–(13′) are satisfied by A^+. For example,

$$AA^+A = AZASA = ASA = A.$$

$$(AA^+)^{\mathrm{T}} = (AZAS)^{\mathrm{T}} = (AS)^{\mathrm{T}} = AS = AZAS = AA^+. \qquad \text{Q.E.D.}$$

COROLLARY 2 If A is a real symmetric idempotent matrix, $A^+ = A$.

PROOF Replace A^+ by A in the fundamental equations (10′)–(13′) and observe that these equations hold true. Q.E.D.

COROLLARY 3 Let A be any real matrix. Then we have the following properties of its generalized inverse A^+.

$$A^+AA^{\mathrm{T}} = A^{\mathrm{T}} = A^{\mathrm{T}}AA^+ \tag{15}$$

$$(A^+)^+ = A \tag{16}$$

$$(A^+)^{\mathrm{T}} = (A^{\mathrm{T}})^+ \tag{17}$$

$$(A^{\mathrm{T}}A)^{+} = A^{+}(A^{\mathrm{T}})^{+}, \qquad (AA^{\mathrm{T}})^{+} = (A^{\mathrm{T}})^{+}A^{+} \tag{18}$$

$$(A^{+}A)^{+} = A^{+}A, \qquad (AA^{+})^{+} = AA^{+} \tag{19}$$

$$(A^{\mathrm{T}}A)^{+}A^{\mathrm{T}} = A^{+} = A^{\mathrm{T}}(AA^{\mathrm{T}})^{+} \tag{20}$$

$$A(A^{\mathrm{T}}A)^{+}(A^{\mathrm{T}}A) = A. \tag{21}$$

PROOF (15) $A = AA^{+}A = (AA^{+})^{\mathrm{T}}A \Rightarrow A^{\mathrm{T}} = ((AA^{+})^{\mathrm{T}}A)^{\mathrm{T}} = A^{\mathrm{T}}AA^{+}$. Similarly for $A^{\mathrm{T}} = A^{+}AA^{\mathrm{T}}$.

(16) Replacing A by $(A^{+})^{+}$ in Eqs. (10′)–(13′) yields an identical set of equations where A^{+} occupies the position of A in the original equations. Thus for given A^{+}, $(A^{+})^{+}$ is unique in the new equations, while for given A^{+}, A is unique in the original equations. (See Theorem 19.) Hence $(A^{+})^{+} = A$.

(17) $A^{\mathrm{T}} = ((AA^{+})^{\mathrm{T}}A)^{\mathrm{T}} = A^{\mathrm{T}}(A^{+})^{\mathrm{T}}A^{\mathrm{T}}$. On the other hand, substituting A^{T} for A in $A = AA^{+}A$ yields $A^{\mathrm{T}} = A^{\mathrm{T}}(A^{\mathrm{T}})^{+}A^{\mathrm{T}}$. Hence $(A^{+})^{\mathrm{T}} = (A^{\mathrm{T}})^{+}$.

(18) $(A^{\mathrm{T}}A)^{+}$ is the generalized inverse of $A^{\mathrm{T}}A$. Therefore, the following conditions must be fulfilled:

(a) $A^{\mathrm{T}}A(A^{\mathrm{T}}A)^{+}A^{\mathrm{T}}A = A^{\mathrm{T}}A$

(b) $(A^{\mathrm{T}}A(A^{\mathrm{T}}A)^{+})^{\mathrm{T}} = A^{\mathrm{T}}A(A^{\mathrm{T}}A)^{+}$

(c) $(A^{\mathrm{T}}A)^{+}A^{\mathrm{T}}A(A^{\mathrm{T}}A)^{+} = (A^{\mathrm{T}}A)^{+}$

(d) $((A^{\mathrm{T}}A)^{+}A^{\mathrm{T}}A)^{\mathrm{T}} = (A^{\mathrm{T}}A)^{+}A^{\mathrm{T}}A.$

If $A^{+}(A^{\mathrm{T}})^{+}$ is substituted for $(A^{\mathrm{T}}A)^{+}$, both sides of each equation of (a)–(d) are found to assume an identical value, e.g.,

$$\begin{aligned}\text{the left-hand side of (a)} &= A^{\mathrm{T}}AA^{+}(A^{\mathrm{T}})^{+}A^{\mathrm{T}}A = A^{\mathrm{T}}AA^{+}(AA^{+})^{\mathrm{T}}A \\ &= A^{\mathrm{T}}A(A^{+}AA^{+})A = A^{\mathrm{T}}AA^{+}A = A^{\mathrm{T}}A \\ &= \text{the right-hand side of (a).}\end{aligned}$$

Similarly for $(AA^{\mathrm{T}})^{+} = (A^{\mathrm{T}})^{+}A^{+}$.

(19) can be verified in the same way as (18).

(20) $(A^{\mathrm{T}}A)^{+}A^{\mathrm{T}} = A^{+}(A^{\mathrm{T}})^{+}A^{\mathrm{T}} = A^{+}(AA^{+})^{\mathrm{T}} = A^{+}AA^{+} = A^{+}$. Similarly for $A^{\mathrm{T}}(AA^{\mathrm{T}})^{+} = A^{+}$.

(21) The left-hand side $= A(A^{+}(A^{\mathrm{T}})^{+}A^{\mathrm{T}})A = AA^{+}A = A$. Q.E.D.

COROLLARY 4 If A is a real symmetric matrix, then

$$A^{+} = (A^{+})^{\mathrm{T}} \qquad \text{and} \qquad AA^{+} = A^{+}A.$$

PROOF

$$(A^{+})^{\mathrm{T}} = (A^{\mathrm{T}})^{+} = A^{+}, \qquad AA^{+} = A^{\mathrm{T}}(A^{+})^{\mathrm{T}} = (A^{+}A)^{\mathrm{T}} = A^{+}A. \qquad \text{Q.E.D.}$$

THEOREM 20 (Albert, 1972) For any $m \times n$ real matrix A and real $\alpha \neq 0$,

$$A^{+} = \lim_{\alpha \to 0} (A^{\mathrm{T}}A + \alpha^{2}I)^{-1}A^{\mathrm{T}} \tag{22}$$

always exists.

PROOF It can be easily seen that $A^{\mathrm{T}}A + \alpha^2 I$ is nonsingular for any nonzero α. Any $y \in R^m$ is decomposed as

$$y = y_0 + \tilde{y},$$

where $y_0 \in \bar{R}(A)$ and $\tilde{y} \in R(A)^{\perp} = N(A^{\mathrm{T}})$ in view of the projection theorem (Theorem 5 in Section 6.1) and of Corollary 2 to Theorem 16 in Section 6.2. Hence $A^{\mathrm{T}}y = A^{\mathrm{T}}y_0$ and $y_0 = Ax_0$ for some $x_0 \in R^n$. Thus

$$(A^{\mathrm{T}}A + \alpha^2 I)^{-1}A^{\mathrm{T}}y = (A^{\mathrm{T}}A + \alpha^2 I)^{-1}A^{\mathrm{T}}Ax_0.$$

By virtue of Theorem 6 in Section 6.1, the limit of the last expression coincides with the projection $\hat{x}_0$ of x_0 on $\bar{R}(A^{\mathrm{T}}A)$; i.e.,

$$\lim_{\alpha \to 0} (A^{\mathrm{T}}A + \alpha^2 I)^{-1}A^{\mathrm{T}}y = \hat{x}_0.$$

Note that $\bar{R}(A^{\mathrm{T}}A) = \bar{R}(A^{\mathrm{T}})$. (See Exercise 4 in this chapter.) Since

$$x_0 = \hat{x}_0 + \tilde{x}_0,$$

where $\hat{x}_0 \in \bar{R}(A^{\mathrm{T}}) = N(A)^{\perp}$ and $\tilde{x}_0 \in R(A^{\mathrm{T}})^{\perp} = N(A)$, we have

$$y_0 = Ax_0 = A\hat{x}_0.$$

In view of the projection theorem (Theorem 5 in Section 6.1), $y_0 = Ax_0$ is the unique vector satisfying

$$\|Ax_0 - y\| \leqq \|Ax - y\| \qquad \text{for all } x.$$

The vector of minimum norm among these x_0's is unique and orthogonal to $N(A)$, and hence it must be identical with $\hat{x}_0$. By definition, $\hat{x}_0$ is expressed as $\hat{x}_0 = A^+y$. Therefore, the assertion of the present theorem has been verified.

Q.E.D.

Two corollaries to formula (22) are in order.

If A is the diagonal matrix consisting of real $\lambda_1, \lambda_2, \ldots, \lambda_n$, then A^+ is the diagonal matrix consisting of $\lambda_1^+, \lambda_2^+, \ldots, \lambda_n^+$, where

$$\lambda_i^+ = \begin{cases} 0 & \text{if} \quad \lambda_i = 0, \\ 1/\lambda_i & \text{if} \quad \lambda_i \neq 0. \end{cases}$$

If A is an $n \times n$ real symmetric matrix, then

$$A^+ = \lim_{\alpha \to 0} V(\Lambda^2 + \alpha^2 I)^{-1}\Lambda V^{\mathrm{T}} = V\Lambda^+V^{\mathrm{T}}, \tag{23}$$

where Λ is the diagonal matrix consisting of the eigenvalues $\lambda_1, \ldots, \lambda_n$ of A, Λ^+ denotes the diagonal matrix consisting of $\lambda_1^+, \ldots, \lambda_n^+$ mentioned above, and V is an orthogonal matrix consisting of the eigenvectors of A such that $VV^{\mathrm{T}} = I$.

Application 2 (*ridge estimator*) In Application 1 of Section 6.1, if $Q = \sigma^2 I$ $(\sigma \neq 0)$, then the best linear unbiased estimator of β to the model $y = X\beta + \varepsilon$ will be

$$\hat{\beta} = (X^{\mathrm{T}}X)^{-1}X^{\mathrm{T}}y.$$

(For notations, refer to Application 1.) This estimator is equal to the so-called ordinary least-squares estimator of β in the sense that $\hat{\beta}$ minimizes $\|y - X\beta\|$ over all β, where the norm is Euclidean. When X contains some almost linearly dependent columns, we can rely on a generalized least-squares estimator $\tilde{\beta}$ instead of $\hat{\beta}$:

$$\tilde{\beta} = X^{+}y,$$

which is termed the *generalized-inverse estimator* of β. (For details, refer to the corollary to Theorem 25 in Section 6.4.) In view of formula (22), however, we may adopt an alternative estimator of β:

$$\hat{\beta}^{*} = (X^{\mathrm{T}}X + kI)^{-1}X^{\mathrm{T}}y \qquad \text{for some} \quad k \geqq 0,$$

which is said to be the *ridge estimator* of β. $\hat{\beta}^{*}$ is equivalent to $\hat{\beta}$ if $k = 0$. As it is known (cf. Marquardt, 1970) that $\|y - X\hat{\beta}^{*}\|$ is a monotone increasing function of k, and that $\|\hat{\beta}^{*}\|$ is a continuous monotone decreasing function of k such that as k goes to infinity, $\|\hat{\beta}^{*}\|$ tends to zero, an optimal k should be chosen for any problem. (See, for example, Goldstein and Smith (1974).)

Corollary 1 to Theorem 19 provides one method of computing the generalized inverse of a matrix. There are other useful methods, some of which will be explained below.

THEOREM 21 Let A be a real matrix of finite dimension. There are two ways to compute A^{+}. Method 1: Let $Q = A^{\mathrm{T}}A$, solve $Q^{2}Z^{\mathrm{T}} = Q$ for Z^{T}, calculate $Q^{+} = ZQZ^{\mathrm{T}}$, and compute $A^{+} = Q^{+}A^{\mathrm{T}}$. Method 2: Let $Q = AA^{\mathrm{T}}$, solve $Q^{2}Z^{\mathrm{T}} = Q$ for Z^{T}, calculate $Q^{+} = ZQZ^{\mathrm{T}}$, and compute $A^{+} = A^{\mathrm{T}}Q^{+}$.

PROOF Q in either method is symmetric. When Q is substituted for A in (1*) or (2*) in Corollary 1 to Theorem 19, therefore, we have $Q^{2}Z^{\mathrm{T}} = Q$, which is solved for Z^{T}. By the corollary $Q^{+} = ZQZ^{\mathrm{T}}$. Then apply relation (20). Q.E.D.

We may save the computation of A^{+} by choosing method 1 if $A^{\mathrm{T}}A$ has a smaller order than AA^{T} and choosing method 2 otherwise. In a special case, the above theorem reduces to the following.

COROLLARY Let A be an $m \times n$ real matrix. If $\mathrm{rk}(A) = n$, then $A^{+} = (A^{\mathrm{T}}A)^{-1}A^{\mathrm{T}}$ and hence $A^{+}A = I$. If $\mathrm{rk}(A) = m$, then $A^{+} = A^{\mathrm{T}}(AA^{\mathrm{T}})^{-1}$ and hence $AA^{+} = I$.

PROOF If $\mathrm{rk}(A) = n$, $A^{\mathrm{T}}A$ is nonsingular. Hence $(A^{\mathrm{T}}A)^{+}$ is reduced to $(AA^{\mathrm{T}})^{-1}$. Then apply relation (20). Similarly for the case where $\mathrm{rk}(A) = m$. Q.E.D.

THEOREM 22 Let B be an $m \times r$ real matrix of rank r and C be an $r \times n$ real matrix of rank r. Then

$$(BC)^+ = C^+B^+.$$

PROOF By the preceding corollary to Theorem 21, we have

$$C^+B^+ = C^T(CC^T)^{-1}(B^TB)^{-1}B^T.$$

Hence $CC^+B^+B = I$. On the other hand, $BC(BC)^+BC = BC$, implying that $C(BC)^+B = I$. Q.E.D.

COROLLARY An $m \times n$ real matrix A of rank r has generalized inverse of the form

$$A^+ = C^T(CC^T)^{-1}(B^TB)^{-1}B^T,$$

where B is an $m \times r$ matrix and C is an $r \times n$ matrix, both having rank r, such that $BC = A$.

THEOREM 23 Let A be an $m \times n$ real matrix, α be a real column m-vector, and $M(A)$ be the subspace generated by the columns of A. Then the generalized inverse of the $m \times (n + 1)$ matrix $[A:\alpha]$ is the following.

(i) If $\alpha \notin M(A)$,

$$[A:\alpha]^+ = \begin{bmatrix} A^+ - A^+\alpha b \\ b \end{bmatrix}, \qquad \text{where} \quad b = \frac{\alpha^T(I - AA^+)}{\alpha^T(I - AA^+)\alpha}. \tag{24}$$

(ii) If $\alpha \in M(A)$,

$$[A:\alpha]^+ = \begin{bmatrix} A^+ - A^+\alpha\beta \\ \beta \end{bmatrix}, \qquad \text{where} \quad \beta = \frac{\alpha^T(A^+)^TA^+}{1 + \alpha^T(A^+)^TA^+\alpha}. \tag{25}$$

PROOF The results are established by straightforward computations.

(i)

$$[A:\alpha]\,[A:\alpha]^+ = [A:\alpha]\begin{bmatrix} A^+ - A^+\alpha b \\ b \end{bmatrix} = AA^+ + (I - AA^+)\alpha b,$$

which is symmetric because $(I - AA^+)\alpha b$ so

$$[A:\alpha]^+[A:\alpha] = \begin{bmatrix} A^+ - A^+\alpha b \\ b \end{bmatrix}[A:\alpha] = \begin{bmatrix} A^+A - A^+\alpha bA & A^+\alpha - A^+\alpha b\alpha \\ bA & b\alpha \end{bmatrix}$$

$$= \begin{bmatrix} A^+A & 0 \\ 0 & 1 \end{bmatrix},$$

since $bA = \alpha^T(I - AA^+)A/\alpha^T(I - AA^+)\alpha = 0$ in view of $AA^+A = A$, and since $b\alpha = 1$.

$$[A:\alpha]\,[A:\alpha]^+[A:\alpha] = [A:\alpha]\begin{bmatrix} A^+A & 0 \\ 0 & 1 \end{bmatrix} = [A:\alpha].$$

$$[A:\alpha]^+[A:\alpha]\,[A:\alpha]^+ = \begin{bmatrix} A^+A & 0 \\ 0 & 1 \end{bmatrix}\begin{bmatrix} A^+ - A^+\alpha b \\ b \end{bmatrix} = \begin{bmatrix} A^+ - A^+\alpha b \\ b \end{bmatrix}.$$

(ii)

$$[A:\alpha]\,[A:\alpha]^+ = [A:\alpha]\begin{bmatrix} A^+ - A^+\alpha\beta \\ \beta \end{bmatrix} = AA^+ + (I - AA^+)\,\alpha\beta = AA^+,$$

because $AA^+A = A$ and $\alpha \in M(A)$ imply $AA^+\alpha = \alpha$.

$$[A:\alpha]^+[A:\alpha] = \begin{bmatrix} A^+ - A^+\alpha\beta \\ \beta \end{bmatrix}[A:\alpha] = \begin{bmatrix} A^+A - A^+\alpha\beta A & A^+\alpha - A^+\alpha\beta\alpha \\ \beta A & \beta\alpha \end{bmatrix},$$

where $\beta A = \alpha^{\mathrm{T}}(A^+)^{\mathrm{T}}/[1 + \alpha^{\mathrm{T}}(A^+)^{\mathrm{T}}A^+\alpha]$ since $(A^+)^{\mathrm{T}}A^+A = (A^+)^{\mathrm{T}}$ which is obtained by transposing $(A^+A)A^+ = A^+$;

$$A^+\alpha - A^+\alpha\beta\alpha = A^+\alpha/[1 + \alpha^{\mathrm{T}}(A^+)^{\mathrm{T}}A^+\alpha] = A^{\mathrm{T}}\beta^{\mathrm{T}}.$$

Thus $[A:\alpha]^+[A:\alpha]$ is symmetric.

$$[A:\alpha]\,[A:\alpha]^+[A:\alpha] = AA^+[A:\alpha] = [AA^+A : AA^+\alpha] = [A:\alpha].$$

$$\begin{aligned}[A:\alpha]^+[A:\alpha]\,[A:\alpha]^+ &= \begin{bmatrix} A^+A - A^+\alpha\beta A & A^+\alpha(1-\beta\alpha) \\ \beta A & \beta\alpha \end{bmatrix}\begin{bmatrix} A^+ - A^+\alpha\beta \\ \beta \end{bmatrix} \\ &= \begin{bmatrix} (A^+A - A^+\alpha\beta A)(A^+ - A^+\alpha\beta) + A^+\alpha(1-\beta\alpha)\beta \\ \beta A(A^+ - A^+\alpha\beta) + \beta\alpha\beta \end{bmatrix} \\ &= \begin{bmatrix} A^+ - 2A^+\alpha\beta + A^+\alpha\beta\alpha\beta + A^+\alpha(1-\beta\alpha)\beta \\ \beta \end{bmatrix} \\ &= \begin{bmatrix} A^+ - A^+\alpha\beta \\ \beta \end{bmatrix},\end{aligned}$$

in view of $AA^+\alpha = \alpha$, $A^+AA^+ = A^+$, and $\beta AA^+ = \beta$. Q.E.D.

COROLLARY (*Greville recursive algorithm*) Let A_k be the submatrix consisting of the first k columns of a real matrix A, and α_{k+1} be column $k+1$ of A. Then

$$A_{k+1}^+ = \begin{bmatrix} A_k^+ - A_k^+\alpha_{k+1}b_{k+1} \\ b_{k+1} \end{bmatrix}, \tag{26}$$

where

$$b_{k+1} = \frac{\alpha_{k+1}^{\mathrm{T}}(I - A_kA_k^+)}{\alpha_{k+1}^{\mathrm{T}}(I - A_kA_k^+)\alpha_{k+1}} \qquad \text{or} \qquad b_{k+1} = \frac{\alpha_{k+1}^{\mathrm{T}}(A_k^+)^{\mathrm{T}}A_k^+}{1 + \alpha_{k+1}^{\mathrm{T}}(A_k^+)^{\mathrm{T}}A_k^+\alpha_{k+1}},$$

corresponding to $\alpha_{k+1} \notin M(A_k)$ or $\alpha_{k+1} \in M(A_k)$, respectively. To initiate the recursive process, we note that A_1^+ is a null vector if α_1 is a null vector; otherwise A_k^+ can be computed by

$$A_k^+ = C^{\mathrm{T}}(CC^{\mathrm{T}})^{-1}(B^{\mathrm{T}}B)^{-1}B^{\mathrm{T}}, \tag{27}$$

where B is of full column rank and C is of full row rank such that $A_k = BC$.

To conclude this section, we introduce an important theorem concerning the general solution to a system of equations.

THEOREM 24 (*Penrose, second theorem*) Let A, B, C be real matrices. A necessary and sufficient condition for the equations $AXB = C$ to have a solution X is

$$AA^+CB^+B = C, \tag{28}$$

in which case the general solution is

$$X = A^+CB^+ + Y - A^+AYBB^+, \tag{29}$$

where Y is arbitrary.

PROOF Suppose X satisfies $AXB = C$. Then

$$C = AXB = AA^+AXBB^+B = AA^+CB^+B$$

since $A = AA^+A$. Conversely, if $C = AA^+CB^+B$, then a particular solution of $AXB = C$ is $X = A^+CB^+$ since the substitution of the X into AXB yields AA^+CB^+B. For the general solution, we must solve $AXB = 0$. Any expression of the form

$$X = Y - A^+AYBB^+ \tag{30}$$

satisfies $AXB = 0$; and conversely if $AXB = 0$, then $X = X - A^+AXBB^+$. Thus (30) is the general solution of $AXB = 0$, and hence (29) is that of $AXB = C$. Q.E.D.

COROLLARY 1 Let A, B, C be real matrices. The general solution of the system of linear equations $AX = C$ is

$$X = A^+C + (I - A^+A)Y, \tag{31}$$

and that of $XB = C$ is

$$X = CB^+ + Y(I - BB^+), \tag{32}$$

where Y is arbitrary, provided each system of equations has a solution.

PROOF Set $B = I$ in (29) in the former case and $A = I$ in the latter case, respectively. Q.E.D.

COROLLARY 2 Let A be an $m \times n$ real matrix, and y, b be column m-vectors of real constants. The general solution x of a system of linear equations $y = Ax + b$ is

$$x = A^{+}(y - b) + x_1, \tag{33}$$

where x_1 is any element of the nullspace of A.

PROOF Applying (31) to $Ax = y - b$, we have $x = A^{+}(y - b) + (I - A^{+}A)z$, where z is arbitrary. $x_1 \equiv (I - A^{+}A)z$ is an element of the nullspace of A since $Ax_1 = (A - AA^{+}A)z \equiv \theta$. Q.E.D.

Note that $x_1 = \theta$ in (33) if $\text{rk}(A) = n$ since $\dim N(A) = n - \text{rk}(A)$.

6.4 Generalization of the Gauss–Markov Theorem

In Application 1 of Section 6.1, we studied the Gauss–Markov model where it is assumed that the data matrix X has all linearly independent columns and that the error covariance matrix Q is positive definite. We shall generalize the Gauss–Markov model by relaxing these assumptions. In the present section, all vectors are supposed to be column vectors if not mentioned otherwise, and vectors and matrices are all defined over the field of real numbers.

We start with a generalization of the least-squares estimate. Given an n-vector y and an $n \times k$ matrix X of sample data, we seek the k-vector $\tilde{\beta}$ that minimizes $\|y - X\beta\|$ over all k-vectors β, where the norm is taken as Euclidean. In the ordinary least-squares (LS) method, the rank of X is assumed to be equal to k. We now drop this assumption.

THEOREM 25 (*generalized least-squares estimate*) Let y be an n-vector and X be an $n \times k$ matrix of sample data, where $\text{rk}(X)$ is not necessarily equal to k. Then, there exists a k-vector $\tilde{\beta}$ that minimizes $\|y - X\beta\|$ over all k-vectors β, where the norm is Euclidean. The general solution $\tilde{\beta}$ is

$$\tilde{\beta} = X^{+}y + (I - X^{+}X)z, \tag{34}$$

where z is an arbitrary k-vector. Furthermore, the corresponding estimate of y, denoted $\tilde{y} \equiv X\tilde{\beta}$, is uniquely determined by

$$\tilde{y} = XX^{+}y. \tag{35}$$

PROOF By the projection theorem (Theorem 5 in Section 6.1), the unique minimizing vector is $X\tilde{\beta}$ that satisfies

$$(y - X\tilde{\beta} \,|\, x_i) = 0 \qquad \text{for} \quad i = 1, \ldots, k,$$

where x_i is the ith column vector of X. Since the norm is Euclidean, the above expression may be rewritten as

$$X^{\mathrm{T}}(y - X\tilde{\beta}) = \theta \qquad \text{or} \qquad X^{\mathrm{T}}X\tilde{\beta} = X^{\mathrm{T}}y.$$

Then, by Corollary 1 to the second Penrose theorem (Theorem 24 in Section 6.3), we have

$$\tilde{\beta} = (X^{\mathrm{T}}X)^{+}X^{\mathrm{T}}y + (I - (X^{\mathrm{T}}X)^{+}X^{\mathrm{T}}X)z. \tag{34'}$$

Since

$$(X^{\mathrm{T}}X)^{+}X^{\mathrm{T}} = X^{+}(X^{\mathrm{T}})^{+}X^{\mathrm{T}} = X^{+}(X^{+})^{\mathrm{T}}X^{\mathrm{T}} = X^{+}(XX^{+})^{\mathrm{T}} = X^{+}XX^{+} = X^{+},$$

Eq. (34′) is reduced to (34). Thus

$$\tilde{y} = X\tilde{\beta} = XX^{+}y + X(I - X^{+}X)\,z = XX^{+}y. \qquad \text{Q.E.D.}$$

COROLLARY If $\mathrm{rk}(X) = k$, the generalized least-squares estimator $\tilde{\beta}$ in (34) reduces to the ordinary LS estimator

$$\hat{\beta} = (X^{\mathrm{T}}X)^{-1}\,X^{\mathrm{T}}y \tag{36}$$

because of the corollary to Theorem 21 in Section 6.3.

We define two variants of the Gauss–Markov model as follows:

$$(y,\ X\beta,\ Q) \tag{37}$$

is referred to as an *unconstrained Gauss–Markov model* representing

$$y = X\beta + \varepsilon \tag{38}$$

with the properties

$$E(\varepsilon) = \theta, \tag{39}$$

$$E(\varepsilon\varepsilon^{\mathrm{T}}) = Q \qquad (Q \text{ positive semidefinite}), \tag{40}$$

where y is an n-vector, X is an $n \times k$ matrix of sample data, ε is an n-vector of disturbances (or errors), and β is a k-vector of unknown constants. Clearly the expectation of y is

$$E(y) = X\beta, \tag{41}$$

and the dispersion matrix of y is

$$D(y) \equiv E[(y - E(y))\,(y - E(y))^{\mathrm{T}}] = E(\varepsilon\varepsilon^{\mathrm{T}}) = Q. \tag{42}$$

When a linear restriction

$$S\beta = c \qquad (S,\ m \times k;\ c,\ m \times 1) \tag{43}$$

is imposed on the model (37), we have a *constrained Gauss–Markov model*, denoted as

$$(y,\ X\beta\,|\,S\beta = c,\ Q). \tag{44}$$

First, we are concerned with unbiased estimators of these models.

DEFINITION 5 Define a set

$$\Omega \equiv \{\beta : \beta \in R^{k},\ S\beta = c\}\,.$$

As estimator $\hat{\beta}$ of the model (44) is said to be *unbiased with respect to* Ω if

$$E(\hat{\beta}) = \beta \qquad \text{for all} \quad \beta \in \Omega.$$

THEOREM 26 (Schönfeld, 1971) The linear estimator

$$\hat{\beta} = Ky + b \qquad (K,\ k \times n;\ b,\ k \times 1) \tag{45}$$

is unbiased with respect to Ω if and only if

$$(I - KX)(I - S^{+}S) = 0 \tag{46}$$

and

$$b = (I - KX)S^{+}c. \tag{47}$$

PROOF Unbiasedness requires

$$\beta = E(\hat{\beta}) = K \cdot E(y) + b = KX\beta + b,$$

or equivalently

$$(I - KX)\beta = b.$$

In view of the general solution of $\beta \in \Omega$ (cf. (31) in Section 6.3), we have

$$(I - KX)(S^{+}c + (I - S^{+}S)w) = b$$

for an arbitrary $w \in E^{k}$. Hence (46) and (47) follow. Conversely, if (46) and (47) hold, it is easily seen that estimator $\hat{\beta}$ in (45) is unbiased with respect to Ω. Q.E.D.

DEFINITION 6 Let p be a k-vector. $p^{\mathrm{T}}\beta$ is said to be *unbiasedly estimable* under the model (44) if there exists a linear function $h^{\mathrm{T}}y + \gamma$ such that

$$E(h^{\mathrm{T}}y + \gamma) = p^{\mathrm{T}}\beta \qquad \text{for all} \quad \beta \in \Omega, \tag{48}$$

where h is an n-vector and γ is a constant.

THEOREM 27 For a parametric function $p^{\mathrm{T}}\beta$ to be unbiasedly estimable under model (44), it is necessary and sufficient that there exist an m-vector g and an n-vector h such that

$$p^{\mathrm{T}} = h^{\mathrm{T}}X + g^{\mathrm{T}}S, \tag{49}$$

and

$$\gamma = g^{\mathrm{T}}c. \tag{50}$$

PROOF *Necessity* By definition, there is $h^{\mathrm{T}}y + \gamma$ such that

$$h^{\mathrm{T}}X\beta + \gamma = E(h^{\mathrm{T}}y + \gamma) = p^{\mathrm{T}}\beta \qquad \text{for all} \quad \beta \in \Omega.$$

Thus, $\gamma = (p^{\mathrm{T}} - h^{\mathrm{T}}X)(S^{+}c + (I - S^{+}S)w)$ for any $w \in E^{k}$, from which we get $\gamma = g^{\mathrm{T}}c$ where $g^{\mathrm{T}} \equiv (p^{\mathrm{T}} - h^{\mathrm{T}}X)S^{+}$, and

$$(p^{\mathrm{T}} - h^{\mathrm{T}}X)(I - S^{+}S) = 0.$$

Hence (49) follows. (*Sufficiency* is immediate.) Q.E.D.

A simple version of the above theorem is the following.

COROLLARY 1 For a parametric function $p^{\mathrm{T}}\beta$ to be unbiasedly estimable under model (37) by a linear function $h^{\mathrm{T}}y$, it is necessary and sufficient that p belong to the subspace generated by the column vectors of X^{T}, i.e., that there exists an n-vector h such that

$$p = X^{\mathrm{T}}h. \tag{49'}$$

Another equivalence condition for unbiased estimability of model (37) is given below.

COROLLARY 2 A parametric function $p^{\mathrm{T}}\beta$ is unbiasedly estimable under model (37) by a linear function $h^{\mathrm{T}}y$ if and only if

$$p^{\mathrm{T}}X^{+}X = p^{\mathrm{T}}. \tag{51}$$

PROOF Suppose that (51) holds, and put $h^{\mathrm{T}} = p^{\mathrm{T}}X^{+}$. (49′) follows at once. Conversely, if (49′) holds for some h, then in view of (10′),

$$p^{\mathrm{T}}X^{+}X = h^{\mathrm{T}}XX^{+}X = h^{\mathrm{T}}X = p^{\mathrm{T}}. \qquad \text{Q.E.D.}$$

Now we seek the "best" among linear unbiased estimators.

DEFINITION 7 Under model (37), the estimator $h^{\mathrm{T}}y$ of a parametric function $p^{\mathrm{T}}\beta$ is said to be the *best linear unbiased estimator* (BLUE) if

$$E(h^{\mathrm{T}}y) = p^{\mathrm{T}}\beta \tag{48'}$$

and if the variance of $h^{\mathrm{T}}y$

$$V(h^{\mathrm{T}}y) \equiv E(h^{\mathrm{T}}y - p^{\mathrm{T}}\beta)^2$$

achieves the minimum in the class of linear unbiased estimators of $p^{\mathrm{T}}\beta$.

In view of (38) and (49′),

$$h^{\mathrm{T}}y = h^{\mathrm{T}}(X\beta + \varepsilon) = p^{\mathrm{T}}\beta + h^{\mathrm{T}}\varepsilon.$$

Hence, by virtue of (40),

$$V(h^{\mathrm{T}}y) = E(h^{\mathrm{T}}\varepsilon\varepsilon^{\mathrm{T}}h) = h^{\mathrm{T}}Qh. \tag{52}$$

THEOREM 28 Consider the model (37) with $Q = \sigma^2 I$. Then (i) the BLUE of a parametric function $p^{\mathrm{T}}\beta$ is represented as $p^{\mathrm{T}}\hat{\beta}$, where

$$\hat{\beta} = X^{+}y. \tag{53}$$

(ii) The variance of the BLUE and the covariance of the BLUEs of $p^{\mathrm{T}}\beta$ and $q^{\mathrm{T}}\beta$ are

$$V(p^{\mathrm{T}}\hat{\beta}) = \sigma^2 p^{\mathrm{T}}(X^{\mathrm{T}}X)^{+}p, \tag{54}$$

$$\operatorname{Cov}(p^{\mathrm{T}}\hat{\beta}, q^{\mathrm{T}}\hat{\beta}) = \sigma^2 p^{\mathrm{T}}(X^{\mathrm{T}}X)^{+}q. \tag{55}$$

PROOF (i) Since $V(h^{\mathrm{T}}y) = \sigma^2 h^{\mathrm{T}}h$, we minimize $h^{\mathrm{T}}h$ subject to (49′). The general solution of $X^{\mathrm{T}}h = p$ is

$$h^{\mathrm{T}} = p^{\mathrm{T}}X^{+} + w^{\mathrm{T}}(I - XX^{+}) \qquad \text{for an arbitrary } n\text{-vector } w. \tag{56}$$

Thus, by virtue of (11′), (17), (18), and (12′),

$$\begin{aligned} h^{\mathrm{T}}h &= [p^{\mathrm{T}}X^{+} + w^{\mathrm{T}}(I - XX^{+})]\,[(X^{+})^{\mathrm{T}}p + (I - XX^{+})w] \\ &= p^{\mathrm{T}}(X^{\mathrm{T}}X)^{+}p + w^{\mathrm{T}}(I - XX^{+})w, \end{aligned}$$

which is not less than $p^{\mathrm{T}}(X^{\mathrm{T}}X)^{+}p$. Therefore, $h_p \equiv (X^{\mathrm{T}})^{+}p$ is the optimal h. Hence

$$p^{\mathrm{T}}\hat{\beta} = h_p^{\mathrm{T}}y = p^{\mathrm{T}}X^{+}y,$$

from which (53) follows.

(ii) Since $p^{\mathrm{T}}\hat{\beta} = h_p^{\mathrm{T}}y = h_p^{\mathrm{T}}(X\beta + \varepsilon) = p^{\mathrm{T}}\beta + h_p^{\mathrm{T}}\varepsilon$,

$$\begin{aligned}\mathrm{Cov}(p^{\mathrm{T}}\hat{\beta}, q^{\mathrm{T}}\hat{\beta}) &= E[p^{\mathrm{T}}(\hat{\beta} - \beta)(\hat{\beta} - \beta)^{\mathrm{T}}q] = h_p^{\mathrm{T}}E(\varepsilon\varepsilon^{\mathrm{T}})h_q \\ &= h_p^{\mathrm{T}}Qh_q = \sigma^2 p^{\mathrm{T}}X^{+}(X^{\mathrm{T}})^{+}q = \sigma^2 p^{\mathrm{T}}(X^{\mathrm{T}}X)^{+}q.\end{aligned}$$

Similarly for (54). Q.E.D.

COROLLARY An unbiased estimator of σ^2 associated with the BLUE $\hat{\beta}$ in Theorem 28 is

$$\hat{\sigma}^2 = \frac{y^{\mathrm{T}}(I - XX^{+})y}{n - \mathrm{rk}(X)}. \tag{57}$$

PROOF The vector of the residuals is

$$e \equiv y - X\hat{\beta} = (I - XX^{+})y = (I - XX^{+})(X\beta + \varepsilon) = (I - XX^{+})\varepsilon.$$

Note that XX^{+} is symmetric idempotent. Thus

$$E(e^{\mathrm{T}}e) = E[\varepsilon^{\mathrm{T}}(I - XX^{+})\varepsilon] = \sigma^2\,\mathrm{tr}(I - XX^{+}) = \sigma^2(n - \mathrm{rk}(X)),$$

since $\mathrm{tr}(XX^{+}) = \mathrm{rk}(XX^{+}) = \mathrm{rk}(X)$. Q.E.D.

The error covariance matrix Q is now assumed to be positive semidefinite. By Theorem 33 in Section 2.5, there exists a square matrix B such that

$$B^{\mathrm{T}}B = Q. \tag{58}$$

THEOREM 29 Let a parametric function $p^{\mathrm{T}}\beta$ be unbiasedly estimable under model (37) by a linear function $h^{\mathrm{T}}y$ and let

$$\hat{h} \equiv (I - (I - XX^{+})\bar{B}^{+}B)(X^{+})^{\mathrm{T}}p, \tag{59}$$

where B is the matrix satisfying (58) and

$$\bar{B} \equiv B(I - XX^{+}). \tag{60}$$

Then all BLUEs of $p^{\mathrm{T}}\beta$ are of the form $\hat{h}^{\mathrm{T}}y$ with probability 1, and hence the BLUE of $p^{\mathrm{T}}\beta$ is represented as $p^{\mathrm{T}}\hat{\beta}$, where

$$\hat{\beta} = Ky, \tag{61}$$

with

$$E(\hat{\beta}) = X^{+}X\beta \qquad \text{for all} \quad \beta, \tag{62}$$

and

$$K \equiv X^{+}(I - (\bar{B}^{+}B)^{\mathrm{T}}(I - XX^{+})). \tag{63}$$

PROOF For $p^{\mathrm{T}}\beta$ to be unbiasedly estimable by $h^{\mathrm{T}}y$, it is necessary and sufficient that there is a vector h satisfying (49′). The general solution of such an h is given by (56). The variance of $h^{\mathrm{T}}y$ is

$$V(h^{\mathrm{T}}y) = (Bh)^{\mathrm{T}}Bh. \tag{52′}$$

In view of (56) and (60), we have

$$Bh = B(X^+)^{\mathrm{T}}p + \bar{B}w.$$

Thus, the minimum of $(Bh)^{\mathrm{T}}(Bh)$ is zero, when w must fulfill

$$\bar{B}w = -B(X^+)^{\mathrm{T}}p.$$

The general solution of such a w is

$$w = -\bar{B}^+B(X^+)^{\mathrm{T}}p + (I - \bar{B}^+\bar{B})u$$

for an aribitrary n-vector u. The corresponding value of h is obtained by substituting the w into (56), i.e.,

$$\begin{aligned} h &= (X^+)^{\mathrm{T}}p + (I - XX^+)\,((I - \bar{B}^+\bar{B})u - \bar{B}^+B(X^+)^{\mathrm{T}}p) \\ &= \hat{h} + (I - XX^+)\,(I - \bar{B}^+\bar{B})u. \end{aligned}$$

Since, in view of (60) and (10′),

$$E[(h - \hat{h})^{\mathrm{T}}y]^2 = (h - \hat{h})^{\mathrm{T}}B^{\mathrm{T}}B(h - \hat{h}) = u^{\mathrm{T}}(I - \bar{B}^+\bar{B})\bar{B}^{\mathrm{T}}\bar{B}(I - \bar{B}^+\bar{B})u = 0,$$

$(h - \hat{h})^{\mathrm{T}}y = 0$ with probability 1. Thus, the BLUE for $p^{\mathrm{T}}\beta$ is represented as

$$p^{\mathrm{T}}\hat{\beta} = \hat{h}^{\mathrm{T}}y = p^{\mathrm{T}}Ky.$$

And, in view of (38), (39), (63), and (10′),

$$E(\hat{\beta}) = KX\beta = X^+X\beta. \qquad \text{Q.E.D.}$$

Note that we can check the unbiasedness of the estimator $p^{\mathrm{T}}\hat{\beta}$ by virtue of (51), i.e.,

$$E(p^{\mathrm{T}}\hat{\beta}) = p^{\mathrm{T}}\beta \qquad \text{for } \hat{\beta} \text{ satisfying (61).}$$

Denoting

$$H \equiv I - XX^+,$$

and taking account of (20), (60), and (58), we can rewrite K in (63) as

$$\begin{aligned} K &= X^+(I - B^{\mathrm{T}}(\bar{B}^+)^{\mathrm{T}}H) = X^+(I - B^{\mathrm{T}}\bar{B}(\bar{B}^{\mathrm{T}}\bar{B})^+H) \\ &= X^+(I - QH(HQH)^+H). \end{aligned} \tag{63′}$$

If Q is positive definite, estimator $\hat{\beta}$ in (61) takes a simpler form.

COROLLARY 1 Let a parametric function $p^{\mathrm{T}}\beta$ be unbiasedly estimable under model (37) by the linear function $h^{\mathrm{T}}y$. If the error covariance matrix Q is positive definite, the BLUE of $p^{\mathrm{T}}\beta$ is represented as $p^{\mathrm{T}}\hat{\beta}$ where

$$\hat{\beta} = (X^{\mathrm{T}}Q^{-1}X)^+X^{\mathrm{T}}Q^{-1}y, \tag{64}$$

which is regarded as an extended form of the Gauss–Markov estimator $\hat{\beta}$ shown at the end of Section 6.1.

PROOF According to Exercise 8 in Chapter 2, there is a positive definite symmetric matrix B such that

$$B^2 = Q. \tag{58'}$$

Postmultiply (63′) by this B. Then, by virtue of (58′), (20), and Exercise 5 in this chapter, we have

$$KB = X^+B(I - BH(HBBH)^+HB) = X^+B(I - (HB)^+HB) = (B^{-1}X)^+.$$

Applying (20) and (58′) again, therefore, we obtain

$$K = (B^{-1}X)^+B^{-1} = (X^TB^{-1}B^{-1}X)^+X^TB^{-1}B^{-1} = (X^TQ^{-1}X)^+X^TQ^{-1}. \quad \text{Q.E.D.}$$

Corollary 1 implies the following proposition.

COROLLARY 2 Let a parametric function $p^T\beta$ be unbiasedly estimable under model (37) by the linear function h^Ty. If Q is positive definite and if X has rank k, then the BLUE of $p^T\beta$ is represented as $p^T\hat{\beta}$, where

$$\hat{\beta} = (X^TQ^{-1}X)^{-1}X^TQ^{-1}y, \tag{64'}$$

with corresponding error covariance

$$E[(\hat{\beta} - \beta)(\hat{\beta} - \beta)^T] = (X^TQ^{-1}X)^{-1}.$$

This is exactly the Gauss–Markov result obtained in Application 1 in Section 6.1.

Next we turn to the constrained Gauss–Markov model (44) with $\text{rk}(S) = m$. We shall show that it can be converted into an unconstrained Gauss–Markov model, the BLUE of which is to be studied. (Cf. Rao and Mitra (1971).)

THEOREM 30 (i) The constrained Gauss–Markov model (44) with $\text{rk}(S) = m$ is equivalent to the unconstrained Gauss–Markov model

$$(y^*, \tilde{X}\beta^*, Q), \tag{65}$$

where β^* is a $(k-m)$-vector of new parameters,

$$y^* \equiv y - XS^+c, \qquad \tilde{X} \equiv XZ,$$

and Z is a $k \times (k - m)$ matrix whose columns consist of all $k - m$ linearly independent vectors in the nullspace of S.

(ii) Furthermore,

$$\text{rk}(\tilde{X}) = \text{rk}[X^T : S^T] - m. \tag{66}$$

PROOF (i) The general solution of $S\beta = c$ is

$$\beta = S^+c + (I - S^+S)w \qquad \text{for an arbitrary } k\text{-vector } w.$$

Selecting Z as specified above and setting $w = Z\beta^*$, we have

$$\beta = S^+c + Z\beta^* \tag{67}$$

since $SZ = 0$. Then

$$E(y^*) = E(y - XS^+c) = X\beta - XS^+c = XZ\beta^* = \tilde{X}\beta^*,$$

and

$$D(y^*) = E(y^* - \tilde{X}\beta^*)(y^* - \tilde{X}\beta^*)^T = E(\varepsilon\varepsilon^T) = Q,$$

since $y^* - \tilde{X}\beta^* = y - XS^+c - XZ\beta^* = y - X\beta = \varepsilon$. Therefore, model (44) implies model (65). Conversely, assume model (65), i.e., $y^* = \tilde{X}\beta^* + \varepsilon$ with (39) and (40). Then

$$E(y) = E(y^* + XS^+c) = \tilde{X}\beta^* + XS^+c = X(Z\beta^* + S^+c) = X\beta,$$

and

$$\begin{aligned} D(y) &\equiv E[(y - E(y))(y - E(y))^T] = E[(y^* + XS^+c - X\beta)(y^* + XS^+c - X\beta)^T] \\ &= E[(y^* - XZ\beta^*)(y^* - XZ\beta^*)^T] = E(\varepsilon\varepsilon^T) = Q. \end{aligned}$$

(ii) Since $[Z : S^T]$ is a $k \times k$ matrix of full rank, in view of $\text{rk}(S) = m$, $\text{rk}(Z) = k - m$ and of the fact that the columns of Z are linearly independent of those of S^T, and since

$$\begin{bmatrix} X \\ S \end{bmatrix} [Z : S^T] = \begin{bmatrix} XZ & XS^T \\ 0 & SS^T \end{bmatrix},$$

$$\begin{aligned} \text{rk}\begin{bmatrix} X \\ S \end{bmatrix} &= \text{rk}\begin{bmatrix} XZ & XS^T \\ 0 & SS^T \end{bmatrix} = \text{rk}\begin{bmatrix} I & -XS^T(SS^T)^{-1} \\ 0 & I \end{bmatrix}\begin{bmatrix} XZ & XS^T \\ 0 & SS^T \end{bmatrix} \\ &= \text{rk}\begin{bmatrix} XZ & 0 \\ 0 & SS^T \end{bmatrix} = \text{rk}(XZ) + \text{rk}(SS^T) \\ &= \text{rk}(\tilde{X}) + \text{rk}(S). \qquad \text{Q.E.D.} \end{aligned}$$

We define a variation of unbiased estimability and the BLUE for model (65).

DEFINITION 8 Let p be a k-vector. p^TZB^* is said to be unbiasedly estimable under model (65) if there exists a linear function h^Ty^* such that

$$E(h^Ty^*) = p^TZ\beta^* \qquad \text{for all } \beta^*, \tag{68}$$

where h is an n-vector. Moreover, under the same model, the estimator h^Ty^* is said to be the BLUE of the parametric function $p^TZ\beta^*$ if (68) is satisfied and if the variance of h^Ty^* is the minimum in the class of linear unbiased estimators of $p^TZ\beta^*$.

THEOREM 31 For a parametric function $p^TZ\beta^*$ to be unbiasedly estimable under model (65), it is necessary and sufficient (i) that there is an n-vector h satisfying

$$h^{\mathrm{T}}\tilde{X} = p^{\mathrm{T}}Z, \tag{69}$$

or (ii) that

$$p^{\mathrm{T}}Z\tilde{X}^{+}\tilde{X} = p^{\mathrm{T}}Z. \tag{70}$$

(For a proof, refer to Corollaries 1 and 2 to Theorem 27.)
Note that in view of (68) and (69), the variance of $h^{\mathrm{T}}y^*$ becomes

$$V(h^{\mathrm{T}}y^*) = h^{\mathrm{T}}Qh. \tag{71}$$

THEOREM 28′ Consider model (65) with $Q = \sigma^2 I$.

(i) The BLUE of a parametric function $p^{\mathrm{T}}Z\beta^*$ is $p^{\mathrm{T}}Z\hat{\beta}^*$, where

$$\hat{\beta}^* = \tilde{X}^{+}y^*. \tag{72}$$

(ii) The variance of the BLUE is

$$V(p^{\mathrm{T}}Z\hat{\beta}^*) = \sigma^2 p^{\mathrm{T}}Z(\tilde{X}^{\mathrm{T}}\tilde{X})^{+}Z^{\mathrm{T}}p. \tag{73}$$

(iii) The unbiased estimator of σ^2 associated with the BLUE is

$$\hat{\sigma}^2 = \frac{y^{*\mathrm{T}}(I - \tilde{X}\tilde{X}^{+})y^*}{n - \mathrm{rk}(\tilde{X})}. \tag{74}$$

PROOF (i) Putting $Q = \sigma^2 I$ in (71) yields

$$V(h^{\mathrm{T}}y^*) = \sigma^2 h^{\mathrm{T}}h. \tag{71′}$$

Minimize $h^{\mathrm{T}}h$ subject to (69). Proceeding in a similar manner to the proof of Theorem 27, we obtain the optimal h, denoted h_p, as follows:

$$h_p^{\mathrm{T}} = p^{\mathrm{T}}Z\tilde{X}^{+}.$$

Thus, the BLUE of $p^{\mathrm{T}}Z\beta^*$ becomes

$$p^{\mathrm{T}}Z\hat{\beta}^* = h_p^{\mathrm{T}}y^* = p^{\mathrm{T}}Z\tilde{X}^{+}y^*.$$

(ii) Setting h equal to h_p in (71′) and taking account of (18) entail (73).
(iii) The proof of this part is similar to that of the corollary to Theorem 27. Q.E.D.

COROLLARY Interpret the result of Theorem 28′ in terms of model (44). Let $\hat{\beta}$ be the estimator of β corresponding to $\hat{\beta}^*$ in (72), i.e.,

$$\begin{aligned} \hat{\beta} &= S^{+}c + Z\hat{\beta}^* = S^{+}c + Z\tilde{X}^{+}(y - XS^{+}c) \\ &= Z(XZ)^{+}y + (I - Z(XZ)^{+}X)S^{+}c. \end{aligned} \tag{67′}$$

Then $p^{\mathrm{T}}\hat{\beta}$ is a linear unbiased estimator of the parametric function $p^{\mathrm{T}}\beta$ under model (44) with $Q = \sigma^2 I$ and $\mathrm{rk}(S) = m$. The variance of the estimator is the same as (73), i.e.,

$$V(p^{\mathrm{T}}\hat{\beta}) = \sigma^2 p^{\mathrm{T}}Z(Z^{\mathrm{T}}X^{\mathrm{T}}XZ)^{+}Z^{\mathrm{T}}p, \tag{73′}$$

and $\hat{\sigma}^2$ in (74) is rewritten as

$$\hat{\sigma}^2 = \frac{(y - XS^+c)^T(I - XZ(XZ)^+)(y - XS^+c)}{n + m - \text{rk}[X^T : S^T]}. \tag{74'}$$

PROOF Since $p^TZ \cdot E(\hat{\beta}^*) = p^TZ\tilde{X}^+\tilde{X}\beta^* = p^TZ\beta^*$ and by (67), (67′),

$$E(p^T\hat{\beta}) = p^TS^+c + p^TZ \cdot E(\hat{\beta}^*) = p^TS^+c + p^TZ\beta^* = p^T\beta.$$

On the other hand, by (69)

$$\begin{aligned} p^TS^+c + p^TZ\beta^* &= p^TS^+c + h^T\tilde{X}\beta^* = E(p^TS^+c + h^Ty^*) \\ &= E(p^TS^+c + h^T(y - XS^+c)) = E(h^Ty + \gamma), \end{aligned}$$

where $\gamma \equiv (p^T - h^TX)S^+c$. Thus (48) holds. Hence $p^T\hat{\beta}$ is a linear unbiased estimator of $p^T\beta$. The variance of $p^T\hat{\beta}$ becomes (73′) since

$$V(p^T\hat{\beta}) = E[p^T(\hat{\beta} - \beta)(\hat{\beta} - \beta)^Tp]$$

and since

$$\begin{aligned} p^T(\hat{\beta} - \beta) &= p^T(S^+c + Z\hat{\beta}^*) - p^T(S^+c + Z\beta^*) = p^TZ(\hat{\beta}^* - \beta^*) \\ &= p^TZ(\tilde{X}^+(\tilde{X}\beta^* + \varepsilon) - \beta^*) = p^TZ\tilde{X}^+\varepsilon. \end{aligned}$$

(74′) is obtained by substituting (66) and other relations into (74). Q.E.D.

If the error covariance matrix Q is positive semidefinite, we have the following theorem, which is an extension of Theorem 29.

THEOREM 32 Let a parametric function $p^TZ\beta^*$ be unbiasedly estimable under model (65) by a linear function h^Ty^* and let

$$\hat{h}^* = (I - (I - \tilde{X}\tilde{X}^+)\tilde{B}^+B)(\tilde{X}^+)^TZ^Tp, \tag{59'}$$

where B is the matrix satisfying (58) and

$$\tilde{B} \equiv B(I - \tilde{X}\tilde{X}^+). \tag{60'}$$

Then, all BLUEs of $p^TZ\beta^*$ are of the form $(\hat{h}^*)^Ty^*$ with probability 1, and hence the BLUE of $p^TZ\beta^*$ is represented as $p^TZ\hat{\beta}^*$, where

$$\hat{\beta}^* = \tilde{K}y^*, \tag{61'}$$

with

$$E(\hat{\beta}^*) = \tilde{X}^+\tilde{X}\beta^* \qquad \text{for all } \beta^*, \tag{62'}$$

and

$$\begin{aligned} \tilde{K} &\equiv \tilde{X}^+(I - (\tilde{B}^+B)^T(I - \tilde{X}\tilde{X}^+)) \\ &= \tilde{X}^+(I - Q\tilde{H}(\tilde{H}Q\tilde{H})^+\tilde{H}), \qquad \text{where} \quad \tilde{H} \equiv I - \tilde{X}\tilde{X}^+. \end{aligned} \tag{75}$$

In particular, if the error covariance matrix Q is positive definite, $\tilde{K}$ becomes

$$\tilde{K} \equiv (\tilde{X}^TQ^{-1}\tilde{X})^+\tilde{X}^TQ^{-1}. \tag{75'}$$

(The proof is similar to that of Theorem 29 and its Corollary 1.)

COROLLARY Interpret the result of Theorem 32 in terms of model (44). Let $\hat{\beta}$ be the estimator of β corresponding to $\hat{\beta}^*$ in (61′), i.e.,

$$\hat{\beta} = S^+c + Z\hat{\beta}^* = S^+c + Z\tilde{K}(y - XS^+c). \tag{67″}$$

Then $p^T\hat{\beta}$ is a linear unbiased estimator of the parametric function $p^T\beta$ under model (44) with $\text{rk}(S) = m$. The variance of the estimator is

$$V(p^T\hat{\beta}) = p^TZ\tilde{X}^+(Q - Q\tilde{H}(\tilde{H}Q\tilde{H})^+\tilde{H}Q)(Z\tilde{X}^+)^Tp. \tag{76}$$

If Q is positive definite,

$$V(p^T\hat{\beta}) = p^TZ(\tilde{X}^TQ^{-1}\tilde{X})^+Z^Tp. \tag{76′}$$

PROOF The linear unbiasedness of $p^T\hat{\beta}$ will be verified in the same way as in the corollary to Theorem 28′. (The verification of (76) and (76′) is left to the reader.) Q.E.D.

So far we have assumed $\text{rk}(S) = m$ in the constrained Gauss–Markov model (44), which results in an unconstrained G-M model. If $\text{rk}(S) = k$ in model (44), it will be intrinsically a constrained model, to which we need a different approach. (The reader may refer to Schönfeld (1971) for a treatment of the intrinsically constrained Gauss–Markov model.)

6.5 Generalized Linear Equation Economic Systems

As an application of the generalized inverse to economic problems, we shall now discuss a generalization of such linear equation systems as described in Section 4.4.

Consider a linear equation system

$$Ax = y, \tag{77}$$

where $A = [a_{ij}]$ is an $m \times n$ real matrix, $x \equiv \{x_1, \ldots, x_n\} \in E_+^n$, and $y \equiv \{y_1, \ldots, y_m\} \in E_+^m$. This system can be interpreted as an output model where A represents a collection of n activities characterized by the column vectors, x the intensity vector of all activity operations, and y the output vector of m goods. Any positive component in A stands for an output and a negative one an input. When y is given and fixed at $\bar{y}$ as a target, we try to minimize the gap between the actual output Ax and the target $\bar{y}$; so logically we want to obtain $\dot{x}$, say $\bar{x}$, that minimizes $\|Ax - \bar{y}\|$. Such an $\bar{x}$ is not necessarily unique. Then we may intend to get an x^* that has the minimum norm among $\bar{x}$'s; i.e., the inconsistent equation system

$$Ax = \bar{y} \tag{78}$$

is to be approximated by $x = x^*$ such that

$$\|x^*\| \leqq \|\bar{x}\| \qquad \text{for any } \bar{x} \text{ fulfilling} \tag{79}$$

$$\|A\bar{x} - \bar{y}\| \leqq \|Ax - \bar{y}\| \qquad \text{for any } x \in E_+^n. \tag{80}$$

We know that the x^* thus obtained is unique and represented by

$$x^* = A^+\bar{y}, \tag{81}$$

where A^+ is the generalized inverse of A. Throughout this section, we assume $A^+ \geq 0$. (For its equivalents, see Berman and Plemmons (1972).)

The x^* in (81) can be regarded as the best value of the instruments to achieve the given target $\bar{y}$ in system (78). In a simple policy model of Tinbergen type it is assumed that $m = n$, and hence, provided A is nonsingular, (81) reduces to

$$x^{**} = A^{-1}\bar{y}. \tag{81$'$}$$

x^{**} in (81′) satisfies system (78) consistently, while x^* in (81) is not necessarily an exact solution to the consistent system (78). (i) If the number n of activities (or instruments) is less than that m of goods (or target variables, respectively), x^* from (81) cannot attain the preassigned target $\bar{y}$ exactly, but achieves the closest approximation to $\bar{y}$ in the sense formulated by (79) and (80). (ii) If $m < n$ and if A contains m linearly independent activities, then $\text{rk}(A)$ equals m and hence the x^* happens to be the exact solution to consistent system (78), for then we have $AA^+ = I$. (See the corollary to Theorem 21 in Section 6.3.)

Now consider the dual system corresponding to (77):

$$pA = b, \tag{82}$$

where $p \equiv (p_1, \ldots, p_m) \in E_+^m$ denotes the price vector and $b \equiv (b_1, \ldots, b_n) \in E_+^n$, the vector of the "value added" from all activities at the unit level of intensity. Let the value-added vector v be composed of a wage vector wL and profit vector R:

$$b = wL + R, \tag{83}$$

where w stands for the wage rate per unit of labor input; $L \equiv (l_1, \ldots, l_n) \in E_+^n$ and $R \equiv (r_1, \ldots, r_n) \in E^n$ are the vectors of labor requirements and profits, respectively, in each activity at unit intensity. Substitution of (83) in (82) yields

$$pA = wL + R. \tag{84}$$

If the right-hand side of system (84) is preassigned at some value, the system is in general inconsistent.

(i) In the case where $n < m$, the number of prices to be determined is larger than the number of equations in system (84). In this case, by the same reasoning as for (79) and (80), the normalized price vector that best approximates system (84) is given by

$$p^* = (wL + R)A^+. \tag{85}$$

The p^* will satisfy system (84) consistently only if $\text{rk}(A) = n$, for then $A^+A = I$. Note that, if $\text{rk}(A) = n$, the intensity of operation of any activity has nothing to do with the solution p^* in (85) since by Theorem 22 $(AX)^+ = X^{-1}A^+$, where X is defined by (86) below.

(ii) In the case where $m < n$, it is clear that prices depend on the intensities with which the activities are operated. Let X be the diagonal matrix consisting of the intensities:

$$X \equiv \text{diag}(x_1, \ldots, x_n). \tag{86}$$

Postmultiplying (84) by X yields

$$pAX = (wL + R)X. \tag{87}$$

Assuming $\text{rk}(A) = m$, we have, by virtue of the corollary to Theorem 21,

$$(AX)^+ = XA^{\text{T}}[AX^2A^{\text{T}}]^{-1}, \tag{88}$$

and hence the best normalized price vector will be

$$p^* = (wL + R)X^2A^{\text{T}}[AX^2A^{\text{T}}]^{-1}. \tag{89}$$

From the formal point of view, (89) is a special case of (85). In general, whatever the rank of A may be, we can adopt p^* in (85) as the best approximator of p to system (84). Since $A^+ \geq 0$ by assumption, the p^* takes a nonnegative vector value in normal circumstances.

Let us consider the labor value of each good in our production system, and let λ_i stand for the labor contents of a unit of good i. Calling $\Lambda \equiv (\lambda_1, \ldots, \lambda_m)$ the *labor-contents vector*, we define the labor-value vector of all goods as the minimum labor-contents vector per unit of output that best approximates the inconsistent system

$$\Lambda A = L. \tag{90}$$

This system is comparable with system (80) in Section 4.4 where nonjoint production and $m = n$ were assumed. Mathematically our labor-value vector is the best minimizer Λ^* in the sense that

$$\|\Lambda^*\| \leqq \|\bar{\Lambda}\| \qquad \text{for any } \bar{\Lambda} \text{ fulfilling,} \tag{91}$$

$$\|\bar{\Lambda}A - L\| \leqq \|\Lambda A - L\| \qquad \text{for any } \Lambda \in E_+^m. \tag{92}$$

(i) First assume $n < m$ and $\text{rk}(A) = n$. Then, by a discussion parallel to the previous price determination, we have

$$\Lambda^* = LA^+, \tag{93}$$

which takes nonnegative values on the assumption that $A^+ \geq 0$.

(ii) Next assume $m < n$ and $\text{rk}(A) = m$. Then

$$\Lambda^* = LX^2A^{\text{T}}[AX^2A^{\text{T}}]^{-1}, \tag{94}$$

which takes nonnegative values under the assumption that $A^{\mathrm{T}}[AX^2A^{\mathrm{T}}]^{-1} \geq 0$. Substituting (93) and (94) in (85) and (89), respectively, yields

$$p^* = w\Lambda^* + RA^+ \qquad \text{in case } \mathrm{rk}(A) = n, \tag{85'}$$

$$p^* = w\Lambda^* + RX^2A^{\mathrm{T}}[AX^2A^{\mathrm{T}}]^{-1} \qquad \text{in case } \mathrm{rk}(A) = m. \tag{89'}$$

In any case, only if $R = \theta$, is price vector p^* proportional to labor-value vector Λ^*.

Suppose that the wage rate w is set at the subsistence level, so that all wages are to be spent on consumption:

$$w = pC, \tag{95}$$

where $C \equiv \{c_1, \ldots, c_m\} \in E_+^m$ represents the standard consumption pattern by an average laborer per wage rate. Note that (95) here is the same as (85) in Section 4.4. Taking this supposition into account, we obtain from (84) and (77) respectively

$$p[A - CL] = R, \tag{96}$$

$$[A - CL]x = z, \tag{97}$$

where $z \equiv y - CLx$ stands for the vector of surplus outputs. Systems (96), (97) are comparable with (86), (87) in Section 4.4, respectively. Obviously the following holds.

PROPOSITION 1 p in price system (96) is nonnegative for an arbitrary $R \geqq \theta$ if and only if x in quantity system (97) is nonnegative for an arbitrary $z \geqq \theta$. In this case, $[A - CL]^{-1} \geqq 0$.

(i) When $\mathrm{rk}(A) = n$, we get from (96), (97)

$$p[I - C\Lambda^*]A = R, \tag{96'}$$

$$[I - C\Lambda^*]Ax = z \tag{97'}$$

since, by virtue of $A^+A = I$ and (93),

$$[A - CL] = [A - CL]A^+A = [I - C\Lambda^*]A.$$

Then we define the best approximators of p, x as

$$p^* = RA^+[I - C\Lambda^*]^{-1}, \tag{98}$$

$$x^* = A^+[I - C\Lambda^*]^{-1}z, \tag{99}$$

where $C\Lambda^*$ is a nonnegative matrix and $[I - C\Lambda^*]$ is supposed to satisfy the Hawkins–Simon conditions. Thus p^* from (98) and x^* from (99) are nonnegative for $R \geqq \theta$ and $z \geqq \theta$, respectively, on the assumption that $A^+ \geq 0$.

(ii) If $\mathrm{rk}(A) = m$, Λ^* in (94) is not an exact solution but a best approximator to (90), so that (96) postmultiplied by A^+ yields

$$p[I - C\Lambda^*] \cong RA^+ \tag{96''}$$

in view of $AA^+ = I$, and (97) is converted to a best approximation

$$[I - CA^*]Ax \cong z. \tag{97''}$$

Therefore, p^* and x^* defined in (98) and (99) happen to be the solutions to these inconsistent systems (96″) and (97″), respectively. In general, whatever the rank of A is, p^* and x^* from (98) and (99) are the best approximators to (96) and (97), respectively.

We shall be concerned with the relationship between profits (or surplus outputs) and labor exploitation. As in Section 4.4, denote by μ^* the surplus labor per unit of labor input:

$$\mu^* \equiv 1 - A^*C. \tag{100}$$

PROPOSITION 2 Assume $A^+ \geq 0$. Then p^* in (98) and x^* in (99) take nonnegative values for arbitrary $R \geqq \theta$ and $z \geqq \theta$, respectively, if and only if $\mu^* > 0$ or the rate of exploitation $\mu^*/(1 - \mu^*) > 0$.

PROOF $|I - CA^*| = \mu^* > 0$ implies and is implied by the fact that every principal minor of $[I - CA^*]$ is positive, which is equivalent to saying that $p^* \geqq RA^+ \geqq \theta$ and $x^* \geqq A^+z \geqq \theta$ for arbitrary $R \geqq \theta$ and $z \geqq \theta$, respectively. Q.E.D.

So far matrix A has been supposed to contain capital (stock) coefficients as well as current account input and output coefficients. Henceforth we separate from A the matrix B of capital coefficients, denote by π_j the annual rate of profit of capital in the jth activity, and

$$\hat{\pi} \equiv \operatorname{diag}(\pi_1, \ldots, \pi_n). \tag{101}$$

Then R in (84) can be replaced by $pB\hat{\pi}$, resulting in

$$p[A - B\hat{\pi}] = wL. \tag{102}$$

By a similar discussion to (98), we get the best approximator of p for (102) as

$$p^* = wA^*[I - B\hat{\pi}A^+]^{-1}, \tag{103}$$

where $[I - B\hat{\pi}A^+]$ is assumed to be nonsingular. We can verify the following propositions in a similar manner to Propositions 8 and 9 in Section 4.4.

PROPOSITION 3 Assume $w > 0$, $A^* > \theta$, and $H \equiv B\hat{\pi}A^+ \geqq 0$. Then p^* from (103) is positive if and only if $[I - H]$ satisfies the Hawkins–Simon conditions.

PROPOSITION 4 Assume $w > 0$, $A^* > \theta$, and $A^+ \geq 0$. Let ρ^* be the Frobenius root of BA^+ and assume $\rho^* > 0$. Then p^* in (103) is strictly positive if

$$0 < \pi_i < 1/\rho^* \qquad \text{for} \quad i = 1, \ldots, n. \tag{104}$$

Through competition, profit rates may tend to be equalized for every activity, so in equilibrium where $\pi_1 = \cdots = \pi_n \equiv \pi$, system (102) reduces to

$$p[A - \pi B] = wL. \tag{105}$$

π is termed a uniform rate of profit. Then p^* in (103) is reduced to

$$p^* = w\Lambda^*[I - \pi BA^+]^{-1}, \tag{103'}$$

so that Proposition 4 will change into the following.

PROPOSITION 4′ Assume $w > 0$ and $A^+ \geq 0$. Then p^* from (103′) is semipositive for an arbitrary $\Lambda^* \geq \theta$ if

$$0 < \pi < 1/\rho^*. \tag{104'}$$

Furthermore, if π increases within the range (104′), real wage rate w/p_i $(i = 1, \ldots, m)$ will fall.

PROOF Since $[I - \pi BA^+]^{-1} = (1/\pi)[(1/\pi)I - BA^+]^{-1}$, (104′) implies $[I - \pi BA^+]^{-1} \geqq 0$, which in turn implies that the Frobenius root of πBA^+ is less than unity. Hence we have

$$[I - \pi BA^+]^{-1} = I + \sum_{t=1}^{\infty} (\pi BA^+)^t.$$

Thus, clearly the statement holds true. Q.E.D.

If the wage rate is higher than the subsistence level,

$$w = pC + s \qquad \text{for some} \quad s > 0, \tag{106}$$

then (105) becomes

$$p[A - CL - \pi B] = sL. \tag{105'}$$

On the assumption that $\mathrm{rk}(A) = m$, it follows from (105′) that

$$p[I - \pi M] = s\Lambda^*[I - C\Lambda^*]^{-1}, \tag{107}$$

where $[I - C\Lambda^*]$ is assumed to satisfy the Hawkins–Simon conditions and

$$M \equiv BA^+[I - C\Lambda^*]^{-1}. \tag{108}$$

When $\mathrm{rk}(A) = n$, p determined by (107) can be regarded as the best approximation to (105′).

PROPOSITION 5 Assume $A^+ \geq 0$, $\mu^* > 0$, and either $\Lambda^* > \theta$ or indecomposability of M. Then p from system (107) with $s > 0$ takes on a strictly positive value if

$$0 < \pi < 1/\lambda^*, \tag{109}$$

where λ^* is the Frobenius root of M.

PROOF Since $[I - C\Lambda^*]^{-1} \geqq I$ (because $\mu^* > 0$), we have

$$p[I - \pi M] \geqq s\Lambda^*.$$

(109) implies $\lambda^* < 1/\pi$ and hence we get nonnegative $[I - \pi M]^{-1}$, which can be expanded as

$$[I - \pi M]^{-1} = I + \pi M + (\pi M)^2 + (\pi M)^3 + \cdots.$$

Thus, if $\Lambda^* > \theta$, $p \geqq s\Lambda^* > \theta$. Instead, if M is indecomposable together with $\Lambda^* \geq \theta$, then there is some power t such that M^t is a positive matrix, and thereby

$$p \geqq s\Lambda^*[I - \pi M]^{-1} > \theta. \qquad \text{Q.E.D.}$$

Suppose $s = 0$ in (106), so that (95) holds. Then (107) reduces to

$$p[I - \pi M] = \theta. \tag{107'}$$

PROPOSITION 6 Assume $A^+ \geq 0$ and indecomposability of M. If $\mu^* > 0$, then π compatible with a strictly positive vector p in (107′) is positive.

PROOF $\mu^* > 0$ implies nonnegativity of $[I - C\Lambda^*]^{-1}$ and hence of M. Then indecomposability of M ensures $p > \theta$ if and only if $1/\pi = \lambda^*$ (the Frobenius root of M) which is positive. Q.E.D.

Proposition 6 is regarded as a weak version of the fundamental Marxian theorem (Theorem 26′ in Section 4.4) in an economy where joint production and multiple activities are allowed.

The dynamic model (referring to (118′) in Section 4.4) corresponding to (105) is

$$p_{t+1}[A + B] = (1 + \pi)p_t B + wL. \tag{110}$$

The best approximation to (110) will be

$$p_{t+1}^* = (1 + \pi)\, p_t^* K + w\Lambda^*[I + BA^+]^{-1}, \tag{111}$$

where $K \equiv BA^+[I + BA^+]^{-1}$. If p^* in system (111) converges to a stationary equilibrium described by (103′), as t goes to infinity, starting from an arbitrary initial value p_0^*, then system (111) is said to be globally stable.

PROPOSITION 7 Assume $w > 0$, $\Lambda^* \geq \theta$, and $A^+ \geq 0$. Dynamic system (111) is globally stable and p_t^* converges to semipositive p^* in (103′) if π fulfills (104′) and

$$0 < \pi < \frac{1}{\max\limits_j \sum\limits_i |k_{ij}|} - 1, \tag{112}$$

where k_{ij} stands for the (i, j)th component of K.

PROOF If inequality (112) holds, every eigenvalue of $(1 + \pi)K$ is less than unity in modulus. Hence

$$\begin{aligned}\lim_{t\to\infty} p_t^* &= w\Lambda^*[I + BA^+]^{-1}\,[I - (1 + \pi)\,K]^{-1} \\ &= w\Lambda^*[I - \pi BA^+]^{-1}.\end{aligned}$$

Then refer to Proposition 4′. Q.E.D.

Lastly, we consider the dual quantity system corresponding to price system (110), referring to (123) in Section 4.4,

$$[A + B]x_t = (1 + g)^2 Bx_{t-1} + y_t, \tag{113}$$

where g denotes a uniform growth rate of capital goods, x_t the operation-intensity vector, and y_t the consumption vector in period t. The best approximation to (113) will be

$$x_t^* = (1 + g)^2 Fx_{t-1}^* + [I + A^+B]^{-1}A^+y_t, \tag{114}$$

where $F \equiv [I + A^+B]^{-1}A^+B$. Symmetrically to Proposition 7, we have the following.

PROPOSITION 8 Assume $A^+ \geq 0$ and $y_0 \geq \theta$. x_t^* from (114) is globally stable and converges to the unique nonnegative growing equilibrium:

$$\tilde{x}_t^* = [I - gA^+B]^{-1}A^+(1 + g)^t y_0 \tag{115}$$

if y_t ($\geq \theta$) grows at g and if

$$0 < g < \frac{1}{\left(\max_i \sum_j |f_{ij}|\right)^{1/2}} - 1 \qquad \text{and} \qquad g < \frac{1}{\sigma^*}, \tag{116}$$

where f_{ij} stands for the (i, j)th component of F and σ^* the Frobenius root of A^+B.

PROOF If the first half of (116) holds, every eigenvalue of $(1 + g)^2F$ is less than unity in modulus. Hence

$$\begin{aligned}\lim_{t\to\infty} x_t^* &= [I - (1 + g)\, F]^{-1}\, [I + A^+B]^{-1}A^+(1 + g)^t y_0 \\ &= [I - gA^+B]^{-1}A^+(1 + g)^t y_0.\end{aligned}$$

$g < 1/\sigma^*$ ensures $[I - gA^+B]^{-1} \geqq I$. Q.E.D.

EXERCISES

1. Let M_1 and M_2 be mutually orthogonal subspaces of a Hilbert space H, and z be an element of H. Then verify the projection of z on $M \equiv M_1 + M_2$ is the sum of individual projections on M_1 and M_2.

2. Prove the following proposition. Let $y_1, \ldots, y_n$ be linearly independent vectors in a Hilbert space H, let M be the subspace generated by the y_i, and let x be an element of H. Then, (i) the projection of x on M is represented by $x_0 = \sum_{i=1}^n b_i y_i$, where the coefficients are determined by the so-called *normal equations*:

$$\begin{aligned} b_1(y_1 | y_1) + b_2(y_2 | y_1) + \cdots + b_n(y_n | y_1) &= (x | y_1) \\ &\ \ \vdots \\ b_1(y_1 | y_n) + b_2(y_2 | y_n) + \cdots + b_n(y_n | y_n) &= (x | y_n); \end{aligned}$$

and (ii) the minimum "distance" $\|x - x_0\|$ is calculated as

$$\|x - x_0\|^2 = g(y_1, \ldots, y_n, x)/g(y_1, \ldots, y_n),$$

where $g(y_1, \ldots, y_n)$ stands for the Gram determinant of $y_1, \ldots, y_n$ and $g(y_1, \ldots, y_n, x)$ the Gram determinant of $y_1, \ldots, y_n, x$.

3. Let F be a bounded linear transformation from E^n into E^m, and verify

(i) $\mathrm{rk}(A) + \dim N(A) = n$,
(ii) $\mathrm{rk}(A) + \dim N(A^{\mathrm{T}}) = m$,

where A is the $m \times n$ matrix corresponding to F and $N(A)$ denotes the null-space of A.

4. Let A be an arbitrary real matrix of finite dimension, and verify

(i) $R(A) = R(AA^{\mathrm{T}})$,
(ii) $R(A^{\mathrm{T}}) = R(A^{\mathrm{T}}A)$,

where $R(A)$ denotes the range of A.

5. Let A be an $m \times n$ real matrix and B be an $m \times m$ real symmetric non-singular matrix. Verify

$$(B^{-1}A)^+ = A^+B[I - (CB)^+(CB)], \qquad \text{where} \quad C \equiv I - AA^+.$$

6. Prove that a square matrix A is idempotent if and only if there exist Hermitian idempotent matrices B and C such that

$$A = (CB)^+,$$

and that in this case, we have

$$A = BAC.$$

7. Let A, B, C be real matrices of appropriate dimensions such that $AB = CB^+B$, and verify

$$AA^{\mathrm{T}} = CB^+(CB^+)^{\mathrm{T}} + (A - CB^+)(A + CB^+)^{\mathrm{T}}.$$

8. Prove Theorem 32 and its corollary.
9. Prove Proposition 3.
10. Prove Proposition 4.

REFERENCES AND FURTHER READING

Albert, A. (1972). *Regression and the Moore–Penrose Pseudoinverse*. Academic Press, New York.

Ben-Israel, A., and Charnes, A. (1963). "Contributions to the Theory of Generalized Inverses," *SIAM Journal on Applied Mathematics* **11**, 667–699.

Ben-Israel, A., and Greville, T. N. E. (1974). *Generalized Inverses: Theory and Applications*. Wiley (Interscience), New York.

Berman, A., and Plemmons, R. J. (1972). "Monotonicity and the Generalized Inverse," *SIAM Journal on Applied Mathematics* **22**, 155–161.

Boullion, T. L., and Odell, P. L. (1971). *Generalized Inverse Matrices*. Wiley (Interscience), New York.

Chipman, J. S. (1964). "On Least Squares with Insufficient Observations," *Journal of American Statistical Association* **59**, 1078–1111.

Chipman, J. S., and Rao, M. M. (1964). "Projections, Generalized Inverses, and Quadratic Forms," *Journal of Mathematical Analysis and Applications* **9**, 1–11.

Goldstein, M., and Smith, A. F. M. (1974). "Ridge-type Estimators for Regression Analysis," *Journal of Royal Statistical Society* **36**, 284–291.

Graybill, F. A., Meyer, C. D., and Painter, R. J. (1966). "Note on the Computation of the Generalized Inverse of a Matrix," *SIAM Review* **8**, 522–524.

Greville, T. N. E. (1959). "The Pseudoinverse of a Rectangular or Singular Matrix and its Application to the Solution of Systems of Linear Equations," *SIAM Review* **1**, 38–43.

Greville, T. N. E. (1960). "Some Applications of the Pseudoinverse of a Matrix," *SIAM Review* **2**, 15–22.

Luenberger, D. G. (1969). *Optimization by Vector Space Methods*. Wiley, New York.

Marquardt, D. W. (1970). "Generalized Inverse, Ridge Regression, Biased Linear Estimation, and Nonlinear Estimation," *Technometrics* **12**, 591–612.

Penrose, R. (1955). "A Generalized Inverse for Matrices," *Proceedings of the Cambridge Philosophical Society* **51**, 406–413.

Penrose, R. (1956). "On Best Approximate Solutions of Linear Matrix Equations," *Proceedings of the Cambridge Philosophical Society* **52**, 17–19.

Rao, C. R., and Mitra, S. K. (1971). *Generalized Inverse of Matrices and Its Applications*. Wiley, New York.

Schönfeld, P. (1971). "Best Linear Minimum Bias Estimation in Linear Regression," *Econometrica* **39**, 531–544.

Schönfeld, P. (1975). "A Note on Least Squares Estimation and the BLUE in a Generalized Linear Regression Model," *Journal of Econometrics* **3**, 189–197.

Spivey, W. A., and Tamura, H. (1970). "Generalized Simultaneous Equation Models," *International Economic Review* **11**, 216–225.

Tinbergen, J. (1952). *On the Theory of Economic Policy*, 2nd ed. North-Holland Publ., Amsterdam.

Yoshida, K. (1965). *Functional Ayalysis*. Springer-Verlag, Berlin.

Chapter 7

Optimization under Economic Equation Constraints

7.1 Differentials and Extrema

First, we introduce two kinds of differentials which are to be frequently referred to in optimization problems.

DEFINITION 1 Let F be a transformation from a vector space X into a normed (vector) space Y with domain D and x be an element of D. If there exists a limit for each $h \in X$ with $x + vh \in D$ and $v \in R^1$

$$\lim_{v \to 0} \frac{F(x + vh) - F(x)}{v} \equiv \delta F(x; h), \tag{1}$$

then F is said to be *Gateaux differentiable* at x and $\delta F(x; h)$ is called the *Gateaux differential* of F at x (with increment h).

The limit $\delta F(x; h)$ is taken in the sense of norm convergence in Y, i.e.,

$$\left\| \frac{1}{v} [F(x + vh) - F(x)] - \delta F(x; h) \right\| \to 0 \qquad \text{as} \quad v \to 0.$$

This expression can be rewritten as

$$\|F(x + vh) - F(x) - v \cdot \delta F(x; h)\| = o(v) \tag{2}$$

because the notation $g(v) = o(v)$ means that $\lim_{v \to 0} g(v)/v = 0$, where g is a real-valued function and $o(\,\cdot\,)$ is called the *Landau's* o-symbol.

DEFINITION 2 Let X, Y be normed spaces, let $F \colon X \to Y$, and F be defined on an open subset D of X. For $x \in D$, if there exists a linear and continuous operator F_x of h such that $F_x(h) \in Y$ and

$$\lim_{||h||\to 0} \frac{||F(x+h) - F(x) - F_x(h)||}{||h||} = 0 \tag{3}$$

for each $h \in X$ with $x + h \in D$, then F is said to be *Fréchet differentiable* at x, $F_x(h)$ is called the *Fréchet dieffrential* of F at x (with increment h), and F_x is termed the *Fréchet derivative* of F at x. F_x is alternatively expressed as $F'(x)$. As x varies over D, the correspondence of $F'(x)$ with x defines a transformation (cf. p. 185 for the space $B(X, Y)$)

$$F' \colon D \to B(X, Y) \tag{4}$$

since $F_x(h) \in Y$ and since $F'(x)$ is linear and continuous in $h \in X$.

THEOREM 1 Let F be a transformation defined on an open domain D of a normed space X and be Fréchet differentiable at x. Then (i) its Fréchet derivative at x is unique and (ii) the Fréchet differential of F at x is equal to its Gateaux differential at x.

PROOF (i) Suppose both F_x and G_x are the Fréchet derivatives of F at x. Since

$$||F_x(h) - G_x(h)|| \leqq ||F(x+h) - F(x) - F_x(h)|| + |-1|\,||F(x+h) - F(x) - G_x(h)||,$$

$$\lim_{||h||\to 0} \frac{||F_x(h) - G_x(h)||}{||h||} = 0 \qquad \text{for each } h \in X \quad \text{with } x + h \in D. \tag{1*}$$

Given $h \in X$, $||F_x(h) - G_x(h)||$ is bounded, and $||F_x(h) - G_x(h)||/||h||$ is invariant of any scalar multiplication of h. Hence, there is a nonnegative number c_h such that $||F_x(h) - G_x(h)|| = c_h||h||$. Thus it follows from (1*) that

$$0 = \lim_{t\to 0} \frac{||F_x(th) - G_x(th)||}{||th||} = c_h,$$

implying $||F_x(h) - G_x(h)|| = 0$ for each h.

(ii) The limit (3) implies $||F(x + vh) - F(x) - vF_x(h)|| = o(v)$, while the Gateaux differential $\delta F(x;\, h)$ satisfies (2). Hence $F_x(h) = \delta F(x;\, h)$. Q.E.D.

We consider a necessary condition for a functional to achieve a maximum or a minimum.

DEFINITION 3 Let f be a real-valued functional defined on a subset S of a normed space X. If there is an open sphere U containing $x^0 \in S$ such that

$$f(x) \leqq f(x^0) \qquad \text{for all} \quad x \in S \cap U, \quad x \neq x^0,$$

then f is said to achieve a *local* (or *relative*) *maximum* at x^0. Likewise a local minimum can be defined. *Extremum* is used to refer to either a local (or global) maximum or minimum. (Cf. Definition 7.) The set on which an extremum problem is defined is called the *admissible set*.

THEOREM 2 Let f be a Fréchet differentiable real-valued functional on a subset S of a normed space X. If f has an extremum at $x^0 \in S$, then its Gateaux differential at x^0 will vanish.

PROOF For each $h \in X$ with $x^0 + vh \in S$, $f(x^0 + vh)$ is a real-valued function of the real variable v. This function must achieve an extremum at $v = 0$, i.e.,

$$\frac{d}{dv} f(x^0 + vh)\Big|_{v=0} = 0.$$

By definition,

$$\frac{d}{dv} f(x + vh)\Big|_{v=0} = \lim_{v \to 0} \frac{1}{v} [f(x + vh) - f(x)] = \delta f(x; h). \qquad \text{Q.E.D.}$$

DEFINITION 4 A point at which the Gateaux differential of functional f vanishes is termed a *stationary point* of f.

THEOREM 3 If a transformation F defined on an open subset D of a normed space X is Fréchet differentiable at x, then F is continuous at x.

PROOF In view of the openness of D, the expression (3) can be rewritten as follows: Given $\varepsilon > 0$, there is an open sphere $U(x; \delta) \equiv \{u: \|x - u\| < \delta, \delta > 0\}$ such that

$$x + h \in U(x; \delta) \qquad \text{implies} \qquad \|F(x + h) - F(x) - F_x(h)\|/\|h\| < \varepsilon.$$

In other words, for every h satisfying $\|h\| < \delta$,

$$\|F(x + h) - F(x)\| - \|F_x(h)\| \leqq \|F(x + h) - F(x) - F_x(h)\| < \varepsilon \|h\|.$$

Since F_x is linear and continuous, $F_x(h)$ is bounded, i.e., there is a finite number $N > 0$ such that $\|F_x(h)\| < N\|h\|$. Therefore, given $\varepsilon > 0$ there exist $\delta > 0$ and finite $N > 0$ such that

$$\|F(x + h) - F(x)\| < (\varepsilon + N)\|h\| \qquad \text{for each } h \text{ satisfying } \|h\| < \delta.$$

This implies that F is continuous at x. (Refer to the following remark.)

Q.E.D.

Remark The last part of the above proof is essentially identical with the *uniform Lipschitz condition*; i.e., there exist $\delta > 0$ and $M > 0$ such that

$$\|F(z) - F(x)\| \leqq M \|z - x\| \qquad \text{for each } x, z \text{ satisfying } \|z - x\| < \delta. \tag{5}$$

This condition is sufficient for F to be continuous at x.

If the original transformation f is a functional on a normed space X, the Fréchet derivative $f'(x)$ is said to be the *gradient* of f at $x \in X$, and denoted alternatively by $\nabla f(x)$. Let f be a functional defined on the real n-space R^n with domain D. If there is the limit

$$\lim_{v \to 0} \frac{f(x + ve^j) - f(x)}{v} \equiv \frac{\partial f(x)}{\partial x_j} \equiv f_j(x)$$

for $x \equiv (x_1, \ldots, x_n) \in D$, a real variable v, and the jth unit vector e^j in R^n with $x + ve^j \in D$, then $f_j(x)$ is called the partial derivative of f at x with respect to x_j. Given $\varepsilon > 0$, if there is $\delta > 0$ such that

$$|f_j(x) - f_j(x^0)| < \varepsilon \qquad \text{for } x \text{ satisfying } \|x - x^0\| < \delta, \tag{6}$$

then f_j is said to be continuous at x^0.

DEFINITION 5 Let F be a transformation from R^n into Euclidean m-space E^m and assume that the ith component $F^i(x)$ of $F(x)$ has partial derivative $F^i_j(x)$ at x with respect to the jth component of x ($i = 1, \ldots, m$; $j = 1, \ldots, n$). The matrix

$$\begin{bmatrix} F^1_1(x) & F^1_2(x) & \cdots & F^1_n(x) \\ F^2_1(x) & F^2_2(x) & \cdots & F^2_n(x) \\ \vdots & \vdots & & \vdots \\ F^m_1(x) & F^m_2(x) & \cdots & F^m_n(x) \end{bmatrix} \equiv F'(x) \tag{7}$$

is termed the *Jacobian matrix* of F at x. In case $n = m$, the determinant of $F'(x)$ is well defined and called the *Jacobian* of F at x. If $F^i_j(x)$ is continuous at x for each i and j, F is said to be *continuously differentiable* at x.

THEOREM 4 Let F be a transformation from E^n into E^m and assume that F is continuously differentiable at x. Then the Fréchet differential of F at x with increment $h \in E^n$ is

$$F_x(h) = F'(x)h, \tag{8}$$

where $F'(x)$ is that in (7).

PROOF F_x in (8) is linear and continuous in h. It is necessary to verify only that it satisfies the limit (3). (The verification is left as an exercise for the reader.) Q.E.D.

For example, when $F(x) = Px + w$, we have $F'(x) = P$ since

$$F'(x)h = F_x(h) = \delta F(x; h) = Ph.$$

Let f be a Fréchet differentiable real-valued functional on an open subset S of E^n. If f has an extremum at $x^0 \in S$, then in view of Theorems 1, 2, and 4,

$$f'(x^0)h = 0 \qquad \text{for every} \quad h \in E^n, \quad x^0 + h \in S,$$

or equivalently

$$f'(x^0) = \theta, \tag{9}$$

where $f'(x^0)$ is the gradient of f at x^0.

There are two useful rules concerning Fréchet derivatives.

THEOREM 5 Let X, Y be normed spaces and F, G be transformations from X into Y. If both F and G have Fréchet differentials at $x \in X$, then $\alpha F + \beta G$ has a Fréchet differential at x and

$$(\alpha F + \beta G)'(x) = \alpha F'(x) + \beta G'(x), \tag{10}$$

where α and β are constant scalars.

(The proof is left to the reader.)

THEOREM 6 Let X, Y, Z be normed spaces, let D, S be open subsets of X, Y, respectively, and let

$$G\colon\ D \to S \qquad \text{and} \qquad F\colon\ S \to Z.$$

If G and F have Fréchet differentials at $x \in D$ and at $y \equiv G(x) \in S$, respectively, then $T \equiv FG$ has a Fréchet differential at x and

$$T'(x) = F'(y)\, G'(x) \quad \text{(the chain rule).} \tag{11}$$

PROOF For $g \in Y$ and $h \in X$ with $x + h \in D$,

$$\begin{aligned} &\frac{\|T(x+h) - T(x) - F'(y)\, G'(x)h\|}{\|h\|} \\ &\qquad \leqq \frac{\|T(x+h) - T(x) - F'(y)g\|\;\|g\|}{\|g\|\;\|h\|} \\ &\qquad\qquad + \frac{\|F'(y)(g - G'(x)h)\|\;\|g - G'(x)h\|}{\|g - G'(x)h\|\;\|h\|}. \end{aligned} \tag{2*}$$

Put $g \equiv G(x+h) - G(x)$. Then $\|g - G'(x)h\| = o(\|h\|)$. Since

$$T(x+h) - T(x) = FG(x+h) - FG(x) = F(y+g) - F(y),$$

$$\|T(x+h) - T(x) - F'(y)g\| = \|F(y+g) - F(y) - F'(y)g\| = o(\|g\|).$$

$F'(y)$ is a continuous linear transformation. Hence it is bounded, i.e., there is a finite positive number M such that

$$\|F'(y)(g - G'(x)h)\| \leqq M\,\|g - G'(x)h\|.$$

By Theorem 3, G is continuous at x; i.e., given $\varepsilon > 0$ there are $\delta > 0$ and finite $N > 0$ such that

$$\|g\| < (\varepsilon + N)\|h\| \qquad \text{for} \quad \|h\| < \delta.$$

As $\|h\|$ tends to zero, therefore, $\|g\|$ converges to zero, and in view of (2*)

$$\lim_{\|h\|\to 0} \frac{\|T(x+h) - T(x) - F'(y)\, G'(x)h\|}{\|h\|} \leqq 0. \qquad \text{Q.E.D.}$$

7.2 The Euler Equation, the Ramsey Path, and Concave Functionals

In classical calculus of variations we find an extremum problem that is concerned with an *extremal* (function) and has wide applicability to economic optimization problems over time.

Recall that $C[a, b]$ with real constants $a < b$ represents the set of all continuous real-valued functions on a closed interval $[a, b]$, and define a function J on $X \equiv C[a, b]$ by

$$J(x) = \int_a^b f(x(t), \dot{x}(t), t)\, dt \qquad \text{for} \quad x \in C[a, b], \tag{12}$$

where $\dot{x}(t) \equiv dx/dt$, and f is a real-valued functional in x, $\dot{x}$, and t. We seek a function $x \in X$ that maximizes the value of $J(x)$. Let S be the admissible set in X for our maximizing problem. By Theorem 2 in Section 7.1, if x^0 is the maximizing point in S, we have the following extremum condition:

$$\delta J(x^0; h) = 0 \tag{13}$$

for $h \in X$ with $x^0 + vh \in S$ for $v \in (0, 1)$. Assuming that partial derivatives $f_x \equiv \partial f/\partial x$ and $f_{\dot{x}} \equiv \partial f/\partial \dot{x}$ exist, we can show

$$\delta J(x; h) = \int_a^b [f_x h + f_{\dot{x}} \dot{h}]\, dt \tag{14}$$

since

$$\begin{aligned}
\delta J(x; h) &= \lim_{v \to 0} \frac{1}{v} \left[\int_a^b f(x + vh, \dot{x} + v\dot{h}, t)\, dt - \int_a^b f(x, \dot{x}, t)\, dt \right] \\
&= \lim_{v \to 0} \frac{1}{v} \int_a^b [f(x + vh, \dot{x} + v\dot{h}, t) - f(x, \dot{x}, t)]\, dt \\
&= \frac{d}{dv} \int_a^b f(x + vh, \dot{x} + v\dot{h}, t)\, dt \,|_{v=0} \\
&= \int_a^b \frac{d}{dv} f(x + vh, \dot{x} + v\dot{h}, t)\,|_{v=0}\, dt \\
&= \int_a^b [f_x h + f_{\dot{x}} \dot{h}]\, dt.
\end{aligned}$$

The Gateaux differential in (14) is found to be a Fréchet differential. (The verification is left to the reader.) Thus the extremum condition (13) can be rewritten as

$$\int_a^b [f_x^0 h + f_2^0 \dot{h}]\, dt = 0 \tag{13'}$$

for $h \in X$ with $x^0 + vh \in S$ for $v \in (0, 1)$, where

$$f_x^0 \equiv f_x(x, \dot{x}, t)|_{x=x^0}, \qquad f_{\dot{x}}^0 \equiv f_{\dot{x}}(x, \dot{x}, t)|_{x=x^0}.$$

First, we consider the case where both the initial value $x(a)$ and the terminal value $x(b)$ are fixed. Then, for any $x + vh$ fulfilling these boundary conditions, the function $h \in X$ must vanish at a and b, i.e.,

$$h(a) = h(b) = 0. \tag{15}$$

LEMMA 1 Let G be a continuous function on a closed interval $[a, b]$, and h be a Gateaux differentiable function on the interval satisfying conditions (15). If $\int_a^b G(t)\dot{h}(t)\,dt = 0$, then $G(t)$ is constant for all $t \in [a, b]$.

PROOF Let c be a constant satisfying

$$\int_a^b (G(\tau) - c)\,d\tau = 0,$$

and define h as

$$h(t) = \int_a^t (G(\tau) - c)\,d\tau.$$

Then h satisfies our assumption. Since $\dot{h}(t) = G(t) - c$, we have

$$\begin{aligned}\int_a^b (G(t) - c)^2\,dt &= \int_a^b (G(t) - c)\dot{h}(t)\,dt \\ &= \int_a^b G(t)\dot{h}(t)\,dt - c(h(b) - h(a)) = 0.\end{aligned}$$

Hence $G(t) \equiv c$ on $[a, b]$. Q.E.D.

THEOREM 7 Let $f_{\dot{x}}^0$ in (13′) be a continuous function on a closed interval $[a, b]$, and h be a Gateaux differentiable function on the interval satisfying conditions (15). If Eq. (13′) holds, then

$$f_x^0 = \frac{d}{dt} f_{\dot{x}}^0 \qquad \text{for all} \quad t \in [a, b]. \tag{16}$$

Equation (16) is called the *Euler equation*.

PROOF Integrating $\int_a^b f_x^0\, h\,dt$ by parts yields

$$\int_a^b f_x^0 h\,dt = F(t)h(t)]_a^b - \int_a^b F(t)\dot{h}(t)\,dt = -\int_a^b F(t)\dot{h}(t)\,dt,$$

where $F(t) \equiv \int_a^t f_x^0(\tau)\,d\tau$. Thus, Eq. (13′) is rewritten as

$$\int_a^b (f_{\dot{x}}^0 - F(t))\dot{h}(t)\,dt = 0.$$

By Lemma 1, therefore, we have $f_{\dot{x}}^0 \equiv F(t) + c$, where c is a constant. Hence (16) follows. Q.E.D.

Thus, the Euler equation (16) is a condition for function J in (12) to achieve an extremum under fixed boundary conditions.

Next we consider the same extremum problem in the case where the terminal condition is not fixed; viz., the end point β in time and the terminal value $x(\beta)$ of x are not rigidly predetermined. In particular, we are interested in the search for a terminal situation $(\beta, x(\beta))$ such that $x(\beta)$ be located along some target curve $g(\beta)$.

Assume that the end point β is variable with respect to a parameter p; i.e.,

$$\beta = b(p) \qquad \text{with} \quad db/dp \neq 0.$$

Let $x(t)$ be an extremal, and consider its variant

$$x(t(p)) \equiv x(t) + ph(t), \tag{17}$$

where $h \in X$ with $h(a) = 0$. Accordingly, we put

$$g(b(p)) \equiv x(b(p)) + ph(b(p)), \tag{18}$$

and redefine function J on $X \equiv C[a, b(p)]$ by

$$J(x, p) \equiv \int_a^{b(p)} f[x(t(p)), \dot{x}(t(p)), t]\, dt, \tag{19}$$

where $\dot{x}(t(p)) \equiv \dot{x}(t) + p\dot{h}(t)$. Since the desired extremal $x(t)$ will be obtained when p is set equal to zero, a necessary condition for our extremum problem is

$$\left.\frac{dJ(x, p)}{dp}\right|_{p=0} = 0, \tag{20}$$

to which the following lemma is applied.

LEMMA 2 Let ψ be a functional of two real variables p and t, and assume that ψ and $\partial\psi/\partial p$ are continuous with respect to these variables. Define a function Ψ by

$$\Psi(p) \equiv \int_{a(p)}^{b(p)} \psi(p, t)\, dt.$$

Then

$$\frac{d\Psi(p)}{dp} = \int_{a(p)}^{b(p)} \frac{\partial\psi}{\partial p}\, dt + \frac{db(p)}{dp}\psi(p, b(p)) - \frac{da(p)}{dp}\psi(p,a(p)).$$

(The proof of Lemma 2 may be found in most standard textbooks on calculus.)

Thus, in view of (17) and (19),

$$\left.\frac{dJ(x, p)}{dp}\right|_{p=0} = \int_a^b f_x(x(t), \dot{x}(t), t)h(t)\, dt + \int_a^b f_{\dot{x}}(x(t), \dot{x}(t), t)\dot{h}(t)\, dt$$
$$+ b'f(x(b), \dot{x}(b), b), \tag{21}$$

where $b \equiv b(0)$ and $b' \equiv db(p)/dp|_{p=0}$. Integrating by parts and taking into account that $h(a) = 0$, we reduce the second term on the right-hand side of (21) to

$$f_{\dot{x}}(x(b), \dot{x}(b), b)h(b) - \int_a^b \frac{df_{\dot{x}}}{dt} h(t)\, dt,$$

where $f_{\dot{x}} \equiv f_{\dot{x}}(x(t), \dot{x}(t), t)$. Hence condition (20) is expressed as

$$0 = \int_a^b \left[f_x(x(t), \dot{x}(t), t) - \frac{df_{\dot{x}}}{dt} \right] h(t)\, dt + f_{\dot{x}}(x(b), \dot{x}(b), b)h(b) + f(x(b), \dot{x}(b), b)\, b'. \tag{20'}$$

Upon differentiating (18) with respect to p and setting p equal to zero, we get

$$\dot{g}(b)b' - \dot{x}(b)b' = h(b). \tag{18'}$$

On the other hand, $x(t)$ is an extremal for J in (19) when $p = 0$, and hence it satisfies the Euler equation. In view of this fact, (18′) and $b' \neq 0$, (20′) is reduced to

$$[f(x(t), \dot{x}(t), t) + (\dot{g}(t) - \dot{x}(t)) f_{\dot{x}}(x(t), \dot{x}(t), t)]_{t=b} = 0. \tag{22}$$

This is called the *transversality condition*, which must be fulfilled at an end point in time. In the special case where $g(b(p))$ is constant for any $b(p)$, (22) reduces to

$$[f(x(t), \dot{x}(t), t) - \dot{x}(t)\, f_{\dot{x}}(x(t), \dot{x}(t), t)]_{t=b} = 0. \tag{22'}$$

The above discussions are summarized as follows.

THEOREM 8 Let f be a real-valued functional of $x \in C[a, b]$, $t \in [a, b]$, and $\dot{x} \equiv dx/dt$ for a real variable $b > a$. Assume that the partial derivatives $f_x \equiv \partial f/\partial x$, $f_{\dot{x}} \equiv \partial f/\partial \dot{x}$ exist, that $f_{\dot{x}}$ is continuous in t, and that h is a Gateaux differentiable function on $[a, b]$ satisfying $h(a) = 0$. If the terminal value $x(b)$ should be located along a given curve $g(b)$, then the extremum condition for $x(t)$ maximizing the value of function J in (12) is that the Euler equation (16) and the transversality condition (22) (or (22′) in case $g(b)$ is constant for all b) be satisfied by $x(t)$.

Application 1 (*Ramsey model—a two-sector case*) We consider an optimal theory of accumulation in a closed economy intending to maximize the utility of per capita consumption over time under the following assumptions.

A.1 There are two kinds of goods, viz., consumption good C and investment good V, each of which is producible by a fixed-proportion function of capital input only, say at time t

$$C(t) = \alpha K_1(t), \tag{23}$$

$$V(t) = \beta K_2(t), \tag{24}$$

where α, β are positive constants, K_1 and K_2 stand for capital inputs in the consumption-good and investment-good sectors, respectively, and total capital $K = K_1 + K_2$.

A.2 Labor (= population) L is constant and always larger than its demand. Hence labor cannot be a binding factor of production.

A.3 Output of new investment good is all distributed to production sectors. We allow free transferability of old capital. Hence the distribution percentage 100λ of V to the consumption-good sector may take any value.

We denote by $\dot{y}$ the derivative of a variable y with respect to time t.

In view of assumptions A.1 and A.3, we obtain

$$\dot{C}(t) = \alpha V(t) - (\alpha/\beta)\dot{V}(t) \tag{25}$$

by substitution of

$$\dot{C} = \alpha\dot{K}_1 = \alpha\lambda V \qquad \text{and} \qquad \dot{V} = \beta\dot{K}_2 = \beta(1-\lambda)V.$$

Since $\dot{K} = V$, (25) is rewritten as

$$d\dot{K}/dt = \beta\dot{K} - (\beta/\alpha)\dot{C}. \tag{25$'$}$$

Integrate (25′) over a closed interval $[0, \tau]$ for a positive τ, and we have

$$\dot{K}(\tau) - \dot{K}(0) = \beta(K(\tau) - K(0)) - (\beta/\alpha)(C(\tau) - C(0)),$$

into which

$$\dot{K}(0) = \beta K_2(0), \qquad K(0) = K_1(0) + K_2(0), \qquad \text{and} \quad C(0) = \alpha K_1(0)$$

are substituted to entail

$$c(t) \equiv C(t)/L = \alpha k(t) - (\alpha/\beta)\dot{k}(t) \qquad \text{for} \quad t > 0, \tag{26}$$

where $k \equiv K/L$ and $\dot{k} \equiv \dot{K}/L$.

Our objective is to maximize

$$\int_0^T U(c)\, dt, \tag{27}$$

where U stands for total utility and T the end point in time. Suppose that the initial condition $K(0)$ is given and constant, that the terminal value $K(T)$ is fixed at a target K^*, though the end point T is not fixed, and that

$$K(t) < K^* \qquad \text{for} \quad t \in [0, T).$$

Replace k in (26) by $k^* \equiv K^*/L$. Then $c^* \equiv \alpha k^*$ is the target value of c. $B \equiv U(c^*)$ is referred to as the *satiation* or *Bliss*. Since $U(c(t)) < B$ for $t \in [0, T)$, our objective function can be expressed as

$$\int_0^T [U(\alpha k(t) - (\alpha/\beta)\dot{k}(t)) - B]\, dt. \tag{27$'$}$$

The Euler equation for this problem is

$$\frac{\partial U}{\partial k} = \frac{d}{dt}\left[\frac{\partial U}{\partial \dot{k}}\right],$$

from which it follows that

$$\dot{c}(t) = -\beta\frac{u(c)}{u'(c)} > 0 \qquad \text{for} \quad t > 0 \tag{28}$$

since we assume a decreasing marginal utility:

$$u(c) > 0 \qquad \text{and} \qquad u'(c) < 0 \qquad \text{for} \quad c > 0, \tag{29}$$

where $u \equiv dU/dc$ and $u' \equiv du/dc$. Moreover, transversality condition (22′) is applicable to our problem; i.e.,

$$U(T) - B + (\alpha/\beta)\dot{k}(T)u(T) = 0, \tag{30}$$

where $U(T) \equiv U(\alpha k(T) - (\alpha/\beta)\dot{k}(T))$ and $u(T) \equiv u(\alpha k(T) - (\alpha/\beta)\dot{k}(T))$.

Now we shall show that all the above assumptions and conditions determine a unique $\dot{k}(t)$ as

$$\dot{k}(t) = \frac{\beta(B - U(c))}{\alpha u(c)} > 0 \qquad \text{for} \quad t \in [0, T). \tag{31}$$

In view of (26) and (28), respectively, we know

$$\ddot{k} \equiv \ddot{K}/L = \beta\dot{k} - (\beta/\alpha)\dot{c} \qquad \text{and} \quad \dot{u} = u'\dot{c} = -\beta u.$$

Therefore

$$d(u\dot{k})/dt = \dot{u}\dot{k} + u\ddot{k} = -(\beta/\alpha)u\dot{c} = -(\beta/\alpha)\dot{U},$$

which is integrated to result in

$$u(t)\dot{k}(t) = \int d(u\dot{k}) = -(\beta/\alpha)\int \dot{U}\,dt = -(\beta/\alpha)(U(t) - \delta),$$

where δ is an integration constant. Condition (30) ensures that $\delta = B$.

By virtue of (31) and (26), we get the value of $k(t)$ corresponding to $\dot{k}$ in (31) as follows:

$$\tilde{k}(t) = \frac{1}{\alpha}\left(c + \frac{B - U(c)}{u(c)}\right) \qquad \text{for} \quad t \in [0, T), \tag{32}$$

which traces the so-called *Ramsey path* of accumulation. The derivative of $\tilde{k}$ in (32) with respect to c is known to be positive in view of (29). Dividing $K(0)$ into $K_1(0)$ and $K_2(0)$, we determine $c(0) = \alpha K_1(0)/L$. Thus the Ramsey path of $\tilde{k}$ relative to c can be illustrated as in Fig. 3.

(The reader may refer to Samuelson and Solow (1956) for a study of the Ramsey path in a many-goods model.)

In the preceding application the Euler equation and transversality condition, as extremum conditions, together with assumption (29) ensure a maximum for the objective function (27). In general, if the function U is concave,

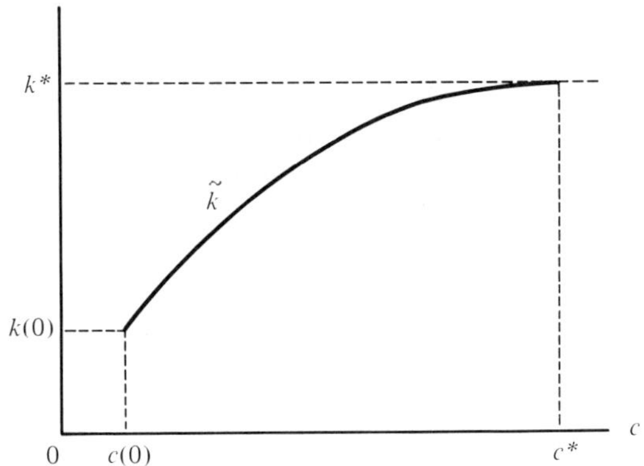

FIGURE 3. Ramsey path.

then the extremum conditions are found to be sufficient to ensure a global maximum.

DEFINITION 6 A real-valued functional f defined on a convex subset D of a vector space X is said to be *concave* if

$$\alpha f(x) + (1 - \alpha) f(x^0) \leqq f(\alpha x + (1 - \alpha) x^0) \tag{33}$$

for any $x, x^0 \in D$ and $\alpha \in [0, 1]$. If strict inequality holds in (33) for any $\alpha \in (0, 1)$ whenever $x \neq x^0$, f is said to be *strictly concave*. When f is a concave functional on a convex subset D of X, $g \equiv -f$ is termed a *convex functional* on D. That is, g is a convex functional on D if it is real-valued and satisfies

$$\alpha g(x) + (1 - \alpha) g(x^0) \geqq g(\alpha x + (1 - \alpha) x^0) \tag{34}$$

for any $x, x^0 \in D$ and $\alpha \in [0, 1]$. If strict inequality holds in (34) for any $\alpha \in (0, 1)$ whenever $x \neq x^0$, g is said to be *strictly convex*. (Refer to Fig. 4.)

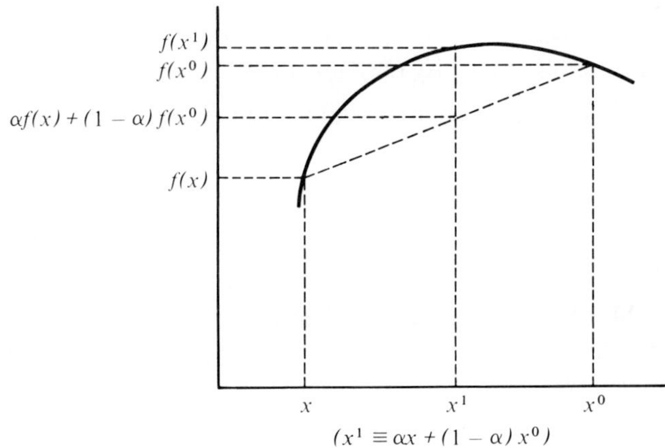

FIGURE 4. Strict concavity.

It follows from (33) that

$$f(x) - f(x^0) \leqq [f(x^0 + \alpha(x - x^0)) - f(x^0)]/\alpha \tag{35}$$

for $x, x^0 \in D$ and $\alpha \in (0, 1]$. Let f be Fréchet differentiable at $x^0 \in D \subset E^n$. Then the differential of f at x^0 with increment $x - x^0$ is

$$\delta f(x^0; x - x^0) \equiv \lim_{\alpha \to 0} [f(x^0 + \alpha(x - x^0)) - f(x^0)]/\alpha = f'(x^0)(x - x^0). \tag{36}$$

Combining (35) and (36), we assert that if f is a concave functional on a convex subset D of E^n, having partial derivative with respect to each component of x at $x^0 \in D$, then

$$f(x) - f(x^0) \leqq f'(x^0)(x - x^0) \qquad \text{for} \quad x \in D. \tag{37}$$

Similarly, for a convex functional g on D having gradient $g'(x)$,

$$g(x) - g(x^0) \geqq g'(x^0)(x - x^0) \qquad \text{for} \quad x, x^0 \in D. \tag{38}$$

Conversely, if (37) holds for each $x, x^0 \in D$, then f can be shown to be concave. For $\alpha \in [0, 1]$,

$$f(x) - f(\alpha x + (1 - \alpha)x^0) \leqq (1 - \alpha)f'(\alpha x + (1 - \alpha)x^0) \cdot (x - x^0),$$

$$f(x^0) - f(\alpha x + (1 - \alpha)x^0) \leqq -\alpha f'(\alpha x + (1 - \alpha)x^0) \cdot (x - x^0).$$

Multiplying the first inequality by α, the second one by $1-\alpha$, and adding give (33).

Similarly for the convex case. Thus we have

THEOREM 9 Let f, g be real-valued differentiable functionals on an open convex set D in E^n. f is concave if and only if inequality (37) holds for each $x, x^0 \in D$, and g is convex if and only if inequality (38) holds.

COROLLARY Let f, g be real-valued differentiable functionals on an open convex set D in E^n. f is strictly concave if and only if inequality (37) holds with strict inequality for each $x, x^0 \in D$, $x \neq x^0$, and g is strictly convex if and only if inequality (38) holds with strict inequality.

DEFINITION 7 Let f be a real-valued functional defined on a subset S of a normed space X. If

$$f(x) \leqq f(x^0) \qquad \text{for all} \quad x, x^0 \in S, \quad x \neq x^0,$$

then f is said to achieve a *global maximum* at x^0. A global minimum can be defined with the reverse inequality sign.

THEOREM 10 Let f be a real-valued functional defined on E^n and assume that f is differentiable at x^0. If f is concave (convex) on a convex set D in X containing x^0, then

$$f'(x^0) = \theta \tag{39}$$

is necessary and sufficient for $f(x^0)$ to be a global maximum (minimum) on D.

PROOF Necessity is already known. (37) and (39) yield $f(x) \leqq f(x^0)$ for all $x \in D$. Q.E.D.

It is easily checked that if U in Application 1 above is a concave functional, then the integral (27) is also concave with respect to c. Hence, by Theorem 10, extremum conditions are enough to ensure a global maximum for the integral.

Next an equivalence condition for concavity of a real-valued functional is to be provided when it is twice differentiable on a Euclidean space as defined below.

DEFINITION 8 Let f be a real-valued functional defined on an open set D in E^n, and let x be in D. f is said to be *twice differentiable* at x if there exists a real-valued functional w of h such that

$$f(x+h) - f(x) - f'(x)h - \tfrac{1}{2} h^{\mathrm{T}} f''(x)h = w(x;h)\|h\|^2,$$

$$\lim_{h \to \theta} w(x;h) = 0,$$

for each $h \in E^n$ with $x + h \in D$, where $f'(x)$ is the gradient of f at x and $f''(x)$ is called the *Hessian* of f at x, representing the symmetric matrix of order n whose (i, j)th component is

$$f_{ij} \equiv \partial^2 f(x)/\partial x_i \, \partial x_j = \partial^2 f(x)/\partial x_j \, \partial x_i \qquad \text{for} \quad i, j = 1, \ldots, n.$$

LEMMA 3 (*Taylor expansion of second order*) Let f be a twice-differentiable real-valued functional on an open convex set D in E^n, and let x, $x + h$ be in D. Then

$$f(x+h) - f(x) = f'(x)h + \tfrac{1}{2} h^{\mathrm{T}} f''(x + \alpha h)h$$

for some real scalar $\alpha \in (0, 1)$.

(The proof of Lemma 3 may be found in standard textbooks on calculus.)

THEOREM 11 Let f be a twice-differentiable real-valued functional on an open convex set D in E^n. f is concave on D if and only if $f''(x)$ is negative semidefinite on D (where $f''(x)$ stands for the Hessian of f at x), i.e., for each $x \in D$

$$h^{\mathrm{T}} f''(x)h \leqq 0 \qquad \text{for all} \quad h \in E^n; \tag{n}$$

f is convex on D if and only if $f''(x)$ is positive semidefinite on D, i.e., for each $x \in D$

$$h^{\mathrm{T}} f''(x)h \geqq 0 \qquad \text{for all} \quad h \in E^n. \tag{p}$$

PROOF We shall prove only for the concave case. (The convex case can be proved similarly.)

"*If*" *part* Inequality (n) is taken into consideration on the right-hand side of the equation in Lemma 3, entailing

$$f(x+h) - f(x) \leqq f'(x)h \qquad \text{for} \quad x,\ x + h \in D.$$

Thus, f is concave in view of Theorem 9 above.

"Only if" part Let x be in D and let h be in E^n. Since D is open, there is a positive number $\bar{\beta}$ such that $x + \beta h \in D$ for $\beta \in (0, \bar{\beta})$. The concavity of f at x implies

$$f(x + \beta h) - f(x) - \beta f'(x)h \leqq 0.$$

But, since f is twice differentiable at x,

$$f(x + \beta h) - f(x) - \beta f'(x)h = \tfrac{1}{2}\beta^2 h^{\mathrm{T}} f''(x)h + \beta^2 w(x; \beta h)\|h\|^2.$$

Hence, by taking the limit of the right-hand side of the above equation as β goes to zero, we have inequality (n). Q.E.D.

COROLLARY Let f be a twice-differentiable real-valued functional on an open convex set D in E^n. A sufficient condition that f be strictly concave on D is that $f''(x)$ be negative definite on D, and a sufficient condition that f be strictly convex on D is that $f''(x)$ be positive definite on D.

We remark that there are some relationships between a twice-differentiable quasi-concave functional f (as defined in Section 8.4) and the matrix

$$\begin{bmatrix} 0 & f'(x) \\ f'(x)^{\mathrm{T}} & f''(x) \end{bmatrix},$$

which is called the *bordered Hessian* of f at x. (See Theorem 30 in Section 8.4.)

Lastly, refer to Katzner (1970) for other relations between concave (or convex) functionals and their Hessians; and see Stigum (1968) and Newman (1969) for interesting theorems on linear homogeneous concave functionals.

7.3 Contraction Mappings, the Implicit Function Theorem, Univalence Theorems, and a Nonlinear Price System

In many optimization problems we encounter a set of implicit functions representing constraints and rely on the implicit function theorem, which is one of the main topics in this section. We start with the mean value inequality theorem, go through the contraction mapping theorem, and reach the implicit function theorem. Then we touch on univalence theorems, which are of great use in showing the existence of a unique solution of some nonlinear economic systems.

LEMMA 4 (*mean value theorem for functionals*) Let f be a Fréchet differentiable functional on an open subset K of E^n. If the segment joining two elements x and y of K belongs to K, there exists a real number $\alpha \in (0, 1)$ such that

$$f(y) = f(x) + f'(\alpha x + (1 - \alpha)y) \cdot (y - x).$$

(For a proof, see for example Apostol (1957, p. 117).)

THEOREM 12 (*mean value inequality theorem*) Let X, Y be normed spaces, and F be a transformation from X into Y with open domain D. Assume F is Fréchet differentiable on D. Given $x \in D$ and $h \in X$, if $x + \beta h \in D$ for all $\beta \in [0, 1]$, then

$$\|F(x + h) - F(x)\| \leqq \|h\| \sup_{0<\beta<1} \| F'(x + \beta h)\|.$$

PROOF By Theorem 46 in Section 5.6, there is a nonzero $y^* \in Y^*$ such that

$$\| y^*\| \, \|F(x + h) - F(x)\| = y^*(F(x + h) - F(x)). \tag{3*}$$

Define a function f for $\beta \in [0, 1]$ by $f(\beta) \equiv y^*(F(x + \beta h))$. By the chain rule, the derivative of f at β is $f'(\beta) = y^*(F'(x + \beta h)h)$. By Lemma 4 above, there is $\beta \in (0, 1)$ such that $f(1) - f(0) = f'(\beta)$, i.e.,

$$y^*(F(x + h) - F(x)) = y^*(F'(x + \beta h)h). \tag{4*}$$

By the definition of norm,

$$| y^*(F'(x + \beta h)h)| \leqq \| y^*\| \, \|F'(x + \beta h)h\| \leqq \| y^*\| \, \|F'(x + \beta h)\| \, \|h\|.$$

Thus, taking (3*) and (4*) into consideration, we get

$$\|F(x + h) - F(x)\| \leqq \|h\| \, \|F'(x + \beta h)\| \qquad \text{for some} \quad \beta \in (0, 1). \quad \text{Q.E.D.}$$

DEFINITION 9 Let S be a subset of a normed space and F be a transformation from S into S. If there exists a number $\alpha \in [0, 1)$ such that

$$\|F(x) - F(y)\| \leqq \alpha \, \|x - y\| \qquad \text{for all } x, y \in S, \tag{40}$$

then F is said to be a *contraction mapping*.

Example 1 A transformation F having $\|F'(x)\| \leqq \alpha < 1$ on a convex subset S of a normed space is a contraction mapping. For, by the mean value inequality theorem, for any x, $y \in S$

$$\|F(x) - F(y)\| \leqq \sup_{0<\beta<1} \|F'(\beta x + (1 - \beta)y)\| \, \|x - y\| \leqq \alpha \, \|x - y\|.$$

Example 2 Define a transformation F on unitary n-space U^n by

$$F(x) = Ax + c,$$

where $A = [a_{ij}]$ is an $n \times n$ matrix and x, c are column n-vectors. If $\sum_{i=1}^n \times \sum_{j=1}^n |a_{ij}|^2 < 1$, then F is a contraction mapping. For, by the definition of norm and the Cauchy–Schwarz inequality,

$$\|F(x) - F(y)\|^2 = \sum_{i=1}^n \left| \sum_{j=1}^n a_{ij}(\xi_j - \eta_j) \right|^2 \leqq \sum_i \sum_j |a_{ij}|^2 \, \|x - y\|^2,$$

where ξ_j, η_j stand for the jth components of x, $y \in U^n$, respectively, and $(\sum_i \sum_j |a_{ij}|^2)^{1/2}$ plays the role of α in (40).

THEOREM 13 Define a transformation F on a normed space X of dimension n by

$$F(x) = Ax + c,$$

where $A = [a_{ij}]$ is an $n \times n$ matrix and x, c are n-tuple column vectors. Specify the norm of $x \in X$ as

$$\|x\| = \max_{1 \leq i \leq n} |x_i|,$$

where $|x_i|$ stands for the modulus of x_i, the ith component of x. Then F is a contraction mapping if and only if

$$\sum_{j=1}^{n} |a_{ij}| < 1 \qquad \text{for} \quad i = 1, \ldots, n. \tag{41}$$

PROOF *Sufficiency* The ith component of $F(x)$ is represented as

$$F_i(x) = \sum_j a_{ij} x_j + c_i.$$

Therefore, by our specification of norm,

$$\begin{aligned} \|F(x) - F(y)\| &= \max_i |F_i(x) - F_i(y)| = \max_i \left|\sum_j a_{ij}(x_j - y_j)\right| \\ &\leqq \max_i \sum_j |a_{ij}(x_j - y_j)| = \max_i \sum_j |a_{ij}|\,|x_j - y_j| \\ &\leqq \alpha \max_j |x_j - y_j| = \alpha \|x - y\| \qquad \text{for} \quad x, y \in X, \end{aligned}$$

where $\alpha = \max_i \sum_j |a_{ij}| < 1$ and y_j stands for the jth component of y.

Necessity Let F be a contraction mapping. Then there exists $\alpha \in [0, 1)$ such that

$$\max_i |F_i(x) - F_i(y)| \leqq \alpha\, |x_p - y_p| \qquad \text{for all} \quad x, y \in X,$$

where $|x_p - y_p| = \max_j |x_j - y_j|$. It follows that

$$\left|\sum_j a_{ij}(x_j - y_j)\right| \leqq \alpha\, |x_p - y_p| < |x_p - y_p| \qquad \text{for all} \;\; i \;\; \text{and all } x, y. \tag{5*}$$

Suppose, to the contrary, there exists an integer $q \in \{1,2, \ldots, n\}$ such that $\sum_j |a_{qj}| \geqq 1$. And choose x, y such that

$$x_j - y_j = \begin{cases} 1 & \text{if} \quad a_{qj} > 0, \\ 0 & \text{if} \quad a_{qj} = 0, \\ -1 & \text{if} \quad a_{qj} < 0. \end{cases}$$

Then we have

$$\left|\sum_j a_{qj}(x_j - y_j)\right| = \sum_j |a_{qj}| \geqq 1 = |x_p - y_p|,$$

contradicting (5*). Q.E.D.

THEOREM 14 (*contraction mapping theorem*) If F is a contraction mapping on a closed subset S of a Banach space, there is a unique point x_0

$\in S$ satisfying $F(x_0) = x_0$, which can be reached by successive approximation:

$$x_{t+1} = F(x_t), \tag{42}$$

starting from an arbitrary initial point in S. The point x_0 is termed the *fixed point* of F.

PROOF Select an arbitrary element x_1 of S and define a sequence $\{x_t\}$ from S by the formula (42). Then for some $\alpha \in (0, 1)$,

$$\|x_{t+1} - x_t\| = \|F(x_t) - F(x_{t-1})\| \leqq \alpha \|x_t - x_{t-1}\|.$$

By an iterative substitution, we have $\|x_{t+1} - x_t\| \leqq \alpha^{t-1}\|x_2 - x_1\|$. Hence for an integer $k \geqq 1$,

$$\begin{aligned}\|x_{t+k} - x_t\| &\leqq \sum_{i=0}^{k-1} \|x_{t+i+1} - x_{t+i}\| \leqq \sum_{i=0}^{k-1} \alpha^{t+i-1} \|x_2 - x_1\| \\ &\leqq \frac{\alpha^{t-1}}{1-\alpha} \|x_2 - x_1\|.\end{aligned}$$

Thus $\|x_{t+k} - x_t\| \to 0$ as $t \to \infty$ (whence $t + k \to \infty$); i.e., $\{x_t\}$ is a Cauchy sequence. Since S is a closed subset of a Banach space, the sequence converges to a unique limit x_0 in S. It remains to show that $x_0 = F(x_0)$. In view of (42), for an element x_t of the sequence

$$\begin{aligned}\|x_0 - F(x_0)\| &\leqq \|x_0 - x_t\| + \|F(x_{t-1}) - F(x_0)\| \\ &\leqq \|x_0 - x_t\| + \alpha \|x_{t-1} - x_0\|.\end{aligned}$$

As t goes to infinity, the right-hand side of the above inequality approaches zero. Q.E.D. (The proof is due to Luenberger (1969).)

We remark that an inequality in the above proof implies

$$\|x_{k+1} - x_1\| \leqq \frac{1}{1-\alpha} \|x_2 - x_1\| \qquad \text{for} \quad k \geqq 1, \quad \alpha \in [0, 1). \tag{43}$$

DEFINITION 10 Let X and Y be normed spaces, and let there be associated with each $y \in Y$ a transformation Q_y mapping a subset S of X into S. We say that Q_y is continuous with respect to y at the point $y_0 \in Y$ if for an arbitrary sequence $\{y_n\} \subset Y$ convergent to y_0,

$$Q_{y_n}(x) \to Q_{y_0}(x) \qquad \text{for all} \quad x \in S, \quad \text{as} \quad y_n \to y_0. \tag{44}$$

Let the system of equations

$$Q_y(x) = x \tag{45}$$

have a unique solution x_y^* for each $y \in Y$. We say that the solution of (45) depends continuously on y in the vicinity of y_0 if for an arbitrary sequence $\{y_n\} \subset Y$ convergent to y_0,

$$x_{y_n}^* \to x_{y_0}^* \qquad \text{as} \quad y_n \to y_0.$$

LEMMA 5 Let X be a Banach space, Y be a normed space, and S be a closed subset of X. If for each $y \in Y$, the transformation Q_y mentioned above satisfies

$$\|Q_y(x) - Q_y(x')\| \leqq \alpha \|x - x'\| \qquad \text{for all} \quad x, \; x' \in S \subset X, \tag{46}$$

for an $\alpha \in [0, 1)$, and if Q_y is continuous with respect to y at $y_0 \in Y$, then the solution of system (45) depends continuously on y in the vicinity of y_0.

PROOF Let y be an element of Y and construct a solution x_y^* of system (45) as the limit of a sequence $\{x_k\}$ such that

$$x_{k+1} = Q_y(x_k), \qquad k = 1, 2, \ldots,$$

where $x_1 \equiv x_{y_0}^*$. Since $x_{y_0}^* = Q_{y_0}(x_{y_0}^*)$, we have by (43)

$$\|x_y^* - x_{y_0}^*\| \leqq \frac{1}{1 - \alpha} \|x_2 - x_1\| = \frac{1}{1 - \alpha} \|Q_y(x_{y_0}^*) - Q_{y_0}(x_{y_0}^*)\|.$$

The continuity of x_y^* in the vicinity of y_0 follows from this inequality and (44). Q.E.D.

THEOREM 15 (*implicit function theorem*) Let X, Y, Z be Banach spaces with $\dim X = \dim Z$ and F be a Fréchet differentiable transformation from an open set $D \subset X \times Y$ into Z. Denote by $F_x'(x, y)$ the Fréchet derivative of F with respect to x at (x, y). Clearly, $F_x'(x, y) \in B(X, Z)$. If (x_0, y_0) is a point in D at which $F(x_0, y_0) = \theta$, $F_x'(x_0, y_0)$ exists and is continuous, and if inverse operator $T \equiv [F_x'(x_0, y_0)]^{-1}$ exists, then there are a sphere $S(y_0; \delta)$ $\subset Y$ and a unique continuous transformation G mapping $S(y_0; \delta)$ into X, which possesses the properties:

$$G(y_0) = x_0 \tag{47}$$

$$F(G(y), y) = \theta \qquad \text{for} \quad y \in S(y_0; \delta). \tag{48}$$

PROOF Let θ_x and θ_y be the origins (null vectors) of X and Y, respectively, and suppose without loss of generality that $x_0 = \theta_x$ and $y_0 = \theta_y$. Given $y \in Y$, we define a set of elements

$$D_y \equiv \{x : x \in X, (x, y) \in D\},$$

and define an operator Q_y on D_y by

$$Q_y(x) \equiv x - TF(x, y).$$

We shall show that given $\varepsilon > 0$ there exists a $\delta > 0$ such that Q_y maps a closed sphere $U(\theta_x; \varepsilon)$ into itself for all y with $\|y\| < \delta$. For this purpose we consider the Fréchet differential of Q_y at $\bar{x} \in U(\theta_x; \varepsilon)$ with increment h:

$$Q_y'(\bar{x})h = h - TF_x'(\bar{x}, y)h = -T(F_x'(\bar{x}, y) - F_x'(\theta_x, \theta_y))h.$$

Then, by Theorem 38 in Section 5.5

$$\|Q_y'(\bar{x})\| \leqq \|T\| \, \|F_x'(\bar{x}, y) - F_x'(\theta_x, \theta_y)\|.$$

In view of the assumption that F'_x is continuous at (θ_x, θ_y), the second factor of the above inequality can be made as small as we please. So, by choosing ε and δ sufficiently small, it can be arranged such that

$$\|Q'_y(\bar{x})\| \leqq \alpha < 1 \qquad (\|y\| < \delta, \quad \|\bar{x}\| \leqq \varepsilon). \tag{6*}$$

Consider $Q_y(\theta_x)$. Since $F(\theta_x, \theta_y) = \theta$,

$$\|Q_y(\theta_x)\| = \|TF(\theta_x, y)\| \leqq \|T\| \, \|F(\theta_x, y) - F(\theta_x, \theta_y)\|,$$

and in view of the continuity of F at (θ_x, θ_y) (cf. Theorem 3 in Section 7.1), the right-hand side of the above inequality can be made as small as we like by decreasing δ. We suppose that δ is reduced to such an extent that

$$\|Q_y(\theta_x)\| \leqq \varepsilon\,(1 - \alpha) \qquad (\|y\| < \delta). \tag{7*}$$

Thus, if $\|y\| < \delta$ and $\|x\| \leqq \varepsilon$, then by (6*), (7*), and the mean value inequality theorem,

$$\begin{aligned} \|Q_y(x)\| &\leqq \|Q_y(\theta_x)\| + \|Q_y(x) - Q_y(\theta_x)\| \\ &\leqq \varepsilon(1 - \alpha) + \|x\| \sup_{0<\beta<1} \|Q'_y(\beta x)\| \leqq \varepsilon(1 - \alpha) + \varepsilon\alpha = \varepsilon, \end{aligned}$$

proving our assertion.

The operator Q_y maps the closed sphere $U(\theta_x; \varepsilon)$ into itself, while, by the mean value inequality theorem and (6*), we have

$$\begin{aligned} \|Q_y(x_1) - Q_y(x_2)\| &\leqq \|x_1 - x_2\| \sup_{0<\beta<1} \|Q'_y(\beta x_1 + (1 - \beta)x_2)\| \\ &\leqq \alpha\, \|x_1 - x_2\| \end{aligned}$$

for $x_1, x_2 \in U(\theta_x; \varepsilon)$. Therefore, Q_y is a contraction mapping and hence there exists a unique fixed point $x_y^* \in U(\theta_x; \varepsilon)$ satisfying

$$x_y^* = Q_y(x_y^*) \equiv x_y^* - TF(x_y^*, y),$$

i.e., $F(x_y^*, y) = \theta$. Since x_y^* is unique for each $y \in S(y_0; \delta)$ and since $F(x_0, y_0) = \theta$, x_y^* must be equal to x_0 for $y = y_0$. Define an operator G on $S(y_0; \delta)$ by

$$G(y) \equiv Q_y(x_y^*).$$

Then $G(y_0) = x_0$.

The continuity of G on $S(y_0; \delta)$ is verified as follows. Q_y is a contraction mapping for each $y \in S(y_0; \delta)$, and Q_y is continuous with respect to y at y_0 since F is continuous on D which contains (x_0, y_0). Thus we can apply Lemma 5 and know that the solution $x_y^* \equiv G(y)$ depends continuously on $y \in S(y_0; \delta)$.

Let H be a continuous transformation mapping $S(y_0; \delta)$ into X and possessing properties (47) and (48). Then given $\varepsilon > 0$ there exists an $\eta > 0$ such that $H(y) = x_y^* = G(y)$ for each y with $\|y\| < \eta$ since the fixed point x_y^* of

Q_y for each $y \in S(\theta_y; \delta)$ is unique in $U(\theta_x; \varepsilon)$. Thus G is a unique transformation on $S(y_0; \eta)$. Q.E.D.

(The above proof is parallel to that in Kantorovich and Akilov (1964).) From this follows a univalence theorem.

THEOREM 16 (*local univalence theorem*) Let F be a continuous transformation from an open set $D \subset E^n$ into E^n, and assume F is differentiable on D. If x_0 is a point in D at which $F(x_0) = y_0$ and the Jacobian matrix of F at x_0 is continuous and nonsingular, then there is a sphere $U \equiv U(x_0; \varepsilon)$ where F is univalent, i.e., $F(x_1) = F(x_2)$ for $x_1, x_2 \in U$ implies $x_1 = x_2$.

PROOF By the implicit function theorem, there is a sphere $S(y_0; \delta) \subset E^n$ and a unique continuous transformation $G: S(y_0; \delta) \to E^n$ such that $G(y_0) = x_0$ and $F(G(y)) = y$ for each $y \in S(y_0; \delta)$. Hence $G = F^{-1}$ and G is one-to-one. Thus there exists a sphere $U \equiv U(x_0; \varepsilon) \subset \{x: x = F^{-1}(y) \text{ for } y \in S(y_0; \delta)\}$ such that if $x_1 \neq x_2$ for $x_1, x_2 \in U$, then $y_1 \neq y_2$ where $F^{-1}(y_1) = x_1$ and $F^{-1}(y_2) = x_2$; i.e., $F(x_1) = F(x_2)$ for $x_1, x_2 \in U$ implies $x_1 = x_2$. Q.E.D.

There is a very useful theorem of global univalence provided by Gale and Nikaido (1965) and stated below.

THEOREM 17 (*global univalence theorem*) Let W be a closed rectangular region $\{x : x \in E^n, p \leqq x \leqq q \text{ for } -\infty < p \leqq q < \infty\}$ of E^n, and F be a transformation from W into E^n. Assume that F is differentiable on W and that the Jacobian matrix of F is a P-matrix for each x in W. Then F is univalent on W, i.e., $F(x_1) = F(x_2)$ for $x_1, x_2 \in W$ implies $x_1 = x_2$.

(For the definition of a P-matrix, refer to Definition 9 in Section 1.3; and for the proof of Theorem 17, see Application 2 in Section 8.2.)

Remark A global univalence theorem was provided by Inada (1971) for a transformation F, as defined in Theorem 17, whose Jacobian matrix has all positive principal minors of odd order and all negative principal minors of even order at each point x in the definition domain and is continuous in x.

Lastly, we apply the global univalence theorem to prove the existence of a unique solution to a nonlinear price system.

Application 2 (*a nonlinear Leontief price system*) Industry j is supposed to produce good j subject to the production function

$$x_j = a_j \prod_{i=1}^{n+1} x_{ij}^{a_{ij}} \qquad (j = 1, \ldots, n), \tag{8*}$$

where x_j stands for the output of good j, x_{ij} the input of good i (in particular $x_{n+1,j}$ is the labor input), and a_j, a_{ij} are technical coefficients, all taking nonnegative values, in industry j. Denoting by p_i the price of good i and by p_{n+1} the wage rate, we have the profits z_j in industry j:

$$z_j = p_j x_j - \sum_{i=1}^{n+1} p_i x_{ij} \qquad (j = 1, \ldots, n).$$

Maximizing z_j subject to (8*) yields

$$a_{ij} = p_i x_{ij}/p_j x_j \qquad (i = 1, \ldots, n, n+1;\ \ j = 1, \ldots, n), \tag{9*}$$

which implies that a_{ij} is equal to the current-account input coefficient in money terms. Assuming that z_j is nonnegative for each j, we define

$$\alpha_j \equiv 1 - \sum_{i=1}^{n+1} a_{ij} \geqq 0 \qquad (j = 1, \ldots, n). \tag{10*}$$

Taking account of (9*) and then (10*) in the right-hand side of (8*), we get

$$x_j = b_j (p_j x_j)^{1-\alpha_j} \prod_{i=1}^{n+1} p_i^{-a_{ij}} \qquad (j = 1, \ldots, n), \tag{11*}$$

where $b_j \equiv a_j \prod_{i=1}^{n+1} a_{ij}^{a_{ij}}$. We also assume that the demand for each good is met by its current output:

$$x_i = \sum_{j=1}^{n} x_{ij} + c_i \qquad (i = 1, \ldots, n), \tag{12*}$$

where c_i stands for the final demand for good i. Multiply (12*) by p_i and take (9*) into consideration. Then we have

$$p_j x_j = \sum_{k=1}^{n} f_{jk} p_k c_k = \sum_{k=1}^{n} p_k m_{jk} \qquad (j = 1, \ldots, n), \tag{13*}$$

where $[f_{jk}] \equiv [I - A]^{-1}$, $A \equiv [a_{ij}]$, and $m_{jk} \equiv f_{jk} c_k$. Multiplying (11*) by p_j and taking (13*) into account yield

$$p_j b_j \prod_{i=1}^{n+1} p_i^{-a_{ij}} = \left(\sum_{k=1}^{n} p_k m_{jk} \right)^{\alpha_j} \qquad (j = 1, \ldots, n),$$

the logarithmic form of which is given by

$$\ln p_j - \sum_{i=1}^{n} a_{ij} \ln p_i = q_j + \alpha_j \ln \left(\sum_{k=1}^{n} p_k m_{jk} \right) \qquad (j = 1, \ldots, n), \tag{14*}$$

where $q_j \equiv a_{n+1,j} \ln p_{n+1} - \ln b_j$. (14*) can be rewritten as

$$F(\ln p) = q, \tag{15*}$$

where $\ln p \equiv \{\ln p_1, \ldots, \ln p_n\}$, $q \equiv \{q_1, \ldots, q_n\}$, and

$$F(\ln p) \equiv \begin{bmatrix} 1 - a_{11} & -a_{21} \cdots & -a_{n1} \\ -a_{12} & 1 - a_{22} \cdots & -a_{n2} \\ \vdots & & \vdots \\ -a_{1n} & \cdots & 1 - a_{nn} \end{bmatrix} \begin{bmatrix} \ln p_1 \\ \vdots \\ \ln p_n \end{bmatrix} - \begin{bmatrix} \alpha_1 \ln (\sum_k p_k m_{1k}) \\ \vdots \\ \alpha_n \ln (\sum_k p_k m_{nk}) \end{bmatrix}. \tag{16*}$$

By the global univalence theorem, a sufficient condition for the existence of a unique solution $\ln p$ to system (15*) for a given q is that the Jacobian matrix $F'(\ln p)$ is a P-matrix; i.e., every principal minor of $F'(\ln p)$ is positive. We shall show that it is the case. The (i, j)th component of $F'(\ln p)$ is obtained from (16*) as

$$F_j^i(\ln p) \equiv \frac{\partial F^i(\ln p)}{\partial \ln p_j} = \begin{cases} 1 - a_{ii} - \alpha_i \xi_{ii} & \text{for} \quad i = j, \\ -a_{ji} - \alpha_i \xi_{ij} & \text{for} \quad i \neq j, \end{cases}$$

where

$$\xi_{ij} \equiv \frac{\partial \ln(\sum_k p_k m_{ik})}{\partial \ln p_j} = \frac{1/\sum_k p_k m_{ik}}{1/p_j} \frac{\partial(\sum_k p_k m_{ik})}{\partial p_j} = \frac{p_j m_{ij}}{\sum_k p_k m_{ik}}.$$

Hence

$$\sum_{j=1}^{n} \xi_{ij} = 1 \qquad (i = 1, \ldots, n). \tag{17*}$$

The sum of the ith row of $F'(\ln p)$ is

$$\sum_{j=1}^{n} F_j^i(\ln p) = 1 - \sum_{j=1}^{n} a_{ji} - \alpha_i = a_{n+1,i} > 0,$$

in view of (17*) and (10*). Moreover, $a_{ji} + \alpha_i \xi_{ij}$ are all nonnegative. Thus, the $n \times n$ matrix $[a_{ji} + \alpha_i \xi_{ij}]$ satisfies the Solow condition (ii) of Theorem 12 in Section 4.2, and thereby $F'(\ln p)$ fulfills the H-S conditions in view of the Metzler lemma (Lemma 2 in Section 4.1). (For a related empirical study, see Morishima and Murata (1972).)

7.4 The Lagrange Multiplier Theory under Equality Constraints

This section is devoted to Lagrange multiplier theory, i.e., necessary conditions for a local maximum or minimum under equality constraints.

THEOREM 18 (*Lagrange multiplier theorem*) Let f be a real-valued functional on E^n, and G a transformation from E^n into E^m with $m < n$. Assume that f achieves a local maximum or minimum under the constraint $G(x) = \theta$ at the point $x^0 \in E^n$, that f and G are continuously differentiable on an open set D containing x^0, and that the Jacobian matrix $G'(x^0)$ of G at x^0 has rank m. Then there exists $\lambda \in E^m$ such that

$$f'(x^0) + \lambda G'(x^0) = \theta, \tag{49}$$

implying that the Lagrangian function $L(x) \equiv f(x) + \lambda G(x)$ is stationary at x^0.

PROOF Rewrite (49) as

$$f_j(x^0) + \sum_{i=1}^{m} \lambda_i G_j^i(x^0) = 0 \qquad \text{for} \quad j = 1, \ldots, n, \tag{49'}$$

where $f_j(x^0)$ stands for the jth component of the gradient $f'(x^0)$ and $G_j^i(x^0)$ the (i, j)th component of the matrix $G'(x^0)$. Consider the first m equations in (49′):

$$\sum_{i=1}^{m} \lambda_i G_j^i(x^0) = -f_j(x^0) \qquad (j = 1, \ldots, m). \tag{18*}$$

This system has a unique solution $\lambda = (\lambda_1, \ldots, \lambda_m)$ since the matrix $[G_j^i(x^0)]$ $(i, j = 1, \ldots, m)$ is nonsingular by hypothesis. We shall show that for this λ, the remaining $n - m$ equations in (49′) are also satisfied.

Since $m < n$, every point $x \in E^n$ can be written in the form

$$x = \{z; y\},$$

where $z \in E^m$ and $y \in E^{n-m}$. In the remainder of this proof we write z for $\{x_1, \ldots, x_m\}$ and y for $\{x_{m+1}, \ldots, x_n\}$. Hence $x^0 = \{z^0; y^0\}$. Applying the implicit function theorem (Theorem 15 in Section 7.3), we know that there exist an $(n - m)$-dimensional sphere $S_0 \equiv S(y^0; \delta)$ and a unique continuous mapping $t \equiv \{t^1, \ldots, t^m\} : S_0 \to E^m$ such that

$$t(y^0) = z^0 \qquad \text{and} \qquad G(t(y), y) = \theta \qquad \text{for} \quad y \in S_0.$$

Correspondingly, $f(x)$ is now expressed as $f(t(y), y)$ for $y \in S_0$. We define new functions $F: E^{n-m} \to E^1$ and $H: E^{n-m} \to E^m$ as

$$F(y) \equiv f(T(y)) \qquad \text{and} \qquad H(y) \equiv G(T(y)),$$

where $T(y) \equiv \{t(y), y\}$ for y restricted to the set S_0, whence $T: S_0 \to E^n$. Since the transformation H so defined is identically zero on S_0, $H'(y)$ is identically zero on S_0. By the chain rule (Theorem 6 in Section 7.1), we can compute $H'(y^0) = 0$ as

$$0 = H'(y^0) = G'(x^0)T'(y^0),$$

or equivalently

$$0 = \begin{bmatrix} \sum_{j=1}^{m} G_j^1 t_{m+1}^j + G_{m+1}^1 & \cdots & \sum_{j=1}^{m} G_j^1 t_n^j + G_n^1 \\ \vdots & & \vdots \\ \sum_{j=1}^{m} G_j^m t_{m+1}^j + G_{m+1}^m & \cdots & \sum_{j=1}^{m} G_j^m t_n^j + G_n^m \end{bmatrix}, \tag{19*}$$

where $G_j^i \equiv G_j^i(x^0)$ and $t_k^i \equiv (\partial t^i/\partial x_k)|_{y=y^0}$ for $i, j = 1, \ldots, m; k = m + 1, \ldots, n$.

By continuity of t, there is a sphere $U(y^0) \subset S_0$ such that $y \in U(y^0)$ implies $\{t(y), y\} \in V(x^0)$, where $V(x^0)$ is the sphere on which $f(x) \leqq f(x^0)$ or $f(x) \geqq f(x^0)$ holds. Hence for $y \in U(y^0)$, we have either $F(y) \leqq F(y^0)$ or $F(y) \geqq F(y^0)$; i.e., F has a local maximum or minimum at the interior point y^0. Thus $F'(y)$ must vanish at y^0. Using the chain rule, therefore, we have

$$\theta = \left(\sum_{j=1}^{m} f_j(x^0)t_{m+1}^j + f_{m+1}(x^0), \ldots, \sum_{j=1}^{m} f_j(x^0)t_n^j + f_n(x^0)\right). \tag{20*}$$

Premultiply (19*) by $\lambda = (\lambda_1, \ldots, \lambda_m)$ satisfying (18*) and add the result to (20*). Then

$$\sum_{j=1}^{m}\left[f_j(x^0) + \sum_{i=1}^{m} \lambda_i G_j^i(x^0)\right] t_k^j + f_k(x^0) + \sum_{i=1}^{m} \lambda_i G_k^i(x^0) = 0$$

for $k = m+1, \ldots, n$. The expression in square brackets in this equation vanishes because of the way $\lambda_1, \ldots, \lambda_m$ were defined. Thus we are left with

$$f_k(x^0) + \sum_{i=1}^{m} \lambda_i G_k^i(x^0) = 0 \qquad \text{for} \quad k = m+1, \ldots, n. \qquad \text{Q.E.D.}$$

Application 3 Let f be a real-valued functional in the variables x_{ij} ($i = 1, \ldots k; j = 1, \ldots, n$) and denote by $f(X)$ the value of f at $X = [x_{ij}]$, a $k \times n$ matrix. We want to get the extremum conditions for $f(X)$ achieving a local maximum or minimum under the constraints:

$$\sum_{i=1}^{k} c_{hi} x_{ij} = b_{hj} \qquad \text{for} \quad h = 1, \ldots, p; \quad j = 1, \ldots, n,$$

which can be rewritten as

$$CX = B, \tag{50}$$

where $C \equiv [c_{hi}]$, a $p \times k$ matrix, and $B \equiv [b_{hj}]$, a $p \times n$ matrix. The corresponding Lagrangian function is

$$L(X) = f(X) + \sum_{j=1}^{n} \sum_{h=1}^{p} \lambda_{hj}\left(\sum_{i=1}^{k} c_{hi} x_{ij} - b_{hj}\right) = f(X) + \operatorname{tr}[\Lambda(CX - B)], \tag{51}$$

where $\Lambda \equiv [\lambda_{hj}]$, an $n \times p$ matrix. Thus, by Theorem 18, the extremum conditions are obtained as

$$0 = \frac{\partial L(X)}{\partial x_{ij}} = f_{ij}(X) + \sum_{h=1}^{p} c_{hi} \lambda_{hj} \qquad \text{for all } i, j;$$

or equivalently

$$0 = [f_{ij}(X)] + C^{\mathrm{T}} \Lambda^{\mathrm{T}}, \tag{52}$$

where $f_{ij}(X) \equiv \partial f(X)/\partial x_{ij}$ and $[f_{ij}(X)]$ is $k \times n$.

Application 4 Consider a calculus of variations problem having the constraints

$$K_i = \int_a^b k^i(x(t), \dot{x}(t), t)\, dt \qquad \text{for} \quad i = 1, \ldots, m, \tag{53}$$

where K_i is constant and k^i is a real-valued functional of x, $\dot{x}$, and t. We assume that partial derivatives $k_x^i \equiv \partial k^i/\partial x$, $k_{\dot{x}}^i \equiv \partial k^i/\partial \dot{x}$ exist, and that $k_{\dot{x}}^i$ is continuous in t. If the value of function J in (12) of Section 7.2 is maximized under the constraints (53), with all the assumptions stated in Theorem 8, then, by defining the Lagrangian function ϕ as

$$\phi(x, \dot{x}, t) \equiv f(x, \dot{x}, t) + \sum_{i=1}^{m} \lambda_i k^i(x, \dot{x}, t), \tag{54}$$

we will have a variation of Euler equation:

$$\frac{\partial \phi}{\partial x} = \frac{d}{dt}\left(\frac{\partial \phi}{\partial \dot{x}}\right), \tag{55}$$

and the transversality condition (22) (or (22′)) where f is replaced by ϕ.

(The verification is left to the reader.)

7.5 Second-Order Conditions for Local Maxima and Demand Laws

The Lagrange multiplier theory explained in the preceding section provides a necessary condition for a real-valued functional f on E^n to achieve an extremum under a set of equality constraints $G(x) = \theta$, where $G\colon E^n \to E^m$ and f, G are assumed to be continuously differentiable. This section is concerned with sufficiency conditions for f to achieve a local maximum or a minimum under the same constraints.

We begin by redefining a local maximum under equality constraints.

DEFINITION 3′ Let $f\colon E^n \to E^1$ and $G\colon E^n \to E^m$, and assume that f, G are twice differentiable, i.e., that $f(x)$ and each component of $G(x)$ have second derivatives with respect to the ith component x_i of x. If there exists an open sphere S centered at x^0 with a positive radius such that

$$f(x^0) > f(x) \qquad \text{for all} \quad x \in S \cap X, \quad x \neq x^0, \tag{56}$$

where $X \equiv \{x\colon x \in E^n,\ G(x) = \theta\}$, then we say that f has a (*strong* or *strict*) *local maximum* at x^0 under the constraint $G(x) = \theta$.

Define a Lagrangian function L on E^n by

$$L(x) \equiv f(x) + \lambda G(x), \tag{57}$$

where f, G are the same transformations as above and $\lambda \in E^m$. Then (56) is equivalent to

$$L(x^0) > L(x) \qquad \text{for all} \quad x \in S \cap X, \quad x \neq x^0. \tag{58}$$

Since L is continuous in view of Theorem 3 in Section 7.1,

$$L_{ij}^0 = L_{ji}^0 \equiv \partial^2 L(x)/(\partial x_j \partial x_i) \qquad \text{at} \quad x^0.$$

Denoting by $L''(x^0)$ the Hessian of L, i.e., the symmetric matrix of order n whose (i, j)th component is L_{ij}^0, we have

$$L(x) = L(x^0) + L'(x^0)(x - x^0) + \tfrac{1}{2}(x - x^0)^{\mathrm{T}} L''(x^0)(x - x^0) + r(x - x^0),$$

where $L'(x^0) = \theta$ (the extremum condition) and $\lim_{x \to x^0} r(x - x^0) = 0$. Thus there exists a sphere S as mentioned above such that $L(x) < L(x^0)$ if

$$(x - x^0)^T L''(x^0)(x - x^0) < 0 \qquad \text{for all} \quad x \in S, \tag{59}$$

where $x - x^0$ represents a deviation from x^0. This deviation, denoted u, should not violate the constraint $G(x) = \theta$, i.e., it must satisfy

$$G'(x^0)u = \theta. \tag{60}$$

Therefore we get the following sufficiency condition for our local maximum problem:

$$u^T L''(x^0)u < 0 \qquad \text{for all nonzero } u \in E^n \text{ satisfying (60);} \tag{61}$$

in other words $L''(x^0)$ is negative definite for all u satisfying (60). Condition (61) may be termed the *second-order condition* for a local maximum since the extremum condition is often referred to as the first-order condition. Similarly, the second-order condition for a local minimum under the same constraint is the positive definiteness of the relevant Hessian for all u satisfying (60).

If there is no constraint, the second-order condition of achieving a local maximum (or a local minimum) for f is reduced to that the Hessian of f be negative definite (or positive definite). Then we can apply Theorem 35 and its corollary in Section 2.5, which is recapitulated as follows: Let $A = [a_{ij}]$ be a real symmetric matrix of order n. A is positive definite if and only if all the principal minors of A take on positive values; i.e.,

$$a_{ii} > 0, \qquad \begin{vmatrix} a_{ii} & a_{ij} \\ a_{ij} & a_{jj} \end{vmatrix} > 0, \qquad \ldots, \qquad |A| > 0 \qquad (i \neq j). \tag{62}$$

A is negative definite if and only if all the principal minors of odd orders take on negative values and all the principal minors of even orders take on positive values; i.e.,

$$a_{ii} < 0, \qquad \begin{vmatrix} a_{ii} & a_{ij} \\ a_{ij} & a_{jj} \end{vmatrix} > 0, \qquad \ldots, \qquad (-1)^n |A| > 0 \qquad (i \neq j). \tag{63}$$

If the above matrix A represents the Hessian of our functional f, the second-order condition of achieving a local maximum for f without constraint is equivalent to (63), and that for a local minimum is equivalent to (62).

Application 5 Consider a maximizing problem. Let x_i be the input of the ith production factor to produce output by quantity Q, and p_i the price of the factor in terms of output ($i = 1, \ldots, n$). (The price of output is unity.) We search for the first-order and second-order conditions for maximizing profits π:

$$\pi = Q - \sum_{i=1}^{n} p_i x_i$$

for given prices, subject to a production function

$$Q = f(x_1, x_2, \ldots, x_n),$$

where f is assumed to be twice differentiable with respect to the x_i. This problem can be transformed into an unconstrained maximum one:

$$\text{Maximize} \quad \pi = f(x_1, \ldots, x_n) - \sum_{i=1}^{n} p_i x_i,$$

whose first-order condition is

$$\frac{\partial \pi}{\partial x_i} = \frac{\partial f}{\partial x_i} - p_i = 0 \qquad \text{for} \quad i = 1, \ldots, n, \tag{64}$$

i.e., the extremum is attained at $x^0 \equiv \{x_1^0, \ldots, x_n^0\}$ where the marginal product of a factor has value equal to its price. Its second-order condition is obtained as follows by applying (63):

$$f_{ii} < 0, \qquad \begin{vmatrix} f_{ii} & f_{ij} \\ f_{ij} & f_{jj} \end{vmatrix} > 0, \qquad \ldots, \qquad (-1)^n |F| > 0 \quad \text{for} \quad i, j = 1, \ldots, n, \tag{65}$$

where $f_{ij} \equiv \partial^2 f/(\partial x_i\, \partial x_j)$ evaluated at x^0, and

$$|F| \equiv \begin{vmatrix} f_{11} & f_{12} \cdots f_{1n} \\ f_{12} & f_{22} \cdots f_{2n} \\ \vdots & \vdots \quad \vdots \\ f_{1n} & f_{2n} \cdots f_{nn} \end{vmatrix}.$$

Note that in this example we exclude the cases where $|F|$ vanishes. One of these cases occurs when f is homogeneous of degree one, for then

$$\partial f(cx)/\partial(cx_i) = \partial f(x)/\partial x_i \qquad \text{for a real scalar } c \text{ and } i = 1, \ldots, n,$$

and differentiating this equation with respect to c and putting $c = 1$ yield

$$\sum_{j=1}^{n} f_{ij} x_j = 0 \qquad \text{for} \quad i = 1, \ldots, n,$$

which results in $|F| = 0$ in view of $x \equiv \{x_1, \ldots, x_n\} \neq \theta$.

Let F_i denote the cofactor of f_{ii} in $|F|$, $F_{i \cdot j}$ the cofactor of f_{jj} in F_i, $F_{i \cdot j \cdot k}$ the cofactor of f_{kk} in $F_{i \cdot j}$, and so forth. Then condition (65) is equivalent to

$$\frac{F_i}{|F|} < 0, \qquad \frac{F_{i \cdot j}}{|F|} > 0, \qquad \frac{F_{i \cdot j \cdot k}}{|F|} < 0, \qquad \ldots \qquad \text{for all different } i, j, k. \tag{65$'$}$$

Let F_{ij} be the cofactor of f_{ij} in $|F|$ for $i, j = 1, \ldots, n$. (Hence $F_{ii} \equiv F_i$.) In view of (16) and (18) in Section 1.1, we have

$$\begin{vmatrix} F_{ii} & F_{ji} \\ F_{ij} & F_{jj} \end{vmatrix} = |F| F_{i \cdot j}, \qquad \begin{vmatrix} F_{ii} & F_{ji} & F_{ki} \\ F_{ij} & F_{jj} & F_{kj} \\ F_{ik} & F_{jk} & F_{kk} \end{vmatrix} = |F|^2 F_{i \cdot j \cdot k}, \qquad \ldots .$$

Thus, condition (65′) is also equivalent to

$$\frac{F_{ii}}{|F|} < 0, \qquad \begin{vmatrix} F_{ii}/|F| & F_{ji}/|F| \\ F_{ij}/|F| & F_{jj}/|F| \end{vmatrix} > 0, \qquad \begin{vmatrix} F_{ii}/|F| & F_{ji}/|F| & F_{ki}/|F| \\ F_{ij}/|F| & F_{jj}/|F| & F_{kj}/|F| \\ F_{ik}/|F| & F_{jk}/|F| & F_{kk}/|F| \end{vmatrix} < 0, \quad \ldots \tag{65''}$$

for all different $i, j, k = 1, \ldots, n$. Condition (65″) is obviously a necessary and sufficient condition for

$$\sum_{i=1}^{n} \sum_{j=1}^{n} \frac{F_{ij}}{|F|} \xi_i \xi_j < 0 \qquad \text{for any nonzero } n\text{-vector } x, \tag{66}$$

where $x \equiv \{\xi_1, \ldots, \xi_n\}$. Condition (65″) also ensures the negative definiteness of any subquadratic form of (66); i.e., for integer m, $1 \leqq m \leqq n$,

$$\sum_{i=1}^{m} \sum_{j=1}^{m} \frac{F_{ij}}{|F|} \xi_i \xi_j < 0 \qquad \text{for any nonzero } m\text{-vector } x, \tag{66'}$$

where $x \equiv \{\xi_1, \ldots, \xi_m\}$.

Let us examine the effects of changes in factor prices upon the inputs of factors in the vicinity of the equilibrium where profit has been maximized. Differentiating

$$\partial f/\partial x_j = p_j \qquad \text{for} \quad j = 1, \ldots, n$$

with respect to p_i, we get

$$\begin{bmatrix} f_{11} & \cdots & f_{1n} \\ \vdots & & \vdots \\ f_{1n} & \cdots & f_{nn} \end{bmatrix} \begin{bmatrix} \partial x_1/\partial p_i \\ \vdots \\ \partial x_n/\partial p_i \end{bmatrix} = \begin{bmatrix} 0 \\ \vdots \\ 1 \\ \vdots \\ 0 \end{bmatrix} \quad \begin{matrix} \text{(at the } i\text{th position)} \\ \text{for} \quad i = 1, \ldots, n, \end{matrix}$$

from which it follows that

$$\partial x_j/\partial p_i = F_{ij}/|F| \qquad \text{for} \quad i, j = 1, \ldots, n.$$

Taking these into account, and replacing ξ_i by p_i in (66′), we have

$$\sum_{i=1}^{m} \sum_{j=1}^{m} p_i p_j \frac{\partial x_j}{\partial p_i} < 0 \qquad \text{for integer } m,\ 1 \leqq m \leqq n \tag{67}$$

and for any nonzero price vector $p \equiv \{p_1, \ldots, p_m\}$. In particular

$$\partial x_i/\partial p_i = F_{ii}/|F| < 0, \tag{68}$$

which means that the input whose price has risen must decline. Suppose p_i is positive. Accordingly, if output remains constant, the total amount of inputs of the factors other than the ith factor is found to rise; i.e.,

$$\sum_{j=1, j \neq i}^{n} p_j \frac{\partial x_j}{\partial p_i} > 0 \tag{69}$$

since the partial derivative of $Q = f(x_1, \ldots, x_n)$ with respect to p_i is set equal to zero:

$$\sum_{j=1}^{n} \frac{\partial f}{\partial x_j} \frac{\partial x_j}{\partial p_i} = \sum_{j=1}^{n} p_j \frac{\partial x_j}{\partial p_i} = 0. \tag{70}$$

Next suppose that prices $p_1, p_2, \ldots, p_m$ have risen and that the other prices remain unchanged. When the quantity of output is constant, the total amount of inputs of $x_{m+1}, x_{m+2}, \ldots, x_n$ must be increased since

$$\sum_{i=1}^{m} \sum_{j=m+1}^{n} \frac{p_j \partial x_j}{\partial p_i / p_i} > 0 \qquad \text{for integer} \quad m, \quad 1 \leqq m \leqq n, \tag{71}$$

which is obtained, in view of (70), by substituting

$$\sum_{j=1}^{m} p_j \frac{\partial x_j}{\partial p_i} = - \sum_{j=m+1}^{n} p_j \frac{\partial x_j}{\partial p_i}$$

into (67). Obviously (71) is a generalization of (69).

The preceding example is essentially a local maximum problem without constraint. Now we turn to a local maximum problem under a finite number of equality constraints: Maximize $f(x)$, subject to $g^j(x) = 0$ for $j = 1, \ldots, m$; $m < n$, where f, g^j are twice-differentiable real-valued functionals on E^n.

Let $L''(x^0)$ be the Hessian of the Lagrangian function $L(x)$ in (57). The (i, k)th component of $L''(x^0)$ is now represented by

$$\psi_{ik} \equiv \frac{\partial^2 f(x)}{\partial x_i \, \partial x_k} + \sum_{j=1}^{m} \lambda_j \frac{\partial^2 g^j(x)}{\partial x_i \, \partial x_k} \qquad \text{for} \quad i, k = 1, \ldots, n, \tag{72}$$

evaluated at the x^0 where the first-order condition is satisfied. In view of (61), the second-order condition is that $L''(x^0)$ is negative definite for all $u \in E^n$ satisfying linear constraints

$$g_x^j(x^0) u = 0 \qquad \text{for} \quad j = 1, \ldots, m,$$

where $g_x^j(x^0)$ stands for the gradient of g^j at x^0. Represent by B the $m \times n$ matrix consisting of all these gradients for $j = 1, \ldots, m$,

$$B \equiv \begin{bmatrix} g_x^1(x^0) \\ \vdots \\ g_x^m(x^0) \end{bmatrix}, \tag{73}$$

and denote $L''(x^0)$ by A. Then the second-order condition may be rewritten as

$$u^{\mathrm{T}} A u < 0 \qquad \text{for all } u \in E^n \text{ satisfying } Bu = \theta. \tag{74}$$

To (74) we may apply Theorem 36 in Section 2.5. Instead, we simplify the constraints, and consider the case where there is only one constraint $g(x) = 0$, where g is a real-valued functional on E^n. To this simple case we apply the corollary to Theorem 36 in Section 2.5. Then, the Hessian of the Lagrangian function $L(x) \equiv f(x) + \lambda g(x)$ is positive definite for all $u \in E^n$ satisfying $g'(x^0)u = 0$ if and only if

$$\begin{vmatrix} 0 & \psi_1 & \psi_2 \\ \psi_1 & \psi_{11} & \psi_{12} \\ \psi_2 & \psi_{12} & \psi_{22} \end{vmatrix} < 0, \quad \begin{vmatrix} 0 & \psi_1 & \psi_2 & \psi_3 \\ \psi_1 & \psi_{11} & \psi_{12} & \psi_{13} \\ \psi_2 & \psi_{12} & \psi_{22} & \psi_{23} \\ \psi_3 & \psi_{13} & \psi_{23} & \psi_{33} \end{vmatrix} < 0, \quad \ldots,$$

$$\begin{vmatrix} 0 & g'(x^0) \\ g'(x^0)^{\mathrm{T}} & L''(x^0) \end{vmatrix} < 0, \tag{75}$$

where ψ_{ij} is defined in (72) and $g'(x^0) \equiv (\psi_1, \ldots, \psi_n), \psi_i \equiv g_i'(x^0)$. The Hessian of $L(x)$ is negative definite for all $u \in E^n$ satisfying $g'(x^0)u = 0$ if and only if

$$\begin{vmatrix} 0 & \psi_1 & \psi_2 \\ \psi_1 & \psi_{11} & \psi_{12} \\ \psi_2 & \psi_{12} & \psi_{22} \end{vmatrix} > 0, \quad \begin{vmatrix} 0 & \psi_1 & \psi_2 & \psi_3 \\ \psi_1 & \psi_{11} & \psi_{12} & \psi_{13} \\ \psi_2 & \psi_{12} & \psi_{22} & \psi_{23} \\ \psi_3 & \psi_{13} & \psi_{23} & \psi_{33} \end{vmatrix} < 0, \quad \ldots,$$

$$(-1)^n \begin{vmatrix} 0 & g'(x^0) \\ g'(x^0)^{\mathrm{T}} & L''(x^0) \end{vmatrix} > 0. \tag{76}$$

(75) and (76) are second-order conditions for $f(x)$ to achieve a local minimum and a local maximum, respectively, under a single constraint $g(x) = 0$, where f, g are twice-differentiable real-valued functionals on E^n. Similarly, (55) or (56), and (58) in Section 2.5 are second-order conditions for a local minimum and a local maximum, respectively, under m constraints $g^j(x) = 0$ $(j = 1, \ldots, m)$.

Application 6 Let us represent by

$$g(x_1, x_2, \ldots, x_n) = 0 \tag{77}$$

a production relationship where some of the x_i designate outputs and the other x_i are the factor inputs required. If the ith good is an output in (77), x_i takes on a positive value, while if the jth good is an input, x_j takes on a negative value. g is assumed to be twice differentiable. Then the profit accruing from (77) is

$$\pi = \sum_{j=1}^{n} p_j x_j,$$

where p_j stands for the price of good j. Given all the prices, the first-order conditions of maximizing π under the constraint (77) are

$$p_j + \lambda g_j = 0 \quad \text{for} \quad j = 1, \ldots, n, \tag{78}$$

where $g_j \equiv \partial g/\partial x_j$ and λ is a Lagrange multiplier. (77) and (78) determine the equilibrium values of $x_1, \ldots, x_n$ and λ. In order for these values to achieve the local maximum at the equilibrium, the following second-order conditions must be fulfilled at the equilibrium:

$$\begin{vmatrix} 0 & g_1 & g_2 \\ g_1 & \lambda g_{11} & \lambda g_{12} \\ g_2 & \lambda g_{12} & \lambda g_{22} \end{vmatrix} > 0, \quad \begin{vmatrix} 0 & g_1 & g_2 & g_3 \\ g_1 & \lambda g_{11} & \lambda g_{12} & \lambda g_{13} \\ g_2 & \lambda g_{12} & \lambda g_{22} & \lambda g_{23} \\ g_3 & \lambda g_{13} & \lambda g_{23} & \lambda g_{33} \end{vmatrix} < 0, \quad \ldots, \quad (-1)^n |G| > 0, \tag{79}$$

where $g_{ij} \equiv \partial^2 g/(\partial x_i\, \partial x_j)$ and

$$|G| \equiv \begin{vmatrix} 0 & g_1 & g_2 & \cdots & g_n \\ g_1 & \lambda g_{11} & \lambda g_{12} & \cdots & \lambda g_{1n} \\ g_2 & \lambda g_{12} & \lambda g_{22} & \cdots & \lambda g_{2n} \\ \vdots & \vdots & \vdots & & \vdots \\ g_n & \lambda g_{1n} & \lambda g_{2n} & \cdots & \lambda g_{nn} \end{vmatrix}.$$

Note that in this example we exclude the cases where $|G|$ vanishes. One of these cases occurs when g is homogeneous of degree zero, for then we have

$$\sum_{i=1}^{n} g_i x_i = 0,$$

and differentiating this with respect to x_j yields

$$g_j + g_{1j}x_1 + \cdots + g_{nj}x_n = 0 \qquad \text{for} \quad j = 1, \ldots, n,$$

which results in $|G| = 0$ by adding $(1/\lambda)\sum_{i=1}^{n} x_i \cdot$(column $i + 1$ of $|G|$) to the first column of $|G|$.

Denoting by G_{ij} th cofactor of λg_{ij} in $|G|$ and proceeding in the same way as Application 5, we know in view of (79)

$$\sum_{i=1}^{m} \sum_{j=1}^{m} \frac{G_{ij}}{|G|} \xi_i \xi_j < 0 \qquad \text{for any nonzero } x \equiv \{\xi_1, \ldots, \xi_m\}, \tag{80}$$

for integer m, $1 \leq m \leq n$; and

$$G_{ii}/|G| < 0. \tag{81}$$

Let us examine the effects of changes in prices upon the equilibrium values. Differentiating (77) and (78) with respect ot p_i, we have

$$\partial x_j/\partial p_i = -G_{ij}/|G| \qquad \text{for} \quad i, j = 1, \ldots, n.$$

Substitution from these into (80), together with replacement of ξ_i by p_i $(i = 1, \ldots, n)$, yields

$$\sum_{i=1}^{m} \sum_{j=1}^{m} p_i p_j \frac{\partial x_j}{\partial p_i} > 0 \qquad \text{for any nonzero } p \equiv \{p_1, \ldots, p_m\}, \tag{82}$$

for integer m, $1 \leqq m \leqq n$. In particular

$$\partial x_i/\partial p_i = -G_{ii}/|G| > 0, \tag{83}$$

implying that if a product price has risen, its output is to be increased, and that if a factor price has risen, its input is to decline.

It follows from (77) and (78) that

$$\sum_{j=1}^{n} p_j \frac{\partial x_j}{\partial p_i} = -\lambda \sum_j g_j \frac{\partial x_j}{\partial p_i} = 0. \tag{84}$$

Assuming p_i is positive and taking (83) into account, we have

$$\sum_{j=1,\, j\neq i}^{n} p_j \frac{\partial x_j}{\partial p_i} < 0. \tag{85}$$

This means that total amount of all the factor inputs and outputs except good i must fall if the price of the latter has risen.

Suppose that goods $1, \ldots, m$ represent products and goods $m+1, \ldots, n$ factors in (77). In view of (84),

$$\sum_{j=1}^{m} p_j \frac{\partial x_j}{\partial p_i} = \sum_{j=m+1}^{n} p_j \frac{\partial(-x_j)}{\partial p_i}.$$

Thus (82) can be expressed as

$$\sum_{i=1}^{m} \sum_{j=m+1}^{n} p_i p_j \frac{\partial(-x_j)}{\partial p_i} > 0, \tag{82$'$}$$

which means that if all product prices have risen, the total amount of factor inputs must increase. Since

$$\partial x_j/\partial p_i = -G_{ij}/|G| = -G_{ji}/|G| = \partial x_i/\partial p_j,$$

(82′) will be rewritten as

$$\sum_{j=m+1}^{n} \sum_{i=1}^{m} p_j p_i \frac{\partial x_i}{\partial p_j} < 0, \tag{82$''$}$$

which means that if all factor prices have risen, the total amount of products must decline.

We remark that the above conclusions are derived from the profit-maximizing behavior of a price-taking firm engaged in joint production.

Concluding this section, we shall weaken the local maximum in Definition 3′ by replacing (56) by

$$f(x^0) \geqq f(x) \qquad \text{for all} \quad x \in S \cap X, \quad x \neq x^0, \tag{56$'$}$$

and say that f has a *weak local maximum* at x^0. In this case, the Hessian of the Lagrangian function L defined in (57) must be negative semidefinite. Thus, in view of Theorem 11 in Section 7.2, we have the following.

THEOREM 19 Let the Lagrangian function L defined in (57) be concave (or convex) on S. Then, the function L being stationary at x^0 is sufficient for f to have a weak local maximum (or minimum, respectively) at x^0.

EXERCISES

1. Prove Theorem 4.

2. Prove Theorem 5.

3. Let f be a functional on a normed space X. An element f^* of the dual of X is called a *subgradient* of f at x^0 if

$$f(x) \geqq f(x^0) + [x - x^0; f^*] \qquad \text{for all} \quad x \in X.$$

Show that when f has a gradient at x^0, any subgradient of f is equal to the gradient.

4. Let $X = C[a, b]$, where a, b are real numbers with $a < b$. Define $f(x) \equiv \int_a^b g(x(t), t)\, dt$ on X and assume that $g_x(x, t) \equiv \partial g(x, t)/\partial x$ exists and is continuous with respect to x and t. Show that the Gateaux with increment $h \in X$

$$\delta f(x; h) = \int_a^b g_x(x, t) h(t)\, \mathrm{dt}$$

is a Fréchet differential.

5. Assume that national product Y is obtainable as a function of capital K and labor L:

$$Y = F(K, L),$$

where F is linear homogeneous in K and L, and that labor is fully employed and grows at a constant rate. Then maximize the utility of per capita consumption over time to derive a Ramsey rule of accumulation.

6. Let $A = [a_{ij}]$ be an $n \times n$ constant matrix and let c be a constant n-vector. Show that $\sum_{i=1}^{n} |a_{ij}| < 1$ $(j = 1, \ldots, n)$ is sufficient for $F(x) \equiv Ax + c$ being a contraction mapping.

7. Prove the following second contraction mapping theorem: Let S be a closed subset of a Banach space and F be a continuous transformation from S into S. If F^p is a contraction mapping for some positive integer $p > 1$, there is a unique point $x_0 \in S$, satisfying $F(x_0) = x_0$, that can be obtained by successive approximation

$$x_{t+1} = F^p(x_t),$$

starting from an arbitrary initial point in S.

8. Prove the following inverse function theorem: Let D be an open subset of E^n and F be a transformation from D into E^n. Assume that F is continuously differentiable on D and that the Jacobian matrix of F at x_0 is nonsingular. Then there exists a continuous transformation G defined on a sphere $S(y_0; \delta)$ centered at $y_0 \equiv F(x_0)$ with $R(G) \subset D$ such that $G(F(x)) = x$ for $x \in R(G)$, where $R(G)$ denotes the range of G.

9. Let X be a Banach space and let F be a bounded linear transformation from X into X. Verify that if $\|F\| \equiv \alpha < 1$, then $(I - F)^{-1}$ exists and $\|(I - F)^{-1}\| < 1/(1 - \alpha)$, where I is the identity operator.

10. Verify Application 4 in Section 7.4.

REFERENCES AND FURTHER READING

Akhiezer, N. I. (1962). *The Calculus of Variations* (English translation). Ginn (Blaisdell), New York.

Apostol, T. M. (1957). *Mathematical Analysis*. Addison-Wesley, Reading. Massachusetts.

Gale, D., and Nikaido, H. (1965). "The Jacobian Matrix and Global Univalence of Mappings," *Mathematishe Annalen* **159**, 81–93; (1968), in *Readings in Mathematical Economics* (P. Newman, ed.), Vol. I. Johns Hopkins Press, Baltimore, Maryland.

Hadley, G., and Kemp, M. C. (1971). *Variational Methods in Economics*. North-Holland Publ., Amsterdam.

Hicks, J. R. (1939). *Value and Capital*. Oxford Univ. Press, London and New York.

Inada, K. (1971). "The Production Coefficient Matrix and the Stolper–Samuelson Condition," *Econometrica* **39**, 219–239.

Kantorovich, L. V., and Akilov, G. P. (1964). *Functional Analysis in Normed Spaces* (English translation). Pergamon, Oxford.

Katzner, D. W. (1970). *Static Demand Theory*. Macmillan, New York.

Kolmogorov, A. N., and Fomin, S. V. (1957). *Elements of the Theory of Functional Analysis* (English translation), Vol. I. Graylock Press, Rochester.

Luenberger, D. G. (1969). *Optimization by Vector Space Methods*. Wiley, New York.

Morishima, M., and Murata, Y. (1972). "An Input–Output Analysis of Disguised Unemployment in Japan, 1951–1965," in *The Working of Econometric Models* (Morishima *et al.*, eds.), pp. 241–300. Cambridge Univ. Press, London and New York.

Newman, P. (1969). "Some Properties of Concave Functions," *Journal of Economic Theory* **1**, 291–314.

Ramsey, F. P. (1928). "A Mathematical Theory of Saving," *Economic Journal* **38**, 543–559; (1969), in *Readings in the Modern Theory of Economic Growth* (G. E. Stiglitz and H. Uzawa, eds.). MIT Press, Cambridge, Massachusetts.

Sagan, H. (1969). *Introduction to the Calculus of Variations*. McGraw-Hill, New York.

Samuelson, P. A., and Solow, R. M. (1956). "A Complete Capital Model Involving Heterogeneous Capital Goods," *Quarterly Journal of Economics* **70**, 537–562.

Stigum, B. P. (1968). "On a Property of Concave Functions," *Review of Economic Studies* **35**, 413–416.

Chapter 8

Optimization in Inequality Economic Systems

8.1 Hyperplanes and Separation Theorems

We start with the definition of a hyperplane in terms of a linear variety.

DEFINITION 1 A subspace M of a vector space X or a linear variety $x_0 + M$ for an element x_0 of X not in M such that the subspace generated by $x_0 + M$, denoted $[x_0 + M]$, is identical with X is called a *hyperplane* in X. An M with the above property is referred to as a maximal proper subspace of X. When P is a hyperplane in X represented as

$$P = x_0 + M \qquad \text{for} \quad x_0 \notin M, \tag{1}$$

any subspace of X containing P is nothing but X and hence P is said to be a maximal (proper) linear variety in X.

It should be clear that when a hyperplane P in a vector space X is represented as (1), P does not contain the origin θ of X; while if P is equal to a maximal proper subspace, then P contains θ. Note that, since a subspace or a linear variety is a convex cone, so is a hyperplane.

There is another way of defining a hyperplane in view of Theorem 1:

THEOREM 1 P is a hyperplane in a vector space X if and only if there exists a nonzero linear functional f on X such that

$$P = \{x : x \in X, f(x) = c\} \qquad \text{for a real constant } c. \tag{2}$$

Furthermore, to each hyperplane that contains no origin there corresponds a unique nonzero linear functional f satisfying (2) with nonzero c.

PROOF (i) Suppose P is a hyperplane in X. Let $P = x_0 + M = \{x :$

$x = x_0 + m, m \in M\}$, where M is a subspace of X and x_0 is an element of X not in M. Then $[x_0 + M] = X$. An element x of $[x_0 + M]$ is uniquely represented as $x = bx_0 + m$, where b is a scalar and m is a vector in M. Define for a nonzero constant c a linear functional f such that $f(bx_0 + m) = cb$. Then $f(x_0 + m) = c$ and $f(m) = 0$, and hence $P = \{x : x \in X, f(x) = c\}$; and in the case $P = M$, we have $P = \{x : x \in X, f(x) = 0\}$.

Suppose that g is any other linear functional satisfying $P = \{x : x \in X, g(x) = c, c =$ the same nonzero constant as before$\}$. Then we have

$$P \subset \{x : x \in X, f(x) = g(x)\} = \{x : x \in X, (f - g)(x) = 0\} \equiv G,$$

where G is a subspace of X since

$$\begin{aligned}(f - g)(\alpha x_1 + \beta x_2) &= f(\alpha x_1 + \beta x_2) - g(\alpha x_1 + \beta x_2) \\ &= \alpha(f - g)(x_1) + \beta(f - g)(x_2)\end{aligned}$$

for $x_1, x_2 \in G$ and scalars α, β. Any subspace containing the hyperplane P must be equal to X, whence $G = X$, i.e., $\{x : x \in X, (f - g)(x) = 0\} = X$. Thus, $f = g$ on X.

(ii) Let f be a nonzero linear functional on X and let $M = \{x : x \in X, f(x) = 0\}$. It is clear that M is a subspace of X. Let $x_0 \in X$ with $f(x_0) = 1$, wherefore $x_0 \notin M$. Then for any element x of $X, f(x - f(x)x_0) = f(x) - f(x) f(x_0) = 0$ implying that $x - f(x)x_0 \in M$, or $x = f(x)x_0 + m$ with $m \in M$, and hence x belongs to $[x_0 + M]$. Thus $X \subset [x_0 + M]$, whereas apparently $[x_0 + M] \subset X$. Therefore $[x_0 + M] = X$, i.e., M is a maximal proper subspace of X and $x_0 + M$ and M are hyperplanes on X. Now for any nonzero constant c, select an element x_1 of X for which $f(x_1) = c$. Then x_1 is not in M and

$$\{x : x \in X, f(x) = c\} = \{x : x \in X, f(x - x_1) = 0\} = x_1 + M$$

because $x - x_1 \in M$ implies that $x = x_1 + m$ with $m \in M$. Thus, $x_1 + M$ is a maximal proper linear variety in X, and hence a hyperplane in X. Q.E.D.

THEOREM 2 Let f be a nonzero linear functional on a normed vector space X. Then, the hyperplane P defined by (2) is closed for every constant c, called the value of the hyperplane, if and only if f is continuous on X.

PROOF *Sufficiency* Suppose f is continuous on X, in particular at $x \in X$; i.e., $x_n \to x$ implies $f(x_n) \to f(x)$. Let $\{x_n\}$ be a sequence from P convergent to $x \in X$. Then $c = f(x_n) \to f(x)$ and thus $f(x) = c$. Hence $x \in P$, implying that P is closed.

Necessity Suppose the hyperplane P defined by (2) is closed. It can also be represented as $P = x_0 + M$ or $P = M$ where $[x_0 + M] = X$ with $M \equiv \{x : x \in X, f(x) = 0\}$ and x_0 is an element of X not in M. Since P is closed, M is a closed subspace. Let $\{x_n\}$ be a sequence from X convergent to $x \in X$.

Since $X = [x_0 + M]$, x_n and x have unique representations: $x_n = b_n x_0 + m_n$, $x = bx_0 + m$ for m_n, $m \in M$. Let $d = \inf_{y \in M} \|x_0 + y\|$. d is positive because $x_0 \notin M$ which is closed. Let $y = (m_n - m)/(b_n - b)$. This y is apparently an element of M. Thus

$$|b_n - b| d \leqq |b_n - b| \|x_0 + y\| = \|(b_n - b) x_0 + m_n - m\| = \|x_n - x\|.$$

Since d is positive, $x_n \to x$ implies $b_n \to b$, and hence

$$f(x_n) = b_n f(x_0) + f(m_n) = b_n f(x_0) \to bf(x_0) = f(x).$$

Therefore, f is continuous at x. Q.E.D.

Now we define the half-spaces determined by a hyperplane.

DEFINITION 2 Let f be a nonzero continuous linear functional on a normed space X and c any real constant. Due to the continuity of f we can define closed half-spaces as

$$\begin{aligned} &\textit{closed negative half-space} \equiv \{x : f(x) \leqq c\}, \\ &\textit{closed positive half-space} \equiv \{x : f(x) \geqq c\}. \end{aligned}$$

The intersection of these half-spaces is the hyperplane having value c. Similarly, the hyperplane separates the open half-spaces

$$\begin{aligned} &\textit{open negative half-space} \equiv \{x : f(x) < c\}, \\ &\textit{open positive half-space} \equiv \{x : f(x) > c\}. \end{aligned}$$

The positiveness or negativeness of half-spaces is only a matter of convention. Indeed, if the signs of f and c are reversed in the above definition, a positive half-space and a negative one will interchange their names without changing their substance.

Clearly, each half-space defined above is a convex set, and a closed half-space determined by a hyperplane containing the origin is a convex cone with vertex at the origin.

A Hilbert space H has a one-to-one correspondence with its dual space H^* in such a manner that $f(x) = (x|y)$ for a unique $f \in H^*$ and a unique $y \in H$. Therefore, a hyperplane $P = \{x : f(x) = c\}$ in a Hilbert space is represented as

$$P = \{x : (x|y) = c,\ x \in H\} \qquad \text{for a unique } y \in H. \tag{3}$$

In particular, since the dual of Euclidean n-space E^n is nothing but E^n itself, a hyperplane in E^n or in the real n-space R^n is expressed as

$$P = \left\{x = (x_1, \ldots, x_n) : \sum_{i=1}^{n} \alpha_i x_i = c,\ x_i \in R^1\right\} \tag{4}$$

for a given nonzero real vector $\alpha = (\alpha_1, \ldots, \alpha_n)$ and a given real scalar c. Let $q = (q_1, \ldots, q_n)$ be an arbitrary point in P. Then we have $\sum_{i=1}^{n} \alpha_i (x_i - q_i) = 0$ for $x \in P$, which implies that α is orthogonal to the subspace $P - q$ and hence to the hyperplane P. Thus α is termed the *normal vector* to the hyperplane P defined by (4). A closed positive half-space determined by P in Euclidean n-space E^n is written as

$$B = \left\{x = (x_1, \ldots, x_n) : \sum_{i=1}^{n} \alpha_i x_i \geqq c,\ x_i \in R^1\right\}, \tag{5}$$

and any element x of B satisfies

$$\sum_{i=1}^{n} \alpha_i(x_i - q_i) \geqq 0 \qquad \text{for} \quad (q_1, \ldots, q_n) \in P. \tag{6}$$

Since $\sum_{i=1}^{n} \alpha_i(x_i - q_i) = \|\alpha\|\,\|x - q\| \cos \omega$, where ω stands for the angle between α and $x-q$, (6) implies that $\cos \omega \geqq 0$ or equivalently $-\pi/2 \leqq \omega \leqq \pi/2$. Hence B is identical to the closed half-space containing the normal vector α to the separating hyperplane P.

Consider a system of linear equations

$$\sum_{j=1}^{n} a_{ij} x_j = c_i \qquad \text{for} \quad i = 1, \ldots, m,$$

where the a_{ij} and c_i are real constants. Its solution space in R^n is the intersection of all the hyperplanes

$$P_i \equiv \left\{x = (x_1, \ldots, x_n) : \sum_{j=1}^{n} a_{ij} x_j = c_i,\ x_i \in R^1\right\} \qquad \text{for} \quad i = 1, \ldots, m.$$

Since each P_i is a convex set, so is their intersection. Similarly, the solution space of the following system of linear inequalities in R^n

$$\sum_{j=1}^{n} a_{ij} x_j \geqq c_i \qquad \text{for} \quad i = 1, \ldots, m, \tag{7}$$

is equal to the intersection of the closed positive half-spaces determined by P_i in R^n, and hence a convex set. Furthermore, if the c_i in (7) are all zero, its solution space in R^n is a convex polyhedral cone. Obviously the solution space of the corresponding homogeneous linear equations in R^n is also a convex polyhedral cone.

Next we define supporting half-spaces and hyperplanes for a convex set.

DEFINITION 3 Let P and K be a closed hyperplane and a convex set, respectively, in a normed space. If K is contained in one of the closed half-spaces determined by P, the half-space is referred to as a *supporting half-space* for K. If, in addition, P contains a point of the closure $\bar{K}$, P is said to be a *supporting hyperplane* or simply a *support* for K.

Several basic theorems concerning supporting half-spaces and hyperplanes are in order.

THEOREM 3 Let K be a closed convex set in a normed space. Then K is identical with the intersection of all the supporting half-spaces for K.

PROOF We know that a half-space is a convex set and that the intersection of an arbitrary collection of closed convex sets is closed and convex. Thus, the intersection of all the closed half-spaces containing K is the smallest closed convex set containing K, which is nothing but K. Q.E.D.

(The following three theorems are parallel to the presentation in Day (1958) and Luenberger (1969).) (Refer to p. 187 for the expression $[v; x^*]$ below.)

THEOREM 4 Let K and V be a convex set and a linear variety in a real normed space X, respectively, and assume that

$$\mathring{K} \neq \varnothing \qquad \text{and} \qquad V \cap \mathring{K} = \varnothing,$$

where $\mathring{K}$ stands for the interior of K and $\varnothing$, the empty set. Then there is a closed hyperplane P in X such that

$$P \supset V \qquad \text{and} \qquad P \cap \mathring{K} = \varnothing;$$

in other words, there exist a nonzero continuous linear functional x^* in the dual X^* of X and a nonzero constant c such that $[v; x^*] = c$ for all $v \in V$ and $[k; x^*] < c$ for all $k \in \mathring{K}$.

PROOF By an appropriate translation we assume that the null vector θ is an interior point of K. Then $\mathring{K} = \{x : x \in X, p_K(x) < 1\}$, where p_K is the Minkowski functional of K defined on X. Let M be the subspace generated by V. Then V can be regarded as a hyperplane in M. (Note that $\theta \notin V$.) Therefore, there is a unique nonzero linear functional f defined on M such that $V = \{x : x \in M, f(x) = 1\}$. Since $V \cap \mathring{K} = \varnothing$, we have $f(v) = 1 \leqq p_K(v)$ for $v \in V$. Thus for given $b > 0$, $f(bv) = b \leqq bp_K(v) = p_K(bv)$ for $v \in V$; while for given $b \leqq 0$, $f(bv) = b \leqq 0 \leqq p_K(bv)$ for $v \in V$. Hence, $f(x) \leqq p_K(x)$ for $x \in M$ since $x = b_1v_1 + b_2v_2$ for $v_1, v_2 \in V$.

Since p_K is a continuous sublinear functional, by the Hahn–Banach theorem (the real case) there exists an extension x^* of f from M to X such that $[x; x^*] \leqq p_K(x)$ for $x \in X$ and $[v; x^*] = f(v) = 1$ for $v \in V$. Let $P = \{x : x \in X, [x; x^*] = 1\}$. Since p_K is continuous and $[x; x^*] \leqq p_K(x)$ on X, x^* is continuous and hence P is a closed hyperplane. Lastly $[k; x^*] < 1$ for $k \in \mathring{K}$ because $p_K(k) < 1$ for the k. Q.E.D.

THEOREM 5 (*support theorem*) Let K be a convex set in a real normed space X and assume that its interior $\mathring{K}$ is not empty. Let z be an element of X not in $\mathring{K}$. Then there is a supporting hyperplane $P = \{x : x \in X, [x; x^*] = [z; x^*] \neq 0\}$ for K such that

$$[k; x^*] \leqq [z; x^*] \qquad \text{for all} \quad k \in K,$$

where $x^* \in X^*$.

PROOF Construct a linear variety V in X such that

$$z \in V \qquad \text{and} \qquad V \cap \mathring{K} = \varnothing.$$

Then, by the preceding theorem, there exists a closed hyperplane $P = \{x : x \in X, [x; x^*] = c\}$, where $x^* \in X^*$ and c is a nonzero constant such that

$$[v; x^*] = c \quad \text{for} \quad v \in V \qquad \text{and} \qquad [k; x^*] < c \quad \text{for} \quad k \in \mathring{K}.$$

Apparently $[z; x^*] = c$. Since any accumulation point of $\mathring{K}$ must lie in the set $\{x : [x; x^*] \leqq c\}$, so does K. Q.E.D.

COROLLARY Let K be a nonempty *open* convex set in a real normed space X and let z be an element of X not in K. Then there exists a nonzero continuous linear functional $x^* \in X^*$ such that

$$[k; x^*] < c = [z; x^*] \qquad \text{for all} \quad k \in K,$$

where c is a nonzero constant.

Now we come to a separation theorem on a normed space.

THEOREM 6 (*Eidelheit separation theorem*) Let K_1, K_2 be convex sets in a real normed space X such that $\mathring{K}_1 \neq \varnothing$ and $\mathring{K}_1 \cap K_2 = \varnothing$. Then there is a closed hyperplane P separating K_1 from K_2 such that

$$[y; x^*] \leqq [z; x^*] \qquad \text{for all} \quad y \in K_1 \quad \text{and } z \in K_2, \tag{8}$$

where x^* is a nonzero continuous linear functional belonging to X^*.

PROOF Let $K \equiv K_1 + (-K_2) = \{x : x = y - z, y \in K_1, z \in K_2\}$ which is convex. Since $\mathring{K}_1 \neq \varnothing$, we know that $\mathring{K} \neq \varnothing$. $\mathring{K}_1 \cap K_2 = \varnothing$ implies that $\theta \notin \mathring{K}$. Thus, by the support theorem, there is a nonzero continuous linear functional x^* such that $[x; x^*] \leqq [\theta; x^*] = 0$ for $x \in K$, or equivalently (8) holds. Consequently, there is a real constant c for which

$$\sup_{y \in K_1} [y; x^*] \leqq c \leqq \inf_{z \in K_2} [z; x^*].$$

The desired hyperplane is $P = \{x : x \in X, [x; x^*] = c\}$. Q.E.D.

COROLLARY 1 Let K_1 and K_2 be convex sets in a real normed space X and let K_1 be nonempty and *open*. If

$$K_1 \cap K_2 = \varnothing,$$

then there is a nonzero continuous linear functional $x^* \in X^*$ such that

$$\sup_{y \in K_1} [y; x^*] < c \leqq \inf_{z \in K_2} [z; x^*],$$

where c is a real constant.

PROOF Define $K = K_1 + (-K_2)$. Then K is nonempty, open, and convex; and $\theta \notin K$. Thus, in view of the corollary to the support theorem, we have, by putting $z = \theta$,

$$[k; x^*] < [\theta; x^*] = 0 \qquad \text{for} \quad k \in K.$$

Hence $[y; x^*] < [z; x^*]$ for $y \in K_1$, $z \in K_2$. Q.E.D.

COROLLARY 2 Let K be a closed convex set in a real normed space X and suppose K does not contain $x \in X$. Then there exists for K a supporting half-space that does not contain x.

PROOF Let $d = \inf_{k \in K} \|x - k\|$, which is positive since K is closed. Let U be an open sphere centered at x with radius $d/2$. Noticing that $U \neq \varnothing$ and $U \cap K = \varnothing$, we can apply the separation theorem (Theorem 6) to U and K. Thus, there exists a nonzero continuous linear functional $x^* \in X^*$ such that

$$\sup_{u \in U} [u; x^*] \leqq \inf_{k \in K} [k; x^*].$$

Since x is the center of U, we have

$$[x; x^*] < [k; x^*] \qquad \text{for} \quad k \in K. \qquad \text{Q.E.D.}$$

THEOREM 7 (*separation theorem on a Euclidean space*) Let K be a convex set in Euclidean n-space E^n such that K has no intersection with the interior of $E^n_+ \equiv \{x : x \in E^n,\ x \geqq \theta\}$. Then there is a closed hyperplane M separating K from E^n_+ defined as

$$M \equiv \{x : x \in E^n,\ (x \mid y) = 0\} \qquad \text{for some} \quad y \leqq \theta$$

satisfying $(k \mid y) \geqq 0$ for $k \in K$. (Refer to Fig. 5.)

PROOF Let $B = E^n_+ + (-K) = \{x : x = r - k,\ r \in E^n_+,\ k \in K\}$. Observe that B is convex, that $\mathring{B}$ is nonempty and that $\theta \notin \mathring{B}$. Then, by the support theorem, there is a nonzero vector $y \in E^n$ such that

$$(r - k \mid y) \leqq 0 \qquad \text{for} \quad r \in E^n_+ \text{ and } k \in K, \tag{9}$$

and (9) holds in particular for r and k satisfying $r - k > \theta$. Thus $y \leqq \theta$. Hence, $\sup_{r \in E^n_+}(r \mid y) = (\theta \mid y) = 0$. By the separation theorem (Theorem 6),

$$\inf_{k \in K} (k \mid y) \geqq \sup_{r \in E^n_+} (r \mid y).$$

Therefore, we get $(k \mid y) \geqq 0$ for $k \in K$, and the desired separating hyperplane is the closed subspace M defined above. Q.E.D.

COROLLARY Let K be a convex set in E^n_+. Then, there is a closed hyperplane M separating K from $E^n_- \equiv \{x : x \in E^n,\ x \leqq \theta\}$ defined as

$$M \equiv \{x : x \in E^n,\ (x \mid y) = 0\} \qquad \text{for some} \quad y \geqq \theta$$

such that $(k \mid y) \geqq 0$ for $k \in K$.

PROOF Observe that K has no intersection with the interior of E^n_-, and define $B = E^n_- + (-K)$. Then, proceed in the same manner as Theorem 7, taking account of the fact that B is a nonpositive convex set. Q.E.D.

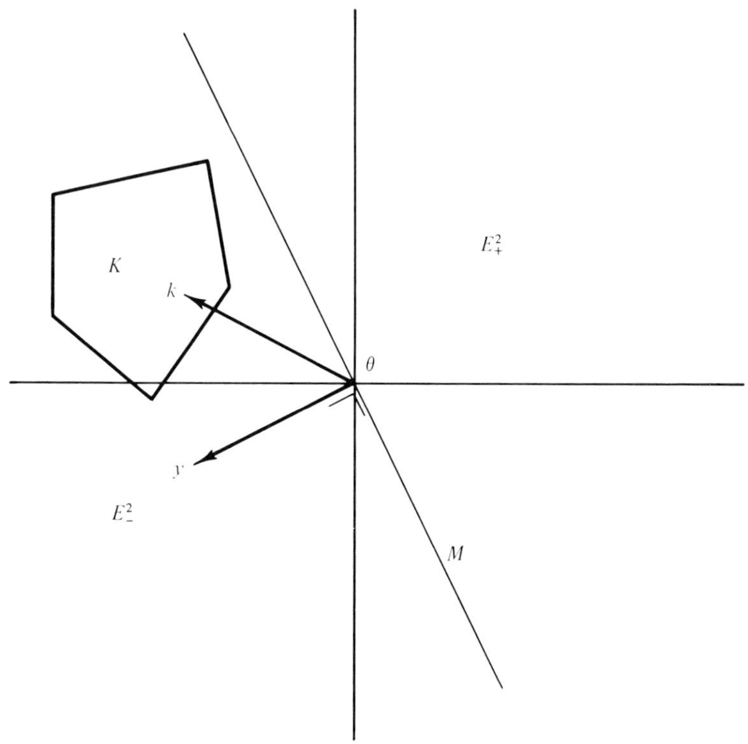

FIGURE 5. Separation on E^2.

The following theorem and its corollaries are to be proved with the help of the separation theorems.

THEOREM 8 Let K be a convex set in Euclidean n-space E^n, and define

$$K^{\#} = \{x : x \in E^n, (k \mid x) \geqq 0 \text{ for all } k \in K\}, \tag{10}$$

$$K^{\#\#} = \{y : y \in E^n, (x \mid y) \geqq 0 \text{ for all } x \in K^{\#}\}. \tag{11}$$

Then

(i) $K^{\#}$ and $K^{\#\#}$ are closed convex cones.
(ii) $K \subset K^{\#\#}$.
(iii) If K is a closed convex cone, then $K = K^{\#\#}$.

PROOF (i) Let x, y be elements of $K^{\#}$. Then

$$(k \mid \alpha x) = \alpha(k \mid x) \geqq 0 \qquad \text{for all} \quad k \in K \text{ and } \alpha \geqq 0.$$

Hence $\alpha x \in K^{\#}$ for $\alpha \geqq 0$. Next, given $\beta \in [0, 1]$,

$$(k \mid \beta x + (1 - \beta)y) = (k \mid \beta x) + (k \mid (1 - \beta)y) \geqq 0 \qquad \text{for all} \quad k \in K.$$

Hence $\beta x + (1 - \beta)y \in K^{\#}$ for $\beta \in [0, 1]$. Thus $K^{\#}$ is a convex cone (with vertex at the origin).

Let $\{x_m\}$ be a sequence from $K^{\#}$ convergent to $x \in E^n$. By the continuity of inner product,

$$0 \leqq \lim_{m\to\infty} (k \mid x_m) = (k \mid x) \qquad \text{for all} \quad k \in K.$$

Hence x belongs to $K^{\#}$, implying that $K^{\#}$ is closed.

Since $K^{\#}$ has been found to be convex, $K^{\#\#}$ may be shown to be a closed convex cone in a similar fashion.

(ii) Given $k \in K$, $(k \mid x) \geqq 0$ for all $x \in K^{\#}$. Hence $k \in K^{\#\#}$.

(iii) We shall show that $K \supset K^{\#\#}$. Let x be an element of E^n not in K. By Corollary 2 to the separation theorem (Theorem 6), there is for K a supporting half-space that does not contain x, or equivalently there is a nonzero vector $y \in (E^n)^* = E^n$ such that

$$(x \mid y) < (\alpha k \mid y) \qquad \text{for all} \quad k \in K \text{ and } \alpha \geqq 0$$

since K is a cone. Putting $\alpha = 0$, we have $(x \mid y) < 0$. Then we select a nonzero $y \in E^n$ such that

$$\inf_{k\in K} (k \mid y) = 0.$$

This y is an element of $K^{\#}$ and hence $(x \mid y) < 0$ implies $x \notin K^{\#\#}$. Q.E.D.

A symmetric proposition holds as follows.

COROLLARY 1 Let K be a convex set in E^n and define

$$\tilde{K}^{\#} = \{x : x \in E^n, (k \mid x) \leqq 0 \text{ for all } k \in K\}, \tag{10'}$$

$$\tilde{K}^{\#\#} = \{y : y \in E^n, (x \mid y) \leqq 0 \text{ for all } x \in \tilde{K}^{\#}\}. \tag{11'}$$

Then

(i′) $\tilde{K}^{\#}$ and $\tilde{K}^{\#\#}$ are closed convex cones.
(ii′) $K \subset \tilde{K}^{\#\#}$.
(iii′) If K is a closed convex cone, then $K = \tilde{K}^{\#\#}$.

(The proof proceeds in a similar manner to Theorem 8.)

COROLLARY 2 Let K be a closed convex cone in E^n, and define $\tilde{K}^{\#}$ and $\tilde{K}^{\#\#}$ as in (10′) and (11′). K contains no semipositive element if and only if $\tilde{K}^{\#}$ contains a positive vector.

PROOF (i) Suppose $\tilde{K}^{\#}$ contains no positive vector. Applying the separation theorem on a Euclidean space to $\tilde{K}^{\#}$, we see that there is a closed hyperplane separating K from E^n_+ such that for some vector $y \leq \theta$,

$$x^{\mathrm{T}} y \geqq 0 \qquad \text{for all} \quad x \in \tilde{K}^{\#}.$$

Thus $-y$ is an element of $\tilde{K}^{\#\#}$. Since $K = \tilde{K}^{\#\#}$, $\theta \leq -y \in K$.

(ii) If there exists a positive vector x in $\tilde{K}^{\#}$, then for any semipositive vector u, we have $u^{\mathrm{T}}x > 0$. Hence u does not belong to $\tilde{K}^{\#\#}$. Since $K \subset \tilde{K}^{\#\#}$, u cannot be an element of K. Q.E.D.

To conclude this section, we apply Theorem 8 to the proof of a relationship between two minimum cost functions.

Application 1 (Uzawa, 1964) Consider a single product firm producing its output y from a combination of n inputs $x = \{x_1, \ldots, x_n\} \geqq \theta$. Assume the input prices $p = (p_1, \ldots, p_n) \geqq \theta$ are given from outside of the firm. Denote by $\Omega(y)$ the set of all input vectors that can produce at least y, and assume:

(A-1) For each $y \geqq 0$, $\Omega(y)$ is nonempty and closed.
(A-2) For each $y \geqq 0$, $\Omega(y)$ is convex.
(A-3) $x \in \Omega(y)$ and $x^* > x$ imply $x^* \in \Omega(y)$.
(A-4) $y^0 \geqq y^1$ implies $\Omega(y^0) \subset \Omega(y^1)$.

We define the minimum cost for y as

$$c(p, y) \equiv \min_x \{px : x \in \Omega(y)\},$$

where px represents $\sum_{i=1}^n p_i x_i$. Furthermore, we introduce a set $\Gamma(y)$ associated with $c(p, y)$:

$$\Gamma(y) \equiv \{x : px \geqq c(p, y) \text{ for all } p \geqq \theta\},$$

and define the minimum cost on $\Gamma(y)$

$$c^*(p, y) \equiv \min_x \{px : x \in \Gamma(y)\}.$$

We shall show that $c^*(p, y)$ coincides with $c(p, y)$ if the latter satisfies the conditions

(A-5) $c(p, y)$ is defined for any $p \geqq \theta$ and $y > 0$ and is continuous and linear homogeneous with respect to p.

(A-6) $c(p, y)$ is a concave functional with respect to p.

Let B be the set in E^{n+1} defined by

$$B \equiv \{(p, \alpha) : p \geqq \theta,\ \alpha \geqq -c(p, y)\}.$$

It is easy to see that B is a closed convex cone in view of conditions (A-5) and (A-6). Thus, by Theorem 8, we have

$$B = B^{\#\#},$$

where $B^{\#} \equiv \{\{x, \beta\} : px + \alpha\beta \geqq 0 \text{ for all } (p, \alpha) \in B\}$, and $B^{\#\#} \equiv \{(p, \alpha);\ px + \alpha\beta \geqq 0 \text{ for all } \{x, \beta\} \in B^{\#}\}$. From the definitions of $\Gamma(y)$ and $B^{\#}$, it follows that

$$B^{\#} = \{\{x, \beta\} : \beta = 0,\ x \geqq \theta \text{ or } \beta > 0,\ x/\beta \in \Gamma(y)\},$$

since $x/\beta \in \Gamma(y)$ implies $px \geqq \beta c(p, y)$. Hence

$$B^{\#\#} = \{(p, \alpha) : p \geqq \theta, \alpha \geqq -px \text{ for all } x \in \Gamma(y)\}.$$

$B = B^{\#\#}$, therefore, implies $c(p, y) = c^*(p, y)$.

8.2 Dual Linear Relations and Gale–Nikaido Theorems

In this section we assemble theorems on dual systems of linear equations and inequalities and include a nonlinear extension at the end. We begin with the most fundamental lemma.

LEMMA 1 (*Farkas lemma*) Let A be an $m \times n$ real matrix, and let b, $x \in E^n$ be column vectors. Then there is a nonnegative column vector $y \in E^m$ such that $A^{\mathrm{T}}y = b$ if and only if $b^{\mathrm{T}}x \geqq 0$ for x satisfying $Ax \geqq \theta$.

PROOF (i) Suppose there is a $y \geqq \theta$ such that $b = A^{\mathrm{T}}y$. Then $b^{\mathrm{T}}x = y^{\mathrm{T}}Ax \geqq 0$ for x satisfying $Ax \geqq \theta$. (ii) Let a^i be the ith column vector of A^{T}, and generate a closed convex polyhedral cone K:

$$K \equiv \{k : k = \sum_{i=1}^{m} \beta_i a^i \text{ for } \beta_i \geqq 0 \ (i = 1, \ldots, m)\}.$$

$Ax \geqq \theta$ implies $x^{\mathrm{T}}a^i \geqq 0$ for $i = 1, \ldots, m$, and hence $x^{\mathrm{T}}k \geqq 0$ for all $k \in K$. Thus, by definition (10), an x satisfying $Ax \geqq \theta$ is an element of $K^{\#}$. Therefore, $b^{\mathrm{T}}x \geqq 0$ for x satisfying $Ax \geqq \theta$ implies $b \in K^{\#\#}$, where $K^{\#\#}$ is defined by (11). Since $K = K^{\#\#}$ by Theorem 8 above, b is represented as

$$b = \sum_{i=1}^{m} y_i a^i \qquad \text{for} \quad y_i \geqq 0 \qquad (i = 1, \ldots, m),$$

i.e., there exists a nonnegative column vector $y = \{y_1, \ldots, y_m\}$ such that $b = A^{\mathrm{T}}y$. Q.E.D.

For an intuitive understanding of the Farkas lemma, we depict the a^i by arrows in Fig. 6 in the case where $m = 3$ and $n = 2$, and draw vectors c^1, c^2 at right angles to a^1, a^2, respectively. Since $x^{\mathrm{T}}a^i \geqq 0$ means that the angle between x and a^i is not larger than 90 degrees and not less than -90 degrees in view of (7) in Section 5.1, the cone $c^1\theta c^2$ represents the feasible area of x satisfying $x^{\mathrm{T}}a^i \geqq 0$ for all i. In order that $b^{\mathrm{T}}x \geqq 0$ holds for any x belonging to this area, b must lie in the cone $a^1\theta a^2$.

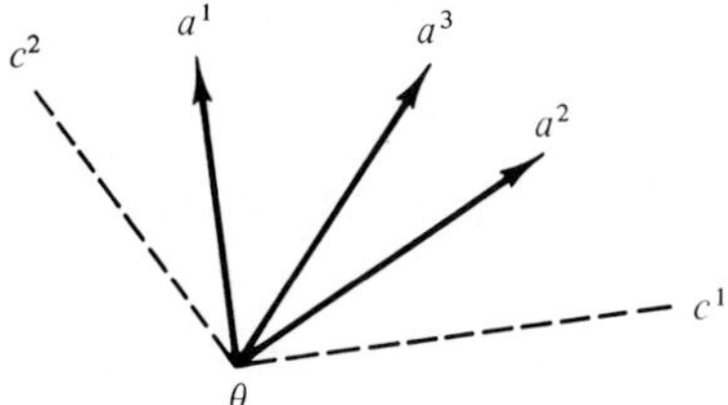

FIGURE 6. Farkas lemma.

An immediate result from the Farkas lemma is the following duality.

THEOREM 9 (*Farkas theorem*) Exactly one of the following alternatives holds: Either

$$A^{\mathrm{T}}y = b \text{ has a nonnegative solution } y, \tag{12}$$

or

$$Ax \geqq \theta \text{ and } b^{\mathrm{T}}x < 0 \text{ have a solution,} \tag{13}$$

where the notations A, x, b, and y are those defined in the Farkas lemma.

PROOF The contrapositive statement of $b^{\mathrm{T}}x \geqq 0$ for x satisfying $Ax \geqq \theta$ is that $b^{\mathrm{T}}x < 0$ for some x satisfying $Ax \geqq \theta$. Then apply the Farkas lemma. Q.E.D.

There are many other important dual systems of linear relations, which will be stated in the subsequent theorems where we use the same notations as in the Farkas lemma. (The following five theorems are due to Gale (1960).)

THEOREM 10 (*solutions of linear inequalities*) Exactly one of the following alternatives holds: Either

$$A^{\mathrm{T}}y \geqq b \text{ has a solution,} \tag{14}$$

or

$$Ax = \theta \text{ and } b^{\mathrm{T}}x = 1 \text{ have a nonnegative solution.} \tag{15}$$

PROOF (i) Inequality (14) cannot have any solution if there exists a nonnegative vector x satisfying (15). For otherwise we have a contradiction: $x^{\mathrm{T}}A^{\mathrm{T}}y = 0 \geqq 1$.

(ii) If $\left[\begin{smallmatrix} A \\ b^{\mathrm{T}} \end{smallmatrix}\right] x = \left[\begin{smallmatrix} \theta \\ 1 \end{smallmatrix}\right]$ have no nonnegative solution, then by the Farkas theorem, we can assert that there exist a vector y and a scalar c satisfying

$$[A^{\mathrm{T}}, b] \begin{bmatrix} y \\ c \end{bmatrix} \geqq \theta \qquad \text{and} \qquad \theta y + c = c < 0,$$

and this assertion implies, by setting $z = y/(-c)$, that there is a vector z such that $A^{\mathrm{T}}z \geqq b$. Q.E.D.

THEOREM 11 (*nonnegative solutions of linear inequalities*) Exactly one of the following alternatives holds: Either

$$A^{\mathrm{T}}y \leqq b \text{ has a nonnegative solution,} \tag{16}$$

or

$$Ax \geqq \theta \text{ and } b^{\mathrm{T}}x < 0 \text{ have a nonnegative solution.} \tag{17}$$

PROOF (i) If inequalities (17) have a nonnegative solution x, then (16) has no nonnegative solution because

$$y^{\mathrm{T}}Ax \leqq b^{\mathrm{T}}x < 0 \qquad \text{and} \qquad Ax \geqq \theta$$

imply that y cannot be nonnegative.

(ii) If (16) has no nonnegative solution, then since it can be rewritten as $A^{\mathrm{T}}y + z = b$ where z is a nonnegative vector, $[A^{\mathrm{T}}, I]\left[\begin{smallmatrix} y \\ z \end{smallmatrix}\right] = b$ has no nonnegative solution. By the Farkas theorem, therefore, there exists x such that

$$\begin{bmatrix} A \\ I \end{bmatrix} x \geqq \theta \qquad \text{and} \qquad b^{\mathrm{T}}x < 0. \qquad \text{Q.E.D.}$$

THEOREM 12 (*semipositive solutions of homogeneous inequalities*) Exactly one of the following alternatives holds: Either

$$Ax \leqq \theta \text{ has a semipositive solution,} \tag{18}$$

or

$$A^{\mathrm{T}}y > \theta \text{ has a nonnegative solution.} \tag{19}$$

PROOF (i) If (18) has a semipositive solution, we have $y^{\mathrm{T}}Ax > 0$, which together with inequality (18) implies that y cannot be nonnegative.

(ii) Suppose (18) has no semipositive solution. Then

$$\begin{bmatrix} A \\ -e^{\mathrm{T}} \end{bmatrix} x \leqq \begin{bmatrix} \theta \\ -1 \end{bmatrix}$$

has no nonnegative solution, where $e^{\mathrm{T}} \equiv (1, \ldots, 1)$. This means, by Theorem 11, that there exist a nonnegative vector y and a nonnegative scalar c such that

$$[A^{\mathrm{T}}, -e]\begin{bmatrix} y \\ c \end{bmatrix} \geqq \theta \qquad \text{and} \qquad \theta y - c = -c < 0,$$

or that there exists y such that $A^{\mathrm{T}}y \geqq ce > \theta$. Q.E.D.

COROLLARY If A is a nonsingular square matrix, exactly one of the following alternatives holds: Either

$$Ax \leqq \theta \text{ has a semipositive solution,} \tag{18'}$$

or

$$A^{\mathrm{T}}y > \theta \text{ has a semipositive solution.} \tag{19'}$$

PROOF In view of Theorem 12, it suffices to show that if $A^{\mathrm{T}}y > \theta$ has a nonnegative solution, it must be semipositive. Setting $z \equiv A^{\mathrm{T}}y$, we get $y^{\mathrm{T}} = z^{\mathrm{T}}A^{-1}$. Suppose $y = \theta$. Then, since $z > \theta$, $|A^{-1}|$ must vanish, contradicting $|A| \neq 0$. Q.E.D.

THEOREM 13 (*semipositive solutions of homogeneous equations*) Exactly one of the following alternatives holds: Either

$$Ax = \theta \text{ has a semipositive solution,} \tag{20}$$

or

$$A^{\mathrm{T}}y > \theta \text{ has a solution.} \tag{21}$$

PROOF (i) If (20) has a semipositive solution x, then $A^{\mathrm{T}}y > \theta$ has no solution because otherwise we have a contradiction: $0 = x^{\mathrm{T}}A^{\mathrm{T}}y > 0$.

(ii) If (20) has no semipositive solution, then

$$\begin{bmatrix} A \\ e^{\mathrm{T}} \end{bmatrix} x = \begin{bmatrix} \theta \\ 1 \end{bmatrix}$$

has no nonnegative solution, where $e^{\mathrm{T}} \equiv (1, \ldots, 1)$. Hence by the Farkas theorem, there exist a vector y and a scalar c such that

$$[A^{\mathrm{T}}, e] \begin{bmatrix} y \\ c \end{bmatrix} \geqq \theta \qquad \text{and} \qquad \theta y + c = c < 0.$$

This implies that there exists a solution y such that

$$A^{\mathrm{T}}y \geqq -ce > \theta. \qquad \text{Q.E.D.}$$

COROLLARY Let L be the subspace generated by $a^1, a^2, \ldots, a^m$, where a^i stands for the ith column vector of A^{T}:

$$L = \{z : z = A^{\mathrm{T}}y,\ y \in E^m\}, \tag{22}$$

and let

$$L^{\perp} = \{x : x \in E^n,\ x^{\mathrm{T}}z = 0 \text{ for all } z \in L\}. \tag{23}$$

Then, exactly one of the following alternatives holds: Either L contains a positive vector, or $L^{\perp}$ contains a semipositive vector.

PROOF (i) Suppose that L contains no positive vector, or equivalently that there is no solution y to $A^{\mathrm{T}}y > \theta$. Then by the preceding theorem there exists a semipositive vector x satisfying $Ax = \theta$, i.e., $x^{\mathrm{T}}a^i = 0$ for $i = 1, \ldots, m$, and hence $x \in L^{\perp}$.

(ii) Suppose $L^{\perp}$ contains a semipositive x satisfying $x^{\mathrm{T}}A^{\mathrm{T}}y = \theta$ for each $y \in E^m$. Then $Ax = \theta$ for $x \geq \theta$. By the preceding theorem, therefore, $A^{\mathrm{T}}y > \theta$ has no solution y. Q.E.D.

THEOREM 14 (*positive solutions of homogeneous equations*) Exactly one of the following alternatives holds: Either

$$Ax = \theta \text{ has a positive solution}, \tag{24}$$

or

$$A^{\mathrm{T}}y \geq \theta \text{ has a nonzero solution}. \tag{25}$$

PROOF (i) Suppose $Ax = \theta$ has a positive solution x. Then $x^{\mathrm{T}}A^{\mathrm{T}}y = 0$ for every $y \in E^m$, which entails $y = \theta$ as the unique solution of $A^{\mathrm{T}}y \geq \theta$.

(ii) Suppose $A^{\mathrm{T}}y \geq \theta$ has only the trivial solution $y = \theta$; i.e., L defined by (22) does not contain any semipositive vector $z \equiv A^{\mathrm{T}}y$. By the corollary to Theorem 13, $L^{\perp}$ defined by (23) contains a semipositive vector $x = \{\xi_1, \xi_2,$

$\ldots, \xi_n\}$. Suppose $\xi_i = 0$ and all the other components of x are positive. Then $a_i y$ can assume any number since $\xi_i a_i y = 0$ for all $y \in E^m$, where a_i stands for the ith row vector of A^{T}. Hence it is possible that $A^{\mathrm{T}}y \geqq \theta$ has a nonzero solution. Therefore, the semipositive vector x must indeed be positive. Q.E.D.

THEOREM 15 (*Tucker theorem*) The dual systems

$$A^{\mathrm{T}}y \geqq \theta \qquad \text{and} \qquad Ax = \theta \qquad \text{with} \quad x \geqq \theta \tag{26}$$

possess a pair of solutions y and x such that

$$A^{\mathrm{T}}y + x > \theta. \tag{27}$$

PROOF (i) If $Ax = \theta$ has only the trivial solution $x = \theta$, then by Theorem 13, $A^{\mathrm{T}}y > \theta$ has a solution. Hence (27) is satisfied.

(ii) If $Ax = \theta$ has a positive solution, then by Theorem 14, $A^{\mathrm{T}}y = \theta$. Hence (27) is satisfied.

(iii) We shall show below that when $Ax = \theta$ has a semipositive solution $x \geq \theta$, $\not> \theta$, our assertion holds. In this case, by Theorem 13, $A^{\mathrm{T}}y > \theta$ has no solution. Define a set of integers $J(y) = \{j : [A^{\mathrm{T}}y]_j > 0\}$, where $[A^{\mathrm{T}}y]_j$ stands for the jth component of $A^{\mathrm{T}}y$. Thus $J(y)$ is a subset of $N \equiv \{1, 2, \ldots, n\}$. The number of elements of $J(y)$ will be maximized for some $y = \hat{y}$. If $J(\hat{y}) = \varnothing$ (empty), $A^{\mathrm{T}}y \geqq \theta$ has only trivial solution and, by Theorem 14, $Ax = \theta$ has $x > \theta$. This is the same case as (ii). Note that always $J(\hat{y}) < N$. For, if $J(\hat{y}) = N$, then $A^{\mathrm{T}}\hat{y}$ would be strictly positive, which has been denied. Assume that $J(\hat{y})$ contains k integers $(0 < k < n)$. We have to find a solution $x = \{x_1, \ldots, x_n\}$ of $Ax = \theta$ such that $x_j > 0$ for $j \notin J(\hat{y})$ while $x_i \geqq 0$ for $i \in J(\hat{y})$. We may assume that $J(\hat{y}) = \{1, 2, \ldots, k\}$. A is accordingly partitioned into $A = [C, B]$ where C and B are matrices of dimensions $m \times k$ and $m \times (n - k)$, respectively. x is similarly partitioned into $\{x_C, x_B\}$. It suffices to show that $B^{\mathrm{T}}y \geq \theta$ has no solution, for then $Bx_B = \theta$ has $x_B > \theta$ by Theorem 14. Suppose to the contrary that y satisfies $B^{\mathrm{T}}y \geq \theta$. Recall $B^{\mathrm{T}}\hat{y} = \theta$ and $C^{\mathrm{T}}\hat{y} > \theta$. Define a new vector $\tilde{y} \in E^m$ by

$$\tilde{y} \equiv \mu\hat{y} + y, \qquad \text{where} \quad \mu > \max_{1 \leqq j \leqq k} (-[C^{\mathrm{T}}y]_j/[C^{\mathrm{T}}\hat{y}]_j).$$

Then, $C^{\mathrm{T}}\tilde{y} = \mu C^{\mathrm{T}}\hat{y} + C^{\mathrm{T}}y > \theta$, and $B^{\mathrm{T}}\tilde{y} = \mu B^{\mathrm{T}}\hat{y} + B^{\mathrm{T}}y = B^{\mathrm{T}}y \geq \theta$. Therefore, $J(\tilde{y})$ contains more integers than $J(\hat{y})$, contradicting the definition of $J(\hat{y})$. Q.E.D.

COROLLARY 1 There exists a pair of vectors $x, y \geqq \theta$ such that

$$Ax \leqq \theta, \qquad A^{\mathrm{T}}y \geqq \theta, \qquad y - Ax > \theta, \qquad x + A^{\mathrm{T}}y > \theta. \tag{28}$$

PROOF Apply Theorem 15 to the dual systems

$$[I, A]^{\mathrm{T}}y \geqq \theta \qquad \text{and} \qquad [I, A]\begin{bmatrix} w \\ x \end{bmatrix} = \theta \qquad \text{with} \qquad \begin{bmatrix} w \\ x \end{bmatrix} \geqq \theta.$$

Then there exists a set of solutions such that

$$[I, A]^{\mathrm{T}} y + \begin{bmatrix} w \\ x \end{bmatrix} > 0,$$

i.e., $A^{\mathrm{T}} y + x > 0$ and $y - Ax = y + w > 0$. Q.E.D.

COROLLARY 2 If

$$Ax \leqq 0, \qquad x \geqq 0 \tag{29}$$

have only the trivial solution $x = 0$, then

$$A^{\mathrm{T}} y > 0 \qquad \text{has} \qquad y > 0. \tag{30}$$

PROOF Put $x = 0$ in Corollary 1 above. Q.E.D.

We can show as a corollary to the following theorem that if A is a P-matrix, (30) always holds. (See Definition 9 in Section 1.3 for a P-matrix.)

THEOREM 16 (*Gale–Nikaido, first theorem*) If A is an $n \times n$ P-matrix, then the inequalities (29) have only the trivial solution.

PROOF We proceed by induction on n. For $n = 1$, the statement holds true obviously. Assume that it is true for any principal submatrix, of order $n - 1$, of A. Since A is a P-matrix, the diagonal elements of $A^{-1} \equiv [b_{ij}]$ are all positive. Hence each column of A^{-1}, say its first column vector $b^1 \equiv \{b_{11}, \ldots, b_{n1}\}$, has some positive components. Let $x \equiv \{\xi_1, \ldots, \xi_n\} \geqq 0$ and let

$$\min_{b_{i1}>0} (\xi_i / b_{i1}) \equiv \xi_k / b_{k1} \equiv c.$$

Then $c \geqq 0$, $y \equiv x - cb^1 \equiv \{\eta_1, \ldots, \eta_n\} \geqq 0$, and $\eta_k = 0$. Note that

$$Ay = Ax - cAb^1 = Ax - ce^1 \leqq 0,$$

where $e^1 \equiv \{1, 0, 0, \ldots, 0\}$ (the first unit vector), since $Ax \leqq 0$. Let $\tilde{A}$ be the principal submatrix of A after deleting its kth row and column, and $\tilde{y}$ be the $(n - 1)$-vector obtained from y by deleting its kth component. Then, we have $\tilde{A}\tilde{y} \leqq 0$ and $\tilde{y} \geqq 0$. Since $\tilde{A}$ is a P-matrix, it follows from our induction assumption that $\tilde{y} = 0$. Hence $y = 0$, in view of $\eta_k = 0$. Thus $Ax = ce^1 \geqq 0$, which, combined with $Ax \leqq 0$, yields $Ax = 0$. By the nonsingularity of A, therefore, we have $x = 0$. Q.E.D.

By Theorem 16 and Corollary 2 to Theorem 15, we get the following at once.

COROLLARY 1 If A is a P-matrix, (30) always holds.

Another corollary to Theorem 16 is

COROLLARY 2 If A is a P-matrix, there is a positive scalar m such that for all nonnegative vectors x of a fixed positive norm, some component of Ax is equal to, or larger than, m.

PROOF Let a_i be the ith row of A and $f(x) \equiv \max_i a_i x$. Then $f(x)$ is continuous on a bounded, closed set S of all nonnegative vector x of a fixed positive norm. $f(x)$ can attain a minimum m on the set S. (Refer to Theorem 19 in Section 5.2.) Note that $x \in S$ cannot be null. Thus, by Theorem 16 above, there is some index i for which $a_i x > 0$, and hence m must be positive. Q.E.D.

We shall extend Theorem 16 to the nonlinear case.

THEOREM 17 (*Gale–Nikaido, second theorem*) Let W be a closed rectangular region $\{x : x \in E^n, p \leqq x \leqq q \text{ for } -\infty < p \leqq q < \infty\}$ in E^n, and F be a transformation from W into E^n. Assume that F is differentiable on W and that the Jacobian matrix $J(x)$ of F is a P-matrix for each x in W. Then for any $x, a \in W$,

$$F(x) \leqq F(a), \qquad x \geqq a \tag{31}$$

have only the solution $x = a$.

PROOF Let X be the set of all solutions of (31). Differentiability of F implies

$$\lim_{x \to a} \frac{\|F(x) - F(a) - J(a)(x - a)\|}{\|x - a\|} = 0. \tag{$*$}$$

Since $J(a)$ is a P-matrix, by Corollary 2 to Theorem 16, some component of $J(a)(x - a)/\|x - a\|$ is as great as a positive constant for all $x \geq a$. In view of $(*)$, some component of $F(x) - F(a)$ must be positive, i.e., $F(x) \nleq F(a)$, for all $x \geq a$ in the vicinity of a. In other words, (31) holds only for $x = a$ in the vicinity of a. Thus a is an isolated point of X.

We must show that X contains only the single point $\{a\}$. We proceed by mathematical induction on n of E^n. For the case $n = 1$, by the mean value theorem for functions, there exists some $\beta \in (0, 1)$ such that

$$F(x) - F(a) = F'(x^*)(x - a) \qquad \text{for} \quad x^* = \beta x + (1 - \beta)a.$$

In view of $F'(x^*) > 0$, therefore, the only solution x to inequalities (31) is the point a.

Assuming the result for $n - 1$, we consider the case for n. Suppose that X contains a second point b ($\neq a$) fulfilling (31). Clearly $b \geq a$. Define a bounded set

$$Q = \{x : b \geqq x \geqq a,\ F(x) \leqq F(a)\},$$

and the complement of $\{a\}$ in Q, denoted $Q \setminus \{a\}$, which is not empty because of the inclusion of b and is found to be closed since F is continuous and since a is an isolated point. So there exists a vector $\bar{x}$ in $Q \setminus \{a\}$ such that the sum of its components, as a continuous function, takes a minimum over $Q \setminus \{a\}$. Clearly, there is no other vector x in $Q \setminus \{a\}$ for which $x \leq \bar{x}$. Since $\bar{x} \geq a$, there are only two situations possible: (i) $\bar{x} > a$ and (ii) $\bar{x} \not> a$. It will be shown that either situation entails a contradiction, whereby proving that $X \equiv \{a\}$.

(i) $\bar{x} > a$. Since $J(\bar{x})$ is a P-matrix, by Corollary 1 to Theorem 16, there is a vector $h < \theta$ for which $J(\bar{x})h < \theta$. We can choose a positive number t such that

$$x(t) = \bar{x} + th > a.$$

Thus $\bar{x} > x(t) > a$, so that $x(t)$ lies in W since a and $\bar{x}$ do so. Furthermore, by the differentiability of F, we have

$$F(x(t)) - F(\bar{x}) - tJ(\bar{x})h = o(t\|h\|),$$

and hence

$$\frac{F(x(t)) - F(\bar{x})}{t\|h\|} - \frac{J(\bar{x})h}{\|h\|}$$

can be made as small as we please by letting t approach zero. This implies, in view of $J(\bar{x})h < \theta$, that

$$F(x(t)) < F(\bar{x}) \leqq F(a).$$

Thus we know that $x(t)$ belongs to $Q \setminus \{a\}$, contradicting the minimality of $\bar{x}$ mentioned above.

(ii) $\bar{x} \not> a$. At least one component of $\bar{x} = (\bar{\xi}_i)$ equals the corresponding component of $a = (\alpha_i)$. By renumbering equations and variables simultaneously, we may assume that $\bar{\xi}_1 = \alpha_1$. Define a new differentiable transformation

$$\hat{F}\colon \hat{W} \to E^{n-1}$$

by the formulas

$$\hat{F}(\xi_2, \ldots, \xi_n) = \{\hat{F}_i(\xi_2, \ldots, \xi_n)\}$$

and

$$\hat{F}_i(\xi_2, \ldots, \xi_n) = F_i(\alpha_1, \xi_2, \ldots, \xi_n) \qquad \text{for} \quad i = 2, 3, \ldots, n,$$

where ξ_i denotes the ith component of x and

$$\hat{W} \equiv \{(\xi_2, \ldots, \xi_n) : (\alpha_1, \xi_2, \xi_3, \ldots, \xi_n) \in W\}.$$

The Jacobian matrix of this new transformation is again a P-matrix and

$$\hat{F}_i(\bar{\xi}_2, \ldots, \bar{\xi}_n) \leqq \hat{F}_i(\alpha_2, \ldots, \alpha_n) \qquad \text{for} \quad i = 2, 3, \ldots, n,$$

$$\bar{\xi}_i \geqq \alpha_i \qquad \text{for} \quad i = 2, 3, \ldots, n.$$

Therefore, we have $\bar{\xi}_i = \alpha_i$ $(i = 2, 3, \ldots, n)$ by our induction assumption. This contradicts $\bar{x} \neq a$. Q.E.D.

With the help of Theorem 17, we can easily prove the global univalence theorem.

Application 2 (*proof of the global univalence theorem* (Theorem 17 in Section 7.3)) Let a, b be elements of the closed rectangular region W defined in

Theorem 17 above such that $F(a) = F(b)$. We must show that $a = b$. Let α_i, β_i be the ith components of a, b, respectively, and suppose, after reordering, that

$$\alpha_i \leqq \beta_i \quad \text{for} \quad i \leqq k, \qquad \alpha_i \geqq \beta_i \quad \text{for} \quad i > k.$$

In case $k = n$, we observe that $F(a) = F(b)$ and $a \leqq b$, whence by Theorem 17 we have $a = b$. The case $k = 0$ can be treated likewise. In case $0 < k < n$, define the transformation T_k: $E^n \to E^n$ by

$$T_k(\xi_1, \ldots, \xi_n) = (\xi_1, \ldots, \xi_k, -\xi_{k+1}, \ldots, -\xi_n),$$

where ξ_i stands for the ith component of $x \in E^n$. Then T_k is one-to-one on E^n and $T_k^{-1} = T_k$. Furthermore, the range of T_k over W, denoted $T_k(W)$, is again a closed rectangular region. Denote $a^* \equiv T_k(a)$ and $b^* \equiv T_k(b)$. Let G: $T_k(W) \to E^n$ be the composite transformation defined by $G = T_k F T_k$. Then we know that $a^* \leqq b^*$ and $G(a^*) = G(b^*)$ since

$$G(a^*) = T_k F T_k(a^*) = T_k F(a) = T_k F(b) = G(b^*).$$

Moreover, the Jacobian matrix of G is a P-matrix since it is obtained from that of F by changing the signs of its rows and the corresponding columns simultaneously. Hence by Theorem 17 we have $a^* = b^*$, which implies $a = b$. Q.E.D.

8.3 The von Neumann Economic System and Maximal Paths

As typical dual systems of linear inequalities, we shall study at length the expanding economic model initiated by von Neumann (1937).

Consider an m-commodity economy where there are n activities (or processes), each of which is characterized by a set of factor inputs and a set of production outputs. We represent the jth activity by a pair of two vectors, i.e., input vector a^j and output vector b^j:

$$a^j \equiv \begin{bmatrix} a_{1j} \\ a_{2j} \\ \vdots \\ a_{mj} \end{bmatrix} \quad \text{and} \quad b^j \equiv \begin{bmatrix} b_{1j} \\ b_{2j} \\ \vdots \\ b_{mj} \end{bmatrix}, \tag{32}$$

where a_{ij} stands for the input of commodity i and b_{ij} the output of commodity i per unit of intensity in activity j. Assembling all a^j and b^j for $j = 1, 2, \ldots, n$, we define the input matrix A and the output matrix B as follows:

$$A \equiv [a^1, a^2, \ldots, a^n] = \begin{bmatrix} a_1 \\ \vdots \\ a_m \end{bmatrix}, \qquad B \equiv [b^1, b^2 \ldots, b^n] = \begin{bmatrix} b_1 \\ \vdots \\ b_m \end{bmatrix}, \tag{33}$$

where

$$a_i \equiv (a_{i1}, \ldots, a_{in}), \quad b_i \equiv (b_{i1}, \ldots, b_{in}) \quad \text{for} \quad i = 1, \ldots, m. \tag{34}$$

Note that labor is treated as a commodity, that capital stocks are included in factor inputs, and that capital goods left over after they are employed in production are regarded as outputs.

The following three assumptions are basic:

Inputs and outputs are all nonnegative:

$$a_{ij} \geqq 0, \quad b_{ij} \geqq 0 \qquad \text{for} \quad i = 1, \ldots, m; \quad j = 1, \ldots, n. \tag{35}$$

Each activity contains at least one positive input:

$$a^j \geq 0 \qquad \text{for} \quad j = 1, \ldots, n. \tag{36}$$

Each commodity can be produced by some activity:

$$b_i \geq 0 \qquad \text{for} \quad i = 1, \ldots, m. \tag{37}$$

Let x_j denote the intensity with which activity j is operated and let p_i be the price of commodity i. Define an overall intensity by a column vector $x \equiv \{x_1, x_2, \ldots, x_n\}$, and price vector as $p \equiv (p_1, p_2, \ldots, p_m)$. If something of value is produced in the economy, we have

$$pBx > 0. \tag{38}$$

Two factors are introduced: an expansion factor α and a profit factor β. The former designates one plus an expansion rate when each activity grows at a uniform rate, i.e.,

$$\alpha x(t) = x(t + 1), \tag{39}$$

where t stands for a period in time. Assuming that the output in period t is available for use in period $t + 1$, we have

$$Ax(t + 1) \leqq Bx(t), \tag{40}$$

meaning that the demand for each commodity cannot exceed its availability. If (39) and (40) are combined, we get

$$\alpha Ax \leqq Bx. \tag{41}$$

Profit factor β is supposed to be equal to one plus a uniform rate of profit. If the proceeds from an activity exceed its cost and the profit associated with β, the intensity of the activity will be enhanced to the point where no extra profit accrues. Thus, competition will eventually bring forth the following situation.

$$\beta pA \geqq pB. \tag{42}$$

First, we are interested in finding the largest α and the smallest β such that (41) and (42) hold with semipositive x and p, respectively.

THEOREM 18 Let A, B, x, and p be those defined above, and suppose that the basic assumptions (35)–(37) are satisfied. Then

(i) the set of α satisfying (41) with $x \geq 0$, and the set of β satisfying (42) with $p \geq 0$ are both nonempty.

(ii) There exist a maximum α, denoted α^*, and a minimum β, denoted β^*, in these sets respectively. α^* and β^* are both positive.

(iii) $\alpha^* \geqq \beta^*$.

PROOF (i) We normalize x and p such that the sum of the components of each vector equals unity. Define the set

$$S_\beta \equiv \left\{\beta : p[\beta A - B] \geqq 0 \text{ for some } p \geq 0, \sum_{i=1}^{m} p_i = 1\right\}.$$

If we put $p_i = 1/m$ for all i, then $pA > 0$ in view of (36). Hence for sufficiently large $\beta > 0$, we have $p[\beta A - B] > 0$, implying that S_β is nonempty. Similarly for the nonemptiness of the set S_α defined as

$$S_\alpha \equiv \left\{\alpha : [\alpha A - B]\, x \leqq 0 \text{ for some } x \geq 0, \sum_{j=1}^{n} x_j = 1\right\}.$$

(ii) Let β be an element of S_β and let p qualify for that β in the definition of S_β. Consider the jth component of the resulting vector $p[\beta A - B]$, i.e., $\beta \sum_i p_i a_{ij} - \sum_i p_i b_{ij}$. Summing over j and changing the order of summation yield

$$\beta \sum_i p_i \sum_j a_{ij} \geqq \sum_i p_i \sum_j b_{ij} > 0$$

since $\sum_j b_{ij} > 0$ (in view of (37)) and some p_i is positive. Thus β must be positive. Then it follows that

$$\max_i \frac{\sum_j a_{ij}}{\sum_j b_{ij}} \geqq \frac{\sum_i p_i \sum_j a_{ij}}{\sum_i p_i \sum_j b_{ij}} \geqq \frac{1}{\beta} > 0.$$

Hence $1/\beta$ is bounded above, or β is bounded below by a positive number.

Next we show that S_β is closed. Consider a sequence $\{\beta_t\}$ from S_β convergent to a limit β_0. Let $\{p^t(\beta_t)\}$ be a sequence of p corresponding to $\{\beta_t\}$ such that all elements of $\{p^t(\beta_t)\}$ belong to the closed set $P \equiv \{p : p \geq 0$ and $\sum_{i=1}^m p_i = 1\}$, and let $\{p^{t*}\}$ be a subsequence of $\{p^t(\beta_t)\}$ convergent to $p^0 \in P$. The sequence $\{\beta_t^*\}$ of β corresponding to $\{p^{t*}\}$ must converge to β_0 since otherwise $\{\beta_t\}$ would have two limit points. Thus

$$\lim_{t\to\infty} p^{t*}[\beta_t^* A - B] \quad \text{exists and equals} \quad p^0[\beta_0 A - B] \geqq 0$$

because $p[\beta A - B]$ is continuous in p and β and is nonnegative.

Since S_β is closed and bounded from below, there is a minimum $\beta > 0$ in S_β. Similarly for the existence of α^* in S_α.

(iii) Let $C \equiv B - \alpha^* A$. The inequality $Cx > 0$ has no nonnegative solution, for if x were such a solution, then we would have $\alpha^* Ax < Bx$, or

$$(\alpha^* + \delta)Ax \leqq Bx$$

for some positive δ, so that α^* would not be maximal. Now apply Theorem 12, and we know that there is a $p \geq \theta$ such that $pC \leqq \theta$, or equivalently

$$\alpha^* pA \geqq pB.$$

Thus it follows from the definition of β^* that $\alpha^* \geqq \beta^*$. Q.E.D.

From the above proof of (iii) follows immediately a proposition, which is stated as statement (i) in the following corollary.

COROLLARY (i) For α^* defined above, there is a $p \geq \theta$ such that

$$p[\alpha^* A - B] \geqq \theta.$$

(ii) For β^* defined above, there is an $x \geq \theta$ such that

$$[\beta^* A - B]x \leqq \theta.$$

(The proof of (ii) is left as an exercise for the reader.)

THEOREM 19 There exist semipositive vectors $\tilde{x} \equiv \{\xi_1, \ldots, \xi_n\}$ and $\tilde{p} = (\pi_1, \ldots, \pi_m)$ associated with α^* defined in Theorem 18 such that:

(i) $[\alpha^* A - B]\tilde{x} \leqq \theta$ and $\tilde{p}[\alpha^* A - B] \geqq \theta$;

(ii) $\tilde{p}[\alpha^* A - B]\tilde{x} = 0$; i.e., if $\alpha^* a_i \tilde{x} < b_i \tilde{x}$, then $\pi_i = 0$, and if $\alpha^* \tilde{p} a^j > \tilde{p} b^j$, then $\xi_j = 0$; and

(iii) $\tilde{p} B \tilde{x} > 0$.

PROOF (i) According to Corollary 1 to Theorem 15 (Tucker theorem) in Section 8.2, for any real matrix C there exists a pair of nonnegative vectors x, p such that

$$Cx \leqq \theta, \qquad pC \geqq \theta, \qquad p^{\mathrm{T}} - Cx > \theta, \qquad x^{\mathrm{T}} + pC > \theta. \qquad (*)$$

Put $x = \tilde{x}$, $p = \tilde{p}$, and $C = \alpha^* A - B$. Suppose $\tilde{p} = \theta$. Then we get, from the third inequality in $(*)$, $[\alpha^* A - B]\tilde{x} < \theta$, implying that there can exist an $\alpha > \alpha^*$ in S_α, contradicting the definition of α^*. Hence $\tilde{p}$ cannot be null. Next suppose $\tilde{x} = \theta$. Then it follows from the fourth inequality in $(*)$ that $\tilde{p}[\alpha^* A - B] > \theta$, which is postmultiplied by $x^* \geq \theta$ to entail

$$\tilde{p}[\alpha^* A - B]x^* > 0,$$

where x^* stands for the vector x qualified for α^*, i.e., it satisfies $[\alpha^* A - B]x^* \leqq \theta$. Premultiplying the last inequality by $\tilde{p} \geqq \theta$ yields

$$\tilde{p}[\alpha^* A - B]x^* \leqq 0.$$

But this is impossible. Hence $\tilde{x}$ cannot be null.

(ii) Put $x = \tilde{x}$, $p = \tilde{p}$, and $C = \alpha^* A - B$ in the first two inequalities in $(*)$, premultiply the first inequality by $\tilde{p}$ and postmultiply the second by $\tilde{x}$.

(iii) Rearranging $\tilde{x}$, $\tilde{p}$ such that

$$\tilde{x} = \begin{bmatrix} \tilde{x}_1 \\ \tilde{x}_2 \end{bmatrix} \qquad \text{and} \qquad \tilde{p} = [\tilde{p}_1, \tilde{p}_2],$$

where $\tilde{x}_1 > \theta$, $\tilde{x}_2 = \theta$, $\tilde{p}_1 > \theta$, $\tilde{p}_2 = \theta$. Rearranging A and B conformably, we rewrite the equation in (ii) as

$$[\tilde{p}_1, \tilde{p}_2] \begin{bmatrix} \alpha^* A_{11} - B_{11}, & \alpha^* A_{12} - B_{12} \\ \alpha^* A_{21} - B_{21}, & \alpha^* A_{22} - B_{22} \end{bmatrix} \begin{bmatrix} \tilde{x}_1 \\ \tilde{x}_2 \end{bmatrix} = 0,$$

and hence

$$\tilde{p}_1[\alpha^* A_{11} - B_{11}]\, \tilde{x}_1 = 0. \tag{**}$$

If $\tilde{p}B\tilde{x} = 0$, then $\tilde{p}_1 B_{11} \tilde{x}_1 = 0$ and hence $B_{11} = 0$ in view of $\tilde{p}_1 > \theta$ and $\tilde{x}_1 > \theta$. Then (**) implies $A_{11} = 0$. On the other hand, it follows from the third inequality in (*) that if $\tilde{p}_2 = \theta$ then $C_2 \tilde{x} < \theta$, where C_2 is the submatrix consisting of the rows of C corresponding to $\tilde{p}_2$. Therefore,

$$[\alpha^* A_{21} - B_{21}]\, \tilde{x}_1 < \theta.$$

Thus, in view of $A_{11} = B_{11} = 0$, we can pick an $\alpha > \alpha^*$ in S_α, contradicting the definition of α^*. Hence $\tilde{p}B\tilde{x}$ cannot be zero. Q.E.D.

We can similarly prove

THEOREM 19′ There exist semipositive vectors x^0, p^0 associated with β^* defined in Theorem 18 such that:

(i) $[\beta^* A - B]x^0 \leqq \theta$ and $p^0[\beta^* A - B] \geqq \theta$;
(ii) $p^0[\beta^* A - B]x^0 = 0$; and
(iii) $p^0 B x^0 > 0$.

The expression

$$p[\gamma A - B]x = 0 \tag{43}$$

can be interpreted as an identity in national accounting. Let $\gamma \equiv 1 + r$ (r, profit rate), $A \equiv K + D + W$ (K, capital coefficient matrix; D, current account input coefficient and depreciation matrix; and W, laborers' consumption matrix), and $B \equiv Q + K$ (Q, current output coefficient matrix). Then (43) may be rewritten as

$$p[Q - D]x = rpAx + pWx, \tag{43′}$$

where the left-hand side represents net national product; the first term on the right denotes profits and the second term wages.

We guess from Theorem 19 and Theorem 19′ that there are several pairs of semipositive vectors x, p satisfying

$$\gamma Ax \leqq Bx, \qquad \gamma pA \geqq pB, \qquad \text{and} \qquad pBx > 0, \tag{44}$$

for different values of the factor γ. (43) follows at once. We refer to $x, p \geq \theta$

satisfying (44) as the economic solutions to $\gamma A - B$. Our next concern is the relationship between the economic solutions and the factor γ. Theorem 19 implies that α^* is the maximum possible factor for which economic solutions exist, and Theorem 19′ implies that β^* is the minimum possible factor for which economic solutions exist. If there are semipositive vectors x, p and a nonnegative scalar γ satisfying (44), the triplet (x, p, γ) may be termed a von Neumann equilibrium.

Let us interpret our problem in terms of matrix game theory. A matrix game refers to a two-person, zero-sum game where players I and II control the rows and columns, respectively, of an $m \times n$ payoff matrix $A = [a_{ij}]$. Define two strategy sets of $p = (p_1, \ldots, p_m)$ and $x = \{x_1, \ldots, x_n\}$ (refer to Fig. 7):

$$P \equiv \left\{p : p \in E^m, \sum_{i=1}^{m} p_i = 1, p_i \geqq 0 \quad (i = 1, \ldots, m)\right\},$$

$$X \equiv \left\{x : x \in E^n, \sum_{j=1}^{n} x_j = 1, x_j \geqq 0 \quad (j = 1, \ldots, n)\right\},$$

and denote by $K(p, x)$ the payoff for player I when strategies p, x are chosen:

$$K(p, x) = pAx = \sum_{j=1}^{n} \sum_{i=1}^{m} a_{ij} p_i x_j. \tag{45}$$

Because of the zero-sum assumption, $-K(p, x)$ is the payoff for player II.

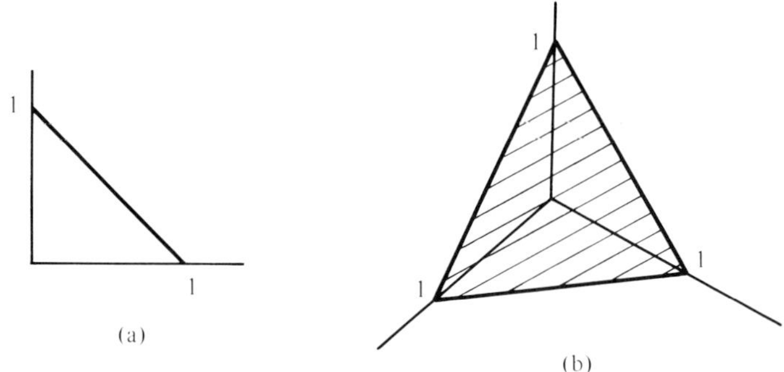

FIGURE 7. (a) P or X in case $m = n = 2$; (b) P or X in case $m = n = 3$.

If player I chooses strategy p, the minimum possible payoff that he gains for any strategy x adopted by player II will be

$$f(p) = \min_{x \in X} K(p, x), \tag{46}$$

and the minimum possible payoff for player II, when he chooses strategy x, is

$$g(x) = \min_{p \in P} [-K(p, x)] = \max_{p \in P} K(p, x). \tag{47}$$

Note that the last term in (47) can be regarded as the maximum possible loss for player II in case he chooses x. Suppose that player I tries to maximize the minimum possible payoff $f(p)$ and player II tries to minimize the maximum possible loss $g(x)$ by maneuvering their own strategies p, x respectively. Since f and g are continuous functionals on bounded, closed sets P and X, respectively, they achieve a maximum and a minimum on these sets. Denote

$$v_1 = \max_{p \in P} f(p), \tag{48}$$

$$v_2 = \min_{x \in X} g(x). \tag{49}$$

Then we know at once that

$$v_1 \leqq v_2 \tag{50}$$

since (46) and (47) imply

$$f(p) \leqq K(p, x) \leqq g(x) \qquad \text{for} \quad p \in P, \quad x \in X. \tag{51}$$

We shall show that in fact $v_1 = v_2$ for any payoff matrix A. In general, if $v_1 = v_2$ holds, the game is said to be *strictly determined* and v $(\equiv v_1)$ is termed the *value* of the game. $p^0 \in P$ such that $K(p^0, x) \geqq v$ for all $x \in X$ is called an *optimal strategy* for player I, and $x^0 \in X$ such that $K(p, x^0) \leqq v$ for all $p \in P$ is said to be an optimal strategy for player II.

LEMMA 2 A matrix game is strictly determined, i.e., $v_1 = v_2$.

PROOF It suffices to show that $v_1 \geqq v_2$ in view of (50). For the game with payoff matrix $A = [a_{ij}]$, $f(p)$ and $g(x)$ are reduced to the following, with (45) taken into consideration,

$$f(p) = \min_{1 \leqq j \leqq n} \sum_{i=1}^{m} a_{ij} p_i, \tag{46$'$}$$

$$g(x) = \max_{1 \leqq i \leqq m} \sum_{j=1}^{n} a_{ij} x_j. \tag{47$'$}$$

Because of (48), therefore, there is no solution $p \in P$ such that

$$v_1 < \sum_{i=1}^{m} a_{ij} p_i \qquad \text{for all} \quad j = 1, \ldots, n.$$

Thus, the subset $\tilde{K}$ of E^n defined as

$$\tilde{K} = \{k : k = pA - v_1 e,\ p \in P\},$$

where $e \equiv (1, 1, \ldots, 1) \in E^n$, contains no interior point of E^n_+. Furthermore, $\tilde{K}$ is found to be convex since for $k^1, k^2 \in \tilde{K}$ and $\alpha \in [0, 1]$,

$$\begin{aligned} \alpha k^1 + (1 - \alpha)k^2 &= \alpha(p^1 A - v_1 e) + (1 - \alpha)(p^2 A - v_1 e) \\ &= (\alpha p^1 + (1 - \alpha) p^2)A - v_1 e, \end{aligned}$$

where $\alpha p^1 + (1 - \alpha)p^2$ belongs to P for $p^1, p^2 \in P$, in view of the fact that P

is a convex set. Hence, according to Theorem 7 in Section 8.1, there is a closed hyperplane

$$H \equiv \{h : h \in E^n, (h \mid y) = 0\} \qquad \text{for some} \quad y \leq \theta$$

such that H separates $\tilde{K}$ from E^n_+ and

$$(k \mid y) \geqq 0 \qquad \text{for all} \quad k \in \tilde{K}.$$

Multiplying y by an appropriate negative value ν, we have

$$\hat{x} \equiv \nu y = (\hat{x}_1, \ldots, \hat{x}_n) \in X,$$

satisfying $(k \mid \hat{x}) \leqq 0$ for $k \in \tilde{K}$. Thus, for any $p \in P$,

$$pA\hat{x} - v_1 = (pA \mid \hat{x}) - v_1(e \mid \hat{x}) = (pA - v_1 e \mid \hat{x}) \leqq 0,$$

implying that

$$g(\hat{x}) \equiv \max_i \sum_j a_{ij}\hat{x}_j \leqq v_1.$$

(Cf. (47′).) On the other hand, $g(\hat{x}) \geqq v_2$ by virtue of (49). Hence we get $v_1 \geqq v_2$. Q.E.D.

Remark Rewriting $f(p)$, $g(x)$ as $K(p, x^0)$, $K(p^0, x)$, respectively, we have

$$K(p^*, x^0) \equiv \max_{p \in P} f(p) = \min_{x \in X} g(x) \equiv K(p^0, x^*).$$

Although there is no reason that $p^* = p^0$ and $x^* = x^0$ should always hold, we must have $p^* = p^0$ and $x^* = x^0$ when the game is determined. Then

$$K(p, x^0) \leqq K(p^0, x^0) \leqq K(p^0, x) \qquad \text{for} \quad p \in P, x \in X, \tag{52}$$

where $K(p^0, x^0)$ stands for the value of a matrix game. The pair (p^0, x^0) is called the *saddle-point solution* to functional K if (52) holds. (See Fig. 8.)

Henceforth, *matrix game A* refers to a matrix game with payoff matrix A where the maximizing player I controls its rows and the minimizing player

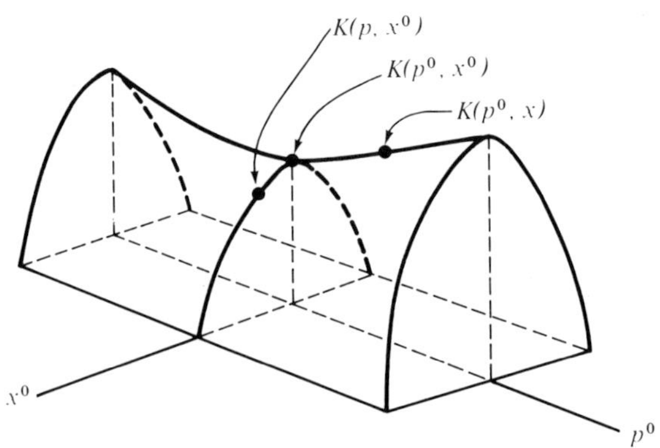

FIGURE 8. Saddle point $K(p^0, x^0)$.

II controls its columns, and the strategies under control of players I, II are restricted to P, X respectively. Also we denote by $v(A)$ the value of matrix game A.

LEMMA 3 Let A, B be the matrices defined in (33), and assume that conditions (35)–(37) are satisfied. Then

$$v(A) > 0 \qquad \text{and} \qquad v(-B) < 0. \tag{53}$$

PROOF Letting $f(p)$ denote the minimum payoff that player I expects when he chooses p, we have from (48) and (46′)

$$v(A) = \max_{p \in P} f(p) = \max_{p \in P} \min_{j} \sum_{i} a_{ij} p_i.$$

Let $\sum_i a_{ik} p_i = \min_j \sum_i a_{ij} p_i \geqq 0$, and by setting p_h equal to one for h such that a_{hk} is the largest among the a_{ik}, we get $a_{hk} = \max_{p \in P} \sum_i a_{ik} p_i$. a_{hk} is positive if condition (36) holds.

A procedure similar to the above verifies that $v(-B) < 0$. We shall sketch the procedure:

$$v(-B) = \min_{x \in X} g(x) = \min_{x \in X} \max_{i} \sum_{j} (-b_{ij})\, x_j,$$

where $g(x)$ denotes the maximum possible loss that player II expects when he chooses strategy x. Let

$$\sum_{j} (-b_{gj})\, x_j = \max_{i} \sum_{j} (-b_{ij})\, x_j.$$

Then $-b_{gk} \equiv \min_{x \in X} \sum_j (-b_{gj}) x_j$, which is negative if condition (37) holds. Q.E.D.

Let us rewrite the first two inequalities in (44) as

$$C_\gamma x \leqq 0, \qquad pC_\gamma \geqq 0, \tag{44′}$$

where $C_\gamma \equiv \gamma A - B$. Considering C_γ as a matrix game, we see clearly that the value $v(C_\gamma)$ of the game equals zero if (44′) holds. The $\gamma \geqq 0$ for which inequalities (44′) hold for some $p \in P$ and $x \in X$ is called an *allowable* γ in C_γ, and the p and x are said to be *optimal* in C_γ. Note that for an allowable γ in C_γ and the associated p and x

$$pC_\gamma x = 0. \tag{54}$$

THEOREM 20 Assume that conditions (35)–(37) are satisfied. Then there is at least one positive allowable γ in C_γ, and $pBx > 0$ for p and x associated with the γ.

PROOF Assuming that γ is nonnegative, we multiply C_γ by $1/(1 + \gamma)$. Then the inequalities in (44′) change to

$$C_k x \leqq 0, \qquad pC_k \geqq 0, \tag{44″}$$

where $C_k \equiv kA - (1 - k)B$ and $k \equiv \gamma/(1 + \gamma)$ with $0 \leqq k < 1$. We search for k such that (44″) holds for some $x \in X$ and $p \in P$. The value $v(C_k)$ of matrix game C_k is a continuous function of k. Since $A \geqq 0$ and $B \geqq 0$, $v(C_k)$ is a monotone increasing function of k. By our assumption and Lemma 3,

$$v(C_0) = v(-B) < 0 \qquad \text{and} \qquad v(C_1) = v(A) > 0.$$

By continuity there exists at least one k, $0 < k < 1$, such that $v(C_k) = 0$, or equivalently at least one positive γ such that $v(C_\gamma) = 0$. Let p^*, x^* be vectors associated with such a γ. Then, in view of (45), (48), (51), (53), and (54),

$$p^* B x^* = \gamma p^* A x^* \geqq \gamma v_1 = \gamma v(A) > 0. \qquad \text{Q.E.D.}$$

LEMMA 4 Let γ^1 and γ^2 ($> \gamma^1$) be two distinct allowable values in C_γ. Then any $\gamma \in [\gamma^1, \gamma^2]$ is allowable in C_γ. Furthermore, if p^1 is an optimal strategy in matrix game C_{γ^1} and x^2 is an optimal strategy in matrix game C_{γ^2}, then the pair (p^1, x^2) is optimal in matrix game C_γ for any $\gamma \in [\gamma^1, \gamma^2]$.

PROOF Since p^1 is an optimal strategy,

$$p^1 C_{\gamma^1} x \geqq v(C_{\gamma^1}) = 0 \qquad \text{for all} \quad x \in X.$$

Hence $p^1 C_{\gamma^1} \geqq \theta$. For $\gamma \geqq \gamma^1$, therefore,

$$p^1 C_\gamma = p^1 C_{\gamma^1} + p^1(\gamma - \gamma^1) A \geqq \theta. \tag{1*}$$

Thus we have

$$p^1 C_\gamma x \geqq 0 \qquad \text{for all} \quad x \in X. \tag{2*}$$

Similarly, for $\gamma \leqq \gamma^2$, we have

$$C_\gamma x^2 = C_{\gamma^2} x^2 + (\gamma - \gamma^2) A x^2 \leqq \theta, \tag{3*}$$

and

$$p C_\gamma x^2 \leqq 0 \qquad \text{for all} \quad p \in P. \tag{4*}$$

From (1*) and (3*), we can say that $\gamma \in [\gamma^1, \gamma^2]$ is an allowable value in C_γ. (2*) and (4*) imply that (p^1, x^2) is optimal in matrix game C_γ for any $\gamma \in [\gamma^1, \gamma^2]$. Q.E.D.

THEOREM 20′ Assume that conditions (35)–(37) are satisfied. Then there are at most $\min(m, n)$ allowable γ's for which economic solutions to C_γ exist, where m, n are the dimensions of matrix B.

PROOF By Theorem 20, there is a positive allowable γ for which economic solutions (p, x) to C_γ exist, i.e., $pBx > 0$, implying that

$$\gamma p a^j x_j = p b^j x_j > 0 \qquad \text{for some } j.$$

This, in turn, implies $pa^j > 0$ and $p_i b_{ij} x_j > 0$ for some i, j. Let γ^1, γ^2 ($> \gamma^1$) be two distinct allowable values in C_γ, and let (p_i, x_j), (p_h, x_k) be the pairs of components of the economic solutions (p, x) corresponding to γ^1, γ^2, respectively, such that

$$p_i b_{ij} x_j > 0 \qquad \text{and} \qquad p_h b_{hk} x_k > 0. \tag{5*}$$

We shall show that $i \neq h$ and $j \neq k$. Suppose to the contrary that $j = k$. By Lemma 4, there is an optimal p in matrix game C_γ for $\gamma \in [\gamma^1, \gamma^2]$, implying that

$$pC_{\gamma^1}^j \geqq 0 \qquad \text{and} \qquad pC_{\gamma^2}^j \geqq 0 \qquad \text{for} \quad j = 1, \ldots, n,$$

where C_γ^j stands for the jth column of C_γ. Now

$$pC_{\gamma^2}^k = pC_{\gamma^2}^j = pC_{\gamma^1}^j + (\gamma^2 - \gamma^1)\, pa^j > 0$$

since the second term on the right-hand side of the equation is positive. Hence we must have $x_k = 0$ in view of the fact that $pC_{\gamma^2}^k x_k = 0$, contradicting (5*). Thus $j \neq k$. Similarly for $i \neq h$.

Since to each allowable γ for which economic solutions exist there corresponds a positive component b_{ij} of B, and since the indices of any two such b components corresponding to different allowable γ's are pairwise distinct, it is clear that the maximum number of such allowable γ's is equal to $\min(m, n)$. Q.E.D.

So far we observe that α^* and β^* defined in Theorem 18 are the largest and the smallest allowable factors, respectively, among possible allowable values in C_γ. Next we shall show that if the model described above is irreducible, then a unique allowable factor exists, i.e., $\alpha^* = \beta^*$.

DEFINITION 4 Consider the model $[A, B]$, where A, B are the matrices in (33) satisfying conditions (35)–(37). The model is said to be *reducible* if there exist subsets $M_1, M_2\ (\neq \varnothing)$ of index set $M = \{1, 2, \ldots, m\}$ and subsets N_1, N_2 of index set $N = \{1, 2, \ldots, n\}$ such that

$$M_1 \cup M_2 = M, \qquad M_1 \cap M_2 = \varnothing, \qquad N_1 \cup N_2 = N, \qquad N_1 \cap N_2 = \varnothing,$$

that $a_{ij} = 0$ for every $i \in M_2$ and $j \in N_1$, and that for each $i \in M_1$, $b_{ij} > 0$ for some $j \in N_1$; in other words, if it is possible to produce each good $i_1 \in M_1$ without consuming any good $i_2 \in M_2$. If there is no proper subset M_1 of M that satisfies the above requirements, we say that the model $[A, B]$ is *irreducible.*

THEOREM 21 (Gale, 1960) Assume conditions (35)–(37) are satisfied. If the model $[A, B]$ is irreducible, then $\alpha^* = \beta^*$, where α^*, β^* are those defined in Theorem 18.

PROOF Since $\alpha^* \geqq \beta^*$ by Theorem 18, it suffices to verify that $\alpha^* \leqq \beta^*$. By the same theorem, there exist $x \geq \theta$ such that $\alpha^* Ax \leqq Bx$ and $p \geq \theta$ such that $\beta^* pA \geqq pB$. Therefore,

$$\alpha^* pAx \leqq pBx \leqq \beta^* pAx. \tag{6*}$$

Let M_1 be $\{i : b_i x > 0\}$. By taking N_1 as $\{j : x_j > 0\}$, we must have $a_{ij} = 0$

for every $i \in M_2$ and $j \in N_1$ since otherwise we would get some $i \in M_2$ for which $a_i x > 0$ and $b_i x = 0$, and hence we could not have $\alpha^* a_i x \leqq b_i x$ for all $i \in M$. Now from the irreducibility assumption, $M_2 = \varnothing$ follows, whence $Bx > \theta$. Since $p \geq \theta$, $pBx > 0$, implying $pAx > 0$ and hence $\alpha^* \leqq \beta^*$ in view of (6*). Q.E.D.

A consequence of Theorem 21 is that any von Neumann system with more than one allowable factor must be reducible. However, the converse is not true, i.e., that von Neumann system be structurally reducible is not sufficient for the economy to have more than one allowable factor, as the reader may easily check by constructing an example.

An important model in which the allowable factor γ in (44) exists uniquely is the nonjoint production case, provided by Morishima (1961), where each activity produces only one commodity; i.e., the output matrix B takes the form

$$B = \begin{bmatrix} 1 & \cdots & 1 & 0 & \cdots & 0 & \cdots & 0 & \cdots & 0 \\ 0 & \cdots & 0 & 1 & \cdots & 1 & & \vdots & & \vdots \\ & & & 0 & \cdots & 0 & & & & \\ \vdots & & \vdots & \vdots & & \vdots & & 0 & \cdots & 0 \\ \underbrace{0 \quad \cdots \quad 0}_{n_1} & & & \underbrace{0 \quad \cdots \quad 0}_{n_2} & & & & \underbrace{1 \quad \cdots \quad 1}_{nm} & & \end{bmatrix} \tag{55}$$

where nj is an integer no less than one and $n1 + n2 + \cdots + nm = n$. Conformably with the above definition of B, the input matrix A is rewritten as

$$A = [a^{11}, \ldots, a^{n1}, a^{12}, \ldots, a^{n2}, \ldots, a^{1m}, \ldots, a^{nm}], \tag{56}$$

where a^{ij} denotes the input vector associated with activity ij of industry j. Let $A_s \equiv [a^{s1}, a^{s2}, \ldots, a^{sm}]$ stand for any $m \times m$ matrix whose jth column represents an input vector available to industry j. The number of all possible such nonnegative matrices is $n1 \times n2 \times \cdots \times nm$. Consider the system (44) with matrices B, A specified as in (55), (56) respectively, and assume (a) there is a unique indecomposable square matrix A_e among all the above A_s matrices such that $\lambda_e < \lambda_s$, where λ_e and λ_s denote the Frobenius roots of A_e and A_s, respectively. Then, the left and right eigenvectors p_e and $x_e^* \equiv (x_{e1}^*, \ldots, X_{em}^*)$ of A_e associated with $\lambda_e\,(> 0)$ are both positive. Define a column n-vector x_e as

$$\text{the } ij\text{th component of } x_e = \begin{cases} x_{ej}^* & \text{if } \; ij = ej, \\ 0 & \text{if } \; ij \neq ej. \end{cases}$$

Note that

$$\lambda_e p_e = p_e A_e, \qquad Bx_e = x_e^*, \qquad \lambda_e x_e^* = A_e x_e^* = Ax_e. \tag{7*}$$

THEOREM 22 (Morishima, 1961) The above specified system (44) with assumption (a) has a solution such that $x = x_e$, $p = p_e$, and $\gamma = 1/\lambda_e$. Furthermore, if (x, p, γ) is a triplet satisfying the system (44), then $x = c_x x_e$, $p = c_p p_e$, and $\gamma = 1/\lambda_e$, where c_x and c_p are positive scalars; i.e., the von Neumann equilibrium is unique in the sense that the equilibrium output and price rays are uniquely determined, associated with a unique allowable factor.

PROOF Let A_f be a matrix A_s that does not contain any of the activities in A_e. To begin, we establish

$$\lambda_e p_e < p_e A_f. \tag{8*}$$

Suppose, to the contrary, that some components of $\lambda_e p_e$, say the first k components, are greater than or equal to the corresponding components of $p_e A_f$. Replacing the first k columns of A_e by those of A_f, we get A_g such that

$$\lambda_e p_e \geqq p_e A_g.$$

Then, letting λ_g ($\geqq 0$) be the Frobenius root of A_g, and x_g^* ($\geq \theta$) be the associated right eigenvector, we have

$$\lambda_e p_e x_g^* \geq p_e A_g x_g^* = \lambda_g p_e x_g^* \geqq 0,$$

contradicting $\lambda_e < \lambda_g$. Hence (8*) must hold true.

From (7*) and (8*), it follows that

$$\lambda_e p_e B \leqq p_e A, \qquad \lambda_e B x_e = A x_e, \qquad \text{and} \qquad p_e B x_e = p_e x_e^* > 0, \tag{9*}$$

which imply that $(x_e, p_e, 1/\lambda_e)$ is a von Neumann equilibrium.

Let (x, p, γ) be a triplet satisfying our system (44), i.e., x and p are semipositive vectors and γ is a nonnegative scalar satisfying (44). Then, taking (9*) into account, we have

$$\gamma p_e A x \leqq p_e B x \leqq p_e A x/\lambda_e, \tag{10*}$$

$$\gamma p A x_e \geqq p B x_e = p A x_e/\lambda_e. \tag{11*}$$

Since $p_e A > \theta$ (cf. (36)) and $pAx_e = \lambda_e p B x_e > 0$ (cf. $Bx_e = x_e^* > \theta$), (10*) implies $\gamma \leqq 1/\lambda_e$ and (11*) implies $\gamma \geqq 1/\lambda_e$. Hence $\gamma = 1/\lambda_e$.

Once $\gamma = 1/\lambda_e$ is established, the inequality in (11*) holds with equality. This means $\lambda_e p x_e^* = p A_e x_e^*$ in view of (7*), or

$$\lambda_e p = p A_e \tag{12*}$$

since $x_e^* > \theta$. A_e is indecomposable and hence p in (12*) must be positive and proportionate to p_e ($> \theta$), i.e., $p = c_p p_e$ for some $c_p > 0$. Similarly (10*) holds with equality, i.e., $\lambda_e p_e B x = p_e A x$, which together with (8*) implies that the ijth component of x must be zero if $ij \neq ej$, and hence Bx is equal to $y_e^* \equiv \{y_{e1}^*, \ldots, y_{em}^*\}$ such that $Ax = A_e y_e^*$. Since $p_e > \theta$, we get

$$\lambda_e y_e^* = A_e y_e^*. \tag{13*}$$

Indecomposability of A_e guarantees that y_e^* in (13*) is positive and proportionate to x_e^*, i.e., $y_e^* = c_x x_e^*$ for some $c_x > 0$. Thus $x = c_x x_e$. Q.E.D.

We conclude this section with a brief introduction to a maximal path in von Neumann balanced growth equilibria. Let us define a triplet (y, p, γ) as a von Neumann equilibrium if there is a nonnegative (indeed, positive) γ for which x, p are semipositive vectors such that

$$\gamma Ax \leqq \gamma y \leqq Bx, \qquad \gamma pA \geqq pB, \qquad pBx > 0. \tag{44†}$$

This definition implies the relations in (44) and $py > 0$. The set of all feasible pairs of input vector y and output vector z in our von Neumann economy will be defined as

$$Y = \{\{y, z\} : y \geqq Ax,\ \ z \leqq Bx \text{ for some } x \in E_+^n\}. \tag{57}$$

This set Y is found to be a convex polyhedral cone with vertex at the origin in E_+^{2m}, with $\{a^i, b^i\}$, $i = 1, \ldots, n$, being its extreme points since they are supposed to be all independent and efficient, where a^i, b^i are as in (32).

The set of the price vectors (p, q) that yield nonpositive profit to each activity with reference to Y is

$$Y^\# = \{(p, q) : py \geqq qz \text{ for all } \{y, z\} \in Y\}, \tag{58}$$

which is a closed convex cone in view of Theorem 8 in Section 8.1 since $Y^\#$ can be redefined as

$$Y^\# = \{(p, q) : (p, q \mid y, -z) \geqq 0 \text{ for all } \{y, -z\} \in Y_-\},$$

where Y_- stands for the convex polyhedral cone

$$Y_- = \{\{y, -z\} : y \geqq Ax,\ z \leqq Bx \text{ for some } x \in E_+^n\}.$$

Since $\{y, \theta\} \in Y$ for any $y \geqq \theta$, $(p, q) \in Y^\#$ implies that p is nonnegative. Given a price vector $(p, q) \in Y^\#$,

$$F(p, q) = \{\{y, z\} : \{y, z\} \in Y \text{ and } py = qz\} \tag{59}$$

represents the set of input and output vectors for which neither profit nor loss is obtained. Clearly, $F(p, q)$ is a convex cone with vertex at the origin. If the triplet (y, p, γ) is a von Neumann equilibrium mentioned above, then

$$\{y, \gamma y\} \in F(\gamma p, p) \qquad \text{and} \qquad py > 0.$$

Let $P\gamma$ be the set of p that appear in a von Neumann equilibrium with γ, and define the von Neumann facet for γ as

$$F\gamma = \bigcap_{p \in P\gamma} F(\gamma p, p), \tag{60}$$

which is a convex cone.

For a fixed target output vector $\bar{y} = \{\bar{y}_1, \ldots, \bar{y}_m\} \geq \theta$, we try to have as large an output in as close proportion to $\bar{y}$ as possible at a given end point τ in time. This can be done by maximizing the function

$$\eta(y(\tau)) \equiv \min_i \,(y_i(\tau)/\bar{y}_i) \qquad \text{for} \quad i \text{ such that } \bar{y}_i > 0, \tag{61}$$

where $y(\tau) = \{y_1(\tau), \ldots, y_m(\tau)\}$ stands for a final-state output vector. A τ-period path $(y(0), y(1), \ldots, y(\tau))$ is said to be feasible if

$$(y(t), y(t+1)) \in Y \qquad \text{for} \quad t = 0, 1, \ldots, \tau - 1, \tag{62}$$

and the path is said to be maximal with respect to $\bar{y}$ if it is feasible and if for any other feasible path $(z(0), z(1), \ldots, z(\tau))$ with $z(0) = y(0)$, $\eta(y(\tau)) \geqq \eta(z(\tau))$.

Theorem 23 below provides a criterion that must be satisfied by maximal paths; i.e., if a path stays outside a prescribed vicinity of $F\gamma$ for more than some finite number of periods, then it will not be able to be maximal. We use the following definitions:

$$\begin{aligned} d(z, w) &\equiv \left\| \frac{z}{\|z\|} - \frac{w}{\|w\|} \right\| && \text{for} \quad z, w \neq \theta \quad \text{(with Euclidean norm);} \\ &= 1 && \text{for} \quad z = \theta \text{ or } w = \theta. \end{aligned} \tag{63}$$

$$d(z, F\gamma) \equiv \inf_{w \in F\gamma} d(z, w). \tag{63'}$$

THEOREM 23 (*Radner–McKenzie theorem*) Let (y^*, p^*, γ) be a von Neumann equilibrium and let $(y(0), \ldots, y(\tau))$ be a maximal path with respect to $\bar{y}$ where $\bar{y}_i > 0$ implies $y_i^* > 0$ and $p^*\bar{y} > 0$. Then for any $\delta > 0$, there is a positive integer τ_1 such that the number of periods in which

$$d(\{y(t), y(t+1)\}, F\gamma) > \delta$$

cannot exceed τ_1.

(The reader should refer to McKenzie (1967) for the proof of Theorem 23 as well as for related topics.)

The maximal path in terms of y may be redefined in terms of x. In view of (57), (62), and (61), given the initial endowment $y(0)$ and a semipositive target vector $\bar{y}$, the maximal path $(y(0), \ldots, y(\tau))$ with $y(t) \geqq \theta$ for all t must satisfy

$$y(t-1) \geqq Ax(t),\ y(t) \leqq Bx(t) \quad \text{for some} \quad x(t) \geqq \theta, \quad t = 1, \ldots, \tau; \tag{62'}$$

and maximize

$$\eta \equiv \min_i \,(y_i(\tau)/\bar{y}_i) \qquad \text{for} \quad i \text{ such that } \bar{y}_i > 0. \tag{61'}$$

It follows from (61′) that $\eta\bar{y} \leqq y(\tau)$. Thus, by virtue of (62′), the maximal path can be redefined in terms of x; i.e. the $(x(1), \ldots, x(\tau))$ satisfying the problem: Maximize $\eta \geqq 0$ subject to

$$\begin{aligned} &Ax(1) \leqq y(0), && Ax(t+1) \leqq Bx(t) && \text{for} \quad t = 1, 2, \ldots, \tau - 1, \\ &\eta\bar{y} \leqq Bx(\tau), && x(t) \geqq \theta && \text{for} \quad t = 1, 2, \ldots, \tau. \end{aligned}$$

Since η is nonnegative, the maximand can be multiplied by an arbitrary positive scalar ρ without any effect on the solution to the above maximum problem, which can then be restated as

Problem (M) Maximize $\rho\eta \geqq 0$ subject to

$$\begin{bmatrix} A & 0 & 0 & \cdots & 0 & \theta \\ -B & A & 0 & & 0 & \theta \\ 0 & -B & A & & \vdots & \vdots \\ \vdots & & & \ddots & 0 & \theta \\ 0 & \cdots & 0 & -B & A & \theta \\ 0 & \cdots & 0 & 0 & -B & \bar{y} \end{bmatrix} \begin{bmatrix} x(1) \\ x(2) \\ \vdots \\ \\ x(\tau) \\ \eta \end{bmatrix} \leqq \begin{bmatrix} y(0) \\ \theta \\ \vdots \\ \\ \theta \\ \theta \end{bmatrix} \tag{64}$$

and

$$\{x(1), \ldots, x(\tau), \eta\} \geqq \theta,$$

where 0 denotes a zero matrix and θ is a column zero vector. The scalar ρ in Problem (M) is set equal to λ_e^τ in relation to the maximal path in the nonjoint production case as assumed in Theorem 22. (Refer to Section 8.5 for further discussion.)

For other theoretical developments of the von Neumann expanding economy, the reader may refer to Koopmans (1964), Morishima (1969), and articles in Bruckmann and Weber (1971) and in Łoś and Łoś (1974).

8.4 Kuhn–Tucker Theorems, Concave and Quasi-Concave Programming

This section is devoted to Kuhn–Tucker (K-T) theorems and the related concave and quasi-concave programming. To prove K-T theorems we start with a rather general theorem, which is useful also for generalizations of K-T theorems.

THEOREM 24 Let f be a real-valued functional on Euclidean n-space E^n and G a transformation from E^n into E^m and assume that f and G have partial derivatives on E^n. If x^0 is a finite point in E^n such that

$$G(x^0) \leqq \theta \qquad \text{and} \qquad G(x^0) + G'(x^0)h < \theta \qquad \text{for some } h \in E^n, \tag{65}$$

where $G'(x^0)$ is the Jacobian matrix of G at x^0, and

$$f(x^0) \geqq f(x) \qquad \text{for any } x \in E^n \qquad \text{satisfying } G(x) \leqq \theta, \tag{66}$$

then there exists a nonnegative vector $y^0 \in E^m$ such that the Lagrangian function

$$L(x, y^0) \equiv f(x) - y^0 G(x)$$

is stationary at x^0, i.e.,

$$L_x(x^0, y^0) \equiv f'(x^0) - y^0 G'(x^0) = \theta, \tag{67}$$

where $f'(x^0)$ denotes the gradient of f at x^0. Furthermore,

$$L_y(x^0, y^0)y^0 \equiv y^0 G(x^0) = 0. \tag{68}$$

PROOF Define the following sets in $E^1 \times E^m$:

$$K_1 = \{k : k = (s, z),\ s \geqq 0,\ z \leqq \theta,\ z \in E^m\},$$
$$K_2 = \{k : k = (r, y),\ r \leqq f'(x^0)h,\ y \geqq G(x^0) + G'(x^0)h \text{ for some } h \in E^n\}.$$

K_1 is obviously a convex cone with vertex at $(0, \theta)$. K_2 is a convex cone with vertex at $k^0 = (0, G(x^0))$ because K_2 is clearly convex and because $\alpha r \leqq f'(x^0)\alpha h$, $\alpha(y - G(x^0)) \geqq G'(x^0)\alpha h$ for any nonnegative scalar α, implying that if $c \equiv (r, y - G(x^0)) \in C$, then $\alpha c \in C$, where C is a cone. We shall show that K_2 does not contain any interior point of K_1. Suppose to the contrary that $(r, y) \in K_2$ with $r > 0$, $y < \theta$. Then there exists $h \in E^n$ such that $f'(x^0)h > 0$, $G^0 \equiv G(x^0) + G'(x^0)h < \theta$. Let E^m_- be the negative orthant of E^m. There exists an open sphere in E^m_- centered at G^0 with some positive radius ρ. Then, for $\beta \in (0, 1)$, βG^0 is the center of an open sphere of radius $\beta\rho$ contained in E^m_-. Since $(1 - \beta)G(x^0) \leqq \theta$, $G(x^0) + G'(x^0)\beta h = (1 - \beta)G(x^0) + \beta G^0 < \theta$. By the definition of the differential of G, we have for a fixed $h \in E^n$

$$\|G(x^0 + \beta h) - G(x^0) - G'(x^0)\beta h\| = o(\beta).$$

Hence, for a sufficiently small $\beta > 0$, we get $G(x^0 + \beta h) \leqq \theta$. For the same h and β, we have, in view of $f'(x^0)h > 0$ and by the definition of the differential of f,

$$f(x^0 + \beta h) - f(x^0) > 0 \qquad \text{with} \quad G(x^0 + \beta h) \leqq \theta,$$

which contradicts (66).

Since K_1, K_2 are convex sets in $E^1 \times E^m$ such that K_1 has interior points and K_2 contains no interior point of K_1, by the separation theorem (Theorem 6) there is a closed hyperplane separating K_1 and K_2; i.e., there exists nonzero $(\sigma, \lambda) \in E^1 \times E^m$ such that

$$s\sigma + (z \mid \lambda) \leqq \delta \qquad \text{for all} \quad (s, z) \in K_1, \tag{69}$$

$$r\sigma + (y \mid \lambda) \geqq \delta \qquad \text{for all} \quad (r, y) \in K_2. \tag{70}$$

Since $(0, \theta)$ belongs to both K_1 and K_2, $\delta = 0$. Then it follows from (69) that $\sigma \leqq 0$ and $\lambda \geqq \theta$. Furthermore, σ cannot be zero, or else it follows from (70) that

$$(y \mid \lambda) \geqq 0 \qquad \text{for all} \quad y \geqq G(x^0) + G'(x^0)h \quad \text{for any } h \in E^n;$$

in particular $(G(x^0) + G'(x^0)h \mid \lambda) \geqq 0$ for any $h \in E^n$. However, λ is semipositive and $G(x^0) + G'(x^0)h < 0$ for some $h \in E^n$. (See (65).) Thus $(G(x^0) + G'(x^0)h \,|\, \lambda) < 0$ for some $h \in E^n$, which is a contradiction. Therefore, σ is negative. Define $y^0 \equiv -\lambda/\sigma$.

In view of the definition of K_2 and of inequality (70) where $\sigma < 0$ and $\delta = 0$, we have

$$f'(x^0)h \leqq (G(x^0) + G'(x^0)h \,|\, y^0) \qquad \text{for all} \quad h \in E^n. \tag{71}$$

Putting $h = 0$ in (71) yields

$$(G(x^0) \,|\, y^0) \geqq 0. \tag{72}$$

On the other hand, $G(x^0) \leqq 0$ and $y^0 \geqq 0$ imply

$$(G(x^0) \,|\, y^0) \leqq 0. \tag{73}$$

From (72) and (73) it follows that $(G(x^0) \,|\, y^0) = 0$, or equivalently $y^0 G(x^0) = 0$. Then, from (71), we obtain

$$L_x(x^0, y^0)h = [f'(x^0) - y^0 G'(x^0)]h \leqq 0 \qquad \text{for all} \quad h \in E^n.$$

For a fixed $h \in E^n$, $L_x(x^0, y^0)\alpha h \geqq 0$ for any $\alpha < 0$, while $L_x(x^0, y^0)\alpha h \leqq 0$ for the same α, since $\alpha h \in E^n$. This implies (67). Q.E.D.

COROLLARY 1 (*Kuhn–Tucker necessity theorem for maximum problems*) Consider the problem:

$$\text{Maximize } f(x) \qquad \text{subject to} \quad G(x) \leqq 0 \text{ and } x \geqq 0, \tag{74}$$

where $f\colon E^n \to E^1$ and $G\colon E^n \to E^m$; f, G have partial derivatives. If x^0 is a finite maximizer fulfilling a condition termed a *constraint qualification*:

$$G(x^0) + G'(x^0)h < 0 \qquad \text{for some} \quad h > -x^0, \tag{75}$$

then there exists a nonnegative vector $y^0 \in E^m$ for which

$$L_x(x^0, y^0) = f'(x^0) - y^0 G'(x^0) \leqq 0, \tag{76}$$

$$L_y(x^0, y^0)y^0 = y^0 G(x^0) = 0, \tag{77}$$

$$L_x(x^0, y^0)x^0 = [f'(x^0) - y^0 G'(x^0)]x^0 = 0, \tag{78}$$

where $L_x(\cdot)$ and $L_y(\cdot)$ designate the gradients of the following Lagrangian function with respect to x and y, respectively:

$$L(x, y) \equiv f(x) - yG(x). \tag{79}$$

PROOF The constraints in problem (74) are expressed as

$$F(x) \equiv \begin{bmatrix} G(x) \\ -x \end{bmatrix} \leqq 0, \qquad F\colon E^n \to E^{m+n}.$$

Then, condition (75) is equivalent to

$$F(x^0) + F'(x^0)h < 0, \qquad \text{where} \quad F'(x^0) \equiv \begin{bmatrix} G'(x^0) \\ -I \end{bmatrix}.$$

Thus, by Theorem 24, there exists a nonnegative vector $(y^0, w^0) \in E^m \times E^n$ such that

$$f'(x^0) - (y^0, w^0)F'(x^0) = \theta, \tag{80}$$

$$(y^0, w^0)F(x^0) = 0. \tag{81}$$

(76) follows immediately from (80). Since $y^0G(x^0) \leqq 0$ and $w^0x^0 \geqq 0$, (81) implies $y^0G(x^0) = w^0x^0 = 0$. Finally,

$$[f'(x^0) - y^0G'(x^0)]x^0 = [f'(x^0) - y^0G'(x^0) + w^0]x^0 = 0. \qquad \text{Q.E.D.}$$

Remark $y^0G(x^0) = 0$, together with $y^0 \geqq \theta$ and $G(x^0) \leqq \theta$, imply that $y_j^0 = 0$ if $G(x^0)_j < 0$, and that $G(x^0)_j = 0$ if $y_j^0 > 0$, where y_j^0, $G(x^0)_j$ stand for the jth components of y^0, $G(x^0)$, respectively. Similarly, (76), (78), and $x^0 \geqq \theta$ imply that the derivative of the Lagrangian (79) (evaluated at the maximum) with respect to x_i, the ith component of x, must vanish if $x_i^0 > 0$ and that $x_i^0 = 0$ if the derivative takes on a negative value.

COROLLARY 2 (*Kuhn–Tucker necessity theorem for minimum problems*) Let y^* be an optimal solution to the problem:

$$\text{Minimize } \psi(y) \qquad \text{subject to} \quad H(y) \geqq \theta \text{ and } y \geqq \theta, \tag{82}$$

where ψ: $E^m \to E^1$ and H: $E^m \to E^n$; ψ, H have partial derivatives on E^m. Assume y^* is a finite minimizer fulfilling a constraint qualification:

$$H(y^*) + H'(y^*)q > \theta \qquad \text{for some } q > -y^*. \tag{83}$$

Then there exists a nonnegative vector $x^* \in E^n$ for which

$$\Lambda_y(x^*, y^*) = \psi'(y^*) - x^*H'(y^*) \geqq \theta, \tag{84}$$

$$\Lambda_x(x^*, y^*)x^* = x^*H(y^*) = 0, \tag{85}$$

$$\Lambda_y(x^*, y^*)y^* = [\psi'(y^*) - x^*H'(y^*)]y^* = 0, \tag{86}$$

where $\Lambda_x(\cdot)$, $\Lambda_y(\cdot)$ represent the gradients of the following Lagrangian function with respect to x, y, respectively:

$$\Lambda(x, y) \equiv \psi(y) - xH(y). \tag{87}$$

(The verification is easy in view of Corollary 1.)

For a related theorem on necessary optimality conditions in the presence of equality and inequality constraints, refer to Mangasarian and Fromovitz (1967) and Mangasarian (1969).

Now we define a concave mapping whose limited form is a concave functional as introduced in Section 7.2.

DEFINITION 5 Let F be a transformation from E^n into E^m with domain D. If the domain D is a convex subset of E^n and if

$$\alpha F(x) + (1 - \alpha)F(x^0) \leqq F(\alpha x + (1 - \alpha)x^0) \tag{88}$$

for any x, $x^0 \in D$ and $\alpha \in [0, 1]$, then F is said to be a *concave mapping* on D.

If the inequality sign in (88) is reversed, then F will be a *convex mapping*. Furthermore, if strict inequality holds in (88) for any $\alpha \in (0, 1)$ whenever $x \neq x^0$, F is said to be a *strictly concave mapping*. Similarly, we can define a *strictly convex mapping*.

If F is a concave mapping on a convex subset D of E^n having Jacobian matrix $F'(x^0)$ at $x^0 \in D$, then

$$F(x) - F(x^0) \leqq F'(x^0)(x - x^0) \qquad \text{for} \quad x \in D. \tag{89}$$

Conversely, if (89) holds for each x^0, $x \in D$, F is concave as in Theorem 9 of Section 7.2. Similarly, F is a differentiable convex mapping on a convex subset D of E^n if and only if

$$F(x) - F(x^0) \geqq F'(x^0)(x - x^0) \qquad \text{for} \quad x,\ x^0 \in D. \tag{90}$$

It should be noted that if F is a concave mapping from E^n into E^m with convex domain D, then the set

$$C_y \equiv \{x : x \in D,\ F(x) \geqq y\} \qquad \text{for each } y \in E^m$$

is convex because for x^1, $x^2 \in C_y$ we have

$$x^* = \alpha x^1 + (1 - \alpha)x^2 \in D \qquad \text{for} \quad \alpha \in [0, 1],$$

and

$$F(x^*) \geqq \alpha F(x^1) + (1 - \alpha)F(x^2) \geqq \alpha y + (1 - \alpha)y = y.$$

Likewise, if F is a convex mapping from E^n into E^m with convex domain D, then the set

$$V_y \equiv \{x : x \in D,\ F(x) \leqq y\} \qquad \text{for each } y \in E^m$$

is convex.

We remark also that when f is a concave functional and G is a convex mapping on a convex subset D of E^n,

$$L(x, y^0) \equiv f(x) - y^0 G(x) \qquad \text{for} \quad y^0 \geqq \theta$$

is a concave functional on D, and that when f and G are a convex functional and a concave mapping, respectively, on a convex subset D of E^n,

$$L(x, y^0) \equiv f(x) - y^0 G(x) \qquad \text{for} \quad y^0 \geqq \theta$$

is a convex functional on D.

We are in a position to verify a Kuhn–Tucker theorem easily.

THEOREM 25 (*Kuhn–Tucker, second theorem*) Let f be a real-valued concave functional on a convex set $K \subset E^n_+ \equiv \{x : x \in E^n,\ x \geqq \theta\}$, and let $G: E^n \to E^m$ be a convex mapping on K, both being differentiable on K. Consider the problem:

$$\text{Maximize} \quad f(x) \qquad \text{subject to} \quad G(x) \leqq \theta \text{ and } x \in K \subset E^n_+. \tag{91}$$

(i) Assume that there exists a positive $x^1 \in K$ for which $G(x^1) < \theta$. If x^0 is an optimal solution, which is finite, of this maximum problem, then there exists a $y^0 \in E^m_+$ such that (76)–(78) hold.

(ii) Conversely, the existence of $y^0 \in E^m_+$ satisfying (76)–(78) with $x^0 \in K$ is sufficient for x^0 to be a finite optimal solution of the maximum problem above. (The assumption in (i) may be termed a strong *Slater condition.*)

PROOF (i) By our assumption on G and x^1, we have

$$G(x^0) + G'(x^0)(x^1 - x^0) \leqq G(x^1) < \theta,$$

which fulfills condition (75) in Corollary 1 to Theorem 24.

(ii) Since f is a differentiable concave functional on K,

$$f'(x^0)(x - x^0) \geqq f(x) - f(x^0) \qquad \text{for} \quad x, x^0 \in K;$$

and since G is a differentiable convex mapping on K,

$$G'(x^0)(x - x^0) \leqq G(x) - G(x^0) \qquad \text{for} \quad x, x^0 \in K.$$

Thus, for a nonnegative $y^0 \in E^m$, we have

$$[f'(x^0) - y^0G'(x^0)](x - x^0) \geqq f(x) - f(x^0) - y^0[G(x) - G(x^0)],$$

or in view of (77) and (78),

$$f(x^0) + [f'(x^0) - y^0G'(x^0)]x \geqq f(x) - y^0G(x).$$

Taking (76) into account, therefore, we know that for $G(x) \leqq \theta$ and $x \geqq \theta$,

$$f(x^0) \geqq f(x^0) + [f'(x^0) - y^0G'(x^0)]x \geqq f(x) - y^0G(x) \geqq f(x). \quad \text{Q.E.D.}$$

A symmetric proposition below can be proved similarly.

COROLLARY Let ψ be a real-valued convex function on a convex set $S \subset E^m_+$, and let $H: E^m \to E^n$ be a concave mapping on S, both differentiable on S. Consider the problem:

$$\text{Minimize} \quad \psi(y) \qquad \text{subject to} \quad H(y) \geqq \theta \text{ and } y \in S \subset E^m_+. \tag{92}$$

(i) Assume that there exists a positive $y^1 \in S$ for which $H(y^1) > \theta$. If y^* is an optimal solution to this minimum problem, then there exists an $x^* \in E^n_+$ such that (84)–(86) hold.

(ii) Conversely, the existence of $x^* \in E^n_+$ satisfying (84)–(86) with $y^* \in S$ is sufficient for y^* to be an optimal solution of the minimum problem above.

Application 3 Consider a quadratic programming problem:

$$\text{Maximize} \quad cx - \tfrac{1}{2}x^{\mathrm{T}}Qx \qquad \text{subject to} \qquad Ax \leqq b \text{ and } x \geqq \theta, \tag{91$'$}$$

where $x \in E^n_+$ to be determined, c is $1 \times n$, b is $m \times 1$, A is $m \times n$, and Q is $n \times n$ symmetric and positive semidefinite. $x^{\mathrm{T}}Qx$ is a convex functional on E^n_+ since for $x, z \in E^n_+$ and $\alpha \in (0, 1)$,

$$\begin{aligned}(1-\alpha)x^{\mathrm{T}}Qx+\alpha z^{\mathrm{T}}Qz &= x^{\mathrm{T}}Qx+\alpha x^{\mathrm{T}}Q(z-x)+\alpha(z-x)^{\mathrm{T}}Qx\\&\quad+\alpha(z-x)^{\mathrm{T}}Q(z-x)\\&\geqq x^{\mathrm{T}}Qx+\alpha x^{\mathrm{T}}Q(z-x)+\alpha(z-x)^{\mathrm{T}}Qx\\&\quad+\alpha^2(z-x)^{\mathrm{T}}Q(z-x)\\&=\{x+\alpha(z-x)\}^{\mathrm{T}}Q\,\{x+\alpha(z-x)\}\\&=\{(1-\alpha)x+\alpha z\}^{\mathrm{T}}Q\,\{(1-\alpha)x+\alpha z\}.\end{aligned}$$

Hence $cx-\frac{1}{2}x^{\mathrm{T}}Qx$ is a concave functional on E_{+}^{n}. Assume that there is a positive $x\in E_{+}^{n}$ for which $Ax<b$ and that the maximizer x^0 to the problem (91′) is finite. By Theorem 25(i), there is a $y^0\in E_{+}^{m}$ such that

$$c-x^{0\mathrm{T}}Q-y^0A\leqq\theta,\qquad y^0(Ax^0-b)=0,\qquad (c-x^{0\mathrm{T}}Q-y^0A)x^0=0,$$

since $\partial(cx)/\partial x=c^{\mathrm{T}}$, $\partial(x^{\mathrm{T}}Qx)/\partial x=2Qx$, and $\partial(Ax)/\partial x=A$.

A generalization of a Kuhn–Tucker theorem is given next.

THEOREM 26 Let f be a real-valued differentiable concave functional on a convex subset K of E^n and let G: $E^n\to E^m$ be a differentiable convex mapping on K. Assume that there exists an $x^1\in K$ for which $G(x^1)<\theta$. x^0 is a maximizer of $f(x)$ over K subject to $G(x)\leqq\theta$ if and only if there exists a $y^0\in E_{+}^{m}$ satisfying the saddle-point condition

$$L(x^0,y)\geqq L(x^0,y^0)\geqq L(x,y^0)\qquad\text{for}\quad x\in K,\quad y\in E_{+}^{m},\tag{93}$$

where $L(x,y)\equiv f(x)-yG(x)$. (Note that the sufficiency does not require differentiable concavity and convexity of f and G, respectively.)

PROOF *Necessity* By assumption,

$$G(x^0)+G'(x^0)(x^1-x^0)\leqq G(x^1)<\theta.$$

Hence, by Theorem 24, there is a $y^0\geqq\theta$ such that

$$L_x(x^0,y^0)=f'(x^0)-y^0G'(x^0)=\theta\qquad\text{and}\qquad y^0G(x^0)=0.$$

Since $L(x,y^0)$ is concave on K for $y^0\geqq\theta$,

$$L(x,y^0)-L(x^0,y^0)\leqq L_x(x^0,y^0)\,(x-x^0)=0\qquad\text{for}\quad x\in K,$$

and

$$L(x^0,y)-L(x^0,y^0)=-\,yG(x^0)\geqq0\qquad\text{for}\quad y\in E_{+}^{m}.$$

Sufficiency (93) implies

$$yG(x^0)\leqq y^0G(x^0)\qquad\text{for}\quad y\in E_{+}^{m}.\tag{$*$}$$

Thus,

$$\begin{aligned}&(y^1+y^0)G(x^0)\leqq y^0G(x^0)\qquad\text{for}\quad y^1\geqq\theta\\&\Rightarrow y^1G(x^0)\leqq0\Rightarrow G(x^0)\leqq\theta\Rightarrow y^0G(x^0)\leqq0.\end{aligned}$$

On the other hand, setting $y = \theta$ in (*) above, we get $0 \leqq y^0 G(x^0)$. Therefore, $y^0 G(x^0) = 0$. Assume $G(x) \leqq \theta$. Then, for $y^0 \in E_+^m$,

$$f(x^0) = L(x^0, y^0) \geqq L(x, y^0) = f(x) - y^0 G(x) \geqq f(x). \qquad \text{Q.E.D.}$$

LEMMA 5 Let f be a real-valued differentiable concave functional defined on a convex subset K of E^n. A sufficient condition for $x^0 \in K$ to maximize f over K is that

$$f'(x^0)x \leqq 0 \qquad \text{for all} \quad x \in K, \tag{94}$$

and

$$f'(x^0)x^0 = 0. \tag{95}$$

PROOF Since f is concave, $f(x) - f(x^0) \leqq f'(x^0)(x - x^0)$ for $x, x^0 \in K$. Hence, (94) and (95) ensure $f(x) - f(x^0) \leqq 0$. Q.E.D.

THEOREM 26′ (*Kuhn–Tucker, third theorem*) Let f be a real-valued differentiable concave functional on a convex subset K of E_+^n and let $G: E^n \to E^m$ be a differentiable convex mapping on K. Assume that there exists a positive vector $x^1 \in K$ for which $G(x^1) < \theta$. Then, a necessary and sufficient condition for $x^0 \in K$ to satisfy

$$f(x^0) \geqq f(x) \qquad \text{subject to} \qquad G(x) \leqq \theta \quad \text{and} \quad x \in K,$$

is that there exists a $y^0 \in E_+^m$ satisfying the saddle-point condition (93)

$$L(x^0, y) \geqq L(x^0, y^0) \geqq L(x, y^0) \qquad \text{for} \quad x \in K, \quad y \in E_+^m,$$

where $L(x, y) \equiv f(x) - yG(x)$. (Note that the sufficiency does not require differentiable concavity and convexity of f and G, respectively.)

PROOF *Necessity* By our assumption on G and x^1, we have

$$G(x^0) + G'(x^0)(x^1 - x^0) \leqq G(x^1) < \theta,$$

which fulfills condition (75) in Corollary 1 to Theorem 24. Hence, there exists $y^0 \in E_+^m$ such that (76)–(78) hold. Conditions (76) and (78) correspond to (94) and (95), respectively, and the Lagrangian functional L is concave on K. Thus, by Lemma 5,

$$L(x^0, y^0) \geqq L(x, y^0) \qquad \text{for} \quad x \in K.$$

Condition (77) ensures

$$L(x^0, y) - L(x^0, y^0) = -yG(x^0) \geqq 0 \qquad \text{for} \quad y \in E_+^m.$$

The proof of sufficiency is the same as that of Theorem 26. Q.E.D.

If constraints change, the optimal solution will shift accordingly. The following theorem provides a rule for this kind of shift in solution.

THEOREM 27 (*sensitivity theorem*) Let f be a real-valued differentiable concave functional on a convex set $K \subset E^n$ and let $G: E^n \to E^m$ be a differentiable convex mapping on K. Assume that there exists some $x \in K$ for which $G(x) < \theta$, and that for given $z \in E^m$ there exists some $x \in K$ for which $G(x) - z < \theta$. Suppose x^0 is a finite optimal solution to the problem

$$\text{Maximize } f(x) \qquad \text{subject to} \quad G(x) \leqq \theta \text{ and } x \in K \subset E^n; \tag{91*}$$

and suppose x^1 is a finite optimal solution to the problem

$$\text{Maximize } f(x) \qquad \text{subject to} \quad G(x) - z \leqq \theta \text{ and } x \in K. \tag{96}$$

Let $y^0, y^1 \in E_+^m$ be the Lagrange multipliers associated with these problems (91*), (96) respectively. Then we have

$$y^0 z \geqq f(x^1) - f(x^0) \geqq y^1 z. \tag{97}$$

PROOF Since x^0 is a maximizer to problem (91*), by Theorem 26,

$$f(x^0) - y^0 G(x^0) \geqq f(x) - y^0 G(x) \qquad \text{for} \quad x \in K.$$

Setting $x = x^1$ and taking accout of $y^0 G(x^0) = 0$, we have

$$f(x^1) - f(x^0) \leqq y^0 G(x^1) \leqq y^0 z.$$

Similarly, since x^1 is a maximizer to problem (96),

$$f(x^1) - y^1[G(x^1) - z] \geqq f(x) - y^1[G(x) - z] \qquad \text{for} \quad x \in K.$$

Setting $x = x^0$ and taking account of $y^1[G(x^1) - z] = 0$, we have

$$f(x^1) - f(x^0) \geqq y^1 z - y^1 G(x^0) \geqq y^1 z. \qquad \text{Q.E.D.}$$

Remark $(y^1 - y^0)z \leqq 0$ derived from (97) may be termed the *LeChatelier principle*. (Refer to Leblanc and Moeseke (1976), Eichhorn and Oettli (1972) and Kusumoto (1977) for further developments of this subject.)

Next we turn to the study of the duality relations corresponding to the maximum problem (91*). Define a functional F on the set

$$Z \equiv \{z : z \in E^m, G(x) \leqq z \quad \text{for some } x \in K \subset E^n\}$$

by the formula

$$F(z) \equiv \max\{f(x) \text{ subject to } G(x) \leqq z, x \in K \subset E^n\}. \tag{98}$$

Since $F(z)$ is nondecreasing,

$$\max\{f(x) \text{ subject to } G(x) \leqq \theta, x \in K\} \leqq F(z) \qquad \text{for} \quad z \geqq \theta.$$

Letting x^0 denote the optimal solution to the maximum problem (91*), therefore, we know that

$$f(x^0) = \min_{z \geqq \theta} F(z). \tag{99}$$

Corresponding to the primal functional F above, we define the dual functional ψ on E_+^m by

$$\psi(y) \equiv \max_{x \in K}\{f(x) - yG(x)\}. \tag{100}$$

ψ is found to be a convex functional since for $y^1, y^2 \in E_+^m$ and $\alpha \in [0, 1]$,

$$\begin{aligned}\psi(\alpha y^1 + (1-\alpha)y^2) &= \max_K \{f(x) - \alpha y^1 G(x) - (1-\alpha)y^2 G(x)\} \\ &= \max_K \{\alpha(f(x) - y^1G(x)) + (1-\alpha)(f(x) - y^2G(x))\} \\ &\leqq \alpha\psi(y^1) + (1-\alpha)\psi(y^2).\end{aligned}$$

Imposing concavity on f and convexity on G, we have the following.

THEOREM 28 (*duality theorem*) Let f be a real-valued concave functional on a convex subset K of E^n, and let $G\colon E^n \to E^m$ be a convex mapping on K, both being differentiable on K. Assume that there is some $x^1 \in E^n$ for which $G(x^1) < \theta$ and that $f(x^0) \equiv \max\{f(x) \text{ subject to } G(x) \leqq \theta,\ x \in K\}$ is finite. Then

$$f(x^0) = \min_{y \geqq \theta} \psi(y) \equiv \psi(y^0), \tag{101}$$

and x^0 maximizes $f(x) - y^0G(x)$ for $x \in K$.

PROOF For $y \geqq \theta$,

$$\begin{aligned}\max_{x\in K}\{f(x) - yG(x)\} &\geqq \max_{x\in K}\{f(x) - yG(x) \text{ subject to } G(x) \leqq \theta\} \\ &\geqq \max_{x\in K}\{f(x) \text{ subject to } G(x) \leqq \theta\}.\end{aligned}$$

Thus we get

$$\min_{y\geqq\theta} \psi(y) \geqq f(x^0).$$

By Theorem 24, there exists $y^0 \geqq \theta$ for which $y^0G(x^0) = 0$ and $f'(x) - y^0G'(x) = \theta$; $f(x) - y^0G(x)$, as a concave functional on K, achieves a maximum at x^0, in view of Lemma 5. Hence

$$f(x^0) \equiv \max_{x\in K}\{f(x) \text{ subject to } G(x) \leqq \theta\} = \max_{x\in K}\{f(x) - y^0G(x)\} = \psi(y^0).$$

Q.E.D.

Under the assumptions in Theorem 28, therefore, we obtain the optimal value $f(x^0)$ of the objective function for the maximum problem (91*) by solving the following dual problem:

$$\min_{y\geqq\theta}\max_{x\in K}\{f(x) - yG(x)\}. \tag{102}$$

Since

$$\max_{x\in K}\{f(x) - yG(x)\} \geqq f(x) - yG(x) \geqq f(x) \qquad \text{for} \quad G(x) \leqq \theta, \quad y \geqq \theta,$$

if the primal problem (91*) has the optimal value $f(x^0) = +\infty$, then the dual problem must be essentially infeasible. Also from (101) it follows that

$$\min_{y\geqq\theta}\psi(y) = f(x^0) \geqq \{f(x) \text{ subject to } G(x) \leqq \theta,\ x \in K\}.$$

Hence if the optimal value to the dual problem is $-\infty$, the primal problem is infeasible.

Application 3′ The dual problem corresponding to the quadratic programming problem (91′) in Application 3 is

$$\min_{y \geqq \theta} \max_{x \geqq \theta} g(x, y), \tag{102′}$$

where $g(x, y) \equiv cx - \frac{1}{2}x^{\mathrm{T}}Qx - y(Ax - b)$, which is a concave functional on E_{+}^{n} for each $y \geqq \theta$. Thus, the maximizer $x \geqq \theta$ of $g(x, y)$ needs only satisfy

$$g_x(x, y) = c - x^{\mathrm{T}}Q - yA = \theta \qquad \text{for each} \quad y \geqq \theta. \tag{103}$$

Substituting (103) into (102′) yields an alternative form of the dual problem:

$$\min_{y \geqq \theta} \{\tfrac{1}{2}x^{\mathrm{T}}Qx + yb\} \qquad \text{for any } x \geqq \theta \qquad \text{satisfying (103)}. \tag{104}$$

If Q is positive definite, we have from (103)

$$x^{\mathrm{T}} = (c - yA)Q^{-1},$$

which is substituted into the minimand of (104) to entail

$$\begin{aligned} \tfrac{1}{2}x^{\mathrm{T}}Qx + yb &= \tfrac{1}{2}(c - yA)Q^{-1}(c - yA)^{\mathrm{T}} + yb \\ &= \tfrac{1}{2}yBy^{\mathrm{T}} + yd + \tfrac{1}{2}cQ^{-1}c^{\mathrm{T}}, \end{aligned}$$

where $B \equiv AQ^{-1}A^{\mathrm{T}}$ and $d \equiv b - AQ^{-1}c^{\mathrm{T}}$. Thus the variable x has been eliminated from the minimand. Hence the dual problem reduces to

$$\min_{y \geqq \theta} \{\tfrac{1}{2}yBy^{\mathrm{T}} + yd\} + \tfrac{1}{2}cQ^{-1}c^{\mathrm{T}}. \tag{105}$$

Since Q^{-1} is positive definite, B is at least positive semidefinite. Therefore, the minimand of (105) is convex. (Cf. Theorem 11 in Section 7.2.)

Now we introduce the concept of quasi-concave mappings, which leads to quasi-concave programming.

DEFINITION 6 Let F be a transformation from E^n into E^m with a convex set $D \subset E^n$ as its domain. If

$$F(x) \geqq F(x^0) \qquad \text{implies} \qquad F(\alpha x + (1 - \alpha)x^0) \geqq F(x^0), \tag{106}$$

or equivalently

$$F(\alpha x + (1 - \alpha)x^0) \geqq \min\,[F(x), F(x^0)], \tag{106′}$$

with equality only when $x = x^0$, for any $\alpha \in [0, 1]$ and $x, x^0 \in D$, then F is said to be a *quasi-concave mapping* on D. If

$$F(x) \leqq F(x^0) \qquad \text{implies} \qquad F(\alpha x + (1 - \alpha)x^0) \leqq F(x^0), \tag{107}$$

or equivalently

$$F(\alpha x + (1 - \alpha)x^0) \leqq \max[F(x), F(x^0)], \tag{107′}$$

with equality only when $x = x^0$, for any $\alpha \in [0, 1]$ and $x, x^0 \in D$, then F is said to be a *quasi-convex mapping* on D. A *quasi-concave functional* F is a quasi-concave transformation F mapping E^n into E^1. Furthermore, if strict inequality holds in (106) or (107), i.e., if

$$F(x) \geqq F(x^0) \qquad \text{implies} \qquad F(\alpha x + (1-\alpha)x^0) > F(x^0), \tag{108}$$

or

$$F(x) \leqq F(x^0) \qquad \text{implies} \qquad F(\alpha x + (1-\alpha)x^0) < F(x^0), \tag{109}$$

for any $\alpha \in (0, 1)$ and $x, x^0 \in D$ with $x \neq x^0$, then F is said to be a *strictly quasi-concave mapping* on D or a *strictly quasi-convex mapping* on D, respectively.

If F is quasi-concave, then $-F$ is quasi-convex, and vice versa.

Any concave mapping is a quasi-concave mapping, but the converse is not true generally. (For cases where the converse holds true, refer to Newman (1969) and to Cox (1973).)

If F is a quasi-concave mapping on a convex set $D \subset E^n$ having Jacobian matrix $F'(x^0)$ at $x^0 \in D$, then from (106)

$$F(x) \geqq F(x^0) \qquad \text{implies} \qquad F'(x^0)(x - x^0) \geqq \theta \qquad \text{for} \quad x \in D; \tag{110}$$

and for a differentiable quasi-convex mapping F on D, from (107)

$$F(x) \leqq F(x^0) \qquad \text{implies} \qquad F'(x^0)(x - x^0) \leqq \theta \qquad \text{for} \quad x \in D, \tag{111}$$

since $F'(x^0)(x - x^0) = \lim_{\alpha \to 0} [F(x^0 + \alpha(x - x^0)) - F(x^0)]/\alpha$ for $\alpha \in (0, 1)$ and $x, x^0 \in D$ with $x \neq x^0$. For a strictly quasi-concave (or strictly quasi-convex) mapping F, (110) (or (111)) holds with strict inequalities. Clearly, the converse holds true.

Examples (1) Any monotonic function of one variable is quasi-concave. (2) Any linear transformation is quasi-concave. (3) Nonlinear functionals defined on E_+^n such as a utility function or prduction function are supposed to be quasi-concave in economics.

THEOREM 29 (Arrow and Enthoven, 1961) Let f be a real-valued quasi-concave functional on E_+^n and let $G\colon E^n \to E^m$ be a quasi-concave mapping on E_+^n, both being differentiable on E_+^n. Consider the problem:

$$\text{Maximize } f(x) \qquad \text{subject to} \quad G(x) \geqq \theta \text{ and } x \in E_+^n. \tag{91''}$$

$x^0 \in E_+^n$ with $G(x^0) \geqq \theta$ is a finite optimal solution to this problem if there exists $y^0 \in E_+^m$ such that

$$f'(x^0) + y^0 G'(x^0) \leqq \theta, \tag{76'}$$

$$y^0 G(x^0) = 0, \tag{77'}$$

$$[f'(x^0) + y^0 G'(x^0)]x^0 = 0, \tag{78'}$$

and if one of the following conditions (a)–(d) is satisfied:

(a) f is concave on E_+^n;
(b) $f_i^0 \equiv (\partial f/\partial x_i)|_{x=x^0} < 0$ for at least one index i;
(c) $f_j^0 \equiv (\partial f/\partial x_j)|_{x=x^0} > 0$ for some index j such that $x_j^* > 0$ for $x^* \in E_+^n$, $G(x^*) \geqq \theta$;
(d) $f'(x^0) \neq \theta$ and f is twice differentiable in a neighborhood of x^0.

Conditions (76′)–(78′) are also necessary for x^0 to be a finite optimal solution to problem (91″), provided

(e) $G(x^*) > \theta$ for a positive $x^* \in E^n$

and provided either one of the following conditions is satisfied:

(a′) G is concave on E_+^n;
(b′) every row of $G'(x)$ is nonzero for each $x \in E_+^n$ with $G(x) \geqq \theta$.

The set of conditions (e) and (a′) together with the differentiability of G or the set of conditions (e) and (b′) together with the differentiability and quasi-concavity of G makes up a constraint qualification (abbreviated as CQ). The first CQ is designated as CQ1 and the second as CQ2.

PROOF Taking (76′), (78′), and $y^0 \geqq \theta$, (77′), (110) into account in the first and second terms, respectively, on the right-hand side of the identity

$$f'(x^0)(x - x^0) = (f'(x^0) + y^0G'(x^0))(x - x^0) - y^0G'(x^0)(x - x^0),$$

we know that

$$G(x) \geqq \theta, \quad x \in E_+^n \qquad \text{imply} \qquad f'(x^0)(x - x^0) \leqq 0. \tag{112}$$

We shall show below that $f(x^0) \geqq f(x)$ when one of the conditions (a)–(c) is fulfilled. (We omit the proof for case (d), for which the reader should refer to Arrow and Enthoven (1961).)

(a) *f is concave on E_+^n* $f(x^0) \geqq f(x)$ follows at once from (37) in Section 7.2 and (112).

(b) *$f_i^0 < 0$ for at least one i* Let $x^1 \equiv x^0 + e^i$, where $e^i \equiv \{0, \ldots, 0, e, 0, \ldots, 0\} \in R^n$ with e (> 0) in the ith position such that $x^1 \in E_+^n$ and $G(x^1) \geqq \theta$. Then

$$f'(x^0)(x^1 - x^0) = f'(x^0)e^i = f_i^0 e < 0, \qquad x^1 \geqq \theta. \tag{113}$$

For any $x \in E_+^n$ with $G(x) \geqq \theta$ and $\alpha \in [0, 1]$, let

$$x(\alpha) \equiv (1 - \alpha)x + \alpha x^1, \qquad x^0(\alpha) \equiv (1 - \alpha)x^0 + \alpha x^1.$$

$x(\alpha) \in E_+^n$, and $G(x(\alpha)) \geqq G(x) \geqq \theta$. Then

$$f'(x^0)(x^0(\alpha) - x^0) = \alpha f'(x^0)(x^1 - x^0) < 0 \qquad \text{for} \quad \alpha > 0,$$

due to (113), and

$$f'(x^0)(x(\alpha) - x^0(\alpha)) = (1 - \alpha)f'(x^0)(x - x^0) \leqq 0 \quad \text{for} \quad \alpha \leqq 1,$$

due to (112). Adding these two equations, we get

$$f'(x^0)(x(\alpha) - x^0) < 0 \qquad \text{for} \quad 0 < \alpha \leqq 1,$$

and from (110) it follows that $f(x(\alpha)) < f(x^0)$. As α approaches zero, $x(\alpha)$ tends to x, and so $f(x) \leqq f(x^0)$.

(c) *$f_j^0 > 0$ for some j such that $x_j^* > 0$ for $x^* \in E_+^n$, $G(x^*) \geqq \theta$* If we exclude case (b), $f'(x^0)x^0 > 0$ and (c) will be found to be equivalent. Obviously, $f'(x^0)x^0 > 0$ implies (c). Conversely, if condition (c) is fulfilled, $f'(x^0)x^* > 0$ since excluding (b) means $f'(x^0) \geqq \theta$. Putting $x = x^*$ in (112), therefore, we have $0 < f'(x^0)x^* \leqq f'(x^0)x^0$.

For any $x \in E_+^n$ with $G(x) \geqq \theta$, let

$$x(\alpha) \equiv (1 - \alpha)x \qquad \text{and} \qquad x^0(\alpha) \equiv (1 - \alpha)x^0.$$

Then

$$f'(x^0)(x^0(\alpha) - x^0) = -\alpha f'(x^0)x^0 < 0 \qquad \text{for} \quad \alpha > 0,$$
$$f'(x^0)(x(\alpha) - x^0(\alpha)) = (1 - \alpha)f'(x^0)(x - x^0) \leqq 0 \qquad \text{for} \quad \alpha \leqq 1.$$

Thus, adding these

$$f'(x^0)(x(\alpha) - x^0) < 0 \qquad \text{for} \quad 0 < \alpha \leqq 1.$$

As α approaches zero, there exists some α^* such that $x(\alpha) \in E_+^n$ and $G(x(\alpha)) \geqq \theta$ for all $\alpha \leqq \alpha^*$. Hence from (110),

$$f(x(\alpha)) < f(x^0) \qquad \text{for all} \quad \alpha \leqq \alpha^*.$$

Since $x(\alpha)$ tends to x as α goes to zero, $f(x) \leqq f(x^0)$.

(The proof for case (d) is omitted.)

Let us turn to the necessity. *CQ*1 guarantees, by virtue of (89),

$$G(x^0) + G'(x^0)(x^* - x^0) \geqq G(x^*) > \theta \qquad \text{for a positive } x^*.$$

Hence, by Corollary 1 to Theorem 24, we get conditions (76′)–(78′).

Assume *CQ*2 and consider the set

$$S^0 \equiv \{x : G(x) \geqq G(x^0) \text{ and } x \geqq \theta\}.$$

S^0 is a nonempty convex set because for $x \in S^0$ and $\alpha \in (0, 1]$,

$$G(\alpha x + (1 - \alpha)x^0) \geqq G(x^0)$$

and $\alpha x + (1 - \alpha)x^0 \geqq \theta$. Further, we have

$$G'(x^0)(x - x^0) \geqq \theta \qquad \text{for} \quad x \in S^0.$$

Let $g^j(x)$ be the jth component of $G(x)$ and let $g_x^j(x^0)$ be the gradient of $g^i(x)$ at x^0. By definition, for index k for which $g^k(x^0) = 0$,

$$g_x^k(x^0)(x - x^0) = \lim_{\alpha \to 0} \frac{1}{\alpha} g^k(x^0 + \alpha(x - x^0)).$$

Thus, if for some k such that $g^k(x^0) = 0$,

$$g_x^k(x^0)(x - x^0) = 0 \qquad \text{for} \quad x \neq x^0,$$

then

$$\lim_{\alpha \to 0} \frac{1}{\alpha} g^k(x^0 + \alpha(x - x^0)) = 0 \qquad \text{for} \quad x \neq x^0,$$

which, together with $g^k(x^0) = 0$, implies that $g_x^k(x^0) = \theta$, contradicting condition (b′). Therefore, for each k such that $g^k(x^0) = 0$,

$$g_x^k(x^0)(x - x^0) > 0 \qquad \text{for} \quad x \in S^0 \text{ with } x \neq x^0.$$

S^0 may contain a point x^* satisfying condition (e). Hence

$$G(x^0) + G'(x^0)(x - x^0) > \theta \qquad \text{for some positive } x \in S^0,\ x \neq x^0.$$

Then, by Corollary 1 to Theorem 24, we get conditions (76′)–(78′). Q.E.D.

Remark The assumption in Theorem 29 that $G(x)$ is quasi-concave was used only to establish that, for all x in the constraint set $S \equiv \{x : G(x) \geqq \theta,\ x \geqq \theta\}$ or in the set $S^0 \equiv \{x : G(x) \geqq G(x^0),\ x \geqq \theta\}$,

$$g_x^j(x^0)(x - x^0) \geqq 0 \qquad \text{for index } j \text{ for which } g^j(x^0) = 0.$$

But for this purpose it suffices that S or S^0 be a convex set. For then, $(1 - \alpha)\, x^0 + \alpha x$ belongs to S or S^0, respectively, for $\alpha \in [0, 1]$, whence

$$G^j(\alpha) \equiv g^j((1 - \alpha)x^0 + \alpha x) \geqq 0 \qquad \text{for} \quad \alpha \in [0, 1].$$

Further, for $\alpha = 0$, the left-hand side becomes $g^j(x^0) = 0$, so that the derivative with respect to α at $\alpha = 0$ must be nonnegative, i.e.,

$$\left.\frac{dG^j(\alpha)}{d\alpha}\right|_{\alpha=0} = g_x^j(x^0)(x - x^0) \geqq 0.$$

Concluding this section, we provide some relationships among quasi-concave functionals, their bordered Hessians, and global maximum.

THEOREM 30 (Arrow and Enthoven, 1961) Let f be a twice-differentiable real-valued functional on E^n.

(i) If f is quasi-concave on E_+^n, then for each $x \in E_+^n$,

$$(-1)^r H_r(x) \geqq 0 \qquad \text{for} \quad r = 1, \ldots, n,$$

where $H_r(x)$ stands for the determinant of order $r + 1$ obtained from the bordered Hessian $[H]$ defined below, by deleting its last $n - r$ rows and columns:

$$[H] \equiv \begin{bmatrix} 0 & f'(x) \\ f'(x)^{\mathrm{T}} & f''(x) \end{bmatrix}.$$

(ii) A sufficient condition for f to be quasi-concave on E^n is that for each $x \in E^n$,

$$(-1)^r H_r(x) > 0 \qquad \text{for} \quad r = 1, \ldots, n.$$

(Note that in (i) x belongs to E_+^n and that in (ii) x can be any point in E^n, contrary to the original Theorem 5 of Arrow and Enthoven (1961).)

PROOF (i) If $f'(x^0) = \theta$ for $x^0 \in E_+^n$, then $H_r(x^0) = 0$ and the necessary condition is obviously satisfied. If $f'(x^0) \neq \theta$ for $x^0 \in E_+^n$, consider the problem:

$$\text{Maximize } f(x) \qquad \text{subject to} \quad f'(x^0)x^0 \geqq f'(x^0)x, \; x \geqq \theta.$$

Defining $G(x) \equiv f'(x^0)(x^0 - x) \geqq 0$, we know that conditions (76′)–(78′) are fulfilled with Lagrange multiplier $y^0 = 1$. Hence, by virtue of Theorem 29, x^0 is found to be an optimal solution to the problem mentioned above. On the other hand, since f is quasi-concave, if $f'(x^0)(x^0 - x) > 0$, then $f(x^0) > f(x)$ for $x \geqq \theta$, in view of (110). Thus, in effect $f(x^0)$ is the weak local maximum of $f(x)$ under the constraints $f'(x^0)(x^0 - x) = 0$, $x \geqq \theta$. Taking account of the fact that the relevant Lagrange multiplier is unity, we get

$$(-1)^r H_r(x^0) \geqq 0, \qquad \text{for} \quad r = 1, \ldots, n,$$

in view of the equivalence conditions (76) in Section 7.5 for a local maximum.

(ii) According to the corollary to Theorem 36 in Section 2.5, $(-1)^r H_r(x) > 0$ holds for all r if and only if $h^{\mathrm{T}} f''(x) h < 0$ for all $h \in E^n$ such that $f'(x)h = 0$. Hence, twice differentiability of f at any point $x^0 \in E^n$ implies that for x sufficiently close to x^0 and satisfying $f'(x^0)(x - x^0) = 0$, we have $f(x) < f(x^0)$, in view of Definition 8 in Section 7.2. That is, $f(x^0)$ is a strict local maximum of $f(x)$ subject to $f'(x^0)(x - x^0) = 0$. Let x^1 be any point in E^n for which

$$f'(x^0)x^1 \leqq f'(x^0)x^0. \tag{$*$}$$

We shall prove that $f(x^0)$ is a global constrained maximum subject to ($*$). Let $x(\alpha) \equiv (1 - \alpha)x^0 + \alpha x^1$, and $F(\alpha) \equiv f[x(\alpha)]$. Then let $\bar{\alpha}$ be the largest value of α for which $F(\bar{\alpha})$ takes its minimum in the interval [0, 1]. We shall show that $\bar{\alpha} < 1$ leads to a contradiction.

If $0 < \bar{\alpha} < 1$, then $F'(\bar{\alpha}) = 0$ because $F(\bar{\alpha})$ is a minimum. If $\bar{\alpha} = 0$, then $F'(0) = f'(x^0)(x^1 - x^0) \geqq 0$. But from ($*$) above, $F'(0) \leqq 0$, so that $F'(0) = 0$. Hence, in either case, $F'(\bar{\alpha}) = 0$, or equivalently

$$f'[x(\bar{\alpha})]\,(x^1 - x^0) = 0 \qquad \text{if} \quad 0 \leqq \bar{\alpha} < 1. \tag{$**$}$$

Since $x(\bar{\alpha} + \beta) - x(\bar{\alpha}) = \beta(x^1 - x^0)$, it follows from ($**$) that

$$f'[x(\bar{\alpha})]\,(x(\bar{\alpha} + \beta) - x(\bar{\alpha})) = 0 \qquad \text{for all } \beta. \tag{$***$}$$

But, by assumption, ($***$) implies that $f[x(\bar{\alpha})]$ is a strict local maximum of $f(x)$ subject to $f'[x(\bar{\alpha})]\,(x - x(\bar{\alpha})) = 0$, so that

$$f[x(\bar{\alpha} + \beta)] < f[x(\bar{\alpha})] \qquad \text{for sufficiently small } \beta > 0.$$

This contradicts the definition of $\bar{\alpha}$. It follows that we cannot have $\bar{\alpha} < 1$, so that $\bar{\alpha} = 1$ and in particular, $F(1) \leqq F(0)$, or equivalently $f(x^1) \leqq f(x^0)$.

We have thus shown that the point x^0 in E^n maximizes $f(x)$ subject to $f'(x^0)(x - x^0) \leqq 0$. Now, let x^0 and x^1 be any two points in E^n, and let x^2 be a convex combination of them. Then, we must have either

$$f'(x^2)x^0 \leqq f'(x^2)x^2 \qquad \text{or} \qquad f'(x^2)x^1 \leqq f'(x^2)x^2.$$

Since x^2 maximizes $f(x)$ subject to $f'(x^2)(x - x^2) \leqq 0$, we must then have either

$$f(x^2) \geqq f(x^0) \qquad \text{or} \qquad f(x^2) \geqq f(x^1),$$

and, in either case, $f(x^2) \geqq \min[f(x^0), f(x^1)]$, so that $f(x)$ is quasi-concave. Q.E.D.

Concerning quasi-convex functionals, a proposition holds parallel to statement (ii) in Theorem 30.

THEOREM 30′ A sufficient condition for a twice-differentiable functional f to be quasi-convex on E^n is that for each $x \in E^n$,

$$H_r(x) < 0 \qquad \text{for} \quad r = 1, \ldots, n.$$

(The proof proceeds similarly to that of the previous theorem, *mutatis mutandis.*)

THEOREM 31 (Ponstein, 1967) (i) A local maximum of a strictly quasi-concave functional $f(x)$ is at the same time a global maximum.

(ii) A local minimum of a strictly quasi-convex functional $f(x)$ is at the same time a global minimum.

PROOF We shall prove (i) only. ((ii) can be proved similarly, *mutatis mutandis.*) Let $f(x^0)$ be a local maximum and suppose that it is not a global maximum. Then there is an x^1 such that $f(x^1) > f(x^0)$, which means, by (108), that

$$f(\alpha x^1 + (1 - \alpha)x^0) > f(x^0) \qquad \text{for} \quad \alpha \in (0, 1).$$

Thus, there exists an x^2 arbitrarily close to x^0 such that $f(x^2) > f(x^0)$. But this contradicts the assumption that $f(x^0)$ is a local maximum. Q.E.D.

For other interesting theorems on quasi-concavity, refer to Katzner (1970).

Application 4. (*quasi-concave programming*) Given a budget B and prices $p_1, \ldots, p_n$, a consumer is supposed to maximize his utility $u(x)$ for some consumption vector $x \in E_+^n$ on the constraint set

$$D \equiv \left\{x : g(x) \equiv B - \sum_{i=1}^{n} p_i x_i \geqq 0,\ x \in E_+^n\right\}.$$

Suppose u is quasi-concave on D. Obviously, D is a convex set and g is quasi-concave. Assume that he has not reached the satiation point, and thereby condition (c) is satisfied for the function u. It is clear that there is a positive x^* satisfying condition (e) for the function g, and that $g'(x) = -(p_1, \ldots, p_n)$

$\neq \theta$ (condition (b')). Thus, applying Theorem 29, we know that a necessary and sufficient condition for x^0 to maximize $u(x)$ on the set D is that there is a positive scalar λ^0 such that

$$u_i^0 \leqq \lambda^0 p_i \qquad \text{for} \quad i = 1, \ldots, n, \tag{114-1}$$

$$\sum_{i=1}^{n} p_i x_i^0 = B, \tag{114-2}$$

$$\sum_{i=1}^{n} (u_i^0 - \lambda^0 p_i) x_i^0 = 0. \tag{114-3}$$

Combining (114-1), (114-3) with $x_i^0 \geqq \theta$, we have

$$\text{if} \quad x_j^0 > 0, \qquad \text{then} \quad u_j^0 = \lambda^0 p_j; \tag{115-1}$$

$$\text{if} \quad u_i^0 < \lambda^0 p_i, \qquad \text{then} \quad x_i^0 = 0. \tag{115-2}$$

Interpreting λ^0 as the marginal utility of money, (115-2) means that in case the marginal utility of commodity i is less than that of money, there is no demand for the commodity. (115-1) means that the commodities consumed in the optimal program are such that their marginal utilities are equalized to λ^0.

For applications of Kuhn–Tucker theorems to economic development, refer to Chenery and Uzawa (1958), Gale (1967), and Hansen and Koopmans (1972), among others. For an application of the K-T necessity theorem to a firm behavior problem, see Averch and Johnson (1962); a related theorem on Lagrange multiplier values was supplied by Zajac (1972).

8.5 Duality in Linear Programming, the Morishima Turnpike Theorem, and Other Related Problems

We shall utilize the second Kuhn–Tucker theorem and other relevant theorems from the previous section to derive duality relations in linear programming problems, and then apply these relations to some optimal production programmes.

A typical maximum problem of linear programming is:

$$\text{Maximize } cx \qquad \text{subject to} \quad Ax \leqq b \text{ and } x \geqq \theta,$$

which is henceforth expressed as

$$\max_{x \geqq \theta} \{cx : Ax \leqq b\}, \tag{116}$$

where $x \in E^n$ is to be determined, $c \equiv (c_1, \ldots, c_n)$ is a row vector, $b \equiv \{b_1, \ldots, b_m\}$ is a column vector, and A is an $m \times n$ matrix, all of real constants.

Assume that there exists a positive column vector $x \in E^n$ for which $Ax < b$, and note that since cx and $Ax - b$ are linear in $x \geqq \theta$, they are concave as well as convex on E^n_+. Then applying Theorem 28, we have the dual problem corresponding to the primal problem (116) as follows:

$$\min_{y \geqq \theta} \max_{x \geqq \theta} \{cx - y(Ax - b)\}. \tag{117}$$

The minimand of (117) can be rewritten

$$L(y) \equiv \max_{x \geqq \theta} \{(c - yA)x\} + yb,$$

which becomes equal to yb if $c \leqq yA$ (putting $x = \theta$) and to infinity otherwise. Suppose the primal problem (116) has a finite optimal value $f(x^0) = cx^0$. Then $L(y)$ must be finite in view of (101), and hence the dual problem can now be expressed as

$$\min_{y \geqq \theta} \{yb : yA \geqq c\}. \tag{118}$$

Moreover, in view of (101), denoting by x^0, y^* the optimal solutions to (116), (117) respectively, we have

$$y^*b \equiv \min_{y \geqq \theta} \{yb : yA \geqq c\} = \max_{x \geqq \theta} \{cx : Ax \leqq b\} \equiv cx^0, \tag{119}$$

while in general

$$\{yb : yA \geqq c, y \geqq \theta\} \geqq \{cx : Ax \leqq b, x \geqq \theta\}. \tag{120}$$

The second Kuhn–Tucker theorem (Theorem 25 (i)) applied to problem (116) ensures the existence of $y^0 \geqq \theta$ such that

$$c - y^0 A \leqq \theta, \qquad y^0 b = y^0 A x^0 = cx^0, \tag{121}$$

which imply not only that y^0 is a feasible vector of y satisfying the constraints in the dual problem (118), but also that $y^0 = y^*$ (the optimal solution), with (119) taken into consideration.

The above results may be summarized as

THEOREM 32 (*duality theorem for canonical linear programming*)

(i) Let $x^0 \in E^n_+$ be an optimal solution to the primal problem (116):

$$\max_{x \geqq \theta} \{cx : Ax \leqq b\}.$$

Assume that there exists a positive $x \in E^n$ for which $Ax < b$. If the optimal value cx^0 of problem (116) is finite, there exists an optimal solution $y^0 \in E^m_+$ to the associated dual problem (118):

$$\min_{y \geqq \theta} \{yb : yA \geqq c\},$$

such that (121) holds:

$$c \leqq y^0 A, \qquad y^0 b = y^0 A x^0 = cx^0.$$

(ii) Conversely, let $y^0 \in E^m_+$ be an optimal solution to problem (118), providing a finite value $y^0 b$. Assume that there is a positive $y \in E^m_+$ for which $yA > c$. Then there exists an optimal solution $x^0 \in E^n_+$ to problem (116) such that

$$Ax^0 \leqq b, \qquad cx^0 = y^0Ax^0 = y^0b. \tag{122}$$

In either case (i) or (ii), we have

$$(c - y^0A)x^0 = 0 \quad \text{with} \quad x^0 \geqq \theta, \quad c - y^0A \leqq \theta; \tag{123}$$

and

$$y^0(Ax^0 - b) = 0 \quad \text{with} \quad y^0 \geqq \theta, \quad Ax^0 - b \leqq \theta; \tag{124}$$

which imply

$$x_j^0 = 0 \quad \text{if} \quad c_j < y^0a^j; \qquad c_i = y^0a^i \quad \text{if} \quad x_i^0 > 0; \tag{123$'$}$$

and

$$y_j^0 = 0 \quad \text{if} \quad a_jx^0 < b_j; \qquad a_ix^0 = b_i \quad \text{if} \quad y_i^0 > 0; \tag{124$'$}$$

where x_j^0, y_j^0, c_j, b_j stand for the jth components of x^0, y^0, c, b, respectively, a^j denotes the jth column and a_j the jth row of matrix A. (123) and (124) are referred to as the *complementary slackness conditions.*

Remark A contraposition of Theorem 32 can be stated as follows: Assume the existence of $x > \theta$ such that $Ax < b$, and let x^0 be an optimal solution to the primal problem (116). If the set $\{y : yA \geqq c, y \geqq \theta\}$ is empty, or equivalently, if the dual problem (118) is essentially infeasible, then cx^0 is not finite, i.e., the set $\{cx : Ax \leqq b, x \geqq \theta\}$ is not bounded from above. Note that the converse also holds true. (See the paragraph immediately after Theorem 28 in Section 8.4.)

Now we study dual relations regarding some variants of canonical linear programming.

COROLLARY 1 Consider the problem

$$\max_{x \geqq \theta} \{cx : A_1x \leqq b_1, A_2x = b_2\}, \tag{125}$$

where A_1 is $(m - k) \times n$, A_2 is $k \times n$, b_1 is $(m - k) \times 1$, b_2 is $k \times 1$, and the others are those defined before. (125) can be rewritten

$$\max_{x \geqq \theta} \{cx : \bar{A}x \leqq \bar{b}\} \qquad \text{where} \quad \bar{A} \equiv \begin{bmatrix} A_1 \\ A_2 \\ -A_2 \end{bmatrix} \quad \text{and} \quad \bar{b} \equiv \begin{bmatrix} b_1 \\ b_2 \\ -b_2 \end{bmatrix}. \tag{125$'$}$$

Suppose (125′) has a finite solution x^0. Then, by Theorem 32, there exists an optimal solution $\bar{y}^0 \in E^{m+k}_+$ to the associated dual problem

$$\min_{\bar{y} \geqq \theta} \{\bar{y}\bar{b} : \bar{y}\bar{A} \geqq c\}, \qquad \text{where} \quad \bar{y} \equiv (y, y_2, y_3); \tag{126$'$}$$

or, by putting $z \equiv y_2 - y_3$, there is a pair of optimal vectors $y^0 \in E_+^{m-k}$, $z^0 \in E^k$ to the dual problem

$$\min_{y \geqq \theta, z \in E^k} \{yb_1 + zb_2 : yA_1 + zA_2 \geqq c\}, \tag{126}$$

such that

$$c - y^0A_1 - z^0A_2 \leqq \theta, \quad y^0(A_1x^0 - b_1) = 0, \quad (c - y^0A_1 - z^0A_2)x^0 = 0. \tag{127}$$

Hence the complementary slackness conditions in this case are written

$$(c - y^0A_1 - z^0A_2)x^0 = 0 \quad \text{with} \quad x^0 \geqq \theta, \quad c - y^0A_1 - z^0A_2 \leqq \theta; \tag{128}$$

and

$$y^0(A_1x^0 - b_1) = 0 \quad \text{with} \quad y^0 \geqq \theta, \quad A_1x^0 - b_1 \leqq \theta. \tag{129}$$

COROLLARY 2 Similarly, when the primal problem specified as

$$\max_{x \geqq \theta} \{cx : Ax = b\} \tag{130}$$

has a finite optimal solution x^0, its associated dual problem assumes the form

$$\min_{y \in E^m} \{yb : yA \geqq c\}, \tag{131}$$

and has an optimal solution y^0 such that (123) holds:

$$(c - y^0A)x^0 = 0 \quad \text{with} \quad x^0 \geqq \theta, \quad c - y^0A \leqq \theta.$$

COROLLARY 3 Multiplying cx in (130) by -1 and setting $p = -c$, we convert (130) into

$$\min_{x \geqq \theta} \{px : Ax = b\}. \tag{132}$$

Accordingly, its associated dual problem becomes

$$\max_{y \in E^m} \{yb : yA \leqq p\}. \tag{133}$$

If problem (132) has a finite optimal solution x^0, then there exists an optimal vector y^0 to problem (133) such that

$$(p - y^0A)x^0 = 0 \quad \text{with} \quad x^0 \geqq \theta, \quad p - y^0A \geqq \theta. \tag{134}$$

By virtue of the second Kuhn–Tucker theorem (Theorem 25 (ii)) and its corollary (ii), we have a sufficient condition for optimality to each of the above mentioned problems.

PROPOSITION 1 (*sufficiency for canonical linear programming*) If there is a pair of vectors $y^0 \in E_+^m$ and $x^0 \in E_+^n$ such that

$$Ax^0 - b \leqq \theta, \quad c - y^0A \leqq \theta, \quad cx^0 = y^0b, \tag{135}$$

then x^0, y^0 are finite optimal solutions to problems (116) and (118), respectively.

COROLLARY 1 (i) If there is a pair of vectors $y^0 \in E_+^{m-k}$ and $z^0 \in E^k$ satisfying conditions (127) with $A_1x^0 - b_1 \leqq \theta$ and $x^0 \geqq \theta$, then x^0 is a finite optimal solution of the maximum problem (125).

(ii) If there is an $x^0 \in E_+^n$ satisfying

$$A_1x^0 - b_1 \leqq \theta, \qquad A_2x^0 - b_2 = \theta, \qquad (c - y^0A_1 - z^0A_2)x^0 = 0,$$
$$y^0(A_1x^0 - b_1) = 0, \tag{136}$$

with $c - y^0A_1 - z^0A_2 \leqq \theta$ and $y^0 \geqq \theta$, then the pair (y^0, z^0) is a finite optimal solution of the minimum problem (126).

COROLLARY 2 (i) If there is a $y^0 \in E^m$ satisfying (123), then x^0 is a finite optimal solution of the maximum problem (130). (ii) If there is an $x^0 \in E_+^n$ satisfying

$$Ax^0 - b = \theta, \quad (c - y^0A)x^0 = 0 \qquad \text{with} \quad c - y^0A \leqq \theta, \tag{137}$$

then y^0 is a finite optimal solution of the minimum problem (131).

COROLLARY 3 (i) If there is a $y^0 \in E^m$ satisfying (134), then x^0 is a finite optimal solution of the minimum problem (132). (ii) If there is an $x^0 \in E_+^n$ satisfying

$$Ax^0 - b = \theta, \quad (p - y^0A)x^0 = 0 \qquad \text{with} \quad p - y^0A \geqq \theta, \tag{138}$$

then y^0 is a finite optimal solution of the maximum problem (133).

THEOREM 33. (*saddle-point property of canonical linear programming*) The conditions (135) for canonical linear programming are equivalent to the following saddle-point condition: There exist $x^0 \geqq \theta$, $y^0 \geqq \theta$ such that

$$L(x, y^0) \leqq L(x^0, y^0) \leqq L(x^0, y) \qquad \text{for} \quad x \geqq \theta, \quad y \geqq \theta, \tag{139}$$

where $L(x, y) \equiv cx - y(Ax - b)$.

PROOF Assume that (135) holds. Then, for $x \geqq \theta$ and $y \geqq \theta$,

$$cx^0 - y(Ax^0 - b) \geqq cx^0 = L(x^0, y^0) = y^0b \geqq y^0b + (c - y^0A)x.$$

Conversely, assume the saddle-point condition. $L(x^0, y) \geqq L(x^0, y^0) \Rightarrow$

$$y(Ax^0 - b) \leqq y^0(Ax^0 - b) \qquad \text{for} \quad y \geqq \theta. \tag{$*$}$$

Putting $y = \theta$ in ($*$) yields $y^0(Ax^0 - b) \geqq 0$. ($*$) also provides

$$(y^1 + y^0)(Ax^0 - b) \leqq y^0(Ax^0 - b) \qquad \text{for} \quad y^1 \geqq \theta,$$

$\Rightarrow y^1(Ax^0 - b) \leqq 0 \Rightarrow Ax^0 - b \leqq \theta \Rightarrow y^0(Ax^0 - b) \leqq 0$. Thus we get $y^0(Ax^0 - b) = 0$, and hence for $x \geqq \theta$,

$$y^0b + (c - y^0A)x^0 = cx^0 = L(x^0, y^0) \geqq L(x, y^0) = y^0b + (c - y^0A)x;$$

i.e.,

$$(c - y^0A)x^0 \geqq (c - y^0A)x \qquad \text{for} \quad x \geqq \theta. \tag{$**$}$$

Putting $x = \theta$ in (**) yields $(c - y^0 A)x^0 \geqq 0$. (**) also provides

$$(c - y^0 A)x^0 \geqq (c - y^0 A)(x^0 + x^1) \qquad \text{for} \quad x^1 \geqq \theta,$$

$\Rightarrow (c - y^0 A)x^1 \leqq 0 \Rightarrow c - y^0 A \leqq \theta \Rightarrow (c - y^0 A)x^0 \leqq 0$. Therefore, $(c - y^0 A)x^0 = 0$. Q.E.D.

It is easy to check that condition (139) is also necessary for the existence of a pair of finite optimal solutions x^0, y^0 to linear programming problems (116), (118). Thus, in view of Proposition 1 and Theorem 33, we have

THEOREM 34 Condition (139) or condition (135) is necessary and sufficient for x^0, y^0 to be a pair of finite optimal solutions to canonical linear programming problems (116) and (118), respectively.

Remark Comparing the saddle-point condition (139) with (52) in Section 8.3, we notice a close relationship between canonical linear programming problems and a matrix game. Indeed, if we solve a game with $(m + 1) \times (n + 1)$ payoff matrix

$$B \equiv \begin{bmatrix} -A & b \\ c & 0 \end{bmatrix}$$

for a pair of optimal solutions (ξ^0, η^0) such that

$$\xi^0 \equiv \{\xi_1^0, \ldots, \xi_n^0, \xi_{n+1}^0\} \in \hat{X} \equiv \{\xi : \xi \in E_+^{n+1}, \sum_{j=1}^{n+1} \xi_j = 1, \xi_{n+1} > 0\},$$

$$\eta^0 \equiv \{\eta_1^0, \ldots, \eta_m^0, \eta_{m+1}^0\} \in \hat{Y} \equiv \{\eta : \eta \in E_+^{m+1}, \sum_{i=1}^{m+1} \eta_i = 1, \eta_{m+1} > 0\},$$

where ξ_j, η_i denote the jth component of ξ and the ith component of η respectively, then by defining

$$\tilde{x}_j \equiv \xi_j/\xi_{n+1}, \qquad \tilde{y}_i \equiv \eta_i/\eta_{n+1}, \qquad \tilde{x} \equiv \{\tilde{x}_1, \ldots, \tilde{x}_n\}, \qquad \tilde{y} \equiv (\tilde{y}_1, \ldots, \tilde{y}_m),$$

we have

$$(\tilde{y}^0, 1)B \begin{bmatrix} \tilde{x} \\ 1 \end{bmatrix} \leqq (\tilde{y}^0, 1)B \begin{bmatrix} \tilde{x}^0 \\ 1 \end{bmatrix} \leqq (\tilde{y}, 1)B \begin{bmatrix} \tilde{x}^0 \\ 1 \end{bmatrix},$$

or equivalently

$$L(\tilde{x}, \tilde{y}^0) \leqq L(\tilde{x}^0, \tilde{y}^0) \leqq L(\tilde{x}^0, \tilde{y}) \qquad \text{for} \quad \tilde{x} \geqq \theta, \quad \tilde{y} \geqq \theta. \tag{139'}$$

By Theorem 33, $\tilde{x}^0$ and $\tilde{y}^0$ constitute a pair of optimal solutions of our canonical linear programming problems. Conversely, let (x^0, y^0) be a pair satisfying (139) and define two sets

$$X_* \equiv \left\{x_* : x_* = \{x, 1\} \Big/ \left(\sum_1^n x_i + 1\right), x \in E_+^n\right\},$$

$$Y_* \equiv \left\{y_* : y_* = (y, 1) \Big/ \left(\sum_1^m y_i + 1\right), y \in E_+^m\right\}.$$

Then we have $L(x_*, y_*^0) \leqq L(x_*^0, y_*^0) \leqq L(x_*^0, y_*)$ for $x_* \in X_*$, $y_* \in Y_*$; i.e., (x_*^0, y_*^0) is the saddle-point solution to matrix game B.

Utilizing the saddle-point property of the solutions to canonical linear programming problems, some sensitivity rules can be established for optimal solutions with respect to parametric vectors.

THEOREM 35 (*sensitivity theorem for canonical linear programming*) Let x^0 and y^0 be the optimal solutions to (116) and (118), respectively. If vectors c and b vary by Δc and Δb, respectively, the corresponding change in the optimal solutions, denoted Δx and Δy, will be such that

$$\Delta c \cdot \Delta x - \Delta y \cdot \Delta b \geqq 0, \tag{140}$$

$$c \cdot \Delta x - \Delta y \cdot b \leqq y^0 \cdot \Delta b - \Delta c \cdot x^0. \tag{141}$$

PROOF Define $L(x, y) \equiv cx - y(Ax - b)$ and $L^*(x, y) \equiv (c + \Delta c)x - y(Ax - b - \Delta b)$. By Theorem 34 we have

(i) $L(x^0, y^0 + \Delta y) \geqq L(x^0, y^0)$,

(ii) $L(x^0, y^0) \geqq L(x^0 + \Delta x, y^0)$,

(iii) $L^*(x^0 + \Delta x, y^0) \geqq L^*(x^0 + \Delta x, y^0 + \Delta y)$,

(iv) $L^*(x^0 + \Delta x, y^0 + \Delta y) \geqq L^*(x^0, y^0 + \Delta y)$;

or equivalently

(i′) $\Delta y(b - Ax^0) \geqq 0$,

(ii′) $(y^0 A - c)\Delta x \geqq 0$,

(iii′) $\Delta y[A(x^0 + \Delta x) - b - \Delta b] \geqq 0$,

(iv′) $[c + \Delta c - (y^0 + \Delta y)A]\Delta x \geqq 0$.

Adding (i′)–(iv′) yields (140). Then, $cx^0 = y^0 b$ and $(c + \Delta c)(x^0 + \Delta x) = (y^0 + \Delta y)(b + \Delta b)$ provide

$$y^0 \cdot \Delta b - \Delta c \cdot x^0 = c \cdot \Delta x - \Delta y \cdot b + \Delta c \cdot \Delta x - \Delta y \cdot \Delta b$$
$$\geqq c \cdot \Delta x - \Delta y \cdot b. \qquad \text{Q.E.D.}$$

COROLLARY In Theorem 35, if $\Delta c \neq \theta$ and $\Delta b = \theta$, then we have

$$\Delta c \cdot \Delta x \geqq 0, \tag{140-1}$$

$$\Delta y \cdot b - c \cdot \Delta x \geqq \Delta c \cdot x^0. \tag{141-1}$$

If $\Delta c = \theta$ and $\Delta b \neq \theta$, then we have

$$\Delta y \cdot \Delta b \leqq 0, \tag{140-2}$$

$$c \cdot \Delta x - \Delta y \cdot b \leqq y^0 \cdot \Delta b. \tag{141-2}$$

Remark (140-1) implies that the optimal vector x tends to vary in the same direction as the changes in c; and (140-2) implies that the optimal vector y tends to vary in the opposite direction to the changes in b. (140-1) and (140-2) may be termed the *LeChatelier–Samuelson inequalities*.

Another sensitivity theorem is given next.

THEOREM 36 (*technological changes*) Let x^0 and y^0 be optimal solutions to (116) and (118), respectively. If matrix A varies by ΔA, the corresponding changes in the optimal solutions, denoted Δx and Δy, will be such that

$$c \cdot \Delta x = \Delta y \cdot b, \tag{142}$$

$$y^0 A \cdot \Delta x \geqq \Delta y \cdot A x^0, \tag{143}$$

$$y^0 \cdot \Delta A \cdot \Delta x \leqq \Delta y \cdot \Delta A \cdot x^0. \tag{144}$$

PROOF Apply the duality principles in (135) to the optimal solutions after the variation in A took place. In particular, we have

$$(y^0 + \Delta y)[(A + \Delta A)(x^0 + \Delta x) - b] = 0,$$

$$[c - (y^0 + \Delta y)(A + \Delta A)](x^0 + \Delta x) = 0.$$

Adding these equations and taking account of (135) yield (142). From (i′) and (ii′) in the proof of Theorem 35, it follows that

$$(y^0 A - c)\Delta x + \Delta y(b - Ax^0) \geqq 0.$$

Then, taking (142) into account, we obtain (143) at once. Defining

$$L^{**}(x, y) \equiv cx - y[(A + \Delta A)x - b],$$

and considering the following saddle-point condition:

$$L^{**}(x^0 + \Delta x, y^0) \geqq L^{**}(x^0, y^0 + \Delta y),$$

together with (142) and (143), we get (144). Q.E.D.

COROLLARY Assume that in Theorem 36 the only nonzero element in ΔA is $\Delta a_{ij} < 0$, and that $x_j^0 > 0$ and $y_i^0 > 0$. Then, we have

$$\Delta x_j / x_j^0 \geqq \Delta y_i / y_i^0. \tag{145}$$

PROOF In this case (144) is reduced to

$$y_i^0 \cdot \Delta a_{ij} \cdot \Delta x_j \leqq \Delta y_i \cdot \Delta a_{ij} \cdot x_j^0. \qquad \text{Q.E.D.}$$

(145) means that when a technological coefficient a_{ij} associated with a scarce input i and an active activity j is decreased, *ceteris paribus*,the induced relative change in the level of the activity that is directly involved cannot be exceeded by the relative change in the efficiency price (or the marginal productivity) of the input directly involved.

Now we shall apply the preceding theorems on linear programming to optimal production programmes.

Application 5 (*Morishima turnpike problem*) In this problem frequent use is made of basic properties of linear programming. Recalling the notations in Theorem 22 of Section 8.3, we restate Problem (M) at the end of that section with λ_e^τ replacing ρ.

Problem (M) Maximize $\lambda_e^\tau \eta$ subject to

$$Ax(1) \leqq y(0), \qquad Ax(t+1) \leqq Bx(t) \qquad \text{for} \quad t = 1, \ldots, \tau - 1, \tag{146}$$

$$\eta \bar{y} \leqq Bx(\tau), \qquad \eta \geqq 0, \qquad x(t) \geqq \theta \qquad \text{for} \quad t = 1, \ldots, \tau. \tag{147}$$

The dual problem corresponding to this Problem (M) is

Problem (m) Minimize $p(0)y(0)$ subject to

$$(p(0), p(1), \ldots, p(\tau)) \begin{bmatrix} A & 0 & \cdots & 0 & \theta \\ -B & A & & 0 & \theta \\ 0 & -B & \ddots & & \vdots \\ \vdots & & & & \\ 0 & & -B & A & \theta \\ 0 & \cdots & 0 & -B & \bar{y} \end{bmatrix} \geqq (\theta^{\mathrm{T}}, \ldots, \theta^{\mathrm{T}}, \lambda_e^\tau)$$

and $(p(0), p(1), \ldots, p(\tau)) \geqq \theta^{\mathrm{T}}$; or equivalently, minimize $p(0)y(0)$ subject to

$$p(t)A \geqq p(t+1)B \qquad \text{for} \quad t = 0, 1, \ldots, \tau - 1, \tag{148}$$

$$p(\tau)\bar{y} \geqq \lambda_e^\tau, \qquad p(t) \geqq \theta^{\mathrm{T}} \qquad \text{for} \quad t = 0, 1, \ldots, \tau. \tag{149}$$

In order to prove the lemmas below, we need the following assumptions:

(A-1) A_e is an indecomposable matrix among all square matrices A_s defined in Section 8.3 and is unique in the sense that the Frobenius root λ_e of A_e is less than that of any other A_s.

(A-2) A_e is primitive.

(A-3) For each good i and time t there is at least one activity sj in some industry j such that its ith element $a_i^{sj} > 0$ with $\tilde{x}_{sj}(t) > 0$ for any optimal path $(\tilde{x}(1), \ldots, \tilde{x}(\tau))$.

(A-2) prevents $(A_e)^k$ from becoming decomposable for some integer $k > 0$.

LEMMA 6 Assume (A-1) and semipositive vectors $y(0)$ and $\bar{y}$. Let the objective function $p(0)y(0)$ of Problem (m) achieve a minimum at $p(0) = p_\tau(0)$. Then every component of $p_\tau(0)$ is bounded from above even if the programming period τ is extended to infinity.

PROOF Let p_e be the positive eigenvector of A_e associated with λ_e such that $p_e\bar{y} = 1$. We know that $p(t) = \lambda_e^t p_e$ $(t = 0, 1, \ldots, \tau)$ is a feasible solution to Problem (m) in view of (7*) and (8*) in Section 8.3. Thus $p_\tau(0)y(0) \leqq p(0)y(0) = p_e y(0)$ holds for this feasible solution. Q.E.D.

LEMMA 7 Assume (A-3) and strictly positive vectors $y(0)$ and $\bar{y}$. Let

$(\tilde{p}(0), \tilde{p}(1), \ldots, \tilde{p}(\tau))$ be an optimal solution to Problem (m); let a^{kj} be an activity of industry j such that for time t

$$\tilde{p}(t)a^{kj} = \min[\tilde{p}(t)a^{1j}, \ldots, \tilde{p}(t)a^{nj}];$$

and denote $\tilde{A}_t \equiv [a^{k1}, a^{k2}, \ldots, a^{km}]$. Then

$$\tilde{p}(t+1) = \tilde{p}(t)\tilde{A}_t \leqq \tilde{p}(t)A_s \qquad \text{for} \quad t = 0, 1, \ldots, \tau - 1,$$

where A_s stands for any square matrix as defined after (56) in Section 8.3.

PROOF Let $\{\tilde{x}(1), \ldots, \tilde{x}(\tau), \tilde{\eta}\}$ be an optimal solution to Problem (M). Any feasible solution $p(0)$ is semipositive, since if $p(0)$ were the zero vector, all $p(t)$'s would be zero for $t = 1, \ldots, \tau$ in view of (148), contradicting (149). With $y(0) > \theta$ and $\tilde{p}(0) \geq \theta$ taken into consideration, it follows from

$$\lambda_e^\tau \tilde{\eta} = \tilde{p}(0)y(0) > 0$$

that $\tilde{\eta} > 0$. This, together with $\bar{y} > \theta$, ensures $B\tilde{x}(\tau) > \theta$ by virtue of (147). Thus, for $t = \tau$

$$\{\tilde{x}_{1j}(t), \ldots, \tilde{x}_{nj}(t)\} \geq \theta \qquad \text{for each} \quad j = 1, \ldots, m. \tag{150}$$

By assumption (A-3), therefore, we get $A\tilde{x}(\tau) > \theta$, which in turn implies $B\tilde{x}(\tau - 1) > \theta$ in view of (146), and hence (150) for $t = \tau - 1$. Proceeding similarly, we know after all that (150) holds for all $t = 1, \ldots, \tau$; i.e., for each t there is kj such that $\tilde{x}_{kj}(t) > 0$. Then, the complementary slackness conditions (cf. Theorem 32) require that for each j and t

$$\tilde{p}_j(t+1) = \tilde{p}(t)a^{kj} \leqq \tilde{p}(t)a^{sj} \qquad \text{for} \quad sj \neq kj. \qquad \text{Q.E.D.}$$

The following two lemmas are not related to linear programming, so we omit their proofs. (Refer to Morishima (1961) or (1964, pp. 165–169).)

LEMMA 8 Assume (A-1) and (A-2). Let a^{rj} be an activity of industry j such that

$$p(t)a^{rj} = \min[p(t)a^{1j}, \ldots, p(t)a^{nj}],$$

and denote $A_t \equiv [a^{r1}, a^{r2}, \ldots, a^{rm}]$. If any path starting from an arbitrary $p(0) \geq \theta$ satisfies

$$p(t+1) = p(t)A_t, \tag{151}$$

it eventually approaches the von Neumann price ray, i.e.,

$$p(t) \to \omega\lambda_e^t p_e > \theta \qquad \text{as} \quad t \to \infty.$$

LEMMA 9 Assume (A-1) and (A-2). Let K be a prescribed neighboring cone of the von Neumann price ray, let $p(t, p(0))$ be the path (151) starting from a point $p(0) \geq \theta$, and let $t(p(0))$ be the minimum period in time that $p(t, p(0))$ comes into K and remains within it thereafter. For any specified K and any point $p^* \geq \theta$, there exists a sphere centered at p^* such that if $p(0)$ belongs to the sphere, $t(p(0))$ does not exceed a finite time period t_*.

We are in a position to establish a famous turnpike theorem, in the proof of which we utilize again the duality theorem of canonical linear programming.

THEOREM 37 (*Morishima turnpike theorem*) Assume (A-1)–(A-3). Let the initial stock vector $y(0)$ and the target output vector $\bar{y}$ be strictly positive. If the programming period τ is sufficiently large, the maximal path $x(t)$ determined by Problem (M) will most of the time remain within a preassigned vicinity of the von Neumann operation-intensity vector.

PROOF Let $p_\tau(0)$ be such $p(0)$ that minimizes $p(0)y(0)$. We know that $p_\tau(0)$ is semipositive in the proof of Lemma 7 and is bounded from above componentwise for $\tau = 1, 2, \ldots$. Let P^0 be the smallest proper subset of E_+^m that contains $p_\tau(0)$ for $\tau = 1, 2, \ldots$. For each point p^{*i} in P^0, let $U(p^{*i})$ be a sphere centered at p^{*i} such that if $p(0)$ belongs to the sphere, the minimum time that $p(t, p(0))$ comes into K (a prescribed neighboring cone of the von Neumann price ray) and remains within it thereafter does not exceed a finite time period t_{*i}. Since P^0 is closed and bounded, it can be covered by a finite subcollection of $U(p^{*i})$, say $U(p^{*1})$, $U(p^{*2})$, . . ., and $U(p^{*k})$, by virtue of Heine–Borel theorem. (Refer, for example, to Apostol (1957, p. 53).) Let $\tau_* \equiv \max[t_{*1}, t_{*2}, \ldots, t_{*k}]$. τ is supposed to be so large that $\tau_* + 1 < \tau$. Then for t in $[\tau_*, \tau]$, $p(t, p_\tau(0))$ remains within the cone K. Taking account of the fact that for each $p \in K$, $pA_e < pA_f$ holds (cf. (8*) in Section 8.3), we have

$$p(t+1, p_\tau(0)) = p(t, p_\tau(0))A_e < p(t, p_\tau(0))A_f \tag{152}$$
$$\text{for} \quad t = \tau_*, \tau_* + 1, \ldots, \tau - 1.$$

Note that $p(t, p_\tau(0))$ is an optimal solution to Problem (m) since a path (151) starting with $p(0) = p_\tau(0)$ is optimal in view of Lemma 7. Thus it follows from (152) and the complementary slackness conditions that the components of the optimal solution $\tilde{x}(t)$ to Problem (M) corresponding to any activites other than those in A_e take zero values for all t in $[\tau_* + 1, \tau]$. Hence the first inequality in (147) and the second inequality in (146) reduce to

$$\tilde{\eta}\bar{y} \leqq \tilde{x}(\tau), \qquad A_e\tilde{x}\,(t+1) \leqq \tilde{x}(t) \qquad \text{for} \quad t = \tau_* + 1, \ldots, \tau - 1,$$

where $\tilde{x}(t) = \{\tilde{x}_{e1}(t), \ldots, \tilde{x}_{em}(t)\}$, the same activities as in the von Neumann operation-intensity vector x_e^*. (Cf. Theorem 22 in Section 8.3.) Since p_e is strictly positive, K can be taken such that any point in K is strictly positive. Then $p(t, p_\tau(0)) > \theta$ for all t in $[\tau_*, \tau]$, and thereby

$$A_e\tilde{x}(t+1) = \tilde{x}(t) \qquad \text{for} \quad t = \tau_* + 1, \ldots, \tau - 1; \qquad \tilde{x}(\tau) = \tilde{\eta}\bar{y} > \theta, \tag{153}$$

in view of the complementary slackness conditions again.

By setting

$$\tilde{x}(t) = \tilde{\eta}\tilde{y}(\tau - t) \qquad \text{for} \quad t = \tau_* + 1, \ldots, \tau, \tag{154}$$

with $\tilde{y}(0) = \bar{y}$, we can rewrite (153) as

$$A_e\tilde{y}(s - 1) = \tilde{y}(s) \qquad \text{for} \quad s = 1, 2, \ldots, \tau - \tau_* - 1. \tag{153'}$$

Since A_e is indecomposable and primitive,

$$\tilde{y}(s) \to c\lambda_e^s x_e^* \qquad \text{as} \quad s \to \infty,$$

where c is a constant scalar and x_e^* is the right eigenvector of A_e associated with λ_e. (See Application 2 in Section 4.3.) In other worlds, there is a finite integer s^* such that $\tilde{y}(s)$ remains within an assigned vicinity of the von Neumann intensity vector for all $s \geqq s^*$. Thus, if τ is sufficiently large, (whereby so is $\tau^{1/2}$) the $\tilde{y}(s)$ satisfying (153′) remains within the vicinity for all s in $[\tau^{1/2}, \tau - \tau_* - 1]$, and hence the optimal path $\tilde{x}(t)$ in (154) remains within the preassigned vicinity of the von Neumann operation-intensity (= output) vector for all t in $[\tau_* + 1, \tau - \tau^{1/2}]$. Lastly we note that

$$\lim_{\tau\to\infty} (\tau - \tau^{1/2} - \tau_* - 1)/\tau = 1,$$

since $\lim_{\tau\to\infty} (\tau^{1/2} + \tau_* + 1)/\tau = \lim_{\tau\to\infty} \tau^{-1/2} = 0$. Q.E.D.

Application 6 (*Gale nonsubstitution problem*) Gale (1960) proved the so-called nonsubstitution theorem with the help of the following proposition.

PROPOSITION 2 Let A be an $m \times n$ real matrix with $m < n$, and consider the problem:

Find an $x \in E_+^n$ that minimizes px subject to $Ax = b$, where $p \in E^n$ and $b \in E^m$. (155)

We call a set of independent columns a^i of A an *optimal basis* if there is an optimal x to (155) depending on these columns. Let A^0 be an optimal basis for (155). Then $\bar{x}$ ($\geq \theta$) such that $A^0\bar{x} = b$ is said to be a *basic optimal vector* for (155). Now consider the new problem:

$$\text{Minimize } px \text{ subject to } Ax = b^* \ (b^* \neq b) \text{ and } x \in E_+^n. \tag{156}$$

Then, if A^0 is a feasible basis for (156), it is in fact an optimal basis for (156).

PROOF Let x^0 be a finite optimal vector in E_+^n for problem (155) depending on A^0 and let y^0 be an optimal solution to the problem dual to problem (155). By Corollary 3 to Theorem 32,

$$\text{if} \quad y^0a^i < p_i, \qquad \text{then} \quad x_i^0 = 0, \tag{157}$$

where p_i, x_i^0 stand for the ith components of p, x^0, respectively. Let x^* be a feasible vector for problem (156) depending on A^0. Then, by hypothesis, $x_i^* = 0$ whenever $x_i^0 = 0$. Hence

$$\text{if} \quad y^0a^i < p_i, \qquad \text{then} \quad x_i^* = 0. \tag{157'}$$

Furthermore, taking (134) into account, we know that

$$\text{if} \quad x_j^* > 0, \qquad \text{then} \quad y^0 a^j = p_j \tag{158}$$

since $x_j^* > 0$ holds only if $x_j^0 > 0$. Conditions (157′) and (158) ensure that x^* is a finite optimal solution to problem (156) by virtue of Corollary 3(i) to Proposition 1. Q.E.D.

Consider the nonjoint production system

$$y = [B - A]x, \quad lx \leqq 1 \quad \text{for some} \quad x \in E_+^n, \tag{159}$$

where B, A are those defined by (55), (56) in Section 8.3, x and y are an intensity vector and a net output vector respectively, and l denotes the vector of input requirements of a single primary factor, labor per unit intensity of each activity,

$$l \equiv (l_{11}, \ldots, l_{n1}, l_{12}, \ldots, l_{n2}, \ldots, l_{1m}, \ldots, l_{nm}).$$

The output space Y is defined as the set of all nonnegative y satisfying (159); i.e.,

$$Y = \{y : y = [B - A]x \geqq \theta, \, lx \leqq 1 \text{ for some } x \in E_+^n\}. \tag{160}$$

"Technique σ" is defined by an $m \times m$ matrix A_σ composed of some columns of A and the corresponding l_σ of l such that the corresponding $m \times m$ submatrix of B is the identity matrix I. And technique σ is said to be *viable* (or *productive*) if there exists a $z \in E_+^m$ such that

$$[I - A_\sigma]z > \theta \qquad \text{and} \qquad l_\sigma z \leqq 1.$$

LEMMA 10 If A_σ is viable, then for any $y \in E_+^m$,

$$[I - A_\sigma]\, x_\sigma = y \tag{161}$$

has a unique solution $x_\sigma \in E_+^m$.

PROOF Immediate from Hawkins–Simon theorem and its Corollary 1 in Section 2.4. Q.E.D.

THEOREM 38 (*Gale nonsubstitution theorem*) In system (159), if some $x \geq \theta$ produces $y > \theta$, there exists a viable technique σ such that the simple model (161) of Leontief type has the same output space Y as that defined by (160).

PROOF Let $\bar{y}$ be a positive vector in the output space Y and consider the problem:

$$\text{Find an } x \in E_+^n \text{ that minimizes } lx \text{ subject to } [B - A]x = \bar{y}. \tag{162}$$

Let $\bar{x}$ be a basic optimal vector for (162). Then $\bar{x}$ depends on at most m columns of $[B - A]$. Since $\bar{y} > \theta$, $\bar{x}_{sj}$ (the jth component of $\bar{x}$) must be positive for some index sj. Let A_σ be the $m \times m$ matrix composed of columns a^{sj} of A. Clearly A_σ is viable.

Let y^* be any other vector in Y. By Lemma 10, there is a unique $x^* \geqq \theta$ such that

$$[I - A_\sigma]x^* = y^*.$$

By virtue of Proposition 2, x^* is also optimal; i.e., $l_\sigma x^*$ minimizes lx among all x satisfying

$$[B - A]x = y^*.$$

Since y^* belongs to Y, there is some $x \in E_+^n$ that produces y^* and for which $lx \leqq 1$. Hence we know $l_\sigma x^* \leqq 1$. Thus

$$Y \subset Y_\sigma \equiv \{y : y = [I - A_\sigma]x \geqq \theta,\ l_\sigma x \leqq 1 \text{ for some } x \in E_+^m\}.$$

It is obvious that $Y_\sigma \subset Y$. Q.E.D.

Application 7 (*Bruno fundamental duality*) Bruno (1969) observed the identity of the optimal transformation surface with the factor price surface in a heterogeneous capital model, utilizing the duality theorem of canonical linear programming. Given the total supply of labor force L, we want to maximize the sum of consumption and investment evaluated in terms of consumption good, under the assumption that one consumption good and n ($\geqq 1$) capital goods ($=$ production goods) exist in the closed economy and that each good is producible by only a single activity characterized by a set of input coefficients of labor and capital goods, say $\{a_{0j}, a_{1j}, \ldots, a_{nj}\}$ for the jth (good) sector ($j = 0, 1, \ldots, n$), where the 0th sector means consumption good sector, a_{0j} is the labor coefficient, and a_{ij} ($i = 1, \ldots, n$) are the capital coefficients for sector j. The physical constraints on production can be summarized as

$$A\hat{H}k \leqq k, \tag{163}$$

where

$$A \equiv \begin{bmatrix} a_{00} & a_{01} & \cdots & a_{0n} \\ a_{10} & a_{11} & \cdots & a_{1n} \\ \vdots & \vdots & & \vdots \\ a_{n0} & a_{n1} & \cdots & a_{nn} \end{bmatrix}, \qquad k \equiv \begin{bmatrix} 1 \\ k_1 \\ \vdots \\ k_n \end{bmatrix},$$

$\hat{H} \equiv \operatorname{diag}(c, h_1, \ldots, h_n)$, $c \equiv C/L$, $h_i \equiv I_i/K_i$, $k_i \equiv K_i/L$, and C, I_i, K_i denote consumption, investment of capital good i ($=$ the demand for good i), endowment of capital good i, respectively. Hence the left-hand side of (163) represents the demand for goods, while the right-hand side the supply of goods. We want to determine $\hat{R} \geqq 0$ such that $p\hat{H}k$ is maximized under constraints (163), where $p \equiv (1, p_1, \ldots, p_n)$ is the vector of prices in terms of consumption good.

The dual problem corresponding to the above maximum problem is to determine $\hat{R} \geqq 0$ such that $p\hat{R}k$ is minimized under the constraints

$$p\hat{R}A \geqq p, \tag{164}$$

where $\hat{R} \equiv \operatorname{diag}(w, r_1, \ldots, r_n)$, w stands for wage rate in terms of consumption good, and r_i gross rate of return of capital good i.

By the optimal transformation surface we mean the set of all semipositive vectors $h \equiv \{c, h_1, \ldots, h_n\}$ such that production takes place at the full-utilization level for an arbitrary $k \neq \theta$; i.e., (163) holds with the equality sign. Hence at any point on the optimal transformation surface we have

$$|A\hat{H} - I| = 0. \tag{165}$$

The factor price surface is the set of all semipositive vectors $r \equiv \{w, r_1, \ldots, r_n\}$ such that every activity is operated with zero excess profit for an arbitrary $p \neq \theta$; i.e., (164) holds with the equality sign. Hence at any point on the factor price surface

$$|A^{\mathrm{T}}\hat{R} - I| = 0. \tag{166}$$

It is easily checked that the two polynomials (165) and (166) possess identical structure.

To conclude this section, we mention other important applications of linear programming to economics.

Application 8 (*Manne development program*) Manne (1970) applied Proposition 1 (sufficiency for canonical linear programming) directly to the proof of the optimality of his infinite horizon development plan.

Application 9 (*Morishima generalized fundamental Marxian theorem*) Morishima (1974) generalized the fundamental Marxian theorem stated in Section 4.4 to the case where joint production and multiple activities are allowed, relying on the duality theorem of canonical linear programming.

Application 10 (*Kornai planning in a socialist economy*) Kornai (1967) applied extensively linear programming theory to long-range sectoral and nationwide planning problems in a socialist economy.

EXERCISES

1. Let K be a closed convex set in E^n, define the set $M \subset E^{n+1}$ of nonnegative values of, and the associated normal vectors to, hyperplanes that bound K:

$$M \equiv \{(a, c) : ax \leqq c,\ c \geqq 0 \text{ for all } x \in K\},$$

and define the set dual to M:

$$K^* \equiv \{(x, -w) : ax - cw \leqq 0 \text{ for all } (a, c) \in M\}.$$

Then show the following

PROPOSITION E1 (Cass, 1974)

(i) $K = \{x:(x, -1) \in K^*\} = \{x:(x, -w) \in K^*, w \leqq 1\}$,
(ii) $M = \{(a, c): ax - cw \leqq 0 \text{ for all } (x, -w) \in K^*\}$.

2. Let K, M, K^* be those defined above in Exercise 1 with new notation: for nonnegative integers m, n with $m \leqq n$,

$$(z, -y) \equiv x, \qquad z \in E^m, \quad y \in E^{n-m} \qquad \text{(column vectors);}$$
$$(\mu, \lambda) \equiv a, \qquad \mu \in E^m, \quad \lambda \in E^{n-m} \qquad \text{(row vectors).}$$

Consider the problems:

(P) Maximize μz subject to $(z, -y) \in K$, $y \leqq \bar{y}$;
(D) Minimize $\lambda\bar{y} + c$ subject to $(\mu, \lambda, c) \in M$, $\lambda \geqq \theta$,

where μ, $\bar{y}$ are given constants. Define $(z^*, -y^*)$ as a regular optimal solution to (P) if

$$\lambda^*(\bar{y} - y^*) = 0 \qquad \text{and} \qquad \mu z^* - \lambda^* y^* = c^*$$

for some $(\mu, \lambda^*, c^*) \in M$, $\lambda^* \geqq \theta$.

Then show the following

PROPOSITION E2 (Cass, 1974) (i) Any feasible solution to (P) has value no greater than the value of any feasible solution to (D), and both problems have optimal solutions with equal values if and only if (P) has a regular optimal solution. (ii) $(z^*, -y^*)$ is a regular optimal solution to (P) if and only if $(z^*, -y^*, \lambda^*)$ is a saddle point of the Lagrangian $\mu z + \lambda(\bar{y} - y)$ for $(z, -y) \in K$, $\lambda \geqq \theta$.

3. Prove Theorem 19′.

4. Show that in the von Neumann economic system, the equilibrium growth rate $= rs$, where $r =$ rate of profit, and $s =$ capitalists' propensity to save.

5. Let A be a skew-symmetric matrix, i.e., $A^{\mathrm{T}} = -A$, and prove the following statements: (i) the matrix game A has value $v(A) = 0$; (ii) the optimal strategy for player I is identical with that for player II; and (iii) p^0 is an optimal strategy of the matrix game A if and only if $p^0 A \geqq \theta$.

6. Prove Theorem 23.

7. Let f: $E^n \to E^1$ and G: $E^n \to E^m$ be positively homogeneous of degree $r \neq 0$ on a convex cone K, and be concave and convex, respectively. Show that x^0 is a maximizer of $f(x)$ over K subject to $G(x) \leqq \theta$ if and only if there exists a $y^0 \in E_+^m$ satisfying the saddle-point condition (93). (Refer to Moeseke (1974).)

8. Prove the following fourth Kuhn–Tucker theorem. Let $L(x, y)$ be a differentiable transformation from $E^n \times E^m$ into R. Denote by L_x^0 and L_y^0 the derivatives of L at (x^0, y^0) with respect to x and y, respectively. If some $x^0 \geqq \theta$ and $y^0 \geqq \theta$ satisfy

(i) $L_x^0 \leqq \theta, \quad L_x^0 x^0 = 0,$
(ii) $L_y^0 \geqq \theta, \quad L_y^0 y^0 = 0,$
(iii) $L(x, y^0) \leqq L(x^0, y^0) + L_x^0 \cdot (x - x^0) \quad$ for $x \geqq \theta,$
(iv) $L(x^0, y) \geqq L(x^0, y^0) + L_y^0 \cdot (y - y^0) \quad$ for $y \geqq \theta;$

then

$$L(x^0, y) \geqq L(x^0, y^0) \geqq L(x, y^0) \qquad \text{for} \quad x \geqq \theta, y \geqq \theta.$$

9. Let $u(x)$ be a differentiable real-valued concave functional of $x \equiv \{x_1, \ldots, x_n\} \in E_+^n$, and consider the problem of maximizing $u(x)$ subject to $\sum_{i=1}^n p_i x_i \leqq M$ and $x_i \geqq 0$ $(i = 1, \ldots, n)$, where p_i $(i = 1, \ldots, n)$ and M are positive constants. Applying the second Kuhn–Tucker theorem to the problem, derive the following: The optimal solution $x^0 = \{x_1^0, \ldots, x_n^0\}$ satisfies

$$\sum_{i=1}^n p_i x_i^0 = M \qquad \text{and} \qquad u_i(x^0) = \lambda p_i \qquad \text{for} \quad x_i^0 > 0, \quad \lambda > 0,$$

where $u_i(x^0)$ denotes the partial derivative of $u(x)$ at x^0 with respect to x_i.

10. Prove the following theorem. (Refer to Afriat (1973).) If a column vector $\{\bar{x}^0, \bar{x}^1, \ldots, \bar{x}^r\} \in E_+^{n_0} \times E_+^{n_1} \times \cdots \times E_+^{n_r}$ is an optimal solution to the problem

$$\begin{aligned} \text{Maximize} \quad & p^0 x^0 + p^1 x^1 + \cdots + p^r x^r \\ \text{subject to} \quad & A^0 x^0 + A^1 x^1 + \cdots + A^r x^r \leqq q, \\ & b^0 x^0 \leqq c^0, \quad b^1 x^1 \leqq c^1, \ldots, b^r x^r \leqq c^r, \\ & x^0 \in E_+^{n_0}, \quad x^1 \in E_+^{n_1}, \ldots, x^r \in E_+^{n_r}, \end{aligned}$$

and if a row vector $(\bar{u}, \bar{v}^0, \bar{v}^1, \ldots, \bar{v}^r) \in E_+^m \times E_+^{m_0} \times E_+^{m_1} \times \cdots \times E_+^{m_r}$ is an optimal solution to the dual

$$\begin{aligned} \text{Minimize} \quad & uq + v^0 c^0 + v^1 c^1 + \cdots + v^r c^r \\ \text{subject to} \quad & uA^0 + v^0 b^0 \geqq p^0, \\ & uA^1 + v^1 b^1 \geqq p^1, \\ & \vdots \\ & uA^r + v^r b^r \geqq p^r, \\ & u \in E_+^m, \quad v^0 \in E_+^{m_0}, \quad v^1 \in E_+^{m_1}, \ldots, v^r \in E_+^{m_r}, \end{aligned}$$

then $\bar{x}^i$ is an optimal solution to the problem

$$\begin{aligned} \text{Maximize} \quad & (p^i - \bar{u}A^i)\, x^i \\ \text{subject to} \quad & b^i x^i \leqq c^i, \quad x^i \in E_+^{n_i} \qquad (i = 0, 1, \ldots, r), \end{aligned}$$

and $\{\bar{x}^0, \bar{x}^1, \ldots, \bar{x}^r\}$ is an optimal solution to the problem

$$\begin{aligned} \text{Maximize} \quad & (p^0 - \bar{v}^0 b^0)x^0 + (p^1 - \bar{v}^1 b^1)x^1 + \cdots + (p^r - \bar{v}^r b^r)x^r \\ \text{subject to} \quad & A^0 x^0 + A^1 x^1 + \cdots + A^r x^r \leqq q, \\ & x^0 \in E_+^{n_0}, \quad x^1 \in E_+^{n_1}, \ldots, x^r \in E_+^{n_r}, \end{aligned}$$

where $n_0, n_1, \ldots, n_r, m, m_0, m_1, \ldots, m_r$ are arbitrary positive integers.

REFERENCES AND FURTHER READING

Abadie, J. (ed.) (1957). *Nonlinear Programming*. North-Holland Publ., Amsterdam.

Afriat, S. N. (1973). "A Theorem on Shadow Prices," *Econometrica* **41**, 1197–1199.

Apostol, T. M. (1957). *Mathematical Analysis*. Addison-Wesley, Reading, Massachusetts.

Arrow, K. J., and Enthoven, A. C. (1961). "Quasi-Concave Programming," *Econometrica* **29**, 779–800.

Arrow, K. J., Hurwicz, L., and Uzawa, H. (eds.) (1958). *Studies in Linear and Nonlinear Programming*. Stanford Univ. Press, Stanford, California.

Arrow, K. J., Hurwicz, L., and Uzawa, H. (1961). "Constraint Qualification in Maximization Problems," *Naval Research Logistics Quarterly* **8**, 175–191.

Averch, H., and Johnson, L. L. (1962). "Behavior of the Firm under Regulatory Constraint," *American Economic Review* **52**, 1052–1169.

Bailey, M. J. (1955). "A Generalized Comparative Statics in Linear Programming," *Review of Economic Studies* **23**, 236–240.

Beckmann, M. J. (1955). "Comparative Statics in Linear Programming and the Giffen Paradox," *Review of Economic Studies* **23**, 232–235.

Bruckmann, G., and Weber, W. (eds.) (1971). *Contributions to the von Neumann Growth Model*. Springer-Verlag, Berlin and New York.

Bruno, M. "Fundamental Duality Relations in the Pure Theory of Capital and Growth," *Review of Economic Studies* **36**, 39–53.

Cass, D. (1974). "Duality: a Symmetric Approach from the Economist's Vantage Point," *Journal of Economic Theory* **7**, 272–295.

Chenery, H. B., and Uzawa, H. (1958). "Non-linear Programming in Economic Developments," in Arrow, Hurwicz, and Uzawa (1958), *op. cit.*, pp. 203–229.

Cox, J. C. (1973). "A Theorem on Additively-Separable, Quasi-Concave Functions," *Journal of Economic Theory* **6**, 210–212.

Dantzig, G. B. (1963). *Linear Programming and Extensions*. Princeton Univ. Press, Princeton, New Jersey.

Day, M. M. (1958). *Normed Linear Spaces*. Springer-Verlag, Berlin and New York.

Diewert, W. E. (1973). "Functional Forms for Profit and Transformation Functions," *Journal of Economic Theory* **6**, 284–316.

Eichhorn, W., and Oettli, W. (1972). "A General Formulation of the LeChatelier–Samuelson Principle," *Econometrica* **40**, 711–717.

Gale, D. (1960). *The Theory of Linear Economic Models*. McGraw-Hill, New York.

Gale, D. (1967). "On Optimal Development in a Multi-Sector Economy," *Review of Economic Studies* **34**, 1–18.

Gale, D., Kuhn, H. W., and Tucker, A. W. (1951). "Linear Programming and the Theory of Games," in *Activity Analysis of Production and Allocation* (T. C. Koopmans, ed.), pp. 317–329. Wiley, New York.

Gale, D., and Nikaido, H. (1965). "The Jacobian Matrix and Global Univalence of Mappings," *Mathematishe Annalen* **159**, 81–93; (1968), in *Readings in Mathematical Economics* (P. Newman, ed.), Vol.I. Johns Hopkins Press, Baltimore, Maryland.

Geoffrion, A. M. (1971). "Duality in Nonlinear Programming: A Simplified Applications-Oriented Development," *SIAM Review* **13**, 1–37.

Hansen, T., and Koopmans, T. C. (1972). "On the Definition and Computation of a Capital Stock Invariant under Optimization," *Journal of Economic Theory* **5**, 487–523.

Howe, C. W. (1960). "An Alternative Proof of the Existence of General Equilibrium in a von Neumann Model," *Econometrica* **28**, 635–639.

Intriligator, M. D. (1971). *Mathematical Optimization and Economic Theory*. Prentice-Hall, Englewood Cliffs, New Jersey.

Karlin, S. (1959). *Mathematical Methods and Theory in Games, Programming and Economics*, Vol.I. Addison-Wesley, Reading, Massachusetts.

Katzner, D. W. (1970). *Static Demand Theory*. Macmillan, New York.

Kemeny, J. G., Morgenstern, O., and Thompson, G. L. (1956). "A Generalization of the von Neumann Model of an Expanding Economy," *Econometrica* **24**, 115–135.

Koopmans, T. C. (1964). "Economic Growth at a Maximal Rate," *Quarterly Journal of Economics* **78**, 355–394; (1967), in *Activity Analysis in the Theory of Growth and Planning* (E. Malinvaud and M. O. L. Bacharach, eds.). Macmillan, New York.

Kornai, J. (1967). *Mathematical Planning of Structural Decisions* (English translation). North-Holland Publ., Amsterdam.

Kuhn, H. W., and Tucker, A. W. (1951). "Nonlinear Programming," in *Proceedings of the Second Berkeley Symposium on Mathematical Statistics and Probability* (J. Neyman, ed.), pp. 481–492. Univ. of California Press, Berkeley, California; (1968), in *Readings in Mathematical Economics* (P. Newman, ed.), Vol. I. Johns Hopkins Press, Baltimore, Maryland.

Kusumoto, S. (1977). "Global Characterization of the Weak LeChatelier–Samuelson Principles and Its Applications to Economic Behaviour, Preferences, and Utility—'Embedding' Theorems," *Econometrica* **45** (forthcoming).

Leblanc, G., and Moeseke, P. V. (1976). "The LeChatelier Principle in Convex Programming," *Review of Economic Studies* **43**, 143–147.

Łoś, J., and Łoś, M. W. (eds.) (1974). *Mathematical Models in Economics*. North-Holland Publ., Amsterdam.

Luenberger, D. G. (1969). *Optimization by Vector Space Methods*. Wiley, New York.

Luenberger, D. G. (1973). *Introduction to Linear and Nonlinear Programming*. Addison-Wesley, Reading, Massachusetts.

McKenzie, L. W. (1967). "Maximal Paths in the von Neumann Model," in *Activity Analysis in the Theory of Growth and Planning* (E. Malinvaud and M. O. L. Bacharach, eds.), pp. 43–63. Macmillan, New York.

Mangasarian, O. L. (1969). *Nonlinear Programming*. McGraw-Hill, New York.

Mangasarian, O. L., and Fromovitz, S. (1967). "The Fritz John Necessary Optimality Conditions in the Presence of Equality and Inequality Constraints," *Journal of Mathematical Analysis and Applications* **17**, 37–47.

Manne, A. S. (1970). "Sufficient Conditions for Optimality in an Infinite Horizon Development Plan," *Econometrica* **38**, 18–38.

Moeseke, P. V. (1974). "Saddlepoint in Homogeneous Programming without Slater," *Econometrica* **42**, 593–596.

Morishima, M. (1961). "Proof of a Turnpike Theorem: The 'No Joint Production Case'," *Review of Economic Studies* **28**, 89–97.

Morishima, M. (1964). *Equilibrium Stability and Growth*. Oxford Univ. Press, London and New York.

Morishima, M. (1969). *Theory of Economic Growth*. Oxford Univ. Press, London and New York.

Morishima, M. (1974). "Marx in the light of Modern Economic Theory," *Econometrica* **42**, 611–632.

von Neumann, J. (1937). (English translation, 1945) "A Model of General Economic Equilibrium," *Review of Economic Studies* **13**, 1–9.

Newman, P. (1969). "Some Properties of Concave Functions," *Journal of Economic Theory* **1**, 291–314.

Nikaido, H. (1968). *Convex Structures and Economic Theory*. Academic Press, New York.

Ponstein, J. (1967). "Seven Kinds of Convexity," *SIAM Review* **9**, 115–119.

Radner, R. (1961). "Paths of Economic Growth that Are Optimal with Regard only to Final States: A Turnpike Theorem," *Review of Economic Studies* **28**, 98–104.

Robinson, S. M. (1973). "Irreducibility in the von Neumann Model," *Econometrica* **41**, 569–573.

Rockafellar, R. T. (1970). *Convex Analysis*. Princeton Univ. Press, Princeton, New Jersey.

Samuelson, P. A. (1946). "Comparative Statics and the Logic of Economic Maximizing," *Review of Economic Studies* **14**, 41–43.

Samuelson, P. A. (1949). "The LeChatelier Principle in Linear Programming," RAND Corporation Research Memorandum; (1966), in *The Collected Scientific Papers of Paul A. Samuelson* (J. E. Stiglitz, ed.), Vol. 1, pp. 638–650. MIT Press, Cambridge, Massachusetts.

Samuelson, P. A. (1947). *Foundations of Economic Analysis*. Harvard Univ. Press, Cambridge, Massachusetts.

Takayama, A. (1974). *Mathematical Economics*. Dryden Press, Hinsdale, Illinois.

Thompson, G. L. (1956). "On the solution of a Game-Theoretic Problem," in *Linear Inequalities and Related Systems* (H. W. Kuhn and A. W. Tucker, eds.), pp. 275–284. Princeton Univ. Press, Princeton, New Jersey.

Tucker, A. W. (1956). "Dual Systems of Homogeneous Linear Relations," in *Linear Inequalities and Related Systems* (H. W. Kuhn and A. W. Tucker, eds.), pp. 3–18. Princeton Univ. Press, Princeton, New Jersey.

Uzawa, H. (1964). "Duality Principles in the Theory of Cost and Production," *International Economic Review* **5**, 216–220.

Valentine, F. A. (1964). *Convex Sets*. McGraw-Hill, New York.

Weil, R. L. (1970). "Solutions to the Decomposable von Neumann Model," *Econometrica* **38**, 276–280.

Wolfe, P. (1961). "A Duality Theorem for Nonlinear Programming," *Quarterly of Applied Mathematics* **19**, 239–244.

Zajac, E. E. (1972). "Lagrange Multiplier Values at Constrained Optima," *Journal of Economic Theory* **4**, 125–131.

Chapter 9

Optimal Control of Dynamical Economic Systems

9.1 Pontryagin Maximum Principle: Necessity and Sufficiency

One of the most powerful techniques of optimal control is the so-called Pontryagin maximum principle. (Refer to Pontryagin *et al.* (1962).) The principle may be summarized as Theorems 1–3, where we use the notation

$x \equiv (x_1, \ldots, x_n)$ an n-vector of state variables,

$v \equiv (v_1, \ldots, v_m)$ an m-vector of control variables,

$y \equiv (y_1, \ldots, y_n)$ an n-vector of auxiliary variables.

These vectors are supposed to vary with continuous time $t \in [a, b]$, $a < b \leqq +\infty$. (For discrete-time cases, see the second half of Section 9.4.)

DEFINITION 1 If a function $u(t)$ on $[a, b]$ has a finite number of discontinuous points, if it is differentiable on each segment between discontinuous points, and if there exist bounded limits at each discontinuous point τ:

$$u(\tau - 0) \equiv \lim_{t \to \tau, t < \tau} u(t) \qquad \text{and} \qquad u(\tau + 0) \equiv \lim_{t \to \tau, t > \tau} u(t),$$

then u is said to be *piecewise continuous* on $[a, b]$. If the control vector function v is piecewise continuous on a prescribed time interval, it is called an *admissible control* on the interval.

THEOREM 1 (*Pontryagin maximum principle—the free final state case*) Let v belong to a prescribed subset Ω of a normed space, and let $v = v^*$ be an admissible control on a fixed time interval $[a, b]$ that maximizes

$$J = \int_a^b f^0(x, v)\,dt \tag{1}$$

subject to the constraints on state variable vector x

$$\dot{x}_i = f_i(x, v) \qquad \text{for} \quad i = 1, \ldots, n \tag{2}$$

and

$$x(a) = \text{constant}. \tag{3}$$

Assume that f^0 and $F \equiv \{f_1, \ldots, f_n\}$ are continuously Fréchet differentiable with respect to x and that F satisfies a uniform Lipschitz condition. (Refer to (5) in Section 7.1.) Then there exists an auxiliary variable vector y such that for each t, $v^*(t)$ maximizes the Hamiltonian function

$$H(x, v, y) \equiv f^0(x, v) + \sum_{i=1}^{n} y_i f_i(x, v), \tag{4}$$

the y_i ($i = 1, \ldots, n$) satisfy

$$\dot{y}_i = -\partial H/\partial x_i \qquad \text{(evaluated along the optimal trajectory)}, \tag{5}$$

and a transversality condition holds:

$$y_i(b) = 0 \qquad \text{for} \quad i = 1, \ldots, n. \tag{6}$$

THEOREM 2 (*Pontryagin maximum principle—the fixed final state case*) Let v belong to a prescribed subset Ω of a normed space, and let $v = v^*$ be an admissible control on a time interval $[a, b]$, where b is not fixed, that maximizes (1) subject to (2) and

$$x(a) = \text{constant}, \qquad x(b) \geqq x^b \equiv (x_1^b, \ldots, x_n^b) \tag{3'}$$

for a given nonnegative x^b. Assume that f^0 and $F \equiv \{f_1, \ldots, f_n\}$ are continuously Fréchet differentiable with respect to x and that F satisfies a uniform Lipschitz condition. Then, there exists an auxiliary variable vector y such that for each t, $v^*(t)$ maximizes the Hamiltonian function (4), y_i ($i = 1, \ldots, n$) satisfy (5), and a transversality condition holds:

$$y_i(b)[x_i(b) - x_i^b] = 0, \qquad y_i(b) \geqq 0 \qquad \text{for} \quad i = 1, \ldots, n. \tag{6'}$$

THEOREM 3 (*Pontryagin maximum principle—the time optimal case*) Let v belong to a prescribed subset Ω of a normed space, and let $v = v^*$ be an admissible control on a time interval $[a, b]$, where b is not fixed, that minimizes $b - a$ subject to (2) and

$$x(a) = \text{constant}, \qquad x(b) \geqq x^b, \qquad x(b) \ngtr x^b. \tag{3''}$$

Assume that $F \equiv \{f_1, \ldots, f_n\}$ is continuously Fréchet differentiable with respect to x and that F satisfies a uniform Lipschitz condition. Then, there exists an auxiliary variable vector y such that for each t, $v^*(t)$ maximizes the Hamiltonian function

$$H(x, v, y) \equiv \sum_{i=1}^{n} y_i f_i(x, v), \tag{4'}$$

the y_i ($i = 1, \ldots, n$) satisfy (5), and the transversality condition (6′) holds.

Remark Along the optimal trajectory that satisfies the Pontryagin maximum principle, the value of the Hamiltonian function is found to be invariant for all $t \in [a, b]$.

We shall sketch a proof of the above Pontryagin maximum principle. In order to do this, two lemmas are needed.

LEMMA 1 Let μ be a finite constant and let $[a, b]$ be an interval on a real line. If

$$z(t) \leqq \mu \int_a^t (z(\tau) + w(\tau))\, d\tau \qquad \text{for} \quad t \in [a, b], \tag{7}$$

where z, w are nonnegative-valued functions on $[a, b]$, then

$$z(t) \leqq \mu e^{\mu(b-a)} \int_a^b w(\tau)\, d\tau \qquad \text{for} \quad t \in [a, b]. \tag{8}$$

PROOF It follows from (7) that

$$z(t) \leqq \mu \int_a^t (z(\tau_1) + w(\tau_1))\, d\tau_1, \tag{1*}$$

$$\mu z(\tau_1) \leqq \mu^2 \int_a^{\tau_1} (z(\tau_2) + w(\tau_2))\, d\tau_2,$$

$$\vdots$$

$$\mu^\nu z(\tau_\nu) \leqq \mu^{\nu+1} \int_a^{\tau_\nu} (z(\tau_{\nu+1}) + w(\tau_{\nu+1}))\, d\tau_{\nu+1}.$$

Thus

$$\mu \int_a^t z(\tau_1)\, d\tau_1 \leqq \mu^2 \int_a^t \int_a^{\tau_1} (z(\tau_2) + w(\tau_2))\, d\tau_2\, d\tau_1, \tag{2*}$$

$$\vdots$$

$$\mu^\nu \int_a^t \int_a^{\tau_1} \cdots \int_a^{\tau_{\nu-1}} z(\tau_\nu)\, d\tau_\nu \cdots d\tau_1 \leqq \mu^{\nu+1} \int_a^t \int_a^{\tau_1} \cdots \int_a^{\tau_\nu} (z(\tau_{\nu+1}) + w(\tau_{\nu+1}))\, d\tau_{\nu+1} \cdots d\tau_1. \tag{ν + 1*}$$

Add inequalities (1*), (2*), . . ., (ν + 1*), . . ., to infinity, on each side. Then, after cancellations, we have

$$z(t) \leqq \mu \int_a^t w(\tau_1)\, d\tau_1 + \mu^2 \int_a^t \int_a^{\tau_1} w(\tau_2)\, d\tau_2\, d\tau_1 + \cdots$$

$$+ \mu^{\nu+1} \int_a^t \cdots \int_a^{\tau_\nu} w(\tau_{\nu+1})\, d\tau_{\nu+1} \cdots d\tau_1$$

$$+ \cdots + \lim_{\nu\to\infty} \mu^{\nu+1} \int_a^t \cdots \int_a^{\tau_\nu} z(\tau_{\nu+1})\, d\tau_{\nu+1} \cdots d\tau_1$$

$$\leqq \mu \int_a^t w(\tau_1)\, d\tau_1 + \mu^2 \int_a^t d\tau_1 \int_a^t w(\tau_2)\, d\tau_2$$

$$+ \cdots + \mu^{\nu+1} \int_a^t \cdots \int_a^{\tau_{\nu-1}} d\tau_\nu \cdots d\tau_1 \int_a^t w(\tau_{\nu+1})\, d\tau_{\nu+1} + \cdots$$

$$= \mu \int_a^t w(\tau)\, d\tau \cdot (1 + \mu(t-a) + \cdots + \mu^\nu (t-a)^\nu/\nu! + \cdots) + Z,$$

where $Z \equiv \mu \lim_{\nu\to\infty} (\mu^\nu (t-a)^\nu/\nu!) \int_a^{\tau_\nu} z(\tau_{\nu+1})\, d\tau_{\nu+1} = 0$ since

$$\lim_{\nu\to\infty} \frac{\mu^\nu (t-a)^\nu}{\nu!} = \lim_{\nu\to\infty} \frac{(\mu(t-a)e)^\nu}{(2\pi)^{1/2}\nu^{\nu+1/2}} = 0$$

(cf. Stirling's formula) and since $\tau_\nu \to a$ as $\nu \to \infty$. Therefore

$$z(t) \leqq \mu e^{\mu(t-a)} \int_a^t w(\tau)\, d\tau \qquad \text{for} \quad t \in [a, b],$$

from which (8) follows. Q.E.D.

LEMMA 2 (Luenberger, 1969) Let X and V be normed vector spaces. Let $G(x, v)$ be a transformation from $X \times V$ into X and let $g(x, v)$ be a real-valued functional on $X \times V$. Assume that G and g are Fréchet differentiable with respect to x, that $G(x, v) = \theta$ defines a unique function $x = x(v)$, and that $x(v)$ satisfies a uniform Lipschitz condition (see (5) in Section 7.1); i.e., there exist $\sigma > 0$ and $\mu > 0$ such that

$$\|x(v) - x(u)\| \leqq \mu \|v - u\| \qquad \text{for} \quad v, u \text{ satisfying } \|v - u\| < \sigma. \tag{9}$$

Let Ω be a prescribed subset of V and define a Lagrangian function

$$L(x, v, y) \equiv g(x, v) + yG(x, v) \tag{10}$$

for $x \in X$, $v \in \Omega$ and $y \in X^*$, where X^* stands for the dual of X. Further, we assume g_x is continuous on $X \times \Omega$. If y^* is a solution of

$$g_x(x(u), u) + y^* G_x(x(u), u) = \theta, \tag{11}$$

then for any $v \in \Omega$

$$J[u] - J[v] = L(x(u), u, y^*) - L(x(u), v, y^*) + o(\|v - u\|), \tag{12}$$

where $J[u] \equiv g(x(u), u)$.

PROOF Since g is Fréchet differentiable with respect to x,

$$|g(x(u), v) - g(x(v), v) - g_x(x(v), v) \cdot (x(u) - x(v))| = o(\|x(u) - x(v)\|),$$

or equivalently

$$g(x(u), v) - g(x(v), v) = g_x(x(v), v) \cdot (x(u) - x(v)) + o(\|x(u) - x(v)\|)$$

$$\begin{aligned}&= g_x(x(u), u) \cdot (x(u) - x(v))\\ &\quad + (g_x(x(v), v) - g_x(x(u), u)) \cdot (x(u) - x(v))\\ &\quad + o(\|x(u) - x(v)\|).\end{aligned}$$

The continuity of g_x on $X \times \Omega$ ensures the existence of a constant M such that for $v, u \in \Omega$,

$$|g_x(x(v), v) - g_x(x(u), u)| \leqq M(\|x(v) - x(u)\| + \|v - u\|).$$

This, together with (9), implies that as $u \to v$, $x(u)$ tends to $x(v)$ and hence $g_x(x(u), u)$ tends to $g_x(x(v), v)$. Thus, we get

$$g(x(u), v) - g(x(v), v) = g_x(x(u), u) \cdot (x(u) - x(v)) + o(\|u - v\|).$$

Considering the identity

$$J[v] - J[u] = g(x(v), v) - g(x(u), v) + g(x(u), v) - g(x(u), u),$$

we finally obtain

$$\begin{aligned}J[v] - J[u] = g(x(u), v) - g(x(u), u) + g_x(x(u), u) \cdot (x(v)\\ - x(u)) + o(\|v - u\|).\end{aligned} \tag{13}$$

Likewise, since G is Fréchet differentiable with respect to x and since

$$\theta = G(x(v), v) - G(x(u), v) + G(x(u), v) - G(x(u), u),$$

$$[G(x(u), v) - G(x(u), u)] \to G_x(x(v), v) \cdot (x(u) - x(v)) \qquad \text{as} \quad x(u) \to x(v).$$

$G(x(v), v) = \theta$ for all $v \in \Omega$ implies

$$G_x(x(v), v) \cdot (x(u) - x(v)) = G_x(x(u), u) \cdot (x(u) - x(v)).$$

Thus, in view of (9),

$$\|G(x(u), v) - G(x(u), u) - G_x(x(u), u) \cdot (x(u) - x(v))\| = o(\|v - u\|).$$

For the y^* satisfying (11), therefore, we have

$$y^*G(x(u), v) - y^*G(x(u), u) + g_x(x(u), u) \cdot (x(u) - x(v)) = o(\|v - u\|). \tag{14}$$

Combining (13) and (14) and taking (10) into account, we have (12). Q.E.D.

We shall follow mainly Luenberger (1969) to sketch a proof of Theorem 1.

PROOF OF THEOREM 1 First we introduce two spaces:

$$X \equiv C^n[a, b] \qquad \text{and} \qquad V \equiv L_1^m[a, b], \tag{*}$$

where

$$C^n[a, b] \equiv \{x: x = (x_1, \ldots, x_n), x_i = \text{a real-valued continuous function on } [a, b], i = 1, \ldots, n\}$$

with norm

$$\|x\| = \max_{a \leq t \leq b} \left(\sum_{i=1}^{n} (x_i(t))^2 \right)^{1/2}, \tag{15}$$

and

$$L_1^m[a, b] \equiv \{v : v = (v_1, \ldots, v_m), v_i = \text{a real-valued function on } [a, b]\}$$

with norm

$$\|v\| = \int_a^b \sum_{i=1}^{m} |v_i(t)| \, dt. \tag{16}$$

These spaces are found to be normed vector spaces. State variable vector x and control variable vector v are supposed to belong to the above-mentioned X and a prescribed subset Ω of V, respectively.

Define

$$F(x, v) \equiv \{f_1(x, v), \ldots, f_n(x, v)\},$$

$$G(x, v) \equiv x(t) - x(a) - \int_a^t F(x(\tau), v(\tau)) \, d\tau, \tag{17}$$

$$g(x, v) \equiv \int_a^b f^0(x(t), v(t)) \, dt. \tag{18}$$

Let $x, x + \Delta x$ correspond to $v, v + \Delta v$, respectively, in $\{(x, v) : G(x, v) = \theta\}$. Then, by virtue of (17) and $\Delta x(a) = \theta$,

$$\begin{aligned} \theta &= G(x + \Delta x, v + \Delta v) - G(x, v) \\ &= \Delta x(t) - \int_a^t [F(x + \Delta x, v + \Delta v) - F(x, v)] \, d\tau. \end{aligned}$$

Hence, using the Euclidean norm, we have for $t \in [a, b]$,

$$\begin{aligned} \|\Delta x(t)\| &= \left\| \int_a^t [F(x + \Delta x, v + \Delta v) - F(x, v)] \, d\tau \right\| \\ &\leqq \int_a^t \|F(x + \Delta x, v + \Delta v) - F(x, v)\| \, d\tau \\ &\leqq \int_a^t \mu(\|\Delta x(\tau)\| + \|\Delta v(\tau)\|) \, d\tau \qquad \text{(in view of (5) in Section 7.1)} \\ &\leqq \mu e^{\mu(b-a)} \int_a^b \|\Delta v(\tau)\| \, d\tau \qquad \text{(by Lemma 1).} \end{aligned} \tag{19}$$

Since in view of (16),

$$\int_a^b \|\Delta v(\tau)\| \, d\tau = \int_a^b \left(\sum_{i=1}^{m} (\Delta v_i(\tau))^2 \right)^{1/2} d\tau \leqq \int_a^b \sum_{i=1}^{m} |\Delta v_i(\tau)| \, d\tau \equiv \|\Delta v\|,$$

and since in view of (15),

$$\|\Delta x(t)\| = \left(\sum_{i=1}^{n} (\Delta x_i(t))^2 \right)^{1/2} \leqq \max_{a \leq t \leq b} \left(\sum_{i=1}^{n} (\Delta x_i(t))^2 \right)^{1/2} \equiv \|\Delta x\|,$$

it follows from (19) that

$$\|\Delta x\| \leqq K\|\Delta v\|, \qquad \text{where} \quad K \equiv \mu e^{\mu(b-a)};$$

i.e., x satisfies a uniform Lipschitz condition.

By virtue of (17) and (18), the Lagrangian function (10) is now reduced to

$$L(x, v, y) = \int_a^b f^0(x, v)\, d\tau, \tag{20}$$

since in view of (2)

$$\int_a^t F(x, v)\, d\tau = \int_a^t \dot{x}\, d\tau = x(t) - x(a).$$

On the other hand, by virtue of (4) and (2),

$$\begin{aligned} \int_a^b H(x, v, y)\, dt &= \int_a^b f^0(x, v)\, dt + \int_a^b y\dot{x}\, dt \\ &= \int_a^b f^0(x, v)\, dt - \int_a^b \dot{y}x\, dt - y(a)x(a) + y(b)x(b) \end{aligned} \tag{21}$$

since

$$\int_a^b y\dot{x}\, dt = yx]_a^b - \int_a^b \dot{y}x\, dt.$$

It follows from (20) and (21) that

$$\begin{aligned} \int_a^b [H(x, u, y) - H(x, v, y)]\, dt &= \int_a^b [f^0(x, u) - f^0(x, v)]\, dt \\ &= L(x, u, y) - L(x, v, y). \end{aligned} \tag{22}$$

Let x^* be an optimal x and let y^* be the associated auxiliary variable vector y. Then, in analogy with the Lagrange multiplier theorem (Theorem 18 in Section 7.4), we know

$$L_x(x^*, v^*, y^*) \equiv g_x(x^*, v^*) + y^*G_x(x^*, v^*) = \theta. \tag{23}$$

Since g_x and G_x are linear and continuous in $h \in X$, so is L_x. Taking (17) and (18) into account, we represent the differential of L with respect to x with increment h as

$$\delta L_x(h) \equiv \int_a^b f_x^0 h\, d\tau + yh - y\int_a^t F_x h\, d\tau,$$

where f_x^0 is the gradient of f^0 and

$$F_x \equiv \begin{bmatrix} f_{11} & f_{12} & \cdots & f_{1n} \\ \vdots & \vdots & & \vdots \\ f_{n1} & f_{n2} & \cdots & f_{nn} \end{bmatrix}, \qquad f_{ij} \equiv \partial f_i/\partial x_j \quad (i, j = 1, \ldots, n).$$

The presentation of y acting on $h \in X$ is

$$yh = \int h\,dy = \int_a^b \dot{y}h\,dt.$$

Similarly,

$$\begin{aligned} y\int_a^t F_x h\,d\tau &= \int_a^b \dot{y}\int_a^t F_x h\,d\tau \cdot dt \\ &= y\int_a^t F_x h\,d\tau\,]_a^b - \int_a^b yF_x h\,dt \\ &= \int_a^b (y(b) - y(t))\,F_x h\,dt. \end{aligned}$$

Thus

$$\delta L_x(h) = \int_a^b (f_x^0 + \dot{y} - y(b)F_x + yF_x)h\,dt. \tag{24}$$

$\delta L_x(h)$ must vanish for $x = x^*$, $v = v^*$, $y = y^*$, and for any $h \in X$. Hence the term inside the parentheses on the right-hand side of (24) must vanish; i.e., along the optimal trajectory

$$\dot{y} = -f_x^0 - yF_x + y(b)F_x. \tag{25}$$

With the boundary condition $y(b) = \theta$, Eq. (25), now reduced to (5), defines a unique function $y(t)$ for $t \in [a, b]$.

Since y^* satisfies (24), applying Lemma 2 to the present problem and taking (22) into consideration, we get for any $v \in \Omega$

$$J[v^*] - J[v] = \int_a^b [H(x^*, v^*, y^*) - H(x^*, v, y^*)]\,dt + o(\|v - v^*\|). \tag{26}$$

We shall show that (26) implies

$$H(x^*, v^*, y^*) \geqq H(x^*, v, y^*) \qquad \text{for any} \quad v \in \Omega \text{ and } t \in [a, b]. \tag{27}$$

Suppose to the contrary that there exist $u \in \Omega$ and $t_1 \in [a, b]$ such that

$$H(x^*(t_1), v^*(t_1), y^*(t_1)) < H(x^*(t_1), u(t_1), y^*(t_1)).$$

In view of the continuity of H, there exist $\sigma < 0$ and an interval $[a', b']$ containing t_1 such that

$$H(x^*(t), v^*(t), y^*(t)) - H(x^*(t), u(t), y^*(t)) < \sigma \qquad \text{for } t \in [a', b'].$$

Let $v(t)$ be the piecewise continuous function equal to $u(t)$ on $[a', b']$ and equal to $v^*(t)$ outside $[a', b']$. Then

$$\begin{aligned} &\int_a^b [H(x^*, v^*, y^*) - H(x^*, v, y^*)]\,dt \\ &\qquad = \int_{a'}^{b'} [H(x^*, v^*, y^*) - H(x^*, u, y^*)]\,dt \\ &\qquad < \int_{a'}^{b'} \sigma\,dt = \sigma\,(b' - a'). \end{aligned}$$

Thus, from (26),

$$J[v^*] - J[v] < \sigma (b' - a') + o(\|v - v^*\|).$$

But $\|v - v^*\| = o([b' - a'])$ since $v(t) = v^*(t)$ for $t \notin [a', b']$. Hence, by selecting $[a', b']$ sufficiently small, $J[v^*] - J[v]$ can be made negative, contradicting the optimality of v^*. Q.E.D.

Remark (*on the proof of Theorems* 2 *and* 3) Imposing an additional boundary condition (3′) necessitates the requirement (6′) since in analogy with the second Kuhn–Tucker theorem (Theorem 25 in Section 8.4), maximization of $L(x, v, y)$ under the constraints

$$x(b) - x^b \geqq \theta \qquad \text{and} \qquad x(b) \geqq \theta,$$

will entail the existence of $y(b) \geqq \theta$ such that

$$y(b)[x(b) - x^b] = 0.$$

Theorem 3 can be obtained by putting $f^0 \equiv -1$ in Theorem 2.

Perhaps it is more important for applying the Pontryagin maximum principle to economic systems to know that those conditions stated in the principle also constitute a part of the sufficiency conditions for it. Thus we shall next verify these sufficiency conditions rigorously. Turning now to sufficient conditions for the Pontryagin maximum principle, one will notice that the sufficient conditions turn out to be equal to the hypotheses stated in the principle plus concavity assumptions on some mappings and that the problem treated in our sufficiency theorem below is more general than the preceding Pontryagin maximum principle. We follow Mangasarian (1966) to prove the theorem. [In Theorems 4, 5, and 6, spaces X and V are as in (*).]

THEOREM 4 (*sufficiency for maximum principle*) Consider the problem of maximizing

$$J[x, v] \equiv \int_a^b f^0(x, v)\, dt + s(x(b)) \tag{28}$$

subject to

$$\dot{x} = F(x, v), \tag{29}$$

$$x(a) = \text{constant}, \tag{30}$$

$$Q(x(b)) \geqq \theta, \tag{31}$$

where $x(\in X)$ and $v(\in V)$ represent a state variable n-vector function and a control variable m-vector function, respectively, defined on the real interval $[a, b]$, f^0 is a functional of x and v, s means an evaluation function of the final state, F is a transformation from $X \times V$ into X, and Q is a transformation from X into E^r, regulating the final state. Let v be an admissible control on $\Omega \subset V$. Define the Hamiltonian

$$H(x, v, y) \equiv f^0(x, v) + yF(x, v), \tag{32}$$

where x and y are continuous on $[a, b]$. Assume that f and F are differentiable in (x, v), that f^0 and yF are concave in (x, v) on $[a, b]$ and that Q and s are differentiable and concave in $x(b)$. If there exist x^*, v^*, y, and z ($\geqq \theta$) satisfying relations (29)–(31) and

$$\dot{y} = -\partial H^*/\partial x \equiv -H_x^* = -f_x^* - yF_x^*, \tag{33}$$

$$\theta = \partial H^*/\partial v \equiv H_v^* = f_v^* + yF_v^*, \tag{34}$$

$$zQ^* = 0, \tag{35}$$

$$y(b) = \partial(s + zQ)/\partial x(b)|_{x^*(b)} = s_{x(b)}^* + zQ_{x(b)}^*, \tag{36}$$

where $H^* \equiv H(x^*, v^*, y)$, $f^* \equiv f^0(x^*, v^*)$, $F^* \equiv F(x^*, v^*)$, $Q^* \equiv Q(x^*(b))$, $s^* \equiv s(x^*(b))$, and we use the convention that $H_x \equiv \partial H/\partial x$ and the like, then x^*, v^* will maximize (28) subject to (29)–(31).

PROOF Let f^* denote $f^0(x^*, v^*)$. For any $x \in X$, $v \in \Omega$,

$$
\begin{aligned}
&J[x, v] - J[x^*, v^*] \\
&= \int_a^b (f^0 - f^*)\, dt + s - s^* \\
&\leqq \int_a^b [f_x^*(x - x^*) + f_v^*(v - v^*)]\, dt + s_{x(b)}^*(x(b) - x^*(b)) && (3^*) \\
&= \int_a^b [-(yF_x^* + \dot{y})(x - x^*) - yF_v^*(v - v^*)]\, dt \\
&\quad + (y(b) - zQ_{x(b)}^*)(x(b) - x^*(b)) && (4^*) \\
&= \int_a^b [yF_x^*(x^* - x) + yF_v^*(v^* - v) - y(F^* - F)]\, dt \\
&\quad + zQ_{x(b)}^*(x^*(b) - x(b)) && (5^*) \\
&\leqq zQ_{x(b)}^*(x^*(b) - x(b)) && (6^*) \\
&\leqq zQ^* - zQ && (7^*) \\
&\leqq 0, && (8^*)
\end{aligned}
$$

where the following relations are supposed to be taken into consideration:

in (3*): differentiability and concavity of f^0 and s;
in (4*): (33), (34), and (36);
in (5*): (29), (30), and continuity of x, x^*, and y, with

$$\int_a^b \dot{y}(x^* - x)\, dt = y(x^* - x)]_a^b - \int_a^b y(\dot{x}^* - \dot{x})\, dt;$$

in (6*): differentiability and concavity of yF;
in (7*): differentiability and concavity of Q;

in (8*): (35), $z \geqq \theta$, and (31). Q.E.D.

Remark 1 (33) need not be satisfied at discontinuous points of v.

Remark 2 The concavity assumption of yF in Theorem 4 can be replaced by the following assumption:

$$y \geqq \theta \qquad \text{and} \qquad \text{concavity of } F. \tag{37}$$

Remark 3 If $x(b) \geqq x^b$ (fixed), we put

$$Q(x(b)) = x(b) - x^b.$$

Then, (35), (36), and $z \geqq \theta$ yield

$$(y(b) - s^*_{x(b)})(x(b) - x^b) = 0, \qquad y(b) - s^*_{x(b)} \geqq \theta. \tag{38}$$

In particular, if the function s does not exist, (38) reduces to

$$y(b)(x(b) - x^b) = 0, \qquad y(b) \geqq \theta, \tag{38'}$$

which is nothing but the transversality condition in Theorem 2.

Remark 4 (34) together with the concavity of H implies that H^* is the maximum value of all $H(x, v, y)$.

In view of Theorem 4 and the remarks above, we know that any policy satisfying all the hypotheses in the Pontryagin maximum principle is optimal, provided some mappings are differentiable and concave. This proviso could be modified without changing its effect, as is seen in the following theorem.

THEOREM 5 (Arrow and Kurz, 1970) Let $v = v(x, y)$ be the solution v (an admissible control on $\Omega \subset V$) to the problem of maximizing (32) for specified values of x and y, and denote

$$\bar{H}(x, y) \equiv f^0(x, \bar{v}(x, y)) + yF(x, \bar{v}(x, y)) \geqq H(x, v, y) \qquad \text{for} \quad v \in \Omega.$$

If $\bar{H}(x, y)$ is concave in x for given y on $[a, b]$, then any policy satisfying all the hypotheses in the Pontryagin maximum principle (Theorem 1, 2, or 3) is optimal.

PROOF Let x^* be the solution x of

$$\dot{x} = F(x, \bar{v}(x, y)), \; x(a) = \text{constant}, \qquad \text{for given } y.$$

By the concavity of $\bar{H}(x, y)$ in x for given y on $[a, b]$,

$$\bar{H}(x, y) \leqq \bar{H}(x^*, y) + \bar{H}_x(x^*, y)(x - x^*)$$

for any x, y satisfying the constraints. By definition and (29),

$$H(x, v, y) = f^0(x, v) + y\dot{x}$$

and in particular

$$\bar{H}(x^*, y) = H(x^*, \bar{v}^*, y) = f^0(x^*, \bar{v}^*) + y\dot{x}^*,$$

where $\bar{v}^* \equiv \bar{v}(x^*, y)$. We have also

$$-\dot{y} = \bar{H}_x(x^*, y).$$

Thus we get

$$f^0(x^*, \bar{v}^*) + y\dot{x}^* - \dot{y}(x - x^*) \geqq f^0(x, v) + y\dot{x},$$

or equivalently

$$f^0(x^*, \bar{v}^*) - f^0(x, v) \geqq y(\dot{x} - \dot{x}^*) + \dot{y}(x - x^*).$$

Integrating this inequality on $[a, b]$ yields

$$\int_b^a (f^0(x^*, \bar{v}^*) - f^0(x, v))\, dt \geqq y(x - x^*)]_a^b = y(b)(x(b) - x^*(b)) \tag{39}$$

since $x(a) =$ constant.

In the case where the final state is free, there is a boundary condition $y(b) = 0$. Then it follows from (39) that

$$\int_a^b f^0(x^*, \bar{v}^*)\, dt \geqq \int_a^b f^0(x, v)\, dt. \tag{40}$$

In the case where the final state is specified as

$$x(b) \geqq x^b \qquad \text{(fixed)},$$

there is a transversality condition (38′), and hence (40) holds as well since

$$y(b)(x(b) - x^*(b)) = y(b)(x(b) - x^b) - y(b)(x^*(b) - x^b) = 0. \qquad \text{Q.E.D.}$$

Lastly, we shall supply sufficient conditions for a separable case of the maximum principle, referring to Mangasarian (1966).

THEOREM 6 (*sufficiency for the maximum principle—a separable case*) Consider the problem of maximizing

$$\int_a^b (f^0(x) + g^0(v))\, dt + s(x(b)) \tag{41}$$

subject to

$$\dot{x} = F(x) + G(v), \tag{42}$$

$$x(a) = \text{constant}, \tag{43}$$

$$Q(x(b)) \geqq \theta, \tag{44}$$

where x ($\in X$) and v ($\in V$) represent a state variable n-vector function and a control variable m-vector function, respectively, defined on the real interval $[a, b]$, f^0 and g^0 are functionals of x and v, respectively, s denotes an evaluation function of the final state, F and G are transformations from X into X and from V into X, respectively, and Q is a transformation from X into E^r, regulating the final state. Let v be an admissible control on $\Omega \subset V$ and y be an auxiliary n-vector function. Assume that x, y are continuous on $[a, b]$, that f^0 and F are differentiable in x, that f^0 and yF are concave in x on $[a, b]$ and that Q and s are differentiable and concave in $x(b)$. If there exist x^*, v^*, y, and z ($\geqq \theta$) satisfying relations (42)–(44) and

$$-\dot{y} = f_x^0(x^*) + yF_x(x^*), \tag{45}$$

$$g^0(v^*) + yG(v^*) \geqq g^0(v) + yG(v) \qquad \text{for} \quad v \in \Omega, \tag{46}$$

$$zQ(x^*(b)) = 0, \tag{47}$$

$$y(b) = \partial(s + zQ)/\partial x(b)\,|_{x^*(b)}, \tag{48}$$

then x^* and v^* will maximize (41) subject to (42)–(44).

(The proof proceeds similarly to that of Theorem 4.)

For inequality constraint cases, see Hestenes (1965) and Mangasarian (1966).

9.2 Optimal Accumulation of Nontransferable Capital

Application 1 in Section 7.2 dealt with optimal accumulation of capital in a two-sector economy, where capital good is supposed to be transferable freely between the two sectors. As an application of the Pontryagin maximum principle, we now study optimal accumulation of capital under the assumption that capital goods once installed in one sector cannot be transferred to another sector of the economy. We confine ourselves to a two-sector model, i.e., an economy that consists of a consumption-good sector and an investment-good sector alone. Let C, V denote output of consumption good and that of investment good, respectively. Each good is supposed to be producible by a fixed-proportion function of capital input only: at time t

$$C(t) = \alpha K_1(t), \tag{49}$$

$$V(t) = \beta K_2(t), \tag{50}$$

where α, β are positive constants, K_1 and K_2 stand for capital inputs in the consumption-good sector and in the investment-good sector, respectively. In the background of (49) and (50), there is an implicit assumption that labor is not a binding factor of production. Let $K \equiv K_1 + K_2$, and let λ be the allocation ratio of new investment good V to the consumption-good sector. Hence $1 - \lambda$ is the allocation ratio to the investment-good sector. Since we do not allow any transfer between sectors of old capital good already installed, the value of λ is restricted:

$$0 \leqq \lambda \leqq 1. \tag{51}$$

Assuming labor L remains constant, we denote

$$c(t) \equiv C(t)/L, \qquad v(t) \equiv V(t)/L, \qquad k(t) \equiv K(t)/L.$$

Also we make the convention that $\dot{y}$ stands for the derivative of a variable y

with respect to t. Thus, differentiating the per capita version of (49) and (50) with respect to t, we have

$$\dot{c} = \alpha \dot{K}_1/L = \alpha\lambda v, \qquad c \geqq 0, \tag{52}$$

$$\dot{v} = \beta \dot{K}_2/L = \beta(1 - \lambda)v, \qquad v \geqq 0, \tag{53}$$

with (51) and the initial conditions

$$c(0) = c_0 \quad \text{(constant)}, \qquad v(0) = v_0 \quad \text{(constant)}. \tag{54}$$

Under these conditions, we try to maximize

$$\int_0^\infty (U(c) - B)\, dt, \tag{55}$$

where U denotes total utility and B the satiation level, which is never exceeded by $U(c)$.

In applying the Pontryagin maximum principle to this problem, we treat λ as a control variable and c, v as state variables. The corresponding Hamiltonian function is now defined as

$$\begin{aligned} H &\equiv U(c) - B + \alpha p_1 v\lambda + \beta p_2 v(1 - \lambda) \\ &= U(c) - B + \beta p_2 v + (\alpha p_1 - \beta p_2)v\lambda, \end{aligned} \tag{56}$$

where p_1, p_2 are auxiliary variables associated with c and v, respectively, and are interpreted as the shadow prices of these goods. According to Theorem 1, the necessary conditions for our problem are

$$\dot{p}_1 = -\partial H/\partial c = -dU/dc \equiv -u, \tag{57}$$

$$\dot{p}_2 = -\partial H/\partial v = -\beta p_2 + (\beta p_2 - \alpha p_1)\lambda, \tag{58}$$

$$H \text{ is maximized with respect to } \lambda, \tag{59}$$

$$p_1(\infty) = p_2(\infty) = 0 \qquad \text{(transversality condition)}, \tag{60}$$

where u denotes marginal utility. In view of (51) and (56), the λ that maximizes H will be

$$\lambda = 1 \qquad \text{if} \quad \alpha p_1 > \beta p_2, \tag{59-1}$$

$$\lambda = 0 \qquad \text{if} \quad \alpha p_1 < \beta p_2, \tag{59-2}$$

$$0 \leqq \lambda \leqq 1 \qquad \text{if} \quad \alpha p_1 = \beta p_2. \tag{59-3}$$

Further, we assume

$$U \text{ is a concave function}, \tag{61}$$

$$p_1(t) \geqq 0, \quad p_2(t) \geqq 0 \qquad \text{for all } t. \tag{62}$$

Then, according to Theorem 4, we know that conditions (57)–(62) constitute sufficient conditions for our maximum problem. We note that for the maximizer λ,

$$0 = \partial H/\partial \lambda = (\alpha p_1 - \beta p_2)v$$

holds, and hence

$$\alpha p_1 = \beta p_2 \qquad \text{if maximizer } \lambda \in (0, 1) \tag{59-4}$$

since $v > 0$ for $\lambda \in (0, 1)$. Thus, condition (58) implies

$$\dot{p}_2 = -\alpha p_1 \qquad \text{if} \quad \lambda = 1, \tag{58-1}$$

$$\dot{p}_2 = -\beta p_2 \qquad \text{if} \quad \lambda \in [0, 1), \tag{58-2}$$

in view of (59-4).

We have the following proposition.

PROPOSITION 1 (Dasgupta, 1969) We can maintain

$$\alpha p_1 = \beta p_2 \tag{63}$$

over an interval of time if and only if the shadow prices satisfy

$$p_1 = u/\beta, \tag{64}$$

$$p_2 = \alpha u/\beta^2. \tag{65}$$

Moreover, during this period our economy with nontransferable capital obeys the condition

$$\dot{c}(t) = -\beta u(c)/u'(c) > 0, \tag{66}$$

where we assume

$$u(c) > 0, \quad u'(c) \equiv du/dc < 0 \qquad \text{for} \quad c > 0. \tag{67}$$

Note that (66) is identical with the necessary condition for optimal accumulation of transferable capital. (See (28) in Section 7.2.)

PROOF It follows from (64) and (57) that

$$u'\dot{c}/\beta = \dot{p}_1 = -u,$$

which is nothing but (66). Necessity is proved as follows. (63) implies $\alpha\dot{p}_1 = \beta\dot{p}_2$, in which (57), (58-1), (58-2) are taken into account, entailing:

(i) if $\lambda = 1$, then $u = \beta p_1$, which together with (63) implies (65);

(ii) if $\lambda \in [0, 1)$, then $\alpha u = \beta^2 p_2$, which together with (63) implies (64).

Sufficiency is immediate. Q.E.D.

We remark that the Hamiltonian function of our problem takes a constant value, say H^*, at all times on the optimal path of accumnlation. Denote the optimal value of λ by λ^*. If $\lambda^* \in (0, 1)$, we have

$$\begin{aligned} H^* &= U(c) - B + \beta p_2 v && \text{(in view of (59-4))} \\ &= U(c) - B + (\alpha/\beta)uv && \text{(in view of Proposition 1).} \end{aligned}$$

Thus, the corresponding optimal v ($\equiv \dot{k}$), denoted v^*, is given by

$$v^* = \beta(B + H^* - U)/\alpha u, \tag{68}$$

which traces an optimal path. The path determined by (68) may be termed the *Euler path* associated with H^*. The value of H^* can be set equal to zero by choosing the initial prices $p_1(0)$, $p_2(0)$ appropriately. Then, (68) is reduced to the Ramsey rule of accumulation:

$$\tilde{v} = \beta(B - U(c))/\alpha u(c) \geqq 0. \tag{69}$$

(Refer to (31) in Section 7.2.) One should notice that if we want to maintain $\lambda^* \in (0, 1)$ and hence (63) at the final stage of an infinite horizon program, the only optimal path is the Ramsey path where $H^* = 0$, as is seen from the following discussion. From (68), we have $\partial v^*/\partial H^* > 0$, which implies that the greater is H^*, the larger will v^* be, at an arbitrary fixed c. Thus, the path associated with a smaller H^* is more efficient. Furthermore, the path with any positive H^* is inefficient as an infinite program since the path is accumulating capital unnecessarily fast and is inferior to the Ramsey path (where $H^* = 0$) in a Pareto sense. On the other hand, if H^* is negative, the associated path of v^* will collapse onto the c axis in a finite time (see Fig. 9) since there exists a number $\bar{c}$ such that

$$U(c) > B + H^* \qquad \text{for} \quad c > \bar{c}.$$

Such a path cannot be optimal. As an explicit solution to this infinite horizon problem, knowing c_0, we shall reach eventually the optimal path determined by (66) and (69).

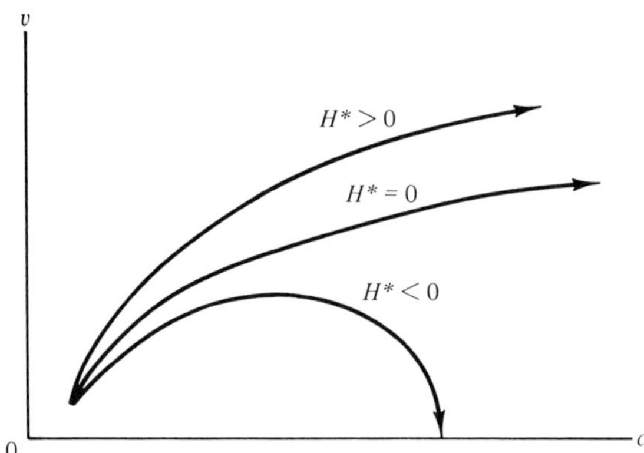

FIGURE 9. Euler paths.

Consider the case where given c_0,

$$v_0 < \tilde{v}(0) = \beta(B - U_0)/\alpha u_0, \tag{70}$$

where $U_0 \equiv U(c_0)$ and $u_0 \equiv u(c_0)$. Then it is best to raise $v(t)$, with $c(t) = c_0$, for an initial period $[0, \tau]$ of the program. (The value of τ will be determined below.) To achieve the purpose, we put the optimal λ equal to zero for the interval:

$$\lambda^*(t) = 0 \qquad \text{for} \quad t \in [0, \tau],$$

and choose $p_2(0)$ such that $H^*(0) = 0$, i.e.,

$$p_2(0) = (B - U_0)/\beta v_0 > 0. \tag{71}$$

Then, in view of (58-2), $p_2(t)$ will change according to the equation

$$p_2(t) = p_2(0)e^{-\beta t} \qquad \text{for} \quad t \in [0, \tau]; \tag{72}$$

and in view of (57) and $c(t) = c_0$, $p_1(t)$ will take the form

$$p_1(t) = -u_0 t + p_1(0) \qquad \text{for} \quad t \in [0, \tau], \tag{73}$$

where $p_1(0)$ is arbitrary. $p_1(0)$ and τ are to be determined such that $\alpha p_1(\tau) = \beta p_2(\tau)$; i.e., taking (71)–(73) into consideration,

$$\alpha p_1(0) = \alpha u_0 \tau + ((B - U_0)/v_0)\, e^{-\beta\tau}. \tag{74}$$

Given $p_1(0)$, τ is therefore uniquely determined. Also it is easily checked that

$$\alpha p_1(t) < \beta p_2(t) \qquad \text{for} \quad t \in [0, \tau). \tag{75}$$

Thus, $p_1(0)$ may be chosen as a nonnegative value less than

$$(B - U_0)/\alpha v_0.$$

When we reach the point τ in time, we switch over to a new phase where $\lambda^*(t) \in (0, 1)$ and we maintain (63). Then our optimal policy obeys the rules (66) and (69) from time period τ on; i.e., we trace the Ramsey path. Note that on the Ramsey path $p_1(\infty) = 0$ and $p_2(\infty) = 0$, satisfying the transversality conditions, since in view of $0 = H^* = U - B + \beta p_2 v$ and (63),

$$\lim_{t\to\infty} p_2(t) = \lim_{t\to\infty} \frac{B - U(t)}{\beta v(t)} = 0 \qquad \text{and} \qquad \lim_{t\to\infty} p_1(t) = \frac{\beta}{\alpha} \lim_{t\to\infty} p_2(t) = 0.$$

Conversely, given c_0, let $v_0 > \tilde{v}(0) = \beta(B - U_0)/\alpha u_0$. Then it is best to increase c, with $v(t) = v_0$, for the initial stage $[0, \tau]$. For this purpose we put $\lambda^*(t) = 1$ and choose $p_1(0)$ such that $H^*(0) = U_0 - B + \alpha p_1(0)v_0 = 0$, i.e.,

$$p_1(0) = (B - U_0)/\alpha v_0 > 0.$$

By a discussion similar to the previous case, we eventually reach the Ramsey path. (The reader should proceed to verify this conclusion.)

Here we note that in the above optimal programs, both c and v increase along the Ramsey path, and that this is possible if and only if the utility function U satisfies

$$-u' > u^2/(B - U) \qquad \text{for all } c. \tag{76}$$

(For a related discussion, see Dasgupta (1969).)

Now we consider the time-optimal problem of minimizing the time T required to attain a target pair of prescribed per capita consumption c^* and investment v^*, starting from initial values $c(0) < c^*$ and $v(0) < v^*$, within the framework of the preceding two-sector economy with population growth at a constant rate $n > 0$. When the population growth is taken into account, we have the following equations instead of (52) and (53):

$$\dot{c} = \alpha\lambda v - nc, \qquad c \geqq 0, \tag{52$'$}$$

$$\dot{v} = (\beta(1 - \lambda) - n)v, \qquad v \geqq 0. \tag{53$'$}$$

The corresponding Hamiltonian function becomes

$$H = (\alpha p_1 - \beta p_2)\lambda v + (\beta - n)p_2 v - np_1 c. \tag{56$'$}$$

Hence, the necessary conditions for our problem are

$$\dot{p}_1 = np_1, \tag{57$'$}$$

$$\dot{p}_2 = (\beta p_2 - \alpha p_1)\lambda + (n - \beta)p_2, \tag{58$'$}$$

together with (59-1)–(59-4) and

$$p_1(T)[c(T) - c^*] = 0, \qquad p_1(T) \geqq 0, \tag{60$'$-1}$$

$$p_2(T)[v(T) - v^*] = 0, \qquad p_2(T) \geqq 0. \tag{60$'$-2}$$

Condition (58′) is alternatively expressed as

$$\dot{p}_2 = np_2 - \alpha p_1 \qquad \text{if} \quad \lambda = 1, \tag{58$'$-1}$$

$$\dot{p}_2 = (n - \beta)p_2 \qquad \text{if} \quad \lambda \in [0, 1). \tag{58$'$-2}$$

We shall adopt the policy $\lambda = 0$ at the beginning of our program through some positive time S by choosing positive $p_1(0)$ and $p_2(0)$ such that

$$\alpha p_1(t) < \beta p_2(t) \qquad \text{for} \quad 0 \leqq t < S, \qquad \text{and} \qquad \alpha p_1(S) = \beta p_2(S). \tag{77}$$

Such a choice of $p_1(0)$ and $p_2(0)$ is possible in view of (57′) and (58′-2), i.e.,

$$\alpha p_1(0) = \beta p_2(0)e^{-\beta S}. \tag{77$'$}$$

During the above-mentioned period, state variables take the following values by virtue of (52′) and (53′):

$$c(t) = c_0 e^{-nt} \qquad \text{for} \quad t \leqq S, \tag{78}$$

$$v(t) = v_0 e^{(\beta - n)t} \qquad \text{for} \quad t \leqq S. \tag{79}$$

The time S denotes the switching point from one phase to the other phase where $\alpha p_1 > \beta p_2$ holds. It will be found appropriate in view of the discussions below to determine the S such that

$$v(S) = v^* e^{n(T - S)}. \tag{80}$$

From (79) and (80) it follows that

$$S = (\ln v^* - \ln v_0 + nT)/\beta. \tag{81}$$

Thus, once T is given, S is subsequently determined by (81). Let τ represent $t - S$ ($t \geqq S$). Then for $\tau > 0$, the policy $\lambda = 1$ is to be adopted consistently with a necessary condition (59-1). For, by virtue of (57′) and (58′-1),

$$\dot{p}_2[\tau] = np_2[\tau] - \alpha p_1(S)e^{n\tau} \qquad \text{for} \quad \tau > 0, \tag{82}$$

where $p_1(S) \equiv p_1[0]$ and the like; and Eq. (82) can be solved as

$$p_2[\tau] = (p_2(S) - \alpha p_1(S)\tau)e^{n\tau} = (1 - \beta\tau)p_2(S)e^{\tau n} \qquad \text{for} \quad \tau > 0, \tag{83}$$

which implies that the growth rate of $p_2[\tau]$ is less than $p_1[\tau]$ $(= p_1(S)e^{n\tau})$, and hence that

$$\alpha p_1[\tau] > \beta p_2[\tau] \qquad \text{for} \quad \tau > 0.$$

The motions of consumption and investment in this phase are

$$\dot{c} = \alpha v - nc \qquad \text{and} \qquad \dot{v} = -nv.$$

Thus, similarly to (83), we can obtain

$$v[\tau] = v(S)e^{-n\tau} \qquad \text{for} \quad \tau > 0, \tag{84}$$

$$c[\tau] = (c(S) + \alpha v(S)\tau)e^{-n\tau} \qquad \text{for} \quad \tau > 0. \tag{85}$$

Note that substitution of (80) in (84) yields

$$v(T) = v[T - S] = v^*. \tag{86}$$

Lastly, we want to determine the minimum time T such that $c(T) = c^*$. Taking account of (78), (80), and (85), we derive

$$c(T) = c[T - S] = c_0e^{-nT} + (T - S)\alpha v^*. \tag{87}$$

Considering (81), (87), and the requirement $c(T) = c^*$, we get the following equation to determine T:

$$c^* = c_0e^{-nT} + \left\{\left(1 - \frac{n}{\beta}\right)T - \frac{1}{\beta}(\ln v^* - \ln v_0)\right\}\alpha v^*. \tag{88}$$

In order to check the optimality of the above proposed policies, it will be easily seen that the value of the Hamiltonian function is invariant for all t and that the function is linear in (c, v), throughout the program. (Refer to Theorem 5.)

Other interesting applications of the Pontryagin maximum principles to capital accumulation are found in Cass (1965), Stoleru (1965), Shell (1967), (1969), Arrow (1968), and Uzawa (1969), among others.

9.3 Controllability of Linear Dynamical Economic Systems: Generalization of the Static Tinbergen Theory of Policy

Some economic systems will be capable of achieving a preassigned target by the control of policy instruments, but others will not. What is the rule to be satisfied by an economic system so that it can attain any given target? This problem was initially raised by Tinbergen (1952) within a static framework. Our concern in the present section is to generalize the Tinbergen rule of policy formation within a linear dynamical framework from the point of view of modern control systems.

The simplest Tinbergen model may be represented as the reduced form

$$x = Fv, \tag{89}$$

where x is an n-vector of target variables, v is an m-vector of policy instruments (or control variables), and F is an $n \times m$ real constant matrix. What is the condition for the existence of v attaining any preassigned target x? This question is answered immediately by

THEOREM 7 System (89) has a solution v for an arbitrary target x if and only if

$$\mathrm{rk}(F) = n. \tag{90}$$

(For a proof, refer to Theorem 28 in Section 2.3.)

(90) may be termed the *static controllability* condition. In order to have (90), it is necessary that the number of rows of F be not greater than that of its columns, i.e., that the number of instruments be equal to or greater than that of target variables. This is the so-called *Tinbergen rule of policy formation.*

Turning to dynamic problems, let us consider an economic system modeled by a linear differential equation system termed a *state-space form*

$$\dot{x}(t) = Ax(t) + Bv(t) \tag{91}$$

with initial condition

$$x(0) = x^0 \quad \text{(constant)}, \tag{92}$$

where x denotes an n-vector of state variables, v an m-vector of control variables, and A, B are real constant matrices of dimensions $n \times n$, $n \times m$, respectively. Referring to the end of Section 3.1, we know that the general solution to system (91) is

$$x(t) = e^{At}\left(x^0 + \int_0^t e^{-A\tau}Bv(\tau)\, d\tau\right). \tag{93}$$

Given a fixed target $x(\beta) = x^1$ for terminal time $\beta > 0$, we want to determine a necessary and sufficient condition for achieving this target in the system mentioned above. We may assume $x^1 = \theta$ (the origin of R^n) without loss of generality since, if $x^1 \neq \theta$, we can consider instead of (91) the system

$$\dot{\xi}(t) = A\xi(t) + Bv(t) \tag{91'}$$

with initial condition

$$\xi(0) = x^0 - e^{-A\beta}x^1 \tag{92'}$$

and target $\xi(\beta) = \theta$. Then $x(t)$ is expressed as

$$x(t) = \xi(t) + e^{A(t-\beta)}x^1 \qquad \text{for nonnegative} \quad t \leqq \beta. \tag{94}$$

Once vector ξ is controllable (as defined below), vector x is also controllable.

DEFINITION 2 System (91) is said to be *state controllable* if state vector x can reach the origin θ of R^n at some time $\beta \geqq 0$ from an arbitrary initial condition (92) by manipulating control variables $v(\tau)$ $(0 \leqq \tau \leqq \beta)$, i.e.,

$$x(\beta) = e^{A\beta}x^0 + \int_0^\beta e^{A(\beta-\tau)} Bv(\tau)\, d\tau = \theta. \tag{95}$$

THEOREM 8 A necessary and sufficient condition for system (91) to be state controllable is that the symmetric matrix

$$P(0, t) \equiv \int_0^t e^{-A\tau}BB^{\mathrm{T}}e^{-A^{\mathrm{T}}\tau}\, d\tau \tag{96}$$

be nonsingular for some time $t \geqq 0$.

PROOF *Sufficiency* Let x^0 be an arbitrary initial state and determine $v(\tau)$ as

$$v(\tau) = -B^{\mathrm{T}}e^{-A^{\mathrm{T}}\tau}P(0, \beta)^{-1}x^0 \qquad \text{for} \quad \tau \in [0, \beta]. \tag{97}$$

Substitution of (97) in (93) and setting $t = \beta$ yield

$$x(\beta) = e^{A\beta}\left(x^0 - \left(\int_0^\beta e^{-A\tau}BB^{\mathrm{T}}e^{-A^{\mathrm{T}}\tau}\, d\tau\right)P(0, \beta)^{-1}x^0\right) = \theta.$$

Necessity If $P(0, t)$ were singular for every $t \geqq 0$, then, since $P(0, t)$ has a zero eigenvalue, there would exist a nonzero vector x such that

$$x^{\mathrm{T}}P(0, t)x = 0 \qquad \text{for an arbitrary} \quad t \geqq 0,$$

which is equivalent to

$$x^{\mathrm{T}}e^{-A\tau}B = \theta \qquad \text{for all} \quad \tau \geqq 0, \tag{9*}$$

in view of (96). On the other hand, since system (91) is controllable, there is a control vector $v(\tau)$, $0 \leqq \tau \leqq \beta$, for some final time $\beta \geqq 0$ such that (95) holds with x^0 replaced by the above-mentioned x corresponding to $t = \beta$. Hence

$$x = -\int_0^\beta e^{-A\tau}Bv(\tau)\, d\tau.$$

Then we have

$$x^{\mathrm{T}}x = -x^{\mathrm{T}}\int_0^\beta e^{-A\tau}Bv(\tau)\, d\tau = 0$$

by virtue of (9*). This implies $x = \theta$, a contradiction Q.E.D.

A more useful equivalence condition for state controllability is the rank condition stated next.

THEOREM 9 System (91) is state controllable if and only if the $n \times (nm)$ matrix

$$P \equiv [B, AB, \ldots, A^{n-1}B] \tag{98}$$

has rank n. P is called the state controllability matrix.

PROOF *"If" part* Suppose that system (91) were not controllable. Then in view of Theorem 8 above, there would be a nonzero vector x such that (9*) holds. Differentiating (9*) k times ($k = 0, 1, 2, \ldots$) successively with respect to τ and then setting $\tau = 0$ yield

$$x^{\mathrm{T}}A^{k}B = \theta \qquad \text{for} \quad k = 0, 1, \ldots, n-1, \tag{10*}$$

or equivalently $x^{\mathrm{T}}P = \theta$, which implies $PP^{\mathrm{T}}x = \theta$. Since x is nonzero, PP^{T} must be singular and hence $\mathrm{rk}(P)$ must be less than n, a contradiction.

"Only if" part Assume system (91) is controllable and suppose $\mathrm{rk}(P) < n$. Then, in view of the above sufficiency proof, proceeding in reverse, there would exist a nonzero x satisfying (10*). By virtue of the Cayley–Hamilton theorem (Theorem 2 in Section 3.2), A^n can be represented as a linear combination of $I, A, A^2, \ldots, A^{n-1}$. Thus each A^{n+j} ($j = 1, 2, \ldots$) is expressible as a linear combination of these matrices A^k ($k = 0, 1, \ldots, n-1$). Therefore, (10*) implies (9*). Then we have

$$0 = \int_0^t (x^{\mathrm{T}}e^{-A\tau}BB^{\mathrm{T}}e^{-A^{\mathrm{T}}\tau}x)\, d\tau = x^{\mathrm{T}}P(0, t)x \qquad \text{for each} \quad t > 0. \tag{11*}$$

Since system (91) is controllable, $P(0, t)$ is nonsingular symmetric for some $t > 0$, and hence (11*) implies $x = \theta$, a contradiction. Q.E.D.

The condition $\mathrm{rk}(P) = n$ in Theorem 9 may be regarded as the *dynamic controllability* condition, as contrasted to condition (90).

An economic system may sometimes be represented by the following state-space form:

$$\dot{x}(t) = Ax(t) + Bv(t), \tag{99}$$

$$y(t) = Cx(t), \tag{100}$$

with initial condition

$$x(0) = x^0 \quad \text{(constant)}, \tag{101}$$

where (99) and (101) are the same as (91) and (92), respectively, y denotes an r-vector of output variables, and C is a real constant matrix of dimension $r \times n$. Given an initial condition (101) and a preassigned target output

$$y(\beta) = y^1 \qquad \text{for some time} \quad \beta \geqq 0,$$

we want to select an appropriate input vector $v(t)$ for $t \in [0, \beta]$, in order to reach the preassigned target. We may put $y^1 = \theta$ by the same reasoning as for $x^1 = \theta$.

DEFINITION 3 The system consisting of (99) and (100) is said to be *output controllable* if output vector y can reach the target $y(\beta) = \theta$ at some time $\beta \geqq 0$, starting from an arbitrary initial condition $y(0) = Cx^0$, by manipulating the control vector $v(\tau)$ $(0 \leqq \tau \leqq \beta)$.

Concerning output controllability, we have the following two equivalence theorems.

THEOREM 8′ A necessary and sufficient condition for system (99), (100) to be output controllable is that the symmetric matrix

$$Q(0, t) \equiv \int_0^t Ce^{A(t-\tau)} BB^{\mathrm{T}} e^{A^{\mathrm{T}}(t-\tau)} C^{\mathrm{T}} \, d\tau \tag{102}$$

be nonsingular for some time $t \geqq 0$.

PROOF *Sufficiency* From (93) and (100), it follows that

$$y(t) = Ce^{At}\left(x^0 + \int_0^t e^{-A\tau} Bv(\tau) \, d\tau\right). \tag{93′}$$

Assume $Q(0, \beta)$ is nonsingular. Determine $v(\tau)$ by

$$v(\tau) = -B^{\mathrm{T}} e^{A^{\mathrm{T}}(t-\tau)} C^{\mathrm{T}} Q(0, \beta)^{-1} Ce^{At} x^0 \qquad \text{for each} \quad t \geqq 0, \tag{97′}$$

and substituting in (93′) to entail $y(\beta) = \theta$.

Necessity If $Q(0, t)$ were singular for every $t \geqq 0$, then there would exist a nonzero y such that

$$y^{\mathrm{T}} Q(0, t) y = 0 \qquad \text{for an arbitrary} \quad t \geqq 0,$$

which is equivalent to

$$y^{\mathrm{T}} Ce^{A(t-\tau)} B = \theta \qquad \text{for all} \quad \tau \geqq 0.$$

Since system (99), (100) is (output) controllable, there is a control vector $v(\tau)$, $0 \leqq \tau \leqq \beta$, for some $\beta \geqq 0$ such that $y(\beta) = \theta$ with $Ce^{A\beta}x^0$ replaced by the above-mentioned y corresponding to $t = \beta$. Hence

$$y = -\int_0^\beta Ce^{A(\beta-\tau)} \, Bv(\tau) \, d\tau.$$

Then we have

$$y^{\mathrm{T}} y = -y^{\mathrm{T}} \int_0^\beta Ce^{A(\beta-\tau)} Bv(\tau) \, d\tau = 0,$$

implying $y = \theta$, a contradiction. Q.E.D.

THEOREM 9′ System (99), (100) is output controllable if and only if the $r \times (nm)$ matrix

$$Q \equiv [CB, CAB, CA^2B, \ldots, CA^{n-1}B] = CP \tag{103}$$

has rank r. Q is called the output controllability matrix.

(The proof is similar to that of Theorem 9.)

Remark As we noted before, output controllability of system (99), (100) implies that it is capable of achieving an arbitrary target output $y(\beta) = y^* \neq \theta$ at any time $\beta > 0$. Indeed,

$$v(\tau) = B^{\mathrm{T}} e^{A^{\mathrm{T}}(\beta-\tau)} C^{\mathrm{T}} Q(0, \beta)^{-1}[y^* - Ce^{A\beta}x^0] \qquad \text{for} \quad \tau \in [0, \beta] \quad (97'')$$

will achieve $y(\beta) = y^*$.

There is a relationship between state controllability and output controllability.

PROPOSITION 2 Assume that $r \leqq n$ in system (99), (100) and that it is state controllable, i.e., $\mathrm{rk}(P) = n$. Then the system is output controllable, i.e., $\mathrm{rk}(CP) = r$ if and only if C has rank r.

PROOF If $\mathrm{rk}(P) = n$ (full row rank) and $\mathrm{rk}(C) = r$, then $\mathrm{rk}(CP) = r$ in view of Theorem 24 in Section 2.3. If $\mathrm{rk}(C) < r$,

$$\mathrm{rk}(CP) \leqq \min\{\mathrm{rk}(C), \mathrm{rk}(P)\} < r. \qquad \text{Q.E.D.}$$

In order to check state controllability, we need not calculate P in (98) but only a matrix with a smaller number of columns in view of

THEOREM 10 Define the $n \times (jm)$ matrix

$$P_j \equiv [B, AB, A^2B, \ldots, A^{j-1}B]. \qquad (98')$$

If j is the least integer such that

$$\mathrm{rk}(P_j) = \mathrm{rk}(P_{j+1}), \qquad (104)$$

then $\mathrm{rk}(P_k) = \mathrm{rk}(P_j)$ for all integers $k > j$, and the j is said to be the *controllability index* of (A, B).

PROOF (104) implies that every column of A^jB is linearly dependent on the columns of P_j. Then every column of $A^{j+1}B$ is linearly dependent on the columns of

$$AP_j = [AB, A^2B, \ldots, A^jB].$$

However, since the columns of A^jB are linearly dependent on P_j, every column of $A^{j+1}B$ is ultimately linearly dependent on P_j. Proceeding similarly for $A^{j+2}B$, $A^{j+3}B$, and so on, one by one successively, we have the above statement. Q.E.D.

COROLLARY Assume that $r \leqq \mathrm{rk}(P_j) = \mathrm{rk}(P_{j+1}) \leqq n$ holds for some $j \leqq n$. Then system (99), (100) is output controllable if and only if $\mathrm{rk}(C) = r$.

(The proof is left to the reader as an exercise.)

According to the Tinbergen rule of policy formation within a static economic model, there must exist as many instruments as target variables to be attained. We shall consider a dynamic version of this rule. For the sake of simplicity, at first we assume that matrix A in system (91) has distinct eigenvalues $\lambda_1, \lambda_2, \ldots, \lambda_n$. Then, by Theorem 16 in Section 1.2, there exists a nonsingular eigenvector matrix M such that

$$M^{-1}AM = \Lambda, \qquad M = [k_1, \ldots, k_n], \qquad M^{-1} = [u_1, \ldots, u_n]^{\mathrm{T}},$$

where $\Lambda = \operatorname{diag}(\lambda_1, \ldots, \lambda_n)$ and k_i, u_i^{T} denote the right, left eigenvectors, respectively, of A associated with λ_i. System (91) is transformed to

$$\dot{w}(t) = \Lambda w(t) + \hat{B}v(t), \tag{105}$$

or equivalently

$$\dot{w}_i(t) = \lambda_i w_i(t) + u_i^{\mathrm{T}} B v(t) \qquad \text{for} \quad i = 1, \ldots, n, \tag{105$'$}$$

where $w(t) \equiv M^{-1}x(t)$ and $\hat{B} \equiv M^{-1}B$. It is obvious from (105′) that the control of each $w_i(t)$ requires at least one nonzero component of the vector $u_i^{\mathrm{T}}B$ since otherwise $w_i(t) = w_i(0) \exp\{\lambda_i t\}$ would not attain an arbitrary target value $w_i(\beta)$. The requirement that there exist at least one nonzero component in each row of $\hat{B}$ in system (105) is designated the *coupling criterion* by Preston (1974). This dynamic criterion does not require so many control variables as target variables, as opposed to the static Tinbergen rule mentioned above. Let b_j be the jth column of matrix B. For a fixed j, if

$$u_i^{\mathrm{T}} b_j \neq 0 \qquad \text{for all} \quad i = 1, \ldots, n, \tag{106}$$

i.e., if any u_i^{T} is not orthogonal to b_j, then the coupling criterion is satisfied, and in this case we need only one instrument $v_j(t)$ in order to have system (91) be state controllable, i.e.,

$$\dot{x}(t) = Ax(t) + b_j v_j(t) \tag{107}$$

be state controllable. Indeed, system (107) satisfies the dynamic controllability condition:

$$\begin{aligned} \operatorname{rk}(P) &= \operatorname{rk}(M^{-1}P) = \operatorname{rk}[M^{-1}b_j, M^{-1}Ab_j, \ldots, M^{-1}A^{n-1}b_j] \\ &= \operatorname{rk}([I, \Lambda, \Lambda^2, \ldots, \Lambda^{n-1}]M^{-1}b_j) = n \end{aligned}$$

since $M^{-1}b_j$ is an all-nonzero-element vector by (106) and since $\lambda_1, \ldots, \lambda_n$ are all distinct. If any one column of matrix B does not satisfy condition (106), we search for two columns b_j, b_h of B such that $M^{-1}(b_j + b_h)$ is an all-nonzero-element vector. If no combination of two columns of B does fulfill this requirement, we proceed to search for some three columns of B satisfying it, and so on. The minimum number of columns of B satisfying the requirement will not exceed n provided

$$\operatorname{rk}(P) = \operatorname{rk}[B, AB, \ldots, A^{n-1}B] = n$$

in view of the fact that $\operatorname{rk}(P) = \operatorname{rk}(M^{-1}P)$. Let $b_1, \ldots, b_j$ be the minimum set of columns of B such that their combination $B_j \equiv \sum_{i=1}^{j} b_i$ satisfies

$$u_i^{\mathrm{T}} B_j \neq 0 \qquad \text{for all} \quad i = 1, \ldots, n. \tag{106$'$}$$

Condition (106′) holds if and only if B_j is linearly dependent on all n right eigenvectors $k_1, \ldots, k_n$ of A since in case

$$B_j = \sum_{i=1}^{n-1} \alpha_i k_i \qquad \text{for nonzero} \quad \alpha_i \quad (i = 1, \ldots, n-1),$$

we have $M^{-1}B_j = \{\alpha_1, \ldots, \alpha_{n-1}, 0\}$. Thus a proposition is obtained.

PROPOSITION 3 Assume matrix A in system (91) has all distinct eigenvalues. A sufficient condition for system (91) to be state controllable is that there exist for the columns of B some combination that is linearly dependent on all n right eigenvectors of A.

COROLLARY Assume that $\mathrm{rk}(C) = r \leqq n$ in system (99), (100) and that matrix A has all distinct eigenvalues. A sufficient condition for this system to be output controllable is that there exist for the columns of B some combination that is linearly dependent on all n right eigenvectors of A.

(This corollary follows directly from Propositions 2 and 3.)

To deal with the general case where the eigenvalues of A are not necessarily distinct, we introduce several new concepts.

DEFINITION 4 The system consisting of

$$\dot{\bar{x}}(t) = \bar{A}\bar{x}(t) + \bar{B}v(t), \tag{99′}$$

$$y(t) = \bar{C}\bar{x}(t), \tag{100′}$$

is said to be (*algebraically*) *equivalent* to system (99), (100) if

$$\bar{x}(t) = Tx(t), \qquad \bar{A} = TAT^{-1}, \qquad \bar{B} = TB, \qquad \bar{C} = CT^{-1}$$

for an $n \times n$ real constant nonsingular matrix T. In this case T is called a *similarity transformation*.

It is clear that system (99), (100) is equivalent to system (99′), (100′) if the latter is equivalent to the former.

THEOREM 11 The (state and output) controllability of a linear, continuous-time dynamical system (99), (100) is invariant under any similarity transformation.

PROOF We shall show that the rank of the controllability matrix is invariant under the matrix T mentioned in Definition 4:

$$\begin{aligned} \mathrm{rk}[\bar{B}, \bar{A}\bar{B}, \ldots, \bar{A}^{n-1}\bar{B}] &= \mathrm{rk}(T[B, AB, \ldots, A^{n-1}B]) \\ &= \mathrm{rk}[B, AB, \ldots, A^{n-1}B]. \end{aligned}$$

$$[\bar{C}\bar{B}, \bar{C}\bar{A}\bar{B}, \ldots, \bar{C}\bar{A}^{n-1}\bar{B}] = [CB, CAB, \ldots, CA^{n-1}B]. \qquad \text{Q.E.D.}$$

DEFINITION 5 A linear dynamical system (99), (100) is said to be *completely controllable* if it is not algebraically equivalent to a system of the type

$$\dot{x}^1(t) = A_{11}x^1(t) + A_{12}x^2(t) + B_1v(t) \tag{108-1}$$

$$\dot{x}^2(t) = A_{22}x^2(t) \tag{108-2}$$

$$y(t) = C_1x^1(t) + C_2x^2(t), \tag{108-3}$$

where x^1 and x^2 are vectors of n_1 and n_2 $(= n - n_1)$ components, respectively.

In other words, system (99), (100) is completely controllable if it is not possible to find a coordinate system in which the state variables are separated into two groups x^1 and x^2 such that the second group is not affected either by the first group or by the control variables of the system. Obviously, in the previous case where matrix A in system (91) has all distinct eigenvalues, if the transformed system (105) satisfies the coupling criterion, the original system (91) is completely controllable.

To system (91) or system (99), (100) where the eigenvalues of matrix A need not be all distinct, we can obtain an equivalent system such that A is transformed into its Jordan canonical form. Then, we know that if the corresponding transform $\hat{B}$ of matrix B satisfies the coupling criterion, the system is completely controllable. Also it is known that the Jordan form of A is equal to $M^{-1}AM$ for a nonsingular matrix M, which may be termed the Jordan transformation matrix of A. (Refer to Theorem 6 in Section 3.2.) Thus, for the general case, we have a proposition similar to Proposition 3.

PROPOSITION 3′ A sufficient condition for system (91) to be state controllable is that there exist for the columns of B some combination that is linearly dependent on all columns of the Jordan transformation matrix of A.

COROLLARY Assume $\text{rk}(C) = r \leqq n$ in system (99), (100). A sufficient condition for this system to be output controllable is that there exist for the columns of B some combination that is linearly dependent on all columns of the Jordan transformation matrix of A.

So far we have dealt with differential systems. But some macroeconomic models are formulated as difference equation systems, where time is treated as a discrete variable. Thus, we now turn to a linear time-invariant system modeled by

$$x(t) = Ax(t-1) + Bv(t), \tag{109}$$

$$y(t) = Cx(t), \tag{110}$$

with initial condition

$$x(0) = x^0 \text{ (constant)}, \tag{111}$$

where variables x, v, y are dependent on discrete time t, and their roles and dimensions are the same as in the differential counterpart (99), (100). Note that any linear difference equation system with constant coefficients can be transformed into a first-order difference-equation system of the type (109). (Refer to Eqs. (110) and (110′) in Section 3.5.)

It is easy to see that the general solution to (109) is obtained as

$$x(t) = A^t x(0) + \sum_{\tau=0}^{t-1} A^\tau B v(t-\tau) \tag{112}$$

by an iterative substitution. Hence the general solution to system (109), (110) is

$$y(t) = CA^t x(0) + \sum_{\tau=0}^{t-1} CA^\tau B v(t-\tau). \tag{113}$$

Controllability of the discrete systems will be defined as before.

DEFINITION 2′ System (109) is said to be *state controllable* if x can reach a preassigned target vector x^1 at some time $\beta \geqq 0$, starting from an arbitrary initial state (111), by manipulating control variables $v(\tau)$ $(1 \leqq \tau \leqq \beta)$, i.e., if

$$x(\beta) = A^\beta x^0 + \sum_{\tau=0}^{\beta-1} A^\tau B v(\beta-\tau) = x^1. \tag{112′}$$

DEFINITION 3′ System (109), (110) is said to be *output controllable* if y can reach a preassigned target vector y^1 at some time $\beta \geqq 0$, starting from an arbitrary initial value $y(0) = Cx^0$, by manipulating control variables $v(\tau)$ $(1 \leqq \tau \leqq \beta)$, i.e., if

$$y(\beta) = CA^\beta x^0 + \sum_{\tau=0}^{\beta-1} CA^\tau B v(\beta-\tau) = y^1. \tag{113′}$$

Rank conditions for controllability of our discrete systems are given below, where β may be replaced by n in view of the Cayley–Hamilton Theorem if $\beta > n$.

THEOREM 12 System (109) is state controllable if and only if the $n \times (\beta m)$ matrix

$$P_\beta \equiv [B, AB, \ldots, A^{\beta-1}B] \tag{114}$$

has rank n. P_β is called the state controllability matrix of system (109).

PROOF (112′) may be rewritten as

$$P_\beta \begin{bmatrix} v(\beta) \\ v(\beta-1) \\ \vdots \\ v(1) \end{bmatrix} = x^1 - A^\beta x^0,$$

to which we apply Theorem 7. Q.E.D.

THEOREM 12′ System (109), (110) is output controllable if and only if the $r \times (\beta m)$ matrix

$$Q_\beta \equiv [CB, CAB, \ldots, CA^{\beta-1}B] = CP_\beta \tag{115}$$

has rank r. Q_β is called the output controllability matrix of system (109), (110).

To conclude this section, we consider the problem of achieving not only a single target but also several targets preassigned successively from $\beta\,(\geqq 0)$ to $\beta + \delta$ $(\delta > 0)$.

DEFINITION 6 System (109), (110) is said to be *perfectly output controllable* (or *functionally reproducible*) if y can trace preassigned targets

$$y(t) = y^*(t) \qquad \text{for} \quad t = \beta, \beta + 1, \ldots, \beta + \delta, \tag{116}$$

starting from an arbitrary initial value $y(0) = Cx^0$, by manipulating control variables $v(\tau)$ $(1 \leqq \tau \leqq \beta + \delta)$, i.e., if

$$y(t) = CA^t x^0 + \sum_{\tau=0}^{t-1} CA^\tau Bv(t - \tau) = y^*(t) \tag{117}$$

for $t = \beta, \beta + 1, \ldots, \beta + \delta$.

Perfect state controllability can be defined similarly.

THEOREM 13 System (109), (110) is perfectly output controllable with respect to preassigned targets (116) if and only if the $(\delta + 1)r \times (\beta + \delta)m$ matrix

$$Q_{\beta+\delta} \equiv \begin{bmatrix} CB & CAB & & \cdots & & CA^{\beta+\delta-1}B \\ 0 & CB & & \cdots & & CA^{\beta+\delta-2}B \\ \vdots & \ddots & \ddots & & & \vdots \\ 0 & \cdots\ 0 & CB & CAB & \cdots & CA^{\beta-1}B \end{bmatrix} \tag{118}$$

has full row rank. $Q_{\beta+\delta}$ is called the perfect output controllability matrix.

(The proof proceeds similarly to that of Theorem 12.)

COROLLARY System (109), (110) is perfectly output controllable only if the number of control variables m satisfies

$$m \geqq (\delta + 1)r/(\beta + \delta). \tag{119}$$

The reader may refer to Brockett and Mesarović (1965) and Aoki (1975) for a parallel theory of perfect controllability of linear differential systems.

9.4 Optimal Stabilization Policy for Linear Dynamical Economic Systems with Quadratic Cost Criteria

In the previous section, we were concerned only with controllability of linear dynamical systems without paying any attention to the cost involved.

If a fixed target is expected to cause an intolerable sacrifice to control it completely, the policy will be replaced by another less costly program, even if the latter may not achieve the target completely. The typical "cost" function for implementing a program will include an item measuring the deviations of state variables from a given target as well as the pecuniary cost of control variables, and is in general specified as an integral over time of a quadratic form:

$$J = x^{\mathrm{T}}(\beta)\Gamma x(\beta) + \int_0^\beta \{x^{\mathrm{T}}(t)\,\Xi x(t) + v^{\mathrm{T}}(t)\Phi v(t)\}\,dt, \tag{120}$$

where $x(t)$ stands for a deviation of the state-variable vector at time t, $v(t)$ is the control-variable vector at time t, Γ and Ξ are symmetric positive semidefinite matrices, and Φ is a symmetric positive definite matrix. Note that the end point β (> 0) is free in (120) since otherwise the criterion function must be reduced to

$$J = \int_0^\beta \{x^{\mathrm{T}}(t)\Xi x(t) + v^{\mathrm{T}}(t)\Phi v(t)\}\,dt. \tag{121}$$

DEFINITION 7 $v(t)$ ($0 \leqq t \leqq \beta$) satisfying the familiar linear differential system (91)

$$\dot{x}(t) = Ax(t) + Bv(t),$$

and minimizing J in (120) (or in (121) when β is fixed) is called an *optimal control*.

Example Along the lines of thought of Phillips (1954), Turnovsky (1973), etc., we consider a stabilization policy for a simple macroeconomic differential system:

$$D = C + I + G \tag{12*}$$

$$C = \rho Y + \delta \qquad (0 < \rho < 1) \tag{13*}$$

$$I = \sigma\dot{Y} - \mu\dot{I} \tag{14*}$$

$$\dot{Y} = \eta(D - Y), \tag{15*}$$

where Greek letters stand for positive constants, D denotes aggregate demand, C is consumption, I is investment, G is government expenditure, Y is aggregate supply, and a dot on a variable indicates its first differentiation with respect to time t. (14*) describes investment behavior and (15*) describes the adjustment in output. By substitution, the present system can be reduced to the following equation in terms of Y and G:

$$\ddot{Y} - \alpha_1\dot{Y} - \alpha_2 Y = \eta\dot{G} + \alpha_3 G + \zeta, \tag{16*}$$

where

$$\alpha_1 \equiv \frac{\sigma\eta}{\mu} - \frac{1}{\mu} - \eta(1-\rho), \qquad \alpha_2 \equiv \frac{-\eta(1-\rho)}{\mu}, \qquad \alpha_3 \equiv \frac{\eta}{\mu}, \qquad \zeta \equiv \frac{\eta\delta}{\mu}.$$

Equation (16*) which describes the movement of Y over time for given values of G and $\dot{G}$ can be regarded as a relation in which Y, $\dot{Y}$, and G are to be determined over time for given values of $\dot{G}$. Letting

$$X \equiv \begin{bmatrix} \dot{Y} \\ Y \\ G \end{bmatrix}, \qquad A \equiv \begin{bmatrix} \alpha_1 & \alpha_2 & \alpha_3 \\ 1 & 0 & 0 \\ 0 & 0 & 0 \end{bmatrix}, \qquad B \equiv \begin{bmatrix} \eta \\ 0 \\ 1 \end{bmatrix}, \qquad Z \equiv \begin{bmatrix} \zeta \\ 0 \\ 0 \end{bmatrix},$$

(16*) is transformed into

$$\dot{X} = AX + B\dot{G} + Z. \tag{17*}$$

Or, in terms of the deviations of Y and G from given target values $\bar{Y}$ and $\bar{G}$ $(\equiv (1-\rho)\bar{Y} - \delta)$, respectively, (17*) may be rewritten

$$\dot{x} = Ax + Bv, \tag{18*}$$

where $x \equiv \{\dot{y}, y, g\}$ a column vector, $y \equiv Y - \bar{Y}$, $g \equiv G - \bar{G}$, $v \equiv \dot{g}$. Starting from an arbitrary initial state $x(0) = \{\dot{y}(0), y(0), g(0)\}$, one intends to manipulate $v(t)$ $(0 \leqq t \leqq \beta)$ such that an appropriate cost criterion is minimized for some end point $\beta\,(>0)$ subject to (18*). In this case, one may simplify matrices, Γ, Ξ, and Φ in (120) as follows:

$$\Gamma = \begin{bmatrix} 0 & 0 & 0 \\ 0 & \gamma_1 & 0 \\ 0 & 0 & \gamma_2 \end{bmatrix}, \qquad \Xi = \begin{bmatrix} 0 & 0 & 0 \\ 0 & \xi_1 & 0 \\ 0 & 0 & \xi_2 \end{bmatrix}, \qquad \Phi = \phi,$$

where lowercase Greek letters denote positive scalars. Thus, the cost function for the present problem is

$$J = \gamma_1 y(\beta)^2 + \gamma_2 g(\beta)^2 + \int_0^\beta [\xi_1 y(t)^2 + \xi_2 g(t)^2 + \phi v(t)^2]\, dt. \tag{19*}$$

What is the optimal control for this problem? The analysis below will show that the optimal control $v^*(t)$ becomes

$$v^*(t) = \frac{-1}{\phi}(\eta, 0, 1)\, S(t) \begin{bmatrix} \dot{y}(t) \\ y(t) \\ g(t) \end{bmatrix}, \tag{20*}$$

where $S(t)$ is a unique positive definite matrix satisfying the so-called Riccati equation.

In view of the Lagrange multiplier theorem (Theorem 18 in Section 7.4), if $v(t)$ minimizes J in (120) subject to (91), then there exists $\lambda(t) \in R^n$ such that the differential of $L(\lambda, x, v)$ defined below vanishes:

$$L(\lambda, x, v) \equiv \tfrac{1}{2} J + \int_0^\beta \lambda^{\mathrm{T}}(t)[Ax(t) + Bv(t) - \dot{x}(t)]\, dt$$

$$= \tfrac{1}{2}x^{\mathrm{T}}(\beta)\Gamma x(\beta) + \lambda^{\mathrm{T}}(0)x(0) - \lambda^{\mathrm{T}}(\beta)x(\beta) + \int_0^\beta [f(x, v, t) + \dot{\lambda}^{\mathrm{T}}(t)x(t)]\, dt,$$

where

$$f(x, v, t) \equiv \tfrac{1}{2}x^{\mathrm{T}}(t)\Xi x(t) + \tfrac{1}{2}v^{\mathrm{T}}(t)\Phi v(t) + \lambda^{\mathrm{T}}(t)[Ax(t) + Bv(t)].$$

Note that in the above equation for $L(\lambda, x, v)$ we took account of the fact that

$$-\int_0^\beta \lambda^{\mathrm{T}}\dot{x}\, dt = \int_0^\beta \dot{\lambda}^{\mathrm{T}}x dt - \lambda x\,]_0^\beta.$$

Thus, we have

$$\theta = \frac{\partial L(\lambda, x, v)}{\partial x(t)} = \int_0^\beta [\Xi x(t) + A^{\mathrm{T}}\lambda(t) + \dot{\lambda}(t)]\, dt,$$

$$\theta = \frac{\partial L(\lambda, x, v)}{\partial v(t)} = \int_0^\beta [\Phi v(t) + B^{\mathrm{T}}\lambda(t)]\, dt,$$

$$\theta = \frac{\partial L(\lambda, x, v)}{\partial x(\beta)} = \Gamma x(\beta) - \lambda(\beta).$$

These equations together with (91) yield

$$\dot{\lambda}(t) = -\Xi x(t) - A^{\mathrm{T}}\lambda(t) \qquad \text{for} \quad t \in [0, \beta] \tag{122}$$

$$v(t) = -\Phi^{-1}B^{\mathrm{T}}\lambda(t) \qquad \text{for} \quad t \in [0, \beta] \tag{123}$$

$$\dot{x}(t) = Ax(t) - B\Phi^{-1}B^{\mathrm{T}}\lambda(t) \qquad \text{for} \quad t \in [0, \beta] \tag{124}$$

$$\lambda(\beta) = \Gamma x(\beta). \tag{125}$$

Put

$$\lambda(t) = S(t)x(t). \tag{126}$$

Then

$$\dot{\lambda}(t) = \dot{S}(t)x(t) + S(t)\dot{x}(t). \tag{127}$$

On the other hand, from (122), (124), and (126)

$$\dot{\lambda}(t) = -\Xi x(t) - A^{\mathrm{T}}S(t)x(t)$$

$$= [-\Xi - A^{\mathrm{T}}S(t) - S(t)A + S(t)B\Phi^{-1}B^{\mathrm{T}}S(t)]x(t) + S(t)\dot{x}(t),$$

which is compared with (127), entailing

$$\dot{S}(t) = -A^{\mathrm{T}}S(t) - S(t)A + S(t)B\Phi^{-1}B^{\mathrm{T}}S(t) - \Xi. \tag{128}$$

(125) and (126) imply

$$S(\beta) = \Gamma. \tag{129}$$

Clearly, the matrix $S(t)$ is symmetric, provided it is unique. System (128) is called the *Riccati (differential) equation.*

THEOREM 14 $v(t)$ $(0 \leqq t \leqq \beta)$ minimizes J in (120) subject to (91) if and only if the Riccati equation (128) with (129) has a unique matrix solution $S(t)$. The optimal control $v(t)$ is

$$v(t) = -\Phi^{-1}B^{\mathrm{T}} S(t)x(t) \qquad \text{for} \quad t \in [0, \beta] \tag{123'}$$

and the associated minimum value of J becomes

$$\min_v J = x^{\mathrm{T}}(0)S(0)x(0). \tag{130}$$

PROOF It suffices to prove the "if" part. (Uniqueness of $S(t)$ is implied by Theorem 15 below.) In view of (129), the following identity holds:

$$\begin{aligned} x^{\mathrm{T}}(\beta)\Gamma x(\beta) &= x^{\mathrm{T}}(t)S(t)x(t)]_0^\beta + x^{\mathrm{T}}(0)S(0)x(0) \\ &= \int_0^\beta \frac{d}{dt}(x^{\mathrm{T}}(t)S(t)x(t))\,dt + x^{\mathrm{T}}(0)S(0)x(0). \end{aligned}$$

Note that

$$\begin{aligned} \frac{d}{dt}(x^{\mathrm{T}}Sx) &= x^{\mathrm{T}}\dot{S}x + \dot{x}^{\mathrm{T}}Sx + x^{\mathrm{T}}S\dot{x} \\ &= x^{\mathrm{T}}\dot{S}x + (x^{\mathrm{T}}A^{\mathrm{T}} + v^{\mathrm{T}}B^{\mathrm{T}})Sx + x^{\mathrm{T}}S(Ax + Bv), \end{aligned}$$

by virtue of (91). Hence

$$\begin{aligned} J &= x^{\mathrm{T}}(0)S(0)x(0) + \int_0^\beta \{x^{\mathrm{T}}(t)[\Xi + \dot{S}(t) + A^{\mathrm{T}}S(t) + S(t)A]x(t) \\ &\quad + v^{\mathrm{T}}(t)B^{\mathrm{T}}S(t)x(t) + x^{\mathrm{T}}(t)S(t)Bv(t) + v^{\mathrm{T}}(t)\Phi v(t)\}\,dt \\ &= x^{\mathrm{T}}(0)S(0)x(0) + \int_0^\beta \{v(t) + \Phi^{-1}B^{\mathrm{T}}S(t)x(t)\}^{\mathrm{T}}\Phi\,\{v(t) \\ &\quad + \Phi^{-1}B^{\mathrm{T}}S(t)x(t)\}\,dt \end{aligned}$$

since by (128)

$$\Xi + \dot{S}(t) + A^{\mathrm{T}}S(t) + S(t)A = S(t)B\Phi^{-1}B^{\mathrm{T}}S(t).$$

Therefore, $v(t)$ in (123′) is the minimizer of J, and (130) follows immediately. Q.E.D.

COROLLARY $v(t)$ $(0 \leqq t \leqq \beta)$ minimizes J in (121) subject to (91) if and only if the Riccati equation (128) with

$$S(\beta) = 0 \quad \text{(zero matrix)}$$

has a unique matrix solution $S(t)$. The optimal control is determined by (123′) and the associated minimum value of J is given by (130), where J is that in (121).

Note that the solution $S(t)$ to the Riccati equation is dependent on the end point β and the matrix Γ; so it is sometimes expressed as $S(t;\Gamma,\beta)$.

The rule formulated by (123′) is termed the *optimal feedback rule* since the optimal control at each point in time is directly connected with the value of state-variable vector at the time.

THEOREM 15 The solution $S(t)=S(t;\Gamma,\beta)$ to the Riccati equation (128) with (129) can be calculated in the following manner. Let

$$K\equiv\begin{bmatrix} A & -B\Phi^{-1}B^{\mathrm{T}} \\ -\Xi & -A^{\mathrm{T}} \end{bmatrix},\qquad \psi(t,\tau)\equiv e^{K(t-\tau)},$$

and decompose

$$\psi(t,\tau)=\begin{bmatrix} \psi_{11}(t,\tau) & \psi_{12}(t,\tau) \\ \psi_{21}(t,\tau) & \psi_{22}(t,\tau) \end{bmatrix} \tag{131}$$

conformably to the above decomposition of K. Then

$$S(t;\Gamma,\beta)=[\psi_{21}(t,\beta)+\psi_{22}(t,\beta)\Gamma][\psi_{11}(t,\beta)+\psi_{12}(t,\beta)\Gamma]^{-1}. \tag{132}$$

PROOF Let $z(t)\equiv\{x(t),\lambda(t)\}$, a column vector. Putting (124) and (122) together, we have

$$\dot{z}(t)=Kz(t),$$

which is integrated from β to t $(<\beta)$, yielding

$$z(t)=\psi(t,\beta)z(\beta).$$

In view of (125) and (126), therefore, we have

$$x(t)=[\psi_{11}(t,\beta)+\psi_{12}(t,\beta)\Gamma]x(\beta),$$
$$S(t)x(t)=\lambda(t)=[\psi_{21}(t,\beta)+\psi_{22}(t,\beta)\Gamma]x(\beta).$$

Hence

$$S(t)[\psi_{11}(t,\beta)+\psi_{12}(t,\beta)\Gamma]x(\beta)=[\psi_{21}(t,\beta)+\psi_{22}(t,\beta)\Gamma]x(\beta),$$

where $x(\beta)$ can be arbitrary. Q.E.D.

Let us examine asymptotic properties of the optimal control solution under the assumption of controllability.

THEOREM 16 Assume the state controllability of system (91). Associated with the optimal control of the system with cost criterion function

$$J=\int_0^\infty\{x^{\mathrm{T}}(t)\Xi x(t)+v^{\mathrm{T}}(t)\Phi v(t)\}\,dt, \tag{133}$$

where Ξ and Φ are assumed to be positive definite matrices, the solution to the Riccati equation is a constant positive definite matrix S satisfying

$$A^{\mathrm{T}}S+SA-SB\Phi^{-1}B^{\mathrm{T}}S+\Xi=0. \tag{134}$$

Furthermore, $[A - B\Phi^{-1}B^{\mathrm{T}}S]$ is a stable matrix, i.e., the motion of state variables regulated by

$$\dot{x}(t) = [A - B\Phi^{-1}B^{\mathrm{T}}S]x(t) \tag{124'}$$

is stable. (Optimal control $v(t) = -\Phi^{-1}B^{\mathrm{T}}Sx(t)$.)

PROOF By virtue of the corollary to Theorem 14, for a finite β,

$$x^{\mathrm{T}}(0)S(0;0,\beta)x(0) = \min_{v} \int_0^\beta \{x^{\mathrm{T}}(t)\Xi x(t) + v^{\mathrm{T}}(t)\Phi v(t)\}\,dt. \tag{21*}$$

Since system (91) is controllable, state vector $x(t)$ can attain the origin of R^n at some time t_1 (> 0), starting from an arbitrary $x(0)$, by selecting appropriate control $v(t)$ $(0 \leqq t \leqq t_1)$. Then put $v(t) = 0$ $(t > t_1)$. This implies that the right-hand side of (21*) is bounded from above for every $\beta(> 0)$, i.e., that there exists a positive definite matrix $\bar{S}$ such that $[S(0;0,\beta) - \bar{S}]$ is negative semidefinite. On the other hand, it is seen from the nature of our problem that the left-hand side of (21*) increases as β rises. Thus, there is the limit

$$S \equiv \lim_{\beta\to\infty} S(0;0,\beta). \tag{22*}$$

Next we show that S is positive definite. Suppose, to the contrary, that S is not positive definite. Then, it follows from (22*) that $S(0;0,\beta)$ is not positive definite for some β (> 0), and hence that there is a nonzero $x(0)$ such that the left-hand side of (21*) equals zero. But this implies that

$$v(t) = \theta, \quad x(t) = \theta \qquad \text{for} \quad t \in [0, \beta],$$

a contradiction.

Lastly, stability of $M \equiv [A - B\Phi^{-1}B^{\mathrm{T}}S]$ is verified. From (134)

$$M^{\mathrm{T}}S + SM = -[\Xi + SB\Phi^{-1}B^{\mathrm{T}}S], \tag{23*}$$

whose right-hand side is negative definite. Hence by the Lyapunov theorem (Theorem 41 in Section 2.5), M is stable. Q.E.D.

A similar analysis of optimal control applies *mutatis mutandis* to a linear dynamical system of the other familiar type:

$$\dot{x}(t) = Ax(t) + Bv(t) \tag{99}$$

$$y(t) = Cx(t) \tag{100}$$

with cost function to be minimized

$$J = y^{\mathrm{T}}(\beta)\Gamma y(\beta) + \int_0^\beta \{y^{\mathrm{T}}(t)\Xi y(t) + v^{\mathrm{T}}(t)\Phi v(t)\}\,dt, \tag{120'}$$

where Γ, Ξ, and Φ are positive semidefinite matrices as before, of appropriate dimensions.

THEOREM 14′ $v(t)$ $(0 \leqq t \leqq \beta)$ minimizes J in (120′) subject to (99), (100) if and only if the Riccati equation below has a solution $S(t)$:

$$\dot{S}(t) = -A^{\mathrm{T}}S(t) - S(t)A + S(t)B\Phi^{-1}B^{\mathrm{T}}S(t) - C^{\mathrm{T}}\Xi C \tag{128'}$$

with

$$S(\beta) = C^{\mathrm{T}}\Gamma C. \tag{129'}$$

The optimal control $v(t)$ is provided by (123′), the associated behavior of state variables $x(t)$ is governed by (124′), and the minimum value of J is given by (130).

In order to have an explicit movement of $x(t)$ regulated by (124′), we need the initial value $x(0)$. In the present system, what is observed in general are output vectors $y(\tau)$ for all τ. So we search for a condition for obtaining $x(0)$ from these output data.

DEFINITION 8 System (99), (100) is said to be *observable* if $x(0)$ is uniquely determined from output data $y(\tau)$ $(0 \leqq \tau \leqq \beta)$ for some $\beta(> 0)$.

An equivalence theorem for observability given below is parallel to Theorem 8′.

THEOREM 17 A necessary and sufficient condition for system (99), (100) to be observable is that the symmetric matrix.

$$R(0, t) \equiv \int_0^t e^{A^{\mathrm{T}}\tau}C^{\mathrm{T}}Ce^{A\tau}\, d\tau \tag{135}$$

be nonsingular for some time $t \geqq 0$.

PROOF *Sufficiency* From (93′) in Section 9.3

$$Ce^{A\tau}x(0) = y(\tau) - C\int_0^\tau e^{A(\tau-\sigma)}Bv(\sigma)\, d\sigma.$$

Premultiply both sides of this equation by $e^{A^{\mathrm{T}}\tau}C^{\mathrm{T}}$ and integrate from 0 to t. Then

$$R(0, t)x(0) = \int_0^t e^{A^{\mathrm{T}}\tau}C^{\mathrm{T}}y(\tau)\, d\tau - R(0, t)\int_0^t e^{-A\sigma}Bv(\sigma)\, d\sigma$$
$$+ \int_0^t R(0, \sigma)e^{-A\sigma}Bv(\sigma)\, d\sigma,$$

from which $x(0)$ is uniquely determined since $R(0, t)$ is nonsingular.

(The proof of necessity is similar to that of Theorem 8, and is left to the reader.) Q.E.D.

Observability is found to stand in a dual situation against state controllability.

THEOREM 18 Consider the following system (136), (137) dual to system (99), (100):

$$\dot{x}^*(t) = -A^{\mathrm{T}}x^*(t) - C^{\mathrm{T}}v^*(t), \tag{136}$$

$$y^*(t) = B^{\mathrm{T}}x^*(t). \tag{137}$$

Then, (i) system (99), (100) is observable if and only if system (136) is state controllable; (ii) system (99) is state controllable if and only if system (136), (137) is observable.

PROOF (i) By Theorem 17, system (99), (100) is observable if and only if $R(0, t)$ in (135) is nonsingular for some time $t \geqq 0$, which is nothing but an equivalence condition for system (136) being state controllable. (Refer to Theorem 8 in Section 9.3.)

(The proof of statement (ii) proceeds in a similar manner.) Q.E.D.

There is a rank condition for observability parallel to Theorem 9.

THEOREM 19 System (99), (100) is observable if and only if the $n \times (nr)$ matrix

$$R \equiv [C^{\mathrm{T}}, A^{\mathrm{T}}C^{\mathrm{T}}, \ldots, (A^{\mathrm{T}})^{n-1}C^{\mathrm{T}}] \tag{138}$$

has rank n. Here R is called the observability matrix.

(The proof is similar to that of Theorem 9.)

Utilizing the rank condition for observability, we can verify the following theorem of asymptotic properties of optimal control for the present system.

THEOREM 16′ Assume that system (99), (100) is state controllable and observable. Associated with the optimal control of the system with cost criterion function

$$J = \int_0^\infty \{y^{\mathrm{T}}(t)\Xi y(t) + v^{\mathrm{T}}(t)\Phi v(t)\}\, dt, \tag{133′}$$

where Ξ and Φ are assumed to be positive definite matrices, the solution to the Riccati equation is a constant positive definite matrix S satisfying

$$A^{\mathrm{T}}S + SA - SB\Phi^{-1}B^{\mathrm{T}}S + C^{\mathrm{T}}\Xi C = 0. \tag{134′}$$

Furthermore, $[A - B\Phi^{-1}B^{\mathrm{T}}S]$ is a stable matrix.

The proof proceeds in a manner similar to that of Theorem 16. [For a related observer problem, see Luenberger (1971).]

Now we consider the optimal control problem of discrete type

$$x(t) = Ax(t-1) + Bv(t) \tag{109}$$

with cost criterion function to be minimized

$$J = x^{\mathrm{T}}(\beta)\Gamma x(\beta) + \sum_{t=1}^{\beta}\{x^{\mathrm{T}}(t-1)\Xi x(t-1) + v^{\mathrm{T}}(t)\Phi v(t)\}, \tag{139}$$

where Γ, Ξ, and Φ are assumed to be constant positive semidefinite matrices with Φ positive definite.

Let $J(\beta, 1)$ be the J in (139) where $x(t)$ $(t = 1, 2, \ldots, \beta)$ are replaced by

$$x(t) = A^t x(0) + \sum_{\tau=0}^{t-1} A^\tau B v(t - \tau). \tag{112}$$

Then, our problem is reduced to minimizing $J(\beta, 1)$ with respect to $v(t)$ ($t = 1, 2, \ldots, \beta$). We shall approach this minimum problem from Bellman's *principle of optimality* of the theory of dynamic programming, which may be stated as follows:

An optimal policy has the property that at each point in time, the remaining decisions must constitute an optimal policy with regard to the state resulting from the preceding decisions. (Refer to Bellman (1957).)

Given ρ ($= 1, 2, \ldots, \beta$), define

$$J(\beta, \rho) = x^{\mathrm{T}}(\beta)\Gamma x(\beta) + \sum_{t=\rho}^{\beta} \{x^{\mathrm{T}}(t - 1)\Xi x(t - 1) + v^{\mathrm{T}}(t)\Phi v(t)\} \tag{140}$$

with $x(t)$ ($t = \beta, \beta - 1, \ldots, \rho$) replaced by

$$x(t) = A^{t-\rho+1} x(\rho - 1) + \sum_{\tau=0}^{t-\rho} A^\tau B v(t - \tau). \tag{141}$$

Then, $J(\beta, \rho)$ is expressed only in terms of $x(\rho - 1)$ and $v(t)$ ($t = \rho, \ldots, \beta$). Denoting

$$f_\beta(x(\rho - 1)) \equiv \min_{v(t);t=\rho,\ldots,\beta} J(\beta, \rho) \qquad \text{for} \quad \rho = 1, 2, \ldots, \beta, \tag{142}$$

we have

$$f_\beta(x(0)) = \min_{v(1)} [H(1) + f_\beta(x(1))], \tag{143}$$

where

$$H(1) \equiv x^{\mathrm{T}}(0)\Xi x(0) + v^{\mathrm{T}}(1)\Phi v(1).$$

The more general form of (143) will be

$$f_\beta(x(0)) = \min_{v(t);t=1,\ldots,\sigma} [H(\sigma) + f_\beta(x(\sigma))] \qquad \text{for} \quad \sigma = 1, 2, \ldots, \beta - 1, \tag{143'}$$

where

$$H(\sigma) \equiv \sum_{t=1}^{\sigma} \{x^{\mathrm{T}}(t - 1)\Xi x(t - 1) + v^{\mathrm{T}}(t)\,\Phi v(t)\}.$$

Equation (143′) is the fundamental relation representing the principle of optimality within the context of our problem.

Hence, we determine the optimal control $v(t)$ ($t = 1, 2, \ldots, \beta$) such that they minimize $J(\beta, \rho)$ for all $\rho = 1, 2, \ldots, \beta$. As for the calculation of $v(t)$, we proceed backward from $t = \beta$ to $t = 1$ one by one successively. First, the differential of $J(\beta, \beta)$ with respect to $v(\beta)$ is set equal to zero, yielding

$$B^{\mathrm{T}}\Gamma\{Ax(\beta - 1) + Bv(\beta)\} + \Phi v(\beta) = \theta,$$

which is solved as

$$v(\beta) = -K(\beta)x(\beta - 1), \tag{144-1}$$

where

$$K(\beta) \equiv [B^{\mathrm{T}}\Gamma B + \Phi]^{-1}B^{\mathrm{T}}\Gamma A. \tag{145-1}$$

Second, the differential of $J(\beta, \beta - 1)$ with respect to $v(\beta - 1)$ is equalized to zero, taking account of (145–1) and

$$v(\beta) = -K(\beta)\{Ax(\beta - 2) + Bv(\beta - 1)\}.$$

Then we obtain

$$B^{\mathrm{T}}S(\beta - 1)Ax(\beta - 2) + [B^{\mathrm{T}}S(\beta - 1)B + \Phi]v(\beta - 1) = \theta, \tag{146}$$

where

$$S(\beta - 1) \equiv A^{\mathrm{T}}\Gamma[A - BK(\beta)] + \Xi.$$

It follows from (146) that

$$v(\beta - 1) = -K(\beta - 1)x(\beta - 2), \tag{144-2}$$

where

$$K(\beta - 1) \equiv [B^{\mathrm{T}}S(\beta - 1)B + \Phi]^{-1}B^{\mathrm{T}}S(\beta - 1)A. \tag{145-2}$$

It may be deduced from the above procedure that all the optimal control vectors $v(t)$ $(t = 1, 2, \ldots, \beta)$ take the form

$$v(t) = -K(t)x(t - 1), \tag{144}$$

where

$$K(t) \equiv [B^{\mathrm{T}}S(t)B + \Phi]^{-1}B^{\mathrm{T}}S(t)A, \tag{145}$$

$$S(t - 1) \equiv A^{\mathrm{T}}S(t)[A - BK(t)] + \Xi \tag{147}$$

with

$$S(\beta) = \Gamma. \tag{148}$$

$K(t)$ in (145) is termed the *gain matrix*, and (147) is called the *Riccati difference equation*, whose solution $S(t)$ is a symmetric matrix. Substitution of (144) in (109) yields the behavior of optimal state vectors:

$$x(t) = [A - BK(t)]x(t - 1). \tag{149}$$

Thus we have the following theorem as the discrete counterpart of Theorem 14.

THEOREM 20 $v(t)$ $(t = 1, 2, \ldots, \beta)$ minimizes J in (139) subject to (109) if and only if the Riccati difference equation (147) with (148) has a unique matrix solution $S(t)$. The optimal control $v(t)$ is determined by (144), the corresponding behavior of state variables is governed by (149), and the associated minimum value of J becomes

$$\min_v J = x^{\mathrm{T}}(0)S(0)x(0). \tag{150}$$

PROOF It suffices to prove the "if" part. Eliminating Γ and Ξ in (139) with (147) and (148) taken into consideration, we have

$$\begin{aligned} J = x^{\mathrm{T}}(0)S(0)x(0) + \sum_{t=1}^{\beta} \{&x^{\mathrm{T}}(t)S(t)x(t) + v^{\mathrm{T}}(t)\Phi v(t) \\ &+ x^{\mathrm{T}}(t-1)[A^{\mathrm{T}}S(t)BK(t) - A^{\mathrm{T}}S(t)A]x(t-1)\}. \end{aligned} \tag{139$'$}$$

Then, put

$$A^{\mathrm{T}}S(t)B = K^{\mathrm{T}}(t)[B^{\mathrm{T}}S(t)B + \Phi],$$
$$Ax(t-1) = x(t) - Bv(t)$$

on the right-hand side of (139′), yielding

$$\begin{aligned} J = x^{\mathrm{T}}(0)S(0)x(0) + \sum_{t=1}^{\beta}\{&v^{\mathrm{T}}(t)\Phi v(t) + 2v^{\mathrm{T}}(t)B^{\mathrm{T}}S(t)x(t) \\ &+ x^{\mathrm{T}}(t-1)K^{\mathrm{T}}(t)[B^{\mathrm{T}}S(t)B + \Phi]K(t)x(t-1) - v^{\mathrm{T}}(t)B^{\mathrm{T}}S(t)Bv(t)\}. \end{aligned}$$

Since

$$\begin{aligned} B^{\mathrm{T}}S(t)x(t) &= B^{\mathrm{T}}S(t)\{Ax(t-1) + Bv(t)\} \\ &= [B^{\mathrm{T}}S(t)B + \Phi]K(t)x(t-1) + B^{\mathrm{T}}S(t)Bv(t), \end{aligned}$$

we finally obtain

$$\begin{aligned} J = x^{\mathrm{T}}(0)S(0)x(0) + \sum_{t=1}^{\beta} \{&v(t) + K(t)x(t-1)\}^{\mathrm{T}}[B^{\mathrm{T}}S(t)B \\ &+ \Phi]\{v(t) + K(t)x(t-1)\}. \qquad \text{Q.E.D.} \end{aligned}$$

COROLLARY $v(t)$ $(t = 1, 2, \ldots, \beta)$ minimizes

$$J = \sum_{t=1}^{\beta}\{x^{\mathrm{T}}(t-1)\Xi x(t-1) + v^{\mathrm{T}}(t)\Phi v(t)\}, \tag{151}$$

where Ξ is positive semidefinite and Φ is positive definite, subject to (109), if and only if the Riccati difference equation (147) with

$$S(\beta) = 0 \quad \text{(zero matrix)}$$

has a unique matrix solution $S(t)$. The optimal control $v(t)$ is determined by (144), the corresponding behavior of state variables is governed by (149), and the associated minimum value of J is given by (150).

The optimal solution of our discrete system has the following asymptotic properties, as contrasted to Theorem 16.

THEOREM 21 Assume the state controllability of system (109). Associated with the optimal control of the system with cost criterion function

$$J = \sum_{t=1}^{\infty} \{x^{\mathrm{T}}(t-1)\Xi x(t-1) + v^{\mathrm{T}}(t)\Phi v(t)\}, \tag{152}$$

where Ξ and Φ are assumed to be positive definite matrices, the solution to the Riccati difference equation (147) becomes a constant positive definite matrix S satisfying

$$S = A^{\mathrm{T}}S[A - BK] + \Xi, \tag{153}$$

where

$$K \equiv [B^{\mathrm{T}}SB + \Phi]^{-1}B^{\mathrm{T}}SA. \tag{154}$$

Equation (153) can be rewritten as

$$S = [A - BK]^{\mathrm{T}}S[A - BK] + K^{\mathrm{T}}\Phi K + \Xi. \tag{153$'$}$$

Furthermore, the corresponding behavior of state variables governed by

$$x(t) = [A - BK]x(t-1) \qquad (t = 1, 2, \ldots) \tag{155}$$

is asymptotically stable. (Optimal control $v(t) = -Kx(t-1)$.)

PROOF The proof is parallel to that of Theorem 16, except for the stability problem, which alone will be verified below.

Since S is positive definite,

$$V(t) \equiv x^{\mathrm{T}}(t)Sx(t) \tag{156}$$

is a positive definite quadratic form. Using (155) and (153′), we find

$$\begin{aligned} V(t) - V(t-1) &= x^{\mathrm{T}}(t-1)[(A - BK)^{\mathrm{T}}S(A - BK) - S]x(t-1) \\ &= -x^{\mathrm{T}}(t-1)[\Xi + K^{\mathrm{T}}\Phi K]x(t-1) \\ &< 0 \qquad \text{for all nonzero } x(t-1). \end{aligned}$$

Thus, $V(t)$ in (156) is regarded as a Lyapunov function with respect to the difference equation (155). (Refer to the remark on Lyapunov theorem at the end of Section 2.5.) $V(t) < V(t-1)$ for all t implies that $x(t)$ tends to the origin of R^n as t goes to infinity. Q.E.D.

Remark (Refer to Pindyck (1973).) The above finite-horizon discrete-time optimal control problem can alternatively be resolved by applying the Lagrange multiplier theorem (Theorem 18 in Section 7.4). Define

$$G(y) \equiv \begin{bmatrix} x(1) & - & Ax(0) & - & Bv(1) \\ x(2) & - & Ax(1) & - & Bv(2) \\ \vdots & & & & \\ x(\beta) & - & Ax(\beta-1) & - & Bv(\beta) \end{bmatrix} = \theta, \qquad y \equiv \begin{bmatrix} x(1) \\ \vdots \\ x(\beta) \\ v(1) \\ \vdots \\ v(\beta) \end{bmatrix},$$

and the Lagrangian function

$$L(y, p) \equiv J(y) - pG(y),$$

where $J(y)$ is the J in (139) and p is a row $n\beta$-vector

$$p \equiv (p(1), p(2), \ldots, p(\beta)),$$

$p(t)$ is $1 \times n$ for each t. Referring to Theorems 10 and 19 in Chapter 7, we know that since the Lagrangian L is convex, a sufficient condition for y to be an optimal solution is that L be stationary at y for some p, i.e.,

$$p^{\mathrm{T}}(\beta) - 2\Gamma x(\beta) = \theta \qquad \text{(transversality condition)}$$

$$p^{\mathrm{T}}(t) - 2\Xi x(t) - A^{\mathrm{T}}p^{\mathrm{T}}(t+1) = \theta \qquad (t = 1, \ldots, \beta - 1)$$

$$2\Phi v(t) + B^{\mathrm{T}}p^{\mathrm{T}}(t) = \theta \qquad (t = 1, \ldots, \beta).$$

We make the assumption that $p(t)$ is of the form

$$p^{\mathrm{T}}(t) = 2S(t)x(t)$$

with $S(\beta) = \Gamma$. Substituting this into the last two equations, we get

$$S(t)x(t) = \Xi x(t) + A^{\mathrm{T}}S(t+1)x(t+1), \qquad v(t) = -\Phi^{-1}B^{\mathrm{T}}S(t)x(t).$$

The last equation is substituted in (109), yielding (149)

$$x(t) = [I + B\Phi^{-1}B^{\mathrm{T}}S(t)]^{-1}Ax(t-1) = [A - BK(t)]x(t-1)$$

since

$$[I + B\Phi^{-1}B^{\mathrm{T}}S(t)]^{-1} = I - B[B^{\mathrm{T}}S(t)B + \Phi]^{-1}B^{\mathrm{T}}S(t).$$

Then, substituting (149) into the other equation above, we obtain the Riccati difference equation (147). Lastly, the optimal control vector (144) is derived as follows:

$$\begin{aligned} v(t) &= -\Phi^{-1}B^{\mathrm{T}}S(t)[I - B[B^{\mathrm{T}}S(t)B + \Phi]^{-1}B^{\mathrm{T}}S(t)]Ax(t-1) \\ &= -\Phi^{-1}[I - B^{\mathrm{T}}S(t)B\,[B^{\mathrm{T}}S(t)B + \Phi]^{-1}]B^{\mathrm{T}}S(t)Ax(t-1) \\ &= -[B^{\mathrm{T}}S(t)B + \Phi]^{-1}B^{\mathrm{T}}S(t)Ax(t-1), \end{aligned}$$

making use of the identity

$$I - M(M+N)^{-1} = N(M+N)^{-1} \qquad \text{for square matrices } M, N.$$

When the state-space form is represented by

$$x(t+1) = Ax(t) + Bv(t) \tag{109†}$$

and cost function is specified as

$$J = x^{\mathrm{T}}(\beta)\Gamma x(\beta) + \sum_{t=0}^{\beta-1}\{x^{\mathrm{T}}(t)\Xi x(t) + v^{\mathrm{T}}(t)\Phi v(t)\}, \tag{139†}$$

the optimal control (144) must be replaced by

$$v(t) = -K(t+1)x(t) \tag{144†}$$

with the other elements remaining unchanged.

It is noted that from the above remark we may induce the minimum principle for discrete-time dynamical systems as contrasted to the Pontryagin maximum principle for continuous-time dynamical systems. That is, necessary conditions for minimizing $J(x, v)$ in the system

$$x(t+1) - x(t) = f(x(t), v(t)) \qquad (t = 0, 1, \ldots, \beta - 1)$$

with a given initial state $x(0)$ are

$$p(\beta) = \partial J(x, v)/\partial x(\beta) \qquad \text{(transversality condition)}$$

$$p(t+1) - p(t) = -\ \partial H/\partial x(t) \qquad (t = 1, \ldots, \beta - 1)$$

$$\partial H/\partial v(t) = \theta \qquad (t = 0, \ldots, \beta - 1)$$

where H is the Hamiltonian function

$$H \equiv J(x, v) + \sum_{t=0}^{\beta-1} p(t+1)\, f(x(t), v(t)).$$

(For the Pontryagin maximum principle for discrete-time systems with a free right end point, refer to Propoi (1965).)

Example The discrete version of the previous Phillips model may be written as

$$D(t) = C(t) + I(t) + G(t) \tag{24*}$$

$$C(t) = \rho Y(t) + \delta \qquad (0 < \rho < 1) \tag{25*}$$

$$I(t) = \sigma \Delta Y(t) - \mu I(t-1) \tag{26*}$$

$$\Delta Y(t) \equiv Y(t) - Y(t-1) = \eta(D(t-1) - Y(t-1)), \tag{27*}$$

where we use the same notations as in system (12*)–(15*). By substitution, we have immediately

$$D(t) = \rho Y(t) + \delta + \sigma(Y(t) - Y(t-1)) - \mu I(t-1) + G(t), \tag{28*}$$

$$I(t-1) = D(t-1) - \rho Y(t-1) - \delta - G(t-1), \tag{29*}$$

$$D(t-1) = (1/\eta)(Y(t) - (1-\eta)Y(t-1)). \tag{30*}$$

Substituting in (28*) from (29*) and (30*), we finally obtain

$$Y(t+1) - \alpha_1 Y(t) - \alpha_2 Y(t-1) = \eta G(t) + \alpha_3 G(t-1) + \zeta, \tag{31*}$$

where

$$\alpha_1 \equiv 1 - \mu - \eta(1-\rho) + \eta\sigma, \qquad \alpha_2 \equiv \mu(1 - \eta(1-\rho)) - \eta\sigma,$$

$$\alpha_3 \equiv \eta\mu, \qquad \zeta \equiv \delta\eta(1+\mu).$$

Letting

$$X(t) \equiv \begin{bmatrix} G(t) \\ Y(t) \\ Y(t+1) \end{bmatrix}, \qquad A \equiv \begin{bmatrix} 0 & 0 & 0 \\ 0 & 0 & 1 \\ \alpha_3 & \alpha_2 & \alpha_1 \end{bmatrix}, \qquad B \equiv \begin{bmatrix} 1 \\ 0 \\ \eta \end{bmatrix}, \qquad Z \equiv \begin{bmatrix} 0 \\ 0 \\ \zeta \end{bmatrix}, \tag{32*}$$

(31*) is transformed into

$$X(t) = AX(t-1) + BG(t) + Z. \tag{33*}$$

Or, in terms of the deviations of Y and G from given target equilibrium values $\bar{Y}$ and $\bar{G}$ ($\equiv (1-\rho)\bar{Y} - \delta$) respectively, (33*) may be rewritten as

$$x(t) = Ax(t-1) + Bg(t), \tag{34*}$$

where $x(t) \equiv \{g(t), y(t), y(t+1)\}$ a column vector, $y(t) \equiv Y(t) - \bar{Y}$, $g(t) \equiv G(t) - \bar{G}$. Equation (34*) is a state-space representation of Eq. (31*). We shall adopt a cost function of the form (151) with Ξ, Φ specified as

$$\Xi = \begin{bmatrix} 0 & 0 & 0 \\ 0 & \xi & 0 \\ 0 & 0 & 0 \end{bmatrix}, \qquad \Phi = \phi,$$

where lowercase Greek letters denote positive scalars, i.e.,

$$J = \sum_{t=1}^{\beta} \{\xi y(t-1)^2 + \phi g(t)^2\}. \tag{35*}$$

Then, optimal control values are calculated as

$$\begin{aligned} g(\beta) &= 0, \\ g(\beta-1) &= 0, \\ g(\beta-2) &= \frac{-\xi\eta}{\xi\eta^2 + \phi}(\alpha_1 y(\beta-2) + \alpha_2 y(\beta-3) + \alpha_3 g(\beta-3)), \end{aligned}$$

and so forth, with Riccati equation solution

$$\begin{aligned} S(\beta-1) &= \Xi, \\ S(\beta-2) &= \mathrm{diag}(0, \xi, \xi), \\ &\vdots \end{aligned}$$

The system of generalized distributed lags will be written as

$$z(t) = \sum_{i=1}^{r} A_i z(t-i) + \sum_{j=0}^{s} B_j u(t-j), \tag{157}$$

where $z(t)$ is a column n-vector of endogenous variables in period t, $u(t)$ is a column m-vector of policy instruments in period t, A_i is an $n \times n$ real constant matrix, and B_j is an $n \times m$ real constant matrix. Equation (157) can be regarded as the general form of (31*) in terms of the deviations from target equilibrium. The corresponding state-space representation is

$$x(t) = \tilde{A}x(t-1) + \tilde{B}u(t), \tag{158}$$

where

$$x(t) \equiv \begin{bmatrix} u(t-s+1) \\ \vdots \\ u(t-1) \\ u(t) \\ z(t-r+1) \\ \vdots \\ z(t-1) \\ z(t) \end{bmatrix}, \qquad \tilde{A} \equiv \begin{bmatrix} 0 & I & & 0 & 0 & \cdots & & 0 \\ \vdots & \ddots & \ddots & & \vdots & & & \vdots \\ & & 0 & I & 0 & \cdots & & 0 \\ 0 & \cdots & 0 & 0 & 0 & \cdots & & 0 \\ 0 & \cdots & & 0 & 0 & I & & 0 \\ \vdots & & & \vdots & \vdots & \ddots & \ddots & \\ 0 & \cdots & & 0 & 0 & \cdots & 0 & I \\ B_s & \cdots & & B_1 & A_r & \cdots & A_2 & A_1 \end{bmatrix},$$

$$\tilde{B} \equiv \begin{bmatrix} 0 \\ \vdots \\ 0 \\ I \\ 0 \\ \vdots \\ 0 \\ B_0 \end{bmatrix}. \tag{159}$$

We shall adopt a cost criterion function of the form

$$J = \sum_{t=1}^{\infty} \left\{ \sum_{i=1}^{r} z^{\mathrm{T}}(t-i)\, \Xi_i z(t-i) + \sum_{j=1}^{s} u^{\mathrm{T}}(t-j) \Xi_{r+j} u(t-j) \right. \\ \left. + u^{\mathrm{T}}(t) \Phi u(t) \right\},$$

where Ξ_i $(i = 1, 2, \ldots, r+s)$ and Φ are all constant positive definite matrices, or equivalently

$$J = \sum_{t=1}^{\infty} \{x^{\mathrm{T}}(t-1) \Xi x(t-1) + u^{\mathrm{T}}(t) \Phi u(t)\}, \tag{160}$$

where

$$\Xi \equiv \operatorname{diag}(\Xi_{r+s}, \ldots, \Xi_{r+1}, \Xi_r, \ldots, \Xi_1). \tag{161}$$

Then, by virtue of Theorem 21, the optimal input of instruments is determined by

$$u(t) = -Kx(t-1), \tag{162}$$

and the associated behavior of vector $x(t)$ governed by

$$x(t) = [\tilde{A} - \tilde{B}K]x(t-1) \tag{163}$$

is stable, where

$$K \equiv [\tilde{B}^{\mathrm{T}} S \tilde{B} + \Phi]^{-1} \tilde{B}^{\mathrm{T}} S \tilde{A}, \tag{164}$$

and S is the solution to

$$S = \tilde{A}^{\mathrm{T}} S [\tilde{A} - \tilde{B} K] + \Xi. \tag{165}$$

We note that system (158) is controllable since there exists some positive integer j such that

$$\mathrm{rk}[\tilde{B}, \tilde{A}\tilde{B}, \tilde{A}^2\tilde{B}, \ldots, \tilde{A}^{j-1}\tilde{B}] = sm + rn.$$

(For controllable canonical forms, refer to Chen (1970).)

To conclude this section, we extend the preceding results concerning optimal control of system (109) to the following state-space form:

$$x(t) = Ax(t-1) + Bv(t) \tag{109}$$

$$y(t) = Cx(t) \tag{110}$$

with initial condition

$$x(0) = x^0 \quad \text{(constant)}. \tag{111}$$

THEOREM 20′ A necessary and sufficient condition for $v(t)$ $(t = 1, 2, \ldots, \beta)$ to be the minimizer of

$$J = y^{\mathrm{T}}(\beta)\Gamma y(\beta) + \sum_{t=1}^{\beta} \{y^{\mathrm{T}}(t-1)\Xi y(t-1) + v^{\mathrm{T}}(t)\Phi v(t)\}, \tag{166}$$

where Γ, Ξ, and Φ are positive semidefinite matrices with Φ positive definite, subject to system (109), (110) with (111), is that the Riccati difference equation

$$S(t-1) = A^{\mathrm{T}} S(t)[A - BK(t)] + C^{\mathrm{T}} \Xi C \tag{147′}$$

with

$$S(\beta) = C^{\mathrm{T}} \Gamma C, \tag{148′}$$

where

$$K(t) = [B^{\mathrm{T}} S(t) B + \Phi]^{-1} B^{\mathrm{T}} S(t) A, \tag{145′}$$

has a unique matrix solution $S(t)$. The optimal control $v(t)$ is determined by

$$v(t) = -K(t)x(t-1), \tag{144′}$$

the corresponding behavior of state variables is governed by

$$x(t) = [A - BK(t)]x(t-1), \tag{149′}$$

and the associated minimum value of J becomes

$$\min_{v} J = x^{\mathrm{T}}(0) S(0) x(0). \tag{150′}$$

COROLLARY $v(t)$ $(t = 1, 2, \ldots, \beta)$ minimize

$$J = \sum_{t=1}^{\beta} \{y^{\mathrm{T}}(t-1)\Xi y(t-1) + v^{\mathrm{T}}(t)\Phi v(t)\}, \tag{166′}$$

where Ξ is positive semidefinite and Φ is positive definite, subject to system (109), (110) with (111), if and only if the Riccati difference equation (147′) with

$$S(\beta) = 0 \quad \text{(zero matrix)}$$

has a unique matrix solution $S(t)$. The optimal control $v(t)$ is determined by (144′), the corresponding behavior of state variables is governed by (149′), and the associated minimum value of J is given by (150′).

The rank condition for observability of the present difference equation system will be found to be the same as that of the previous differential equation system since we have from (110) and (113)

$$\begin{bmatrix} y(0) \\ y(1) - CBv(1) \\ y(2) - CBv(2) - CABv(1) \\ \vdots \\ y(n-1) - \sum_{\tau=0}^{n-2} CA^{\tau}Bv(n-\tau-1) \end{bmatrix} = \begin{bmatrix} C \\ CA \\ CA^2 \\ \vdots \\ CA^{n-1} \end{bmatrix} x(0).$$

DEFINITION 8′ System (109), (110) is said to be *observable* if $x(0)$ is uniquely determined from output data $y(\tau)$ ($\tau = 0, 1, \ldots, \beta$) for some positive integer β.

THEOREM 19′ System (109), (110) is observable if and only if matrix R in (138) has rank n.

Thus a theorem parallel to Theorem 21 is obtained for our discrete system.

THEOREM 21′ Assume that system (109), (110) is state controllable and observable. Associated with the optimal control of the system with cost criterion function

$$J = \sum_{t=1}^{\infty} \{y^{\mathrm{T}}(t-1)\Xi y(t-1) + v^{\mathrm{T}}(t)\Phi v(t)\}, \tag{167}$$

where Ξ and Φ are positive definite, the solution to the Riccati difference equation (147′) becomes a constant positive definite matrix S satisfying

$$S = A^{\mathrm{T}}S[A - BK] + C^{\mathrm{T}}\Xi C, \tag{168}$$

where

$$K \equiv [B^{\mathrm{T}}SB + \Phi]^{-1}B^{\mathrm{T}}SA. \tag{154′}$$

Furthermore, $[A - BK]$ is a stable matrix in the sense of (96) on p. 94.

(For the proof, refer to Dorato and Levis (1971).)

For further theoretical development along these lines, see Aoki (1974) and Wonham (1967) among others. For stochastic control problems, the reader may refer to Wonham (1968), Caines and Mayne (1970), Turnovsky (1973), and Chow (1975). For macroeconomic models of stabilization policy, refer to Theil (1964), Pindyck (1973), and Friedman (1975).

9.5 Realization of Controllable and Observable Linear Dynamical Systems

This section supplements the preceding two sections with regard to controllability and observability of linear dynamical systems.

In Sections 9.3 and 9.4, controllability or observability conditions are shown for linear dynamical systems with constant coefficients. If such a system is noncontrollable (or nonobservable), is it possible to transform the original system into a controllable (or observable) one that inherits the input–output properties of the former? Considering a discrete-time system:

$$x(t) = Ax(t-1) + Bv(t), \qquad y(t) = Cx(t), \tag{169}$$

or a continuous-time system:

$$\dot{x}(t) = Ax(t) + Bv(t), \qquad y(t) = Cx(t), \tag{169$'$}$$

where A $(n \times n)$, B $(n \times m)$, and C $(r \times n)$ are constant coefficient matrices, we characterize its input–output properties by

$$M_i \equiv CA^iB \qquad (i = 0, 1, 2, \ldots)$$

which are termed *Markov parameter matrices*. Our present transformation problem is to obtain a new discrete-time system:

$$\bar{x}(t) = \bar{A}\bar{x}(t-1) + \bar{B}v(t), \qquad y(t) = \bar{C}\bar{x}(t), \tag{170}$$

or a continuous-time system:

$$\dot{\bar{x}}(t) = \bar{A}\bar{x}(t) + \bar{B}v(t), \qquad y(t) = \bar{C}\bar{x}(t), \tag{170$'$}$$

that is controllable and/or observable, such that

$$\bar{C}\bar{A}^i\bar{B} = M_i \qquad (i = 0, 1, 2, \ldots)$$

for a given infinite sequence of Markov parameter matrices M_i.

DEFINITION 9 Given an infinite sequence of $r \times m$ Markov parameter matrices

$$M \equiv \{M_i \ (i = 0, 1, 2, \ldots)\}, \tag{171}$$

if we find a triplet $(A, B, C)_n$ such that

$$M_i = CA^iB \qquad (i = 0, 1, 2, \ldots),$$

then we say that M is realizable and that the triplet is a *realization* of M, where $(A, B, C)_n$ represents system (169) or (169′) with n being termed the dimension of the system. Any two such triplets that are realizations of M are said to be *zero-state equivalents*. If there is no positive integer n' less than n such that triplets $(A, B, C)_n$ and $(A', B', C')_{n'}$ are zero-state equivalents, then $(A, B, C)_n$ is called a *minimal realization* of M.

The minimal realization problem is found to be closely related to controllability and observability of realizing systems.

DEFINITION 10 Referring to Theorem 10 in Section 9.3, the least positive integers μ and ν such that

$$\mathrm{rk}(P_\mu) = \mathrm{rk}(P_{\mu+1}), \tag{172}$$

$$\mathrm{rk}(R_\nu) = \mathrm{rk}(R_{\nu+1}), \tag{173}$$

are termed the *controllability index* and *observability index*, respectively, of $(A, B, C)_n$, where

$$P_j \equiv [B, AB, A^2B, \ldots, A^{j-1}B], \tag{174}$$

$$R_k \equiv [C^{\mathrm{T}}, A^{\mathrm{T}}C^{\mathrm{T}}, (A^{\mathrm{T}})^2C^{\mathrm{T}}, \ldots, (A^{\mathrm{T}})^{k-1}C^{\mathrm{T}}]. \tag{175}$$

For convenience, P_j in (174) and R_k in (175) will be called the j-controllability matrix and k-observability matrix, respectively, of $(A, B, C)_n$.

Note that $\mathrm{rk}(P_\mu)$ in (172) or $\mathrm{rk}(R_\nu)$ in (173) is not necessarily equal to n, the dimension of system $(A, B, C)_n$. By Theorem 12 in Section 9.3 and by Theorem 19′ in Section 9.4, $(A, B, C)_n$ is (state) controllable if and only if $\mathrm{rk}(P_\mu) = n$, and it is observable if and only if $\mathrm{rk}(R_\nu) = n$. When P_μ or R_ν has rank less than n, system $(A, B, C)_n$ may be reduced to some controllable or observable system via a transformation.

DEFINITION 4′ System $(\bar{A}, \bar{B}, \bar{C})_n$ is said to be (*algebraically*) *equivalent* to system $(A, B, C)_n$ if

$$\bar{A} = T^{-1}AT, \qquad \bar{B} = T^{-1}B, \qquad \bar{C} = CT \tag{176}$$

for an $n \times n$ real constant nonsingular matrix T. In this case, T is called a *similarity transformation*, and sometimes we write

$$(A, B, C)_n \xrightarrow{T} (\bar{A}, \bar{B}, \bar{C})_n. \tag{176′}$$

Remarks (1) Algebraically equivalent systems are zero-state equivalents since

$$CA^iB = \bar{C}\bar{A}^i\bar{B} \qquad \text{for} \quad i = 0, 1, 2, \ldots,$$

where $\bar{A}$, $\bar{B}$, $\bar{C}$ are those in (176). (2) $\bar{P}_j = T^{-1}P_j$ and $\bar{R}_k = T^{\mathrm{T}}R_k$ where $\bar{P}_j$ and $\bar{R}_k$ are the j-controllability matrix and the k-observability matrix, respectively, of $(\bar{A}, \bar{B}, \bar{C})_n$.

THEOREM 22 The ranks of P_j in (174) and R_k in (175) and the controllability and observability indices of $(A, B, C)_n$ are invariant under any similarity transformation.

(For the proof, refer to that of Theorem 11 in Section 9.3.)

First, we show a system decomposition containing a controllable zero-state equivalent subsystem.

THEOREM 23 (Silverman, 1971) Let μ be the controllability index of system $(A, B, C)_n$. (Cf. Definition 10.) If

$$\mathrm{rk}(P_\mu) = q \leqq n,$$

then $(A, B, C)_n$ is algebraically equivalent to $(\bar{A}, \bar{B}, \bar{C})_n$ whose coefficient matrices have the forms

$$\bar{A} = \begin{bmatrix} \bar{A}_{11} & \bar{A}_{12} \\ 0 & \bar{A}_{22} \end{bmatrix}, \qquad \bar{B} = \begin{bmatrix} \bar{B}_1 \\ 0 \end{bmatrix}, \qquad \bar{C} = [\bar{C}_1, \bar{C}_2] \tag{177}$$

where $\bar{A}_{11}$ is $q \times q$, $\bar{B}_1$ is $q \times m$, and $\bar{C}_1$ is $r \times q$; and $(\bar{A}_{11}, \bar{B}_1, \bar{C}_1)_q$ is a (state) controllable zero-state equivalent of $(A, B, C)_n$.

PROOF Let T_1 be an $n \times q$ matrix composed of basis vectors for the column space of P_μ, let T_2 be any $n \times (n - q)$ matrix such that matrix $T \equiv [T_1, T_2]$ is nonsingular, and transform $(A, B, C)_n$ via this T to $(\bar{A}, \bar{B}, \bar{C})_n$ where $\bar{A}$, $\bar{B}$, $\bar{C}$ are those defined in (176). The $n \times q$ matrix AT_1 is a submatrix of $P_{\mu+1}$, each column of which is represented by a linear combination of the column vectors of T_1 since the column space of $P_{\mu+1}$ coincides with a part or the whole of the column space of P_μ. Hence,

$$\text{the first } q \text{ columns of } \bar{A} = T^{-1}AT_1 = T^{-1}T_1\bar{A}_{11} = \begin{bmatrix} \bar{A}_{11} \\ 0 \end{bmatrix}$$

for some $q \times q$ matrix $\bar{A}_{11}$. Also, B is a submatrix of P_μ, whence

$$\bar{B} = T^{-1}B = T^{-1}T_1\bar{B}_1 = \begin{bmatrix} \bar{B}_1 \\ 0 \end{bmatrix}$$

for some $q \times m$ matrix $\bar{B}_1$. $(\bar{A}_{11}, \bar{B}_1, \bar{C}_1)_q$ is a zero-state equivalent of $(A, B, C)_n$ because

$$CA^iB = \bar{C}_1\bar{A}_{11}^i\bar{B}_1 \qquad \text{for} \quad i = 0, 1, 2, \ldots.$$

Lastly, in view of Theorem 22, $\hat{P}_\mu \equiv [\bar{B}_1, \bar{A}_{11}\bar{B}_1, \ldots, (\bar{A}_{11})^{\mu-1}\bar{B}_1]$ has rank q since

$$[\bar{B}, \bar{A}\bar{B}, \ldots, (\bar{A})^{\mu-1}\bar{B}] = \begin{bmatrix} \hat{P}_\mu \\ 0 \end{bmatrix}. \qquad \text{Q.E.D.}$$

Remark The decomposition in (177) is of the same form as that in (108) in Definition 5 in Section 9.3. Thus, for a completely controllable system $(A, B, C)_n$, $\mathrm{rk}(P_\mu) = n$ must hold.

The dual form of Theorem 23 is given next.

THEOREM 23′ (Silverman, 1971) Let ν be the observability index of system $(A, B, C)_n$. If

$$\operatorname{rk}(R_\nu) = q \leqq n,$$

then $(A, B, C)_n$ is algebraically equivalent to $(\bar{A}, \bar{B}, \bar{C})_n$ whose coefficient matrices have the forms

$$\bar{A} = \begin{bmatrix} \bar{A}_{11} & 0 \\ \bar{A}_{21} & \bar{A}_{22} \end{bmatrix}, \qquad \bar{B} = \begin{bmatrix} \bar{B}_1 \\ \bar{B}_2 \end{bmatrix}, \qquad \bar{C} = [\bar{C}_1, 0], \tag{178}$$

where $\bar{A}_{11}$ is $q \times q$, $\bar{B}_1$ is $q \times m$, and $\bar{C}_1$ is $r \times q$; and $(\bar{A}_{11}, \bar{B}_1, \bar{C}_1)_q$ is an observable zero-state equivalent of $(A, B, C)_n$.

(The proof is similar to that of Theorem 23 above.)

A main decomposition theorem is now presented.

THEOREM 24 (*Kalman decomposition theorem*) Let μ and ν be the controllability index and the observability index of system $(A, B, C)_n$. If

$$\operatorname{rk}(R_\nu^{\mathrm{T}} P_\mu) = q \leqq n, \tag{179}$$

then $(A, B, C)_n$ is algebraically equivalent to $(\bar{A}, \bar{B}, \bar{C})_n$ whose coefficient matrices have the forms

$$\bar{A} = \begin{bmatrix} \bar{A}_{11} & 0 & \bar{A}_{13} \\ \bar{A}_{21} & \bar{A}_{22} & \bar{A}_{23} \\ 0 & 0 & \bar{A}_{33} \end{bmatrix}, \qquad \bar{B} = \begin{bmatrix} \bar{B}_1 \\ \bar{B}_2 \\ 0 \end{bmatrix}, \qquad \bar{C} = [\bar{C}_1, 0, \bar{C}_3], \tag{180}$$

and $(\bar{A}_{11}, \bar{B}_1, \bar{C}_1)_q$ is a (state) controllable and observable zero-state equivalent of $(A, B, C)_n$. Moreover, if u and v are the least positive integers such that

$$\operatorname{rk}(R_v^{\mathrm{T}} P_u) = q, \tag{181}$$

then they are the controllability index and the observability index, respectively, of $(\bar{A}_{11}, \bar{B}_1, \bar{C}_1)_q$.

PROOF In view of Theorem 22 in Section 2.3, it follows from (179) that

$$n \geqq \operatorname{rk}(P_\mu) \equiv \tilde{q} \geqq q, \qquad n \geqq \operatorname{rk}(R_\nu) \equiv q' \geqq q$$

with either $\tilde{q} = q$ or $q' = q$. Applying Theorem 23 to $(A, B, C)_n$, we have an algebraically equivalent system $(\tilde{A}, \tilde{B}, \tilde{C})_n$ whose coefficient matrices have the forms

$$\tilde{A} = \begin{bmatrix} \tilde{A}_{\mathrm{I}} & \tilde{A}_{\mathrm{II}} \\ 0 & \tilde{A}_{33} \end{bmatrix}, \qquad \tilde{B} = \begin{bmatrix} \tilde{B}_{\mathrm{I}} \\ 0 \end{bmatrix}, \qquad \tilde{C} = [\tilde{C}_{\mathrm{I}}, \tilde{C}_3],$$

where $\tilde{A}_{\mathrm{I}}$ is $\tilde{q} \times \tilde{q}$, $\tilde{B}_{\mathrm{I}}$ is $\tilde{q} \times m$, and $\tilde{C}_{\mathrm{I}}$ is $r \times \tilde{q}$; and $(\tilde{A}_{\mathrm{I}}, \tilde{B}_{\mathrm{I}}, \tilde{C}_{\mathrm{I}})_w$ is a (state) controllable zero-equivalent of $(A, B, C)_n$, where w denotes $\tilde{q}$. Note that

$$\tilde{P}_\mu \equiv [\tilde{B}, \tilde{A}\tilde{B}, \ldots, (\tilde{A})^{\mu-1}\tilde{B}] = \begin{bmatrix} \tilde{P}_{\mathrm{I}_\mu} \\ 0 \end{bmatrix},$$

where the $\tilde{q} \times (\mu m)$ matrix

$$\tilde{P}_{\mathrm{I}_\mu} \equiv [\tilde{B}_\mathrm{I}, \tilde{A}_\mathrm{I}\tilde{B}_\mathrm{I}, \ldots, (\tilde{A}_\mathrm{I})^{\mu-1}\tilde{B}_\mathrm{I}]$$

has rank $\tilde{q}$.

Let σ be the observability index of $(\tilde{A}_\mathrm{I}, \tilde{B}_\mathrm{I}, \tilde{C}_\mathrm{I})_w$. Clearly $\sigma \leqq \nu$. Let

$$\tilde{R}_{\mathrm{I}_\sigma} \equiv [\tilde{C}_\mathrm{I}^\mathrm{T}, \tilde{A}_\mathrm{I}^\mathrm{T}\tilde{C}_\mathrm{I}^\mathrm{T}, \ldots, (\tilde{A}_\mathrm{I}^\mathrm{T})^{\sigma-1}\tilde{C}_\mathrm{I}^\mathrm{T}].$$

Then

$$\mathrm{rk}(\tilde{R}_{\mathrm{I}_\sigma}) \equiv \bar{q} \leqq q' \leqq n.$$

Applying Theorem 23′ to $(\tilde{A}_\mathrm{I}, \tilde{B}_\mathrm{I}, \tilde{C}_\mathrm{I})_w$, we have an algebraically equivalent system $(\bar{A}_\mathrm{I}, \bar{B}_\mathrm{I}, \bar{C}_\mathrm{I})_w$ whose coefficient matrices have the forms

$$\bar{A}_\mathrm{I} = \begin{bmatrix} \bar{A}_{11} & 0 \\ \bar{A}_{21} & \bar{A}_{22} \end{bmatrix}, \qquad \bar{B}_\mathrm{I} = \begin{bmatrix} \bar{B}_1 \\ \bar{B}_2 \end{bmatrix}, \qquad \bar{C}_\mathrm{I} = [\bar{C}_1, 0],$$

where $\bar{A}_{11}$ is $\bar{q} \times \bar{q}$, $\bar{B}_1$ is $\bar{q} \times m$, and $\bar{C}_1$ is $r \times \bar{q}$; and $(\bar{A}_{11}, \bar{B}_1, \bar{C}_1)_{\bar{q}}$ is an observable zero-state equivalent of $(\tilde{A}_\mathrm{I}, \tilde{B}_\mathrm{I}, \tilde{C}_\mathrm{I})_w$. Since the $\tilde{q} \times (\mu m)$ matrix

$$\bar{P}_{\mathrm{I}_\mu} \equiv [\bar{B}_\mathrm{I}, \bar{A}_\mathrm{I}\bar{B}_\mathrm{I}, \ldots, (\bar{A}_\mathrm{I})^{\mu-1}\bar{B}_\mathrm{I}] = \begin{bmatrix} \bar{P}_{1\mu} \\ \bar{P}_{2\mu} \end{bmatrix}$$

has rank $\tilde{q}$ in view of the above note, the $\bar{q} \times (\mu m)$ matrix

$$\bar{P}_{1\mu} \equiv [\bar{B}_1, \bar{A}_{11}\bar{B}_1, \ldots, (\bar{A}_{11})^{\mu-1}\bar{B}_1]$$

has rank $\bar{q}$. Hence, system $(\bar{A}_{11}, \bar{B}_1, \bar{C}_1)_{\bar{q}}$ is controllable. Thus we get a similarity transformation T such that

$$(A, B, C)_n \xrightarrow{T} (\bar{A}, \bar{B}, \bar{C})_n$$

whose coefficient matrices have the forms (180) and $(\bar{A}_{11}, \bar{B}_1, \bar{C}_1)_q$ is a controllable and observable zero-equivalent of $(A, B, C)_n$. It remains to show that $\bar{q} = q$. Let $\bar{P}_\mu$ and $\bar{R}_\nu$ be the μ-controllability matrix and the ν-observability matrix of $(\bar{A}, \bar{B}, \bar{C})_n$. $\bar{P}_\mu$ and $\bar{R}_\nu$ are partitioned conformably with the forms (180) as follows:

$$\bar{P}_\mu \equiv [\bar{B}, \bar{A}\bar{B}, \ldots, (\bar{A})^{\mu-1}\bar{B}] = \begin{bmatrix} \bar{P}_{1\mu} \\ \bar{P}_{2\mu} \\ 0 \end{bmatrix},$$

$$\bar{R}_\nu \equiv [\bar{C}^\mathrm{T}, \bar{A}^\mathrm{T}\bar{C}^\mathrm{T}, \ldots, (\bar{A}^\mathrm{T})^{\nu-1}\bar{C}^\mathrm{T}] = \begin{bmatrix} \bar{R}_{1\nu} \\ 0 \\ \bar{R}_{3\nu} \end{bmatrix}.$$

Taking account of the fact that

$$\bar{P}_\mu = T^{-1}P_\mu, \qquad \bar{R}_\nu = T^{\mathrm{T}}R_\nu,$$

we know that

$$\bar{R}_{1\nu}^{\mathrm{T}}\bar{P}_{1\mu} = \bar{R}_\nu^{\mathrm{T}}\bar{P}_\mu = R_\nu^{\mathrm{T}}P_\mu. \tag{182}$$

Thus, by (179)

$$\mathrm{rk}(\bar{R}_{1\nu}^{\mathrm{T}}\bar{P}_{1\mu}) = q.$$

But by controllability and observability of $(\bar{A}_{11}, \bar{B}_1, \bar{C}_1)_{\bar{q}}$,

$$\mathrm{rk}(\bar{R}_{1\nu}^{\mathrm{T}}\bar{P}_{1\mu}) = \bar{q}.$$

Therefore $\bar{q} = q$. The controllability and observability indices of $(\bar{A}_{11}, \bar{B}_1, \bar{C}_1)_q$ are the least positive integers u, v such that (181) holds, in view of (182). Q.E.D.

THEOREM 25 Let $(A, B, C)_n$ be a realization of an infinite sequence of Markov parameter matrices M in (171). Let μ and ν be the controllability index and observability index, respectively, of system $(A, B, C)_n$, and let P_μ, R_ν be its μ-controllability and ν-observability matrices. Then the following three statements are equivalent: (1) $(A, B, C)_n$ is controllable and observable; (2) $\mathrm{rk}(R_\nu^{\mathrm{T}}P_\mu) = n$; and (3) $(A, B, C)_n$ is a minimal realization of M.

PROOF The equivalence of (1) and (2) is obvious. From Theorem 24, we know that (3) implies (2) since if $\mathrm{rk}(R_\nu^{\mathrm{T}}P_\mu) < n$, a lower order realization can be found. It remains to show that (2) implies (3). Suppose that (2) holds and $(A, B, C)_n$ is not minimal. Then by definition there exists a triplet $(\bar{A}, \bar{B}, \bar{C})_{\bar{n}}$ with $\bar{n} < n$ realizing M, i.e.,

$$CA^iB = \bar{C}\bar{A}^i\bar{B} \qquad \text{for} \quad i = 0, 1, 2, \ldots.$$

Thus $R_\nu^{\mathrm{T}}P_\mu = \bar{R}_\nu^{\mathrm{T}}\bar{P}_\mu$ where

$$\bar{P}_\mu \equiv [\bar{B}, \bar{A}\bar{B}, \ldots, (\bar{A})^{\mu-1}\bar{B}], \qquad \bar{R}_\nu \equiv [\bar{C}^{\mathrm{T}}, \bar{A}^{\mathrm{T}}\bar{C}^{\mathrm{T}}, \ldots, (\bar{A}^{\mathrm{T}})^{\nu-1}\bar{C}^{\mathrm{T}}].$$

But $\bar{R}_\nu^{\mathrm{T}}$ has only $\bar{n}$ columns. Hence,

$$n = \mathrm{rk}(R_\nu^{\mathrm{T}}P_\mu) = \mathrm{rk}(\bar{R}_\nu^{\mathrm{T}}\bar{P}_\mu) \leqq \bar{n} < n,$$

which is a contradiction. Q.E.D.

THEOREM 26 If $(A, B, C)_n$ and $(\bar{A}, \bar{B}, \bar{C})_n$ are two different minimal realizations of an infinite sequence of $r \times m$ Markov parameter matrices M in (171), then these systems are algebraically equivalent to each other.

PROOF By Theorem 25, $(A, B, C)_n$ and $(\bar{A}, \bar{B}, \bar{C})_n$ are controllable and observable. Let μ, u be controllability indices of these systems and ν, v be their observability indices. Put

$$\sigma \equiv \max\{\mu, u, \nu, v\},$$

and let P_σ, $\bar{P}_\sigma$ and R_σ, $\bar{R}_\sigma$ be σ-controllability and σ-observability matrices of these systems, respectively. Then

$$\mathrm{rk}(P_\sigma) = \mathrm{rk}(\bar{P}_\sigma) = \mathrm{rk}(R_\sigma) = \mathrm{rk}(\bar{R}_\sigma) = n, \tag{36*}$$

$$CP_\sigma = \bar{C}\bar{P}_\sigma, \qquad R_\sigma^{\mathrm{T}}B = \bar{R}_\sigma^{\mathrm{T}}\bar{B}, \tag{37*}$$

$$R_\sigma^{\mathrm{T}}P_\sigma = \bar{R}_\sigma^{\mathrm{T}}\bar{P}_\sigma. \tag{38*}$$

Thus, we have from (37*) and (36*)

$$C = \bar{C}\bar{P}_\sigma P_\sigma^+ \qquad \text{and} \qquad B = (R_\sigma^{\mathrm{T}})^+\bar{R}_\sigma^{\mathrm{T}}\bar{B}, \tag{39*}$$

where P_σ^+ and $(R_\sigma^{\mathrm{T}})^+$ are the generalized inverses of P_σ and R_σ^{T},

$$P_\sigma^+ \equiv P_\sigma^{\mathrm{T}}(P_\sigma P_\sigma^{\mathrm{T}})^{-1}, \qquad (R_\sigma^{\mathrm{T}})^+ \equiv (R_\sigma R_\sigma^{\mathrm{T}})^{-1}R_\sigma$$

by virtue of the corollary to Theorem 21 in Section 6.3. Furthermore,

$$(R_\sigma^{\mathrm{T}})^+\bar{R}_\sigma^{\mathrm{T}}\bar{P}_\sigma P_\sigma^+ = I$$

in view of (38*). Putting

$$T \equiv \bar{P}_\sigma P_\sigma^+ = \bar{P}_\sigma P_\sigma^{\mathrm{T}}(P_\sigma P_\sigma^{\mathrm{T}})^{-1},$$

we know that T is a nonsingular $n \times n$ matrix. Thus (39*) is rewritten as

$$C = \bar{C}T \qquad \text{and} \qquad B = T^{-1}\bar{B}.$$

Lastly, since

$$R_\sigma^{\mathrm{T}}AP_\sigma = \bar{R}_\sigma^{\mathrm{T}}\bar{A}\bar{P}_\sigma,$$

we have

$$A = T^{-1}\bar{A}T. \qquad \text{Q.E.D.}$$

DEFINITION 11 Define the sequence of *Hankel matrices* for a given infinite sequence of $r \times m$ Markov parameter matrices M in (171) as

$$H_{k,s} \equiv \begin{bmatrix} M_0 & M_1 & \cdots & M_{s-1} \\ M_1 & M_2 & & M_s \\ \vdots & \vdots & & \vdots \\ M_{k-1} & M_k & \cdots & M_{k+s-2} \end{bmatrix} \qquad \text{for} \quad k, s = 1, 2, \ldots. \tag{183}$$

THEOREM 27 (Silverman, 1971) An infinite sequence of $r \times m$ Markov parameter matrices M in (171) is realizable if and only if there exist positive integers μ, ν and n such that

$$\mathrm{rk}(H_{\nu,\mu}) = \mathrm{rk}(H_{\nu+1,\mu+j}) = n \qquad \text{for} \quad j = 0, 1, 2, \ldots. \tag{184}$$

In this case, n is the dimension of a minimal realization $(A, B, C)_n$ of M.

PROOF *"Only if" part* Since $M_i = CA^iB$ $(i = 0, 1, 2, \ldots)$,

$$H_{k,s} = R_k^{\mathrm{T}}P_s \qquad \text{for} \quad k, s = 1, 2, \ldots.$$

Letting ν and μ be the observability index and the controllability index of the realization, respectively, we have

$$\text{rk}(H_{\nu+i,\mu+j}) = \min\{\text{rk}(P_\mu), \text{rk}(R_\nu)\} \qquad \text{for} \quad i, j = 0, 1, 2, \ldots.$$

"If" part Let h_{pq} denote the (p, q)th component of the Hankel matrix. From the form (183),

$$h_{r+i,j} = h_{i,m+j} \qquad \text{for} \quad i, j = 1, 2, \ldots, \tag{40*}$$

where r and m are the dimensions of Markov parameter matrices.

We shall construct an explicit realization of M. Let G_μ denote the submatrix formed from the first n linearly independent rows of $H_{\nu,\mu}$ and let G_μ^* be the submatrix of $H_{\nu+1,\mu}$ positioned r rows below G_μ (i.e., if the ith row of G_μ is the jth row of $H_{\nu+1,\mu}$, then the ith row of G_μ^* is the $(j + r)$th row of $H_{\nu+1,\mu}$). The following four matrices are then uniquely defined as submatrices of $H_{\nu+1,\mu}$:

F: the nonsingular $n \times n$ matrix formed from an arbitrary set of n linearly independent columns of G_μ.

F^*: the $n \times n$ matrix occupying the same column positions in G_μ^* as does F in G_μ.

F_1: the $r \times n$ matrix occupying the same column positions in $H_{1,\nu}$ as does F in G_μ.

F_2: the $n \times m$ matrix occupying the first m columns of G_μ.

Postmultiplying G_μ by a permutation matrix π so as to assemble a set of n linearly independent columns to columns 1 through n, we have

$$F = G_\mu D, \qquad F^* = G_\mu^* D, \qquad F_1 = H_{1,\mu} D \qquad \text{for an arbitrary } \pi, \tag{41*}$$

where $D^{\mathrm{T}} \equiv [I, 0, \ldots, 0]\pi^{\mathrm{T}}$, an $n \times (\mu m)$ matrix. Define $A \equiv F^*F^{-1}$. Then, $AF = F^*$ and (41*) imply

$$G_\mu^* = AG_\mu.$$

We extend or restrict this equation such that

$$G_j^* = AG_j \qquad \text{for} \quad j = 1, 2, \ldots, \tag{42*}$$

where $G_1 = F_2$. It is clear that

$$G_{j+1} = [F_2, G_j^*] \qquad \text{for} \quad j = 1, 2, \ldots \tag{43*}$$

since the submatrix positioned m rows to the right of a given submatrix in the Hankel matrix is the same as the submatrix positioned r rows below it by (40*). By (42*), therefore,

$$G_{j+1} = [F_2, AG_j] = [F_2, AF_2, AG_{j-1}^*]. \tag{44*}$$

Defining $B \equiv F_2$, it follows by repeated application of (42*) and (43*) that

$$G_j = [B, AB, \ldots, A^{j-2}B, A^{j-1}B] \qquad \text{for} \quad j = 1, 2, \ldots. \tag{45*}$$

Defining $C \equiv F_1F^{-1}$ and taking (41*) into account, we get

$$CG_\mu = H_{1,\mu}$$

Extend this as

$$CG_j = H_{1,j} \qquad \text{for} \quad j = 1, 2, \ldots. \tag{46*}$$

From (45*) and (46*)

$$H_{1,j} = [CB, CAB, \ldots, CA^{j-1}B] \qquad \text{for} \quad j = 1, 2, \ldots.$$

On the other hand,

$$H_{1,j} = [M_0, M_1, \ldots, M_{j-1}] \qquad \text{for} \quad j = 1, 2, \ldots.$$

Thus,

$$M_i = CA^iB \qquad \text{for} \quad i = 0, 1, 2, \ldots.$$

We have proved, therefore, that the triplet

$$(F^*F^{-1}, F_2, F_1F^{-1})_n \tag{185}$$

realizes M if (184) holds. (184) and (185) imply that μ and ν are the controllability index and the observability index, respectively, of system (185) and that the system is a minimal realization of M, by Theorem 25. Q.E.D.

The sufficiency proof of Theorem 27 suggests an algorithm for the computation of a minimal realization of a given infinite sequence of Markov parameter matrices. For algorithms of this computation problem, refer to Ho and Kalman (1966) and Rissanen (1971). We present below Rissanen's algorithm for the case where

$$r \leqq m \leqq n. \tag{186}$$

In this case, the condition (184) will hold for the integers ν, μ such that $\nu \geqq \mu$, in view of the dimension of $H_{\nu,\mu}$. Thus we consider the following Hankel matrix of rank n:

$$H_{\nu,\nu} = \begin{bmatrix} h_{11} & h_{12} & \cdots & h_{1,\nu m} \\ h_{21} & h_{22} & \cdots & h_{2,\nu m} \\ \vdots & \vdots & & \vdots \\ h_{\nu r,1} & h_{\nu r,2} & \cdots & h_{\nu r,\nu m} \end{bmatrix}. \tag{187}$$

This matrix can be expressed as a product of two matrices:

$$H_{\nu,\nu} = \Gamma_{\nu\nu} \cdot \Lambda_{\nu\nu}, \tag{188}$$

where $\Lambda_{\nu\nu}$ is a $\nu m \times \nu m$ triangular matrix with ones on its main diagonal:

$$\Lambda_{\nu\nu} \equiv \begin{bmatrix} 1 & \lambda_{12} & \lambda_{13} & \cdots & \lambda_{1,\nu m} \\ 0 & 1 & \lambda_{23} & & \lambda_{2,\nu m} \\ \vdots & 0 & 1 & & \vdots \\ & & \ddots & \ddots & \\ 0 & 0 & \cdots & 0 & 1 \end{bmatrix}; \tag{189}$$

and $\Gamma_{\nu\nu}$ is a $\nu r \times \nu m$ matrix of rank n:

$$\Gamma_{\nu\nu} = \begin{bmatrix} \Gamma_1 & \Theta \\ \Gamma_2 & \Theta \\ \vdots & \vdots \\ \Gamma_\nu & \Theta \end{bmatrix}, \tag{190}$$

in which

$$\Gamma_{i+1} \equiv \begin{bmatrix} \gamma_{ir+1,1} & \cdots & \gamma_{ir+1,n} \\ \gamma_{ir+2,1} & \cdots & \gamma_{ir+2,n} \\ \vdots & & \vdots \\ \gamma_{ir+r,1} & \cdots & \gamma_{ir+r,n} \end{bmatrix} \qquad (i = 0, 1, \ldots, \nu - 1),$$

and Θ stands for an $r \times (\nu m - n)$ zero matrix.

Note that if the first $m \times m$ principal submatrix of $\Lambda_{\nu\nu}$ is denoted Λ_m, then we have for each Markov parameter matrix M_i

$$M_i = \Gamma_{i+1} \begin{bmatrix} \Lambda_m \\ 0 \end{bmatrix} \qquad (i = 0, 1, 2, \ldots, \nu - 1), \tag{191}$$

where 0 stands for an $(n - m) \times m$ zero matrix.

From (188), we know that for $i = 1, 2, \ldots, \nu r$,

$$\begin{aligned} \gamma_{i1} &= h_{i1} \\ \gamma_{i2} &= h_{i2} - \gamma_{i1}\lambda_{12} \\ \gamma_{i3} &= h_{i3} - \gamma_{i1}\lambda_{13} - \gamma_{i2}\lambda_{23} \\ &\vdots \\ \gamma_{ij} &= h_{ij} - \sum_{k=1}^{j-1} \gamma_{ik}\lambda_{kj} \qquad (j = 1, 2, \ldots, n). \end{aligned} \tag{192}$$

Letting $s(1)$ be the least positive integer i such that $h_{i1} \neq 0$, we put $\gamma_{s(1),j} = 0$ for $j = 2, 3, \ldots, n$. Thus λ_{12} and all the γ_{i2} are to be computed. Next, letting $s(2)$ be the least positive integer i such that $\gamma_{i2} \neq 0$, we put $\gamma_{s(2),j} = 0$ for $j = 3, 4, \ldots, n$. Thus $\lambda_{13}, \lambda_{23}$, and all the γ_{i3} are to be computed. Proceeding this way, we can compute all the λ's and γ's, by utilizing (192), though we need not compute all, as seen from (195) below.

Now, let Λ_n be the first $n \times n$ principal submatrix of $\Lambda_{\nu\nu}$, and let Λ_n^* be the $n \times n$ submatrix of $\Lambda_{\nu\nu}$ composed of its rows 1 through n and columns $m + 1$ through $m + n$. Then, in view of (40*),

$$\Gamma_{i+1}\Lambda_n = \Gamma_i\Lambda_n^*,$$

whence

$$\Gamma_{i+1} = \Gamma_i\Lambda_n^*\Lambda_n^{-1} \qquad (i = 1, 2, \ldots). \tag{193}$$

Substituting (193) repeatedly in (191), we get

$$M_i = \Gamma_1(\Lambda_n^* \Lambda_n^{-1})^i \begin{bmatrix} \Lambda_m \\ 0 \end{bmatrix} \qquad (i = 0, 1, \ldots, \nu - 1). \tag{194}$$

Therefore, the minimal realization is given by the triplet:

$$\left(\Lambda_n^* \Lambda_n^{-1}, \begin{bmatrix} \Lambda_m \\ 0 \end{bmatrix}, \Gamma_1\right)_n. \tag{195}$$

Lastly, we shall provide the formula for computing the Markov parameter matrices from a general distributed-lag system:

$$y(t) = \sum_{i=1}^{p} A_i y(t-i) + \sum_{j=0}^{s} B_j v(t-j), \tag{196}$$

where $y(t)$ is a column r-vector of endogenous variables in period t, $v(t)$ is a column m-vector of policy instruments in period t, A_i is an $r \times r$ real constant matrix, and B_j is an $r \times m$ real constant matrix.

Rewrite (196) as

$$[I - A_1 z^{-1} - A_2 z^{-2} - \cdots - A_p z^{-p}]\, y(t) = [B_0 + B_1 z^{-1} + \cdots + B_s z^{-s}]\, v(t), \tag{197}$$

where z^{-i} is the lag operator defined by

$$z^{-i} y(t) = y(t-i), \qquad z^{-i} v(t) = v(t-i),$$

with $z^0 = 1$. On the other hand, assuming that the system (196) is stable, we obtain the following form of $y(t)$ by an iterative substitution:

$$y(t) = \sum_{i=0}^{\infty} M_j z^{-i} v(t), \tag{198}$$

where M_i is an $r \times m$ matrix. The form (198) may be termed the *final form.* (Refer to Theil and Boot (1962).) Comparing (197) with (198), we have

$$\left[I - \sum_{i=1}^{p} A_i z^{-i}\right] \sum_{j=0}^{\infty} M_j z^{-j} = \sum_{j=0}^{s} B_j z^{-j}, \tag{199}$$

from which it follows that

$$M_0 = B_0 \tag{200-1}$$

$$M_j = B_j + \sum_{i=1}^{j} A_i M_{j-i} \qquad \text{for} \quad j = 1, 2, \ldots, s, \tag{200-2}$$

$$M_j = \sum_{i=1}^{j} A_i M_{j-i} \qquad \text{for} \quad j = s+1, s+2, \ldots, \tag{200-3}$$

where $A_i = 0$ for $i > p$. This is the formula for computing the Markov parameter matrices associated with the distributed-lag system (196). In order to obtain a minimal realization, we need not compute all the M_j by the formula.

Only those M_j ($j = 0, 1, 2, \ldots$) sufficient to establish condition (184) are needed.

Example Consider the distributed-lag equation (31*), neglecting its constant term. The equation is then rewritten

$$(1 - \alpha_1 z^{-1} - \alpha_2 z^{-2}) Y(t) = (\eta z^{-1} + \alpha_3 z^{-2}) G(t). \tag{47*}$$

By virtue of the above formulas (200), we compute the Markov parameter matrices (which are scalars in the present case) associated with (47*):

$$M_0 = 0, \qquad M_1 = \eta, \qquad M_2 = \alpha_3 + \alpha_1 \eta,$$

$$M_j = \alpha_1 M_{j-1} + \alpha_2 M_{j-2} \qquad (j = 3, 4, \ldots).$$

Thus, knowing that $r = m = 1$ and that the dimension n of a minimal realization of the Markov matrices is equal to three, we consider the following Hankel matrix:

$$H_{4,4} = \begin{bmatrix} 0 & \eta & M_2 & M_3 \\ \eta & M_2 & M_3 & M_4 \\ M_2 & M_3 & M_4 & M_5 \\ M_3 & M_4 & M_5 & M_6 \end{bmatrix},$$

which can be expressed as

$$H_{4,4} = \begin{bmatrix} \gamma_{11} & \gamma_{12} & \gamma_{13} & 0 \\ \gamma_{21} & \gamma_{22} & \gamma_{23} & 0 \\ \gamma_{31} & \gamma_{32} & \gamma_{33} & 0 \\ \gamma_{41} & \gamma_{42} & \gamma_{43} & 0 \end{bmatrix} \begin{bmatrix} 1 & \lambda_{12} & \lambda_{13} & \lambda_{14} \\ 0 & 1 & \lambda_{23} & \lambda_{24} \\ 0 & 0 & 1 & \lambda_{34} \\ 0 & 0 & 0 & 1 \end{bmatrix}.$$

Note that for this example

$$\Lambda_1 = 1, \qquad \Gamma_1 = (\gamma_{11}, \gamma_{12}, \gamma_{13}),$$

$$\Lambda_3 = \begin{bmatrix} 1 & \lambda_{12} & \lambda_{13} \\ 0 & 1 & \lambda_{23} \\ 0 & 0 & 1 \end{bmatrix}, \qquad \Lambda_3^* = \begin{bmatrix} \lambda_{12} & \lambda_{13} & \lambda_{14} \\ 1 & \lambda_{23} & \lambda_{24} \\ 0 & 1 & \lambda_{34} \end{bmatrix}.$$

By the formula (192) and its accompanying procedure, we compute

$$\gamma_{11} = 0, \qquad \gamma_{12} = \eta, \qquad \gamma_{13} = 0,$$

$$\lambda_{12} = M_2/\eta, \qquad \lambda_{13} = M_3/\eta, \qquad \lambda_{14} = M_4/\eta,$$

$$\lambda_{23} = M_2/\eta, \qquad \lambda_{24} = M_3/\eta,$$

$$\lambda_{34} = \frac{\eta M_5 - M_2 M_4 - (M_3)^2 + M_3 (M_2)^2/\eta}{\eta M_4 - 2 M_2 M_3 + (M_2)^3/\eta}.$$

Taking these results into consideration, we obtain the minimal realization

$$\left(\Lambda_3^* \Lambda_3^{-1}, \begin{bmatrix}1\\0\\0\end{bmatrix}, (0, \eta, 0)\right)_3 .$$

EXERCISES

1. Prove Theorem 6.

2. Verify that in case $v_0 > \tilde{v}(0)$ in the paragraph after (75) in Section 9.2, the indicated policy will lead to the Ramsey path.

3. Show that Eq. (82) is solved as (83).

4. Verify that (11*) in Section 9.3 implies $x = \theta$.

5. Prove the corollary to Theorem 10.

6. Verify that the minimum number of columns of matrix B whose combination satisfies (106′) will not exceed n, provided $\operatorname{rk}(P) = n$, where P is the matrix defined by (98).

7. Prove Theorem 19.

8. In the limiting case where B_j ($j = 1, 2, \ldots, s$) are all zero in (157), show that even if Φ in (160) is zero, the motion of endogenous variables associated with an optimal policy is stable.

9. Prove Theorem 21′.

10. Consider the problem of minimizing the quadratic loss function in terms of the deviations of variables from their targets:

$$J = (x(\beta) - a(\beta))^{\mathrm{T}} \Gamma (x(\beta) - a(\beta)) + \sum_{t=1}^{\beta} \{(x(t-1) - a(t-1))^{\mathrm{T}} \times \Xi (x(t-1) - a(t-1)) + (v(t) - b(t))^{\mathrm{T}} \Phi (v(t) - b(t))\} \tag{E1}$$

subject to the discrete-time system with exogenous variables:

$$x(t) = Ax(t-1) + Bv(t) + c(t) \qquad \text{(with } x(0) \text{ constant)}, \tag{E2}$$

where $a(t)$, $b(t)$ are targets for $x(t)$, $v(t)$, respectively, and $c(t)$ is a vector of exogenous variables. Other notations in (E1), (E2) are those conventional ones used in the text. Applying Bellman's principle of optimality to the present problem, deduce the following optimal control: for $t = \beta, \beta - 1, \beta - 2, \ldots, 2, 1$ backward in time

$$v(t) = -K(t)\, x(t-1) - k(t), \tag{E3}$$

where letting $e(t)$ denote $c(t) - a(t)$,

$$k(t) \equiv [B^{\mathrm{T}} S(t) B + \Phi]^{-1} \Big(B^{\mathrm{T}} \Big\{ S(t)e(t) + L(t+1)S(t+1)e(t+1) + L(t+1)L(t+2)S(t+2)e(t+2) + \cdots + \prod_{\tau=1}^{\beta-t} L(\beta - \tau + 1) S(\beta) e(\beta) \Big\} - \Phi b(t)$$

$$+ B^{\mathrm{T}}\Big\{K^{\mathrm{T}}(t+1)\Phi b(t+1) + L(t+1)K^{\mathrm{T}}(t+2)\Phi b(t+2) + L(t+1)L(t+2)K^{\mathrm{T}}(t+3)\Phi b(t+3) + \cdots + \prod_{\tau=1}^{\beta-t-1} L(\beta-\tau)K^{\mathrm{T}}(\beta)\Phi b(\beta)\Big\}\Big), \tag{E4}$$

$K(t)$, $S(t-1)$ are those defined in (145), (147) respectively in the text, and

$$L(t) \equiv [A - BK(t)]^{\mathrm{T}}. \tag{E5}$$

REFERENCES AND FURTHER READING

Aoki, M. (1973). "On Sufficient Conditions for Optimal Stabilization Policies," *Review of Economic Studies* **40**, 131–138.

Aoki, M. (1974). "Non-Interacting Control of Macroeconomic Variables: Implications on Policy Mix Considerations," *Journal of Econometrics* **2**, 261–281.

Aoki, M. (1975). "On a Generalization of Tinbergen's Condition in the Theory of Policy to Dynamic Models," *Review of Economic Studies* **42**, 293–296.

Arrow, K. J. (1968). "Applications of Control Theory to Economic Growth," *Lectures in Applied Mathematics* **12**, Part 2, 85–119.

Arrow, K. J., and Kurz, M. (1970). *Public Investment, the Rate of Return, and Optimal Fiscal Policy*. Johns Hopkins Press, Baltimore, Maryland.

Athans, M., and Falb, P. L. (1966). *Optimal Control: An Introduction to the Theory and Its Applications*. McGraw-Hill, New York.

Bellman, R. (1957). *Dynamic Programming*. Princeton Univ. Press, Princeton.

Bellman, R. (1967). *Introduction to the Mathematical Theory of Control Processes*, Vol. I. Academic Press, New York.

Brockett, R. W., and Mesarović, M. D. (1965). "The Reproducibility of Multivariable Systems," *Journal of Mathematical Analysis and Applications* **11**, 548–563.

Caines, P. E., and Mayne, D. Q. (1970). "On the Discrete Time Matrix Riccati Equation of Optimal Control," *International Journal of Control* **12**, 785–794.

Canon, M. D., Cullum, C. D. Jr., and Polak, E. (1970). *Theory of Optimal Control and Mathematical Programming*. McGraw-Hill, New York.

Cass, D. (1965). "Optimum Growth in an Aggregative Model of Capital Accumulation," *Review of Economic Studies* **32**, 233–240.

Chen, C. T. (1970). *Introduction to Linear System Theory*. Holt, New York.

Chow, G. C. (1975). *Analysis and Control of Dynamic Economic Systems*. Wiley, New York.

Dasgupta, P. S. (1969). "Optimal Growth When Capital Is Non-Transferable," *Review of Economic Studies* **36**, 77–88.

Dorato, P., and Levis, A. H. (1971). "Optimal Linear Regulators: The Discrete-Time Case," *IEEE Transactions on Automatic Control* **16**, 613–620.

Fel'dbaum, A. A. (1965). *Optimal Control Systems*. Academic Press, New York.

Friedman, B. M. (1975). *Economic Stabilization Policy: Methods in Optimization*. North-Holland Publ., Amsterdam.

Halkin, H. (1966). "A Maximum Principle of the Pontryagin Type for Systems Described by Nonlinear Difference Equations," *SIAM Journal on Control* **4**, 90–111.

Hestenes, M. R. (1965). "On Variational Theory and Optimal Control Theory," *SIAM Journal on Control* **3**, 23–48.

Ho, B. L., and Kalman, R. E. (1966). "Effective Construction of Linear State-Variable Models From Input/Output Functions," *Regelungstechnik* **12,** 545–548.

Holtzman, J. M., and Halkin, H. (1966). "Directional Convexity and the Maximum Principle for Discrete Systems," *SIAM Journal on Control* **4,** 263–275.

Kalman, R. E. (1960). "Contributions to the Theory of Optimal Control," *Boletin Sociedad Matematica Mexicana, 2nd Ser.* **5,** 102–119.

Kalman, R. E. (1963). "Mathematical Description of Linear Dynamical Systems," *SIAM Journal on Control* **1,** 152–192.

Kalman, R. E., Ho, Y. C., and Narandra, K. S. (1962). "Controllability of Linear Dynamical Systems," *Contributions to Differential Equations* **1,** 189–213.

Kamien, M. I., and Schwartz, N. L. (1971). "Sufficient Conditions in Optimal Control Theory," *Journal of Economic Theory* **3,** 207–214.

Lee, E. B., and Markus, L. (1967). *Foundations of Optimal Control Theory.* Wiley, New York.

Leitmann, G. (1966). *An Introduction to Optimal Control.* McGraw-Hill, New York.

Luenberger, D. G. (1969). *Optimization by Vector Space Methods.* Wiley, New York.

Luenberger, D. G. (1971). "An Introduction to Observers," *IEEE Transactions on Automatic Control* **16**, 596–602.

Mangasarian, O. L. (1966). "Sufficient Conditions for the Optimal Control of Nonlinear Systems," *SIAM Journal on Control* **4,** 139–152.

Phillips, A. W. (1954). "Stabilization Policy in a Closed Economy," *Economic Journal* **64,** 290–323.

Pindyck, R. S. (1973). *Optimal Planning for Economic Stabilization.* North-Holland Publ., Amsterdam.

Pontryagin, L. S., Boltyanskĭi, V. G., Gamkrelidze, R. V., and Mishchenko, E. F. (1962). *The Mathematical Theory of Optimal Processes* (English translation). Wiley (Interscience), New York.

Preston, A. J. (1974). "A Dynamic Generalization of Tinbergen's Theory of Policy," *Review of Economic Studies* **41,** 65–74.

Propoi, A. I. (1965). "The Maximum Principle for Discrete Control Systems," *Automation and Remote Control* **26,** 1164–1177.

Rissanen, J. (1971). "Recursive Identification of Linear Systems," *SIAM Journal on Control* **9**, 420–430.

Shell, K. (ed.) (1967). *Essays on the Theory of Optimal Economic Growth.* MIT Press, Cambridge, Massachusetts.

Shell, K. (1969). "Applications of Pontryagin's Maximum Principle to Economics," in *Mathematical Systems Theory and Economics* (H. W. Kuhn and G. P. Szegö, eds.), Vol. 1, pp. 241–292. Springer-Verlag, Berlin.

Silverman, L. M. (1971). "Realization of Linear Dynamical Systems," *IEEE Transactions on Automatic Control* **16**, 554–567.

Stoleru, L. G. (1965). "An Optimal Policy for Economic Growth," *Econometrica* **33,** 321–348.

Theil, H. (1964). *Optimal Decision Rules for Government and Industry.* North-Holland Publ., Amsterdam.

Theil, H., and Boot, J. C. G. (1962). "The Final Form of Econometric Equation Systems," *Review of the International Statistical Institute* **30,** 136–152.

Tinbergen, J. (1952). *On the Theory of Economic Policy,* 2nd ed. North-Holland Publ., Amsterdam.

Tse, E. (1971). "On the Optimal Control of Stochastic Linear Systems," *IEEE Transactions on Automatic Control* **16,** 776–785.

Turnovsky, S. J. (1973). "Optimal Stabilization Policies for Deterministic and Stochastic Linear Economic Systems," *Review of Economic Studies* **40**, 79–95.

Turnovsky, S. J. (1974). "The Stability Properties of Optimal Economic Policies," *American Economic Review* **64**, 136–148.

Uzawa, H. (ed.) (1969). "Symposium on the Theory of Economic Growth," *Journal of Political Economy* **77**(4), Part II.

Wonham, W. M. (1967). "On Pole Assignment in Multi-Input Controllable Linear Systems, *IEEE Transactions on Automatic Control* **12**, 660–665.

Wonham, W. M. (1968). "On a Matrix Riccati Equation of Stochastic Control," *SIAM Journal on Control* **6**, 681–697.

Zabczyk, J. (1975). "On Optimal Stochastic Control of Discrete-Time Systems in Hilbert Space," *SIAM Journal on Control* **13**, 1217–1234.

Author Index

Numbers in italics refer to pages on which the complete references are listed.

A

Abadie, J., *340*
Afriat, S. N., 339, *340*
Aitkens, A. C., *31*
Akhiezer, N. I., *272*
Akilov, G. P., 258, *272*
Albert, A., 200, 212, *236*
Aoki, M., 371, 389, *403*
Apostol, T. M., 175, 182, *196*, 252, *272*, 333, *340*
Arrow, K. J., 62, *64*, 129, 159, *160*, 317, 318, 320, 321, *340*, 353, 355, 361, *403*
Athans, M., *403*
Averch, H., 323, *340*

B

Bailey, M. J., *340*
Barnett, S., *103*
Bear, D., 98, 99, *103*
Beckmann, M. J., *340*
Bellman, R., *64*, *103*, 380, *403*
Benavie, A., *103*
Ben-Israel, A., *236*
Berge, C., *196*
Berman, A., 229, *236*
Black, J., *64*
Block, H. D., 159, *160*
Bodewig, E., *64*
Boltyanskii, V. G., *404*
Boot, J. C. G., 400, *404*
Boullion, T. L., *236*
Bowden, R., *103*
Brockett, R. W., 371, *403*
Bruckmann, G., 306, *340*
Bruno, M., 336, *340*
Burmeister, E., 144, 145, *160*

C

Caines, P. E., 389, *403*
Canon, M. D., *403*
Cass, D., 338, *340*, 361, *403*
Charnes, A., *236*
Chen, C. T., 388, *403*
Chenery, H. B., 323, *340*
Chipman, J. S., *237*
Chitre, V., *160*
Chow, G. C., 390, *403*
Conlisk, J., 99, 101, 102, *103*
Cox, J. C., 317, *340*
Cullum, C. D. Jr., *403*

D

Dantzig, G. B., *340*

Dasgupta, P. S., 357, 359, *403*
Day, M. M., 277, *340*
Debreu, G., *65*, 113, *160*
Diewert, W. E., *340*
Dobell, A. R., 144, 145, *160*
Dorato, P., 389, *403*
Dunford, N., *197*

E

Eichhorn, W., 314, *340*
Enthoven, A. C., 317, 318, 320, 321, *340*

F

Falb, P. L., *403*
Fel'dbaum, A. A., *403*
Fiedler, M., 29, *65*
Fisher, F. M., *160*
Fomin, S. V., 192, *197*, *272*
Friedman, B. M., 390, *403*
Fromovitz, S., 309, *341*
Fujimoto, T., 115, *161*
Fuller, A. T., 90, *103*

G

Gale, D., 28, *31*, *160*, 258, *272*, 284, 301, 323, 334, *340*
Gamkrelidze, R. V., *404*
Gandolfo, G., *103*
Gantmacher, F. R., *31*, *65*, 92, *103*, *160*
Geoffrion, A. M., *341*
Goldberg, S., *103*
Goldstein, M., 214, *237*
Graybill, F. A., *237*
Greville, T. N. E., *236*, *237*

H

Hadley, G., *31*, *272*
Hahn, F. H., 129, 159, *160*
Halkin, H., *403*, *404*
Hansen, T., 323, *341*
Hawkins, D., *65*
Helmberg, G., *197*
Herstein, I. N., 113, *160*
Hestenes, M. R., 355, *403*
Hicks, J. R., 79, *103*, 115, 123, *160*, 272
Ho, B. L., 398, *404*
Ho, Y. C., *404*
Hoffman, K., *65*
Holtzman, J. M., *404*
Horwich, G., *160*
Howe, C. W., *341*
Hurwicz, L., 129, 159, *160*, *340*

I

Inada, K., 258, *272*
Intriligator, M. D., *341*

J

Johnson, C. R., *65*
Johnson, L. L., 323, *340*
Jorgenson, D. W., *160*

K

Kalman, R. E., 398, *404*
Kamien, M. I., *404*
Kantorovich, L. V., 258, *272*
Karlin, S., 136, *160*, *341*
Katzner, D. W., 252, *272*, 322, *341*
Kemeny, J. G., *341*
Kemp, M. C., *31*, *272*
Kennedy, C., 154, *160*
Keynes, J. M., *103*
Klein, E., 133, *160*, *197*
Kolmogorov, A. N., 192, *197*, *272*
Koopmans, T. C., 306, 323, *341*
Kornai, J., 337, *341*
Kuhn, H. W., *340, 341*
Kunze, R., *65*
Kurz, M., 353, *403*
Kusumoto, S., 314, *341*

L

Lancaster, K., *31*, *160*
Lancaster, P., *197*
Lang, S., *31*, 73, *103*
La Salle, J., *65*
Leblanc, G., 314, *341*
Lee, E. B., *404*
Lefschetz, S., *65*
Leitmann, G., *404*
Leontief, W. W., 115, *160*
Levis, A. H., 389, *403*

Łoś, J., 306, *341*
Łoś, M. W., 306, *341*
Luenberger, D. G., 192, *197*, 201, 203, *237*, 255, *272*, 277, *341*, 346, 347, 379, *404*

M

McKenzie, L. W., 23, *31*, 114, 159, *160*, 305, *341*
McManus, M., 62, *64*
Mangasarian, O. L., 309, *341*, 351, 354, 355, *404*
Mann, H. B., *65*
Manne, A. S., 337, *341*
Markus, L., *404*
Marquardt, D. W., 214, *237*
Marx, K., *160*
Mayne, D. Q., 389, *403*
Mesarović, M. D., 371, *403*
Metzler, L. A., 115, *161*
Meyer, C. D., *237*
Mishchenko, E. F., *404*
Mitra, S. K., 224, *237*
Moeseke, P. V., 314, 338, *341*
Morgenstern, O., *341*
Morimoto, Y., *64*
Morishima, M., 115, 120, 147, 152, 153, *161*, 260, *272*, 302, 303, 306, 332, 337, *341*, *342*
Mosak, J. L., *161*
Mukherji, A., 155, 157, 160, *161*
Mundell, R. A., 159, *161*
Murata, Y., *161*, 260, *272*

N

Narandra, K. S., *404*
Negishi, T., 129, 159, *161*
Neumann, J. von, 291, *342*
Newman, P., 252, *272*, 317, *342*
Nikaido, H., 28, *31*, *65*, *161*, 258, *272*, *340*, *342*
Nosse, T., 120, *161*

O

Odell, P. L., *236*
Oettli, W., 314, *340*
Okishio, N., *161*

P

Painter, R. J., *237*
Pearce, I. F., 102, *103*
Penrose, R., *237*
Phillips, A. W., 372, *404*
Pindyck, R. S., 383, 390, *404*
Plemmons, R. J., 229, *236*
Polak, E., *403*
Ponstein, J., 322, *342*
Pontryagin, L. S., *103*, 343, *404*
Preston, A. J., 367, *404*
Propoi, A. I., 385, *404*
Pták, V., 29, *65*

Q

Quirk, J., 156, 157, *161*

R

Radner, R., *342*
Ramsey, F. P., *272*
Rao, C. R., 224, *237*
Rao, M. M., *236*
Rissanen, J., 398, *404*
Robinson, S. M., *342*
Rockafellar, R. T., *342*

S

Sagan, H., *272*
Samuelson, P. A., 79, 94, 95, 103, *104*, 147, *160*, *161*, *162*, 248, *272*, *342*
Saposnik, R., *161*
Sato, R., 136, *161*
Schönfeld, P., 219, 228, *237*
Schwartz, J. T., *197*
Schwartz, N. L., *404*
Seneta, E., *161*
Seton, F., *162*
Shell, K., 361, *404*
Shilov, G. E., *65*
Silverman, L. M., 392, 393, 396, *404*
Simon, H. A., *65*
Simmons, G. F., *197*
Smith, A. F. M., 214, *237*
Solow, R. M., 149, *162*, 248, *272*
Spivey, W. A., *237*
Stigum, B. P., 252, *272*

Stoleru, L. G., 361, *404*
Storey, C., *103*

T

Takayama, A., *342*
Tamura, H., *237*
Theil, H., 390, 400, *404*
Thompson, G. L., *341*, *342*
Tinbergen, J., *237*, 362, *404*
Tse, E., *404*
Tsukui, J., *162*
Tucker, A. W., *340*, *341*, *342*
Turnovsky, S. J., 372, 389, *405*

U

Uekawa, Y., 23, 29, 30, *31*
Uzawa, H., 159, *162*, 282, 323, *340*, *342*, 361, *405*

V

Valentine, F. A., *342*

W

Walras, L., *162*
Weber, W., 306, *340*
Wegge, L. L., *31*
Weil, R. L., *342*
Weizsäcker, C. C. von, 147, *162*
Wolfe, P., *342*
Wolfstetter, E., *162*
Wonham, W. M., 389, *405*

Y

Yaari, M. E., *65*
Yoshida, K., 192, *197*, *237*

Z

Zabczyk, J., *405*
Zajac, E. E., 323, *342*

Subject Index

A

Acceleration principle, 79
Accumulation point, 173
Activity of production, 291
Adherent point, 172
Adjoint
 of matrix, 6
 of transformation, 205
Admissible control, 343
Admissible set, 240
Affine subspace, 36
Algebraic dual, 186
Algebraically equivalent system, 368, 391
Allowable factor, 299
Angle between vectors, 169, 276
Annihilating polynomial, 72
Auxiliary variables, 343

B

Basic optimal vector, 334
Basis, 34
Basis solutions, 66
Banach space, 176
Bellman's principle of optimality, 380
Best linear unbiased estimator (BLUE), 204, 221, 225
Bialternate product, 90
Bliss, 247
Bordered Hessian, 252, 320
Bounded set, 174
 transformation, 184
Bruno fundamental duality, 336

C

Calculus of variations, 243
Capital coefficient, 79, 146, 232
 matrix of, 144, 232
Cauchy–Schwarz inequality, 31, 168
Cauchy sequence, 175
Cayley–Hamilton theorem, 72
Chain rule, 242
Characteristic equation, 67, 79
 polynomial, 14, 70
 root, 13
 vector, 13
Circulating capital, 146
Closed set, 172
Closure, 172
 point, 172
Cofactor, 5
Column dominance, 21
Column dominant diagonal (d.d.), 21
Column-sum condition, 96
Column-sum norm, 100
Companion matrix, 12
Complement
 of good, 151
 of set, 172
Complementary slackness conditions, 325

Completely controllable system, 368
Complete set, 176
Complex space, 33
Concave functional, 249
Concave mapping, 309
Cone, 37
Congruent modulo, 196
Conjugate, 16, 53
Constraint qualification, 308, 309, 318
Continuous transformation, 174, 255
Continuously differentiable transformation, 241
Contraction mapping, 253
Contraction mapping theorem, 254
  second theorem, 271
Control variables, 343, 362
Controllability index, 366, 391
Convergence, 173
Convex combination, 38
Convex cone, 38
Convex cover, 37
Convex functional, 249
Convex hull, 37
Convex mapping, 310
Convex polyhedral cone, 38
Convex polyhedron, 38
Convex set, 37
Correspondence principle, 95, 126
Coset, 196
Cost criterion function, 372
Countable set, 180
Coupling criterion, 367
Cramer's rule, 8
Cumulated multiplier, 84

D

Decomposable matrix, 110, 111, 117
De Morgan's formulas, 173
Dense set, 181
Determinant, 3
  of partitioned matrices, 9, 11–13
Diagonalization of matrix, 18, 54, 77
Difference operator, 79
Differential operator, 66
Dimension, 36, 390
Direct sum, 39
Dispersion matrix, 219
Distance between vectors, 169
Distributed-lag systems, 97, 101, 137, 386, 400
Dominant diagonal (d.d.), 21
D-stable matrix, 62
Dual functional, 314
Dual problem, 315, 324
Dual quantity system, 141, 150, 235
Dual (space), 187
Duality theorem, 315
  for linear programming, 324
  for linear relations, 284–288
Dynamic controllability condition, 364
Dynamic programming, 380

E

Economic solution, 296
Eidelheit separation theorem, 278
Eigenvalue, 13, 90
  generalized, 19
Eigenvector, 13
  generalized left (or right), 20
  left (or right), 17
Elasticity law, 121
Element-sum condition, 96
Elementary divisor, 74
Elementary row operations, 49
Equivalent modulo, 196
Equivalent system, 368, 391
Euclidean algorithm, 73
Euclidean distance, 169
Euclidean length of vector, 169
Euclidean norm, 166
Euclidean space, 166
Euler equation, 244
  under constraints, 263
Euler path, 358
Expansion factor, 292
Extending reproduction, 142
Extension of linear functional, 192
Extremal (function), 243
Extreme point, 38
Extremum, 239

F

Factor price surface, 337
Farkas lemma, 283
Farkas theorem, 284

Feasible path, 305
Field, 32
Final form, 400
Finite convex cone, 38
Finite-dimensional subspace, 34
First-order condition for maximum, 264
Fixed capital, 146
Fixed point, 255
Frobenius root, 107
Frobenius theorem, 107–115, 131–136
  generalized, 152
Full-cost pricing, 140
Functional, 186
Functionally reproducible system, 371
Fundamental matrix, 71
Fundamental Marxian theorem, 147, 234
  generalized, 337
Fréchet differentiable transformation, 239
Fréchet differential, 239
Fréchet derivative, 239

G

Gain matrix, 381
Gale–Nikaido theorems
  first, 288
  on global univalence, 257, 289
  on *P*-matrix, 28
  second, 289
Gale nonsubstitution theorem, 335
Gateaux differentiable transformation, 238
Gateaux differential, 238
Gauss–Markov estimator, 203
  extended form of, 224
Gauss–Markov model, 203
  constrained, 219
  unconstrained, 219
Gauss–Markov theorem, 203
  generalizations of, 221–227
Generalized inverse, 208–217
  computation of, 214
  of matrix, 210
  of transformation, 209
Generalized-inverse estimator, 214
General solution
  of equation system, 217
  of linear difference equations, 79, 82
  of linear differential equations, 66, 67, 68, 70, 71
  of linear equations, 50, 217
  to minimizer of Euclidean distance, 208
  to state-space form, 362, 370
Global maximum (or minimum), 250
Global univalence theorem
  by Gale and Nikaido, 258, 290
  by Inada, 258
Globally stable system, 149, 234
Gradient, 240
Gram determinant, 171
Gram matrix, 171
Gram–Schmidt procedure, 170
Greville recursive algorithm, 216
Gross substitutes (strong or weak), 215

H

Hadamard matrix, 22
Hahn–Banach theorem, 192–195
  complex case, 193
  real case, 192
  simple version, 194
Hamiltonian (function), 344
Hankel matrix, 396
Hawkins–Simon (H–S) conditions, 52
Hawkins–Simon theorem, 52
Hessian, 251
Hicks conditions, 123
Hicksian law, 121
Hicksian matrix, 153
Hilbert space, 177
H-matrix, 27
Homogeneous of degree *h*, 129
Homogeneous functions, 129
  Euler theorem on, 129
Hyperplane, 273
  separating, 276
  supporting, 276

I

Idempotent matrix, 64
Identity matrix, 6
Identity operator, 206
Impact multiplier, 83
Implicit•function theorem, 256
Imprimitive matrix, 130
Indecomposable matrix, 110, 111
Infimum (or inf), xvii

Inner product, 18, 166
Inner product space, 166
Input matrix, 148, 291
Interior, 171
Interior point, 171
Intersection of sets, 172, 173
Inverse
 of matrix, 8
 of partitioned matrices, 9, 10
Inverse function theorem, 271
Inverse transformation, 180
Irreducible model, 301
Isolated point, 173
Isomorphic space, 183
Isomorphism, 134, 183

J

Jacobian, 241
Jacobian matrix, 155, 241
Jacobi's ratio theorem, 7
Joint production, 234, 270
Jordan form of matrix, 76
Jordan transformation matrix, 76, 369

K

Kakeya theorem (generalized), 136
Kalman decomposition theorem, 393
Keynesian system, 82
Kernel, 40
Kornai planning, 337
Kuhn–Tucker theorems
 fourth, 338
 generalized, 312
 necessity, 308, 309
 second, 310
 third, 313

L

Labor-contents vector, 230
Labor exploitation factor, 142
Labor-value vector, 140, 230
Lag operator, 400
Lagged multipliers, 84
Lagrange multiplier theorem, 260
Lagrangian (function), 260, 262, 308, 344
Lancaster lemma, 111
Landau's o-symbol, 238
Laplace expansion, 6, 105
Least-squares (LS) estimator
 generalized, 214, 219
 ordinary, 214, 219
LeChatelier principle, 314
LeChatelier–Samuelson inequalities, 329
Leontief inverse, 116
 Samuelson theorem on, 119
Leontief model, 115, 335
 production system, 51
Linear combination, 38
Linear difference equation, 79
Linear differential equation, 66
Linear functional, 186
Linear homogeneous function, 129
Linear mapping, 40
Linear programming, 323–329
Linear space, 32
Linear subspace, 34
 generated (or spanned), 34
Linear transformation, 40
Linear variety, 36
 generated, 36
Linearly dependent (or independent) vectors, 17, 34
Local maximum (or minimum), 239
 strong (or strict), 263
 weak, 270
Local univalence theorem, 258
Long-run equilibrium, 81
Long-run equilibrium multiplier, 85
Lyapunov function, 63
 of discrete type, 381
Lyapunov theorem, 63

M

Manne development program, 337
Mapping, 39
Marginal productivity, 330
Marginal utility, 248, 323, 356
Markov parameter matrices, 390
Matrix game, 296, 298, 326
Matrix norm, 100
Maximal path, 305
Maximum (or minimum), 175
Maximum linear variety, 273
Maximum proper subspace, 273
Mean value inequality theorem, 253

Mean value theorem, 252
Metzler lemma, 109
Metzler theorems
first, 124
second, 126
Metzlerian law, 120
Metzlerian matrix, 152
Minimal polynomial, 72
Minimal realization, 391
Minimum principle for discrete system, 385
Minkowski functional, 190
Minkowski matrix, 27
M-matrix, 64
Modified Routh–Hurwitz conditions, 92
Modified Routh–Hurwitz theorem, 92
Modulus, 21, 165
Morishima matrix, 152
extended, 154
Morishima turnpike theorem, 333
Mosak theorem, 127

N

Negative definite matrix, 56
Negative dominant diagonal (d.d.), 26
Negative half-space, 275
Negative quasi-definite matrix, 61
Negative semidefinite matrix, 56
Neighborhood, 171
Net national product, 295
(von) Neumann equilibrium, 296, 304
(von) Neumann facet, 304
(von) Neumann price ray, 332
Nonjoint production, 302, 335
Nonnegative definite matrix, 56
Nonpositive definite matrix, 56
Nonsubstitution theorem, 334
Nonsingular matrix, 8
Norm, 165
of matrix, 100
Normal equations, 235
Normal vector, 275
Normalized price vector, 230
Normed (vector) space, 165
of bounded linear transformations, 185
NP-matrix, 27
Null vector, 8, 13, 33
Nullity, 46
Nullspace, 40, 46, 207

O

Observable system, 378, 389
Observability index, 391
Observability matrix, 379
One-to-one correspondence, 180
One-to-one transformation, 180
Onto transformation, 180
Open set, 171
Optimal basis, 334
Optimal control, 372
Optimal feedback rule, 376
Optimal strategy, 297
Optimal transformation surface, 337
Orthogonal complement, 198
Orthogonal matrix, 31, 54
Orthogonal vectors, 18, 198
Orthonormal basis, 170
Orthonormalized vector, 54
Output controllable system, 365, 370
Output controllability matrix, 365, 371
Output matrix, 291
Output variables, 364

P

Parallelogram law, 169
Partial derivative, 241
Particular solutions, 47, 66, 79, 81, 82
Payoff matrix, 296
Penrose theorems
first, 210
second, 217
Perfect output controllability matrix, 371
Perfectly output controllable system, 371
Perfectly stable market, 123
Permutation matrix, 31, 110
Perron root, *see* Frobenius root
Phillips stabilization model, 372, 385
Piecewise continuous function, 343
P-matrix, 27
Polynomial of matrix, 16, 73
Pontryagin maximum principle
fixed final state case, 344
free final state case, 343
Sufficiency theorems, 349, 351–355
time optimal case, 344
Positive definite matrix, 56
Positve half-space, 275

Positive quasi-definite matrix, 61
Positive semidefinite matrix, 56
Positively homogeneous function, 129
Price adjustment, 122
Price system, 141, 231
  nonlinear, 258
Primitive matrix, 130
Principal minor, 15
Process of production, 115, 291
Production function, 258, 264
  fixed-proportion, 246, 355
Productive technique, 335
Profit factor, 292
Projection, 200
Projection theorem
  on linear variety, 202
  on subspace, 200
Propensity to save, 79, 336
Pseudoinverse, *see* Generalized inverse
Pythagorean theorem, 198

Q

Quadratic cost function, 372
Quadratic form, 55
Quadratic programming, 311, 316
Qualitatively *D*-stable matrix, 156
Qualitatively stable matrix, 156
Quasi-concave functional, 317
Quasi-concave mapping, 316
Quasi-concave programming, 322
Quasi-convex functional, 315
Quasi-convex mapping, 317
Quasi-dominant diagonal (q.d.d.), 23
Quasi-Frobenius root, 152
Quotient space, 196

R

Radner–McKenzie theorem, 305
Ramsey model, 246
Ramsey path, 248, 358
Ramsey rule of accumulation, 271, 358
Range, 40, 207
Rank, 16, 43, 44
Rank condition
  for controllability, 363, 370
  for observability, 379, 389
Rank theorem, 44
Rate of exploitation, 142, 232
Rate of profit, 146
Real part, 88
Real space, 33
Realization, 390
Rectangular region, 258
Reducible model, 301
Regular matrix, 8
Relative maximum (or minimum), 239
Relative stability, 140
Reverse the sign of a vector, 28
Riccati (differential) equation, 375
Riccati difference equation, 381
Ridge estimator, 214
Rissanen's algorithm, 398
Routh–Hurwitz conditions, 92
Row dominance, 21
Row dominant diagonal, 21
Row-equivalent matrix, 49
Row-reduced echelon matrix, 49
Row-sum condition, 96
Row-sum norm, 100

S

Saddle-point condition, 312, 327
Saddle-point solution, 298, 329
Samuelson's multiplier–accelerator model, 79
Satiation, 247, 356
Scalar multiplication, 33
Second-order condition for maximum, 264
Segment, 37
Sensitivity theorem, 313
  for linear programming, 329
Separable space, 181
Separation theorem, *see* Eidelheit separation theorem
  on Euclidean space, 279
Set of all continuous real-valued functions, 33, 165
Shadow price, 357
Similar matrix, 13
Similarity transformation, 368, 391
Sign-symmetric matrix, 155
Singular matrix, 8
Skew-symmetric matrix, 338
Slater condition, 311
Solow conditions, 117
Solow dynamic price system, 149
Solow theorem, 117

Solutions
  of homogeneous equations, 285, 286
  of homogeneous inequalities, 285
  of linear inequalities, 284
Solution space
  for linear equations, 47, 276
  for linear inequalities, 276
Solvability of linear equations, 48
Spectral norm, 103
Sphere, 171
S-stable matrix, 62
Stabilization policy, *see* Phillips stabilization model
Stable (or stability) matrix, 62, 85, 88, 89, 155
Stable system in the large, *see* Globally stable system
State controllable system, 363, 370
State controllability matrix, 364, 370
State variables, 343, 362
State-space form, 362, 364
  discrete version of, 367
Static controllability condition, 362
Stationary point, 240
Strategy sets, 296
Strictly concave mapping, 249, 310
Strictly convex mapping, 249, 310
Strictly determined game, 297
Strictly quasi-concave mapping, 317
Strictly quasi-convex mapping, 317
Subgradient, 271
Sublinear functional, 189
Subspace, 34
  generated (or spanned), 34
  proper, 34
Sufficiency
  for linear programming, 325
  for maximum principle, 351, 354
Sum of sets, 38
Sum-of-squares condition, 96
Supermultiplier, 81
Support, 276
Support theorem, 277
Supporting half-space, 276
Supporting hyperplane, 276
Supremum (or sup), xvii
Surplus labor, 142, 232
Surplus output vector, 141, 231
Sylvester inequality, 64
System decomposition, 392–393

T

Target variables, 362
Tâtonnement process, 159
Taylor expansion of second order, 251
Technological changes, 330
Time-optimal problem, 360–361
Tinbergen policy model, 229, 362
Tinbergen rule of policy formation, 362, 366
Tinbergenian (condition), 94
  sufficient conditions for, 96–101
Trace of matrix, 16, 204
Transversality condition, 246, 344
Transformation, *see* Mapping
Transition matrix, 42
Transpose, 4, 167
Triangle inequality, 165
Triangular matrix, 88
Tucker theorem, 287
Twice-differentiable functional, 251

U

U-1 condition, 29
U-2 condition, 30
Unbiased estimator, 219
Unbiasedly estimable parameter, 220
Unconstrained maximum, 265
Uniform Lipschitz condition, 240
Uniform rate
  of profit, 146, 233
  of return, 146
Union of sets, 172, 173
Unit sphere, 172
Unit vectors, 15, 189
Unitary space, 167
Univalent transformation, 180
Utility, 247, 322, 356

V

Value
  of a hyperplane, 274
  of a matrix game, 297
Vandermonde determinant, 5, 67
Vector, 32
Vector addition, 32
Vector space, 32
Viable technique, 335

W

Walras law, 127
Weierstrass approximation theorem, 182

Z

Zero-state equivalent, 390
Zero vector, *see* Null vector

A B 7 C 8 D 9 E 0 F 1 G 2 H 3 I 4 J 5